The Football 100

The Football 100

Mike Sando, Dan Pompei, and
The Athletic NFL Staff

The Athletic

WM

WILLIAM MORROW
An Imprint of HarperCollins*Publishers*

FIRST EDITION

Library of Congress Cataloging-in-Publication Data

Title: The football 100 / [by the writers of] The Athletic.
Other titles: Football one hundred | Athletic (New York, N.Y.)
Description: First edition. | New York, N.Y. : William Morrow, [2023] | Includes index.
Identifiers: LCCN 2023007380 (print) | LCCN 2023007381 (ebook) | ISBN 9780063329096 (hardcover) | ISBN 9780063329089 (ebook)
Subjects: LCSH: Football players—United States—Biography. | Football—United States—History.
Classification: LCC GV939.A1 F54 2023 (print) | LCC GV939.A1 (ebook) | DDC 796.3320922—dc23/eng/20230216
LC record available at https://lccn.loc.gov/2023007380
LC ebook record available at https://lccn.loc.gov/2023007381

ISBN 978-0-06-332909-6

23 24 25 26 27 LBC 5 4 3 2 1

Contents

Testimonials   vii

Introduction   xi

The List   1

The Shooting Stars   617

The Future Top 100?   627

Appendix: The 100   631

Appendix: The 100 by Team   633

Photograph Credits   637

Index   639

Testimonials

Bruce Smith

The feeling that you get, playing the best of the best, is a rush that's unexplainable.

The two most important positions on a football team are the quarterback and the pass rusher. That's how you build a franchise. So if you got the ball in your hands, it doesn't matter if you're John Elway or a backup; it still goes down as one sack or one forced fumble.

But there's more significance against the all-time greats. You crave it more.

You have your favorite guys you want to get to. For me, it was Dan Marino. He was a legend even while we were still playing. He had the quickest release in the game and eyes in the back of his head. He could manipulate the pocket like nobody else, just to buy a second more time. As difficult as it was to get to him, particularly when Don Shula went out and drafted Richmond Webb ninth overall because they couldn't slow me down, it was exhilarating to go up against him. Marino was the least-sacked quarterback, but I got him the most.

I lined up on the right side, which meant I got to face a lot of fantastic offensive linemen on the blind side, but there was only one Anthony Muñoz. I didn't go against him often, but Muñoz was considered the best left tackle who ever played. Facing him was an opportunity to shine. You know that when you compete against guys like that, you appreciate the dedication, the consistency, all the adversity and injuries that had been overcome to reach that high level of play.

I'm sure it felt the same for guys like Derrick Thomas, using his instincts and timing to get off the ball and do exceptional things against opponents with incredible athletic ability. I can remember getting to Joe Montana several times to the point he would look at me and say, "You again!" while I was getting off him. Or I would hear him cussing some of his offensive linemen.

That's your job, to rattle the quarterback. Those are the memories you look back on and think, *Wow, that's pretty cool*. This book is filled with stories from the trenches: the memories, reflections, and insights of the best to ever lace them up.

While you're playing, things can be a blur, and you don't always do a great job of reflecting. You're living in the ups and the downs. But it's so fulfilling to be considered among so many other legends. That's a proud legacy I left behind for others to chase.

—Bruce Smith, Hall of Fame defensive end

Mike Ditka

Greatness has a lot to do with attitude: the will to play, the will to excel, and the will to do more than you are required to do in practice and in games.

I've spent my life in football. I played the game for the love of the game. I loved it and played it hard. I asked no quarter, gave no quarter. What I had, you got. If it wasn't enough, I'm sorry, but I gave you what I had.

That's what I asked of myself for twelve years as a player in the National Football League, and it's what I asked of others in nine years as an assistant coach and fourteen years as a head coach. That's what helped me and my teammates and players win four NFL championships.

It's an honor to be included in lists like this, but I never want to assume I was better than anybody. I don't believe I was the greatest tight end. I think John Mackey was. He had more speed than me and was a little better receiver than me. I couldn't do all the things he could, and he couldn't do all the things I could. But we were probably two of the best in our time.

A lot of people put me in a position to succeed. If the Steelers had drafted me, I would have been a linebacker. Instead, it was the Bears, and coach George Halas said I was going to play tight end. He and his assistant Luke Johnsos used me in a way that no tight end had been used before.

Before then, tight ends were blockers more than anything, extensions of the offensive line. Then when people saw what I was doing and what Mackey was doing, they started using tight ends more as receivers. They realized the tight end could be a hell of a target. People began throwing to tight ends more and more, and I'm grateful for having been a part of that.

The commitment to excellence is what separates great ones—but this list is all the great players. The differences between them are so small.

I played with, or against, so many of the great ones: Deacon Jones, Merlin Olsen, Dick Butkus, Ray Nitschke. Nobody hit harder than those last two.

But the greatest player I ever saw was Walter Payton. He wasn't just a great halfback—he was a great football player. There wasn't anything he couldn't do. He played the game with a relentless pursuit of excellence. He didn't think anybody could bring him down.

Today, of course, so much emphasis is on the quarterback. You can say Tom Brady is the best quarterback. He did everything he could do and just kept winning. But determining the best in history, comparing players from different eras, is so difficult, and it's a part of what makes this project so special. Was Brady better than Dan Marino or Johnny Unitas?

Unitas wasn't supposed to be great. He was a ninth-round pick who was cut by the Steelers before he ever played a game. Then he became one of the greatest of all time. Why? He had a great will, the will to be the best. People don't get to be great by accident. It has a lot to do with determination and the effort you put into it. That's what this book is all about. It's a testament to football greatness. The players on this list have one thing in common: They had the will, and they were able to impose it on their opponents. That's how you get to be one of the greats.

—Mike Ditka, Hall of Fame tight end and coach

Introduction

By Dan Pompei and Mike Sando

It took Tom Brady's seventh Super Bowl victory, this one with a new franchise, for the pro football world to unite around a generally accepted premise: Brady is the greatest NFL quarterback of the modern era, and probably ever. *Probably*. Therein lies the challenge of the most irresistible exercise in sports: ranking the all-time greats.

When we set out to identify the 100 best NFL players of all time, we had many thousands to choose from, considering more than 27,000 have played in an NFL game, more than 2,700 have been selected for the Pro Bowl, nearly 1,200 have been voted first-team All-Pro, and 320 have been inducted into the Pro Football Hall of Fame.

How did we do it?

There is no magic formula, but our decades covering and researching the game, including long stints on the Pro Football Hall of Fame selection committee, gave us an advantage we leveraged to the fullest possible extent in these pages.

The process started in the spring of 2021 when The Athletic convened a panel of four senior writers who were also selectors for the Pro Football Hall of Fame (Ed Bouchette, Jeff Duncan, Dan Pompei, and Mike Sando) and Lisa Wilson, an editorial director who has watched the NFL closely for decades. We began with a list of the most decorated players, pulling those with the most Pro Bowls, All-Pro selections, greatest statistical seasons (and careers), and of course all enshrinees of the Pro Football Hall of Fame. From there, we embarked on a series of discussions and reduction votes spread across two months. Eventually, we came up with a list that was published by The Athletic over a series of months. More than one year later, we crafted a revised list for this book.

Everyone has opinions about who are the greatest players, but compiling a list of 100 players is full of challenges, and we wrestled with all of them.

Perhaps the most challenging part was comparing players from different eras. The typical metrics to judge a wide receiver like Don Hutson, who played in the 1930s and '40s, can't be compared to the typical metrics to evaluate a receiver like Julio Jones, from the current era. Rules have changed to promote passing. Seasons are longer. Strategies have evolved.

Sando solved some of this with wide receivers and running backs by evaluating where they ranked among their peers during their best years. For wide receivers, that meant calculating where they ranked in yardage within a season over each player's eight best seasons. For running backs, whose careers are generally shorter, Sando focused on scrimmage yards during each player's six most productive seasons. We then used the findings as a general guide before making some tweaks we felt were warranted.

We also had to guard against recency bias. The two of us have watched football for a combined nine decades, and covered it for six decades. We knew more about players we had seen and had written about, and even players who were active in our childhoods, than we did about players from the early days of the NFL. The inclination is to give more credence to those we were familiar with, but we tried to even the playing field between players from different eras—to look at Otto Graham through the same lens as Tom Brady.

Positional bias was another potential sticking point. We could have had a list of 100 quarterbacks, given their outsize impact on game outcomes, but that wouldn't be fair to so many great players at less prominent positions. We wound up with 20 quarterbacks compared to three centers, an attempt to account for positional value without going overboard.

Great players are more widely recognized when they are a part of great teams. That's why there are 14 Vince Lombardi–era Green Bay Packers with busts in the Pro Football Hall of Fame, plus Lombardi himself. Only five of those Packers Hall of Famers—Herb Adderley, Willie Davis, Forrest Gregg, Ray Nitschke, and Bart Starr—made our list as we strove to look at more than championship rings. Dick Butkus and Gale Sayers never played in the postseason, but both made our top 100 and are ranked relatively high.

Sayers was an instructive case study because he played in only 68 games, which is 158 fewer than all-time rushing leader Emmitt Smith. We had to weigh brilliant, brief careers against lengthy, impressive bodies of work. In this case, there was room for Sayers and Smith, but not for others whose careers were too short or who compiled impressive numbers over long periods without being truly elite for very long.

Other discussions centered around how to consider active players like Patrick Mahomes. Rather than project what these players might do, we focused on what they already have done. When we started the process, Mahomes had not done enough to be included in our top 100. But between putting together the initial and final lists, Mahomes led the Kansas City Chiefs to another Super Bowl title and won a second Most Valuable Player Award. We decided that was enough for Mahomes to make the list. In a decade, we might laugh at where he ranks on the current list. It represents a snapshot in time, and in all likelihood, he will climb ever higher with each passing season.

The most challenging part of the process was deciding who to leave off. There were solid arguments for about 30 players to make the final 10 spots, and we went back and forth about who should make it. We didn't necessarily feel good about leaving off Troy Aikman, Raymond Berry, Derrick Brooks, Mike Singletary, and some other 220 Hall of Fame players who did not quite make the cut.

But in our opinion, our top 100 is the elite of the elite.

The Football 100

100.
Fran Tarkenton

Fran Tarkenton retired with the NFL records for passing completions, yards, and touchdowns.

Position: Quarterback

Teams: Vikings (1961–1966), Giants (1967–1971), Vikings (1972–1978)

By Zak Keefer

In the defining moment of the defining game of his career, on a day that doubled as the most devastating of his life, Fran Tarkenton wanted to go with his gut. He wanted to run it.

It was third-and-short, late in a 1975 divisional playoff game against the Cowboys, Tarkenton's top-seeded and favored Vikings clinging to a 14–10 lead. One first down would seal it. Two measly yards. Move the chains, bleed the clock, inch one step closer to the

Super Bowl, and send Tom Landry and his mighty Cowboys home to Texas.

With all that hanging in the balance, Tarkenton huddled on the sideline with his offensive coordinator, Jerry Burns, and they debated the play call.

The quarterback wanted to roll out right and sprint to the marker. Tarkenton knew he could make it. He was the game's most electric scrambler from the pocket, and he wanted it all—the game, the season—on his legs.

Burns didn't agree. He wanted a handoff to running back Chuck Foreman.

Back and forth they went, and it took some convincing, but eventually Burns relented. The quarterback got his wish.

Then the Cowboys got the stop.

"Dallas had the play read, almost as though they had been a part of the sideline discussion," Tarkenton would write years later in his book *Every Day Is Game Day*.

"We had no chance."

When Dallas defensive back Charlie Waters busted through the line, he had a clear lane to Tarkenton. He wrapped him up for a 3-yard loss, and the Vikings were forced to punt.

By the end of the game, it would prove to be one of the most improbable turns of events in NFL history, not for Dallas's third-down stop but for what would transpire in the game's final minute. First, Dallas quarterback Roger Staubach connected on a fourth-and-17 to wideout Drew Pearson along the sideline, a miraculous completion that Tarkenton still bristles about to this day.

"The receiver should have been called out of bounds," he believes.

Then, even more impossible: with 24 seconds left, Staubach bought time in the pocket, then, from his own 40, heaved the ball as far as his arm would let him. "He just threw the ball over the scoreboard!" CBS's play-by-play announcer shouted on the broadcast. It'd travel 55 yards, somehow nestling into Pearson's hands 4 yards from the end zone. He beat double coverage to make the catch, then scampered in for the winning score.

It was the ultimate stunner—Tarkenton believed the Vikings were on their way to a Super Bowl, and still are among the 12 NFL teams to have never won one—and it came in the most stunning fashion. Most remember Staubach and Pearson's last-second heroics, but more than four decades later, it's the failed third down that haunts Tarkenton most.

Two measly yards.

He wouldn't watch a replay of the game for 30 years.

Staubach admitted to reporters in the victorious locker room that he'd closed his eyes and said a prayer before breaking that last huddle. Thus "Hail Mary" forever became a part of the football lexicon. The Cowboys made it all the way to Super Bowl X, where they lost to the Steelers.

Meanwhile, Tarkenton seethed. He refused to talk with the press after the game. He retreated to the parking lot outside Metropolitan Stadium, where he and two teammates, Grady Alderman and Mick Tingelhoff, had rented a van, expecting to grill out with their families, bask in the win, and watch the second playoff game of the afternoon.

They stood in the Minnesota cold, still stunned by the loss, when legendary announcer Jack Buck punctured the somber silence from the TV broadcast. "We would like to express our condolences to the Tarkenton family for the unexpected death of Fran's father, Dallas Tarkenton, who died this afternoon of a heart attack," Buck said.

Fran hadn't heard yet.

"I was stunned," he remembered. "I found out the same time as the rest of the country."

Dallas Tarkenton, a Methodist minister, had been watching his son play that afternoon from his home in Savannah, Georgia, sitting in a chair when he started to gasp for breath. He was gone by the time they arrived at the hospital.

"He had no clue whether a football was blown up or stuffed, but he watched the games I was playing in and he always supported everything I did," Fran would write.

A gutting playoff loss, then a devastating personal one, all within a few, excruciating hours. Tarkenton would board a flight a few days later, but it wasn't for the NFC Championship Game.

It was for his hometown in Georgia, where he'd have to bury his father.

They despised him. Loathed him. Wanted him wheezing on the turf, writhing in pain, then wobbling back to the sideline.

They didn't simply want to just hit him; they wanted to crush him. They wanted to injure him.

Some wanted him out of the league.

"I always hated Tarkenton, I really did," Rams Hall of Famer Merlin Olsen once told the NFL Network. "I mean, that little wimp would run around out there for hours and hours and hours, and we had to chase him, wherever he went. Sometimes, he'd run 40 yards back and forth and up and down the field. At the end of a game against Tarkenton, your tongue was right on the ground."

Another Hall of Famer who spent too many Sundays chasing Tarkenton around the field, Deacon Jones, once called him "a pain in the ass."

"He'd gamble. He'd run anywhere. He'd be up in the stands if he had to," Jones explained. "He's one man that we tried, desperately, to end his career. We tried—and I must say that in this day and age—we tried desperately to get rid of him. Because on a hot day in the Coliseum, chasing Fran Tarkenton was not what you wanted to do."

Tarkenton was two decades ahead of Randall Cunningham and Steve Young, four ahead of Michael Vick, five ahead of Russell Wilson and Lamar Jackson. He was a trailblazer, a rebel whose gumption made plenty of enemies in his own era but left a path for those who followed.

He changed the game. He showed that quarterbacks can do more.

Before the Georgia kid arrived in the league in 1961 and started dashing from the pocket, refusing to wave the white flag on broken plays, quarterbacks were mostly stationary passers, chained behind the line of scrimmage, told to crumble to the turf and protect the football at all costs. It was an unwritten rule of the era.

Tarkenton didn't abide.

"I made up my mind when I got to pro football that I wasn't going to give up on a play—ever," said the man who'd later title one of his books *Better Scramble Than Lose*.

Early on, Tarkenton scrambled out of necessity. Drafted by the expansion Vikings in 1961, Tarkenton's offensive lines were often slapped-together combinations of has-beens and also-rans, players other teams had either given up on or had no interest in. He played under constant assault.

Tarkenton figured he'd have to improvise to survive.

So he started to run. And he moved the chains, he kept drives alive, and he kept the Vikings competitive.

His style was not immediately accepted. "The scrambler," they came to call him, and it wasn't a compliment.

"When I began my NFL career in 1961, I was a freak," Tarkenton wrote years later in a guest column for the *St. Paul Pioneer Press*. "The reason was simple: I played quarterback and I ran.

"It was not a skill set that was embraced. Plenty of people mocked it, and the rest wrote it off."

The defensive linemen Tarkenton so often left wheezing during and after games came to revile him. Some, like Baltimore Colts legend Gino Marchetti, predicted a swift and painful demise for the audacious young quarterback. Marchetti once told reporters he didn't see Tarkenton lasting two years in the league.

He'd somehow survive 18.

Tarkenton led all quarterbacks in rushing yards in seven of his first eight seasons and was in the top five in each of his first 10 years. By the time he retired in 1978 after two stints with the Vikings and one with the Giants, he'd piled up 3,674 rushing yards, the most ever by a quarterback. The fact that he also owned records for the

most passing yards (47,003) and touchdown passes (342), earned league MVP honors in 1975, and made nine Pro Bowls put him in the conversation as one of the best to ever play the position.

Asked who he wanted to present that 1975 MVP trophy to him, Tarkenton had a little fun with it.

"Gino Marchetti," he said.

More than anything, Tarkenton's legacy came in the convention he defied and the style in which he played. Over 18 seasons, he'd proven quarterbacks could do it differently, not for a game or a season, but an entire career.

"If you look up here at some of the past enshrinees," Tarkenton told the crowd during his Hall of Fame enshrinement in 1986, "you see Doug Atkins, Deacon Jones, and Ray Nitschke. And they were trying to kill me, ladies and gentlemen.

"And that pocket got crowded, and I wanted to get out, and I did."

And in the process, he changed the game. The unwritten rules of pro football would never be the same.

Tarkenton no longer sits atop the all-time rushing list for quarterbacks. He's currently seventh, since passed by the dual-threat quarterbacks his courage and instincts inspired—players who came to define their era, win Super Bowls, and reshape the definition of what a quarterback could do.

There were Cunningham and Young in the late 1980s and 1990s. Vick and Donovan McNabb in the 2000s. Cam Newton and Wilson after that. Now it is the era of Lamar Jackson, a rushing talent so dynamic that the Ravens benched a Super Bowl–winning quarterback, Joe Flacco, inserted Jackson, and completely redesigned their offense around his ability to run.

In his first full year as the starter, Jackson won the MVP.

It was something that would've never happened in Tarkenton's day.

But his was the spark that lit the fuse; Tarkenton's success made it OK for coaches to accept their quarterback's out-of-pocket impro-

visation, OK for general managers and scouts to see it as an attribute instead of a detriment. Running quarterbacks made the game more unpredictable, and therefore more entertaining. A play that was destined to die could be given new life.

Cunningham and Young carried the torch. Vick took it to another level. Now it's part of what makes the best in the modern game—Patrick Mahomes and Aaron Rodgers—so lethal.

"A tidal wave of talent is changing offensive thinking in the league," Tarkenton said of today's game. "Every general manager is out there now, looking for the next runner, looking for a guy who can scramble, extend the play. GMs are looking for all those things that for so long they dismissed or failed to fully understand."

One player helped change that.

And if there's one thing Tarkenton could change about his career, it's that afternoon in December 1975. The third-and-short against the Cowboys. The one that got away.

"People ask me, after all these years, if I still think about it," Tarkenton wrote in *Every Day Is Game Day*.

"The answer is always instantaneous and emphatic: all the time!"

He couldn't summon the courage to watch a replay of the game until 2008, 33 years later. The wound still stung. The ill-fated call on third-and-short—a rollout to the right instead of a handoff—still eats at him.

He wants that call back. He believes it cost him his best chance at a ring.

"There is absolutely no doubt in my mind that decision cost us the game, and an eventual Super Bowl victory, with our greatest team," he wrote. "I should have gone with Burnsie's running play. It hurts to relive it."

That's because the Vikings of the Tarkenton era—or of any era, for that matter—never could quite finish. Three times he led them to the Super Bowl, and each time Minnesota came up short.

For all his success, and for all the influence his convention-bucking style would have in the decades that followed, Tarkenton's never gotten over that.

"I've never had a day go by I don't regret not being able to do something more to help my team win a Super Bowl," he wrote. "We dominated the league in the 1970s. We did as much as Pittsburgh, the 49ers, or the Miami Dolphins of that era. But I didn't realize then, as I do today, how important it is to win the Super Bowl. We did well, but we never won that last one, so we will never be associated with those great teams of the past."

Perhaps one play would've changed all that. Tarkenton's legacy. Vikings history. All of it, forever altered, if they'd picked up 2 measly yards.

99.
Marcus Allen

Marcus Allen was the first NFL player with 10,000 rushing yards and 5,000 receiving yards.

Position: Running Back

Teams: Raiders (1982–1992), Chiefs (1993–1997)

By Daniel Brown

Marcus Allen's college roommate at the University of Southern California frequently volunteered to whip up dinner for the household, but the hard-hitting defensive back wasn't much of a chef. "He had, seriously, maybe a hundred variations of Hamburger Helper," Allen recalled.

But on the field? Ronnie Lott could really get cooking. And by the time the two former USC roomies faced each other in the NFL, it was a Michelin-star feast for the eyes.

It happened on Day 1: in Allen's debut for the Raiders in the 1982 season-opener, Lott had the running back in his sights while rampaging across the grass at Candlestick Park.

"I'm going to light his butt up," Lott remembered thinking years later.

On a toss sweep to the boundary, Allen was so focused on another 49ers defender that he seemed oblivious to Lott's impending blast.

"I'm like, 'Oh, he doesn't see me!'" Lott continued, his voice rising. "I'm coming up at 100 miles an hour and as soon as I get ready to hit him, he does a 360 on me, goes inside, and gets past me!

"And I remember sitting there going, 'How did he see that?! There's no way he saw me!'"

Well, actually . . .

"Ronnie," Allen told him after the play, "I knew where you were the whole time."

Allen rushed for 116 yards and a touchdown that day against the defending Super Bowl champions, a performance that sounded the alarm for the rest of the NFL: if you think you're going to stop Marcus Allen, think again.

For the next 16 seasons, the speedster zipped past defenders with an array of moves that were somehow both balletic and brutish. He had 12,243 career rushing yards, which ranks 14th all-time. He specialized in goal-line effectiveness (123 career touchdowns, third all time) and caught passes with unprecedented success for a running back (he was the first NFL player with 10,000 rushing yards and 5,000 receiving yards).

And if that weren't enough, Allen completed 12 of 27 passes for 282 yards and six touchdowns in his NFL career.

"There are men who train and there are men who have a gift from God," longtime Raiders teammate Lester Hayes recalled. "There's a difference. And God gave Marcus beaucoup testosterone."

Allen was special all right. There's only one player in NFL history whose LinkedIn profile, should he ever need one, would include all of the following: Heisman Trophy, NCAA national championship, Super Bowl title, NFL MVP, and Super Bowl MVP.

Still, it's possible to explain a lot about what made Allen so magical over his wide-ranging career simply by recounting the events of a single day.

No one stood a chance against him on January 22, 1984, beginning with a dutiful parking lot attendant.

The greatest day of Marcus Allen's life was magical from the instant he opened his eyes.

"I had one of the greatest nights of sleep ever," he said, slipping into a dreamlike state all over again. "I was just walking on air. And I remember going to breakfast and just kind of smiling at every-thing, right?"

He's talking about Super Bowl XVIII, where the Raiders put a 38–9 beating on Washington and Allen was the game's MVP in a runaway.

After early meetings that day, players headed over to the stadium. Things weren't as regimented as they are now, so some players took the team bus while others took cabs.

Allen grabbed his keys and Odis McKinney Jr. joined him for a Super Bowl carpool in Allen's rental car.

It proved to be the toughest defense against him all day. Because when the Raiders duo took a last left turn into Tampa Stadium, there was a parking lot attendant stationed at the entrance. As Allen recalled the conversation, he asked her where the players parked, and the attendant responded by asking to see his parking pass.

ALLEN: No, no. Excuse me, miss, seriously. My name is Marcus
   Allen. This is Odis McKinney. We're playing in today's game.
ATTENDANT: Well, do you have a parking pass?
ALLEN: Ma'am, seriously!

ATTENDANT: I don't care who you guys are. You can't get in if
you don't have a parking pass.

This, to borrow a football term, is where the play went off-
schedule. Allen impulsively whipped the car into reverse, parked
against the curb, and switched off the engine.

"Odis looked at me. I looked at him. He grabbed his bag, I
grabbed my bag, and we took off running to the locker room," Allen recalled. "And to this day, I don't know what happened to the
rental car."

Not even that incident, though, could rattle his trancelike vibe.
Allen recalled being the second-to-last Raiders player to take the
field, just before quarterback Jim Plunkett, during the traditionally
epic Super Bowl player introductions.

"I ran out, and I swear I don't think my feet touched the ground,"
Allen said. "I was just gliding."

Allen fumbled on the Raiders' second drive, and even that barely
fazed him. In his hyperfocused state, the ball oozed away so slowly
to Allen's eyes that he remembers reading the commissioner's im-
printed signature—*Pete Rozelle*—as the ball bobbed along the turf.
It was recovered by teammate Charlie Hannah.

"I just kind of looked at it and went back to the huddle," Allen
said. *"Listen, you're fumbling in the Super Bowl?* Most guys would
get nervous, but I was just like, 'No big deal.'"

The big deal—the *huge* deal—would come with 12 seconds left in
the third quarter, with the Raiders comfortably ahead at 28–9. On
a first-and-10 from the Los Angeles 26, Allen took a handoff from
Plunkett and headed wide left into a thicket of defenders before reversing course. All of his skills were on display here: his speed, his
balance, his genius for angles, and a nervous-system response that
somehow blended fight *and* flight.

Once Allen spotted an opening in the middle of the field, he
blasted into the second level and then . . . his otherworldly day
reached its freakiest point.

"I was traveling like warp speed, time travel and stuff like that,"

Allen recalled. "And then I got to approximately the 10-yard line and everything came back to normal speed."

Hayes, who watched the play from the Raiders sideline, still marvels at the way the running back kept pulling away from the defense.

"Darrell Green couldn't catch him!" Hayes said. "Marcus ran a 4.6 40-yard dash, but he had 4.3 feet. That's a blessing."

Allen's 74-yard frolic was the longest touchdown run in Super Bowl history, a mark that stood until Willie Parker went one yard longer for the Steelers in Super Bowl XL. Allen ran for 191 yards, which also set a Super Bowl record that was since broken by Timmy Smith (204 for Washington in Super Bowl XXII).

Never underestimate the power of a good night's sleep.

"It was just amazing," Allen said. "It was like, just one of those days, like, it didn't matter who was out there or what they could do. Nothing could stop me."

Years after a certain Florida-based parking lot attendant tried redirecting Allen, a harried producer at the Pro Football Hall of Fame got the same treatment. He pulled Allen aside during the ceremony and told him they were getting short on time. Cut your speech short, he told him. Then the producer circled back and reminded him a second time.

"Listen here," Allen remembers responding. "I don't care about me, but you'd better get my father on the air."

Harold "Red" Allen was a carpenter. For the six children he helped raise in the San Diego area, he was also a Little League coach, history teacher, guidance counselor, and plenty of other unofficial roles. Along with Gwendolyn, his wife of 56 years, they made sure their kids had an upbringing that looked nothing like Harold's own childhood.

Marcus said his father was around 9 or 10 years old when his mother told him to go get his dad, who was gambling over at a local bar.

"[Harold] walked two miles to go get him and on the way back home, his dad barely said a word to him," Marcus said. "And so, during that walk, he said to himself, 'If I ever have kids, it will never be like that.'"

That is why Allen told the producer to make sure Harold got all the time he needed in 2003 when Marcus asked his father to serve as his Hall of Fame presenter, the person who gets the honor of introducing the inductee onstage and unveiling their bust.

"Isn't that amazing?" Marcus said. "I had this incredible father, and I wanted everyone to know."

One of the lessons Harold imparted to each of his sons when they were young was less than subtle. The carpenter would drag his boys to a building site to show them what his days looked like. This wasn't because he wanted them to follow in his footsteps; it was because he wanted their footsteps to make a hasty retreat in another direction.

"I gave them an option of hammering nails all day long for a living or going to college," Harold said from the stage in Canton. "They chose college."

Allen played at USC as a freshman on the 1978 team that won the national championship. He served as a backup that season to eventual Heisman Trophy–winning running back Charles White. By the time Allen left, he had a Heisman of his own from the 1981 season, when he became the second player in NCAA history to rush for 2,000 yards in a season. ("I didn't realize how important the Heisman Trophy was until everybody who came over to the house said, 'Where's the trophy?'" Allen joked during a 1989 interview on NBC.)

The Raiders took him with the No. 10 pick in the 1982 draft, somehow nabbing him as the third running back taken behind Darrin Nelson (seventh to Minnesota) and Gerald Riggs (ninth to Atlanta). The timing, as usual, proved fortuitous for Allen. The Raiders were about to begin their first season in Los Angeles, having relocated from Oakland. That meant Allen could suddenly pay back his father by taking Harold to *his* workplace.

"For 15 years, my parents were able to drive to Los Angeles to watch me play," he said, accounting for both his USC and Raiders days.

Looking back at his NFL beginnings, Allen remains forever grateful to head coach Tom Flores and so many assistants. But he holds a special place in his heart for his position coach, Ray Willsey. "He liberated me," Allen said.

As a player, Willsey was a defensive back at Cal and his post-college playing career included dabbling in a New Zealand rugby league. On the surface, he had little to offer one of the best running backs the world would ever know. But Willsey knew what talent looked like, and he nurtured it by giving his brash new artist a blank canvas and permission to color outside the lines.

"He really allowed me to play. He never said, 'Marcus, don't reverse field.' He never said, 'Don't do this, don't do that,'" Allen said. "He always said, 'Just make sure you know the down and distance.' 'Make sure you know where the first-down marker is.' He always said these magic words: 'Make sure.'"

Allen rushed for 11 touchdowns in just nine games in his debut season, winning the NFL's Offensive Rookie of the Year award. The next season, in 1983, he began a streak of three consecutive 1,000-yard seasons. Kenny King, a fellow Raiders running back, once described the sensation this way: "I throw a block and feel a brush of air go by me. It's Marcus."

The last of his 1,000-yard seasons came with a flourish as he closed out 1985 with nine consecutive 100-yard games. He captured MVP honors and led the NFL in yards from scrimmage (2,314), even during a year in which the 49ers' Roger Craig had the first 1,000-1,000 season (and 2,066 yards from scrimmage).

And for all Allen's glamour, he never minded doing the lunch-bucket tasks. In fact, he savored it. Listed at 6-foot-2, 210 pounds, he could be monstrous in pass protection.

"That boy had the mentality of an Art Shell or Gene Upshaw,"

Hayes said, referring to a pair of Raiders Hall of Fame offensive line-men. "I mean, jeez, he's taking on linebackers and blitzing free safe-ties. He wouldn't just stonewall them; he'd drive him and pancake him. That was not normal."

But the addition of star running back Bo Jackson in 1987 has-tened the end of Allen's impact with the Raiders. He missed most of the '89 season with a knee injury, wound up sinking on the depth chart, and, by 1992, he had a very public falling-out with owner Al Davis.

"I think he's tried to ruin the latter part of my career, tried to de-value me," Allen told Al Michaels of ABC in an interview that aired at halftime of a Monday night game against the Dolphins. "He's try-ing to stop me from going to the Hall of Fame. They don't want me to play."

By 1993, he was in Kansas City, where he teamed up with Lott's old buddy, Joe Montana. Allen led the AFC with 12 touchdowns that season, at age 33, to capture Comeback Player of the Year honors and earn the last of his six Pro Bowl selections.

He also scored touchdowns in all three of the Chiefs' playoff games that season. He spent five seasons in Kansas City, where his yards-per-carry average of 4.0 was just a tick off the 4.1 yards of his Raiders tenure.

Even with all of the amazing running backs who have played since Allen retired after the 1997 season, only two have more rush-ing touchdowns: Emmitt Smith (164) and LaDainian Tomlinson (145). It helped that Allen brought an artist's creativity to goal-to-go situations. He could bludgeon would-be tacklers, dart through even the narrowest gaps, and, his specialty, simply go airborne. "Marcus could certainly jump over the whole pile as if he was flying," Hayes said.

When Allen went into the Hall of Fame, he did not mention Al Davis in his speech. But it's notable that he called Chiefs owner Lamar Hunt "one of the kindest, most generous, most thoughtful men I ever met in my entire life."

But beyond his father, the biggest thanks Allen gave on that day in Canton went to the guy who used to cook up economical meals when they were two of the biggest men on USC's very big campus.

"I'm very, very fortunate to rub shoulders with a guy who I admire. He was my roommate in college; I've been knowing him a long, long time," Allen said. "I'm talking about Ronnie Lott. He is the one player that has more influence over me than anybody I've ever met and he's truly a blessing in my life."

Here's wishing that if Allen and Lott dined together that night, they found something tastier than Hamburger Helper. And, for goodness' sake, let's hope the place had valet parking.

98.
Patrick Mahomes

Patrick Mahomes won two Super Bowls, two MVP awards, and two Super Bowl MVP awards in his first six NFL seasons.

Position: Quarterback

Team: Chiefs (2017–present)

By Nate Taylor, Rustin Dodd, Jayson Jenks, and Bruce Feldman

During one Kansas City Chiefs special teams walkthrough in the summer of 2022, while other veterans joked around or began cool-down stretches, Patrick Mahomes realized he couldn't wait for the next part of his usual itinerary. With a remote control in his right hand, he gathered a few of his newest receivers—JuJu Smith-Schuster, Marquez Valdes-Scantling, and Justin Watson—

for an impromptu film session to dig into the details of plays the offense ran in practice.

"Don't be surprised if that's a back-shoulder [throw] for me," Mahomes told his teammates on one play.

Click.

"Don't be surprised if I'm coming to [receiver No.] three and not [No.] two on this."

Click.

"In this window, you can throttle down. If you get open right here, you can give me your eyes and I can still throw you the ball."

The more Mahomes spoke, the more players and coaches surrounded him. Offensive coordinator Eric Bieniemy, quarterbacks coach Matt Nagy, and receivers coach Joe Bleymaier nodded and smiled as they watched Mahomes in his newest role: a professor of head coach Andy Reid's offense.

In his three decades in the NFL, with 22 as a head coach, Reid has helped develop several star quarterbacks, including Brett Favre, Donovan McNabb, Michael Vick, and Alex Smith.

When considering all the tasks and responsibilities placed on the position, Reid knows the truth when comparing Mahomes to his previous quarterbacks.

"I'd probably tell you he's ahead," Reid said of Mahomes. "Brett Favre ran the option in high school. Pat Mahomes (threw) the football (almost) every play in college. In high school, he was doing the same type of thing.

"But on top of that, you get this kid that wants to be the best, is willing to work at it, wants you to give them information and is very intelligent. And he's a good leader. He has the full package, but you're *still* going to see growth."

Growth from the place Mahomes ended the 2022 season is both difficult and exhilarating to fathom.

In Mahomes's fifth season as an NFL starter, he passed for 5,250 yards, a career-high, and 41 touchdowns while posting a passer rating of at least 105.2 for the fourth time. The 5,000-yard season was the second of his career, aligning him with Tom Brady and Drew Brees as the only players to accomplish that feat more than once. And he won NFL Most Valuable Player honors for the second time as well.

The season closed with the Chiefs' second Super Bowl victory, both of which have come with Mahomes at quarterback. The second Super Bowl win, against the Philadelphia Eagles in a game in which the Chiefs trailed by 10 points at halftime, was another reminder that a team is never out of a game when he is in it.

"He's the toughest son of a gun you've ever met," tight end Travis Kelce said.

Mahomes had already made a compelling case for being one of the best comeback artists in NFL history before Super Bowl LVII. Prior to that game against the Eagles, he had fallen behind by 10 points in 23 different games in his career, including the playoffs, and the Chiefs' record in those contests was an astonishing 13-10. No other quarterback in NFL history had even approached a .500 record in games when trailing by 10. Mahomes is that rare.

"He's just made different," Nagy says. "We always joke about it. He was made in a lab."

The lab is a playing field, and its equipment is stored as much in Mahomes's mind as in his body.

In fourth grade, Mahomes was paired with Bobby Stroupe, his trainer and the founder and president of Athlete Performance Enhancement Center (APEC). In more than 20 years, Stroupe has trained close to 30 professional athletes, in six different sports, from when they were in elementary school. Mahomes, though, has always been a unique athlete for Stroupe.

The first principle of their training sessions was creativity. Almost every drill and workout needed to create an environment that encouraged Mahomes to use his imagination since his creativity was further developed than his fundamentals.

"I'm not a quarterback coach," Stroupe said. "Most people look at something and say, 'OK, the way this works is A to B.' Patrick's brain doesn't really work that way. He's a problem-solver, but he's open. He doesn't have any bias on how the problem is solved."

Together, they agreed on the same philosophy when Mahomes wanted to be Whitehouse (Texas) High School's quarterback for his junior season: He didn't have to be textbook or robotic to lead his team to victory.

One of the best discoveries Mahomes made on the field is that extending plays by scrambling felt similar to when he was on the basketball court as Whitehouse's point guard. Eventually, as Mahomes learned, one of his teammates would almost always get open. Before Mahomes commanded Whitehouse's Air Raid offense, the team had relied on prototypical pocket passers who could complete throws in rhythm within the structure of how the play is designed.

Stroupe worked to nurture Patrick's arm strength while refining his ability to make off-platform passes so that the techniques could feel comfortable during games. In a 2012 game against John Tyler High (Tyler, Texas), Stroupe watched Mahomes do what has become almost expected these days, a scrambling, one-footed deep pass for a long completion.

"I heard a random dad say, '*He needs to just throw the ball and quit running around!*'" Stroupe said of that night. "I thought, *You just have no idea what you just saw*. It's funny what the eyes see. Some people think something's a mess, and you see something extraordinary."

Sonny Cumbie saw it while looking for someone else.

Cumbie, then the wide receivers coach at Texas Tech University, was at the Sulphur Springs-Whitehouse game in East Texas in Sept. 2012 to check out a receiver he was recruiting for Texas Tech, Dylan Cantrell. Cumbie, who had been a record-setting QB for Texas Tech, marveled at the junior quarterback throwing the ball to Cantrell that rainy night.

The kid would scramble, make the whole defensive line miss, and then find a wide-open receiver. The kid's name was Patrick Mahomes, and he kept doing it all night along, scrambling around, breaking tackles and launching bombs. He did have a longer release, but his arm strength was as impressive as Cumbie had ever seen in a person at a high school game. Cumbie also knew Mahomes played baseball and basketball and was supposedly excellent at both, so he figured he didn't spend all of his time in the offseason working on throwing or playing quarterback. The only question Cumbie had was, why aren't more people recruiting this kid?

That year Texas A&M took a commitment from a five-star QB in Arizona, Kyle Allen. Texas was after Jerrod Heard, the nation's No. 2-ranked dual-threat quarterback. Mahomes, despite having a huge arm and wondrous escapability, seemed to have been an afterthought on the recruiting trail for other schools.

"Kliff (Kingsbury) and I were both just mesmerized by that," Cumbie said. "You watched his highlights and then you'd watch him play, and it's pretty much the same thing as you see now of him running around, making plays with all of the athleticism and arm strength, the arm angles, the ability to create."

Yet many college coaches questioned whether Mahomes had enough of a focus on football, and recruiting services tabbed him as a middle-of-the-road, three-star player. And later NFL evaluators thought his uncommon playing style—he was labeled as a high-risk gunslinger—would keep him from becoming a star.

But Mahomes has always told Stroupe he wanted to keep pushing the limits of what a quarterback can do. Behind their calculated decision, Stroupe has yet to find Mahomes's maximum capabilities, both physical and intellectual.

Mahomes, meanwhile, has always made his most passionate plans work.

"Honestly, I mean, I've thought I was going to be a professional athlete since the moment I can remember," Mahomes said. "I've always believed that if you put in the work and that you put in the time, you could be here, in the NFL or whatever professional sport that is. I'm not trying to sound cocky or too confident, but that's just how my mindset has always been.

"It's gotten me to where I'm at today."

That mindset plays out on the field for teammates, coaches, and fans to see and enjoy.

The first glimpses beyond his high school team came at a Texas Tech practice in the fall of 2014. Mahomes was a freshman. Davis Webb was the starting quarterback. Nic Shimonek was a transfer from Iowa trying to get noticed. One day Shimonek tried to complete a short slant route without looking, which caught the eye of Kingsbury, Texas Tech's head coach. "When did we start practicing this s—?" Kingsbury asked. Truth was, Kingsbury loved it. So the next practice, Mahomes started experimenting.

"Pat f—ing throws a no-look pass," Shimonek said. "I'm like, 'OK, so now you're just going to try to steal my move and like one-up me?' Literally from that point forward, he would make a third-and-7, and I would make a third-and-10 no-look pass, and then he would throw like a 25-yard missile no-look."

Mahomes does this by positioning his head in a certain direction to psychologically manipulate linebackers and safeties in the middle of the field. On some plays, Mahomes appears to stare at a defender, sometimes as long as a second, to get that player to freeze before passing the ball to an open receiver. This is studied. This is practiced.

By his junior season in 2016, Mahomes had accomplished some notable feats. He threw for 598 yards and six touchdowns in one game, lit up Oklahoma's defense for 734 yards and five touchdowns in another. Still, he had yet to attempt a no-look pass in a game.

Texas Tech was 4-5 at the time. The Red Raiders were on the road against Oklahoma State, trying hard to make a bowl game. They trailed by a touchdown with only a few minutes left. Mahomes had just taken a 9-yard sack deep in his own territory. It was third-and-20.

That was the moment he picked to try it out.

Mahomes dropped back, glanced one way, then launched a no-look strike on a deep crossing route, completing a 23-yard pass. On the sideline, Payne Sullins, a sophomore quarterback, turned to Shimonek, the Red Raiders' backup, in disbelief.

"Bro," Sullins said, "he really just did that."

The experimentation has continued in the NFL. Once, at a Chiefs practice, he forced former Chiefs center Austin Reiter to work on taking shotgun snaps on the run. "For fun," Reiter said. Another time, he made running back Damien Williams run routes with his eyes closed. "He really told me, 'Run straight, put your arms out and close your eyes,'" Williams said.

For Mahomes, there is pure joy in trying something crazy, in doing something that has never been done. "He still sees the magic in the world," former Chiefs receiver Chris Conley said.

In another practice, the offense had the ball down near the goal line. Mahomes rolled to his right and flung the ball, behind his back, to the fullback for a touchdown.

"Like a basketball," former Chiefs offensive lineman Jeff Allen said.

No one said anything; it was just Mahomes being Mahomes, having fun, trying something new. "I don't think he's going to do it in a game," Allen said. "But who knows?"

In the leadup to Mahomes's second Super Bowl with the Chiefs, Kurt Warner presented his theory on Mahomes. As a Hall of Fame quarterback, a two-time MVP winner, and a Super Bowl champion with the St. Louis Rams, Warner felt he had watched enough film of Mahomes, in just 35 NFL games at the time, to make a rather bold statement.

"I wonder if we've never seen an entire package like what we've seen with Patrick," Warner said. "He's got the freaky athleticism and arm talent, like Aaron Rodgers. He's got the ability to be accurate and play in the pocket, like other great quarterbacks. The thing for me that separates him, too, is his ability to creatively see the game, which is very unique. Only a few guys have been able to do that.

"There's the potential for him to be the most complete quarterback we may have ever seen in this game."

. . .

Chiefs general manager Brett Veach was a pro and college personnel analyst for the Chiefs in 2014 when he told Reid that Mahomes was the greatest player he'd ever seen—even though Mahomes had started all of four games in college.

Veach loved Mahomes's arm strength, the way he could turn chaos into big plays. But it was Texas Tech's 2015 bowl game against LSU that blew Veach away. Mahomes and the Red Raiders were outmatched at just about every position, yet the quarterback made play after play.

"You see toughness, competitiveness, but you also see a guy who's able to elevate those around him," Veach said later. "I think that's certainly a characteristic of a great quarterback."

After the bowl game, Veach became a full-on evangelist, preaching the good word of Patrick Lavon Mahomes II. He sent Reid clip after clip, sometimes 10 at a time, and raved about Mahomes in scouting meetings, even when the quarterback wasn't the topic of the day. Either Veach or Chris Ballard, then the Chiefs' director of football operations, attended every one of Mahomes's games in 2016.

Reid knew to trust Veach when he loved a guy, as had been the case with both LeSean McCoy and DeSean Jackson in Philadelphia. And in the clips Veach sent him, Reid saw moments when Mahomes defied football logic. He rolled right, looked right, then connected on a throw back to the left—and almost made it look sensible. "Whoa," Reid would say to himself. "That's something."

In early April 2017, Mahomes traveled to Kansas City for a predraft visit with the Chiefs. It was a pivotal moment for Veach, who was eager to see Reid's reaction. The coach had watched the quarterback's tape and been impressed, but now he got to see what Mahomes was made of up close. "He was giving every test he could, just grilling Patrick," says Mitch Holthus, the Chiefs' radio play-by-play announcer. "Andy loved him." One person described the scene in the team's practice facility that day as two football souls coming together. A smiling Reid gave Veach a thumbs up.

Later that month, with the Bills on the clock for their first-round pick, the Chiefs sent their first-round pick (No. 27), a third-round pick, and their 2018 first-round pick to the Bills for the No. 10 pick and the chance to draft Mahomes.

Since that day he has won two MVP awards, two Super Bowls, played in five AFC title games, made five Pro Bowls, thrown 50 touchdown passes in a season, and set the NFL record for total yards in a season. And yet he never stops striving, never stops thinking, never stops growing.

"The hours he spends going over the plays when he's away from the building, it's a tribute to the kid, and he's completely dedicated to it," Reid said. "He's blessed with great vision. He has a mind that is decisive with decision-making. He's blessed with this, but he also works tremendously hard at the job."

He is a father of two and a global brand, and though the end of his career is likely more than a decade away, if not longer, he has also been playing long enough that the finish line is no longer some abstract idea. In 15 or 20 years, when Mahomes looks back at his career, the first thing he wants to do is make sure he has no regrets, that he did everything he could to maximize his talent, that he made everyone around him better, that he never wasted an opportunity to win.

"We take it for granted now because he has an uncanny feel for the game," Veach said of the Chiefs. "His awareness is at such an elite level that it ties all these things together. He's able to have all these people and all this pressure and all this stimulus around him and still play with that mindset, like he's back in the backyard."

97.
Mike Ditka

Mike Ditka was one of the key forefathers of the receiving tight ends who populate the game today.

Position: Tight End
Teams: Bears (1961–1966), Eagles (1967–1968), Cowboys (1969–1972)

By Dan Pompei

Twenty-two years before he guided the famed "Monsters of the Midway" to a dominant Super Bowl victory, Mike Ditka helped make the Chicago Bears the best team in the NFL for the *first* time.

On Sunday, November 24, 1963, the nation mourned. President John F. Kennedy had been assassinated two days earlier, and his body had not yet been laid to rest. The NFL played on, though, and the Bears had to take on the Steelers before a sparse and somber gathering at Forbes Field in Pittsburgh.

It was Ditka's first time playing in front of his hometown fans. First place in the NFL West belonged to the Bears with a 9–1 record, but the Packers were a half-game behind them.

The Bears trailed 17–14 with five minutes left in the game and faced a second-and-36. Quarterback Bill Wade told Ditka to run a corner route, but Ditka asked to run a short hook instead because he was exhausted after catching six prior passes.

"The stress of everything in the game, the fact that it was my first time playing back in Pittsburgh, what the game meant, a lot of things were involved," Ditka wrote in *Ditka: An Autobiography*. "My parents and a lot of relatives were there who had never seen me play. The night before the game everybody had to be at the hotel. I had to meet everybody and say hello to everybody. It gets to be more than it should be. I was probably a little hyper."

Wade threw him a short pass. Steelers linebacker John Reger dove at Ditka and missed. Then Myron Pottios, Glenn Glass, and Clendon Thomas hit him at once, and only Ditka kept running. He made it another 30 yards, where Thomas caught up with him. Then Ditka dragged him another 5 yards to the 15-yard line, where he finally went down. At the end of the 63-yard gain, Ditka lay on the field for several seconds faceup and spread eagle.

"Greatest run I ever saw," Bears running back Rick Casares said.

Roger LeClerc's field goal three plays later tied the score, and the game ended 17–17. If not for Ditka's run, the Bears would likely have lost and finished the regular season a half-game behind the Packers in the standings—and out of the playoffs.

A little more than one month later, Ditka and the Bears beat the Giants 14–10 to win the NFL championship.

Most of the NFL saw Ditka as an intriguing linebacker prospect when he played at Pitt. As a linebacker, tight end, and punter, he had caught just 11 passes as a senior.

The Bears selected him with the fifth pick of the 1961 draft, and George Halas told him of his plans to make him a tight end—but not the kind of tight end anyone had ever seen before. Tight ends before Ditka blocked on nine of 10 plays, give or take. The vision that assistant coach Luke Johnsos had was for Ditka to be a pass catcher.

"Nobody knew what the hell a tight end was," Ditka said. "Halas and Luke Johnsos were designing a lot of plays for me. They had a great concept. In those days, you were covered by a linebacker or safety, and they weren't cover guys. You could beat them."

In Ditka's first NFL season, he caught 56 passes for 1,076 yards—an average of 19.2 yards per catch. He also had 12 touchdown catches, tied for second most in the NFL.

He was different in many ways, and it was evident from his first game when Ditka had a problem with the effort level of his teammate Ted Karras. "Move your fat ass," Ditka said to the guard, according to the *Gary Post-Tribune*. It eventually led to a sideline brawl.

As for opponents, Ditka was even less respectful. After Packers middle linebacker Ray Nitschke knocked Ditka unconscious in a preseason game, Ditka vowed revenge. Ditka's blindside block in a subsequent regular-season game sent Nitschke to the locker room. "It didn't bother me one bit that he got hurt," Ditka said.

Bears defensive end Ed O'Bradovich said Ditka "put the fear of God" in linebackers and defensive backs. And even some fans. When one spectator, who apparently had been trying to quench an insatiable thirst, ran onto the field at the Los Angeles Coliseum in 1966, Ditka threw a right cross that put him on his back.

"He was the meanest, toughest rascal in the league, and I've got the dent in my head to prove it," Steelers safety Clendon Thomas told the *Pittsburgh Press*. "Anytime you came near Ditka, you had to expect forearms and fists. You came away bruised. He was mean, but he was also as talented as anyone I ever lined up against."

In *Ditka: Monster of the Midway*, Bears center Mike Pyle called him "the most intense, motivated football player I had ever seen." Casares said you had to kill him to get him down. "He was one of the first offensive intimidators," Bears receiver Johnny Morris said. "He would go after people like Ray Nitschke. He was the aggressor.

There were so many times I'd see him throw a block, then immediately roll over and go for a second block. Most players, even great ones, are satisfied after they do their job. Not him. He was never satisfied."

Ditka played the way he did because he loved the game. He loved it because it gave him an identity and fame and a living, sure. But he loved it because he found every aspect of it exhilarating—the anticipation and angst, the conflict and collisions, the speed and strategy, the pain and precision, the jolts and jubilation. He once said he played every game like it was his last, a statement no one who ever saw him put his hand in the dirt would take issue with.

"Those 60 minutes when I played, those were special," Ditka said, his eyes still glinting decades later. "I enjoyed the heck out of that. Wrigley Field, I enjoyed the mud, the slop, people throwing beer on us when we lost going into the locker room. It was all good stuff. You turn around, give them a piece of your mind."

At his finest, he was as punishing a two-way tight end that ever lived. He once scored four touchdowns in a game against the Rams in 1963. He caught 13 passes in another, versus Washington one season later. He dislocated his shoulder and wore a harness during the 1964 season, but he still caught 75 passes—more than any other player in the league besides his teammate Johnny Morris.

His career did not follow the typical arc, though. His most productive season statistically was his first. In 1965, at the age of 26, Ditka started to decline. He cracked his arch in a scrimmage but refused to miss any time. That led to altering his gait, which led to hamstring, knee, and hip issues.

Ditka also enjoyed his success a little too much, questioned authority, and flirted with the AFL's Houston Oilers. He subsequently fell out of favor with Halas, who traded him to the Eagles in 1967 for quarterback Jack Concannon.

His two years in Philadelphia were the worst of his career. "If there's such a thing as purgatory on earth, I was there," Ditka wrote in his autobiography. Ditka clashed with coach and general manager Joe Kuharich, continued to have injury issues, and admittedly lost his way. He wrote, "I was about trying to kill myself with the drinking."

Ditka thought he might be finished after the 1968 season when he received a call from Tom Landry. The Cowboys were trading for him and giving him one more chance.

"I was told I'd be a backup, and that hurt," Ditka said. "And that's what I was because I didn't do all I could that first year. But the next year, I started. I worked harder than anyone else in the offseason. Nobody ever worked harder. I ran in my bare feet to toughen my bad foot . . . I could have done anything a 21-year-old kid could do, and I was 30. I dropped my weight 21 pounds until everything was muscle."

Ditka put his career and life back on track in Dallas with Landry's guidance. He was blocking more and catching less, but that was OK because he could block like a third offensive tackle. In his book *Pro Football's 100 Greatest Players*, Hall of Fame coach George Allen said Ditka "seldom missed" as a blocker. He also wrote, "He modeled the tight end position, really, and it hasn't changed much. You just couldn't do much more with it than Ditka did."

The 1971 Cowboys were a team of stars—Roger Staubach threw passes to Bob Hayes and Lance Alworth and was protected by Rayfield Wright and Forrest Gregg. Their Doomsday Defense was led by Herb Adderley, Cliff Harris, Bob Lilly, and Mel Renfro. But as the Cowboys came down the stretch of the 1971 season, it was Ditka who was at the forefront of their charge.

"He was our spiritual leader," Cowboys linebacker Lee Roy Jordan said. "He got across the urgency of competing on every play, how every play was critical." The final touchdown of Super Bowl VI was a 7-yard pass from Staubach to Ditka on a crossing route and put away a 24–3 Cowboys victory.

Ditka was a critical component of championship teams early in his career and late, and he did it in two completely different ways. Like much of America, Ditka evolved from the early 1960s to the early 1970s. He went from being an open-field menace with a crew cut and single-bar face mask to a gritty role player with long hair, thick sideburns that extended past his ear lobes, and a bushy mustache. What didn't change was his ability to set the tone, which in some ways was as significant as his catching and blocking.

Ditka learned bluntness from Halas, and then he learned calm from Landry, both of which were useful when Halas hired him to coach the Bears in 1982. Because of the way he coached, the success he had, and what he stood for, Ditka the coach is celebrated more than Ditka the player.

But he shouldn't be.

Richie Petitbon played in the NFL for 14 years, including six as Ditka's teammate in Chicago, and coached for another 16. "The best player I've ever been around," he said, "was Mike Ditka."

96.
Paul Warfield

Paul Warfield's 20.1 yards per reception ranks No. 1
all time among players with at least 275 career catches.

Position: Wide Receiver
Teams: Browns (1964–1969), Dolphins (1970–1974), Southmen/WFL (1975),
Browns (1976–1977)

By Joseph Person

There's a life-sized statue of Paul Warfield outside his old high school stadium in Warren, Ohio. The bronze statue is flanked by two granite panels listing Warfield's accomplishments. Those have a heavy Ohio flavor, beginning with his days at Warren G. Harding High through Ohio State and his home-state Cleveland Browns.

In truth, they probably could have used a third panel to chronicle all the highlights of one of the NFL's great wide receivers.

Warfield took a couple of southern detours along the way, including three Super Bowl appearances (and two victories) with the Miami Dolphins and a brief stop in Memphis in the failed World Football League. But all roads led back to Ohio, where Warfield finished his career with the Browns and where he has two permanent bronze tributes—the statue in Warren and a bust in Canton at the Pro Football Hall of Fame.

"He was," said Gil Brandt, the Dallas Cowboys' longtime personnel director, "as good as anybody that's ever come into the NFL."

Warfield is a Hall of Famer, a Super Bowl champion, and a home-state hero. But for Brandt, Warfield will always be the one that got away.

Warfield was a "60-minute man" at Ohio State, where he played both ways as a running back and a cornerback. He also competed for the Buckeyes' track team, finishing second in the long jump at the NCAA championships as a sophomore.

Halfway through Warfield's senior season, legendary Ohio State head coach Woody Hayes moved Warfield to end. Warfield caught 22 passes for 266 yards and three touchdowns in 1963 while playing in a Buckeyes' offense that still relied heavily on the running game.

"Woody's pass offense was far from being refined," Brandt said. "They ran an eight-yard square out and a six-yard square in."

That was probably the reason most NFL and AFL teams who sent scouts to Columbus were interested in Warfield as a defensive back. Not Brandt, who asked Hayes if he could come to practice and watch Warfield go through receiver drills.

Hayes instead wanted Brandt to look at tight end Greg Lashutka, who would later become Columbus's mayor. "They throw [Lashutka] about four passes and he drops about two," Brandt said.

Brandt thought Warfield's size (6 feet, 188 pounds) and speed would play well at wide receiver and told Warfield the Cowboys were going to draft him in the first round.

"We drafted on a Monday morning from Chicago. We were going

to use him as a wide receiver. We had a deal cut," Brandt said. "On Monday morning, coach [Tom] Landry said to me: 'You're not gonna be very happy with me. We've just traded our first choice to Pittsburgh for [wideout] Buddy Dial.' And I said, 'Well, I'm sorry to hear that because I thought Paul was going to be a really great player.'"

Two days after the Bills selected Warfield in the fourth round of the AFL draft, the NFL's Browns took him with the 11th pick and brought him and the other draft picks in a couple of months later for what was the NFL's first-ever minicamp. Warfield lined up at both receiver and cornerback during the one-day minicamp and wasn't sure which would be his primary position until he arrived at Cleveland's training camp that summer.

As Warfield was unloading his car, he was summoned to the coaches' offices, where head coach Blanton Collier told Warfield he was a wide receiver. Warfield spent the next month learning the position in a crash course with the late Browns wideout Ray Renfro, who was then the team's receivers coach.

"He was to be my instructor, teacher, or guru, if you will," Warfield recalled. "Over a period of four weeks roughly, he taught me fundamentally the art of pass-pattern execution [and] at that point, really made me as a wide receiver. . . .

"I improved on a few things. But from a fundamental standpoint and concept, I never varied one iota for the most part from what Ray Renfro taught me."

Clearly, it stuck.

As a rookie, Warfield caught a career-high 52 passes in an offense built around running back Jim Brown, whom Warfield called the greatest runner in NFL history. With Brown gaining nearly 1,500 yards on the ground and Warfield totaling 920 through the air (with nine touchdowns), the Browns rolled to the 1964 championship game. There they blanked the Colts, 27–0.

After an injury limited him to one game in 1965, Warfield returned and had four consecutive seasons with at least 700 receiving yards. The stretch included the only 1,000-yard season of his career in 1968, when he led the league with 12 touchdown catches.

The Browns were winning. Warfield was playing for his child-hood team in a city 50 miles northwest of his hometown. Life was good.

And then Browns owner Art Modell traded him to Miami.

"It was a surprise. I had just completed my sixth year and I was comfortable," Warfield said. "I was being traded from a legitimate, contending and championship team—that I played with in '64—of the National Football League, to an expansion team out of the American Football League, which at that point was not considered to be quite on par."

To acquire Warfield, the Dolphins sent Cleveland the No. 3 pick in the 1970 draft, which the Browns used to select Purdue quarterback Mike Phipps.

In seven seasons with the Browns, Phipps finished with two times as many interceptions (80) as touchdowns (40) before being traded to the Bears in 1977 for first- and fourth-round picks. Meanwhile, Warfield cemented his place as one of the game's greatest players with five consecutive Pro Bowl berths and two All-Pro selections in Miami.

Despite playing in a run-dominant offense that featured a trio of talented backs in Larry Csonka, Mercury Morris, and Jim Kiick, Warfield was quarterback Bob Griese's go-to receiver when Dolphins coach Don Shula decided to air it out.

"We were a running team. If he'd been on one of these other teams that threw the ball 40, 45 times a game, his stats would have been way up there," Griese recalled. "And Warfield never complained about that. He was all-in for that. So, you talk about a real team guy that had all of the abilities to get open and catch the ball and run."

When Warfield would run routes for Griese after practice, he would adjust his patterns as if he was facing double coverage—"because he never got single coverage," Griese said.

According to Griese, Warfield's blocking ability was an oft-overlooked part of his game.

"He wouldn't go for the cheap shots, blindside," Griese said. "He'd hit everybody up around their shoulders. And when he hit you, you went down. You ask a bunch of defensive backs, a bunch of safeties, about who was the best blocking wide receiver, and I'm sure they would say Warfield during that era when he played."

The Dolphins made the first of three consecutive Super Bowl appearances after the 1971 regular season and picked up a new fan along the way. As the Dolphins were preparing to face Dallas in Super Bowl VI at Tulane Stadium in New Orleans, President Richard Nixon—who had a compound in Key Biscayne, Florida—reportedly called Shula to suggest he call a down-and-in for Warfield against the Cowboys.

"I said, 'Yeah, that's a good idea,'" the late Shula told Yahoo Sports in 2013.

"He was referring to that slant-in pattern," Warfield said, "and suggesting to Don Shula—which we would have utilized anyway—that we emphasize that pattern."

Griese threw the slant to Warfield on the Dolphins' eighth offensive play, but it was knocked down by Mel Renfro for an incompletion. Dallas would go on to win, 24–3.

But Miami won back-to-back titles beginning in 1972, which Warfield pointed to as his most memorable season, despite his modest, 29-catch total. No wonder: the Dolphins made history with an undefeated season in which they rushed for a then-record 2,960 yards and attempted only 259 passes, which ranked near the bottom of the league statistically.

Miami turned to backup quarterback Earl Morrall for nine games in '72 after Griese was injured. Still, Warfield averaged 20.9 yards a catch and made the Pro Bowl.

Following the third Super Bowl, Warfield, Csonka, and Kiick left Miami for what was then considered big money in the WFL. (Warfield's deal was worth $220,000, according to the *Los Angeles Times*.) All three joined the Memphis Southmen but didn't make it through one season before the league folded.

Warfield returned to Cleveland, retiring at 35 following the 1977 season, his 13th in the NFL. Though his receiving numbers might look paltry in today's pass-happy NFL, Warfield's 20.1 yards-per-catch average ranks among the best in league history. And Brandt believes he would have done even more in Dallas.

"He had unbelievable quickness, unbelievable speed. He had hands that were great," Brandt said. "He would've caught 75 passes for us a year if we would've gotten him."

Warfield, a first-ballot Hall of Fame inductee in 1983, spent six years as an adviser in the Browns' front office before stepping down in 2010. Warfield now lives in Rancho Mirage, California, where he golfs and marvels at the modern NFL offenses.

"The style of play is much, much different," he said. "Much more passing."

Asked about his football legacy, Warfield mentioned how "very fortunate" he was to have played in the NFL with two successful organizations. According to Griese, that humility was present from the moment Warfield showed up in Miami.

"He was a team guy from the get-go," Griese said. "He was a very intelligent guy. He was always a positive guy in the locker room. You know, you run into some of these guys that are not that way. They want the ball all the time and they say, 'Why didn't you throw it to me that time?' or 'I was open this time.' Paul never did that. He was a good guy from the get-go."

95.
Jim Otto

Jim Otto played 15 consecutive seasons as the Raiders' center and closed his career on a streak of 210 consecutive games played.

Position: Center
Team: Raiders (1960–1974)

By Vic Tafur

The story of the Oakland Raiders can't be told without Jim Otto. From his center position, the undersized Otto pushed and led the franchise by example, leaving a trail of sweat and tears.

And a lot of blood.

"I watched him bleed," linebacker Phil Villapiano said. "I mean, every fucking game. Whatever helmet he had on certainly didn't work, because it would come down and smash on top of his nose.

He'd be bleeding every single game. And players on the other team would be like, 'What the fuck is with this guy?!'

"I couldn't believe how much of a beating he took. Jim Otto just out-toughed everybody."

Otto was the only starting center the Raiders ever had from 1960 through 1974, laying his body on the line again and again. He played with every injury imaginable, and needed a muscle relaxant before games just so he could bend over and hike the ball.

The Wausau, Wisconsin, native played in each of his team's 140 regular-season games in the AFL's 10-year history and was a first-team all-league center every season. He was named All-NFL in 1970 and 1971 following the merger, and when he retired, he had started in 210 straight regular-season games.

And Otto led.

Oakland won seven divisional championships from 1967 through 1974.

"If I missed a tackle, I would rather come off the field and have John Madden berate me than look into Jim Otto's eyes," Villapiano said. "Jim Otto demanded perfection from everybody all the time. That's what I loved about him so much."

The first four years of the linebacker's career were Otto's last.

"If I want to be a Raider, I have to be like Jim Otto," Villapiano said. "I have to play like him. I can't fuck up, because Jim Otto doesn't fuck up. Jim Otto will play through pain, injuries ... through anything. That's what he taught me.

"Years later, I became one of the older guys pushing the younger guys and I stopped myself. 'How did I learn this stuff?' I learned it from Jim Otto."

Otto was inducted into the Pro Football Hall of Fame in 1980, having played for the Raiders his entire career. He was a perfect player for Al Davis. While the Raiders owner is famed for saying "Just Win, Baby," Otto told me the first time I met him a dozen years ago, "You show me a good loser, and I will show you a loser."

Otto always pushed himself, from lifting weights his rookie year and putting on 20 pounds to taking his leadership role seriously enough that it meant never coming off the field. When Davis joined the Raiders after previously being an assistant coach with the Chargers, he told Otto how much of a lift it gave the Chargers when Otto left the game with an injury. Otto nodded and made sure it never happened again.

"Pain is a state of mind," Otto told me in 2010.

The 6-foot-2, 230-pound Otto paid a price, no doubt. He has had 74 surgeries, including 28 on his knees, and his lower right leg had to be amputated in 2007. He also had chronic neck pain throughout his career and sustained at least 35 concussions, by his count.

In the 2012 book *The Pain of Glory*, written with longtime *Oakland Tribune* columnist Dave Newhouse, Otto detailed three near-death infections from knee replacement surgeries. He has trouble getting out of bed every day but says, unlike other players have done with their teams, he would never sue the Raiders for more medical help.

"I'm not a wimp-out," he wrote in his book. "Nobody told me I had to play every week. . . . I take responsibility for everything that happened to my body."

Otto said he would have played football for a pat on the back, a bottle of Budweiser, and a sandwich after the game.

"I think about the injuries and I think about all the things I've gone through in my life," Otto told reporters in 2016. "I'm very happy that I'm here. I'm very happy I did what I did. That's what I wanted to do as a little boy in Wausau. I wanted to be a football player like Elroy 'Crazylegs' Hirsch, and that's what I went out to be.

"There were times right now that I'm sore. It gets you thinking you know, did I do right, did I do wrong? Where did I go wrong? And you know, you say a prayer and it all comes back to me: Jim, you did what you wanted to do."

Otto hit opponents before they could hit him, and never stayed down when they did get him.

"Be the best that you can be," Otto wrote in his book. "I love the Raiders and cherished my time there. It was my favorite part of life."

And while Otto didn't win a Super Bowl ring himself, he definitely set the example for younger players, plowing a path for a team that went on to win three Super Bowls in the 10 years after he retired.

"He was tough and he never stopped," Villapiano said. "He could be blocking Joe Greene and he wouldn't care. He would decide before the game that Joe Greene wasn't going to be a factor today, and that's the way it was. I loved . . . I loved Jim's toughness and it carried over to the whole team and we all played like that."

In many ways, it carried over to the entire league, and Otto remains an icon from the NFL's grittier days when players made $300 a game.

"No football player has given more of himself, physically, to the autumn game than Jim Otto," Newhouse said. "He has more replacement parts to his anatomy than any other NFL player, including replacement parts on top of replacement parts. He is half-human, half-machinery."

94.
Steve Van Buren

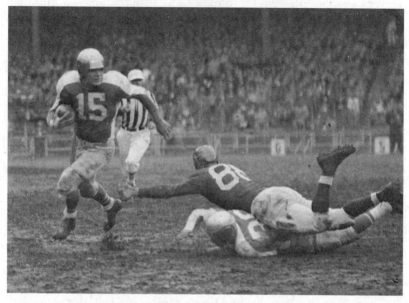

Steve Van Buren transformed the Eagles' fortunes upon his arrival and led the NFL in rushing, scoring, and kickoff returns in 1945.

Position: Running Back
Team: Eagles (1944–1951)

By Zach Berman

Steve Van Buren greeted football immortality with four sentences. He entered the Pro Football Hall of Fame in September 1965, and his presenter—the person who gives a speech introducing a new member at their induction ceremony—spoke longer than he did.

Thank you, Clarke Hinkle, I'm certainly glad to have broken your record. Since you people can't hear too good and I'm not too good a speaker, I won't say much, but it's a great honor to be here. The two days I've spent in Canton will certainly bring me back every year from now on. Thank you very much.

"I'm surprised you got four sentences," said Ray Didinger, the Hall of Fame writer who wrote *The Eagles Encyclopedia* and also worked at NFL Films. "I'm surprised it wasn't Joe Pesci's 'Thank you,' and then sit down."

Van Buren played from 1944 to 1951 and retired as the NFL's all-time leading rusher. He led the league in rushing four times. He won two NFL championships with a Philadelphia Eagles franchise that had never finished better than fourth before his arrival. Yet Van Buren was just as well known for his understated personality.

When Didinger would visit Van Buren in his later years, Van Buren lived in a spartan apartment in Northeast Philadelphia with his cat. There were no vestiges of his greatness, no trophies or memorabilia. He kept photos of his grandchildren, but you wouldn't know he scored the game-winning touchdown in the 1948 championship game, a play that NFL.com ranked as one of the hundred best in league history.

As the legend now goes, Van Buren almost missed his most memorable moment.

The Eagles were scheduled to host the Chicago Cardinals at Shibe Park, later known as Connie Mack Stadium, at 21st Street and Lehigh Avenue in North Philadelphia. A blizzard blanketed the region. Van Buren woke up in his Drexel Hill home, peered out the window, figured the game wouldn't be played, and returned to bed. Coach Greasy Neale called to check on the team's top player. Van Buren said to look outside—there was no way they were going to play.

Still, Neale advised Van Buren to come to the stadium. Van Buren couldn't pull his car out of the driveway, so he turned to public transit. He walked to the bus stop to take the Red Arrow to 69th Street, where he took the Market Street "EL" train to City Hall. He transferred to the Broad Street subway line, heading north to Lehigh Avenue. He then walked eight blocks to the stadium.

The players also needed to help clear the field because so much snow had accumulated on the tarps that the grounds crew was overburdened, delaying the first televised championship.

"And then [Van Buren] scores the winning touchdown and takes public transit home," Didinger said. "There's pro football in 1948."

Van Buren's was the only touchdown that day. The game had been scoreless during an afternoon slog. The yard markers weren't visible because of all the snow. Before the game, captains and coaches consulted referees and agreed they wouldn't dispute where the ball was marked. The footage more closely resembles a backyard game during a blizzard than a Super Bowl. Van Buren broke the tie in the fourth quarter when he rushed five yards around the right tackle into the end zone. He finished with 98 of the team's 232 total yards that day, and teammates carried him off the field on their shoulders.

It might seem like a dose of mythmaking for the player who scored the only touchdown to almost miss the game and need to take the bus to the train to the subway and then walk through a blizzard, like a grandfather claiming to walk miles uphill to school both ways. Didinger said for a different player, that charge might have validity. Not Van Buren.

"He was the most unassuming, naturally humble superstar—I mean true, true superstar—I've ever been around," said Didinger, who first learned of Van Buren's championship journey during an interview in the 1980s. "Because he just didn't view himself that way. . . . It wasn't like some sort of fake humility or anything. He genuinely just said, 'Yeah, I'm a football player.' And whenever you talk to him—and I interviewed him a lot over the years—the hardest thing to do was to get him to talk about himself. He would talk a lot about how great the team was, you know, and how great the line was."

Perhaps humility had something to do with his humble beginnings. According to his page on profootballhof.com, Van Buren was born in Honduras and orphaned at a very early age, ending up living with his grandparents. His bio goes on to say he failed to make his high school team as a 125-pound sophomore, but eventually blossomed as a senior and went on to star at Louisiana State.

When photographers came to practice to take photos of Van Buren, he would never pose alone. He called over Pete Pihos or Al Wistert or Bucko Kilroy, as Pihos once told Didinger. When Didinger wrote *The Eagles Encyclopedia*, he researched countless photographers. Sure enough, Pihos's claim was correct. The only photos found of Van Buren alone were team head shots and photographs from the team. Van Buren passed along any gift certificates he might be given to teammates and avoided the public limelight.

The Eagles won the championship again in 1949 when Van Buren rushed for 196 yards in a 14–0 win over the Los Angeles Rams at the Los Angeles Coliseum. Iconic actor Clark Gable visited the Eagles locker room after the game and approached Van Buren. Gable, who was dubbed "The King of Hollywood," told Van Buren he was the greatest athlete he had ever seen. Van Buren later turned to teammate George Savitsky and asked to learn the identity of the man with the compliment.

"Steve, you ought to get out more," said Savitsky, as explained in Didinger's *The New Eagles Encyclopedia*.

"He was very comfortable in his own skin," Didinger said. "He was proud of what he accomplished. He was not unaware of what he accomplished and he was certainly not unaware of his place in football history, but he just didn't feel he needed to talk about it. He just kind of let the achievements stand for itself."

Those achievements were also significant because of the era in which he played. He was the best running back when the game was built around rushing. He often ran through seven- and eight-man defensive fronts.

When measured against his contemporaries, the production illustrates why Van Buren was so esteemed. He played from 1944 to 1951—an eight-year period during which Van Buren had three of the eight best single-season rushing performances. Wistert told Didinger that the Eagles were a good team during that era, but "Van Buren made us great."

"Watch those old films and you know that Steve Van Buren was something special," former Eagles coach Andy Reid said upon Van Buren's death in 2012. "He was special in person, too, humble about his own accomplishments and encouraging to others."

Didinger was recently asked how Van Buren would have reacted if he could be told that he was ranked among the NFL's top 100 players in 2021.

"Surprised—and he would probably dispute it," Didinger said.

When Didinger interviewed Van Buren in the 1980s about Wilbert Montgomery approaching his Eagles records, Van Buren spoke about how he wanted Montgomery to break the records and said Montgomery was a better player. He suggested that he watched the old footage and saw how slow he was—an opinion that Didinger said isn't accurate. Van Buren used to race with the other running backs at Eagles training camp. One of the players on the team was Clyde Scott, who won a silver medal in the 110 hurdles at the 1948 Olympics. If they ran 100 yards, Scott would win. But if they raced 50 yards, Van Buren would win.

"By today's standards of how we judge players, that everything's on the 40-yard dash, he was faster than an Olympian," Didinger said.

LeSean McCoy later rewrote the franchise's record books, becoming the Eagles' all-time leading rusher and setting the single-season record. That hasn't sullied Van Buren's standing in Eagles history. Didinger attended a 90th birthday party for Van Buren in 2011 at a nursing home in Lancaster, Pennsylvania. Some of the great players in Eagles history were in attendance, including Chuck Bednarik. Van Buren and Bednarik sat next to each other eating birthday cake. Bednarik, known as "Concrete Charlie," wasn't known for deferring to others.

He pointed to Van Buren and said: "You were the greatest Eagle."

Van Buren pointed back to Bednarik and insisted Bednarik was the greatest. They went back and forth, but it said something that the two Hall of Famers held each other in such high esteem.

Despite what Van Buren said at his enshrinement, he didn't make annual trips to Canton. In 2000, the Pro Football Hall of Fame made an effort to bring all the living Hall of Famers to the enshrinement weekend. Van Buren didn't think he needed to make the trip, suggesting nobody would remember him. His family encouraged him to go. Didinger was in the room for a reception at the hotel on the first night. It was full of the greatest players who ever played. Van Buren walked in, and eyes turned toward the door.

"All these guys descend on him, shaking his hand and patting him on the back," Didinger said. "To see all these guys, some of whom were his contemporaries . . . but a lot of them . . . never met him before and knew who he was and saw the way the older guys responded to him. They just surrounded him and made a big deal of it."

For Didinger, the moment represented Van Buren's career. Van Buren tried shunning attention he had nonetheless earned.

93.
Elroy "Crazylegs" Hirsch

Elroy Hirsch (40) was a revelation as a pass catcher
when it was still a relatively small part of the game.

Position: Wide Receiver/Running Back
Teams: Rockets (1946–1948), Rams (1949–1957)

By Bob Kravitz

In 1942, Elroy Hirsch was playing for the University of Wisconsin, and after a game in which he scored multiple touchdowns against the Great Lakes Naval Station team, *Chicago Daily News* writer Francis Powers described his running style:

"His crazy legs were gyrating in six different directions, all at the same time; he looked like a demented duck," he wrote of Hirsch's unusual gait.

And so, the name "Crazylegs" was born.

Hirsch loved the nickname. Beat Elroy, right? Everybody referred to him as "Legs" thereafter. It was that unique running style, his soft hands, his speed and elusiveness that turned the halfback-turned-flanker into one of the 100 greatest NFL players. He was a man before his time who put up monstrous receiving numbers when the NFL was just beginning to transition from 3-yards-and-a-cloud-of-dust to a more wide-open game that featured the forward pass.

He was Tyreek Hill before Tyreek Hill.

Cheetah, meet Crazylegs.

"I wobble," Hirsch said during his time with the Los Angeles Rams from 1949 to 1957. "I picked it up as a kid. I love to run. I used to run home from the movies at night and raced my shadow under the streetlight. They thought I was crazy."

Hirsch's father, Otto, once said, "We lived two miles from school. Elroy ran to school and back, skipping and crisscrossing his legs in the cement blocks of the sidewalks. He said it would make him shiftier."

Dan Daly, a football historian and author of *The National Forgotten League*, called him "the embodiment of swivel-hipness. When he was coming at you, you didn't know which way he was going to go, and he did it with great speed. He was a great runner after he caught the ball. Just watch the highlights from that era and see how well he tracked the deep ball. Norm Van Brocklin, in particular, loved to throw deep. He would adjust to the ball in flight so well, even when he had a guy on his hip, he could make the catch with extended arms, and the first few steps, he was off and nobody was going to catch him. Most of the good ones will slow up just a little bit to catch the ball, but he never did."

Hirsch, a native of Wausau, Wisconsin, played for both Wisconsin and Michigan while in college, leading both teams to No. 3 national rankings. He then served in the Marine Corps from 1944 to 1946 before getting drafted by the NFL, choosing instead to sign with the spectacularly awful Chicago Rockets of the AAFC; Hirsch called signing there the worst mistake of his professional life. He escaped from Chicago, then joined the NFL's Los Angeles Rams, where the blond, crew-cut player became a star in a town filled with stars. He was a speedy, elusive pass catcher with Hollywood good looks that eventually led him to some movie roles, including the classics *Crazylegs, Zero Hour!* and *Unchained*.

Said Daly: "I'll say this: He was a better actor than Frank Gifford."

The numbers he put up were extraordinary, and not just within the context of the 1950s NFL.

In 1951, his best year and one of the greatest years ever produced by a wide receiver, he led the Rams to the NFL title with 1,495 receiving yards, 17 touchdowns (tying Don Hutson's mark in 1942, a mark that lasted 20 years), and amassed 124.6 receiving yards per game, a mark that stood for years until the game opened up after the NFL-AFL merger. In that 1951 season opener, Van Brocklin threw for 554 yards, including 172 yards and four touchdowns to Hirsch. He averaged 51.2 yards per reception on his 17 touchdowns. He was surrounded by talent, including two elite quarterbacks, Van Brocklin and Bob Waterfield, and receiver Tom Fears, all of whom are in the Pro Football Hall of Fame along with Hirsch.

He finished his career with 387 receptions for 7,029 yards and 60 touchdowns, leading to this comment from Michael MacCambridge, author of *America's Game*: "We talk today about yards after the catch, but he would get acres of yards after the catch because he was so elusive in the open field. . . . He could adjust and wind up catching the ball over his shoulder in stride about as well as anyone. If you take a look at the offensive stats in pro football then, he was not just the best in the league, he was head and shoulders above his competition. . . . He was the first true flanker deep threat."

Daly notes that Hirsch's arrival in pro football coincided with teams transitioning from the single wing to the T formation, where a fullback lines up behind the center and quarterback with a halfback on either side. Partly because of that, Hirsch transitioned from his college position of halfback to flanker when he joined the Rams in 1949, and it was a fortuitous period for such a change. Before then, receivers had been utilized for blocking and playing defensive end on the other side of the ball, but the lineup flexibility fostered by the T formation allowed players of Hirsch's skill set and speed to set up wide and play in open space.

"The big change going on in the passing game back then was that receivers were becoming faster, more dangerous threats," Daly said. "Hirsch liked it better than being in motion because it gave him a chance to read the defense before the snap and he could see how they were trying to cover him."

This was a time when the league's offenses were opening up, throwing the ball, scoring big numbers. In 1948, the Eagles, Cardinals, and Bears all averaged more than 30 points per game. It was a time of transition to a new style of game—thanks, largely, to Paul Brown and George Halas—and Hirsch was central to that transition. In a sport that was evolving offensively, Hirsch became a revolutionary figure and was the preeminent pass-catching threat in the league.

Those who saw him play describe him as Willie Mays–like with his ability to adjust to the ball in the air. If you look at the stats, he was head and shoulders above the rest. The 1950s Rams would be the forerunners to the great offenses that would come later, the Air Coryell Chargers and St. Louis's Greatest Show on Turf.

After retirement, he starred in a couple of movies, then became Rams general manager from 1960 to 1969 and was Wisconsin's athletic director from 1969 to 1987. He was inducted into the Hall of Fame in 1967 and the College Football Hall of Fame in 1974. He is also a member of the NFL's 1950s All-Decade team. He passed away at age 80 in 2004.

"There was a growing number of receivers putting up big numbers at that time," Daly said, "but Crazylegs was head and shoulders above the rest. At a time when the game was evolving into more of a passing game, he was far and away the best receiver in the game."

92.
Lenny Moore

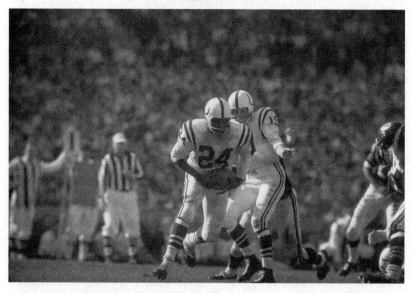

Lenny Moore (24) had a versatility that allowed coaches to maximize their offenses.

Position: Wide Receiver/Running Back
Team: Colts (1956–1967)

By Joseph Person

Watching Lenny Moore's highlights from early in his career—characterized by the black-and-white footage, though he played into the color-TV era—you're struck by this: for every shot of Moore slicing through the defense after taking a handoff in the backfield, there's another of the Baltimore Colts great lined up wide, catching a pass from Johnny Unitas and darting downfield for a big play.

Moore was the NFL's quintessential, dual-threat running back before anyone used that term. But Moore, the former Penn State star and a Pro Football Hall of Famer, was the prototype for the likes of Marcus Allen, Roger Craig, LaDainian Tomlinson, Marshall Faulk, Christian McCaffrey, and every other versatile back who followed him.

"There was a time in the NFL when there wasn't a whole lot of passing going on," said former Colts left tackle Bob Vogel, who played with Moore for five seasons in Baltimore. "It was like college football with a lot of runs, a lot of power runners. And when you found someone who could do both, you put the defense in a real bind."

Moore grew up in Reading, Pennsylvania, and didn't go far for college, starring at Penn State from 1953 to 1955 when Joe Paterno was an assistant coach and the Nittany Lions employed a traditional offense. Moore caught just 13 passes in three seasons at Penn State, but averaged 88 rushing yards a game.

The Colts drafted Moore with the No. 9 pick in 1956, the same year they picked up a 23-year-old free-agent quarterback named John Unitas on a one-year deal worth $7,000, as Peter King pointed out. Though Unitas needed a season to establish himself, Moore hit the ground running, winning Rookie of the Year honors after averaging a league-leading 7.5 yards per carry.

Starting in 1957, Moore caught at least 40 passes for five consecutive seasons as he and Unitas thrived in Weeb Ewbank's passing offense. As a combination halfback/flanker, in the parlance of the times, Moore became a key piece of the Colts' championship teams of 1958 and '59.

Moore caught six passes for 101 yards in the Colts' overtime victory against the Giants in the 1958 championship, played at Yankee Stadium and dubbed "the Greatest Game Ever Played." Moore pulled down three passes for 126 yards and a touchdown when the Colts again beat the Giants in a championship game rematch the following year.

Asked about the '58 championship game, Moore said, "Well, we won. Yeah, the beautiful thing was we won."

Vogel, the offensive tackle from Ohio State, said watching Moore with the football was a beautiful thing . . . provided you were on his team.

"The dynamism that he brought was not only could he break your back as a running back, but then he would come out of the backfield on the pass play with John Unitas throwing the ball and getting it into Lenny's hands," Vogel said. "And you give him any kind of space between him and the defensive back, and it was pretty much decided that the defensive back better pray well because he ain't gonna catch him."

From 1963 to 1965, Moore scored touchdowns in an NFL-record 18 consecutive games, a mark that Tomlinson tied in 2005. Moore is the only NFL player with at least 40 touchdowns both rushing and receiving.

Bill Curry, the former Georgia Tech and Alabama coach, played with Moore for one year in Baltimore in 1967, Moore's final season. So most of Curry's memories of Moore came from watching him on TV.

"You could see a guy that could line up and run the ball inside with power and speed, and then the next thing you know you look out there and he's split out. And you've got a linebacker trying to cover him. Good luck," Curry said. "I remember catches that he made that were just unbelievable. He'd catch the top half of the ball or something, and then run in the end zone. Just those other-worldly plays."

Moore was a five-time All-Pro and was named the league MVP by the Newspaper Enterprise Association in 1964 when he led the NFL with 19 rushing touchdowns (Unitas was the Associated Press MVP that year).

Moore played during a time of racial unrest in the United States and was a victim of discrimination in Baltimore.

In his 2005 autobiography, *All Things Being Equal*, Moore wrote about a banquet at an all-White country club, where as a Black man he was told to use the back entrance, according to the *Baltimore Sun*.

"Being naïve and still riding high on fan adulation after the [1958] championship game, I thought, 'Maybe the VIPs use a special entrance,'" Moore said in the autobiography. "Then it dawned on me that White people probably expected a Black person at the country club to be a server from the kitchen, not a guest."

The racial tensions remain vivid to the 87-year-old Moore. "There were situations that, you know, would come up off and on, racial situations, things of that nature," he said. "But we were able to hang in there."

Curry said Moore welcomed him to the Baltimore locker room after he was traded to the Colts in 1967, adding that Moore's quiet leadership and example during a turbulent time should serve as his lasting legacy off the field.

"In terms of his presence in the locker room in the '60s, that was so important," Curry said. "You can just imagine. We were going through a period not unlike right now, where the racists were loud and cities were burning. It took strong leadership from all the factions on the team. And while Lenny was very quiet, it was impossible to dislike him or to look down your nose at him. He would find something encouraging for everybody, especially the ones of us who were different than him."

Moore, nicknamed "Spats" because of the white tape he would wrap around his cleats and ankles, remained in the Baltimore area after he retired. In part because his career coincided with that of legendary Cleveland Browns running back Jim Brown, some—including the late Don Shula, the Colts' coach for Moore's final five seasons—think Moore's accomplishments have been overlooked.

"Lenny might have been one of the best who's ever played the game," Shula told the *Reading Eagle* in 2003. "I don't think he's ever gotten the recognition. When they talk about the other great backs, he's right there in their league. When we used him as a flanker, he was as good or better than anybody out there. He made some great catches."

Through the years, Moore typically refrained from being drawn into those types of discussions.

"Well, it wasn't really a question. I think I've been blessed," Moore said. "There were things that could have gotten in my way, yeah. We came through a lot of situations. I just thank God for all things that happened. It's pretty hard to say that everything was smooth, but we hung in there."

91.
Willie Davis

Willie Davis (87) played hard and never missed a game in his NFL career.

Position: Defensive End
Teams: Browns (1958–1959), Packers (1960–1969)

By Larry Holder

Siberia" doesn't suit everyone.

That's why when Hall of Fame Browns coach Paul Brown didn't like what he saw from his players, he'd threaten a one-way ticket to his own version of "Siberia": Green Bay.

So you couldn't blame Willie Davis, a Lisbon, Louisiana, native, if his head spun when receiving the news that he'd been traded from the Cleveland Browns to the Packers before the 1960 season.

The defensive end, who spent two years in Cleveland, already had a winding NFL experience.

The Browns selected Davis, a former Grambling standout, in the 15th round of the 1956 draft, but a two-year tenure in the Army kept him from the league until 1958. Brown shifted Davis around within the defensive and offensive line, eventually turning the bullying pass rusher into an offensive tackle by 1959. The experiment ended with Brown trading Davis for flanker A. D. Williams in July 1960.

It turned into what has been dubbed by many as one of the most lopsided trades in NFL history. At the time, though, Davis didn't know what to think. Brown shipped him off because he couldn't cut it. Was he really meant for the NFL?

Legendary Packers head coach Vince Lombardi shifted Davis's emotions upon the player's arrival to Green Bay. Yes, Brown's frustration likely played a role in Davis's trade, but Lombardi also wanted Davis as a defensive end. The confidence from Lombardi catapulted the new Packers player into a relentless defender for the next decade. He retired after the 1969 season, five first-team All-Pros, five Pro Bowls, and five NFL championships later.

"He was a very resilient guy," said Duane Davis, Willie's son (who's also an actor, most notably playing "Alvin Mack" in *The Program*). "He never really concentrated on limitations. He always tried to exploit every opportunity before him. He would always try to turn those negatives into positives. I think that's what really helped him prevail throughout his career. He always challenged himself. He always kind of approached the game from a furious place of passion."

The 1961 NFL championship game against the Giants might have been the ultimate watershed moment for Davis.

He admitted to the *Green Bay Press-Gazette* in March 1962 that he was "an angry young man" when the Packers faced the Giants a few months earlier. He had been passed over for All-Pro and Pro Bowl honors. He was "peeved" heading into that game and "decided to show folks what kind of football Willie Davis could play. I told myself this would be just about the biggest audience I'd ever have watching. It was my chance."

Rookie Greg Larson started at right tackle for the Giants in the title game. Davis beat him so badly that Larson ended up benched. The Giants moved guard Mickey Walker to right tackle. Then Jack Stroud. No one stopped Davis from attacking quarterbacks Y. A. Tittle and Charlie Conerly.

The Packers won their first NFL championship since 1944, clubbing the Giants 37–0. Lombardi won his first NFL title. And Willie Davis landed on the NFL map.

Tittle only went 6 of 20 passing with four interceptions, resulting in a 1.0 passer rating. Conerly played his final game that day in relief of Tittle.

"I never knew how much of a trash-talker he was," said Duane Davis, whose son, Wyatt, was a third-round pick by the Vikings in 2021. "I never knew he had that side to him. Whether it's from his former teammates or those he played against, it was really surprising to hear the trash he talked. I never thought he was a talker.

"He used to always talk about the fact that he was a 'career maker.' He would go up against guys and make them question the career that they had chosen."

Willie Davis followed up his NFL championship accolade with a personal proclamation.

"When football people talk about defensive ends now, they usually mention Gino Marchetti or Andy Robustelli," Willie Davis said in March 1962. "I'm looking to the day when the name of Willie Davis is included. I'll be working hard to get there. That's for sure."

Later that winter, Willie Davis earned the first of his five first-team All-Pro distinctions.

"That's just always how he truly approached things," Duane Davis said.

It's challenging to compute Willie Davis's statistical impact in terms of sack totals, since the NFL did not officially track stats until 1982. Some estimates suggest he had 100–120 sacks during his 10 years in Green Bay.

But Willie Davis's impact extended within the Packers locker room.

"He was that guy that could bring the whole team together," Duane Davis said. "He mixed in with everybody on that team. One of the things that is just so apparent was the emergence of the Black athlete in the NFL."

Only four Black players were in the Packers' team photo in 1960, Davis's first season in Green Bay. By his final season there in 1969, that number jumped to 17.

"One of the interesting things my father and [Packers offensive lineman] Jerry Kramer used to talk about was the fact that they were actually the first two to be interracial roommates in the NFL," Duane Davis said. "They lived with each other during camp and when they traveled. And this was a pretty big deal coming from the South and still had segregation and the civil rights movement was very prevalent. But my father was able to have great relationships with all the players."

Part of Willie Davis's attitude of camaraderie helped cultivate a nickname for him.

"My favorite expression is, 'How are you feeling?'" Willie Davis told the *Green Bay Press-Gazette*. "My teammates turned it around and kept asking me the same thing, as a doctor would inquire of his patient. Finally, they came up with the name 'Dr. Feelgood.'"

Duane Davis never remembered his father discussing the possibility of the Pro Football Hall of Fame much during or after Willie's playing career. It's as if it hit Willie for the first time when he learned he'd be part of the 1981 class headed to Canton.

"I could tell that when he did make it, it blew me away just how ecstatic he was about getting into the Hall of Fame," Duane Davis said. "My father always said to me when I played, and I said it to my son, 'I'm not asking you to be the fastest guy on the team. I'm just always asking you to give your best effort.' That's how he was for me, and that's the same values he placed on both of my sons. Not only with football, but with life in general."

Duane Davis knows he sounds corny when he discusses his father's approach. Still, it's something he believes his father took to heart until he died in 2020.

"When I just think about how he lived his life, even when my dad's health [was] starting to fail, he was always super positive," Duane Davis said. "Truly had a passion for life. When you lose a parent, there's obviously a sense of loss. But . . . one of the things that was such a bright light about my father was just his passion.

"Passion for life, truly living life to the fullest. That's kind of the attitude we've all tried to adopt. As my dad used to say, 'Every day aboveground is a good day.' I try to use that same moniker."

And whatever happened to A. D. Williams, the flanker Brown traded Davis for?

He caught one pass for five yards for Cleveland in 1960. Then Williams moved on to Minnesota the following season, compiling 13 receptions for 174 yards and one touchdown.

Looks like "Siberia" suited Willie Davis perfectly.

90.
Willie Brown

The most special of Willie Brown's 54 career interceptions
clinched a win for the Raiders in Super Bowl XI.

Position: Cornerback

Teams: Broncos (1963–1966), Raiders (1967–1978)

By Tashan Reed

Willie Brown, Charles Woodson, and then-Raiders play-by-play announcer Greg Papa were all on an elevator talking to one another when a polarizing question was posed. Who's the best cornerback in NFL history?

"You're looking at him," Brown said before anyone could answer. Though he laughed, he wasn't joking.

It was a poignant statement given the meager origin of his Hall of Fame career. After playing as a defensive end, linebacker, and tight end at Grambling State from 1959 to 1963, Brown found himself looking for a job. Twice.

Brown went unselected in both the AFL and NFL drafts. He converted to cornerback and signed with the AFL's Houston Oilers but was cut during training camp. That would have been discouraging for anyone, but the Yazoo City, Mississippi, native pushed on. He landed with the Denver Broncos, also of the AFL, and went on to become a starter as a rookie. He played 16 years, including four with the Broncos and 12 with the Raiders.

Both in the AFL and NFL, Brown put together a legendary résumé. From 1963 to 1969, he won an AFL championship, was a five-time AFL All-Star, and was named to All-AFL teams five times. Then, from 1970 to 1978 after he crossed into the NFL, he won a Super Bowl, made the Pro Bowl four times, and was named to All-Pro teams four times. He's not considered by many to be the best corner ever, but he was undoubtedly one of the best corners in pro football history.

"He was humble, but he also was aware of his ability," Papa, now the 49ers play-by-play announcer, said recently after remembering that elevator ride. "He wasn't gonna back down from anybody."

Brown is most known as a player for his 75-yard pick-six to help seal the Raiders' win in Super Bowl XI, but his game went beyond the flash plays. Yes, he racked up 54 interceptions in 204 games, but he was a 6-foot-2, physical, tenacious, press-man corner capable of jamming up opposing receivers at the line of scrimmage, keeping up with them down the field, and shutting them down on a game-by-game basis.

"My job was not catching passes," Brown said at his induction into the Pro Football Hall of Fame in 1984. "My job was to stop the receiver from catching it. If I could have played 15 or 20 years without an interception, that would have been fine. Anything beyond stopping a receiver, that's gravy."

Brown was traded from the Broncos to the Raiders ahead of the 1967 season and had an interception in the Raiders' AFL Championship Game win against the Oilers that season. He'd start at right cornerback from then until he took a backup role in his final season in 1978. He played alongside other great players but was a key factor in the franchise making the playoffs in all but two of his 12 seasons in Oakland.

"To me, he's always been one of the most underrated players in the history of the league," Papa said. "Nobody played the game more completely than Willie with his size and strength. . . . In college he played defensive end, linebacker, tight end, and got converted to corner and revolutionized the sport with his press-man ability that [Raiders owner] Al [Davis] so loved.

"When you think of that great secondary, they had more outlandish characters obviously with Jack [Tatum] and George [Atkinson] and even Skip [Thomas], but Willie was the leader and the captain and the guy that brought it all together."

Even after Brown's playing career ended, he never truly stepped away from the game. The year after he retired, Brown returned to the Raiders as their defensive backs coach and helped the franchise win two more Super Bowls during his tenure from 1979 to 1988. He played a key role in the development of other star defensive backs such as Lester Hayes and Mike Haynes.

Brown stepped away from the Raiders and spent one year as a head coach at Long Beach State (1991) and another at Jordan High School in Los Angeles (1994) before returning to the franchise as the director of staff development in 1995. He'd hold that role until his death in 2019.

Brown might have been more known later in life for his tradition of reminding the audience to wish their moms a Happy Mother's Day while announcing one of the Raiders' picks at the NFL Draft, which has been continued by Charles Woodson and Alec Ingold since his death. It likely came off as a quirky gesture to some who picked up on the trend that Brown set, but it was indicative of his character as a person. He was a mauler as a player but showed another side as a coach and executive.

"Many people know that Willie was a tremendous teammate on the field; I learned as soon as I joined the organization that he was a tremendous teammate off the field as well," former Raiders CEO Amy Trask said. "From the time I joined the organization he supported and encouraged me. I realized soon after joining the organization that Willie was a man I would want with me if ever I was in a street fight. He was also a man who could always make me laugh, even in stressful times when laughter was the furthest thing from my mind."

Brown spent more than three decades with the Raiders as a player, coach, and executive. He displayed a level of commitment and longevity that few have matched.

"It meant everything," Papa said. "He was just constantly around the team, which was comforting for Al to have people that he could trust around when he couldn't be there physically toward the end. But players look up to a guy that was such a great player. The defensive back position has got a little edge to it, and Willie could just keep everybody in line by looking at them."

Brown wasn't officially an on-field coach anymore in his staff development role, but he still attended every practice and spent time working with defensive backs, including Charles Woodson and Rod Woodson. His holistic efforts were particularly appreciated by Al Davis and his family, which could also be said for many others throughout the organization. Given his expansive reach, it's not an understatement to say his legacy will reverberate throughout the Raiders franchise—and the league as a whole—for decades.

89.
Bobby Layne

Bobby Layne was a daring and dynamic quarterback for the Lions and later the Steelers.

Position: Quarterback

Teams: Bears (1948), Bulldogs (1949), Lions (1950–1958), Steelers (1958–1962)

By Nick Baumgardner

With the beginning of a new decade and World War II in the direct rearview, Detroit Lions team president and co-owner Edwin J. Anderson gathered himself for the delivery of a message that was hardly filled with optimism. Anderson was part of an ownership syndicate that had bought the Lions for $165,000. Two years later, they had already lost more than their original investment.

So, in January 1950, Anderson was ready for change—and progress.

"We believe we have strengthened the Lions greatly," Anderson told team brass, per the *Detroit Free Press* in a story published January 25, 1950. "We have a deal now under way that figures to bring us another outstanding player with professional experience.

"If Detroit fans do not support the type of team and the kind of football we will give them in 1950, then we are through. This is the last opportunity."

That last opportunity was a 23-year-old who, at the time of Anderson's announcement, was running a Texas-based sporting goods store with ex-MLB All-Star Sam West. To that point, Layne had delivered only pedestrian results as a football pro two years after an iconic run as a ballyhooed University of Texas quarterback and pitcher.

He went on to earn six Pro Bowl bids and three NFL titles with the Lions before retiring in 1962 as the league's career leader in pass attempts, completions, yards, and touchdowns. His accomplishments with the Lions, and later the Steelers, earned him Hall of Fame enshrinement in 1967.

But in 1950, no one knew what was ahead. Layne was only the representative of what was perhaps a franchise's final hope.

Sports legends are shrouded in so much myth, often beyond hyperbolic. But at least part of Layne's fabled tale as a Lion lives in objective reality. He truly was brought to Detroit to save the franchise. The Lions' ownership group claimed it had enough money for the 1950 season—and nothing else. Many of the franchise's top players did not return after the war, interest waned, and Anderson's group lost more than $200,000 in 1948 and 1949. It was a mess.

Upon signing, Layne became the centerpiece of ownership's final push toward football relevance and financial survival.

He was also—completely and totally—soaked in swagger.

Nothing about Layne's arrival in Detroit, per reports at the time, was easy. Some of that was beyond his control, some of it wasn't. Layne's trade to Detroit almost fell through when fullback Camp Wilson retired. But Layne told Detroit he didn't care what his former team, the New York Bulldogs, got in return. He planned to be a Lion.

Until, of course, he didn't. When the Lions opened camp in August, Layne wasn't there. No one knew why. The *Free Press* reported on August 2, 1950, that, after having been hailed in the press for weeks as the star of the team, Layne had "refused to report."

The following day, Layne—who was one of four QBs on the team—showed up in Ypsilanti for drills. He torched everyone as the focal point of GM/head coach Bo McMillin's T formation, which also included Doak Walker, Layne's prep teammate. The headline that followed?

"Bobby Layne Stamps Self as Lion Luminary in 1950."

As if you didn't already know.

When the lights were bright, so was Layne—even if he could be a roller coaster. He was intercepted in the opening minutes of his Lions career but shrugged it off to throw for better than 75 percent of the team's total offense in a 45–7 win over Green Bay. It was Detroit's first road win over the hated Packers in a decade and the 45 points tied a franchise record. A few weeks later, he fumbled six times before halftime (the offensive line was blamed) and missed a PAT in a 28–27 loss to underdog San Francisco. The reason for the missed PAT? Layne, per the *Free Press*, blamed a high snap.

This would become a theme during Layne's time with the Lions. If Layne was turnover-prone in a game, it was always the offensive line's fault. If Layne pulled a game out of the fire, his narrative was often that he'd done so despite everyone else around him. Walker once famously explained how Layne never—ever—actually lost a football game.

"Time just ran out on him," Walker quipped.

Still, Layne's talent was undeniable, and Detroit became attached to it quickly. It didn't take the "Blond Bomber" long to figure that out, either. He broke the team's single-season passing record eight games into a 12-game season. The Lions went 6-6, but Layne broke every passing record the club had and drew more than 30,000 people for a Thanksgiving home finale in Detroit. The Lions wound up close to break-even—and blamed the lackluster year not on Layne's fumbling, but McMillin's coaching. He "resigned" after three years, taking a swipe at the board on his way out. In reality, the 24-year-old Layne told the Lions it was either McMillin or him. He even admitted it publicly.

"It's true as far as I'm concerned," Layne said.

The following year, Anderson appointed himself general manager. He also promoted backfield assistant Buddy Parker to head coach. Why? Because Parker allowed Layne to essentially call the offense on the field himself. The Lions were Layne's team the minute Anderson made that cryptic announcement in early 1950, and Layne knew it.

Detroit News writer Jerry Green, who has written about the city's sports scene since the 1950s, once pinned local fans' obsession with Layne on their love of the heaviest dose of sports theater possible. An athlete could be hurt, sick, hungover, whatever—but if he performed on the field when it mattered, he was considered a hero.

Away from football, Layne reportedly chewed tobacco constantly. Instead of discreetly entering local bars for a drink, Layne would park his car on the sidewalk out front to make sure everybody knew who would be holding court for the next few (several?) hours. He always went in the front, never the back.

In short order, Layne became—as Green predicted—the perfect made-for-TV football star for Detroit. Forget all the posturing: if there was work to be done, Layne would be there.

"He played without a face mask and he was at his finest against the clock," Green wrote. "When a touchdown drive was necessary, he could make the last two minutes seem an eternity."

Layne broke his leg in three places during a game late in the 1957 season, and the Lions won what remains as their last NFL championship on the back of his replacement, Tobin Rote. The next year, they traded Layne to the Steelers. Though there is no written proof, urban legend persists that Layne declared the Lions would not win for the next 50 years because of his trade. That 50th year was 2008 . . . when the Lions became the first NFL team to go 0-16.

Whether you believe in the "curse" of Bobby Layne, who died in 1986, probably depends on your overall stance on curses. The same might be said for legends. But when a guy gets brought to a town to literally save a football franchise, tells everybody he's going to do it, and then pulls it off?

Thanks to Layne, you know legends can exist.

88.
Darrell Green

Darrell Green was for many years the NFL's fastest man and a key player for the greatest era in his franchise's history.

Position: Cornerback

Team: Washington (1983–2002)

By Ben Standig

D arrell Green's faster-than-a-speeding-bullet velocity fueled his one-team, 20-year career. Yet despite setting NFL records, winning two Super Bowls, finishing as arguably Washington's greatest player, and being among the fastest players the league has ever had, the cornerback never viewed himself as special, let alone Superman.

"It's almost like Clark Kent. I'm just a guy," said Green, a 2008 Pro Football Hall of Fame selection. "I just worked down the street and I lived down the street. I'm in the neighborhood playing with kids and helping kids. Oh, and then on Sunday, then I go and play pro football."

There's nothing modest about Green's preposterously impressive résumé, which includes NFL records of 295 games played by a defender and 19 consecutive seasons with an interception. Drafted in 1983 by the reigning Super Bowl champions, he arrived from Division II Texas A&I (now Texas A&M–Kingsville) as the 28th and final player chosen in the first round and ended his playing days as a seven-time Pro Bowl selection.

In between were superhero moments, starting with a stunning chase-down tackle of Dallas running back Tony Dorsett in Green's first game. In the 1987 playoffs, he sparked a divisional-round road win against Chicago with a 52-yard punt-return touchdown during which he tore rib cartilage while hurdling a potential tackler. The following week, Green batted a fourth-down pass at the goal line inside the final minute to secure an NFC Championship Game victory over Minnesota.

Green's second Super Bowl appearance resulted in his first of two titles as Washington routed Denver 42–10 in Super Bowl XXII. He would earn another ring four years later in a 37–24 win over Buffalo. The Joe Gibbs era ended when the legendary coach retired after the following season, but Green played for another decade. Selected to the NFL's all-decade team for the 1990s, Green finished with franchise records of 54 interceptions and 258 starts before ending his career after the 2002 season at 42.

Green never donned a cape, but his burgundy-and-gold No. 28 jersey made opponents sweat and fans roar.

"Darrell [as a leader] was very vocal," Gibbs said ahead of Green's Hall of Fame induction. "High-quality person. Extremely gifted, obviously. To play speed corner for all of those years . . . is unbelievable."

He was raised with six siblings in a rough part of Houston and drugs, alcohol, a lack of opportunity, and other potential kryptonite lurked everywhere. Green made it to college but dropped out after a close friend died in a car accident. He returned after 18 months. "Three years later, I was a first-round pick," said Green, who was the player drafted after Dan Marino.

It's not hyperbole to declare Green's speed world-class. When Washington general manager Bobby Beathard drafted him, Green could run the 100 meters in 10.08 seconds. That same time a year later would have earned Green a silver medal, behind Carl Lewis, at the 1984 Summer Olympics in Los Angeles.

Green arrived in Washington with that freakish speed—he won the NFL's fastest man competition four times—in a diminutive frame. "He was so impressive, you forgot about his size," Beathard told ESPN in 2008. The leap from Division II to the NFL was massive, and upon joining a Super Bowl–winning team that included wide receiver Art Monk, also a 2008 Hall of Fame inductee, Green quickly grasped that he possessed scant craft for the cornerback position. Perhaps more importantly, he knew the standard approaches to playing the position wouldn't work for him.

Staying afloat against NFL wide receivers meant finding his own unique style.

"I was unorthodox. I was little and I couldn't play the technique, so I developed what I call 'results-nique,'" Green said. "So, I played that 'nique' that got the results. Had I stayed with the [standard] technique, I wouldn't have played one season."

For Green, that meant learning how to play his foes, including NFC East rivals Roy Green and Mike Quick, rather than focusing on backpedaling and other standard cornerback movements. "[I'm] probably the pioneer of truly matching up [one-on-one] on a consistent basis," Green said. Though he declined to name any specific wide receiver as his Lex Luthor, Green said Jerry Rice was the best he faced.

"I'm not Deion [Sanders]. I'm not Rod Woodson. I don't have very many similarities to any of them and how they play," Green said of his contemporaries and those who followed. "I don't know any player in history that I've seen play position-wise (like me). . . . I think that from a football standpoint, you know, I have some unique things."

Champ Bailey, another Hall of Fame cornerback and Washington's first-round pick in 1999, credits Green for helping him learn the league and thrive. While Green didn't force his "results-nique" approach on Bailey, he helped the rookie refine his skill, including the importance of moving his feet and body position rather than worrying about hand placement.

Unlike the flashy Sanders, a future teammate in Washington, Green skipped individual celebrations. That meant he didn't stand out as much despite winning two Super Bowls with Washington, which had an offensive line known as "The Hogs." Green understood such look-at-me bravado, especially from an economic perspective, but that flamboyance wasn't for him. He kept the focus on the game-day task and his family and rolled his dedicated mindset into rigorous twice-daily offseason workouts. "I was 'wax on, wax off' every day of my offseason," Green said.

Green, who passed on an invitation to train for the 1984 U.S. Olympic track team, made a memorable debut on *Monday Night Football* in September 1983 when he sprinted nearly the length of the field to tackle Dorsett. Green caught up with a future Hall of Fame running back—and, in turn, had millions of football fans saying, "Who is he?"

"I was from Texas A&I," Green said. "I'm 5-foot-8¾, 173 pounds. I [played] in NAIA and then two years of NCAA Division II. So, I guarantee you 99 percent of the people that saw me in that moment in that first game did not have any recollection of me."

Washington fans began swooning during that jaw-dropping dash, and their love affair continues four decades later. Green didn't just live and work within the community. Perpetually optimistic and youthful-looking, Green set an example to his legion of fans through his charitable work and an approach to life he believes helped get him to Canton.

Rather than deliver some rah-rah talk about giving a fictitious

120 percent, Green still tells kids or those seeking guidance about the "five 100s." That's the percentage the devout Christian gives to five areas of his life: God; Jewell, his wife of nearly four decades; their four children; his football job; and his charitable outlets, specifically the Darrell Green Foundation and Strong Youth Strong Communities.

"I just had five simple things," Green said. "I dedicated myself to making a simple life out of what can be a complicated life or intrusive life. . . . I did a good job of keeping the noise down."

Beyond the helping hand—there's a new project designed to support children with autism—Green remains a fixture in the greater Washington area as an entrepreneur and in the sports world. He serves as a special assistant to George Mason University athletic director Brad Edwards, who was a starting safety for Washington when it won Super Bowl XXVI.

Special memories continue to come via his dozen grandchildren. He's also pondered a movie about his life, one that began and remains steeped in humility.

Green claims he's more "normal human" than years of attention and accolades—and running a 4.43-second 40-yard dash when he was 50—would suggest.

"I guess that's how I played for 20 years," Green said. "Because I never [drank] the water. . . . All this famous recognition stuff, I'm way more of a guy next door than I am that."

That's exactly what Clark Kent would want everyone to think.

87.
Champ Bailey

Champ Bailey (24) was elected to more Pro Bowls than any defensive back in NFL history.

Position: Cornerback

Teams: Washington (1999–2003), Broncos (2004–2013)

By Lindsay Jones

Champ Bailey and Jake Plummer were hardly strangers when Bailey arrived in Denver in 2004, fresh off one of the biggest player-for-player trades in NFL history. Bailey was already a star, a three-time Pro Bowler with 18 interceptions in his first five NFL seasons with Washington, and five of those picks had come against Plummer.

Now they were going to be teammates. And while the trade meant giving up star running back Clinton Portis, who had back-to-back 1,500-yard seasons and was averaging 5.5 yards per carry in Denver, Plummer was thrilled.

But first, he had to get something off his chest.

"I walked up to Champ, and I told him I used to hate him," Plummer recalled.

Plummer, who had previously played for the Arizona Cardinals in the same division as Washington, shows up plenty of times in a Bailey highlight reel. Bailey's second career interception, a 59-yard pick-six, came against Plummer in October 1999. Plummer recalled chasing Bailey all the way to the end zone and erupting after Bailey seemed to taunt him as he crossed the goal line.

"He held the ball out in front of me like, 'Ha ha, like, nice try.' And that was the closest I ever came to punching somebody in the gut in the end zone," Plummer said.

Plummer can't have been the only NFL quarterback to have felt that way. For 15 years, Bailey combined his incredible athleticism (he ran a 4.28-second 40-yard dash at the 1999 combine, and caught five touchdowns as a two-way player at the University of Georgia) with uncanny field vision and an impeccable work ethic to become one of the NFL's best all-around cornerbacks.

Bailey was a first-ballot selection for the Pro Football Hall of Fame in 2019, five years after playing in his final game with the Broncos. (He spent the 2014 offseason with the Saints but did not make the 53-man roster and retired at age 36.) His statistics and résumé were impeccable: 52 interceptions, four of which were returned for touchdowns; three first-team All-Pro selections; 12 Pro Bowls (a record for a cornerback); and a spot on the 2000s All-Decade team. About the only honor missing from his résumé was Defensive Player of the Year. If that award could be given for multiyear stretches, Bailey might have won it for his domination and production during the 2005 and 2006 seasons.

Over 30 games in those two seasons, Bailey intercepted 18 passes—plus another in the 2005 postseason, despite being infrequently targeted by opposing quarterbacks.

"Teams would come out there and they would throw at me all

game long, and rightfully so. I would do the same thing. And then they'd throw the ball to Champ's side twice a game. Might get a five-yard gain one time. Incomplete another time. And if they tried again, it might be a pick. That type of consistency is not a fluke," said former NFL cornerback Domonique Foxworth, who started seven games at the Broncos' other cornerback spot opposite Bailey in 2005 and was his Denver teammate for three years. "To do that over a course of an entire season is unthinkable."

Bailey's highlights from 2005 included a pick-six in Week 2 to spark a comeback win against Drew Brees and the San Diego Chargers, and another interception he returned for a touchdown against Dallas on Thanksgiving, part of a five-game stretch in which Bailey had a pick. In 2006, Bailey led the NFL with 10 interceptions, including four picks in the final three weeks of the season.

"He was smart, he was physical. He wanted to tackle and you know there was always a big play that was going to happen if he was on the field," said former Broncos safety Nick Ferguson, who shared a defensive backfield with Bailey for four seasons. "It's the same thing I hear when I listen to guys talk about what it was like playing with Peyton Manning; it was just a belief that you were in every single game. With Champ, it was the same thing. You knew you were in every single game. I didn't care what receiver they had, right?"

The most important interception in that two-season stretch and most iconic play of Bailey's career was his interception and 100-yard return against Tom Brady and the Patriots in an AFC divisional playoff game on January 14, 2006.

The athleticism of the play—the way he leaped in front of Patriots receiver Troy Brown in the end zone and the ensuing sprint down the sideline—was impressive enough. But to former Broncos coach Mike Shanahan, what makes that play so incredible was the brains Bailey showed to make it happen.

The Broncos held a 10–6 lead in the final minute of the third quarter, but Brady had driven the Patriots inside Denver's 10-yard line. On third-and-goal, Broncos defensive coordinator Larry Coyer called for zero coverage, with both safeties, Ferguson and John

Lynch, in the box, ready to blitz, which left Bailey and the team's other corners on their islands in man coverage. Typically, in that all-out blitz situation, the cornerbacks weren't supposed to switch off their assigned man. For Bailey, that should have been outside receiver David Givens. But just before the snap, Bailey called an audible for himself after seeing the Patriots' formation: running back Kevin Faulk set off to Brady's right, and Brown in the right slot.

Shanahan said New England had run the formation earlier in the game, and it had resulted in a 33-yard completion to Brown, who had been covered on the play by Denver rookie cornerback Darrent Williams.

This time, the Patriots slipped up. Brady misdiagnosed the blitzing safety—it was Ferguson, not Lynch—and Ferguson flushed Brady to the quarterback's right. Brady rushed a throw to Brown, not expecting that Bailey would have bailed on covering Givens and stayed in the front right portion of the end zone, where Brown was coming on his crossing route.

Bailey jumped the route, caught the ball, and took off down the home sideline. At the 1-yard line, he was sent flying into the sideline from a blindside hit by Patriots tight end Ben Watson, who had taken the perfect angle from the opposite side of the field to chase down Bailey. The Broncos scored on the next play and went on to win the game 27–13.

"He's a smart player and very talented guy who's able to not only cover his guy but see the play that's coming and make a big-time play," Shanahan recalled.

But for Bailey's former teammates and coaches, it wasn't just his in-game domination that made him a Hall of Famer. It was the intensity with which he practiced, his deep understanding not just of defensive coverages, but of quarterback tendencies. It was the way he befriended and mentored so many young teammates and established a professional culture for the Broncos defense that remains to this day, nearly eight years since he last played in Denver. Bailey mentored corners like Foxworth and Chris Harris Jr., who made the Broncos' roster as an undrafted rookie in 2011, then became a defensive leader after Bailey's retirement. Harris Jr., in turn, mentored the next generation of defensive backs, like current Denver All-Pro safety Justin Simmons.

"He set the standard for those young kids around him, and he instilled confidence in the younger players that were below him—he was really good at that—just working with them and making sure they were confident in their abilities and never doubted that they should be there," Plummer said. "Whether they were getting beat or not in practice, or in a game, Champ would be like, 'Nah, let's go. You've got the skills to be here.'"

86.
Buck Buchanan

The towering Buck Buchanan (86) was known for his dominance and durability.

Position: Defensive Tackle
Team: Chiefs (1963–1975)

By Paul Dehner Jr.

In today's game, players possessing rare physical characteristics are perfectly quantified and calculated. Comparable Relative Athletic Scores calculate freakiness of explosion and strength. The GPS tracks game speed and bench press reps show off power.

Those didn't exist when Buck Buchanan entered professional football as the AFL's No. 1 draft pick in 1963.

You quantified athletic freakiness by the words of those tasked with stopping him.

"It was hard to believe somebody so big could be so quick. It was like trying to block a ghost," said late Hall of Fame offensive lineman Gene Upshaw, as relayed to presenter Hank Stram during Buchanan's 1990 Hall of Fame induction. "For the most part, I enjoyed playing against the other guys, but when I played against Buchanan, I couldn't sleep the night before."

Buchanan didn't just leave opposing offensive linemen sleepless during his 13 years spent with the Kansas City Chiefs. At 6-foot-7, nearly 300 pounds playing defensive tackle, he changed the way people thought about football.

"He revolutionized the game," longtime Raiders coach John Madden once said. "Guys that size usually played on the outside. Buck was the first tall guy to play inside."

Buchanan held down the middle of the Chiefs defense for a legendary run of football that included a 64-23-4 record from 1966 to 1971, then appearances in Super Bowls I and IV.

He'd eventually be named an AFL All-Star six times, was twice an AFL champion, a two-time NFL Pro Bowler, and had the one Super Bowl title against the Vikings in 1970. He'd eventually be named to the NFL 100th anniversary all-time team.

The flashy moments, like batting down 16 passes in one season or tossing down Vikings running backs in the Super Bowl, came and went, but the workmanlike reliability of his game made him a legend.

He missed only one game in 13 seasons.

"The only thing I ever tried to do as a football player was be consistent," Buchanan once said. "I never did a lot of spectacular kinds of things. But when we graded out year in and year out, week in and week out, my grades were right there and that's what I prided myself on."

Those grades tell a story of football success, but not the whole story of Junious "Buck" Buchanan. The story of Buchanan goes beyond head slaps and tackles for loss, but into the way in which he compiled those honors and became the first AFL defensive lineman enshrined into the Pro Football Hall of Fame.

"Immediately after learning of my selection, I thought of the many men who had played the sport we love so much," Buchanan said during his Hall of Fame speech. "I also thought about those players, teammates and opponents alike, who had encouraged and challenged me to not only be a very well-rounded athlete, but also a good and decent human being."

The last part lives on in Buchanan's wake as much as any memory of his impact. The native of Gainesville, Alabama, and football and basketball star at A. H. Parker High in Birmingham, Alabama, praised his legendary college coach at Grambling, Eddie Robinson, for molding values that carried his story off the field.

"Coach Robinson taught me love, dedication for my school and my fellow man," Buchanan said.

Robinson once called Buchanan "the finest lineman I have ever seen."

Buchanan's selection at the top of the AFL Draft in 1963 also made him a trailblazer as the first to come out of a small, historically Black college to the top of the league. That didn't occur at that time. Buchanan's career impact assured it wouldn't be the last.

"Buck was able to handle himself the way he was supposed to on the field by dominating people," former Chiefs linebacker Walt Corey once said. "But when he got off the field, he was one of those people that always lent a helping hand."

Following his storied career in Kansas City and after retiring in 1975, Buchanan became an esteemed member of the civic community, specifically with his involvement in the Black Chamber of Commerce, and was dedicated to making life better in the city.

"Buck Buchanan did so much in the Kansas City community that a lot of people didn't know about," former Chiefs quarterback Len Dawson once said. "And he did it all the time that he was playing. He had seen a path he was going to take long before most of us ever see that path—some of us, we never see it."

. . .

As he stood on the podium in Canton, making his Hall of Fame speech in 1990, Buchanan held a secret among the words he shared with the audience. A week earlier he had been diagnosed with cancer. All his family, friends, and former teammates gathered to celebrate his career and enshrinement. Despite holding this debilitating news, he didn't let anybody know in that moment because he knew how happy everyone was to be there celebrating with him.

He didn't want to take a piece of the happiness away from everyone else.

Fitting, in so many ways, the man who was too big a presence to do anything but attract all the attention never wanted it to be about him.

Almost two years after his speech, he passed away at 51. Gone far too soon, leaving levels of community impact unable to feel his finishing touches.

Scholarships and awards in Buchanan's name are littered across the football world, including for best defensive player in the FBS each season. The final message uttered in his Hall speech cut to the core of what Buchanan wanted people to take away from his story and what awards named after him are about.

Whether from a small town in Alabama, a small school not known for churning out top draft picks or not built for the previous definition of a position on the field, he proved lack of precedent doesn't belong in the conversation other than an obstacle to overcome.

"I would like this bronze bust to serve as a greater purpose than a testimony to my football career," Buchanan said in Canton. "I sincerely hope this will stand as a symbol of inspiration to all young people where hard work and honest effort can take you. Being consistent in your work and never quitting until you have reached the finish line will bring you the desired results. Today I am thankful that I am able to cross the finish line. To the young people of all walks of life, I say never give up your hopes and dreams of success."

85.
Clyde "Bulldog" Turner

Clyde "Bulldog" Turner was a core piece of the Bears' rise as a franchise.

Position: Center/Linebacker
Team: Bears (1940–1952)

By Adam Jahns

Centers rarely make the headlines. They clear holes for running backs and protect their quarterbacks.

But centers who also intercept passes as a linebacker get noticed. One of Clyde "Bulldog" Turner's favorite plays of his career was his interception against Washington quarterback Sammy Baugh in the third quarter of the Bears' 56–20 victory on October 26, 1947, at Griffith Stadium in Washington. He picked off Baugh's pass inside Chicago's 5-yard line, then took off.

"I started weaving up that field and picking up blockers," Turner said, according to Michael Barr's *Remembering Bulldog Turner: Unsung Monster of the Midway.* "First thing I know, I'm about in the clear and I got up a head of steam. I'm coming down that sideline, getting my blockers and weaving around.

"I finally decided I'd just dart over to my left, and I did. About that time somebody hit me in the back of the head and jumped on me. Well, it was Sammy Baugh."

Turner and Baugh both attended Sweetwater (Texas) High School. Baugh was five years older and later advised Turner in the NFL, including on his first contract with the Bears.

Chicago drafted Turner out of Hardin-Simmons University (in Abilene, Texas) with the seventh pick in the 1940 draft. Bears coach/owner George Halas met with Turner in April of that year and offered him his first contract. Instead of signing right away, which Halas surely wanted, Turner took his contract home to Texas to discuss it with his father and Baugh.

"Sammy Baugh was the only one I knew that knew anything about pro football," Turner said, according to Barr. "So, being fairly close where I could get ahold of him, I went out to see him."

Baugh advised him to sign. At the time, Turner's deal reportedly made him the highest-paid rookie lineman in the league. And now, years into both of their Hall of Fame careers, Baugh was hanging on Turner's back. As the story goes, Turner carried him seven yards into the end zone. It was officially recorded as a 96-yard touchdown.

No NFL franchise has had more Hall of Fame players than the Bears. They also lead the league in retired numbers. The names are NFL icons: Walter Payton, Dick Butkus, Gale Sayers, Red Grange, Bronko Nagurski, Halas, and others. But Turner also is a member of both elite groups. His No. 66 will never be worn again in Chicago, and he was voted into the Pro Football Hall of Fame in 1966.

Turner was a seven-time All-Pro and a member of the Bears' four championship-winning teams in the 1940s. He's considered one of the best centers of all time, but the 6-foot-1, 237-pounder left his mark on defense, too.

On offense, Turner was a brash, confident blocker who buried his pads and helmet into the chest of would-be tacklers and often made them eat dirt. The Bears' famous T formation turned quarterback Sid Luckman into a household name, but each play started with Turner's snap. Turner joined the Bears the same year as running back George McAfee, the fastest player in the league at the time and an eventual Hall of Famer. Halas acquired McAfee, the No. 2 pick in 1940, from the Philadelphia Eagles.

As a linebacker, Turner led the league with eight interceptions in 1942, a season in which quarterbacks averaged only 20 passes per game. He finished with 21 interceptions in his career, including a 24-yard pick-six in the Bears' famous 73–0 drubbing of Washington in the 1940 championship game. That was his first touchdown. Turner was a tenacious tackler, and some of his hits were legendary. In *George Halas and the Chicago Bears*, author George Vass described Turner as "the Butkus of the 1940s." Bulldog was a true monster for the Monsters of the Midway.

"One day a player jumped on Bill Osmanski's brother after he was down, breaking his back," Halas wrote in his 1979 autobiography, *Halas by Halas*. "Bill told the player he did it deliberately. He replied, 'That's part of football.' Bulldog Turner overheard. On the next punt, Bulldog hit the guy so hard he was carried off."

Facing a combined roster of Cardinals and Steelers on December 3, 1944, the Bears were short on running backs after ejections and turned to Turner. On his first carry, Turner broke loose for a 48-yard touchdown run in a 49–7 victory. It was the only rushing attempt of his 13-year career.

Turner distinguished himself through his intelligence. It was said that he quickly remembered everything about the Bears' offense and defense, including every player's assignment. Turner took the Bears' T formation back with him to Texas and taught it to high school coaches. He also wasn't afraid to challenge Halas, who was ornery and stubborn but also innovative. Turner was proud of who he was as a player.

During the Bears' 73–0 rout of Washington, Halas sent in running back Bob Snyder to tell Turner to botch his long snap on an extra-point attempt. Back then, there was no netting to prevent kicked balls from reaching the stands and becoming souvenirs, and the Bears were running out of balls. Turner refused, but the holder complied, dropping the ball on the attempt.

"The next day in the paper, they say the point was missed due to a bad pass from center," Turner recalled in the *Chicago Tribune* in 1987. "Hell, I never made a bad pass in my life."

Halas would forgive Turner; he always did. After all, Turner, a former cowhand in Texas, was one of Halas's best and favorite players. In Halas's autobiography, he shared the story of how the team figured out Eagles coach Greasy Neale's "elaborate wigwag system" (to signal plays).

"I had an assistant record the position of Greasy's legs and arms on each play," Halas wrote. "In no time I had the code. I gave it to Bulldog Turner. He picked up the messages coming to the quarterback and adjusted our defenses. After a game, Neale said that 'Bulldog is the best @#$%c*& player I have ever seen! He seems to smell where our next play is coming from.'"

Turner's story in the NFL starts with his teeth. He had risen out of relative anonymity at Hardin-Simmons to become a coveted NFL prospect in 1940. In an effort to draft him, Lions owner Dick Richards gave Turner $150 to $200 for some dental work and asked Turner to tell teams that he didn't want to play pro football.

Turner played along and Richards's plan almost worked, as the first five teams in the draft passed on Turner. When it came time for the Lions' selection at No. 6, Richards's ploy blew up because of his own coach.

"Lions coach Gus Henderson, for some inexplicable reason, roared out, 'Doyle Nave of USC,'" Vass wrote in *George Halas and the Chicago Bears.* "Halas, next in line, quick-wittedly claimed, 'Clyde Turner of Hardin-Simmons.'"

Halas's quick action denied the Lions a chance to fix their pick. The Bears had been keen on Turner for a while, and they nabbed the eventual Hall of Famer. Meanwhile, the Lions were stuck with Nave, who didn't even make their team. Henderson was fired and later revealed what Richards did. The NFL fined Richards $5,000 for tampering.

Turner later played a role in the Bears' acquisition of another future Hall of Famer in defensive end Ed Sprinkle, who also played at Hardin-Simmons. Sprinkle earned the reputation as the meanest player in the NFL and was nicknamed "The Claw" for his vicious clotheslines and tackles. In 2020, Sprinkle was voted into the Hall of Fame.

"Bulldog believed in me," Sprinkle said in *Remembering Bulldog Turner: Unsung Monster of the Midway.* "He insisted that I go with him to Chicago and try out for the Bears."

Halas was a stickler for players' weights, and as Turner got older, he developed tricks to keep a few pounds off the scales. He wanted to play at 240 pounds, but Halas wanted him at 232. Turner was caught overweight only once. He was fined, but he earned it back as a bonus. Halas often had tumultuous relationships with his best players, but Turner thought he was treated well. Halas raised Turner's salary, including after his rookie season, and the two were said to have a close relationship.

In 1945, Turner, like many of his Bears teammates, served during World War II. He joined the Air Force but didn't experience any battle action. Instead, he played for the Air Force Superbombers, a football team of service members. When given passes by the Air Force, he would sneak away on a plane and return to the Bears, playing in two games.

Turner was a character both on and off the field—and Halas embraced it. Beer and the Bulldog were a frequent and fun combination. Luckman called him the "champion party boy." Turner would pull out a banjo and sing songs about Texas, and his teammates always remembered his funny stories. He also wasn't afraid to poke fun at Bronko Nagurski when the legend returned to the team in 1943. Off the field and in Chicago's taverns, it was Sprinkle who later helped keep Turner out of trouble.

"He provided so much excitement on and off the field," Halas wrote in his autobiography. "There is a story that one night Bulldog fell from a third-story window of a hotel. An awning broke the fall. As Bulldog brushed himself off, a policeman ran up. 'What happened?' he asked. 'I don't know,' Bulldog is supposed to have replied. 'I just got here myself.'"

Turner considered retirement from the NFL in 1952, but Halas convinced him to return as an assistant. Halas then needed him to play. That season, Turner started 12 games at right tackle, another sign of his amazing versatility. In 1962, Turner succeeded Baugh as the head coach of the New York Titans for a short stint before settling back home in Texas. In 1998, Turner died at age 79 after battling lung cancer.

Barr described Turner's impact on the NFL perfectly in *Remembering Bulldog Turner: Unsung Monster of the Midway*: "Bulldog was a natural at a very violent sport. He had an uncommon combination of size, speed, quickness, and athleticism that only comes along once in a great while. His speed was shocking, especially for a big man. He caused quite a stir when he came into the NFL in 1940 because his kind had never been seen before."

84.
Mel Hein

Mel Hein was part of the Pro Football Hall of Fame's inaugural class.

Position: Center
Team: Giants (1931–1945)

By Ben Standig

Mel Hein never took a break.

"Even as a rookie in 1931, there was no one like him," George Halas, the owner and coach of the Chicago Bears, once said, according to the *New York Times*. "Usually, you look for the rookies on another team and try to take advantage of them. We tried working on Hein, but from the beginning, he was too smart."

If Hein's name doesn't ring a bell, don't fret. After all, the Pro Football Hall of Famer won the NFL's first Most Valuable Player award a long, long time ago. As a member of the Hall's inaugural Class of 1963, Hein's been a part of football lore for decades.

The durable two-way threat for the New York Giants doesn't actually show up on the traditional list of league MVPs that starts with Cleveland Browns running back Jim Brown in 1957. What the first-team All-NFL center from 1933 to 1940 received in 1938, the Gruen Trophy, which was voted on by sportswriters and renamed the following year for NFL commissioner Joe F. Carr, ran its course until 1946. Legendary players such as Don Hutson and Sid Luckman were also honored, but they followed the man who never took a break.

The use of "never" isn't hyperbole unless the nitpickers want to ding Hein, who also played linebacker, because he asked out of a game just once during his 15-year career. Blame a broken nose from a game in 1941 for that rare rest.

"We played 60 minutes in those days," Hein said, according to his Pro Football Hall of Fame bio. "I don't think I would have liked to play just half the time as they do today."

That's how football worked back in the day, long before rosters expanded to 53 and niche roles became a norm even for starters. Bodies wore down over the course of 60 minutes, and for the rank-and-file competitors, the mind would likely follow. The mental game is perhaps what separated a leader during New York's 1934 and 1938 NFL championship seasons from his contemporaries. His exemplary performances allowed his name to resonate decades later.

"The younger generation of Giants rooters know only the name of this legendary linebacker and center of more than half a century ago," famed *New York Times* sports reporter Dave Anderson wrote following Hein's death at 82 in January 1992 from stomach cancer. "But to those of the older generation who remember him, Mel Hein stands with Lawrence Taylor as the two best players in the long history of the Giants franchise."

That initial Pro Football Hall of Fame class included players who resonate even with the modern fans: Hutson, Red Grange, Sammy

Baugh, and Jim Thorpe, along with Halas. Hein was among the 17 players, coaches, and executives enshrined that year and deservedly so. Don't be fooled by his positional oddity.

Picturing an offensive lineman winning the league's top individual honor today is preposterous; since the Associated Press began issuing the award in 1957, only three non-quarterbacks or running backs have been selected as the MVP and none have played tackle, guard, or center. In the 1930s, when single- and double-wing offenses ruled, the man in the middle of the line played a far more substantial role. Those formations relied heavily on pulling linemen as crowded backfields and strong running games were all the rage and very different from the empty sets, wideouts, and pass-oriented offenses that dominate today's game.

Hein was born in 1909 in Redding, California, and raised in Burlington, Washington, a small town in the northwest section of the Evergreen State. An article from the December 10, 1938, edition of the *Spokesman-Review* newspaper that highlighted Hein's MVP selection explained that veteran news photographers unofficially confirmed the sportswriters' selection. "They say that a photographer can watch No. 7, Hein's number, to find out where the play and the ball are going to end up," it reads.

After 170 games—all with the Giants—Hein ended up in the Pro Football Hall of Fame. He earned second-team All-NFL honors five times in addition to the eight first-team selections, according to the Hall of Fame.

"He was absolutely outstanding from the get-go," said Dick Fry, a former sports information director at Washington State, where Hein played from 1928 to 1930. The All-American led Washington State to the Rose Bowl after the 1930 season. Yet without anything akin to the modern scouting apparatus—the NFL Draft would not begin for five more years—pro teams showed little immediate interest in acquiring his services in 1931.

Hein wrote teams seeking a gig. The Providence Steamrollers offered him $125 a game. Hein took the offer, signed the contract, and mailed the document. But when the Giants offered $150 a game, Hein "wired the Providence postmaster, asking him to return the letter," Anderson wrote. "The postmaster intercepted the Steamrollers contract, Hein signed with the Giants and after that 1931 season, the Providence franchise folded."

Identified as a "tall, quiet fellow tipping the scales at 220 pounds" by the *Spokesman-Review* and nicknamed "Cappy" for his 10 years as a Giants captain, Hein also shined defensively. "He rarely plays a game without intercepting at least one pass," the article said.

The Hall of Fame described Hein as "one of the few NFL stars who had the speed and agility to contain" Green Bay's Huston, who set the standard at wide receiver for decades. As for his playing mentality, "Although Mel was thoroughly aggressive and coldly ferocious when it came to blocking and tackling, he was a gentleman player. He rarely lost his temper."

Those gentlemanly instincts stayed with Hein, a member of the NFL's 75th and 100th anniversary all-time teams, off the field.

Fry never saw Hein play, but he interviewed him in 1989 for a book he authored on the school's athletic history. "I knew Mel very well," Fry said in an interview. "He was not only a great football player and athlete, but he was an extremely good human being."

Hein's playing career ended in 1945, but he remained in the sport for decades, including a four-year stint as the head coach at Union College in Schenectady, New York, and a longtime assistant at USC. His son, Mel Jr., once held the United States indoor record in the pole vault.

Thanks to his unique combination of physical stamina, mental acuity, and athletic gifts, Hein soared into football's elite level. Per the *New York Times*, Hein once said, "I can't prove this with any statistics, but I may have played more minutes than anybody in pro football history."

His Hall of Fame trip included an opportunity to swap stories with his fellow inductees.

"I've knocked heads against most of these fellows and you should have heard some of the stories that were told last night," Hein said during his induction speech. "And if any of you people doubt that we're not great, you should have been there. That's the way with football. Whether you're in high school, college, or professional, man, the longer you're away from the sport, the greater you become, and it thrills me to death to think how great I'll be when I'm 100 years old."

83.
Leo Nomellini

Leo Nomellini (73), 49ers legend and part-time professional wrestler, in hot pursuit of Packers fullback Jim Taylor.

Position: Defensive Tackle
Team: 49ers (1950–1963)

By Mike Sando

The greatest defensive lineman in San Francisco 49ers history never played organized sports in high school, working a factory job instead. Leo "The Lion" Nomellini was a U.S. Marine combat veteran before taking his first snap of college football. When his NFL career finished after 14 seasons, he had earned more money on the professional wrestling circuit than he ever earned pinning down Johnny Unitas, Frank Gifford, or Jim Brown.

Prior to becoming a Pro Football Hall of Famer and pro wrestling headliner who filled arenas and felled Gorgeous George with his trademark flying tackle, Nomellini was a Chicago high school student of little means. He supported his immigrant family by working the evening shift, 4 p.m. to midnight, packing lemonade mix for U.S. soldiers. Nomellini went into the service at 18, the same month his father died. The Marine Corps introduced him to football and later delivered him to the Pacific Theater in World War II for the Battle of Okinawa as part of Marine Night Fighter Squadron 542.

No one could have known in those early years that Lio Paolo Nomellini, as 2-year-old Leo's name appears on a 1927 immigration manifest, would stand alone all these decades later. He's the only NFL player to earn Associated Press First-Team All-Pro honors on both offense and defense since the AP began differentiating between sides of the ball in 1951.

Jim Taylor, the Hall of Fame fullback of Green Bay Packers fame, faced many of the great old-school players, including Dick Butkus. He once called Nomellini the "single-most physically imposing" player he ever faced. Hall of Fame coach Bud Grant, who played with Nomellini in college, won an NBA championship as a player, had a 200-yard receiving game in the NFL, and later coached the Minnesota Vikings to four Super Bowls, called Nomellini a "one-of-a-kind" type of player.

"I put him there with Walter Payton and Chuck Bednarik among the players I have seen or gone against," Grant said.

Nomellini, 6-foot-3 and 265 pounds, played 14 NFL seasons, all with the 49ers, and never missed a game. A 10-time Pro Bowl choice, he was an AP First-Team All-Pro tackle six times, twice on offense and four times on defense, despite playing from 1950 to 1963, after the era of two-way players. He was one of 16 players named to the NFL's 50th anniversary team a half-century ago. The 49ers long ago retired his No. 73.

"I truly feel like his story, if you look from beginning to end, what he accomplished, and compare it to today, it is just amazing," Nomellini's daughter, Lane, said of her late father. "What it took to get to that point and to that honor, starting from nothing, really . . ."

• • •

The Immigration Act of 1924 reduced by 80 percent the flow into the United States from outside the Western Hemisphere. It was simultaneously a good time to leave Italy, which was becoming a police state under Mussolini, and a difficult time to enter the U.S. from there.

Nomellini's father, listed as a farm laborer in early paperwork and known to have operated a candy store in Illinois, had fought for the U.S. in World War I and enjoyed citizenship already when the rest of the family immigrated aboard the SS *Conte Rosso*. The ship that transported the Nomellinis to America would later become a troop transport vessel for Mussolini. In 1941, it found the ocean floor, sunk by Royal Navy torpedoes while carrying men to North Africa. By late 1943, when Leo was serving in the Marines, Hitler was running a concentration camp just outside Lucca, Nomellini's hometown, which remains best known for its Renaissance-era protective walls that still stand.

"Canton, Ohio, is thousands of miles from Lucca, Italy, the place where I was born," Nomellini said during his 1969 Hall of Fame speech, "but Canton, Ohio, and the Hall of Fame here is living proof of what opportunity and sportsmanship and America really are."

Growing up in Chicago, Leo reportedly sold newspapers under the steps of train stations before transitioning to the factory job packing lemonade mix as his body took the physical form that would serve him so well on the field. A draft card indicates Leo weighed 206 pounds when registering for the service. He was closer to 250 upon his exit after three years as a Marine.

Nomellini grew into a man with fingers so thick, he required a size 17.5 ring for his Hall of Fame enshrinement, second at the time among Hall of Famers to the size 19 for Bronko Nagurski, Nomellini's friend and occasional tag-team wrestling partner. Those are huge rings in any era, especially for players as lean as Nagurski (226 pounds) and Nomellini (265). Players from the 2019 Super Bowl champion Kansas City Chiefs were typically sized between 10 and

13.5, with the largest an 18, according to Emily McGrath, professional sports program coordinator for Jostens.

"I played sandlot football, but I was not a player in high school," Nomellini said in the 1970s. "My folks weren't rich. It was the Depression. My parents said, 'You'll hurt yourself, ruin your clothes,' but what it really was, if you could make $20 working after school, it was much more productive."

Workers rushed to complete an 8,000-acre Marine air station at Cherry Point, North Carolina, after the Pearl Harbor attack. Nomellini arrived in February 1943 to train for service in the Pacific and was recruited onto the football team by Lieutenant Bill Hopp, who had played at the University of Minnesota and was coaching the "Leathernecks" squad at Cherry Point.

Nomellini had fibbed by telling Hopp he'd been an all-state player in high school. In reality, his interest in football stemmed from watching Pat O'Brien as Knute Rockne and Ronald Reagan as George Gipp in the 1940 film *Knute Rockne, All American.*

The casting might have been better at Cherry Point. Also on that Marine Corps team: future Pittsburgh Steelers Hall of Fame defensive lineman Ernie Stautner, whose family departed Hitler's Germany about when the Nomellinis left Mussolini's Italy. With those two on the same squad, the Leathernecks once routed Wake Forest Army Finance School, 68–6.

Marine Night Fighter Squadron 542 flew air patrols from the Caroline Islands and then deployed for Okinawa, where Nomellini was present for what became the largest amphibious assault in the Pacific. There were 160,000 casualties over 98 days, with bodies strewn in mud so treacherous that tanks could not retrieve them. The stench was notorious, the environment so chaotic that "typhoon of steel" was a common moniker used to describe it. A monument there lists the 240,000 combatants and civilians known to have perished.

There seems to be little documentation of Nomellini's specific experience in the war. Records show he advanced from private to staff sergeant and worked at least part of the time as a clerk. Nomellini shared few details with his family before dying in 2000 at age 76.

"A lot of people in that era, that went in the service for two or three or four years during the war, they came out, they were men," Bud Grant said. "We had some of those on our team. Leo was a man among boys."

Hopp, Nomellini's coach at Cherry Point, had played at Minnesota under coach Bernie Bierman, a World War I Marine captain. That connection was critical for Nomellini in the absence of a high school career. With Hopp's help, Nomellini joined the Gophers after his own service ended in 1946. He was a two-way sensation over the same period Grant starred there. Bierman called Nomellini the closest thing to Nagurski, another Minnesota alum, in sheer physical prowess.

"Leo came out of Chicago, never played football in high school, and I think the advantage of that was, he was never beat up," said Grant, who maintains an office at Vikings headquarters. "Leo was new to football and he was a very raw, raw talent when he came to Minnesota. He was 265 pounds, had extreme strength, and could run. Some guys are quick and fast, but he could outright outrun just about anybody."

In 1948, when Minnesota needed a few points to win the NCAA track and field title, a coach summoned Nomellini to the hammer event, where there were only five competitors for six slots. An athlete from Harvard won with a throw near 171 feet. Nomellini, with no practice, threw the 16-pound weight without employing the customary spin to generate momentum. He simply stood there and hucked the thing as far as he could: 92 feet, 8⅝ inches. Point taken. Title won for Minnesota.

"He was as strong as three bulls," Hall of Fame 49ers teammate

Joe Perry once said. "He'd slap you on the back and knock you 20 feet."

Nomellini would in the current era be a scholarship player poised to profit from "name, image, and likeness" usage under evolving NCAA rules. Back then, he attended Minnesota not on scholarship, but on the GI Bill, living on $120 a month. He earned another $65 monthly counting cash for Northwest Bank, wrapping coins and separating bills. The extra income helped him support his mother and two sisters, who lived with him in the Twin Cities.

"Leo came from nothing, I came from nothing, so we were both poor together," Grant said, "although I learned later that Leo wasn't averse to walking in and saying, 'Hey, coach, I'm broke,' and he'd get something. I wish I'd known that."

The financial picture improved for Nomellini less through his excellence on the football field than through his association with college football teammate Vern Gagne, who won two NCAA wrestling titles and later founded the American Wrestling Association. Gagne drew Nomellini onto the pro circuit in Montana, the Dakotas, and Minnesota.

"I didn't even have enough money to buy shoes [in college]," Nomellini said in 1953. "I was Raggedy Ann on the campus. Ten days after I began [pro] wrestling, I showed up on the campus with a new automobile, and you should have seen the raised eyebrows."

At his peak in the 1950s, Nomellini defeated National Wrestling Alliance heavyweight champ Lou Thesz before 12,000 fans at the Cow Palace in San Francisco. An Associated Press story said Nomellini planned to step away from the 49ers for the 1955 season if he remained the NWA champ at that time. But Thesz, who had lost by disqualification after kicking Nomellini in the face while Nomellini was outside the ring, joined manager Ed "Strangler" Lewis in protesting the outcome (naturally). They claimed rules prevented the title from changing hands when the champion remained on his feet (of course).

The title remained with Thesz. Nomellini remained a 49er,

but he still headlined dozens more wrestling cards into the mid-1960s (he and Thesz met multiple other times, once drawing more than 16,000 to the Cow Palace in a match refereed by the Manassa Mauler, Jack Dempsey).

"Wrestling was real to him," Nomellini's youngest son, Drew, said. "As the story goes, one time my grandmother packed a lunch for Dad and the Sharpe brothers, Ben and Mike, who used to wrestle with him. They were all going to a Sacramento job and they would ride together to save money. Ben ate all the meat out of Leo's sandwich, and they pulled it over in the middle of the trip and started wrestling out there in the middle of a cornfield."

Wrestlingdata.com lists 848 matches for Nomellini against 196 opponents, including Dick the Bruiser, Freddie Blassie, Pat Patterson, Fritz Von Erich, Hard Boiled Haggerty, Bob Orton Sr., and Gorgeous George, whose personal valet would spread rose petals at his feet and spray perfume onto the ring before matches, providing theatrical inspiration for Muhammad Ali and James Brown.

"I loved the wrestling for the roughhousing and the money," Nomellini once said. "I wrestled for five months of every year. It kept me in great shape. . . . I'd have played football for nothing. I just had to play it in an area where I could make money wrestling."

Nomellini earned enough money wrestling to purchase a home for his family in California after the 49ers made him the 11th player chosen in the 1950 draft. Bud Grant was selected 14th that year. Another college teammate, Clayton Tonnemaker, went fourth to Green Bay. It was such a different time. Tonnemaker was United Press All-Pro as a rookie, missed two years while serving in the Korean War, earned All-Pro honors again, and then left the game to become an executive for Cargill.

"Dad's cleats hung in the garage—his damn high-tops hung in the garage," Drew Nomellini said. "I think he just pulled them up, grabbed them, and said, 'I'm going to work.'"

NFL salaries were frequently in four figures at the time.

"Dad always said that when he was drafted by the 49ers, they offered him like one percent of the team or a $500 bonus," Lane Nomellini said. "He took the bonus, because he didn't know if the team was going to make it because it was their first year in the NFL."

An ownership offer might have been made later, after Nomellini defeated Thesz at the Cow Palace in 1955. As Drew Nomellini recalls, his father was earning enough wrestling then to ask general manager Lou Spadia for a raise. Reports at the time suggested Nomellini considered an offer to play in Canada.

Either way, there would be no ownership stake.

The 49ers did present a new 1963 Ford Thunderbird convertible to Nomellini at halftime of his record-setting 159th consecutive game. The car didn't get Nomellini very far along the road to financial freedom. In retirement, Nomellini spent 30 years working at an insurance company. He had a radio show and officiated high school football games.

"When he made the Hall [in 1969], it took off for him and he could make some side money, but it was not an easy battle for my dad," Drew Nomellini said. "He actually reffed a game that I was in. I went up to him one time and said, 'Dammit, this guy is holding me all game.' Dad goes, 'OK, well, why don't you lose your manner, No. 73?' So, I give the guy a head slap, and he threw a flag at me! I'm not kidding. And he was smiling as he was walking off. But you know what? The guy never held me anymore."

Instead of walking away from football following that disputed 1955 wrestling match against Thesz, Nomellini saw his role increase that season. He played left tackle on offense, left defensive tackle in the 4-3, and middle guard in the 5-2, plus duties on special teams, according to film study by football historian T. J. Troup. Nomellini made victory-sealing plays on defense in the final moments of consecutive victories over Chicago and Detroit. He was 31 years old.

"I really like to play football," Nomellini once said. "It's tough and it's hard and no pro football owners can pay a player enough for the punishment they take. You just have to like it—and I do."

Nomellini never missed a game in college or the pros. He was 39 when he retired after 174 consecutive games, then an NFL record.

"You might be good, you might be great for five years, but if you don't have durability, you never achieve greatness," Grant said. "Leo had the durability to play every down, every snap, practice every day."

In an appearance on the 1986 *NFL Crunch Course* video distributed by *Sports Illustrated*, a mustachioed Nomellini smiles wryly while reminiscing about the way the game was played in his day.

Highlight after black-and-white highlight shows players committing gross misdemeanors on the field: leg whips, elbows to the face, kicks to the ribs, takedowns by the face mask, shoves into wooden benches, and all-out fistfights. One clip shows the hulking Nomellini all but decapitating an opposing quarterback with a clothesline strike. An official hurries into position to mark the spot of the ball, never reaching for a flag.

"There wasn't that much dirty play," Nomellini says on the video. "It was rough. Yeah, they were rough. If they could kill you, they'd kill you honestly, OK? But nothing dirty. There's nothing wrong with drawing a little blood here and there, you know."

At one point in the video, Deacon Jones declares that players must know how to "serve justice" to avoid being "kicked around the league."

Former 49ers quarterback Billy Kilmer used to tell a story about a justice-serving Nomellini chasing an opposing offensive lineman out of San Francisco's Kezar Stadium following a game. The opponent had been holding Nomellini and getting away with it, despite Leo's objections. You might say Leo lost his manner.

"The whistle blew, the guy took off," Drew Nomellini said. "Kezar had that old tunnel. He took off toward the tunnel. Leo was chasing him across the field. He got to the other end and the guy locked the gate and all the players were out there and Leo was on the other side.

And they couldn't get the players off the field until they cleared Leo out. He chased him into the locker room. Leo is on the other side, banging on the gate."

Nomellini was a grunter and growler on the field and in the ring. The Lion's roar could intimidate. But those who knew Nomellini best described a gentle soul who loved playing boogie-woogie tunes on the piano, guitar, and harmonica.

"He learned all this musical stuff going into different cities that didn't allow Black players to leave the hotel," Drew Nomellini said. "He was Catholic and married, so he stayed in with the guys and they would teach him how to play 'Sweet Georgia Brown,' tunes like that. You would see him at parties, playing piano. I was blown away."

Years ago, when 49ers alumni gathered at a California Burger King owned by former tackle Len Rohde, they joked about riling the gentle giant before games by calling him on the phone and pretending to be opposing players. The impersonators would insult Nomellini's family on those calls, hoping he would punish the unwitting opponent that week.

"Leo was one of the kindest, gentlest, biggest tough men you'd ever want to meet," former 49ers quarterback Y. A. Tittle once said. "More than that, though, he was a great human being. He never had any bad things to say about anyone. He was a guy you could poke fun at, and he'd poke fun at you."

Lane Nomellini recalls her father's love for kids.

"We'd go to the Elks Club and he would just be like this big float in the middle of the pool and he'd have like 10 little kids hanging on him," she said. "And he would just come up for air and he'd sink back down. He just had kind of a kid-like personality, if you could imagine that, but also loud and kind of scary. He loved people and anyone that knew him loved him, too."

Leo would sometimes bring home wrestling buddies, including William Dee "Haystacks" Calhoun (billed weight: 601 pounds).

"My dad sat on two bar stools, Haystack sat on three," Lane Nomellini said. "Dad would practice wrestling holds on us, on the floor, in front of the TV, watching cartoons. As loud and big as Dad was, he was also very sensitive. He was very dependable, always. With Dad, there was right and wrong and no in-between. He was our rock. As a teenager, I thought he should change his style, get a little more with it. He said this was who he was. He did grow his hair out a tiny bit. As an adult, I appreciate that he was true to himself."

82.
Kellen Winslow

Kellen Winslow had some iron man attributes in the Chargers' Air Coryell offense.

Position: Tight End
Team: Chargers (1979–1987)

By Daniel Popper

Before Travis Kelce, Mark Andrews, and George Kittle, before Jimmy Graham, Zach Ertz, and Rob Gronkowski, before Antonio Gates and Tony Gonzalez, there was Kellen Winslow.

Winslow had a Hall of Fame statistical career—541 catches for 6,741 yards and 45 touchdowns in nine NFL seasons. He topped 1,000 yards three times, including as a second-year player in 1980, when he finished with 1,290 yards, a receiving yards record for tight ends that stood for more than three decades. It was only broken in

2011, when Gronkowski totaled 1,327 yards. To this day, only five tight ends—Kelce, Kittle, Gronkowski, Graham, and Andrews—have ever amassed more receiving yards than Winslow in a season. All four posted their seasons after 2011.

Equally as important to Winslow's legacy is how he shaped the tight end position. Winslow was ahead of his time. Before Winslow, tight ends were big, bulky, and primarily blockers. But under visionary Chargers head coach Don Coryell—the architect of the famed Air Coryell offense—Winslow showcased what a tight end could be in the passing game and laid the groundwork for what the position has become in the modern NFL: first and foremost, a mismatched weapon in the passing game.

As former Coryell assistant Al Saunders said, "The offenses in those days were so run-oriented that a tight end was really an offensive lineman that occasionally caught the football."

Winslow, at 6-foot-5 and 251 pounds with extraordinary athleticism, was a different breed.

He was still a weapon as a blocker, both in the run and as a pass protector. Former Chargers offensive line coach Dave Levy once told Saunders, "If [Winslow] was an offensive tackle, he'd be a Pro Bowl player there also."

"There was nothing that Kellen Winslow could not do in a football environment," Saunders said.

But his true prowess was as a pass catcher. Saunders said Winslow would spend "about five minutes a day" in the run scheme meetings before rejoining the passing game group.

"His size, his ability to run, his ability to catch the ball, was unique, and it would be unique today as well as it was then," Saunders said. "He was a Gronkowski before Gronkowski."

"As many times as we threw the ball to Kellen," Saunders added, "we probably should have thrown it twice as many times."

Coryell and his staff schemed to take advantage of Winslow's skill set—one that has become commonplace in professional football. When Winslow was drafted in 1979, he joined one of the most accurate passers in the league in Hall of Famer Dan Fouts.

"The thing about Coryell is he'd look at a player and see what type of athlete he was and then ask him, 'Do you think you can do this?'" Fouts said. "Or, 'Do you think you can do that?' Or put him in a position to do these different things. And Kellen never shied away from any challenge. So we just kept building. Let's put him out here. Let's move him in motion now. Let's shift him over here. Let him throw a pass. It was all Coryell's genius, but also Kellen carrying it out.

"You have a mismatch basically wherever you put him. You put him out wide, he's bigger than the guy that's guarding him. You put him in tight, he's faster than the guys that are guarding him."

And thus, a new position was born. In modern NFL parlance, the position is known as the "move" or "F" tight end, typically a long and athletic pass-catching tight end who lines up detached from formation.

There was no name for it in the early days of Winslow's career—other than "mismatch."

"Kellen Winslow was a receiver, a tight end, an offensive tackle," said Saunders, who joined Coryell's staff in 1983. "His ability to play in space and the creativity of our offense allowed Kellen to be not only a player that lined up as a traditional true tight end with his hand in the dirt as an inline blocker, but he also stood up and played in the slot. He played as a wide receiver aligned away from the formation."

Defenses were much simpler in the early 1980s. Exotic zone blitzes and coverage looks were rare.

"There was not a lot of creativity from a defensive standpoint," Saunders said. "It was either three-deep zone, two-deep zone, or man-to-man. And when Kellen was in a man-to-man situation, it was a total mismatch because it was either a strong safety or even a linebacker that was one-on-one, and both from a size standpoint, an athletic standpoint, from a speed standpoint, Kellen was the dominant player. And the creativity of Don Coryell's offense allowed him to be in a variety of different positions."

When facing zone, Winslow used his basketball knowledge from his high school days to post up defenders and find open spaces.

He was particularly lethal against three-deep zones, as Coryell's scheme focused on exploiting the seams against those coverages. There was no better player to exploit those areas than Winslow with his combination of size and speed.

"Kellen was probably the first player from the tight end position to be utilized in the seams," Saunders said.

"I was never shy about throwing the ball anywhere near him because his catch radius was phenomenal," Fouts said. "He had long arms and great hands. He could catch the ball high, he could catch it low, he could catch it out in front of him. So I had a lot of targets in one guy."

Winslow, a chess club member in high school, was a chess piece in Coryell's passing offense.

"He was really a smart guy," Fouts said. "Not just football smart, but smart everywhere."

The Chargers sent Winslow in pre-snap motion regularly—something, again, that is a regular occurrence now but was outside-the-box at the time. Sometimes he motioned from one side of the formation inline to the other. Other times, he motioned out of the backfield. He also motioned from inline to out wide or into the slot. This created mismatches against smaller defensive backs or larger, slower linebackers "that defenses couldn't handle," Saunders said.

"Kellen could play anywhere on the line of scrimmage, extended from the formation or in the formation," Saunders said. "We were probably the first team that really utilized tight ends in a movement fashion, not only to determine the coverage but also to get a mismatch that you wanted in a one-on-one situation. He was just exemplary at that."

The defining game of Winslow's career came in the divisional round of the 1981 playoffs. The Chargers defeated the Dolphins, 41–38, in overtime in what has come to be known as the "Epic in Miami." Winslow put forth what is still one of the great individual performances in NFL history, catching 13 passes for 166 yards and a third-quarter go-ahead touchdown.

"The Dolphins just decided to put one guy on him a lot, and that was a mistake," Fouts said. "Sometimes they put two guys on him, and that was a mistake, too."

The Dolphins erased a 24–0 first-quarter deficit before the teams traded punches in the second half. With the game tied 38–38 and seconds remaining in regulation, Winslow blocked Miami's game-winning 43-yard field goal attempt. The Chargers then won the game in overtime on Rolf Benirschke's 29-yard field goal.

Winslow was so exhausted he had to be helped off the field by teammates Eric Sievers and Billy Shields—an iconic clip that has come to represent Winslow's effort and impact as a player.

"He was a fierce competitor and just tough as nails and he wanted to be great on every play," Fouts said. "And he was—many, many times."

Winslow suffered a catastrophic knee injury in 1984 and was never the same player. It eventually forced him to retire in 1987 at 30 years old. He made his fifth and final Pro Bowl that year.

"Had he not had that knee injury, he could have played another six, seven years," said Saunders, who went on to coach Gonzalez in Kansas City for six seasons in the late 1990s and early 2000s. "If you put Kellen in the same positions and did the same things with him that Kelce is doing now, or Tony Gonzalez did for us in Kansas City, the numbers would be astronomical."

Winslow was inducted into the Hall of Fame in 1995.

"He just had more skill, I think, than anybody ever to play that position," Saunders said.

81.
Tony Gonzalez

Tony Gonzalez set the bar for a new generation of tight ends.

Position: Tight End

Teams: Chiefs (1997–2008), Falcons (2009–2013)

By Nate Taylor

Surrounded by cheers from fans, Tony Gonzalez, the super-star tight end who became celebrated for his consistency and longevity, always cherished his routine when he scored a touchdown. The celebration often began with Gonzalez getting up off the ground, in many cases after he jumped higher than two defenders to catch the ball. He used his right hand to palm the ball as if it was a basketball. He focused his eyes on the crossbar above the back of the end zone, imagining it as a basketball rim.

Dunking the ball over the crossbar—over and over and over again for most of his 17 seasons—proved to be the perfect image for Gonzalez's remarkable career.

As a 6-foot-5, two-sport star athlete in college at California, Gonzalez didn't dunk the ball much when he played on the basketball team as an undersized power forward. Gonzalez, though, was quick, powerful, and his determination matched his immense athleticism, all traits that led him to be an All-American tight end during his junior season.

In 2021, Gonzalez told Hall of Fame quarterback Peyton Manning on ESPN's *Peyton's Places* that playing basketball made him a better football player.

"It's right hand/left hand coordination, as you're dribbling all the time," Gonzalez explained to Manning. "It's jumping up and down. It's stopping and going. Very similar types of movements to get open.

"You do an L-cut in basketball. You go to the top of the key and then you pop out. That's what I do on the football field."

With a perfect combination of size (250 pounds), speed, and gifted hands, Gonzalez dominated NFL defenders in multiple ways. He was faster and could outjump most linebackers for the ball. When opposing teams altered their game plans by relying more on a defensive back, Gonzalez countered with his strength, as he would often "box out" a safety in the middle of the field for the ball, the same way he would against a taller player on the basketball court for a rebound.

A large portion of Gonzalez's 111 career touchdowns are highlights of him jumping in the air to catch the ball against double coverage, often leading the league for many seasons if such a statistic was recorded.

"I'm 6-5, and I have a short-man's complex," Gonzalez said in an NFL Films documentary about his career. "I have a chip on my shoulder about being short because I played power forward in Division I basketball. At that position, all those guys are about 6-10.

We've got to have good moves, otherwise it's not going to work. They're going to block our shot.

"So you take that mentality and you put me against a 5-foot-10 defensive back or a 6-foot safety or a 6-2 linebacker, I'm going to kill them."

Gonzalez's Hall of Fame statistics and résumé are unassailable: 14 Pro Bowls, six-time All-Pro, and a spot on the 2000s all-decade team. When he retired after the 2013 season, Gonzalez finished with the second-most receptions (1,325) in league history, behind only Hall of Fame receiver Jerry Rice. He is still the all-time leader in receptions and receiving yards (15,127) by a tight end. Antonio Gates is the lone tight end in league history with more touchdowns (116) than Gonzalez.

"His skill set was so different than any other tight end," quarterback Trent Green said of Gonzalez, his former teammate in Kansas City, in the documentary. "He was always open. He was like, 'If there's somebody on me, just throw up high.' He loved the ball up high."

Growing up in Huntington Beach, California, Gonzalez's football heroes were running backs, superstars such as Marcus Allen and Bo Jackson. Gonzalez wanted to be a running back, too, but his path was altered. Paul Curtis, the freshman coach at Huntington Beach High, convinced Gonzalez to switch from running back to tight end.

"He's the one," Gonzalez said of Curtis in 2019 during his Hall of Fame induction speech. "Thank you for making one of the best decisions you've ever made for me."

The NFL Draft in 1997 was an event in which quarterbacks were not the most coveted prospects. Gonzalez impressed several teams after his workout at the league's scouting combine. A few weeks later, everyone in the NFL was even more intrigued by Gonzalez after he scored a season-high 23 points in an upset win over Villanova to lead California to the Sweet 16 round of the NCAA Tournament.

Steve Mariucci, the San Francisco 49ers' new coach, who had just been hired from Cal, wanted to continue coaching Gonzalez in the NFL. The Dallas Cowboys also wanted to select Gonzalez, which was their plan when discussing a potential trade with the Miami Dolphins, who possessed the 15th overall pick. But the Kansas City Chiefs, led by general manager Carl Peterson and coach Marty Schottenheimer, maneuvered up from No. 18 to 13 in a trade with the Houston Oilers to select Gonzalez.

As a rookie, in his first game against his college coach, Gonzalez helped the Chiefs smash the 49ers. Gonzalez blocked a punt, recovered the ball, and caught a touchdown pass.

"He was a snatcher, a Venus flytrap," Mitch Holthus, the Chiefs' longtime radio play-by-play announcer, said of Gonzalez's receiving skills. "Football at the time had a tight end in a box, like Mike Ditka. This isn't Mike Ditka. Tony was smart, he knew how to get open, and he had the ability to make winning plays that wouldn't necessarily look like winning plays [pre-snap]."

By the end of the 1997 season, the Chiefs' offense started utilizing Gonzalez in ways that, back then, were considered unorthodox. He lined up as the lone receiver on one side in certain formations. He was the slot receiver at times, too. The first time Gonzalez dunked the ball over the crossbar after scoring—as the slot receiver—occurred in the Chiefs' season-ending loss to the Denver Broncos in the divisional round of the playoffs that year.

The worst season for Gonzalez, in terms of individual performance, came in 1998. As a first-time starter, Gonzalez recorded just 59 receptions despite being targeted 102 times. He was down on himself because he led the league with 16 dropped passes.

Gonzalez received encouragement through a letter from his brother, Donnie, who also recommended a book for him to read: *Winning Is a Habit: Vince Lombardi on Winning, Success, and the Pursuit of Excellence.*

"I learned what it takes to be great," Gonzalez said in his induction speech. "I started learning the process, the routine of success, what makes a player great. I changed my whole routine."

At the Chiefs' training facility, Gonzalez caught extra passes before and after each practice. Holthus noticed that Gonzalez was always one of the last players to leave the facility.

"In my 28 years, I would put him up there, maybe top five, when it comes to the hardest-working guys I've seen," Holthus said of Gonzalez. "The thing that was impressive about him is he reached stardom and the work increased instead of decreased. I always admired his work ethic. He did what I've seen all the great pros do: he continued to reinvent himself.

"He was ahead of his time, and not just in the way he revolutionized the position."

Gonzalez polished his training regime, too, especially during the offseason. Holthus credits Gonzalez as being one of the first superstars to be ultra-serious about his nutrition—and how to synchronize it with his training.

"I became a vegan while I was playing," Gonzalez said on the *Pursuit of Healthiness* podcast with NBA star Blake Griffin. "This was back when being a vegan was like, 'What the hell are you talking about?' I started drinking these shakes. I would put spinach and carrots into my shakes. People would literally look at me like I was crazy."

Gonzalez's results were historic. Starting in 1999, he was a Pro Bowler in 14 of the next 15 seasons. He lost just two fumbles in his career and didn't fumble a single time in his final seven seasons. He played in 270 games and missed just two. In addition to conventional passes, the Chiefs gave Gonzalez the ball through screens and the occasional end-around. The Chiefs even let Gonzalez throw a pass, which he completed for a 40-yard gain.

As he transformed the position, Gonzalez improved at one of the position's core principles: he was a trusted blocker throughout his elongated prime.

The Chiefs, however, never won a playoff game with Gonzalez in their uniform. In 2008, Gonzalez was an All-Pro who scored 10 touchdowns on a team that finished with a 2-14 record.

"Of all the things you had to worry about, you didn't worry about Tony," Holthus said. "That's where I think the frustration came in for him. He just kept pedaling the bike. At some point, 11 years into his career, he's thinking, 'Where are we going?' But it didn't keep him from playing well."

Just before the 2009 draft, the Atlanta Falcons traded their 2010 second-round pick to the Chiefs in exchange for Gonzalez. Thomas Dimitroff, the Falcons' general manager at the time, asked Gonzalez to play at least two seasons in Atlanta. Instead, Gonzalez performed well throughout his five seasons with the Falcons. Paired with Matt Ryan, the best quarterback he played with in his career, Gonzalez was the aging veteran who led by example for a contending team.

The Falcons, with Gonzalez in the middle of the field, became one of the best passing teams in the league. Gonzalez's most fulfilling season was in 2012, when the Falcons began the year on the road at Arrowhead Stadium against the Chiefs. Of course, Chiefs fans celebrated Gonzalez by applauding him before kickoff. And of course, the Falcons made sure Gonzalez caught a touchdown pass, which led to him dunking the ball over the crossbar. In the home divisional round playoff game against the Seattle Seahawks, Gonzalez made a clutch 19-yard reception between two defenders that led to the Falcons' game-winning field goal.

"His ability to be comfortable with people on his back and catching [it] was so similar to catching entry passes in basketball," Ryan said of Gonzalez in the documentary. "I just felt like a point guard just throwing that ball down into the post."

The following week, the Falcons fell to the 49ers in the NFC Championship Game. In his final postseason game, Gonzalez was targeted eight times—he made eight receptions for 78 yards and a touchdown.

"There [are] no confetti shots of Tony Gonzalez," Holthus said. "I was always sad about that."

Since his retirement, many of the league's star tight ends—such as Gates, Jimmy Graham, Rob Gronkowski, George Kittle, and Travis Kelce—have thanked Gonzalez for being a trailblazer, someone who was always willing to share advice on how to play the position even better than he did.

"We all have that physical, athletic advantage," Gonzalez told Manning, "because we've been playing basketball our whole lives."

Gonzalez was on the sideline inside Hard Rock Stadium in Miami Gardens, Florida, for Super Bowl LIV, a game that featured Kittle and Kelce. With pride, Gonzalez marveled at Kelce's performance— six receptions (on six targets), 43 yards, and a touchdown—which helped the Chiefs capture the Lombardi Trophy.

Even before red and gold confetti started filling the night's sky, Kelce made sure to dap up and hug Gonzalez, their foreheads touching one another in celebration. Kelce wanted to make sure he included and honored Gonzalez, the greatest tight end, in his most successful moment.

"I remember seeing Tony wearing a pair of Jordans and him actually dunking one over the [crossbar]," Kelce said of Gonzalez in a TV interview. "I thought it was the coolest thing. He's [Michael] Jordan on the field. He was a guy who always had a mismatch on him.

"It's cool to see all that translate onto the football field. [He'll] go down as the greatest tight end to ever play."

80.
Willie Lanier

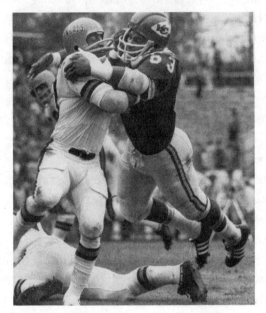

With 45 career interceptions and fumble recoveries,
Willie Lanier (63) had a nose for the ball as a hard-hitting middle linebacker.

Position: Linebacker
Team: Chiefs (1967–1977)

By Larry Holder

Willie Lanier describes his rise into one of the best NFL linebackers in league history as "somewhat unique."

The former Chiefs linebacker admittedly and unabashedly didn't grow up striving to be an athlete in Richmond, Virginia, much less a football player. He didn't attend Morgan State with the intention of being a college football great. The Pro Football Hall of Fame defender simply saw the sport as a pastime for which he excelled, which led to all-time great accolades he never craved.

That makes the statement from Chiefs owner Lamar Hunt during Lanier's Hall of Fame induction speech feel strange given Lanier's personal feelings toward his football life: "His destiny was to be the prototype of his era," Hunt said.

Except it doesn't seem like Lanier looked to become that figure at all. The results simply happened that way.

Lanier, a 1967 second-round pick by Kansas City, emerged as a premier linebacker in only his second season. Imagine a current NFL team with a 6-foot-1, 245-pound linebacker whose style consisted of being a thumping tackler to a rangy sideline-to-sideline mover to a ball hawk in pass coverage. He'd be the dream prototype for the modern game. Tackle statistics weren't official stats during Lanier's career, and there's no doubt Lanier tallied plenty of them. But his penchant for interceptions and creating turnovers stand tall with the all-time greats.

He intercepted 27 passes, two of which went back for touchdowns, and recovered 18 fumbles (forced fumbles also weren't an official statistic). Lanier has no problem boasting about those numbers, which resulted in three first-team All-Pros, eight Pro Bowls, one AFL championship, and one Super Bowl IV trophy.

"If you go back and check about the interceptions, that was done in a 14-game season when the ball was only being thrown 16 or 18 times a game," Lanier recalled. "This is a 16-game schedule where the ball is being thrown 45 to 50 times. I can't imagine if you could extrapolate what the numbers would really have been. I saw that as a focus going into my second year that you win based on turnovers. It creates additional possessions. And a lack of penalties. If you reduce penalties and you produce turnovers, you should win."

Perhaps the most "unique" element of Lanier's game came from how he adapted his playing style . . . and why he did so in the first place.

Lanier was given the name "Contact" his rookie season by teammate Jerry Mays because of his vicious and dangerous tackling style.

But if he continued his "Contact" style, Lanier said, "You and I would not be talking today because I would not have survived."

An incident in late October during his rookie season altered his approach completely.

"I had a blow to the head that did not cause a concussion," Lanier said. "I did not stumble. I played the rest of the game. And a week later in Kansas City I collapsed on the field [October 29, 1967, vs. Denver]. I was out [unconscious] for two hours."

Lanier underwent testing at the Mayo Clinic shortly after the incident. The testing showed Lanier had an undetected subdural hematoma, which is a buildup of blood on the surface of the brain. According to Cedars-Sinai, this can be from a car crash, fall, or violent attack.

"I knew that could kill you," Lanier said.

He came to find out near the end of his career that the medics lost his pulse three times on the way to the hospital, according to what Lanier said the team doctor told him. That part still shocks him, but it also led to a change in his style after the 1967 season that became a defining part of his game.

Lanier returned in 1968 and eventually earned the nickname "Honey Bear" for his bear-hugging tackling methods. Lanier took his head out of tackling, which has become an overarching theme from the NFL for the last few years.

That approach wasn't the norm, or widely accepted by many. Lanier couldn't have cared less about what anyone else said.

"So, I had a blessing from God to give me a way to play the game 90 percent safe," Lanier said. "If not, I would have never played again. But God gave me an understanding of how to play the game. Never to have another concussion, which I did not. Never to use the head or neck when tackling, which I did not. And taking complete care of self. The only thing important was for me to play the next play and play the whole game.

"Winning had nothing to do with it. . . . The reality of it is that had you not been unconscious for two hours, you could be another player or a coach or the owner, I didn't care who it was, I had nothing to say to you about the way I played. Mine was purely taking care of me. And it worked, and the performance went off the charts because I was never injured. I was there for every play."

Lanier paid such strict attention to keeping his head away from danger, especially in practice.

"I'd leave my chin strap unfastened [in practice]," Lanier said. "I would tell any of the players on the field, 'Don't get too close to me. And if you do, I will hurt you.' But I didn't realize how important that was until I was told 10 years later of what really had happened.

"I was caustic. I was caustic with anybody. Coaches, it didn't matter. I will harm you. I will say things to you. I was not kind to you, respectful to you."

Lanier said there was a coach who admonished him for "not sticking his head" into a collision in his ninth or 10th season.

"I said some very bad things, some of them started with the letter *f* in there," Lanier said. "They can take it and put their head in it. I was offended that they would even bring it up. But they didn't have the clarity of understanding that I had about knowing that if I'm unconscious for two hours, and this was what I was doing to do that and your head had anything to do with it, you couldn't be allowed to have your head touch anything!"

After Year 1, Lanier said, "There was certain things that I would not do. Period."

None of this affected his production on game day. It actually enhanced it. Lanier only missed one game the rest of his career. And the statistics rightfully place him among the best defenders in football history.

But while many former NFL players lean on that portion of their life after their playing days are over, Lanier is quite the opposite. He simply views his playing career as one phase of his life. He attended the University of Missouri–Kansas City to receive his MBA, leading to a fruitful career after the NFL. He currently directs the Lanier Group, an investment firm, and works with several charities.

Lanier isn't one to boast about being the first Black player to serve as the middle linebacker and defensive play caller in league history either.

"The reality is for some reason people who looked like me weren't allowed to do it prior to my being there," Lanier said. "So, I wasn't really overjoyed to be proving something to you because people who looked like me couldn't play. That doesn't make me feel better about you. Those were your issues. I was just trying to take advantage of the opportunity."

He admittedly enjoys life more after playing than he did while he played. So much so where you might wonder if he even relishes his accolades from his time in the NFL.

"It's sometimes bittersweet because it was good from an acknowledgment standpoint," Lanier said. "I know that there was another level that I could have had even on top of what was exhibited, which is really fascinating to me. But the individuals and an organizational standpoint, people get a little confused about how you must 'love something that you do.' That makes no sense to me. I love my family. I don't love anything I do from a work standpoint. I don't do that. That's not a requirement in my mind.

"Was I euphoric in terms of being acknowledged because God gave me a skill? I was just doing his work. And his work allowed me to perform. I'm fine with that. But it wasn't about being all of this and all of that."

79.
Roger Staubach

Roger Staubach led Dallas to four NFC Championship wins in nine seasons.

Position: Quarterback
Team: Cowboys (1969–1979)

By Jon Machota

Dating back to the first Super Bowl, there has been a tradition in which just about every Super Bowl MVP has been awarded a brand-new car. It was usually sports cars in the early days.

Bart Starr was given a pair of Chevrolet Corvettes after winning MVP honors during the first two Super Bowls in 1967 and '68. Joe Namath received a Dodge Charger in 1969. Len Dawson went home with a Dodge Challenger in 1970. Chuck Howley got a Charger in 1971.

But Roger Staubach had no use for a sports car after winning MVP of Super Bowl VI in 1972.

Having a wife and three children at the time, the legendary Dallas Cowboys quarterback needed something with more seats. So, he declined the Charger and instead asked for a station wagon. It was a decision that led to some labeling Staubach a square, something that bothered him at the time.

Despite being one of the most famous athletes in the world and having nicknames like "Roger the Dodger," "Captain America," and "Captain Comeback," Staubach didn't crave the spotlight. He preferred spending time with his family over enjoying the nightlife with friends and teammates.

Staubach's all-American image was the focus of a question that led to the most famous response of his career. While sitting down at his Dallas home for an interview with CBS reporter Phyllis George in 1975, Staubach was asked if he enjoys having such a clean image or if it's a burden.

"Everyone in the world compares me to Joe Namath, as far as the idea of off the field, he's single, bachelor swinging," a smiling Staubach responded. "I'm married with a family. He's having all the fun. I enjoy sex as much as Joe Namath, only I do it with one girl. It's still fun. It's the same thing.

"Everybody acts like you're married, and you have a family, so it's not fun. To me, it's unbelievable. That's my life and I enjoy it."

The only reason that quote is still occasionally mentioned is because it seemed somewhat out of character for Staubach. The former Heisman Trophy winner at Navy, who served in Vietnam before returning to have a Hall of Fame NFL career, is exactly who parents wanted their children to emulate.

"He's everything that people think that he is," former Cowboys quarterback and Pro Football Hall of Famer Troy Aikman said during the NFL Network's *A Football Life* documentary on Staubach in 2014. "And that's rare. Roger is held to such a lofty standard that it would be hard for anyone to be able to live up to that. But he does."

Staubach played 11 seasons in Dallas, leading the team to four

Super Bowl appearances and two Super Bowl wins as their starting quarterback. At the time of his retirement in 1979, Staubach had the NFL's all-time highest passer rating at 83.4. He made six Pro Bowls, was named to the 1970s All-Decade team, and never played on a team with a losing record.

His excellence on and off the field combined with his ability to orchestrate heroic comebacks helped turn the Cowboys quarterback position into what is still one of the most visible in all of sports.

"You know in any profession, there are two ways to make a winner," legendary former Cowboys coach Tom Landry said at Staubach's Pro Football Hall of Fame induction in 1985. "How he performs his job and, more importantly, how he performs as a human being. Roger Staubach is an all-pro in both categories. We are here today to honor Roger for his achievements as a professional football player and rightfully so, but if there is a Hall of Fame for people, they better save a spot for him there, too."

When watching highlights from Staubach's career, it's difficult not to wonder how his game would translate to today's style and rules.

The biggest issue he encountered during his time with Landry is that Staubach wanted to call his own plays. He'd likely have a little more freedom to make adjustments today, especially if he was coming off leading his team to a Super Bowl victory in his first full season as a starter, like he did in 1971.

Staubach had the ability to scramble and create something out of nothing at an elite level. Patriots coach Bill Belichick has known Staubach since the early 1960s. Belichick's father was a coach at Navy during Staubach's college career. Before facing the Seattle Seahawks in Super Bowl XLIX, Belichick compared Seahawks star quarterback Russell Wilson to Staubach.

"I remember a lot of Staubach's spectacular running plays where it looked like he was about to get tackled by three or four guys, and he would Houdini it out of there somehow," Belichick said. "You see Wilson doing some of the same things."

When Walter Cronkite announced the breaking news on

March 30, 1980, that Staubach was retiring, the longtime CBS TV news anchor quipped: "The 38-year-old Staubach broke into the National Football League when conventional wisdom held that the only reason for a quarterback to run was sheer terror."

Staubach was still at the top of his game into his 11th and final season, throwing for a career-high 3,586 yards and 27 touchdowns, but a total of 20 concussions during his pro career ultimately forced him into retirement. There's better equipment and rules designed to protect quarterbacks today that would have likely helped him extend his career. Staubach has also noted in previous interviews that receivers are able to run more freely now compared to the beating they would take to get open against the physical defensive play that used to be allowed.

And then there was his late-game heroics that would certainly fit nicely into today's league of parity, where most games come down to the final few possessions.

One of the most famous plays in NFL history was Staubach's "Hail Mary" pass to Drew Pearson to win a 1975 divisional playoff game over the Minnesota Vikings. Staubach brought the Cowboys from behind to win in the last two minutes of overtime 14 times in his career.

When he retired, Staubach's 23 fourth-quarter comebacks were third-most behind only Fran Tarkenton (34) and Johnny Unitas (27).

At the Cowboys' current headquarters, The Star in Frisco, every member of the Cowboys Ring of Honor is recognized outside the facility along what is known as the Ring of Honor Walk. Each member recognized has a list of their accomplishments and a quote about the person at a monument that includes the player's jersey number.

The quote next to Staubach's No. 12 is from Hall of Fame defensive tackle Randy White.

"There was always a chance in any game with Roger out there," White said. "We always believed that if any game was tight, Roger would get the points we needed to win. And he always did."

After his playing career, Staubach started his own commercial real estate company, one that became so successful that it was sold in 2007 for more than $600 million to Jones Lang LaSalle. Staubach then became executive chairman at JLL until his retirement in 2018.

"He was the greatest sports hero of his time," former Cowboys president and general manager Tex Schramm said when Staubach retired, as referenced in the book *The Dallas Cowboys: The Outrageous History of the Biggest, Loudest, Most Hated, Best Loved Football Team in America.*

"The very unique popularity of the Cowboys is based a heck of a lot on Roger Staubach. He was the hero of a nation, not just of the Cowboys, or even the league."

78.
Mike Haynes

Mike Haynes (22) was the first pick of the Patriots in 1976,
and he rewarded that franchise and later the Raiders with his elite play.

Position: Cornerback

Teams: Patriots (1976–1982), Raiders (1983–1989)

By Steve Buckley

On July 26, 1997, Mike Haynes delivered a Pro Football Hall of Fame induction speech that should be taught to every young player who has been asked to consider switching to a new position.

"When I went to Arizona State, I wanted to be a wide receiver," Haynes said on that muggy Saturday afternoon in Canton, Ohio. "Like a lot of kids playing football, you want to see your name in lights and people reading about you in the papers. Well, at wide receiver, quarterback, running back, you can get that, that can happen for you. Not a lineman . . . not at defensive back, usually. It's usually defensive backs getting beat in those news highlights, and some wide receiver is looking pretty good."

While it's true we see many highlights of superhero wide receivers making dazzling grabs that reduce their would-be defenders to doing pratfalls reminiscent of Kramer on *Seinfeld*, Haynes teaches us that you just need to see the right highlights. You need to see his highlights.

Mike Haynes is the former receiver and sometimes quarterback from Marshall High School in Los Angeles who wasn't even planning on a college football career because the college football programs weren't planning on him. But then something fluky happened: he volunteered to play cornerback in a summer high school all-star game for no other reason than that a receiver from another high school was getting all the reps in practice.

To hear Haynes tell it, everything that would come later is a direct result of making the best out of that bad situation.

And by "everything that would come later," here's a partial breakdown:

- Full scholarship to play football at Arizona State
- Two-time All-America selection
- Fifth overall pick by the Patriots in the 1976 NFL Draft
- 46 career interceptions
- Eight Pro Bowl appearances
- Two-time All-Pro selection
- Super Bowl champion with the Raiders, to whom he was traded in 1983 and immediately helped win a title when he intercepted a pass in a 38–9 victory over Washington in Super Bowl XVIII
- Inducted into the Pro Football Hall of Fame in 1997

The way Haynes sees it, the path to being one of the NFL's greatest 100 players began with switching to cornerback for that 1971 summertime high school all-star game.

"You think I'd be in the top 100 if I were a wide receiver?" he asked.

He didn't wait for an answer.

"It's a great question," he said, "but even I don't have an answer to that."

As he spoke, Haynes had just finished his morning workout, a four-times-a-week ritual he undergoes with assorted other retired NFL players in San Diego, where he has been living for years. And before we continue with the receiver-cornerback debate, you need to know that Haynes, 68 at the time of the interview in 2021, is a prostate cancer survivor, which means that now, more than ever, he takes his health seriously. As he likes to put it, "The goal is to live to be 125."

Far-fetched, right? But Haynes is an expert on that word, which brings us back to the receiver-cornerback debate . . . and to the Optimist Bowl.

Its official name was the Optimist Bowl All-Star Football Game, so named because its sponsor was the Elysian Park Optimists Club. The idea was to stage an all-star game using players from unaffiliated Los Angeles high schools.

Each participating school was invited to send two players. Representing Marshall High School were linebacker John Rice . . . and receiver Mike Haynes.

"At practice, I was clearly better than the other wide receiver, but he was All-City and I didn't have any of those awards," is how Haynes remembers it. "And that guy's coach was coaching our team, and that guy's quarterback was the quarterback. They were a unit. They were joined at the hip.

"I figured I'd still get to play, but when we had practice, I didn't get to make any plays," he said. "So, I figured maybe the next day I would. And I again didn't get to make any plays on offense."

Haynes went to the coach and asked if he could play cornerback. The coach agreed.

Haynes worked out on defense for the rest of the week.

"During practice two days before the game, they put the ball on the 6-yard line," Haynes said. "They had these six or seven plays they were going to run against the defense, and every play went away from me and I didn't have anything to show I could play.

"But then on the very last play they ran it on my side of the field," he said. "I ran up and I stuck the running back. I had trouble getting him down, but I was at least able to stop him long enough for the other guys to join in and help me. We got him down and the coach said to me, 'You got the starting job.'"

The game was played on July 4, 1971, at Los Angeles Coliseum, where Haynes would one day burnish his Hall of Fame credentials in the Raiders' defensive backfield. A festive, patriotic crowd of 25,531 turned out, though it's not known how many people were there for the football and how many showed up for the hour-long fireworks display that followed the football. What we do know is that a lot of college scouts were in the stands, and that they weren't there for the pyrotechnics.

"Most of the college scouts were there to watch maybe four or five guys, and I wasn't one of the four or five guys they were there to watch. That's for sure," said Haynes. "Nobody knew anything about me or my little high school and all that."

Haynes remembers making only one mistake that day. He was beaten to the ball by a player named Ike McBee, who would later play at San Jose State. But McBee was whistled for stepping out of bounds on the way to the end zone.

"When they called that, I was like, 'Wow,'" said Haynes. "I got away from the referee and everybody else as quick as I could because I didn't want anybody to ask my opinion. If they had asked me if he stepped out of bounds, I would have said, 'I don't think so.'"

And so, the drive continued. Haynes made an interception.

The game ended. Haynes's team won. He remembers it as being "a huge upset."

In another upset, some of those scouts who had attended the game with plans to watch maybe four or five guys—but not Haynes—were now making inquiries about the learning-on-the-fly cornerback from Marshall High School.

The plan had been to attend a local community college. Instead, he took a year off and then headed for Tempe to play football for the Sun Devils.

"And the extra year actually was a blessing," he said. "I matured a lot during that year. I was young, I was skinny, had a lot of things going on.

"I look back on it all and the way it all happened, and I think, one, everyone was there at that game to see other players. And two, my senior year in high school, we didn't win any games. I didn't play youth football. I didn't even know how to tackle until I got to Arizona State."

It was said at the time that the Optimist Bowl was going to be an annual event, a yearly showcase of high school football talent, but it turns out to have been misplaced optimism. There never was a second Optimist Bowl.

But the one game they did have was just about the best thing that ever happened for Haynes, who, it might be said, was a pessimist about playing college football until the Optimist Bowl came along.

Twenty-six years after the Optimist Bowl, Mike Haynes stood at a podium in Canton, Ohio, trying to hold back the tears.

He failed.

77.
Ted Hendricks

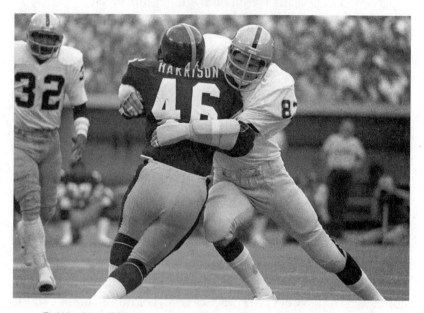

Ted Hendricks (83) had an eccentricity to rival his greatness with the Raiders.

Position: Linebacker

Teams: Colts (1969–1973), Packers (1974), Raiders (1975–1983)

By Dan Pompei

The defensive play call from the sideline was not to the liking of Raiders linebacker Ted Hendricks. So, according to his teammate Howie Long, Hendricks went off script and told Long to do the same. Then, after making a big play, Hendricks requested that Long blame it on him when coaches questioned him, and he, in turn, would blame it on Long.

That was quintessential Hendricks, a nonconformist in every way imaginable.

Unique is a word that is incorrectly used almost always because nearly nothing is unique. Hendricks was unique. He was unique as a player, and he was unique as a person.

That uniqueness made him both famous and great.

It was what Hendricks did between games that made him famous.

"Most Raiders loved to party," quarterback Ken Stabler said according to the book *Snake: The Legendary Life of Ken Stabler.* "But Ted Hendricks was a party all by himself."

Near the start of training camp each season, Hendricks usually livened up the team on the practice fields in Santa Rosa, California. One year, they say he hired a woman wearing a raincoat to interrupt practice and make like Gypsy Rose Lee. Another year, Hendricks borrowed a table with a Cinzano umbrella and some lawn chairs from an Italian restaurant. He set them up on the side of the field, took a seat, and went to work on a pitcher of margaritas while his teammates did up-downs. Then there was the time he wore a black German army helmet with Raider logos on the side, mounted a roan horse, and trotted out to the practice field, holding an orange traffic cone like a lance. He dismounted at the 50 and pronounced himself ready for practice.

"Very strange human," teammate Lyle Alzado told NFL Films, trying to keep a straight face. "Very strange."

Hendricks's antics were not limited to training camp. He attended a retirement party for his coach John Madden with a YIELD sign in his hands that he had knocked over on the way. He said he didn't want to come empty-handed. One Halloween, he wore a helmet carved out of a pumpkin. He sometimes wore masks collected from visits to Renaissance fairs.

However, when he wore a Harlequin mask on the sideline of a 1975 Monday night game, he wasn't trying to be funny.

"I was very upset because I wasn't starting in the lineup and was sitting on the bench," he said in an interview with the Pro Football Hall of Fame's website. "And, I thought I would show my disgust about not being able to play—hide my frustration with a big smile on my mask."

Why was Hendricks on the bench? The NFL had never seen an athlete like him—still hasn't—and coaches didn't know what to do with him.

"One of the problems in the NFL was that coaches were too programmed," he said. "They didn't think I could play linebacker at 214 because no one else was playing the position at 214. Well, that is really quite silly. If you're good, you're good."

That explains why Hendricks fell to the Colts in the second round of the 1969 draft even though he was a three-time All-American at the University of Miami. Hendricks played defensive end in college, but Baltimore coach Don Shula made him a linebacker—a 6-7¾, 214-pound linebacker. Hendricks claimed the title of the tallest linebacker that ever played professional football, and no one has disputed him.

His Colts teammate Bill Curry said he looked like "a series of toothpicks." On Hendricks's first day with the team, Johnny Unitas welcomed him. "I found out later that Unitas was glad to see me because I was the only guy on the team with skinnier legs than his," Hendricks said.

Hendricks's broomstick legs invited cut blocks. But he was adept at jumping over them. They say once, in an attempt to clear teammate Marv Hubbard's cut block in practice, Hendricks kicked Hubbard in the head, earning him the nickname "Kick 'Em in the Head Ted," or "Kick 'Em" for short. Hendricks was known at Miami as "The Mad Stork," a takeoff on the Hurricanes' ibis mascot.

His long limbs hardly were a detriment. In fact, they were part of what made him special. He has said the ability to take long strides gave him range beyond what most others had. Defensive end Clarence Williams, a teammate on the Packers, told Packers.com that Hendricks played with excellent leverage despite his gangly build. "He could get under pads," Williams said.

With 37-inch arms, Hendricks was a wrap-up tackler who almost always brought his man to the ground. He also used his reach to keep blockers from latching on, and from getting clean shots at his legs. And in the day when clotheslining was legal, Hendricks was no friend to Adam's apples.

Hendricks, who could change most lightbulbs without a stepladder, is regarded as the best kick blocker of all time, with 25 on his résumé. He was good at blocking kicks for reasons beyond reach, though.

"Blocking kicks is a knack that some people just seem to have," Raiders specials teams coach Joe Scannella said. "He's got the rare ability to hit and slide his body sideways at the same time."

Throughout Hendricks's career, coaches repeatedly tried to get him to bulk up by lifting weights. He got up to 235, but he never embraced working out. He once had a personal weight rack installed in the Raiders' workout area. At the ends of each of his dumbbells were empty cans, and the rack featured beverage holders.

He looked like he might be susceptible to injuries, but Hendricks played in 215 straight games. Sixty-one percent of those games were with the Raiders, his third team.

After five years in Baltimore, Hendricks had the feeling he no longer belonged because of changes in the coaching staff and roster. He signed a futures contract in August 1974 to play with the Jacksonville Sharks of the WFL in 1975. The Colts subsequently traded him to the Packers, for whom Hendricks played in 1974.

That season may have been his best, as Hendricks had five interceptions and blocked seven kicks. The Sharks went out of business and Hendricks subsequently asked the Packers for a no-cut, guaranteed contract. Bart Starr, who had just taken over as head coach and general manager, refused Hendricks's demand and traded him to the Raiders, who signed him to a three-year, no-cut, guaranteed contract.

He had a bumpy start with the Raiders, but Hendricks made Madden appreciate him in the divisional round of the 1975 playoffs against Cincinnati. With defensive end Tony Cline injured, the Raiders shifted from a 4-3 to a 3-4, which suited Hendricks perfectly. With a three-point lead late in the game, Hendricks sacked Ken Anderson to take the Bengals out of field goal range. "He earned his entire season's salary with that one play," Bengals coach Paul Brown said, according to the book *Badasses: The Legend of Snake, Foo, Dr. Death, and John Madden's Oakland Raiders.*

The sack was Hendricks's fourth of the game. "He played like a madman out there," Raiders owner Al Davis said.

Outside linebackers most often are judged by their pass-rushing skills. Hendricks could rush the passer, but he was much more than a pass rusher. Long calls Hendricks the most complete outside linebacker in history.

"If you were a tight end, you wouldn't want to see me over the top of you during a game," Hendricks said. "If you were a running back, I don't think you'd like to see me just standing there waiting to hit you."

At various times, he played strong-side linebacker, weak-side linebacker, and rover. Davis described Hendricks's well-rounded abilities when presenting him to the Pro Football Hall of Fame: "Ted Hendricks had every endowment, every physical one of the premier linebackers. He could attack the pocket with the greatest of them all . . . but he could play space with devastating efficiency, intercepting passes anywhere on the field. He was near impossible to block at the point of attack, he was one of the first who could actually dictate to the offense, and on fourth down, he could block field goals and punts and extra points like no other player in the history of the game. He was the consummate linebacker, more complete, more all-around than anyone else who played this great game. His records, as well as his play, prove it, and this 6-7 giant was guided by a killer mentality."

It was not luck that Hendricks played on four Super Bowl winners—one with the Colts and three with the Raiders.

He had 26 interceptions and 16 fumble recoveries in his career.

"I can't think of any defensive player who made more big plays for us," Madden said.

Washington coach George Allen called Hendricks "the most

opportunistic player" he ever saw: "He forces as many mistakes as anyone ever did, and he takes advantage of mistakes as well as anyone ever did. . . . He's an amazing athlete, and he's changed our concept of what a linebacker has to be, which is another mark of a great player—that he brings something new to his sport."

Hendricks studied his opponents, but he also studied literature, math, and physics. His brainpower was part of what made him great. Long recalls him coming in on a Monday morning with a hangover and watching film of the Raiders' next opponent while half-awake. He said Hendricks looked at formations and knew what play the opponent would run before the snap.

"Ted Hendricks, one of the smartest players I ever saw," Raiders linebacker Matt Millen said. "He had some limitations, but not from the neck up. He would figure things out. You didn't have to tell him twice."

Madden once said, "Ted's elevator doesn't go all the way to the top."

That helped make him famous.

Another time, Madden said, "Hendricks was brilliant."

That helped make him great.

76.
Art Shell

Art Shell earned All-Pro honors as the Raiders' left tackle for six consecutive seasons.

Position: Offensive Tackle
Team: Raiders (1968–1982)

By Tashan Reed

H arry Schuh pulled Art Shell aside. Practice was over, but the Raiders' veteran starting right tackle wanted the rookie backup offensive tackle to get some extra work in alongside him.

"He didn't have to do that," Shell said of that day in 1968. "But he was gonna work and I was a backup and he knew that, if he got hurt, somebody got to play."

Shell continued the tradition as he grew into a veteran. He helped groom the younger offensive linemen without any trepidation that they could potentially take his job. The coaching staff eventually took notice. One day after another of Shell's post-practice sessions in the mid-1970s, coach John Madden addressed him by a different name.

"John Madden said, 'Hey coach,'" Shell said. "He said, 'You know if you weren't playing, I'd hire you as a coach. I think you could do that.' And, man, he just didn't understand what that did for me."

Team owner Al Davis did the same thing a few days later.

"I'm walking off the field and Al says, 'Hey coach,'" Shell said. "And so, I just walked up to Al and I said, 'When I get through playing, I want to become a coach in this league and I'd like to stay with the Raiders as a coach one day.' He said, 'Look, you continue to do well and do what you're supposed to do and, when it comes time, we'll talk.'"

Following his retirement in 1982, the Raiders hired Shell as their offensive line coach on coach Tom Flores's staff and went on to win the Super Bowl. Six years after that, Shell was promoted to head coach, which made him the first Black head coach in modern NFL history. It was a landmark accomplishment, but Shell had already been inducted into the Pro Football Hall of Fame earlier that year for his vast achievements as a player.

Shell made the Pro Bowl eight times, was named first-team All-Pro twice, second-team All-Pro two other times, and was a two-time Super Bowl champion. Even if the 18-year coaching career that followed never happened, he would have been honored as a football legend. Shell couldn't have foreseen where the sport would take him on either front.

When Art Shell was growing up, the prospect of one day becoming a pro football head coach would have seemed very far away. It was hard enough to find a major college that would recruit him as a *player*, so someday being the man in charge of a team would likely have seemed impossible.

Black people weren't being recruited by White institutions in the

South during the early 1960s. Shell, who was born in 1946 and grew into a star football and basketball player at Bonds-Wilson High School in North Charleston, South Carolina, was unavoidably impacted by the racist practices.

"There was no integration in the school system, so we weren't being recruited," Shell said. "If you wanted to go to a White school, you had to go up North or out West someplace. You weren't being recruited down there."

Shell had lost his mother at 13, but his father managed to put together a good life for him and his four siblings. Despite the rampant segregation at the time, Shell enjoyed his childhood. He took a liking to sports, did well in school, and kept out of trouble. Still, he didn't receive attention from non-HBCU colleges despite being one of the best athletes in the state. Local coaches grew frustrated with such situations and decided to put together an all-star game for Black high school football and basketball players—South Carolina already had this kind of event, but only White people could participate—going into Shell's senior year.

He got invitations to play in both the football and basketball games. Maryland State coach Roosevelt Gilliam and Grambling coach Eddie Robinson both offered him to play football after watching him practice all week and play in the basketball game. Shell was more familiar with Grambling, so that's where he told his dad he was going when he got back home.

Robinson sent him a bus ticket to come to Grambling, Louisiana, the following summer, but Gilliam took a more direct approach: He was driving down from Lancaster, South Carolina, and planning to pick up Shell and other South Carolina–based players and take them with him to Maryland State.

"And I said, 'Coach, my dad hasn't said I can go yet,'" Shell said. "He said, 'Well, I'll come down and talk to your dad.'"

The thing was, Shell didn't want to go to Maryland State. He told his brother that he was going to his friend's house and instructed him to tell Gilliam that he didn't know where he was when he got to their home.

"So, I'm down there with my friend at his house and we were laughing and talking," Shell said. "All of the sudden, my brother comes knocking on the door and he said, 'Art, that coach wants to talk to you.' I said, 'I thought I told you to tell him you didn't know where I was,' and we laughed. So, I go back to the house and the coach says, 'I came to pick you up and I'm gonna take you to Maryland with me.' I said, 'Well, my dad hasn't said I can go and he's not home, he's at work.' And so, he said, 'Well, I'll wait until your dad gets here.'"

Five hours passed before Shell's father got home, but Gilliam was still there. He told him about his intent to take Shell to Maryland State and promised that he would get an education and graduate in four years. Shell's father stood there in silence for a few minutes as he pondered the proposition. Both he and Shell's mother had only gotten a sixth-grade education, and now someone was at his door promising to send their son to college for free. Finally, he responded.

"He said, 'If you promise me that you'll take care of my son and make sure he doesn't get into any trouble, then he can go,'" Shell said. "And that was it. I had nothing else to say; I was on my way to Maryland State."

Shell was reluctant to enroll at Maryland State, but he soon warmed to the idea of going to school, meeting new friends, and putting himself on track to make something of himself. Playing professional football was nowhere near his mind, but he quickly noticed that there were scouts on the sidelines at seemingly every practice. Following his freshman year in 1964, he received questionnaires from the Cowboys and 49ers. After his sophomore year, even more came. In addition to the scouts and questionnaires, he saw teammates like Emerson Boozer get drafted.

"So, I said, 'Hey, there's a chance here,'" Shell said. "But then, in the back of my mind, the only thing I was thinking about was getting my degree and going back and coaching high school and becoming a teacher. That was the No. 1 goal for me. And then, of course, as you go along and move forward in your classes and your grade level, then you realize that the professional ranks are right there and there's an opportunity for you."

By his junior year, Shell thought he could play professionally as long as he stayed healthy and continued to improve. He finished his career as a four-year starter who earned All-America honors twice and was a three-time All-Central Intercollegiate Athletic Association selection. Shell gathered with some teammates to watch the 1968 draft, which was just the second time that the NFL and AFL held a joint draft. Toward the end of the third round, Shell got a call from Raiders scout Ron Wolf.

"He said, 'We just took you in the third round and we're very happy to have you as a member of the Raiders moving forward,'" Shell said. "Then he says, 'Did you expect to get drafted this high?' I said, 'Yeah, I expected to get drafted higher.'"

The Raiders were coming off a 13-1 record and an AFL championship in 1967, so it didn't come as a surprise that Shell started off as a backup. They went on to make the playoffs again in 1968 and 1969, but Shell wasn't complaining about his role on the bench.

"I was an AFL guy because one thing the AFL was doing was giving opportunities to a lot of guys from historically Black schools," Shell said. "I remember rooting for the Raiders and watching Jim Otto and Gene Upshaw as a rookie and the Mad Bomber [Daryle Lamonica]. So, I was happy that I was going to become a Raider. My first two years, I was like an apprentice. I learned the game. I was watching, learning, and trying to get better by honing my skills."

Shell got called up to the starting lineup in 1970, which was the first season following the AFL-NFL merger. In a short amount of time, he'd developed immensely under offensive line coach Ollie Spencer.

"He was a guy who was very patient," Shell said. "He taught techniques that I'd never utilized before. I was fortunate. I always tell people 'til this day: Ollie Spencer is the greatest offensive line coach I can think of being in the league. . . . Ollie was my guy. I love that guy to death. He was a very good communicator with young players. He'd talk to you.

"And I was my own worst critic. Oh boy, I was hard on myself. I'd make a mistake and I even knew it during the game and I knew it after the game. And Ollie would tell me the next day, 'Big Art, you played a hell of a game, man.' I'd say, 'No, Ollie, what about this play here and this play here?' He'd say, 'Big Art, you got to stop that. You played a great game. You can't be perfect. Nobody's perfect. You're gonna make a mistake here and there, but you played great.'"

Shell indeed played great as soon as he took over and would become a Pro Bowl–caliber player by 1972. He worked hard to get to that point but acknowledged that lining up alongside Upshaw, who'd held down the fort at left guard since 1967, helped.

"We formed a bond moving forward where we knew what each other were thinking," Shell said. "During the course of the game, if the defense did something, we would change our blocking scheme because he knew what we were supposed to do. We didn't have to say a word. We didn't have time to say anything, but we could fall into blocking schemes and change them according to what the defense showed us at the last second. So, it was great playing with him; what a great player and a great guy."

The two would eventually become trailblazers off the field, with Upshaw the first Black executive director of the NFL Players Association and Shell's historic coaching stint, but their bond was always rooted in their time in the trenches. Shell remembers those times fondly and in great detail.

"Everybody talks about pass protection. Do you know that the Raiders system was a seven-step drop just about 99 percent of the time?" Shell said. "These people talk about three-step drops and five-step drops today. During the time I played? If we heard something like, '91 quick fire zone,' that was a three-step drop in our system; if we got that three times in a year, we were lucky. I remember we were playing Minnesota in a regular-season game and Daryle Lamonica called a 91 quick fire zone. Now Gene has Alan Page in front of him, so he says, 'Shit, I'ma cut this sucka.' I didn't do that; I just butted up my guy and stood up. So, Gene cut Alan Page and he looked up and Alan Page crawled and jumped over him and Daryle was still holding the damn ball. He looked and said, 'Goddamn, Daryle, it's a three-step drop. The ball is supposed to be gone.' Daryle held the ball and got sacked [laughs]. I said, 'You see why I don't cut? We don't get this play call many times. When you get a call, you can't be going and cutting.' Gene thought he was gonna get a shot in on Alan Page and Alan Page got a sack and, boy, he was so mad."

The two would start alongside each other from 1970 through 1980. During that span, the Raiders made the playoffs eight times and won two Super Bowls.

"Al Davis had an eye for talent," Shell said. "Ron Wolf worked for him and he trained Ron and they had an eye for talent. They knew what they wanted. Al knew what kinds of players he wanted for each position on the team and what was expected of that particular player. He knew the size and he knew the speed that he was looking for from every single player at every position.

"So, he had a mold and you had to fit into that mold. Our teams kept competing and being exciting every year. . . . We had some good teams. We had outstanding coaches. We had outstanding players that played for the Raiders."

One of the most special things about Shell was his durability. He played in his first 156 games, missed five games due to injury, and then played in another 51 consecutive contests. He played 15 years, appeared in 207 regular-season games, started in 169 of those games, and played another 23 playoff games.

"I think you have to be built a certain way," Shell said. "Some guys can be injury prone. I was a pretty big guy. I was a pretty strong guy. Naturally strong; I wasn't a big-time weightlifter. That was not it. My strength came from within. And I think most of our team was built like that. Some lifted a lot of weights and some guys didn't. I ain't care too much for lifting all them damn weights. It was enough just lifting my body, moving forward and driving the sled.

"Big John used to like us to drive that doggone sled, man. That seven-man sled was his baby and we'd push that thing. It'd build your legs up, it'd build your stamina up, and it made you strong at the end of games. We could dig down deep at the end of games and pass protect."

That was made more difficult by the fact that the Raiders' offense was predicated on seven-step drops by the quarterback to allow receivers time to get open down the field. Shell estimated that they might have called plays with a three-step drop just a handful of times per year.

Whether they were under the leadership of Madden or Flores, the Raiders liked to air it out on offense. That put a lot of pressure on the offensive line, but that was simply the way of life for the group.

"If you played for the Raiders on the offensive line, our system was we're gonna hold the ball," Shell said. "And coach was in practice telling the quarterback, 'Hold the ball, hold the ball, hold the ball. Let the receivers get open.' It was all seven-step drops and the receivers running deep routes and the line had to hold. So, you had to be pretty good to play on that offensive line and hold that wall like we did.

"But we were capable of doing that. Nowadays, guys are running three-step drops and five-step drops. Hell, we didn't know what that was."

Shell excelled regardless, but eventually it took a toll on his body. During the first day of training camp going into the 1982 season, the offense called a run play going to his side of the field. He was lined up across from a rookie defensive lineman, came off the ball to make contact, and realized that he couldn't move him. He came back to the huddle and asked Flores to call the same play. The same thing happened.

"I said to myself right then, 'This is it,'" Shell said. "And so, after practice that morning, I walked into Tom's office and I said, 'Tom, I think it's time. It's time for me to let this thing go. I can't do this like I want to anymore. I could hang on, but I don't want to do that.'"

He was ready to retire on the spot, but Flores convinced him to stay on board as the swing tackle that season. After the Raiders lost in the playoffs, he hung up his cleats for good. It was time to transition into coaching.

Shell sat in a meeting room in January 1989 awaiting word of his Hall of Fame selection. But first, he received different news: his father was in the hospital with an illness. A day after learning he would be inducted as a member of the 1989 class, his father died.

Shell would've been devastated regardless of the timing, but it felt particularly cruel to lose his father just after learning about one of the biggest accomplishments of his life. He'd find some semblance of solace when he learned that at least his father knew about it.

"My brother said to me—because Dad was waiting to hear about the Hall of Fame, too—that when they found out that I made the Hall of Fame, they went and told him," Shell said. "And they said he wasn't talking much; it was like he mumbled. But they said when they told him I made the Hall of Fame, in a clear voice he just said, 'That's so nice.' Just like that. That was tough."

Once his father's funeral was over, Shell had to prepare for the 1989 season. Four games into the campaign, another shock wave reverberated through his life when coach Mike Shanahan was fired and he was chosen as the replacement.

Shell guided the team to a 7-5 record that season and led the team to three playoff appearances before he was fired following the 1994 season. (He also later returned for a one-season stint in 2006.) While he hoped for a different ending to his tenure, the significance of it given the history he made as a Black man wasn't lost on him.

"That was big," Shell said. "It was good for everybody that it happened, but it doesn't surprise me. Al Davis was that kind of guy. He cared about his players more than anything else besides his family. He was always wanting to know what was going on in society. We used to talk every now and then to all of the Black players about what was going on in the country. He was aware of it and he was sensitive to some of the things that we were going through as Black people.

"I used to always talk about coaching, and he knew I wanted to coach. But to become the head coach? It shocked a lot of people. It shocked me when he called me on the phone, but it also didn't shock me. Because I'd think if anybody would do it, it'd be him. He saw beyond color. He looked at human beings. He was sensitive to the Black people, but he looked beyond all that crap that was going on and he was sensitive to the human beings that he liked that were part of his organization. That says a lot about him."

Shell had gone from growing up in the Jim Crow South to becoming a Hall of Fame player in the NFL to breaking barriers in the league as a coach. The chances of that all coming together would have seemed impossible to him at the beginning, but none of it was by accident.

"There's a lot of pride in what happened," Shell said. "I'm the type of person that believes things happen because they're supposed to happen. . . . I was just fortunate to be someone to come through that organization and have the opportunities that were given to me to play with some of the greatest players in the history of the National Football League and be associated with one of the best organizations ever in the National Football League."

Shell is undoubtedly right there with the players, coaches, and organization that he loves: one of the best ever.

75.
Lance Alworth

Lance Alworth was the first AFL player inducted into the Pro Football Hall of Fame.

Position: Wide Receiver

Teams: Chargers (1962–1970), Cowboys (1971–1972)

By Matthew Fairburn

Al Davis loved speed. The late owner of the Raiders was infatuated with players who could outrun the opponent and spent a career building teams around the idea that "speed kills" and "you can't teach speed." He chased receivers with scorching 40-yard dash times and quarterbacks with big arms to get them the ball. And it's easy to trace the origins of Davis's love affair with speed to the early 1960s and Lance Alworth.

Davis was the Los Angeles/San Diego Chargers' wide receivers coach from 1960 until 1962. In 1962, the AFL's Oakland Raiders and NFL's San Francisco 49ers both drafted Alworth, a flanker out of the University of Arkansas who earned the nickname "Bambi" because of his graceful long strides and leaping ability as a receiver. Davis played a hand in the Chargers trading multiple players to the Raiders for the right to negotiate with Alworth. Alworth didn't have an agent, but he knew what he wanted was a no-cut contract. The Chargers offered him one with a $20,000 salary and a $10,000 signing bonus over two years. Alworth called the 49ers and said he didn't care about the money, but he wanted a contract that guaranteed his spot on the team. The 49ers said they didn't offer those.

"So, I hung up the phone and never talked to them again," Alworth recalled.

The 49ers lived to regret that. Alworth played in only four games in 1962 because of injury. But Alworth had seven straight seasons with 1,000 yards receiving from 1963 until 1969. He had five seasons with at least 1,200 receiving yards. In the 1960s, Alworth had three of the seven best receiving seasons in terms of yards per game of all players in the AFL and NFL. Even as passing statistics have ballooned in recent years, Alworth, who ended his career in 1972, holds the NFL record with 12 touchdown catches of 70-plus yards. He averaged 75.5 yards per game in his career, which is 11th all time and fifth all time if you exclude active receivers. He also averaged 18.9 yards per reception, the highest mark of any player with at least 10,000 career receiving yards.

Even when teams didn't throw the ball as often as they do now, even when defensive backs could get away with more contact at the line of scrimmage, even when teams played only 14 games in a season, Alworth still amassed numbers that stand up nearly 50 years later.

AFL historian and researcher Todd Tobias said, "If you talk to people that really knew football in the '60s and had watched Lance play and have watched a lot of football in the decades since, Lance is one of the very few guys that almost universally people say he could still be a star today. Whatever qualities he had would translate to the modern game and he would be just fine."

Tobias wrote his master's thesis on then-Chargers coach Sid Gillman, authored a book on the 1960s Chargers, and has dedicated his website, "Tales from the American Football League," to AFL research. He's struck up a friendship with Alworth, and one of his projects involved researching another of Alworth's impressive stats. Alworth couldn't remember exactly how many passes he dropped in his career, but he guessed it was around a dozen. Tobias combed through the official play-by-play accounts of each individual game and counted exactly 12 drops over the course of Alworth's 11-year career in the NFL and AFL.

"It's almost like the position was made for me," Alworth said. "I love to run and I love to catch the ball."

Alworth had a chance coming out of high school to sign a contract with the New York Yankees. Alworth was a star center fielder who loved chasing down fly balls in the outfield. But his parents wanted him to go to school rather than turn pro immediately, and Alworth was more wired for football than baseball anyway.

"In baseball, you don't get any action," Alworth said. "You wait for someone to hit you the ball and you bat every three or four innings. In football, you're busy all the time."

A Mississippi native, Alworth ended up at Arkansas due to unusual circumstances. Ole Miss football coach Johnny Vaught didn't allow his players to be married. Alworth had gotten married in high school and thus could only go to Ole Miss to play baseball. Arkansas offered him the chance to play football and he jumped at it. He played mostly as a halfback at Arkansas, helping the team win or share three Southwest Conference titles.

Once he arrived in San Diego, Gillman shared his vision for Alworth at a new position: flanker. The position proved to be the perfect fit for a player with Alworth's speed, leaping ability, and ball-tracking skills. Gillman once told the *Los Angeles Times*, "He was the greatest combination runner, jumper and catcher I ever saw. His sense of timing was so great that with him out there, we felt that the fly pattern was no more a gamble than a run."

Alworth credits Gillman's offensive genius and the arm of quarterback John Hadl for the gaudy statistics he accumulated during his career. When he watches games now, Alworth wonders what it would have been like to get as many targets as receivers do these days.

"I wish we would have thrown the ball more," Alworth said. "It's not even the numbers. It's just the idea that it would have been a heck of a lot of fun to do. To heck with the numbers, just throw the ball more to me. It's fun!"

The numbers help Alworth find a spot on this list and many other lists of the greatest players in pro football history. But numbers still aren't the perfect way to capture what Alworth meant to the sport. It's difficult to compare statistics from different eras, especially when Alworth played most of his career in the AFL before the AFL and NFL merged. He battled the stigma that the AFL was an inferior league until he became the first AFL player enshrined in the Pro Football Hall of Fame.

When the Cowboys traded for Alworth in 1971, he was about to turn 31 years old. Dallas coach Tom Landry called him into his office and told him, "If you block for me, we'll win a Super Bowl." Alworth said he was willing to block. Landry said, "Good," and walked out of the room.

They did just that, beating the Dolphins 24–3 in Super Bowl VI in January 1972.

Alworth's lasting memory of his time with the Cowboys is that they didn't throw him the ball often. While he may not have been a focal point of the Cowboys' offense, Alworth did catch the first touchdown in the Cowboys' Super Bowl win. That and his blocking helped him become the rare player with an AFL championship and a Super Bowl ring.

In one of his first games with the Cowboys, Alworth was chasing a play away from the ball when he got leveled from behind. When he looked up, a player was standing over him and said, "Welcome to the NFL." Never a trash talker, Alworth found him a few plays later and returned the favor with a hit of his own. Afterward, the opposing player extended his hand for a truce.

That stoic, hard-nosed style of play helped Alworth earn the respect of every cornerback and linebacker he played against. Listen to those who played in both the AFL and NFL and they'll tell you Alworth was arguably the best receiver in either league during that era.

Johnny Sample, who played for four teams across both leagues, wrote in his book, *Confessions of a Dirty Ballplayer*, that Alworth was the best receiver he ever played against.

"He did everything perfectly, and there was no intimidating him," Sample wrote.

"I just couldn't believe that one man could do so many things so well."

Booker Edgerson, who played eight seasons at cornerback for the Buffalo Bills and won two AFL championships, still considers Alworth one of the toughest players he lined up against. Edgerson was covering him in the game in which Alworth set a record by catching a pass in his 96th consecutive game. There's a picture of the catch in the Hall of Fame, which allows Edgerson to joke with his friends that he made it to Canton.

"He had the speed, he had the hands, he had the athletic ability to maneuver his body around a lot," Edgerson said in an interview. "He would be a star now just as he was back then. He was just an outstanding ballplayer. And he had a great attitude. He never once talked trash. That guy is going to continue to be in the top 50 players of all time. I don't care how long the league goes. He was that good."

In Alworth's mind, he never needed to do much talking on the field. The way he went after the football said more than he ever could.

"The main thing is when the ball is thrown, it's mine," Alworth said. "You're not going to get it. I'm going to do whatever I have to do to catch it."

Alworth, who still lives in the San Diego area, said he's amazed by the life he's lived. Asked what it meant to still be considered among the greatest to ever play the game nearly 50 years after he finished playing, Alworth got choked up. He said no specific achievements or games meant as much to him as the friendships he formed and the joy they spread to the fans.

"It's really hard to put into words because you don't really think about what you're doing when you're doing it," Alworth said. "You just go out and do your thing. And do it to the best of your ability. And you know, whatever happens, happens. You thank the good Lord for your ability and just go out and do it. And if you happen to be better than someone else or achieve things more than other people did, then that's fantastic. But you did only because you were given that ability."

74.
Chuck Bednarik

Chuck Bednarik was the No. 1 pick in the 1949 draft
and went on to fourteen great seasons with the Eagles.

Position: Linebacker

Team: Eagles (1949–1962)

By Bo Wulf

There's a scene you can picture that gets to the heart of Chuck Bednarik's legend—even if you never saw him play or know nothing about him. Imagine there's been a change of possession. The respective offensive and defensive units are trotting off the field. From the sidelines, two new groups straggle out and buckle their chin straps. All the while, there's one person in the middle of the field who hasn't moved, a grizzled 35-year-old, No. 60, with his hands on his hips, patiently waiting for 21 lesser men to join him in the fray.

In many ways, Bednarik is something of an avatar for a bygone era. As he often reminded anyone who would listen, he was the last of the 60-minute men. In a tough game for tough men, "Concrete Charlie" might have been the toughest of them all. He was a 10-time All-Pro, a first-ballot Hall of Famer, and the icon in what might be the most famous football photograph of all time.

As longtime general manager Ernie Accorsi succinctly put it, "He was the John Wayne of football."

On the final day of what he announced would be his final season, Bednarik was honored by his longtime team, the Philadelphia Eagles. For "Chuck Bednarik Day," he was joined on the field before the game by his wife and children, gifted with a fancy new color TV, and thanked for everything he'd done as arguably the greatest player in franchise history. He gave a nice speech.

It was December 13, 1959, and the Eagles blew a fourth-quarter lead against Jim Brown and the visiting Cleveland Browns in a 28–21 loss to close the season.

If that had indeed been it, Bednarik would not rank so high on this list. He'd have still been a surefire Hall of Famer, yes, but the legend of Concrete Charlie would not have endured. As the story goes, Bednarik's wife, Emma, gave birth that offseason to the couple's fifth daughter. As he did the math in his head of the forthcoming growth in bills, Bednarik rethought his retirement. After all, he had already moved to center full-time, which was easier on his body, and the team had a chance to be really good with Norm Van Brocklin at quarterback. So, he let the Eagles know he'd be back for the 1960 season.

The Eagles lost the season opener to the Browns before reeling off three wins heading into a rematch with Cleveland in Week 5. During the game, Philadelphia linebacker Bob Pellegrini was carted off the field with a broken leg. Roster sizes were small in those days, and there wasn't much depth at the position. So Buck Shaw, the team's head coach, looked to his starting center, who just so happened to also be a seven-time Pro Bowl linebacker. Shaw asked Bednarik if he'd be willing to go in and replace Pellegrini.

"Fuckin' right I can," Bednarik said, at least as he told it over the years.

In his prime, Bednarik was the league's best middle linebacker. But that spot was occupied now by Chuck Weber, so Bednarik played Pelligrini's spot on the outside, a position he'd never played before. He needed some pre-snap instructions now and then, but he mostly followed his instincts. Go find the ball.

The Eagles won that game and the two that followed, setting up a much-anticipated showdown with the 5-1-1 New York Giants and their glamorous halfback, Frank Gifford. With the game tied 10–10 in the fourth quarter, Bednarik forced a fumble that was returned by defensive back Jimmy Carr for a touchdown to give the Eagles a 17–10 lead. On the ensuing drive, Gifford caught a pass in the middle of the field and angled for the sideline to stop the clock only to be blind-sided by a Bednarik clothesline. Gifford landed on his back and his head snapped back onto the turf while he fumbled the ball, knocking him out cold. Bednarik's celebratory pose was captured for eternity by *Sports Illustrated* photographer John G. Zimmerman.

Bednarik insisted for years he was simply celebrating the game-winning fumble recovery. "This game is fucking over," is the line he often said when retelling the story. He maintained he had no clue Gifford was unconscious on the ground, although that's up for debate. Gifford ended up missing the rest of the season and the entirety of the 1961 season because of the hit, though the two maintained a friendly relationship over the years. "I made you famous, didn't I?" Bednarik remembered Gifford telling him once. "Yes, Frank, I guess you did."

It was all part of the legend.

"I always said if you're going to do something big, do it in New

York," Bednarik wrote. "If that hit happened against any other team or any other player, no one would remember it."

Bednarik credited his fortitude to his childhood in Bethlehem, Pennsylvania. He was the son of Slovakian immigrants, and his father worked at Bethlehem Steel. There wasn't much to do aside from playing ball and getting in fistfights, both of which he did plenty. Then he went off to World War II, where he served as a B-24 bomber in the Eighth Air Force for 30 missions over Germany in 1944 and '45, a badge he wore proudly for the rest of his life.

"Bednarik almost bought it himself when his plane, crippled by flak, skidded off the runway on landing and crashed," John Schulian wrote in *Sports Illustrated* in 1993. "To escape he kicked out a window and jumped 20 feet to the ground. Then he did what he did after every mission, good or bad. He lit a cigarette and headed for the briefing room, where there was always a bottle on the table. 'I was 18, 19 years old,' [Bednarik] says, 'and I was drinking that damn whiskey straight.'"

After the war, he went off to Penn, where he was so good as a two-way player that he became the No. 1 pick in the 1949 NFL Draft. His legacy lives on each year when the Chuck Bednarik Award is doled out to the nation's top collegiate defender.

In the NFL, he became Concrete Charlie, not because of his style of play or chiseled physique, though both were apt. Like most players in those days, he needed some extra money beyond the football paycheck. Every day after practice, he'd head over to his other office at Warner Concrete for his second job as a concrete salesman. He must have been very good at that, too. Imagine needing concrete in Philadelphia in the 1950s and saying no to Chuck Bednarik.

He quickly made a reputation in the NFL, too, playing center, linebacker, and long snapper while earning All-Pro honors from 1950 to '57.

"Talk to the guys from that era about Bednarik, and these are guys who are not easily awed," Ray Didinger, the Hall of Fame sportswriter, said. "They were not saying this because they liked him a whole lot, because they didn't. But there was a genuine admiration bordering on awe for what this guy did."

Toughness was always at the heart of that admiration, and everyone had a story about Concrete Charlie. There was the time Bednarik punched a teammate who was goofing off during warm-ups. Or the time he and Browns offensive lineman Chuck Noll were seen on TV brawling on the field after a game as the credits rolled, only for Bednarik to get a phone call that night from Bert Bell, the league's commissioner, castigating him for ruining the image of the family-friendly game he was trying to sell. Or the time, during an exhibition game, that his biceps muscle came off the bone and slipped to his lower arm.

"Bednarik went to the sideline and went to the trainer and said, 'Where's the tape?'" said Didinger, relaying the story as told to him many times by Tom Brookshier. "And the guy handed him the tape and Bednarik pushed the biceps with his other hand back up into position, taped around his elbow to hold the biceps in place, and went back into the game. And this was an exhibition game."

"Tom said, 'That was Chuck.' The guys on the team just understood he was a different dude."

Later in life, Bednarik was cast as something of a curmudgeon. He objected to the high salaries of players too specialized to ever carry his jock. He mocked Deion Sanders as a two-way player, saying Sanders couldn't tackle Bednarik's wife. A spat with Eagles owner Jeffrey Lurie (later resolved) led him to say he was rooting against the Eagles in their February 2005 Super Bowl appearance against the Patriots.

He never lost his edge. Just ask the poor guy whose neck was on the line during an argument that resulted in the then-68-year-old Bednarik getting fined $250 by the town for choking.

Back to 1960.

After the Gifford hit, the Eagles and Giants played again the following week. Shaw was wary of wearing Bednarik out, so he started a younger player at center. The result was a barrage of pressure from the Giants defense in the first half and a 20–17 halftime deficit for the Eagles. Bednarik went back in at center in the second half, and suddenly Van Brocklin had plenty of time to lead the Eagles to a 31–23 comeback win.

They were in the NFL championship game four games later against Vince Lombardi's Green Bay Packers at Franklin Field, Bednarik's college stomping grounds. Bednarik had won a championship as a rookie with the Eagles in 1949, but he wasn't the protagonist. That was Steve Van Buren's team.

It's important to emphasize that what Bednarik did that day was considered as unthinkable then as it is in hindsight. He was 35, the oldest player on the field, and full-time two-way players were already a thing of the past. "An almost impossible task, even for a young man," Tex Maule wrote in *Sports Illustrated* that year.

Of course, for Bednarik it was possible. There were 142 plays in that game and Bednarik played 139 of them, only taking a breather on the Eagles' kickoffs. With the clock winding down and the Eagles clinging to a 17–13 lead, the Packers were on the edge of the red zone. From the 22-yard line with about 10 seconds left, Bart Starr completed a short pass to All-Pro fullback Jim Taylor, who quickly broke a tackle and darted toward the end zone only to be tackled by who else but Bednarik. As the clock wound down, Bednarik stayed on top of Taylor to cement the victory.

"OK, Jim, you can get up now," Bednarik always said he said.

"Typically, legendary-type seasons or athletes kind of grow over time in the retelling," Didinger said. "You know, 450-foot home runs become 600-foot home runs. He broke 10 tackles on that run when he only broke three. They grow and they grow and they grow in the retelling. I think that Bednarik's legend is one of the few where what he accomplished is actually greater than the legend that followed. Everybody always says he played for 60 minutes, but what's kind of lost in that is, 'Yeah, but he played great for 60 minutes.' It isn't just that he was on the field for 60 minutes, which is a feat in itself for a 35-year-old man. What some people fail to point out is that he played frickin' great.

"To me, that's like Roy Hobbs stuff."

Bednarik ended up playing two more seasons as a center, finally retiring after the 1962 season as an eight-time Pro Bowler. He was inducted into the Pro Football Hall of Fame in 1967 and was named to the league's 50th anniversary team, 75th anniversary team, and 100th anniversary team. He is probably the greatest Eagle ever and his legend has been passed down through generations of fans. He died in 2015.

There's a photo of Bednarik in the postgame locker room of the 1960 championship game that borders on goofy anachronism if you don't know Bednarik. Over his right shoulder, a reporter is interviewing a shirtless Eagle. Bednarik is staring off into the distance, his hair handsomely tousled, his No. 60 jersey still on and his fist mid-pump in celebration. His mouth is smiling as much as it can while juggling both a victory cigar and a customary cigarette. Another mission accomplished.

How, then, to possibly compare Bednarik, the last of an extinct brand of player, to the greats from the modern era? The entirety of his career is overwhelming in scope. In Eagles parlance, he was like Jason Kelce, Seth Joyner, and Jon Dorenbos rolled into one. But could he have even had a career in today's game?

At 6-foot-3, 233, Bednarik was one of the bigger players of his time. With 60 years' worth of advancements in weight training at his disposal, it's fair to think he would have been able to bulk up enough to hang physically. What position would he have played? Would he have been fast enough to play linebacker? Or big enough to play center? Didinger thinks his defensive instincts would have translated to any era. It's a fun hypothetical.

Before he was a three-time general manager, Ernie Accorsi was a football-fanatic kid in Hershey, Pennsylvania. He was 10 when the Eagles moved their training camp to Hershey in 1951 and spent every summer from then on following the team's every move. Then his career gave him an up-close look at football's evolution into the twenty-first century. There might not be anyone alive better suited to answer the question.

"Most likely he's gonna be the center," Accorsi said. "No question in my mind . . . he would have been an All-Pro today, too. First of all, he would have willed it."

On this, Bednarik deserves the last word. And at least one person is lucky he's not around to deliver it in person.

From *Sports Illustrated* in 1993: "[A] stranger asked whether he, Chuck Bednarik, the last of the 60-minute men, could have played in today's NFL. 'I wasn't rude or anything,' he says, 'but inside I was thinking: I'd like to punch this guy in the mouth.'"

73.
Marion Motley

Marion Motley (76) cut an imposing figure as a ball carrier for the Browns.

Position: Running Back
Teams: Browns (1946–1953), Steelers (1955)

By Zac Jackson

Marion Motley was a trailblazer. He was also a punishing runner, an adept blocker and player gifted and instinctive enough to excel on both sides of the ball. In his autobiography, legendary coach Paul Brown wrote that he believed Motley could have been a Hall of Fame–caliber player solely as a linebacker had the Browns not used him on offense.

Giving him the ball, though, worked well for the fledgling Cleveland squad, which won AAFC titles in each of Motley's first four seasons and then won the NFL title in 1950, the franchise's first year in the league. Motley led the NFL in rushing and in yards per attempt in 1950 from his fullback position—the second rushing title he won in his first five seasons after starting his barrier-breaking pro career at the age of 26.

Brown, generally regarded as the godfather of modern football, had long known of Motley's talents. Motley's only losses during his ultra-productive high school career at Canton McKinley came against Brown's fabled Massillon teams. After Motley played briefly in college at South Carolina State and then at Nevada, he joined the Navy and played for Brown at the Great Lakes Naval Training Station. In 1946, Brown and Cleveland's new pro franchise in the AAFC signed Motley and lineman Bill Willis, who became two of the first four Black players to play professional football since a de facto ban had been established in the early 1930s.

Willis had previously played for Brown at Ohio State. Both Motley and Willis ended up in the Pro Football Hall of Fame; Willis served as Motley's presenter when Motley was inducted in 1968. Motley didn't say much at the ceremony, which took place not far from where he'd played high school football. Motley was never much of a public speaker and never sought the spotlight he earned with his bruising running style that pushed those early Browns teams to long-lasting fame.

"The only statistic Marion ever knew was whether we won or lost," Brown wrote in his autobiography. "The man was completely unselfish."

Motley had said he originally believed Brown only invited him to camp with the Browns because Willis needed a roommate, but his talent won out.

And more than 70 years later, some of his numbers are still jarring. Motley ranked among the top 10 rushers five times and twice was named a first-team All-Pro. His 5.7 yards per-carry average still stands as the third-best all time and the best average by a running back. Only quarterbacks Michael Vick and Randall Cunningham have higher per-carry averages.

On October 29, 1951, Motley ran through and around the Pittsburgh Steelers for 188 yards on only 11 carries. His 17.1 yards per-carry average in a single game stood as the NFL record for more than 50 years until Vick broke it in 2002.

Motley rushed for 98 yards and a touchdown in the 1946 AAFC title game and also started at linebacker. In his second season, Motley scored a career-high 10 touchdowns—eight rushing, one receiving, and one on an interception return. He ran for 133 yards and three touchdowns in the 1948 title game, capping a season in which he won his first rushing title and averaged 6.8 yards per touch on 170 touches. Starting in the 1948 season, he played only on the offensive side.

Motley was listed at 6-foot-1, 232 pounds, and power was his game. He was the league's rushing leader in 1948 and 1950, and his eight rushing touchdowns in 1949 also led the league.

"I was as big as the linemen I ran against, so I didn't worry about them," Motley said in a quote that jumps off his Hall of Fame biography page. "And once I ran over a [defensive] back twice, I didn't have to run over him a third time."

Though Motley used his muscle to power through defenders when his number was called in Brown's trap and draw series, he also contributed to the success of the Browns' passing game as a heady blocker and occasional pass catcher. He averaged 18.8 yards per catch on 10 receptions as a rookie and finished his career with seven receiving touchdowns.

A lingering knee injury worsened as Motley's career progressed, and he clearly was not the same player in the back half of his pro career that he was in the first half. Probably not coincidentally, the Browns lost the NFL title game in 1951, '52, and '53. Though Motley announced his retirement in 1954 and did not play that year, he was traded to the Steelers in 1955 and played just six games, totaling two rushing attempts.

Cincinnati Bengals owner Mike Brown was 11 years old in 1946 when his father became coach and part-owner of the Browns. Mike Brown has long referred to Motley as one of his own favorite players and has said his father believed that Motley was the best back he'd ever coached. As for signing Motley and Willis in 1946, Mike Brown has said his father believed the best players should play. Motley and Willis joined the Browns in 1946, a year before Jackie Robinson broke baseball's color barrier.

The Browns adding Motley and Willis was met with public resistance. The team received threatening letters, and Motley talked of dealing with slurs and cheap shots from some opponents.

"Sometimes I wanted to just kill some of those guys, and the officials would just stand right there," Motley said in the book *Legends by the Lake*. "They'd see those guys stepping on us and heard them saying things and just turn their backs. That kind of crap went on for two or three years until they found out what kind of players we were."

In Canton, a street was named after Motley and in August 2022, a statue of Motley (the Marion Motley memorial) was placed in Stadium Park, which sits just a few hundred yards east of the Pro Football Hall of Fame.

Motley was 79 when he died in 1999. Five years earlier, he'd been named a member of the NFL's 75th anniversary team.

"Marion Motley is what the NFL is all about," said longtime Browns tackle and radio broadcaster Doug Dieken. "An NFL city identifies with its players, and the players identify with the city. He represented winning when the Browns were getting started. He represented progress in breaking the color barrier. He fit Cleveland because he grew up an hour south and he didn't have some easy straight-line path to playing for the Browns. He waited, he worked, and people embraced him when he started playing for the Browns.

"Marion was a gentleman to everyone except those poor guys who had to try to tackle him. He was a Hall of Famer in every way he could be."

72.
Mel Blount

Mel Blount had a knack for game-changing plays in the biggest moments for the Steelers.

Position: Cornerback
Team: Steelers (1970–1983)

By Sean Gentille

I magine, for a second, that you're a professional football player.

One day, somebody—your agent, a coach, a reporter—calls you up and says, "Hey, there's a new rule on the books, and it's there because of you."

Why is this happening? Why did the phone ring? For most men, that's been an honor born of bad luck. Jesse James and Calvin Johnson? Congrats. Tweaks to what constitutes a catch didn't put their touchdowns on the board. Tom Brady? He still missed almost all of the 2008 season after a low hit begat a torn ACL.

Things were different in 1978. When the NFL changed the guidelines on what, exactly, a defensive back could do to a receiver—on how he could terrorize them and when—it wasn't due to the misfortune of its namesake. The "Mel Blount Rule" doesn't exist because of something that was done to the Steelers' Hall of Fame cornerback. It exists because of what he did to others.

And the game, at least as we've come to know it, exists because of him, too. After eight seasons, four Super Bowls, three All-Pro nods, one Defensive Player of the Year award, and 35 interceptions, the NFL decided to stop Mel Blount. They tried to stop Mel Blount. Easier said than done for a 6-foot-3, 205-pound, ball-seeking missile.

RULE 8 SECTION 4 ARTICLES 1-4: ILLEGAL CONTACT
Within the area five yards beyond the line of scrimmage, a defensive player may chuck an eligible receiver in front of him. The defender is allowed to maintain continuous and unbroken contact within the five-yard zone, so long as the receiver has not moved beyond a point that is even with the defender.

"He played back in the day when they had no rules, so Mel could just knock the receivers around all over the place," Rod Woodson— another Hall of Fame Steelers cornerback—told the NFL Network in 2019. "So, the competition committee comes together and says, 'You know what? We can't have DBs like this knocking receivers around because they can't get down the field.' So, they [came up with] the 5-yard chuck.

"So, thank you, Mel. Appreciate it."

Woodson's deadpan delivery of that line was impressive. It was also telling; the institution of the five-yard chuck rule didn't just revolutionize the game. It made the life of all defensive backs a little more difficult. Until 1978, they could make contact with receivers until the ball was in the air. In the post–Blount Rule world, the window got smaller. Woodson is old enough to daydream about legalized, downfield harassment. The current generation, for all intents and purposes, doesn't know anything else.

And none of them—not Woodson, not Deion Sanders, not Darrelle Revis, not Patrick Peterson—had to change midstream, as Blount did.

Blount's path to the NFL, all the way back to his youth and upbringing, gives clues as to how he became such an imposing physical presence on the field.

He entered the league as a third-round pick in the 1970 draft, an All-American at cornerback and safety out of Southern University, one of the many future Steelers stars scouted at HBCUs by the legendary Bill Nunn. The Steelers had just finished their second season under Chuck Noll, and their first with Joe Greene and L. C. Greenwood on the roster. With half of "The Steel Curtain" in the fold, it was time to add the star quarterback (Terry Bradshaw) and secondary centerpiece (Blount) for what became the sport's definitive dynasty.

Blount didn't think of playing in the NFL until his junior year, when he switched sides of the ball. He also didn't think much, as a kid who grew up in Georgia and went to college in Louisiana, of heading that far north. "I think every kid that grew up in the South wanted to stay, basically, in the South," Blount said in 2020. "I can remember coming to Pittsburgh after the draft and thinking, 'Oh my God, is this where I have to [live], and the weather.' . . . I didn't really start getting used to the weather until about 10 years after."

In other areas, he was plenty prepared.

"When I came to the [NFL], I just thought, 'Man, what an easy life this is.' Because when we played football in the SWAC, at all-Black colleges, it was physical when you got off the bus," he said. "So, the pro level, I didn't find it to be all that challenging. I was always physical, and I tell people that I'm the youngest of 11 kids.

There were seven boys and four girls, and we all grew up on a farm. It was work every day.

"So, physicality made me who I am."

Blount started 10 of 14 games as a rookie and picked off one pass, starting a streak that would last until the end of his career; in 11 seasons, he never had fewer than one interception, and often had more. Many more. Blount had two picks in 1971 and three in 1972. By 1975, he'd made his first All-Pro team and won Defensive Player of the Year. That season, he had 11 interceptions—still tied for 10th-most in any single season. When he wasn't making life impossible for wide receivers, he was doing the same for quarterbacks.

All the while, the Steelers' success compounded. In Blount's Defensive Player of the Year season, they won their second title, a 21–17 victory over the Cowboys in Super Bowl X.

"He kind of epitomized what Chuck used to tell us all the time: refuse to be denied," Greene told NFL Network. "And he was that guy. The receivers had no routes that they could run. They couldn't get off the line of scrimmage. And when they did, he'd get hands on them and reroute them."

Blount was an off-the-field leader, as well. When Donnie Shell was a rookie in 1974, he found himself playing mostly on special teams packages and as a nickel back, and he wasn't happy. Blount took him to dinner and praised his contributions, regardless of whether they came on kick coverage or not.

"What he did was bring me back in the fold of the team," Shell told former Steelers linebacker Arthur Moats. "I understood the team concept, that everyone has a part to play in it—whether you're out front or not starting and coming off the bench, like I was. He made me feel special."

Shell, a strong safety for all four Steelers Super Bowl teams in the '70s, was inducted into the Hall of Fame in 2021.

The league had seen enough by 1978. The rule outlawing bump-and-run, spearheaded by Dolphins head coach Don Shula, went on the books—and Blount took it personally, not just for what it meant for him as an individual, but what he believed it said about the league's view of the Steelers.

"When that happened, I took it as an insult," Blount said in a March 2021 interview with Peterson and former NFL cornerback Bryant McFadden. "You're putting this rule in because you think that's the only way I can play, and that it's going to slow me down.... They were trying to find ways to slow our defense down."

If that was the goal, the end results didn't change much. The Steelers had two more Super Bowls in their pockets—and Blount three more Pro Bowls—by the dynasty's end.

At the dynasty's start in 1974, the average NFL team completed about 14 of 27 passes for 153 yards per game. In 1979, "the quarterback league" was born, along with another NFL epoch. If it isn't on par with the AFL-NFL merger and the institution of the forward pass, it's close enough. In 2020, the average team completed 22 of 35 passes for 240 yards per game. It's basically impossible to compare today's quarterbacks with those of the '90s, let alone the '60s.

Blount, inducted into the Hall of Fame in 1989, is at peace with it all.

"My kids, my grandkids, they just think it's the coolest thing," he told Peterson and McFadden. "The older I get, the more I appreciate the fact that I had that kind of impact on the game."

As for how Mel Blount would fare now, after more than 40 seasons of NFL life under the rule that exists because of him, and the other changes that have come in its wake?

"I'm coming out of every game, and I'm not lying, with at least two interceptions," he said, "if not more."

71.
LaDainian Tomlinson

LaDainian Tomlinson twice led the NFL in rushing yards and led the league in rushing touchdowns three times.

Position: Running Back

Teams: Chargers (2001–2009), Jets (2010–2011)

By Daniel Popper

Antonio Gates takes a deep breath, almost an overwhelmed sigh, after hearing the question.

What made LaDainian Tomlinson such a special player?

"Oh, man," he says.

Gates takes a few seconds, his mind cycling back through his seven seasons playing alongside Tomlinson in San Diego. Eventually, he settles on one telling story.

There is a specific combo block in football run schemes called a "trey" block, and it involves a tight end and an offensive tackle. The tight end and tackle are taught to double-team the defensive end in front of them, then once that block is secured, the tackle peels off and moves to the second level to take on and shield off the backside linebacker.

This is how the trey block is taught and schemed when you have a typical running back. But Tomlinson, of course, was no typical running back.

As Gates tells it, he and the Chargers' offensive tackles got to a point where the tackle would not peel off to get to the second level. They would simply double-team the defensive end.

"And we would leave a guy for LaDainian," Gates said with a chuckle. "LaDainian was going to make him miss."

"That was a LaDainian Tomlinson rule."

Yes, in many ways, Tomlinson played football by different rules. A gifted athlete with a truly rare combination of speed, strength, and vision, he was an utter nightmare in the open field.

"He could cut on a dime and leave nine-and-a-half cents change," said former Chargers fullback Lorenzo Neal.

Corralling him was as difficult as catching a leaf blowing in a swirling gust. His cuts were so quick, so precise, so otherworldly, he would be through a hole and hurdling toward the end zone quite literally in the blink of an eye.

"If you see the back of 21," Neal said, "it's too late."

When contact did come, Tomlinson's 5-foot-10, 215-pound frame was a stone wall—more like a battering ram.

"He wasn't afraid to run somebody over," said former Chargers center Nick Hardwick.

The end zone was home for Tomlinson during his 11-year Hall of Fame career. He ranks third all-time in total touchdowns with 162, trailing only Jerry Rice and his idol Emmitt Smith.

A single-season record 31 of those touchdowns, 28 of them rushing, came in Tomlinson's MVP season in 2006. He is one of only four non-quarterbacks—all running backs—to win the award this century. Tomlinson was explosive. But he was just as reliable as a touchdown machine in short-yardage situations. Of his 28 rushing touchdowns in 2006, 15 came from 5 yards out or less.

"When you got the ball inside the 2-yard line," the late Chargers head coach Marty Schottenheimer said in Tomlinson's *A Football Life* episode on NFL Network, "everybody in the stands knew what you were going to do with it."

Tomlinson had a counter for whatever a defense tried to do to stop him at the goal line. Leave a crease on the interior? He would get skinny and find it. Lack physicality in the hole? He would run through you. Clog up the line of scrimmage?

"He's going to jump, it seemed like, seven feet over the top of the pile," Hardwick said. "When it's LT over the top, what do you do?"

"LT had this want-to," Neal said. "He's very, very docile. But this guy would kill you on the field."

"It's the mindset that you have to have, being that close," Tomlinson said. "I won't be denied. I will not be stopped for these 2 yards."

Gates recalls the first game of that 2006 season, which was Philip Rivers's first NFL start at quarterback. Rivers only attempted 11 passes.

Tomlinson rushed for 131 yards and a touchdown on 31 carries.

The Chargers won 27–0.

"I was so pissed at the time that we only threw the ball like 10 times," Gates recalled with a smile. "But when you got a guy like LaDainian, that's just what happens."

Schottenheimer and Tomlinson were a perfect pairing. Schottenheimer, who took over as Chargers head coach in 2002 for Tomlinson's second NFL season, wanted to dominate and wear defenses down on the ground. And he had a running back who could bring that vision to life.

"It was everything for my confidence and the type of player I would become," Tomlinson said of Schottenheimer. "I needed that confidence from the head coach to say, 'Hey, we believe in you. We're going to put this ball in your belly and we believe good things are going to happen.'"

It all culminated in that 2006 season for Tomlinson, which remains the most valuable single season for any player in NFL history, according to Pro Football Reference's Approximate Value metric.

"Not only could he run the ball," Hardwick said, "he could run zone, inside zone, outside zone, he could run a pin-and-pull scheme, he could run all the powers and the gap schemes that you wanted to, he's very good at running man schemes, isos, and draws. He could do everything. So, there was never any limitations on, we've got to find a run for LT, we've got to find something to get it going. He just made things happen, so as an offensive lineman, you just blocked what was called to the best of your ability. Our identity was just to smash the ball and not be afraid to call the same run over and over and over again.

"He could also catch the ball really well out of the backfield. His route running was very high-end. And his pass blocking was exceptional too. So, there wasn't even a time that he needed to come off the field because he could do everything."

As the popularity of fantasy football rose in the 2000s, so did Tomlinson's global stardom. He is arguably the greatest fantasy football player ever, and his 2006 season remains the most productive fantasy season of all time, according to Pro Football Reference. The Chargers played the second-ever London game in October 2008 against the Saints. Many fans arrived at Wembley donning Tomlinson jerseys because he had won them fantasy leagues in that remarkable 2006 season.

"The appreciation that I have now removed from it," Tomlinson said of his fantasy legacy, "it's like, man, if I had known what I know back then, I think I could have put up even higher numbers."

Tomlinson finished his career with 13,684 yards rushing, the seventh-most all time. He also caught 624 passes in his career.

"He could have started at receiver in this league," Neal said. "He's that good."

All the while, he maintained a humility that rubbed off on and heavily influenced his teammates and coaches.

"This guy is a better person than he is a player," Neal said.

Tomlinson's most important legacy is in the city of San Diego. The year before Tomlinson was drafted in 2001, the Chargers went 1-15. Three seasons later, in 2004, with Drew Brees at quarterback and Schottenheimer as head coach, the Chargers made the playoffs for the first time since 1995. In 2006, they went 14-2 and earned the top seed in the AFC. In 2007, after the Chargers fired and replaced Schottenheimer with Norv Turner, the Chargers reached the AFC Championship Game—their first appearance in that game since 1994.

The Chargers, who moved to Los Angeles in 2017, have not returned to the AFC title game since.

"We had a winning culture and we had great coaches," Tomlinson said. "And we were always competing for it."

Tomlinson was indispensable on the field. Off the field, he was a pillar in the community, giving out free turkeys to underprivileged families for Thanksgiving, holding football camps, and participating in blood drives, shoe drives, and charity Christmastime shopping sprees.

"In my family the saying was, 'if we have enough, then we have enough to give,'" Tomlinson said.

The Chargers released Tomlinson during the 2010 offseason after nine seasons. He went on to play two seasons with the Jets, including a win over the Patriots in the 2010 playoffs that sent New York to the AFC Championship Game.

"When he left," Gates said, "I was able to really determine how great he was."

Tomlinson's departure from San Diego was considered unceremonious at the time. But he returned in 2012 to retire as a Charger. Tomlinson said he and Chargers owner Dean Spanos came to an agreement that he would retire a Charger before he was released in 2010.

The team retired his jersey in 2015. He was inducted into the Pro Football Hall of Fame in 2017.

"He helped us win a lot of games," Gates said.

70.
Terry Bradshaw

Terry Bradshaw was the first player to quarterback a team to four Super Bowl wins.

Position: Quarterback
Team: Steelers (1970–1983)

By Ed Bouchette

I t took Terry Bradshaw three years to become a winner, and then he never stopped.

The beginning was not pretty. The Steelers made him the first draft choice in 1970 after winning a coin flip with the Bears for that honor. He threw six touchdown passes and 24 interceptions as a rookie, and 13 touchdowns vs. 22 interceptions his second season as Pittsburgh continued its losing ways.

Then came their magical 1972 season when the Steelers went

11-3 as Bradshaw turned the corner. He let loose with the pass that became the Immaculate Reception via Franco Harris that gave the Steelers the first playoff victory in franchise history and put them in the AFC Championship Game. Two years later, Bradshaw and the Steelers won their first of four Super Bowls over six seasons.

Bradshaw overcame his early struggles in Pittsburgh as the first of only two quarterbacks (the other being Joe Montana) with 4-0 Super Bowl records. Steelers founder Art Rooney Sr. spotted his potential from the start.

Said Art Rooney Jr., who headed the team's personnel department that drafted Bradshaw, "My dad told him, 'I saw all the great athletes—Babe Ruth, Jack Dempsey, Red Grange. You're better than all of them,' and he went for it. It took him time."

Joe Greene, Chuck Noll's first draft pick a year before Bradshaw, became one of his biggest and most important supporters. Greene helped lift the young quarterback during his early struggles, and fans and media pleaded for the Steelers to replace him with the other Terry, local hero Terry Hanratty, who played high school football about an hour north of Pittsburgh in Butler. Hanratty was drafted the year before Bradshaw from Notre Dame.

"I had seen Terry [Bradshaw] throw the football in practice from one corner of the end zone to the next and landing that football in a big trash can," Greene said, explaining why he favored him. "I'd seen him throw the football on the line and hear it whistle. I said, 'This guy can throw the football.' And I'd seen him when we were in our infancy and he was getting killed and how tough he was, and standing in the pocket and getting beat up and still making plays. The passes he threw that were intercepted, I always thought that was confidence or overconfidence that he could put the ball where he wanted to. But sometimes it didn't get there because the defense did a better job, the cornerbacks did a better job. But it wasn't like he didn't know. He thought he could do that and many times he did."

Bradshaw, known by teammates and fans alike as the Blond Bomber, threw 212 touchdown passes and 210 interceptions, yet he also finished with a 107-51 record in the regular season and 14-5 in the postseason, including that perfect four-pack in Super Bowls. He earned the league's MVP award in 1978 and two Super Bowl MVPs.

"I think the thing that I'm most proud of as a football player was that I played big in big games," Bradshaw said during the NFL Network's *A Football Life* in 2019.

"He made a lot of big moments happen," teammate Franco Harris concurred on that show.

Bradshaw led the NFL twice in touchdown passes and to this day believes he could have played longer had he treated his right elbow injury and surgery in early 1983 differently. He played just one game that season, famously throwing two touchdown passes in the final game at Shea Stadium that helped put the Steelers in the playoffs.

But he walked off the field clutching his elbow that day never to play again. He was 35. He had torn the ulnar collateral ligament in his right elbow while throwing those TD passes in New York. He visited Dr. Frank Jobe, who developed the famous Tommy John surgery and offered it to Bradshaw back then. Looking back, he wished he had done it and extended his career, maybe won another Super Bowl (the Steelers lost to Dan Marino and the Miami Dolphins in the AFC Championship Game the following season).

"It was really my fault; no one but my own," Bradshaw said. "I should have done Tommy John. I should have done it. Why I didn't do it, I have no idea. . . . Today I would have had the Tommy John, I would have been out a year and I would have come back at 36 and ready to go. That truly is something I regret. I don't know what I was waiting on. Was I waiting on someone to say, 'We want you well'? It was so different back then. I can't say it was anybody's fault but my own."

Bradshaw transferred successfully to what Chuck Noll often called his players' post-NFL careers as their "life's work" as a studio analyst for CBS and then Fox. He has acted in movies, TV commercials, participated in a reality TV show with his daughters, cut albums of songs, and has an ongoing Las Vegas performance act in which he sings and entertains.

What the Steelers and his teammates did not know is that Bradshaw has since said he did not enjoy all that Super Bowl success. He wrote about that over the course of several books, saying what drove him more in those Super Bowls was the fear of losing.

"He had the greatest talent in the world but multiple intangible problems," Rooney Jr. said. "Dick Haley [a former Steelers personnel man] said once, 'You know he loves to fish, but when he's going fishing, he's thinking about fishing, he's not thinking about football.'"

Greene was sad to learn later that Bradshaw did not enjoy all his success.

"I thought Terry was on top of the world when he led the team to the Super Bowl, all four," Greene said. "Then when it came to light that he was not enjoying himself and it wasn't a lot of fun for him—and the relationship between him and Chuck [Noll] wasn't the best—I was disappointed because all I ever wanted to do was play football and have fun. Having fun was winning and we did that, and I thought a number of us teammates enjoyed that experience and I was disappointed for Terry that he didn't enjoy that experience."

Yet during his Hall of Fame speech in 1989, Bradshaw spoke more about his teammates and winning games than he did his other various accomplishments. His philosophy as quarterback was perfectly summed up in the title of his first book, *Looking Deep.*

"My nature was attack, throw it deep," Bradshaw said during his induction in Canton, Ohio. "Anybody can throw wide. Let's go deep. . . . Oh, God, wasn't it fun? Didn't y'all like seeing that stuff fly down there? I mean it was fun! What a ride, what a ride. . . . We, the Steelers, all my boys, all of them, we loved to win. God, we loved to win."

In that vein, Greene recalled how Bradshaw and defensive end Dwight White would have an ongoing back-and-forth during practices, and how one day Bradshaw reminded his teammates about his value to them.

"He and Dwight used to squabble all the time, playfully," Greene recounted. "Dwight would hit him in practice. Bradshaw: 'You're not supposed to hit the quarterback.' Dwight: 'C'mon, Blond Bombah. C'mon, Blond Bombah. C'mon now, why you crying?'

"Blond Bombah, that's what Dwight would call him. And one day Terry got so mad, he said, 'Dwight White, you can lose with him but you can't win without me.'

"That was perfect. That was perfect."

Just like Terry Bradshaw's record in Super Bowls.

69.
Charles Woodson

Charles Woodson was a versatile star in the secondary for the Raiders and Packers.

Position: Defensive Back

Teams: Raiders (1998–2005), Packers (2006–2012), Raiders (2013–2015)

By Vic Tafur

C harles Woodson enjoyed the final leg of the trip to Canton, Ohio, all while making promotional stops for his new batch of bourbon.

The former Raiders and Packers defensive back could probably do something in the salt business as well.

"I always considered myself like seasoning salt," Woodson said in 2021. "You can put seasoning salt on anything and it's going to make it better."

Players in the NFL look up to Woodson—just ask Jalen Ramsey—and there is no secret to his success. Woodson was inducted into the Pro Football Hall of Fame on August 8, 2021. He shared how he was able to be a defensive player who shined on offense in college, then spent 18 years as an impactful cornerback and safety in the NFL, even making the Pro Bowl in his final season at age 39.

"I was a guy each and every week who gave it all I had," Woodson said. "It didn't matter if I was healthy or not. Broken leg in the playoffs. Dislocated my shoulder in the opening week of my 18th year and playing a full season. I left it all on the field. That's what I want people to remember and say about me—there's a reason he's in the Hall of Fame."

Woodson might even raise a glass to himself when he looks back at the offseason of 2006. He had been the Defensive Rookie of the Year with the Raiders in 1998 and was first-team All-Pro in 1999 and 2001 and looking forward to being wooed and thrown money at in free agency, despite missing 10 games the previous season with a broken leg.

"Of course, my thought is I'm going to have people crawling over each other trying to get to me," Woodson said. "I thought I was that type of player, [but] I really didn't have anybody checking for me, and that stung a little bit."

Woodson missed 10 games in 2005 with a broken leg after missing eight games in 2002 with a broken shoulder and four games in 2004 with a knee injury. There were also whispers about his work ethic and his partying in Oakland.

Woodson had made a list of teams he wanted to go to, and Tampa Bay and former Raiders coach Jon Gruden were at the top. His mom lived in Orlando and the proximity excited Woodson. But they weren't interested. Joining a young, up-and-coming defense like Jacksonville also interested Woodson. Nope. Woodson had his agent call Seattle and Atlanta. Crickets.

Finally, Green Bay called.

Green Bay is also really cold and in the middle of nowhere. And Woodson said he had heard from other Black players that it wasn't a great city to live in year-round.

There was no nightlife and nothing to do in Green Bay, Woodson was told.

"That's not the team I wanted calling," Woodson said. "It just got to a point where the writing was on the wall, where if you wanted to play, you're probably going to have to go to Green Bay. That was a tough pill to swallow.

"So, when I got there, I just had that reluctance in my heart and in my spirit, and I just couldn't believe I was in Green Bay. It made me combative off the bat, with really kind of everybody."

The NFL history books clearly show that Woodson settled in, winning the NFL Defensive Player of the Year award in 2009 and a Super Bowl ring the following year. He would set a team record of nine interceptions returned for a touchdown.

In college at Michigan, Woodson won a national championship and a Heisman Trophy in 1997 and the Raiders took him with the fourth overall pick in the 1998 NFL Draft. His list of accomplishments is lengthy—too voluminous to mention all of them. Among them:

- 65 career interceptions (fifth-most in NFL history).
- He holds the record for consecutive seasons of returning an interception for a touchdown at six (2006 to 2011).
- He's tied for No. 2 on the list with Darren Sharper for interceptions returned for touchdowns with 11, trailing Rod Woodson (12).
- Nine Pro Bowl selections, including his first four seasons in the league (1998–2001) as well as his last in 2015.

"I think he's the most talented guy that I ever played with," Packers quarterback Aaron Rodgers said in 2020. "His ability to impact the game was unbelievable. He for sure made me a better player going against him every day in practice. He's one of the most savvy defensive players that I've ever seen on the field. Incredible ability to diagnose routes in real time, fantastic in his disguise."

Woodson had extreme confidence and his speed in diagnosing

plays mentally and then carrying out what he wanted to do physically made him tough to play against. And great to play alongside.

"Once I started playing, got into a few games, and started getting my hands on the ball, things kind of settled down for me," Woodson said. "I just think the football guys I had around me, Al Harris, Nick Collins, Tramon [Williams], and these guys, they made it work for me.

"I just felt we had a great group and through time I was able to work through that thing. I'm here, I'm making plays, you're going to be all right. It got to a peaceful point to where I thought I was going to retire there."

That didn't happen, but Woodson did get married in Green Bay and started a family.

"That was really a time in my life when I was growing as a person," Woodson said. "There was a transition that happened there that was a beautiful transition, if you will, so that time was very special."

Woodson was able to close out his career back in Oakland, where he had the opportunity to instill young players with the same edge that legendary former players such as Willie Brown, George Atkinson, and Cliff Branch had given him.

"I really didn't understand what it meant to be a Raider until I got out there," Woodson said. "My first memories of going out to the facility was hanging around older guys like Willie Brown. Willie Brown was a guy who made sure you understood what it meant to be a Raider.

"The first thing he would always tell us was there were 31 other teams and then there was the Raiders. . . . I knew very early on what I had to bring to the table as a young player, and I had to bring it—by being a tough, physical, fast football player."

Those traits were obvious when you watched Woodson play.

68.
Gene Upshaw

Gene Upshaw was the Raiders' top draft pick in 1967
and starred at guard for fifteen seasons.

Position: Offensive Guard

Team: Raiders (1967–1981)

By Vic Tafur

The Raiders in their heyday rode Highway 63 to the top of the NFL.

"Highway 63," as Raiders running back Mark van Eeghen once called left guard Gene Upshaw, would lead around the edge of the defense with Upshaw's silver-and-black No. 63 jersey then turn up-field as the 6-foot-3, 260-pounder ran through linebackers and defensive backs, blazing a trail for the running back behind him.

"It's sort of nice when you turn the corner and you look into that defensive back's face and he looks a little frightened," Upshaw once said, "because he has 260 pounds coming right at him."

"You could see their eyes get really big," Art Shell said in a phone interview. Shell and Upshaw were teammates in Oakland from 1968 to 1981 and lined up next to each other on the left side of the offensive line for most of that time.

And those opposing players knew it was coming, too.

"I remember one time, playing in Pittsburgh, it was a short-yardage play and we were going to run left," Shell said. "All of a sudden, before the ball was snapped, [defensive tackle] Joe Greene jumped up from the other side and came over to our side. And Joe hollered out, 'They're coming right here, these son of bitches are coming right here!' I am sitting there in my stance thinking that Snake [Kenny Stabler] is going to audible out of this play because the right side is now wide open. Even the linebacker was shaded over to our side. There was nobody on that side.

"So, I am waiting for the audible. And it never came. The ball is hiked, and we got the first down through Joe and all those people. I don't know how, but we did. It was a great feeling when we got into a rhythm and we didn't care if teams knew what was coming, we still did it."

Upshaw had size, speed, and power . . . and tape. He would use four rolls of tape on his padded-up arms to help wield maximum impact, and he would use his huge, bandaged-up thumb to get the last point in on a defensive player's ribs or throat.

"Somehow, his thumb was permanently broken—but just on Sundays," linebacker Phil Villapiano said in a phone interview. "Gene did whatever he had to do to beat you down. He was all about winning."

And the Raiders won plenty. They won two Super Bowls, made the playoffs 11 times, and only had one losing season in Upshaw's 15 years in Oakland.

"Gene was smart, fast, strong, and tough," Shell said. "He had all the ingredients, and he could run like a deer. He could run all day, too."

"When I think about Gene Upshaw, I think about No. 63 pulling," the late Hall of Fame cornerback Willie Brown said in 2008. "A lot of people called it Highway 63. That's what I remember and know about Gene. When he pulled around that left side, it's like a hurricane is coming through. He wiped out everything that was there."

A center and tackle at Texas A&I, Upshaw was moved to guard in 1967 when drafted by the Raiders' Al Davis—as an answer to the Chiefs' dominant Buck Buchanan in the trenches. His rookie year, Upshaw helped lead the Raiders to the Super Bowl, where they lost to the Green Bay Packers.

In fact, Upshaw was the only NFL player to play in a Super Bowl in the 1960s, '70s, and '80s. (The three-decade feat has since been matched by Jerry Rice, Bill Romanowski, and Tom Brady.)

"Gene was a nightmare for us," Vikings Hall of Fame defensive end Carl Eller once said. "He was a tough, rugged guy to play against. Gene was the pilot of that great offense. I hope people remember that."

Eller was a member of the famed Purple People Eaters, Minnesota's fearsome defensive line that also featured Hall of Famer Alan Page, Jim Marshall, and Gary Larsen. But a Raiders offensive line led by Upshaw at left guard and Shell at left tackle kept the Purple People Eaters out of the kitchen in Super Bowl XI.

Running backs Clarence Davis and van Eeghen combined to run for 210 yards on 34 carries and quarterback Kenny Stabler was only sacked once in the 32–14 win.

Upshaw and Shell made up what many think is the best offensive line combination of all time.

The two clicked early—Shell became a full-time starter alongside Upshaw in 1970—and often to the point that they knew what the other was going to do no matter if it was a run or pass play.

Upshaw blocked for Raiders quarterbacks Daryle Lamonica, Stabler, and Jim Plunkett in the Super Bowl XV win over the Eagles. And he only missed one game in 15 seasons.

Upshaw was a vocal leader of both the Raiders—"He never

stopped talking, you would hear him before you could see him," Shell said—and the NFL Players Association, where he later served as the executive director until his death.

Many players looked at the man nicknamed "The Governor" as a coach, and even coach John Madden said he would often go to Upshaw when he was feeling down or needed to talk something out.

Later, coach Tom Flores was the same way.

"Everybody listened to him, myself included," Flores said in a phone interview. "He was a dominant player but also a guiding force who made sure everybody was on the same page and everything was about winning.

"We called him the Governor because he was always talking, always campaigning."

The union was created with Upshaw's help, and as the executive director after retirement, he helped prevent a work stoppage in 2006 and build some financial security for the NFLPA.

"If you look at the history of the NFL, you're going to find out that he was one of the most influential people that the league has known," Madden told reporters in 2008. "He did so much, not only for the players but also for the owners, the teams, and the game of pro football."

Former players go to Truckee, California, every year to play golf and help raise money for the Gene Upshaw Memorial Tahoe Forest Cancer Center. They pay their respects and talk a little football, remembering how nice the view was on Highway 63.

"When you start talking about those old Raider teams everybody just thinks they were a bunch of nuts who just happened to play well together," former linebacker Matt Millen told reporters in 2009. "But Gene played the same way he was as an executive with the players association.

"Gene was very clever. He was a clever player. He was physically gifted and talented, but mentally he was a notch above because Gene would always use you against you."

Upshaw played a big part in keeping the team's characters in line. The five-time All-Pro selection and first-ballot Hall of Famer died of pancreatic cancer in 2008 at the age of 63, three days after being diagnosed.

"He was our leader, and when players were getting ready to get out of line he would say, 'Hey, we have to get so-and-so back in line and not let him get away with what he is doing or with what he is thinking about doing,'" Shell said. "We called him the Governor. We thought he was going to run for office in California. Turns out, running the players association might have been a bigger job than being governor.

"Gene was such a smart person, and I had a great time playing with him. God, I miss him so much."

67.
Earl Campbell

Earl Campbell was one of the most punishing, powerful runners in NFL history.

Position: Running Back
Teams: Oilers (1978–1984), Saints (1984–1985)

By Dan Pompei

Earl Campbell took a handoff from Dan Pastorini and cut to his right. Waiting for the rookie running back in the hole, and sure to tackle him for a loss, was a Los Angeles Rams linebacker who had been named to the Pro Bowl six times.

Isiah Robertson squared up and prepared for contact. But instead of delivering the hit as he had done hundreds of times before, Robertson took one, with Campbell's head buried squarely in his sternum.

It was a collision that was felt from the 23-yard line to the 900 section of the world's first domed stadium. It was felt from Amarillo, Texas, to South Padre Island on the other end of the state. It was felt from the NFL offices to the Pro Football Hall of Fame.

As Robertson dropped on the green carpet, Campbell kept trucking to his right. After his jersey was torn off by a would-be tackler, he finally was brought down by three Rams 16 yards later.

"Earl flat ran over him," an incredulous Pastorini said.

On the CBS broadcast, analyst George Allen, a longtime coach, called it "sledgehammer running."

"The Rams think they're still playing Tony Dorsett," fellow analyst Jim Brown added. The former Cleveland Browns running back later said it might have been the hardest hit he had ever seen.

Rams teammates started referring to Robertson as "Grauman's Chinese Theatre" because he had footprints all over him.

In later years, Campbell said he felt guilty about the collision because of what it did to Robertson's reputation. But it did much more for Campbell's reputation. It let everyone know that defenders trying to tackle the new Oilers running back would pay a price.

"All you can do is close your eyes and hope he doesn't break your helmet," Cowboys safety Cliff Harris said.

Safety Gary Fencik played in the NFL for 12 seasons and started 148 games for the Bears. He had one concussion that he knows about. It came on an attempt to tackle Campbell.

From his stance 8 yards off the line in the I formation, Campbell didn't look like other running backs. He was bowlegged. His shoulders seemed to stretch from hash to hash. Each thigh was like the trunk of a mature oak tree. They put a tape measure around his upper leg halfway between his knee and hip, and it measured 34½ inches. "We make four sizes of thigh pads," Oilers equipment manager Byron Donzis once told ESPN. "Small, medium, large, and Earl Campbell."

Those thighs, and the force with which he could move them, were the difference between Campbell and the rest.

"In my time, I never saw anyone who possessed the power and

speed he had," Steelers great Joe Greene said. "There probably never was one."

It wasn't just power and speed that made Campbell special, though. He had a relentless spirit.

"From my earliest recollection, when I had to play against him three times in college, he refused to go down," Bears Hall of Fame defensive tackle Dan Hampton said. "Other players have had that same type of spirit, but none of them had his power, size, and strength. The entire package was legendary."

Campbell's strength came not from any weight room but from the rose fields of his hometown of Tyler, Texas, where as many as 20 million rosebushes bloom in the heart of football season. Campbell worked harder in those fields than he ever could have with a pair of dumbbells.

He grew up thinking he would be a linebacker—"the Black Dick Butkus," he said—and played the position until his senior year of high school. His coaches thought he would be better at running back and showed him film of Jim Brown to convince him he could deliver punishment on offense as well as on defense. Campbell tried to run like Brown and even imitated the way Brown pretended to be shaken after every run in order to toy with defenders.

Campbell won the Heisman Trophy at the University of Texas and gave many defenders wobbly legs. He also once staggered Bevo, a 1,700-pound longhorn steer, after slamming into him at the end of a run on the sideline at Texas Memorial Stadium.

The Oilers wanted Campbell so much they traded tight end Jimmie Giles and first-, second-, third-, and fifth-round draft picks to the Buccaneers to acquire the first selection in the 1978 NFL Draft.

That run against the Rams was one of many in a remarkable first season. Campbell was voted Rookie of the Year and Offensive Player of the Year. Campbell's coach, Bum Phillips, told *Sports Illustrated* that no one in the previous 20 years had a greater impact on the NFL in his first year other than Commissioner Pete Rozelle. Campbell helped the Oilers to a 35–30 upset of the Dolphins in November by rushing for 199 yards and four touchdowns. Howard Cosell said it was the best Monday night game ever. With the way Campbell fought for extra yards in his rookie year, defenders shredded so many of his jerseys that the league did away with tear-away jerseys after the season.

And then he took it up a notch. He led the league in rushing and was named NFL MVP in his second season.

Campbell made the Oilers—or the "Earlers," as they became known—relevant in ways they had never been. The hottest tickets in Texas were for Oilers games at the Astrodome, where fans waved blue and white pompoms and basked in the "Luv Ya Blue" phenomenon. Campbell led the Oilers to the AFC Championship Game in each of his first two seasons.

In the playoffs, the Oilers had the misfortune of running into the Steelers, who were on their way to winning back-to-back Super Bowls.

"Without Earl Campbell, they were a perennial 7-9, 8-8 team," *Houston Chronicle* columnist Dale Robertson wrote. "Earl single-handedly turned them into a team that could have got to the Super Bowl if they had caught a break. But that Steelers team had nine Hall of Famers. Just bad timing."

No player ever was a better match for his team. In "The Friendly State," they called him "Easy Earl" because he had such a laid-back personality. He could make it from his hometown to Houston in his pickup truck in less than three hours, or from his college town to Houston in two and a half. He wore cowboy boots, quoted Merle Haggard, and sat front and center to listen to Willie Nelson at Gilley's. When Nelson sang "Mamas Don't Let Your Babies Grow Up to Be Cowboys" at the honky-tonk, Campbell joined him onstage and sang along.

The state legislature enshrined Campbell, nicknamed "The Tyler Rose," as an Official State Hero of Texas. The only others to receive the designation were Davy Crockett, the "king of the wild frontier" himself; Stephen F. Austin, known as the father of the state; and Sam Houston, the venerated general from the Texas Revolution.

Campbell earned his designation the hard way. In a 1979 game against the Raiders, Campbell took a handoff on the 1-yard line on a sweep to his right. Jack Tatum, the Raiders safety they called "Assassin," sneaked around another defender and thrust the crown of his helmet under Campbell's chin with a hit so wicked that it snapped Campbell's head back as if he had been rear-ended by a truck. Campbell somehow stayed on his feet and scored; Tatum ended up with a view of the Astrodome ceiling, assuming his vision was functional. "The lick I took from Jack Tatum, that's the only time I ever felt somebody hit me," Campbell said.

It was one of many stunningly violent collisions Campbell was a part of. "He's got absolutely no regard for his body—or anybody else's body," Phillips told *Sports Illustrated*.

In Campbell's first four years in the league, he ran the ball 1,404 times, the most in the NFL. But by his fourth year, when he was just 26, his effectiveness began to diminish. Part of his decline could be attributed to Phillips being replaced by Ed Biles in 1981. Biles preferred a split backfield to the I formation in which Campbell felt comfortable. But the more significant issue was Campbell's body was wearing down.

"He isn't the same Earl Campbell who came into the league," Giants defensive end George Martin said after a game in 1982. "That's obvious. You still have to respect him, even though you can hold him down. The years take a toll on running backs."

In 1984, the Oilers were certain Campbell's best days were gone, but Phillips, then the Saints head coach, still believed in him. The Saints traded a first-round pick to the Oilers, reuniting the coach with the runner. By then, though, Campbell was just another back. He scored one touchdown in 24 games with the Saints.

He should have scored another in the last game of the 1985 season. Campbell broke into the open field from the New Orleans 48-yard line on the Saints' first possession against the Falcons. He sprinted toward the end zone but grabbed the back of his leg at about the 20. He moved more slowly and unevenly to the 7, where he was caught by defensive back Wendell Cason, who knocked the ball out of his hands and recovered in the end zone. It was the last run of Campbell's career. He retired during the 1986 preseason.

In his post-playing days, reminders of what he had done came in the forms of a gold jacket, a retired jersey, a stretch of road named in his honor, and a statue outside his college stadium.

Reminders also came in the forms of back and knee surgeries, arthritis in his hand so severe he could barely make a fist, nerve damage in his legs, memory loss, and panic attacks. Campbell depended on a walker and a wheelchair before he turned 50 and became addicted to painkillers prescribed to treat spinal stenosis. He said he was downing up to 10 OxyContin per day, along with a case of beer.

Campbell spent 44 days in a rehab center in 2009 and kicked his destructive habits. "I had to make a choice between living and dying," he said.

Was it all worth it?

Two years after his last run, he said, "If I had it to do all over again, I'd run the ball the same way. I'd probably even do it harder on certain plays. And I want Bum to give me the ball 30 more times. . . . I loved every minute of it. I loved looking that guy in the eye who was across from me because I know deep down in my heart I'm telling him, 'I'm the best. I've got something to prove on third down.'"

But in *Yards After Contact*, published 34 years after his retirement, he wrote, "Sometimes I tell my wife, 'Shoot, if I knew it was going to hurt like this, I don't know if I'd have [played football].' It's a hell of a price to pay."

What is indisputable is that Earl Campbell paid it. And so did anyone who thought he could take him to the ground.

66.
Ray Nitschke

Ray Nitschke (second from left) spent fifteen years
as a great middle linebacker with the Packers.

Position: Linebacker

Team: Packers (1958–1972)

By Tim Graham

Ray Nitschke spent two decades informing new Pro Football Hall of Famers that none of them is bigger than the rest.

All wear gold jackets, the lone standard for greatness. Neither championships nor individual trophies weighed more.

Nitschke was Canton's conscience.

"He told them how important it was and emphasized there's no one in the Hall of Fame better than anyone else," said fellow.Hall of Famer and Green Bay Packers linebacker Dave Robinson. "We're all equal, going in with 80 percent of the vote. You can't go any higher."

Yet while Nitschke himself would protest the notion, he did rise above the room.

Every year, in a private space only Hall of Famers may enter, Nitschke presided on the first afternoon of induction weekend until his death in March 1998. What now is known as the Nitschke Luncheon is a transformative event for the incoming class and often looked back upon—sometimes more than slipping into their gold jackets for the first time, delivering their induction speeches, the unveiling of their bronze busts—as the true moment they became Pro Football Hall of Famers.

In that room full of alpha males is where Nitschke stood up and explained what it means to join football's greatest team.

"He was a natural-born leader," Hall of Fame right tackle Ron Yary said. "Someone's got to be the leader and step forward, and that was a great quality he had. If you wanted a leader to emulate, you couldn't pick a better person."

Nitschke guided a Packers defense that won five NFL championships, including the first two Super Bowls. He was MVP of the 1962 title game. His No. 66 was the fourth number retired in the franchise's rich history.

Nitschke made only one Pro Bowl team because Detroit Lions middle linebacker Joe Schmidt was a perennial selection from 1954 to 1963. Nitschke was selected in 1964. Then Chicago Bears middle linebacker Dick Butkus went to eight straight.

But in 1969, when Hall of Fame voters honored the NFL's 50th anniversary by naming its 16 best players, Nitschke was one of only five defenders and the lone linebacker. Nitschke also made the NFL's 75th and 100th anniversary rosters.

"Ray Nitschke had a style of play, a personality, a consciousness about being fully imbued into that which brought life to something called professional football," said Hall of Fame linebacker Willie Lanier, the current Nitschke Luncheon master of ceremonies.

"Having played with the Green Bay Packers and the number of

championships they won, the number of Hall of Famers that played for [coach Vince] Lombardi, who happens to have his name on the trophy, seemed to signify a purity of someone who accepted his role in the game and played it with a fervor."

Nitschke was known for his viciousness on the field, a ferocity that welled within him from childhood. His father died in a car accident when Nitschke was 3. Nitschke's mother died from a blood clot when he was 13.

While he wasn't bombing his classes or getting into fistfights, he played quarterback and safety at Proviso High in suburban Chicago. His bad grades and temper couldn't derail such a phenomenal athlete. The St. Louis Browns offered him a baseball contract, but he wanted to play Big Ten football. The University of Illinois converted him to fullback and linebacker.

Nitschke's rage was effectively channeled.

"He wasn't the biggest or the strongest or the smartest," Robinson said. "He definitely wasn't the fastest. But he was a Hall of Famer from the tip of his toes to the top of his head.

"No matter how much he was bleeding, he wouldn't leave the game. Ray played in the 230s, but he hit like he was 300 pounds. He hit you with every ounce of his body. He gave it all to you. He protected his turf."

Yary witnessed the fury before he entered the NFL in 1968 with the Minnesota Vikings as the first draft choice. In that year's Chicago College All-Star Game, played against the reigning NFL champs, a maniacal Nitschke gave Yary a glimpse of what lay ahead in the pros.

"It was a big-time hit," Yary said. "The contact he made with Larry Csonka impressed me, but what I remember was Ray Nitschke getting up and laughing like he just won the $1 million lottery.

"Here's a guy, after all these years, in an exhibition game. That was a statement about how much he loved the game."

Nitschke wasn't merely a hitter. He was a playmaker, recording 25 interceptions and 23 fumble recoveries over his 15 seasons.

Nitschke left his savage persona on the field and occasionally on camera for *The Longest Yard* and Miller Lite commercials. He also was a humanitarian, loved children, and relished being an ambassador for Green Bay and the NFL.

"When he walked off the field and put on his horn-rimmed glasses," Robinson said, "you'd think he was a CPA—unless he took his teeth out."

Cincinnati Bengals left tackle Anthony Muñoz didn't get to hear Nitschke speak at the luncheon. Muñoz was elected in January 1998, six weeks before Nitschke died of a heart attack at 61.

Muñoz, however, had a chance to absorb Nitschke's words.

"We had one-on-one time together, his face right up in my grill," Muñoz said. "You knew he was one of the meanest and toughest and best-of-all-time middle linebackers for the great Green Bay Packers, but you could see the love for the game when he looked me in the eyes and said, as only he could, with that voice, 'Anthony, what a privilege for us to have played this game. There are too many guys who think it was a privilege for the league to have them.'

"That was years and years ago, but I can hear him say it like it was yesterday. His humility and appreciation for having had the opportunity to play in the NFL will always stick in my mind."

The Nitschke Luncheon is a solemn initiation for the new inductees, who are not allowed to speak. As a microphone is passed around the room, elders explain the magnitude of the honor.

"This is the only team you can't get cut from or traded from," Robinson said. "You can't even die from this team. When you die, you're still in the Hall of Fame."

The gravitas is unmistakable. A common response for the muted, new inductees is to look around the room at legends such as Jim Brown, Roger Staubach, and Mean Joe Greene. Reality becomes difficult to fathom.

Andre Reed finally got to his first Nitschke Luncheon in 2014 after eight years of being a finalist.

"It felt like I was in *The Wizard of Oz* or something," Reed said afterward. "I've been trying to get to the Emerald City, and the Emerald City was right in that room. You can't pay your way into that room."

What is said in the room stays in the room.

The men who speak try to recapture Nitschke's message.

"Ray Nitschke most personified what the Hall of Fame really meant," Robinson said. "When he got up to speak, you knew he was speaking from the heart.

"He laid down the law to all the new inductees of what was acceptable and unacceptable, and everybody followed what Ray said."

There was a time when the Hall of Fame allowed NFL commissioner Roger Goodell, family members, or the occasional reporter into the Nitschke Luncheon. Those days are over. The Hall of Famers want to say whatever is on their minds.

For example, when Terrell Owens decided to hold his induction in Chattanooga, Tennessee, the Hall of Famers wanted to speak candidly without fear of retribution or having their remarks appear online. The discussion was heated, but remained private.

The Nitschke Luncheon is like a family reunion and for many Hall of Famers ranks as the favorite part of induction weekend.

Among the recurring themes is that Canton should be treated as their second home. New inductees are encouraged to return every year to help maintain the Hall of Fame's legacy.

"I won't mention any names," Robinson said, "but there are some people that come in and get the gold jacket and never come back. Those are the ones that would piss Ray off. Those are the ones that don't understand what this is all about."

After Nitschke's death, iconic defensive end Deacon Jones took over as master of ceremonies. Lanier took over when Jones died in 2013.

Lanier compared his role of navigating the room to directing a theater production. He knows which Hall of Famers speak with fire, which are circumspect. When a certain message needs to be delivered, Lanier knows who to call upon.

"Bobby Bell, for instance, will make a comment to everyone in the room for them to look around closely and acknowledge the others they see," Lanier said, "because next year a certain number will not be here.

"That becomes a most profound reality. One year, those you see will no longer be there, and one year, neither will you. I have found his comments to be poignant for anybody."

Emotionally impactful is just what Nitschke would appreciate in order to hammer home—as forcefully as stuffing Joe Don Looney in the backfield—what it means to be a Hall of Famer.

A substantial aspect of Nitschke's legacy forever will be respecting the Hall of Fame's legacy. As much as he insisted they all are equals, his passion set him apart.

"He'd be the first to tell you not to put him on a pedestal above all the other linebackers," Robinson said. "Ray wanted everybody to know we're all equal.

"But there was only one Ray Nitschke, and there will never be another."

65.
Walter Jones

Dominant play by Walter Jones (right) landed him in the Pro Football Hall of Fame in 2014.

Position: Offensive Tackle
Team: Seahawks (1997–2008)

By Michael-Shawn Dugar

Mike Baugh and Tag Ribary were at the 1997 NFL Draft in New York celebrating the Seattle Seahawks' selection of cornerback Shawn Springs when they were interrupted by someone working for the league.

"You better get your headset on, your boss is trying to get ahold of you," Baugh, a scouting assistant, says they were told at the time. Baugh was a bit confused. "What?" he replied. "We don't pick for another hour."

Incorrect. Baugh and Ribary, Seattle's assistant director of pro personnel, were about to draft Walter Jones.

Their boss at the time was Randy Mueller, the Seahawks' vice president of football operations, who moments earlier had brokered one of the most significant draft-day deals in team history.

"Randy is *mad*," Baugh recalled, laughing. "He says, 'Get your damn headphones on, we're trading up *right now*.'" Still taken aback, Baugh again replied: "What? We just traded up!"

The 1997 draft was regarded as a six-man class. Seattle believed the top four players were Ohio State left tackle Orlando Pace, USC defensive tackle Darrell Russell, Springs, and Jones. But identifying the top players was the easiest part. For Seattle, acquiring the players would be tricky because of two potential roadblocks.

The first was the draft capital. Coming off a 7-9 season in 1996, Seattle had the 12th pick. In February 1997, Seattle traded quarterback Rick Mirer to the Bears for the 11th pick. The plan was then to use those selections to jump from the top 12 to the top six.

"We had to do whatever we could to maneuver our picks," Mueller said. But that led to the second potential issue: cash. "To have two picks in the top 10 was rare, let alone in the top six," Mueller said. "It was going to cost a lot of money."

In those days, the salary cap was still a new concept (it was implemented in 1994). Teams had a pool of money that could be allocated to rookies, who weren't slotted into predetermined salaries the way today's incoming NFL players are. The rookie wage scale, introduced in the 2011 Collective Bargaining Agreement, ties each draft pick's nonnegotiable, four-year contract to a percentage of the salary cap. Whereas today's rookies are considered inexpensive labor, prospects in the pre–rookie wage scale era could negotiate lucrative contracts, with signing bonuses that immediately put dents in the owners' pockets.

The Seahawks in 1997 were undergoing an ownership change. Ken Behring, who had briefly tried to relocate the franchise to California in 1996, was on his way out. Billionaire Paul Allen, who wouldn't officially purchase the team until the summer of 1997, was on the way in.

"I was dealing with both ownership groups because of the sale," Mueller said. "Ken Behring was the outgoing owner who didn't want to spend money. Paul, he was for it. It was always like I had to negotiate with the two ownership groups to make sure the money was covered."

With Allen willing to foot the bill on the rookie contracts, Seattle on March 28 sent a haul, including the No. 11 pick, to Atlanta for the third overall selection. It was well-known that the Seahawks, desperate for a game-changing defender, would draft Springs.

The plan to draft Jones flew under the radar but it couldn't have been more impactful. Jones would become a Seahawks icon and one of the game's all-time great left tackles. Jones in 1999 was the franchise's first offensive lineman to make the Pro Bowl and led Seattle to its first Super Bowl appearance in the 2005 season while proving to be one of the game's best blockers. He allowed just 23 sacks in 180 regular-season starts. In 12 seasons with the Seahawks, Jones made nine Pro Bowls, four AP All-Pro teams, and was named to the league's All-2000s squad.

He was inducted into the Pro Football Hall of Fame in 2014.

A franchise that at the time was on an eight-year playoff drought was able to change its fortunes by drafting Jones.

"It was giant," Mueller said. "It helped us turn the corner as a playoff team."

Jones's decision to declare for the draft in January 1997 was somewhat of a surprise considering he had played all of one season at Florida State. Because of issues with grades, the Aliceville, Alabama, native began his college career at Holmes Community College in Goodman, Mississippi. Jones was steered there by Florida State, which had unsuccessfully attempted to get him in the door straight out of high school.

Jones, as you might expect from a future Hall of Fame tackle, dominated at HCC, giving up one sack in two years. In 1994, he was voted region MVP, an award seldom given to a player in the trenches, and named the state's best junior college player. The head coach at Holmes said Jones was the best offensive lineman he had ever seen. A 6-foot-5, 285-pound tackle who could run a 4.6 40-yard dash and squat 500 pounds, Jones had received just about every form of praise and every accolade possible on his way out of junior college. He was so athletic he took snaps at tight end and once caught a 40-yard screen pass.

Academic issues forced Jones to redshirt his first year at Florida State, in 1995. And by the time he was eligible to play, the Seminoles had two solid, veteran tackles in Todd Fordham and Tra Thomas. So, although Jones is listed as a starting left tackle for 12 games in 1996, he was actually part of a three-man rotation and would bounce back and forth between left and right tackle—sometimes in the same series.

"I never heard that in my life where you're rotating a tackle in a game," Jones said in a June 2020 interview with NBC Sports Northwest.

Jones didn't mind, though—he was happy to be on the field, competing for a national title against premier competition. But that context makes Mueller's decision to pull the trigger on such a prospect look slightly more courageous, even though Jones was considered one of the draft's best players.

Mueller had worked in Seattle's front office since the early 1980s but was only a few years into his role as VP of football operations. "I think there's an advantage to being young and what you don't know, you don't know," said Mueller, who now has more than three decades of executive experience.

"I read a lot of criticism of that draft of Walt later on, where a lot of veteran-run teams were saying they couldn't have pulled the trigger on a guy with one year at Florida State," Mueller said. "I never even really thought about it. We saw what we saw, we trusted what we saw, and I ran with it. I was probably better off not knowing that it was that risky."

What they saw was stellar left-tackle play from a prospect whose stock only rose as the pre-draft process went on. Seattle's staff was sold immediately. Co–college scouting directors Phil Neri and Mike Allman were on board. Offensive line coach Howard Mudd would beat on Mueller's door every other day with excitement.

"What we all saw was a guy with unbridled power and yet could dance like a bear," Mueller said. "The combination is just perfect."

Baugh recalls watching tape with Mudd and marveling at the way Jones handled Clemson defensive lineman Trevor Pryce, a stud in college who was a first-round pick in the '97 NFL Draft. The Seminoles smoked the Tigers and Jones can be seen mauling defenders throughout the contest—including Pryce, who was drafted 28th overall, then made one All-Pro team and four Pro Bowls.

"I remember Howard saying this is the best knee-bending big man that he had ever seen," said Baugh, now a national scout with the New Orleans Saints. Jones's game film was invaluable to Baugh, then a young scout, for his potential growth as an evaluator.

"You have to know what it looks like," Baugh said. "What does it look like when Jerry Rice transitions at the top of a route? What does it look like when Bruce Smith has hip flexion to bend a corner? It's not just speed, it's bend and pad level. Walter Jones, for me, was that training tape for what bend in the knees, hips, and ankles would look like for a top-flight offensive lineman. And I still fall back on that. Walter was the standard of what an athletic big man can do."

Jones in 12 games with the Seminoles allowed just one sack and was plenty ready for the NFL. But because Jones hadn't *really* gotten to experience a full-time role as a starting left tackle, he was still considering returning to Florida State, which had just gone 11-1 and lost the national championship to Florida. Then one day in the locker room with teammates he saw a pre-draft ranking that had him No. 2 at his position behind Pace, who finished fourth in the Heisman voting. That, along with regular calls from NFL agents, let Jones know how highly he was regarded in league circles.

Still partially undecided in January, Jones attended one of his classes early in the school week and was surprised to learn the professor had assigned a paper due that Friday. Jones had no interest in spending the week slapping together a paper and instead decided to go pro.

Jones was known as a mild-mannered player who played the left tackle position like an angry school bully.

"Walt's a quiet man," Mueller said. "Didn't have a lot to say."

At 6-5, 300 pounds, he ran a 4.63 40-yard dash in front of scouts and made Allman reportedly do a double take looking at his stopwatch. ESPN's Mel Kiper had Jones among the top 10 overall prospects. Tim Ruskell, the Buccaneers' director of college scouting who would later become the GM of the Seahawks, said Jones was a "freakish" athlete for a big man. Longtime NFL executive Gil Brandt said Jones was the most phenomenal player he'd ever seen.

Pace was widely considered the better of the two draft-eligible tackles, but Baugh always felt the gap was small. "To the pros grading the tape you're like, 'Show me the difference,'" he said.

Seattle before the draft had a deal in place with the Jets to move up from No. 12 to No. 6 as long as there wasn't a player Jets coach Bill Parcells wanted in that slot. The morning of the draft, Mueller got a call from Parcells that their deal was off because the Jets were afraid of moving that far back and instead planned to trade with Tampa Bay, which picked eighth.

"But I don't think Tampa at six knows who they want to pick," Parcells told Mueller. "If I was you, I'd call Tampa."

Mueller quickly phoned Bucs GM Rich McKay and brokered a new deal, actually giving up less than the original deal with the Jets. The Seahawks agreed to send pick Nos. 12 and 63 to the Bucs and hold on to their fifth-round pick—but that deal, too, was reliant on Tampa Bay not liking how the board looked when it was on the clock at No. 6.

"We didn't think we were going to pull this off," Mueller said. "I didn't really believe it until it actually happened."

Jones didn't even think Seattle was all that interested. The Seahawks were among a handful of teams Jones visited before the draft and Mudd was the only staffer to interact with their future left tackle. "I don't think I'm going there," Jones told his agent after the visit, during which he watched just one play on film with Mudd before getting a quick tour of the building. "Wasn't nobody there."

Jones and Springs signed six- and seven-year deals, respectively, that cost Allen more than $10 million in signing bonus money. Although it would take a couple more years to end the team's playoff drought, that April weekend in 1997 set the stage for a much-needed franchise pivot. Allman called successfully trading up to get Jones and Springs "dumb luck." Mueller after the draft said, "Maybe the football gods were looking out for us." Head coach Dennis Erickson felt their draft was perfectly executed. NFL pundits were sold as well: much of the post-draft commentary applauded Seattle, which was thought to be in position to start contending after landing its '97 class.

Thanks to a scouting staff that trusted its collective gut, Jones's reluctance to write a criminology paper, and Allen's willingness to open his checkbook, the Seahawks in one day snagged a longtime starting cornerback in Springs, and in Jones, one of the best players in franchise history.

64.

Steve Largent

Steve Largent set NFL records for receptions, receiving yards, and receiving TDs.

Position: Wide Receiver
Team: Seahawks (1976–1989)

By Mike Sando

Steve Largent is one of three NFL players since World War II to retire holding the league records for receptions, receiving yards, and receiving touchdowns. Don Hutson and Jerry Rice are the other two, placing Largent in select company even among Pro Football Hall of Famers.

The greatest players are more than elite producers. They have their own legends, too.

For all the spectacular catches Largent made, the play that defined him as an elite competitor, the one he counts as his personal favorite, had nothing to do with any of his 819 receptions during a 14-year career with the Seattle Seahawks from 1976 to 1989. But to properly explain it, one must first address the play before the play—one that left Largent facedown on the grass unconscious at Mile High Stadium in Denver.

Largent was 34 years old, his career winding down as the 1988 season was beginning. It was Seattle at Denver in Week 1, first-and-10 in the third quarter. Largent ran a slant route into the teeth of the defense, which carried heightened risk back then, before rules prohibited defenders from headhunting defenseless receivers.

As Largent ran his slant route toward the middle, Denver's safety, Mike Harden, slammed his forearm into Largent's face, knocking out Largent's teeth, breaking his face mask, leaving the receiver unconscious and concussed. Harden stood over Largent and exulted, the way Jack Tatum or Ronnie Lott or any of the intimidating hitters might have done back then.

"If that shot [by Harden] is committed today in the National Football League, that player may be suspended for the year," said Joe Vitt, a former Largent-era Seahawks assistant coach who retired from coaching in 2021. "Mike Harden damn near killed Steve Largent. Steve was knocked cold. He was out."

Two minutes passed before doctors brought Largent to a sitting position. Another minute passed before Largent left the field. He would not miss a game, and he would not miss his opportunity for payback.

Fourteen weeks later, in a Sunday night game at the old Kingdome in Seattle, Largent got his revenge spectacularly.

Harden intercepted a pass in the end zone and was returning the ball past the 25-yard line when Largent put him in his crosshairs.

"Largent completely circles the whole perimeter of the field to make sure he has the shot he wants," Vitt recalled.

Largent emerged from out of Harden's view and hit him so hard, the name across the back of Harden's jersey was the first part of him to hit the artificial turf.

"It obviously wasn't premeditated," Largent said at the time, "but it was a Walt Disney situation for me. Storybook. I've never tried to hurt anyone in a game, but I was trying to hit him as hard as I could."

Harden flew one way, legs high in the air, and the football flew to the turf.

"Steve hit him and stood over him, just for a brief second—it seemed like forever," said former Seahawks quarterback Dave Krieg, who threw both passes involving Largent and Harden. "Steve looked over Harden just like Muhammad Ali was looking over Sonny Liston when he first beat him, and then he jumped on the ball. It was such sweet karma, such serendipity."

Largent stood 5-foot-11 and weighed 187 pounds. His timed speed in the 40-yard dash was slow for a wide receiver, somewhere in the 4.6-second range (Rice timed similarly). The Houston Oilers drafted Largent from Tulsa in the fourth round, kept him through four preseason games, and then traded him to the Seahawks, who employed his college offensive coordinator, for an eighth-round draft choice. It was a humble beginning for a player who would land on the NFL's 1980s All-Decade Team and 100th anniversary all-time team.

Largent's secret? In the simplest sense, he got open and caught the ball as well as anyone ever.

"He was as crafty as anybody I could recall," the former NFL linebacker and Green Bay Packers general manager Ted Thompson once said. "He wasn't a big guy, but he knew exactly how to lean on people, and his hands were unbelievable. I would put his hands up against those of anyone."

Largent was unusually proficient in terms of body control, making different routes look the same, maintaining speed in and out of his breaks, leaning to create leverage on defenders and out-quicking them with what might be called competitive speed.

The Hall of Fame receiver and former NCAA long-jump champion James Lofton, who still holds Stanford track records and clocked 10.54 in the 100 meters, tells the story of the time he ran 100s with Largent while on location near UCLA for a Nike photo shoot in the early 1980s.

"Every one we ran, Steve was within like a shoulder length of me, and so this thing about deceptive speed, he was so much faster than what anybody knew," Lofton said. "I remember watching him play and thinking he runs full speed up the field and makes a turn and is still running full speed. It was like he was one of those giant Batmobiles or motorcycles where he would just lean and turn. He was so good in and out of his breaks. That is what made him unique. When you look at his skills, they would transfer so well to today's game, too."

Largent holds up well in an evaluation of elite receiver production across eras. To this end, The Athletic calculated where every receiver with at least 7,000 career yards stood in relation to the league's yardage leader in his eight best seasons. Rice and Hutson tied for the top spot, followed by Randy Moss and Torry Holt. Largent was next at No. 5, followed by Julio Jones, Marvin Harrison, and Lofton.

"You could never believe what he was telling you by the way he was running a route," former Kansas City Chiefs Pro Bowl corner Albert Lewis once said of Largent. "No one sells a route better than Steve. I could never get my hands on him in bump-and-run. He would go at you laterally and quickly get a cushion on you."

Largent played with Seattle when the Seahawks were in an AFC West division packed with Pro Bowl cornerbacks: Lewis and Kevin Ross in Kansas City, Mike Haynes and Lester Hayes on the Raiders, Louis Wright in Denver, and Gill Byrd on the Chargers.

"My 40-yard-dash time is 4.3 and I'm watching Steve *explode* and he is blowing by everybody," Hayes said.

Hayes, a five-time Pro Bowl choice who led the NFL in interceptions with 13 in 1980 and was Defensive Player of the Year, affectionately referred to Largent as "the great Steve Largent" and "the Caucasian Clydesdale" when they were competing against one another from 1977 to 1986.

"Steve Largent is Cooper Kupp's father," Hayes says now, letting loose with cackling laughter. "Steve is 4.6 40-yard dash, but Steve had 4.3 40-yard dash feet. Whew, that boy was blessed. I'm a state champion in track, a sprinter, so I know speed. That explosion and separation, oh, he had the gift from God. That's not normal."

Lots of receivers run fast. They do not all run fast all the time. That also separated Largent at a time when the NFL, instead of legislating dangerous hits out of the game as the case has been in recent years, marketed videotapes featuring devastating hits like the one Largent absorbed from Harden.

"I watched the film, I'm searching a man's heart," Hayes said. "I want to see, will he run a slant and keep running it at full speed? A lot of those guys that I covered, they wouldn't burst on a slant route based upon Jack Tatum is coming, Burgess Owens is coming, Vann McElroy is coming to him and knock your teeth outta your mouth. But Steve Largent ran slant routes at full-speed explosion four, five, six times a game. The boy was blessed with 4.3 feet and maximum testosterone."

Tatum, notorious for the hit that paralyzed former New England Patriots receiver Darryl Stingley, once put out a $1,000 bounty on Largent, according to media reports from the 1980s.

Largent should have been easy to find. Unlike some of the other all-time great receivers, Largent didn't have an elite wingman to serve as a decoy. Rice had John Taylor and later Terrell Owens. Michael Irvin had Alvin Harper. Isaac Bruce and Torry Holt had each other. Largent was the Seattle offense except for a stretch when running back Curt Warner was healthy and dynamic.

There was no question Largent was The Man in Seattle.

Vitt, a Seahawks assistant under Chuck Knox from 1982 to 1991, tells a story from early in Knox's tenure. With the team preparing to face a top opponent, Knox explained to the full squad that there would be five opportunities during the game for either team to make a pivotal play, and that Seattle would need to make at least three of them to have a shot at winning.

"At the end of the presentation, Steve Largent was sitting in the back of this room and raised his hand," Vitt said. "Chuck called on him and Steve says, 'Coach, put me down for two of the three.' I mean, it gave me goose bumps, man."

Another time, Largent missed practice all week after his wife gave birth to son Kramer, who was born with part of his spinal cord exposed. The Largents knew nothing about the condition, known as spina bifida, and they were initially devastated by the news. As the Seahawks prepared for a critical game that week, they built their game plan under the assumption Largent would not play. Wednesday, Thursday, and most of Friday passed without Largent appearing at the team facility.

It was already dark in Seattle on that Friday night when coaches heard a knock on their meeting room door. It was Largent.

"We all get up and hug him and tell him we're so sorry," Vitt recalled. "Steve says, 'Chuck, listen, I need the scripts from Wednesday, Thursday, and Friday practices.' The scripts are the offensive plays that we practiced. Chuck says, 'What for?'"

Largent wanted the scripts so he could practice all the routes he was going to run, in the dark of a chilly November night, two days before kickoff. Many players have played in games shortly after suffering through family emergencies more traumatic than what the Largents endured that week. Still, the memory of that week resonates with Vitt nearly four decades later. Largent caught eight passes for 138 yards even though a penalty negated a 65-yard touchdown grab.

"In the dark, it's cold, he took three days' worth of practice scripts and ran every route with the split, with the precision of the route, coming out of a break," Vitt said. "He did all three practices, the throws that are going to get thrown to him, and about two hours later he came in drenched and he went and played the game and played his ass off. I've never seen anything like it in my life.

"Steve was such an inspiration to everyone he came into contact with. When your best players are your hardest workers and most dependable players in a game, man oh man, that's leadership times 10, and he was that. You talk about a man of character and integrity, he walked the walk and he talked the talk, but let me tell you something, he was a competitor, now. Ask Mike Harden."

63.
Junior Seau

Junior Seau was an eight-time All-Pro and a member of the 1990s All-Decade team.

Position: Linebacker

Teams: Chargers (1990–2002), Dolphins (2003–2005), Patriots (2006–2009)

By Chris Burke

I n the late 1990s, John Parrella used to challenge teammate Rodney Harrison to weekly "liftathons," in which they'd see who could bench-press the most weight relative to their sizes. Parrella weighed about 300 pounds; Harrison was in the 220 range.

Once, Junior Seau walked in as the competition was ongoing. He'd already worked out and had been off watching tape. Parrella guesses that it was around 6 a.m. when he and Harrison decided to poke the bear. "Hey, why aren't you lifting with us?"

Seau, carrying a Red Bull, walked over to Parrella and eyed the bar, loaded up with 500 pounds for Parrella's attempts.

"Hold this," Seau said to Parrella, handing him his drink.

He lay back on the bench, tossed up the 500 pounds, re-racked the bar, and then said only to Parrella: "Give me my Red Bull." And he casually left the room.

"That was no warm-up, already worked out, came in and benched it," Parrella recalled, laughing. "Tell me a guy in the league who's as fast as any receiver in the league—forget about 40 time, he could run with them—was 6-foot-3, 250 pounds, not an ounce of fat, could bench 500 pounds. . . .

"Sometimes, you'd go home and go, 'That guy, he is amazing.' God made him to play football."

There are stories like this littered throughout Seau's 20-year career, which earned him induction into the Pro Football Hall of Fame in 2015. They're also part of the legend he crafted for himself at USC and, before that, at Oceanside (California) High. He was bigger and faster and stronger than anything people had seen, especially after the Chargers let him find a home as an outside linebacker.

When Parrella left the Chargers as a free agent in 2002 and signed with Oakland, the Raiders coaches quizzed him on Seau's game. They pulled up one play, a swing pass out to a back, and asked Parrella what Seau's assignment was in that moment. "Well, he has the running back," Parrella told them—an answer that didn't mesh with film that showed Seau blitzing the A-gap.

So, Parrella explained that Seau had the freedom to blitz there because, in the event that he didn't get to the quarterback, he was fast enough (and confident enough) to change course and chase down the back in the flat.

"I think their quote was: 'You're shitting me,'" Parrella said. "The room was just like, 'You're lying.'"

En route to 1,847 career tackles, 56½ sacks, 18 interceptions, 18 fumble recoveries, and a list of accolades that goes on and on, Seau developed a bit of a reputation for "freelancing" on defense. It was something Bill Belichick had to try to dial back when Seau joined the Patriots at the end of his career. The Chargers, though, mostly rolled with it because Seau's athletic gifts were off the charts, but so too was his understanding of opposing offenses.

During game weeks, he'd spend as much as an extra five or six hours per day studying film, on top of however long his positional sessions lasted. He could call out plays before they happened, both against his own offense in practices and on game days. In defensive meetings, he'd chime in with suggestions for every other spot on the field, because he knew his teammates' roles almost as well as his own.

San Diego's coaching staff went so far as to give him his own audibles—not a change of a play, just a Seau-specific call. If he saw an opportunity to blitz, he could adjust and go.

"Great players feel the game," Seau said on NFL Films' *In Their Own Words* series. "I can feel when you're going to run the ball. I can feel your attitudes, I can feel your demeanor, I can feel the offensive linemen looking at me—I can feel all this. . . . In football, you've got to count on everybody to do their part. On a given Sunday, when you're with Junior, understand he's coming into this game feeling like he's the best and he can't be stopped."

In Week 5 of the 1996 NFL season, the Chargers, at 3-1 and not even two years removed from winning the AFC title, hosted an undefeated Chiefs team for a key rivalry showdown. Seau entered that Sunday at less than 100 percent, slowed by a hamstring injury. "If I have four gears, I'm just kicking it in third," Seau told the Associated Press.

That, the Chiefs found out, was plenty good enough. Late in the first quarter, Seau picked off a Steve Bono pass and helped set up a San Diego field goal—one of nine combined by the two teams. Five minutes into the fourth quarter, the score tied at 19, Seau did it again, leading to what would stand as the game-winning kick. He added 12 tackles and a sack.

A dominant performance, on one-and-a-half legs.

"If Junior Seau isn't one of the best to ever play the game," Chargers coach Bobby Ross said after his team's 22–19 victory, "then I don't know who is."

San Diego couldn't carry over any momentum off that hard-fought result, however, and promptly lost its next three. Seau missed the last of those, a 32–13 drubbing at Seattle, with a knee issue.

By Week 17, the Chargers had nothing left to play for but pride and a shot at .500. Their opponents, the Broncos, already had locked up a division title and the conference's top playoff seed. It was one of those regular-season finales that tend to be forgotten almost as soon as the clock hits zeroes. And, as such, both sides lined up minus a lengthy list of contributors—San Diego, to help its banged-up players get a head start on the offseason; Denver, to rest its key guys for the postseason.

Seau played, but in the second quarter sprained his knee and needed help hobbling off the field. He could have shut it down right there and no one would have blamed him.

Instead, he was back out there for the Broncos' next possession. Two plays into it, Seau recovered a fumble by Denver quarterback Bill Musgrave (who replaced a resting John Elway). A quarter later, Seau dislocated Musgrave's right shoulder on a tackle. He also batted down three passes, and even shifted up and played along the defensive line as the Chargers dealt with a depleted lineup there.

The Chargers won the game 16–10, although the outcome was relatively meaningless. But Seau approached it with the same intensity as he did that Week 5 showdown with Kansas City or his two Super Bowl appearances or . . . well, anytime he stepped on the field, really.

Whenever Junior Seau had a helmet on, his coaches and teammates knew they were going to get everything he had. That was true in San Diego, in Miami, and in New England—the three stops in Seau's playing career.

Seau twice came out of retirement to play for the Patriots, at the behest of Harrison, his longtime Chargers teammate. The second time through, Seau didn't sign on until December 5, after the Patriots found themselves ravaged by injuries. Two days later, on December 7, 2008, he delivered the team's pregame speech ahead of a win at Seattle.

"That guy inspired me more than anybody on this planet," Harrison said on his episode of NFL Films' *A Football Life*. "He outworked everybody I played against or I played with. I asked Junior, 'Why do you run so hard in practice?'

"He says, 'Well, I get paid to practice. I play the games for free.'"

The Chiefs signed Weber State tight end Alfred Pupunu as an undrafted free agent in 1992, and San Diego added him via waivers shortly thereafter. When Pupunu called the Chargers' front office to finalize travel arrangements, they told him that Seau—a burgeoning star heading into his third NFL season—had volunteered to pick him up at the airport.

Pupunu suspects Seau did so because of their shared Polynesian backgrounds—Seau was of Samoan descent; Pupunu was born in Tonga. Either way, Pupunu was excited to have Seau in his corner from the jump. The linebacker's first piece of advice to San Diego's new tight end: bury yourself in the playbook, learn it inside and out.

For Pupunu to stick on the Chargers' roster, he'd had to outwork some of the other hopefuls in that tight end room and that meant never giving an inch, off the field or on it.

"Even when we played basketball at his house," Pupunu recalled, "we would have scratch marks all over our bodies because that's how physical it was. He'd say to me, 'That's all you got? Elevate your game.' Just a friendly basketball game. He was so competitive in everything. He wanted to win."

Pupunu spent parts of seven seasons as a Charger, and he wound up rooming with Seau on the road and at training camp. During two-a-days (back when teams were permitted to hold those in August), while their teammates napped to ready themselves for afternoon practice, Seau would stay up telling jokes and listening to music.

"He was just one of those guys you wanted to be around all the time," Pupunu said. "That guy had so much energy, it was amazing. . . . It was awesome."

You can't talk about Seau without coming to the end. On May 2, 2012, at age 43, Seau died by suicide by shooting himself in the chest. A study of Seau's brain after his death concluded that he suffered from chronic traumatic encephalopathy (CTE), a degenerative disease often linked to head trauma. In 2018, Seau's family settled a wrongful-death lawsuit against the NFL, filed because of that diagnosis (the family opted out of a separate class-action lawsuit against the league, filed by thousands of former players who accused the NFL of negligence in diagnosing and treating concussions).

Seau's death devastated his friends and family, of course, but also the greater community around him.

Oceanside High sits fewer than 40 miles north of San Diego. USC is just 125 miles or so up the coast. Seau was a homegrown, hometown hero even before the Chargers selected him at No. 5 in the 1990 draft.

And, once Seau put on that San Diego uniform, he poured untold time and resources into giving back to those around him. Through its "Shop with a Jock" program and an extremely popular charity golf tournament, the Junior Seau Foundation raised millions of dollars for local youth. As recently as 2015, three years after Seau's death, the foundation donated $500,000 to Rady Children's Hospital Foundation.

Seau held his annual Celebrity Championship golf tournament in March 2012, mere weeks before he died. Dozens of NFL legends attended, including Harrison, Marcus Allen, and Drew Brees.

"One of the biggest accomplishments in my mind was being able to give back to the community through the Junior Seau Foundation," Seau's daughter, Sydney, said during an NFL Network interview at her father's emotional Hall of Fame induction in 2015. "That is where his true legacy lies—giving back to the community that gave him everything. Dad, you gave us your time, your presence, your love, but most of all you gave us your heart. . . .

"You were everything. I hope this induction can exemplify the fact that you are more than just Junior Seau, No. 55 and a buddy. You are a light. . . . I know that his athleticism and talent made him extraordinary enough to make it into the Hall, but it is his passion and heart that make him truly legendary and deserving of this honor."

A year before he was enshrined in the Pro Football Hall of Fame, Seau was voted into the inaugural class of the Polynesian Football Hall of Fame. His son Tyler, choking back tears, spoke on his behalf that evening.

"I'm going to keep it a little short so I don't break down," Tyler said. "I'm going to leave you with a quote that he used to tell each and every one of us after he usually ran us to death on the beach: 'Work hard for today to build our tomorrow and pray for the rest. Stay humble and God bless. Love.'"

62.
Bart Starr

Bart Starr (15) was a three-time NFL passing leader
and was the MVP of the first two Super Bowls.

Position: Quarterback
Team: Packers (1956–1971)

By Zak Keefer

Cherry Starr told a story at her husband's funeral, and it wasn't about Vince Lombardi or the goal-line sneak that clinched the Ice Bowl or all those championships the Packers piled up in the 1960s.

It was about their trash collector back in Green Bay.

Her husband was in the car with their son, Bart Jr., and two neighborhood kids. When Bart saw the town's sanitation truck pull down their street, he hit the brakes, got out, and walked up to the man whose job was to pick up their trash.

Then he thanked him.

"It doesn't matter if it's the president of the United States or the gentleman picking up your trash," Starr later told the kids. "You treat them the same."

That was Starr, a gentleman of the highest order, roundly revered by teammates, coaches, and fans, perhaps as much as any professional football player in history. On the field, he was Tom Brady four decades before Tom Brady: the college quarterback who struggled to get on the field for a big-time program. Starr was benched in his final year at Alabama, throwing one touchdown to go with nine interceptions for a winless Crimson Tide team. Then, like Brady, he was a pro prospect who was severely overlooked and tumbled in the draft (Starr was pick No. 200 in 1956), then a young passer who had to climb the depth chart and earn his keep.

And like Brady would in New England, Starr grew into the unquestioned leader of one of the great dynasties in the history of the sport, forever intertwined with the hard-driving coach with whom he shared so much success. After earning the starting job full-time in 1959, Starr went 9-1 in playoff games and led the Packers to five championships, including three consecutive from 1965 to 1967, something no quarterback has matched since, not even Brady.

Without Starr, there is no Vince Lombardi, certainly not as we remember him. Packers great Paul Hornung once told the team's website that if Bart Starr wasn't his quarterback, the details-obsessed Lombardi would've called every play.

But with Starr under center, he rarely had to.

It was the quarterback's suggestion in the waning, frigid moments of the 1967 NFL championship game—forget the handoff, I'll just run it in—that produced one of the iconic moments in league history. The temperature hovered around 16-below that day in Green Bay, and with the windchill, it dipped to minus-46. The Cowboys led by three with 16 seconds to go, but Starr had driven the Packers down to their opponent's 1-yard line. It was time to finish it.

The winner would punch their ticket to Super Bowl II.

"Fine," Lombardi famously said after Starr suggested the quarterback keeper. "And then let's get the hell out of here."

Starr plowed in. Lombardi celebrated. The Packers were on their way to a third straight championship.

That Lombardi's teams so often grinded out wins in a run-first era probably has overshadowed the fact that Starr was the best passer of his day, a lover of play-action who could heave the football downfield and beat defenses deep.

His story remains remarkable, even all these years later. Legend has it that Starr was only drafted—in the 17th round, no less—because his high school basketball coach knew the Packers' personnel director. But Starr proved after a few seasons that he had the arm to win the job and the mettle to stand up to the new coach.

The quarterback remembered his first meeting with Lombardi, where they worked to install the new offense. An hour in, Lombardi gave the players a break. Starr ran downstairs, found a pay phone, and called his wife.

"Honey, we're gonna start winning," he told her.

He was right.

It's all they'd do for a decade.

And over time, Starr earned the legendary coach's respect in a way few players ever did. Once, after Starr tossed an interception during practice, Lombardi ripped into his quarterback in front of the entire team. Starr marched into Lombardi's office afterward and demanded an apology—and asked that if the coach was going to criticize him, he do it in private so he could maintain the respect of his teammates.

The starting quarterback, Starr believed, couldn't afford to lose the confidence of those he was leading. If he was going to be a coach on the field, he should be treated like it.

"I said, 'Look, coach, I can take all the chewing you wanna dish out,'" Starr said years later. "'I understand that's your personality and that's all well and good. That doesn't bother me.'"

Lombardi agreed.

"He never ever said anything to me in front of them again," Starr said.

His blueprint became The Blueprint for the position, one that scores of quarterbacks would adhere to in the decades that followed as the league's popularity skyrocketed and so did the position's prestige.

This was how Starr saw it: "The quarterback's job is to be a coach on the field. I'd say there are three things a quarterback must have. One, he's got to have the respect of his teammates. Two, his authority must be unquestioned. And three, his teammates must be willing to go to the gates of hell with him."

He checked all the boxes. He set the standard impossibly high, as a quarterback and as a man.

"I don't think Bart Starr made five mistakes in his whole life," Hornung added. "He was just a cut above the rest. He really was."

After his Hall of Fame induction in 1977 and an unsuccessful stint as Packers coach—Starr went 52-76-3 over eight seasons, reaching the playoffs just once—he stayed in touch with his former team in a unique way: by writing handwritten letters to his quarterback successors.

He sent hundreds of letters to Brett Favre and Aaron Rodgers, each of whom came to cherish Starr's input and advice. When Favre, a Mississippi kid who was toiling on the bench for the Atlanta Falcons early in his career, was traded to the Packers in 1992, he didn't even know where Green Bay was.

"But I knew who Bart Starr was," he said years later, "and I knew what he stood for."

The letters kept pouring in once Favre's career took off. After his first win. After his first MVP. After his Super Bowl triumph. And one, Favre would later recall, about the way he wore his hat during a press conference.

"You couldn't help but get a chuckle out of it," Favre said.

Rodgers remembers his first conversation with the Hall of Famer, years before the Packers became his team. "Playing quarterback in Green Bay is about more than winning championships," Starr told him.

There was an expectation, Starr was saying, of leadership, of excellence, of class.

"There was nobody who better exemplified that than Bart," Rodgers said after Starr's passing in 2016. "A true gentleman."

And that, more than anything, is what Cherry Starr wants her husband of 68 years to be remembered for. In the months after his death, she was the one receiving letters, hundreds upon hundreds of them, from fans and friends of Bart from all over the country.

That's when it hit her: his impact was immeasurable.

Each had their own story, a snippet into Bart's kindness or thoughtfulness or goodwill, like those two neighborhood boys back in Green Bay who saw the famous quarterback stop the car just so he could thank the local trash man.

"I've responded to every one of them," Cherry said.

61.
Jonathan Ogden

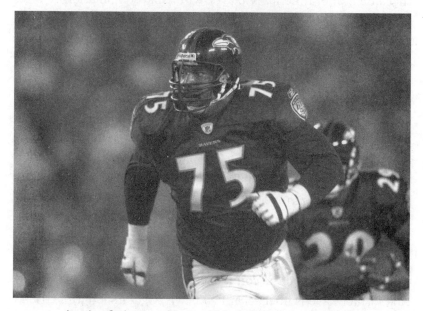

Jonathan Ogden was a five-time All-Pro, an eleven-time Pro Bowler, and a member of the 2000s All-Decade team.

Position: Offensive Tackle

Team: Ravens (1996–2007)

By Jeff Zrebiec

The picture was taken when Jonathan Ogden was a 17-year-old high school senior at the St. Albans School in Washington, D.C. However, a similar scene played out time and time again over the next 16 years, first at UCLA and then in Baltimore.

It depicted Ogden, wearing No. 74 for St. Albans, leading a running back through the hole. Several defenders were in his wake and another one pictured appeared none too interested in a collision with the hulking offensive tackle. Six-foot-7 and more than 300 pounds as a high schooler, Ogden towered over everyone on the field, a man among boys.

It didn't seem fair. A player that big and powerful shouldn't be that quick and athletic. A player with that combination of size, strength, and speed shouldn't also be so smart, savvy, and structured. Yet, that was Ogden, the total package for an offensive tackle, a unique combination of brains and brawn.

"That's the poster child," former Ravens general manager Ozzie Newsome once said.

Ogden was the rarest of NFL stars. He did his job so well and eliminated his counterpart so thoroughly that you barely noticed that he was on the field. Imagine the luxury of not having to worry about the quarterback's blind side, not having to game-plan for some of the league's top edge rushers, not having to commit to double teams or giving the left tackle help?

That was the Ravens' reality for more than a decade with Ogden, all 6-foot-9 and 345 pounds of him, anchoring their offensive line.

"His size gave you the confidence that we could run the world," said former Ravens linebacker Ray Lewis, Ogden's longtime friend and teammate.

Former Ravens head coach Brian Billick often jokes about how easy it was to come up with an offensive game plan when he had Ogden at left tackle: "Run to the left and slide protections to the right."

Ogden made the Pro Bowl 11 times in 12 NFL seasons with the lone exception being his rookie year in 1996, when he started all 16 games at left guard. He moved to left tackle the following season and started a decade-plus run where he was one of the most dominant players in the league at any position. He was still playing at a pretty high level late in his career despite a toe injury that limited his mobility and led to his retirement after the 2007 season.

It wasn't just about his size, though that's where it started. Standing close to Ogden remains a mesmerizing experience. He was so big and powerful that he could absorb a bullrush without giving up ground and consistently knock defenders back in the run game. He was so quick and athletic that he had little trouble getting out of his stance and negating a speed rush or getting to the second level. There was a play during Ogden's rookie year when his assignment was to usher veteran running back Earnest Byner down the field on a screen. The only problem was Byner couldn't stay with Ogden to benefit from his escort.

"I think he kind of changed what we thought was possible at the position because of his physical stature," longtime Cleveland Browns standout tackle Joe Thomas recalled to writer Bob McGinn. "Ogden was athletic like a tight end. It was just so incredible watching [Ogden] move that quickly and with seemingly so little effort on every single play of the game."

He was so flexible that despite often being five or six inches taller than the guy he was trying to block, he had no trouble bending his knees and taking away a defender's leverage. Ogden was a technician, relying on quick, strong hands, nimble feet, and a seemingly limitless wingspan. The options for pass rushers were either limited or nonexistent, depending on whom you talked to.

Ogden was never known as a snarling and trash-talking lineman whose goal was to knock defenders silly. He was considered a gentle giant, content to dominate his man both physically and technically for three hours and then share a laugh with him after the game. Yet, he had no holes.

Former Ravens offensive line coach Jim Coletto noted of Ogden, "If you wanted to build an ideal left tackle, that's the guy you clone. You wouldn't find a better guy."

Ogden was the offensive rock on the Ravens' Super Bowl–winning team during the 2000 season. He paved the way for many of Jamal Lewis's 2,066 rushing yards in 2003. He gave an offense that struggled to find stability at quarterback throughout his tenure an identity and a star to build around.

He was the Ravens' first-ever draft choice, taken fourth in 1996. He was the organization's first first-team All-Pro. He was the Ravens' first homegrown player inducted into the Hall of Fame, making it on his first try. He's also credited in some circles as being the player who contributed to opening the eyes of NFL decision-makers to just how valuable a dominant left tackle could be and how much money they are worth.

Ogden was part of a great era of offensive tackles that also included Tony Boselli, who was drafted the year before him, and Orlando Pace and Walter Jones, who were both drafted a year after him. Standout offensive tackle play ultimately set the stage for teams becoming more open and aggressive with pass-heavy game plans. Ogden, however, would be uncomfortable in getting such credit.

In many ways, he was a reluctant superstar whose easygoing personality and wide array of interests led some NFL decision-makers to question whether he loved football enough to reach his potential. Ogden chose to attend UCLA, largely because the football coaching staff OK'd him to join the Bruins track and field team. He won an NCAA Division I indoor championship in the shot put and had visions at one point of going to the Olympics.

Even after he entered the NFL, Ogden was just as likely to be found walking around team headquarters with a novel in his hand, preferably a sci-fi thriller, than the playbook. When he returned home, he'd watch *Jeopardy!* over a game or sporting event.

Unlike many of his teammates, he didn't embrace the glitz and glamour of being a pro athlete and was known—and often mocked—for his frugality. He signed a six-year, $44 million contract extension in 2000 and a seven-year, $48 million pact in 2004. However, his first luxury car was a used Mercedes-Benz and he bought it about eight years into his NFL career. He eschewed designer suits for a T-shirt or plain polo shirt and jorts. His trademark Afro was always unkempt and he'd relish how much money he'd save by not having to get haircuts. He and his family ultimately set up full-time in Las Vegas, partly because it was a no-income-tax state.

"A Rolex watch? An earring in his ear? That's not his style. With J.O., what you see is what you get," ex-Ravens offensive lineman Wally Williams told the *Baltimore Sun* in a 2007 profile of Ogden. "Here's this big guy with a crazy stare and hair that hasn't been combed since the [1996] pro draft. But there's no detail in his life for which he doesn't have a game plan built for success."

In contrast to Ray Lewis, Ogden wasn't very comfortable out front or being the center of attention. That was apparent before his Hall of Fame induction when Ogden acknowledged how nervous he was to deliver the speech and compared it to "just yanking the Band-Aid off" and getting it over with.

However, he proved to be the perfect complement to Lewis on the other side of the ball. They shared a passion for winning and performing at an elite level. Tossing his helmet and challenging the offensive coordinator to run the ball more was about as demonstrative as Ogden would get, but nobody in Baltimore ever questioned his competitive fire.

Ogden and Lewis also were maniacal about their preparation. Ogden kept a detailed notebook of the top pass rushers, in which he logged observations from film study and experiences playing against them. He regularly consulted it ahead of his individual matchups.

"Football is a hard game. It's hard to play. Jonathan made it look so easy," Newsome said. "I don't know if he even had to sweat half the time when he was out there playing. He played against some very competitive people. He made the game look so easy with the way he played it. That's because of the way he prepared."

Newsome essentially established the foundation for the Ravens organization on April 20, 1996, when he selected Ogden at No. 4 and Lewis at No. 26. The story has been told often. Former Ravens owner Art Modell, looking to drum up excitement for a new fan base after the team moved from Cleveland, badly wanted Newsome to select talented but troubled Nebraska running back Lawrence Phillips. The Ravens already had a competent left tackle in Tony Jones and adding another, even a guy as promising as Ogden, wasn't going to sell tickets.

Newsome and the team's scouting and personnel departments, though, had Ogden as the best and cleanest player in the draft. They graded him as highly as any guy they've ever evaluated. They just never thought they'd have the chance to select him. In fact, Kirk Ferentz, the team's offensive line coach at the time, openly wondered if it was a waste to spend a chunk of time evaluating and getting to know Ogden and his family. He thought for sure that he wouldn't be available to the Ravens.

Wide receiver Keyshawn Johnson went first to the New York Jets and then the Jacksonville Jaguars selected linebacker Kevin Hardy. The Arizona Cardinals had the third pick and they were convinced the Ravens were desperate to get Phillips. At draft headquarters in New York City, the Cardinals had a card that had Phillips's name on it, conveniently placed so the Ravens representative at the draft would see it. They wanted the Ravens to trade up one spot, but Newsome called their bluff.

When the Cardinals selected pass rusher Simeon Rice, Ogden dropped into the Ravens' laps. Modell grudgingly signed off on the pick. The decision solidified the Ravens' best-player-available drafting philosophy that persists to this day and was the first of many selections that earned Newsome a reputation as one of the league's shrewdest drafters and decision-makers.

Years later, as he prepared to present his first-ever draft pick in Canton, Newsome, still basking in the glow of the team's second Super Bowl victory, acknowledged that he probably wouldn't still be employed if he hadn't taken Ogden over Phillips. He knew he had made a good draft pick when he turned in the card for Ogden. He just didn't expect it to turn out that good.

"There are a lot of great offensive linemen, and there are a lot of great players who are in the Hall of Fame that are very deserving," Newsome said, echoing comments made by former Ravens executive James "Shack" Harris. "But I don't know if there's anybody who played the position any better than Jonathan Ogden did."

60.
Joe Schmidt

Joe Schmidt (56) was elected to ten consecutive Pro Bowls and was voted Lions MVP four times by his teammates.

Position: Linebacker

Team: Lions (1953–1965)

By Nick Baumgardner

Football—at least the defensive middle of it—changed forever in the spring of 1956. That was when the Detroit Lions completed a complex four-team trade that centered on coach Buddy Parker's desire to land an athletic defensive tackle.

Parker was in his sixth season as Lions coach, with two NFL championships already in his pocket. But football success was a burden even in the 1950s. A once-powerful offense was suddenly muted in 1955 and a promising defense—anchored by 24-year-old outside linebacker Joe Schmidt—desperately needed a fresh coat of paint after a brutal three-win campaign.

Schmidt, a once unheralded prospect Parker had fallen in love with three years earlier, was going to be a star and the Lions' head coach knew it. He also knew, in order for Schmidt's star to truly shine at linebacker, he needed a better tackle in front of him.

The deal essentially boiled down to the Lions moving offensive lineman Dick Stanfel out of town to make room for New York Giants veteran defensive tackle Ray Krouse. Krouse was exactly what Parker coveted: a 260-pound interior defensive lineman who was best known for his speed and agility. Krouse was the final piece of that trade. But the last step in the plan revolved around Schmidt: the player who would become known as football's first truly elite middle linebacker.

"Schmidt's mobility took some of the load off the defensive backs on pass defense," Parker would explain to the *Detroit Free Press* years later, before getting right to the point. "In fact, his style of play brought about the zone defense, revolving defenses and [the] modern defensive look of pro football."

Schmidt—a member of both the Pro and College Football Halls of Fame, a 10-time Pro Bowler, and a two-time league Defensive Player of the Year—began his career in Detroit with zero notoriety. But by the close of Schmidt's first exhibition season in 1953, Parker had traded star defender Don Doll for draft picks and all but declared Schmidt the future of the defense.

A thinking man's player with football in his blood, Schmidt began his professional career—believe it or not—at 14, playing for his brother John's semipro St. Clair Veterans. Schmidt saw the game differently than most linebackers and was fast enough to do more. At Pitt, Schmidt played for four head coaches and shouldered an abnormal amount of on-field responsibility as the far-and-away top player on a struggling team. In Detroit, when he was freed up to roam, Schmidt became an immediate terror for anything in the backfield that moved.

In those days, most teams used a five-man defensive line with two outside linebackers filling in the extra gaps on either side of the field and one tackle directly over the center. But after the Lions lost their best interior linemen before the 1955 campaign, Schmidt's ability to impact more of the game became limited by his pre-snap alignment as an "outside" linebacker.

After the Lions acquired Krouse in the spring of 1956, Parker switched his outfit to a four-man defensive front. With more agility at the tackle spots, Parker's front was able to control the middle of the line and keep Schmidt free to run. The Lions placed Schmidt directly over the ball, a few yards back off the center. A year earlier, the Lions couldn't stop anything. By December, after 10 games experimenting with Schmidt in the middle of his defense, Parker declared a 42–10 romp over George Halas's Chicago Bears the "greatest the Lions ever have played since I've been here." Schmidt had been calling plays on the field all year, but in this game, his defense forced five turnovers.

The Lions finished 1956 feeling recharged, with a defense—and a new star in Schmidt—as their reliable calling card. The following season, the Lions captured another NFL title. Schmidt's defense held the great Jim Brown to just 69 yards on 20 attempts in a 59–14 championship win over the Cleveland Browns.

Most football historians are quick to point out that Schmidt wasn't the game's first middle linebacker, even though he played some of the position at Pitt. But it quickly became hard to argue he wasn't the first great one.

In T. J. Troup's book *The Birth of Football's Modern 4-3 Defense*, Schmidt explained the detail behind the secret to unlocking Detroit's resurgence—and what made Parker's and Schmidt's system one that basically everyone in the league copied. Schmidt said his calls on the field were prompted by what he thought the opposing quarterback would call based on his film work and overall game-plan studies.

"Joe is responsible for all the defensive signals called on the field. The moves, the strategy, are all his responsibility," Don Shula, then a defensive assistant in Detroit, told the *Free Press* in 1962—

explaining how most linebackers handled the front seven, not the entire field like Schmidt. "We think he's the greatest."

From there, Schmidt keyed on offensive alignment. If an offense was in a split-back formation, he keyed on the back opposite the wide side of the field. If the ball was in the middle of the field, his key became the "triangle" between the center, the two guards, and a fullback. Schmidt's vision from the center of the field allowed him to work from the inside to the outside, helping limit cutback lanes.

Add this to his sure tackling and athleticism, and Schmidt became the type of player other teams envied and attempted to parrot—without much success. The first true "quarterback of the defense," Schmidt was also known as a punishing hitter who almost never missed his target. So much so that repeated and constant shoulder injuries plagued the back half of his career. Still, Schmidt finished his 13-year career with 24 interceptions and 17 fumble recoveries.

Whether he's the greatest Lion in history is subjective, of course. But it's hard to argue he wasn't the best player on the last NFL team in Detroit to win a championship. Shula believed Schmidt was the best overall player in the NFL into the 1960s, and certainly its top defender.

Schmidt's legacy also includes time as the Lions' head coach. He became an assistant for Detroit upon his retirement in 1966, then was elevated to head coach in 1967 at 35 years old. Schmidt went 43-34-7 during a six-year run that featured an early rebuild, a push in the middle, and an eventual plateau that fell short of a title.

More than anything, though, Schmidt's football legacy will be rooted in the advancement of the game. Football's greatest constant—both now and in its earliest days—is change. Players and coaches are the people who create that change by finding ways to do things better and more efficiently than those before them. The list of those who created significant, historical change is small.

But Schmidt is absolutely on it.

59.
Herb Adderley

Over an eleven-year career, Herb Adderley (26)
played for an NFL championship–winning team seven times.

Position: Cornerback

Teams: Packers (1961–1969), Cowboys (1970–1972)

By Connor Hughes

Toni Adderley knew, she just didn't know. To her, Herb was "Dad." To her children, he was "PopPop." She was born in 1968, Year 8 of Herb's 12-year NFL career. So, her memories of his time spent with the Packers and Cowboys aren't of bone-crushing hits, game-sealing interceptions, or Super Bowl championships. Instead, she remembers their homes, friends, and family.

As she grew, Herb's career was seldom a talking point unless someone else brought it up. There wasn't a need to. That's why, while Toni knew her dad played in the NFL and had earned a Hall of Fame jacket, she never truly grasped how incredible he was.

Not until he died in October 2020.

Not until condolences started coming in from people like NFL great Ronnie Lott, Packers president Mark Murphy, and others.

Not until she started reading about everything her dad accomplished.

"I knew he was a great player," Toni said. "Not until then did I know how great."

Hall of Fame Packers linebacker Dave Robinson chuckles about it now. It's among his favorite football stories as it pertains to his close friend Herb. The Packers played the Raiders in Super Bowl II. Green Bay won handily, 33–14. Afterward, Robinson went up to talk to Oakland quarterback Daryle Lamonica.

"He looked at me and said, 'Dave, all week long the coaches told me not to throw it to my right. They said whatever you do, just don't throw it at Adderley. And when we got to that fourth quarter, I hadn't thrown any passes over there. I thought I had lulled you guys to sleep,'" Robinson recalled, laughing.

"He said, 'So we get to the fourth quarter, and I went that way. I wanted to hit Fred [Biletnikoff]. I just didn't believe the coaches. I had to try one. I thought I could get one. So, I did. I went that way.'"

Adderley picked off the pass and returned it 60 yards for a touchdown. The game wasn't ever close, but that touchdown put it away.

"I started laughing," Robinson said. "I told him, 'Daryle, they were right—don't come that way.'"

Deion Sanders is considered by many to be the greatest shutdown cornerback ever. Rod Woodson and Darrell Green are in that discussion, too. As are recent stars like Darrelle Revis and Champ Bailey. Before any of them donned a helmet and pads, though, there was Herb Adderley.

Drafted as a running back out of Michigan State in 1961, Adderley converted to cornerback as a rookie and went on to intercept 48 passes during his career (plus another five in the postseason) and return seven for touchdowns. The Philadelphia native didn't allow a single touchdown during the 1965 regular season. During his 12-year career, Adderley went to five Pro Bowls and was a first-team All-Pro four times. He was voted to the NFL's All-Decade Team, the Packers' 50th anniversary team, and their all-modern era team.

He was Sanders before Sanders . . . Woodson before Woodson . . . Revis before Revis.

"No one used the term 'shutdown' back then," Robinson said. "But he was a shutdown, lockdown corner."

It's not hard for Robinson, who grew up 30 minutes away from Adderley in Moorestown, New Jersey, to recall what made his good friend so special. He had perfect size (6-foot, 205 pounds), tremendous speed, and was so athletic. He played basketball growing up so he could "jump and hurdle" with the best of them and had great control of his body. He had 0-to-60 acceleration. He was a "ball hawk," although no one really called it that back then. He used to play games with the opposing quarterback. He'd leave just enough room between him and the receiver to make it look like he was open. Then, once the quarterback lobbed it in, he'd break on it. It was a gamble—that was fine with Adderley. He might get beat from time to time, but more times than not, he'd win.

He was also smart. Too smart.

"You couldn't run the same play on him twice," Robinson said. "He was so intelligent. Herb was that kind of a guy. He could see it. If we got beat on a play by a team once, we'd go off to the sideline and figure out what happened and how to counter. Herb could just figure it out—just like that. And Herb was always right. I can't ever remember Herb being wrong."

It wasn't just coverage with Adderley, though. He had no problem coming down in the box and playing the run. There was one game, Robinson remembers, where coaches warned Packers players about the opposing running back (Robinson chose not to divulge names). The book on him was that if he got going early, it was nearly impossible to stop him. However, if you got to him early, he tended to run a bit more timid.

Early in the game, this player broke free on a run. Coaches were worried.

Adderley was not.

On the next handoff, he came in from his corner spot and walloped him.

"Herb just crushed him—spun him on his head like a top," Robinson said. "From that point on he ran like a baby. He was intimidated. That was Herb. He intimated the opposition—receivers, runners, quarterbacks. He knew what he was doing.

"People ask me what his best play was, but I never saw him make a bad one."

While Adderley finished the final three years of his career with the Cowboys (he won Super Bowl VI with them), he's most known for his time in Green Bay. There he won five NFL championships, including Super Bowls I and II, and helped establish Green Bay as one of the league's best defensive teams. After Adderley took over as a full-time starter in 1963, the Packers' defenses finished second, second, first, first, third, fourth, and third in points allowed. (Note: NFL and AFL statistics were kept separate until 1970.)

Robinson and Adderley were two of the biggest reasons for that. They played together for seven years and formed a dynamic pairing on the left side of Vince Lombardi's defense. They knew each other perfectly, which allowed them to play seamlessly. Robinson kept linemen off Adderley on run plays.

Adderley knew when Robinson would let go of his underneath coverage for him to pick up—Robinson had the first 10 yards, and Adderley everything after.

They weren't a linebacker and corner, Robinson said, but a single unit. It got to the point where it didn't matter what the coaches said—the two knew their strengths and played to them. If the coaches asked them to do something else, they would change on the fly. Robinson intercepted 27 passes during his career. He credits Adderley with an assist on "at least 15 of them."

"He didn't have to be the big star," Robinson said. "He wanted to be your wingman. And if he needed one—you better be his or you'd be damn sure he'd let you know you weren't.

"That's the way we played. The left hand has to wash the right."

The Packers of the mid-to-late '60s were littered with talent. Robinson and Adderley were two of six Hall of Famers on the defense alone (Ray Nitschke, Willie Davis, Henry Jordan, and Willie Wood the others). The offense featured Bart Starr, Forrest Gregg, Jim Taylor, and Paul Hornung, all coached by the legendary Lombardi.

For that reason, it's sometimes easy to overlook Adderley's excellence. It doesn't help that he played in an era when throwing the ball wasn't nearly as popular as it became in the decades to follow. It could be why his name was omitted from the NFL's 100th anniversary all-time team.

That baffles Packers historian Cliff Christl. He wasn't professionally covering the team then, but he was following it.

"It's written that Lombardi once said that Hornung was the greatest player he ever coached," Christl said. "But I thought Adderley played his position better than anyone else on those Packers teams."

Some of the greats of yesteryear would undeniably struggle in today's game. Not Adderley, who was perfectly suited for today's NFL.

"When you talk about the game's best corners, I think there are only a few guys who could both come up and play the run like they had to in the 1960s, but also run with the receivers in today's NFL," Christl said. "There aren't many who can do that, but also match up physically with guys like Randy Moss, Calvin Johnson, and other big receivers. Herb Adderley is one of those guys.

"He was the prototypical corner when he played, and he would still be the prototypical corner today. He was a perennial All-Pro when he played, and he'd be a perennial All-Pro today."

Nearly a year after Herb Adderley died, his New Jersey condo remained intact. He moved his family back to Philadelphia, where he was born, after he retired from the Cowboys, and then to Jersey after he and his wife divorced. Toni hadn't sold it yet. Herb's passing was still so fresh. It still hurt so much. There are days, Toni said, she struggles. Selling the place her dad last called home? It was a bridge she didn't want to cross.

So, the condo remained how Herb left it, including the loft just above his living room when you walk in the door. That's where he prominently displayed so many tokens and memorabilia from his playing days.

Toni went through them shortly after her dad's passing. She needed to write his obituary. Radio stations had reached out to have her speak about Herb as a player. She needed to familiarize herself—more than ever before—with what he'd accomplished.

She was there for hours. She couldn't believe what she saw.

"I remember looking at it all and just saying, 'Wow,'" Toni said. "I wish I had talked to him more about it."

She found the phone book where Herb had numbers written down for each of his former teammates—so many of them, like Bart Starr, now gone. She found his three Super Bowl rings, and the one from the Pro Football Hall of Fame, where he was enshrined in 1980. There was his Hall of Fame jacket and bust, of course. There was a seemingly endless wall of photos, and even more game balls. There were autographed signs and banners. He had items from his time at Northeast High and Michigan State—things Toni didn't even know existed. There were helmets and jerseys—including a full Cowboys uniform on which Herb had written important dates and autographed the pants.

It's impossible for Toni to recall everything that's there—there's too much.

All of it was a sign of just how impactful her dad was to the game of football.

"When you talk about the great athletes out of Philadelphia— Wilt [Chamberlain] and Kobe [Bryant]," Toni said, "the thing that people have said to me is that my dad deserves to be mentioned with them. He deserves to be called out more often."

58.
Mike Webster

No one played more seasons or games for the Steelers than Mike Webster.

Position: Center

Teams: Steelers (1974–1988), Chiefs (1989–1990)

By Stephen J. Nesbitt

The day Mike Webster was inducted into the Pro Football Hall of Fame in 1997, Terry Bradshaw looked out over a sea of Steelers fans in Canton, Ohio, and talked about his childhood dream. He had dreamed about playing in the NFL and having a championship team around him. Bradshaw said he'd need great receivers, "a little tiny 88" (Lynn Swann) and "a guy out of Alabama A&M" (John Stallworth). He'd need a left tackle who protected his blind side and loved horses (Jon "Cowboy" Kolb). He'd need a fullback, "the Italian

Stallion" (Franco Harris). Bradshaw kept rolling, calling out members of the Steelers' 1970s dynasty one by one. He named the "Steel Curtain" defensive linemen, then head coach Chuck Noll and the late owner Art Rooney Sr.

Then Bradshaw paused.

"What good is a machine if you ain't got a center?" the Hall of Fame quarterback asked. "And oh, did I get a center. I didn't get just any old center. I got the best that's ever played the game. I said to my dream, 'If you're going to give me this guy, make sure he ain't as pretty as me,' and he ain't."

Eight years earlier, at his own enshrinement, Bradshaw had said he'd do anything "to put my hands under Mike Webster's butt just one more time." So, closing his introductory speech in 1997, Bradshaw pulled a football from underneath the podium. "Just one more time," he said, handing the football to Webster. "Just one more snap." Webster removed his suit jacket, crouched, and snapped the ball. The crowd erupted. Bradshaw and Webster hugged. Bradshaw boomed into the microphone, "Ladies and gentlemen, the greatest center in the history of the National Football League: No. 52, Iron . . . Mike . . . Webster!"

If that moment were all you knew about Webster, it would look like a fitting coronation and celebration of a center who won four Super Bowls with the Steelers, played in nine Pro Bowls, and started 150 consecutive games in a 17-year career in Pittsburgh and Kansas City. And it was that.

But for those who knew Webster well, or those who'd read the newspaper articles about his personal and financial problems in the months before the Hall of Fame ceremony, it was only one page in an NFL tragedy. They prayed Webster would make it through his speech. Webster was a broken man. He was separated from his wife, Pam. He had little money. He often slept in his truck. His body was broken and his mental condition worsening. He tried dulling his daily headaches with prescription medications. However, the time around the enshrinement was as close as he'd come to happiness. He started his rambling-yet-coherent 21-minute speech by walking off the stage to hug Pam and their four children at their seats. Later, back at the microphone, Webster wanted to dispel a rumor: he hadn't sold his Super Bowl rings. The crowd cheered.

Webster died five years later. He was 50.

Since then, Webster's football life has been divided into three parts: his playing days, his decline, and his death. Nothing has been written about more than his death. Webster, the first former NFL player diagnosed with chronic traumatic encephalopathy (CTE) by Dr. Bennet Omalu, has become a symbol for the NFL's brain-injury crisis that has carried over into courtrooms and even into cinema in the 2015 film *Concussion*, in which Will Smith starred as Dr. Omalu.

Before all that, standing on the stage in Canton, Webster wanted more than anything to talk about failure. He said his thank-yous: to his wife, his kids, his parents, his in-laws, to the Steelers and the Rooney family, to the Chiefs (for whom Webster played his final two seasons) and owner Lamar Hunt, to his former teammates. Then he skipped right past his life story—his road from the family farm in Tomahawk, Wisconsin, to Rhinelander High School to the University of Wisconsin to cracking the Steelers roster as a fifth-round pick in 1974—and offered life lessons instead.

"We're all in this together, right?" Webster said. "You only fail if you don't finish the game. If you finish, you win. But you don't measure that in the middle of the second or third quarter. You measure it at the end. As long as you keep going, keep trying, keep working, all right? Sometimes you're going to be down. Sometimes you're going to be struggling." Later in the speech, he said, "Don't give up on yourself. Continue to develop. Continue to try. Do not be afraid to fail. Because you're going to fail, believe me. And there's no one keeping score."

The depression and confusion that fogged Webster's mind seemed to lift for a while. He skimped on details but spoke about how he had "embarrassed [himself] over and over and over again," and how others had helped him out. The Steelers—the Rooneys, team staff, and Webster's former teammates—had helped him find places to sleep and quietly paid some bills over the years.

On the field, Webster said, he wouldn't have been close to an NFL-caliber center if he had been afraid to make a mistake. He was too small to be timid. Noll once said Webster wasn't tall enough, didn't weigh enough, but somehow had great playing strength. Webster loved getting up early on practice days to lift in the weight room and sweat up and down the stadium steps.

"He was Paul Bunyan, Pecos Bill, and John Wayne all rolled into one," linemate Tunch Ilkin told the *Pittsburgh Post-Gazette*. "He was bigger than life."

"John Wayne may have been fiction in heroics," Noll told the Pro Football Hall of Fame. "Mike's not fiction."

Webster captained the Steelers' offense for nine seasons, leading the way for Harris and defending Bradshaw. They won Super Bowls IX, X, XIII, and XIV. Webster played 15 seasons and 220 games for the Steelers—more than any player to that point. He played through all manner of injury, with a streak of consecutive starts spanning from 1975 to 1986, when a dislocated elbow sidelined him for four games. In 1989, the Chiefs signed Webster as an assistant offensive line coach. It took him only a few weeks to realize he wasn't ready to retire as a player. He'd start 23 more times over the next two years.

"Hell, I was no ballerina out there," Webster said. "I wasn't pretentious. I worked hard because I was scared. Honest to God, I was scared of the possibility of failure."

He cocked his head.

"And I'm still scared of that," he said.

Over the next five years, Webster's cognitive decline accelerated. Stories leaked out slowly, then all at once after his death. An ESPN series documented Webster missing his son's 10th birthday after taking a cocktail of narcotics; repeatedly stunning himself to sleep with a Taser gun; screaming at strangers at the Amtrak station in Pittsburgh; losing teeth and trying to reattach them with Super Glue; getting arrested for forging prescriptions for Ritalin; losing money in bad business dealings; ranting and rambling on phone calls; getting lost; losing his mind. Once, when a doctor asked if Webster had been in a car accident, he replied, "Yeah, about 350,000 car accidents." Webster's petition for disability benefits began in 1999 and continued for years after his death, according to the *New York Times.*

On September 27, 2002, a crowd of 200 filed into a funeral home on a rainy day in Robinson Township, outside of Pittsburgh. There were the Rooneys, Noll, Bradshaw, Harris, Swann, Kolb, and scores of other former Steelers players and employees. They were there to say goodbye to Webster. He had died of a heart attack, but dementia, depression, and demons had tortured him for years.

At the funeral, which the Steelers paid for, players talked about the first and best part of Webster's football life: the playing days. They talked about his big heart. They talked about his tireless engine and work ethic. They talked about his love for his kids. Within a few years, Webster's story would be at the center of the debate about football and brain injuries, but on that day, friends chose to remember him as "Iron Mike," the toughest player they ever saw.

"Now, when I tell you one more time I'd like to put my hands under his butt, I would," Bradshaw, who gave a eulogy at the funeral, told the *Pittsburgh Post-Gazette* after Webster died. "Now, I'll have to wait until heaven."

57.
John Mackey

John Mackey (88) was a tight end with such power
and speed that he also lined up as the Colts' kick returner.

Position: Tight End

Teams: Colts (1963–1971), Chargers (1972)

By Jeff Zrebiec

Dementia had ravaged his mind and robbed John Mackey of some of his fondest football memories. Yet, there were a few details that never left him.

If you asked him about Super Bowl V and the Colts' 16–13 victory over the Dallas Cowboys in 1971, Mackey would perk up at the thought of one of the most memorable plays from that game.

"That's one thing that he would talk about all the time," said Sylvia Mackey, John's wife. "He was so proud of his 75-yard [touchdown] in Super Bowl V. Even in dementia, he would hold up his Super Bowl ring and say, 'I'm wearing this ring because of that 75-yard [touchdown] in Super Bowl V.' Then, he would hold up his Hall of Fame ring with so much pride.

"Football kind of kept him going even to the end."

The Super Bowl score may have been one of the luckiest of Mackey's 348 catches and 40 touchdowns over 10 professional seasons. Unitas's wobbly and high throw deflected off the outstretched hands of Colts receiver Eddie Hinton and then off Cowboys defensive back Mel Renfro before finding Mackey in stride. The rest is history.

The play, though, exhibited the qualities that made Mackey a transcendent player in the NFL: the wide frame that was such an inviting target for quarterbacks, the anticipation skills and awareness, and the breakaway speed that had never been so evident from a tight end that size.

When Mackey died in July 2011 at the age of 69 after a 10-year battle with frontotemporal dementia, he left behind a dual legacy. His combination of size, strength, and speed revolutionized the tight end position. Not all tight ends had to be glorified offensive linemen, utilized almost exclusively in the running game. Mackey showed that they could be dynamic with the ball in their hands, too. He became the prototype at the position for the modern NFL.

But Mackey's career was never just about receiving. In fact, it was defined by giving, to his teammates, to his football contemporaries, to generations of NFL players who followed and benefited from his courageous and tireless work in promoting—better yet, demanding—fair rights, wages, and pensions for players (current and former).

It's fitting that another thing Mackey remembered were his teammates' numbers since he spent so much energy off the field uplifting his fellow players. He could still rattle off the numbers of many of his beloved Baltimore Colts teammates. He knew that Johnny Unitas wore No. 19, Lenny Moore was No. 24, and Raymond Berry was No. 82. He remembered the non–Hall of Famers, too.

Mackey was the first president of the NFL Players Association following the NFL-AFL merger and he spent three and a half years in that role. Even after he retired from the NFL following the 1972 season, his lone one with the San Diego Chargers, Mackey's advocacy for players never stopped. Sylvia carried on her husband's mission long after his death, saying she got her drive from John.

"It could be said of John, that no one better combined being the greatest at his position all-time and also the greatest leader," said former NFL center Bill Curry, Mackey's longtime Colts teammate and one of his closest friends. "You may argue that there were better leaders. He was certainly one of the greatest one or two presidents of the Players Association that we've ever had. That combination is probably unmatched. In fact, I know it is."

Each January, the John Mackey Award is presented to the top tight end in college football. A few years ago, Sylvia approached the winner at the ceremony and asked him whether he knew her husband's history. "Yeah," the player responded. "He was pretty good, wasn't he?"

Sylvia laughed and nodded at the understatement.

Mackey is one of nine tight ends in the Hall of Fame, and the seven who were enshrined in Canton after him owe a debt of gratitude to the player who changed the way the position was viewed by the league.

Mackey caught only 27 passes in three seasons at Syracuse. He actually got more opportunities as a running back for a team that also had Heisman Trophy winner Ernie Davis. However, Colts head coach Don Shula quickly recognized the impact Mackey could have at tight end after Baltimore drafted him in the second round in 1963. Mackey also found a mentor in the venerable Berry, who worked with him on footwork and route running.

Mackey had more catches (35) and receiving touchdowns (seven) in his first professional season than he did in his entire college career.

"Previous to John, tight ends were big, strong guys like [Mike] Ditka and [Ron] Kramer, who would block and catch short passes over the middle," Shula told the *Baltimore Sun*. "Mackey gave us a tight end who weighed 230, ran a 4.6, and could catch the bomb. It was a weapon other teams didn't have."

Mackey down the seam became a staple of the Colts' offense and defenses couldn't match up. Over his nine-year run with Baltimore, Mackey averaged 16 yards per reception. Thirteen of his 38 regular-season touchdowns covered 50 yards or more.

One of Mackey's signature plays was his 64-yard touchdown reception against the Detroit Lions during the 1966 season. Mackey caught a short pass from Gary Cuozzo and juked one defender before he was surrounded by seven Lions. He shed one tackle attempt, ran over another, and shrugged off another Lion who had jumped on his back. He pushed down his teammate Moore and eluded another would-be tackler on his mad dash to the end zone. It's considered one of the best runs after a catch in football history.

"The guy could outrun the linebacker and run over the safety. How many people can do that?" Curry asked. "You just always had that extra dimension with him. The fact that he weighed 230 pounds, that was another factor. When that's coming at you, you don't really want to hit him."

Curry has long believed that Mackey's big-play ability overshadowed the fact that he was a dominant blocker who had his way with linebackers.

"I don't claim to be objective, but he's the best I've ever seen when you include in-line blocking and being a threat to go the distance every single time he got his hands on the ball," Curry said.

Mackey's ability as a two-way tight end was unmatched among his peers. Yet, it took him until his 15th and final year of eligibility to be inducted into the Pro Football Hall of Fame. Some believe the wait was payback for Mackey's frequent and aggressive challenging of the league and its owners after he became the NFLPA president.

"In his three years as NFLPA president, Mackey was often criticized as too aggressive [favoring confrontation over cooperation] and divisive," former NFL commissioner Paul Tagliabue wrote.

"Sometimes these criticisms accurately described Mackey's actions but misstated his purposes and powerful leadership style."

Not long after taking the NFLPA post, Mackey led a brief strike that netted the players roughly $12 million in pensions and benefits. Two years later, he was the lead plaintiff in a suit that led to the repeal of the "Rozelle Rule," which limited a player's right to free agency.

"He spoke up because he didn't see anybody else doing it and he knew if he saw somebody else doing it, he'd have to step in and tell them how to do it anyway. He used to say, 'I might as well do it myself,'" Sylvia Mackey said. "He took it upon himself to try and do something about the stuff that he knew the other players didn't like."

Ultimately, Mackey encountered a much bigger fight after his football career ended. His battle with dementia shone a more intense light on the violence of the NFL and the long-term health issues experienced by players. Mackey was later discovered to have chronic traumatic encephalopathy.

A decade after Mackey's death, the league's commitment to making the sport safer and taking care of its ex-players remains a hot-button issue. It's a fight Sylvia Mackey's still involved in. With her husband's condition deteriorating, she called on Tagliabue and the league's decision-makers to do more to help former players dealing with illnesses like dementia. The result was the 2007 passing of the "88 plan," named for Mackey's number. The plan provides financial help for care costs of players who are diagnosed with dementia, ALS, or Parkinson's disease.

"I can't even begin to tell you the ripple effect that has had on families," Sylvia said. "When I'm at the Hall of Fame or another football event, people will come up to me and say, 'Sylvia, you don't know what you did for us.' It was something that had to be done. They couldn't let all these famous players die with no dignity. This was happening with too many of us. John always wanted to make sure that the right thing was done for every player."

Mackey's memorial service was attended by football luminaries, former teammates, league and team executives, and Baltimore football fans.

NFL commissioner Roger Goodell spoke at the memorial and summed up the impact of the man they all came to honor.

"John Mackey," he said, "changed the game of football."

56.
Julio Jones

No receiver had more yards—12, 125—in the 2010s than Julio Jones (11), which helped land him on the All-Decade team.

Position: Wide Receiver

Teams: Falcons (2011–2020), Titans (2021), Buccaneers (2022)

By Jeff Schultz

I t started with a sound. Greatness in sports often can be identified by a play or a statistic or a level of career achievement that dazzles even peers. But Julio Jones's greatness was introduced on a practice field during his rookie NFL season, and Terry Robiskie wasn't even watching.

Robiskie heard it. That sound. That rare sound he heard, he felt, only one other time in his four-plus decades as a player and coach.

"In all my years in the NFL, I've had two players that when I'm standing on the sideline I could close my eyes and I can tell you who they are when they run past me," the former longtime coach said. "Only two guys, because the ground vibrates like an earthquake. One was Julio Jones. The other one was a little guy named Bo Jackson. The very first time he ran past me on the practice field, I said, 'This guy's special.' And the ground vibrated."

Jones likely will be a first-ballot Hall of Famer. When he retires, he will be central to every debate on the greatest wide receivers of all time. During his career he exhibited a rare combination of speed, strength, agility, leaping ability, focus, and intelligence, and for most of his career a lack of ego, unusual for one who excelled at the most diva of positions.

"In video games, we used to call it the created player," said Harry Douglas, a former teammate and current ESPN commentator.

"His ability to just stop while running that fast—I'd never seen that before. I was thinking I would tear every ligament in my knee if I tried that," said Roddy White, another former teammate and one of Jones's closest friends.

The first touchdown of Jones's career in 2011 initially was ruled incomplete because officials didn't think a catch was possible. He was surrounded by defenders and on his knees, falling to the ground, as he tried to catch up to Matt Ryan's 50-yard pass. The improbable evidence on the replay corrected the call.

During the first 10 years of his career with the Falcons, he had touchdown catches despite getting flipped upside down (against Green Bay in an NFC Championship Game), reaching back and taking the ball off the top of a defender's head while being smothered in coverage (Carolina), and one-handed while being held and interfered with (New York Jets).

In a non-tormented Atlanta sports world, Jones should have a Super Bowl ring because it was his acrobatic, 27-yard catch with 4:40 left in the Super Bowl and the Falcons leading the Patriots 28–20 that could have, should have, clinched the championship. The visions of Jones making the lunging catch and landing on one foot just inside the right sideline at the New England 22-yard line and somehow holding on to the ball led to Bill Belichick looking up at the video board in Houston to watch the replay with a relatively stunned look on his face. He probably thought the game was over. Instead, this highlight would be drowned out by "Run the Ball" memes as the Falcons failed to run three times, bleed the clock, and kick a likely game-clinching field goal.

What most don't know about that play is the immense pain Jones was in. The man seemed to be born on the weekly injury report. Foot, ankle, hamstring, back, shoulder, ribs, toe—he was one "funny bone" and a red lightbulb nose away from being the poor schlub in the Operation game. In the weeks leading up to the Super Bowl, he was in immense pain from a foot injury that required bunion surgery a month later.

"My toe was just sort of hanging there," he said later. "But I knew if I could take the field, I could do anything. I might not be 100 percent. But 65 or 70 percent is pretty good."

Playing through ailments was something he had been doing since his days at the University of Alabama. He long refused to take painkillers, even after surgery. He had a determination and a resolve that stems in part from his difficult upbringing. He lived in public housing in Foley, Alabama, in a neighborhood surrounded by crime and drugs. His parents split when he was 5 years old, and his mother, Queen Marvin, was a single mother of two who worked far too many hours to try to keep the lights on and food in the fridge.

Jones was born Quintorris Lopez Jones, with a first name that means "Gladiator," his mother told him, but he picked up the nickname of Julio when he was in middle school. Jones had a quiet inner strength and focus that immediately attracted Alabama's new head coach, Nick Saban, who made Jones his first real recruiting gem when he arrived in Tuscaloosa.

There was a balance to Jones's life. On the field, he lived to compete, and he studied and destroyed opponents. He once stayed up all night studying film of Browns cornerback Joe Haden, trying to find a flaw he could exploit.

"He came up to me one day and said, 'I almost called you at 1 a.m.—Joe got bad technique. We're going to be fine,'" Robiskie said. "He knew he had to use his hands more against Joe. He beat Joe so many times that game, but Matt [Ryan] didn't throw to him. But he was open all game." (Jones finished with five catches for 68 yards and a touchdown.)

There was no bragging after that game, or any game. It wasn't Jones's way. Off the field, he was quiet, introspective, spiritual.

His arms were covered with tattoos—skin art that he believed defined him. Down his left arm: symbols of spirituality. Down his right arm: temptations.

"See, over here is my Christian side," he said once, holding out his left arm. "Doves, guardian angels, things like that. Then on my right side, I have vices: things you don't really need but you have, or you just want to have, like cars. I like the roulette table. I like playing cards. Texas Hold 'Em. I'm a pretty good bluffer."

That paid dividends in his route running.

Jones was such a great athlete in high school that he probably could have thrived in elite basketball or track and field. He won state championships in the high jump, long jump, and triple jump. If he stuck with it, he might have been an Olympian. But he gravitated toward football because he preferred to be on a team. Jones's 2008 recruiting class was the start of Alabama's dominance in college football. The Crimson Tide went 36-5 in his three seasons and won a national championship. Jones totaled 179 catches for 2,653 yards and 15 touchdowns at a time when Saban mostly embraced a power running game.

Jones's output was enough for Thomas Dimitroff to know he wanted him.

Dimitroff had been the Falcons' general manager for three seasons. He inherited a franchise that never had consecutive winning seasons and immediately built a roster that went 33-15 with two playoff berths in three years. But Atlanta couldn't win a playoff game, and Dimitroff felt the team needed a game-breaker.

"DeSean Jackson from Philly would continuously kick our ass, and I remember sitting there after the season with Smitty [head coach Mike Smith], saying we need someone on our team like that," Dimitroff said. "We needed someone who could put the defense back on their heels."

Dimitroff locked on to two receivers, Jones and Georgia's A. J. Green. Dimitroff considered both potential Hall of Famers but gave Jones a slight edge because of his strength and felt Jones was a better scheme fit. The problem was both players figured to go early in the 2011 draft, and the Falcons were slotted to pick 26th. Dimitroff started calling around a month before the draft, and Cleveland, at six, was open to a trade. Talks with the Browns heated up about two weeks before the draft, with the two sides agreeing on the framework of a potential deal, and Dimitroff was confident he could get his playmaker.

But Jones wasn't convinced. He balked at meeting with the Falcons a week before the draft in Tuscaloosa because he didn't believe they were serious about trading up 20 spots.

"He felt disconnected," Dimitroff said. "He was thinking, 'Why am I doing this team a favor? How the hell are they going to trade up to get me?'"

So Dimitroff, owner Arthur Blank, and others were sitting in a hotel room across the street from campus, not knowing if Jones was going to show up. But agent Jimmy Sexton cajoled Jones into taking the interview. Dimitroff still felt a chill in the room when he walked in.

"But within five minutes, Terry won him over," Dimitroff said.

Robiskie was the Falcons' receivers coach. Like Jones, he came from a small town (in Louisiana), and they had similar life experiences. The two immediately connected. Jones loosened up and impressed everybody in the room with his maturity and leadership potential.

"From a mental standpoint, he was 35 years old when we got him," Robiskie said. "You know how when you go to a Little League or a Pop Warner game and the kids are 9 years old, but there's one kid who looks like he's 13? That was Julio, except mentally. He didn't fit his age group. He was like my age."

When the meeting was over, Jones left the room, and Robiskie turned to Dimitroff.

"I looked at Thomas, and it was like the day my daughter met her fiancé: Thomas was in love," he said.

Funny thing: despite being a receivers coach, Robiskie had an old-school mindset, and he believed the cost for the Falcons swapping picks with the Browns—a first-rounder in the 2012 draft, a second-rounder, and two fourth-rounders—would be too high. He was against the trade.

"I thought giving up all those picks would hurt us in other places," he said. "But after seeing the look on Thomas's face, I knew he was going to draft Julio no matter what. Then Mr. Blank turned to me and said, 'If we take this guy, what are you going to do? Are you going to quit?' I said, 'No, sir. One day I'll stand up at the podium in Canton, Ohio, and say Julio Jones is the best receiver I've ever coached, and it's great to be here inducting him into the Hall of Fame.'"

The only thing left was the trade. Dimitroff was somewhat torn. He wanted to make the deal, but this move would be extreme, the biggest of his career. On the day of the draft, he left his office and walked to the dorms on the back edge of the team's facility in Flowery Branch, Georgia. He entered his room and then made a phone call to one of his mentors, Bill Belichick. Even though Belichick worked for a different organization, Dimitroff felt he could trust the Patriots' head coach for honest feedback on the potential trade. The two spoke for more than a half hour.

As Dimitroff recalls, Belichick never said, "Don't make the trade." But he did say, "I wouldn't do it." It had nothing to do with Jones as a player but rather the magnitude of a deal that potentially would define the career of a young general manager.

"The bigger-picture message was that this will be attached to the rest of your career, good or bad, and you have to be willing to take that on, and it's not easy," Dimitroff said. "And he was like, 'The media will kill you on this, you know.'"

But Dimitroff made the trade—and drafted arguably the best player in franchise history.

"When people talk about a guy being a smart player, sometimes they're talking about being able to make adjustments," Roddy White said. "But Julio did things at full speed, and he always made the right decision. Being able to make adjustments on the fly like that is something I've never seen a rookie do before."

White led the NFL in receptions the season before Jones was drafted. He could have felt threatened by the move. Instead, he mentored him about the ways of the NFL and how to take care of his body during game weeks and not wear himself down in practice. Jones, in turn, deferred to White as the No. 1 receiver and ingratiated himself to teammates, especially other receivers. White and Jones became close friends. They celebrated birthdays and even their moms' birthdays together. When White's brother was murdered outside a club in Charleston, South Carolina, in 2014, Jones immediately traveled there to be with him.

"He supported me when I needed it the most," White said. "I always appreciated the love from him, and all those guys, and being there for me during that time."

The Falcons released White after the 2015 season, and it was officially Jones's show. He was the star, even if the injuries continued. In the Super Bowl season of 2016, he missed two late-season games with turf toe. But the Falcons were having a special season and a record-breaking offense, run by offensive coordinator Kyle Shanahan and led by quarterback Matt Ryan, who was named the NFL MVP. Jones was not going to come off the field in the postseason.

"Everybody's going through pain right now," he said three days before the NFC Championship Game against Green Bay. "My pain is no different than any of the other guys on the team. Unfortunately for me, I've been dealing with it for weeks now."

He hardly practiced during game week. But on that Sunday, he shredded the Packers for nine catches for 180 yards and two touchdowns.

"He's a beast," Ryan said after the game. "I know he wasn't feeling his best, but he's a warrior."

Or a gladiator.

He played 82 percent of the snaps in the Super Bowl. The catch in the final minutes should have been his crowning achievement, not a painful reminder of the implausible collapse that followed. It would be hung on an imaginary wall in franchise history, for a fan base and a city that had been tortured for most of five decades. It would be forever played on highlight shows revisiting Super Bowl heroes.

Dimitroff was standing on the sideline and watching when Jones got behind defensive back Eric Rowe and made the grab at the Patriots' 22. He was hit with a wave of emotion, not only because the catch may have secured a championship but because Julio was the player who would have tied a ribbon on it—the same player on whom Dimitroff effectively staked his career.

"In my mind, it was the best catch in the history of the world," Dimitroff said. "It was all-encompassing—not just because of the catch but because of what was on the line . . . in my world, anyway. At that point, it was like it all came together in this crazy flash like I was revisiting all the naysayers on Julio Jones. I had encountered a number of those moments over the years after we made the trade. But I saw that catch, and it was like, 'That's why we did it!'"

Too many of these stories don't end well. In the next few years, Jones's relationship with the organization deteriorated. Some of the problems stemmed from Jones's desire for a renegotiated and extended contract. But there were other moments when he felt slighted or disrespected for whatever reasons by all the key figures in the building: Blank, team president Rich McKay, Dimitroff, and new head coach Dan Quinn.

"Julio Jones is not a very trusting person," Robiskie said. "I'm not saying that's wrong. He just doesn't trust a lot of people. I'm the same way. His last two years in Atlanta, he lost trust with some people upstairs. There was a time or two when I had to call him or Face-Time him to go upstairs and see Dan Quinn, and there's no person I can think of in the NFL who I would trust more than Dan Quinn. But he got to the point where he didn't trust anybody upstairs."

Jones is an intensely private person and abhors social media. He hasn't spoken about this publicly.

He asked for a trade after the 2020 season. This coincided nicely with the Falcons' desire to move on, with a new head coach (Arthur Smith) and general manager (Terry Fontenot) coming in. Smith and Jones shared the same agent, so the new coach was familiar with the situation and the fact Jones rarely practiced. Jones's franchise legacy notwithstanding, his presence would not be ideal with a new regime coming in and Smith trying to set a new direction and instill a new personality. The Falcons ultimately traded Jones to Tennessee for a second-round pick.

"Look, he gave us 10 great years," Blank continued. "He's going to be a Hall of Fame player. He was a good teammate for all that period of time. [But] his ability or willingness to practice the way he did early in his career was different. There were some people who were in the building who had an effect on him. He wanted out, and the last thing Coach Smith wants is a player who doesn't want to be here."

"It seemed like there was a shift [in the relationship]," Dimitroff said. "Categorically I believe Julio Jones is a first-ballot Hall of Famer, respectfully to the process. That said, I do not regret the contract we gave Julio, and I was proud of our organization to have the willingness to do so. However, I was a bit taken aback that there would be any issues whatsoever about how the negotiations played out because I thought it was a win-win for both sides."

White, who remains close to Blank and the organization, said, "I wanted that relationship to last forever. In my opinion, he should've been in a Falcons uniform for his entire career. We both know that's not how it works, but I wish they could've figured it out."

Jones was plagued by injuries his next two seasons with Tennessee and Tampa Bay. At 33 years old, he is likely near retirement. His name will hang in the Falcons' Ring of Honor one day with White, Deion Sanders, Claude Humphrey, Tommy Nobis, and others. Relationships will heal. People will remember the athleticism, the highlights, the catch that should have won the Super Bowl. They'll remember the sounds.

"When he passed me, and the ground vibrated, I said, 'I would give up all those picks for him,'" Robiskie said.

55.
Jack Ham

Jack Ham (59) was a six-time All-Pro and made
a key interception that led to the Steelers' first Super Bowl victory.

Position: Linebacker

Team: Steelers (1971–1982)

By Ed Bouchette

If pictures indeed are worth a thousand words, there is no need for dictionaries to describe the position of linebacker in football. They merely could post a photo of Jack Ham.

"That," said Art Rooney Jr., "would be a perfect description."

Rooney was the boss of the Steelers' personnel department when the team drafted Ham in the second round in 1971 from Penn State, which would become known as Linebacker U. Ham was selected six times to an All-Pro first team (plus two second teams) and eight Pro

Bowls, was the NFL Defensive Player of the Year in 1975 according to the *Football News,* was on the 75th and 100th NFL anniversary teams, and made the Pro Football Hall of Fame in his first year of eligibility.

Yet Ham remains somewhat underappreciated. He was not as popular, for example, as fellow linebacker Jack Lambert or others on his own defense. Ham was not big, and he did not scowl over opponents nor mock them. He did not have a sack dance. His comments to the press were often bland. Teammates called him simply "The Hammer."

All he did was perform his job as the Steelers' left outside linebacker to near perfection on his way to pocketing four Super Bowl rings. Lore said Ham never missed a tackle.

"Jack was just such a real smooth athlete," said Joe Greene, who played left tackle in front of Ham. "I never thought of Jack being a physical power player, but he was always in the right place at the right time. And he made the tackles and he made interceptions. He was just an outstanding player. He wasn't flamboyant or anything. He just made plays."

Ham's style of tackling was to wrap up a player and take him down. He did not subscribe to the "kill shot" theory of launching into opponents for the big hit. To Ham, a tackle meant to down the opponent, not so much to punish him. Others could make the big hits and dominate the highlight reels of the day.

It did not prevent him from making the big plays, though. He covered receivers like a safety and finished his career with 32 interceptions, second most among linebackers in the Super Bowl era. Ham intercepted seven passes in his second season when teams played 14 games. His two interceptions helped the Steelers beat Oakland in the 1974 AFC Championship Game, 24–13, and reach their first Super Bowl.

He recovered 21 fumbles over his career, giving him 53 turnovers, the most by a linebacker in history. He also had 25 sacks when they were an unofficial stat and while playing outside linebacker in the

Steelers' 4-3 defense, in which linebackers did not often rush the passer.

"Jack Ham is the greatest of the greatest," Rooney said. "Man alive, how do you get a guy like that? I scouted him by playing and by film. We were really sold on him. Such a superb athlete, a very smart player. Chuck Noll loved that."

Tony Dungy, who briefly played safety for the Steelers in 1977 and 1978 and was a defensive coach for them in Ham's final two seasons, wrote in 2018 that he had "never seen anyone play the outside linebacker position better than Jack Ham. Fundamentals, technique, awareness and athleticism were all exceptional. He was the total package."

Ham stood 6-foot-1 and weighed 225 pounds, and some say he was the fastest Steelers player to run the first 10 yards. He was not an imposing figure and even surprised the man who drafted him when he first saw him in person. Although Rooney scouted him, he never met Ham until after they drafted him.

"We had a dinner and gathering after the draft, the night before they showed up for their physicals," Rooney said of Pittsburgh's 1971 draft class. "This guy knocks on my hotel room door. He comes in and has a black jacket on. I thought he was a bellhop. I scouted him and saw him live but never face-to-face. The guy knocks on the door and says, 'I was told to come here.' I said, 'Do you have a message for me or something?' He said, 'I'm Jack Ham.' My heart sank. I said this guy will hate me for the rest of his life. I thought he was a bellhop.

"The next day were weigh-ins for the rookies. He was very lean in the chest and arms. But he had real big legs. Of course, he became one of our great, great players."

Jerry Hillebrand started for the Steelers at left outside linebacker in 1969 and 1970. He remained there through most of the 1971 preseason, right up until Noll replaced him with Ham for the final tune-up.

"We were playing the Giants up there," Greene said. "Jack started in Jerry Hillebrand's place. I don't know if Hillebrand was hurt, but when Jack got into the lineup, he never left."

Ham intercepted three passes in that game, his first as a starter. He was an immediate starter as a rookie and missed just two games in his first 10 regular seasons. He was voted into the Pro Football Hall of Fame in 1988, his first year of eligibility. Greene said the unassuming Ham even "struggled with the Hall of Fame recognition."

He rarely drew attention to himself. Even in his Pro Football Hall of Fame induction speech, he did not cite his accomplishments but praised teammates and coaches. He has said Lambert was the best linebacker he ever saw and cited others as being better Penn State linebackers.

Asked on a Hall of Fame chat years ago what he considered his favorite accomplishment, Ham responded, "Probably graduating from Penn State with a business degree. I know my parents felt that way! Also, Joe Paterno taught me not to think I was somebody special just because I was a professional football player. It helps keep players from turning into egotistical maniacs."

Ham once said, "I prefer to play consistent, error-free football. If you're doing your job well and defending your area, you might not get tested that often, or get a chance to make big plays."

Ham did it all as well as any linebacker. Just don't ask him about it.

54.
Adrian Peterson

Adrian Peterson was a seven-time first- or second-team All-Pro,
with three NFL rushing titles and one MVP award.

Position: Running Back

Teams: Vikings (2007–2016), Cardinals (2017), Saints (2017), Washington
(2018–2019), Lions (2020), Titans (2021), Seahawks (2021)

By Nick Kosmider

O n November 4, 2007, in the first half when the Vikings were
playing the Chargers, Adrian Peterson ran for 43 yards. Eight
of his 13 carries had totaled 2 or fewer yards. The San Diego defense
felt good about its game plan to that point. After all, the rookie out
of Oklahoma, picked seventh by the Vikings the prior spring, had
rushed for 224 yards against the Bears weeks earlier. Surely, the
Chargers had a better hold on Peterson than that.

"But with Adrian, the sky was the limit because he's always one play away from making a big play," Chiefs offensive coordinator and former Vikings running backs coach Eric Bieniemy recalled in 2019. "That's just the type of player that he is. We had no idea what was going to happen. The only thing that we knew is if you keep giving him the ball, he'll have an opportunity to make something happen."

Peterson finished that game with an NFL-record 296 yards. He ran for 253 yards in the second half, a number that has been eclipsed in an entire game just seven other times in league history. On his second carry of the second half, Peterson torpedoed through a sliver of a hole on the left side, broke one tackle, and then ran away from everyone for a 64-yard touchdown.

That run was the gut punch. Seven of Peterson's 16 carries after that went for at least 10 yards.

Peterson's former teammate Teddy Bridgewater calls it the "keep shooting mentality," the idea that no matter how bleak things may have seemed at any point in a game, the next play always presented the possibility of magic.

"When I was on the team with Adrian, there would be games where he might have 32 carries for 180 yards, 200 yards," Bridgewater said. "The thing that people didn't realize was he might get 1 yard here, 2 yards here, 3 yards there, and then boom, 20-yard run. One yard here, 2 yards here, and boom again. He just kept shooting. That type of mindset is what made him special."

Twelve years later and three months shy of his 35th birthday when he took the ball from Washington quarterback Dwayne Haskins, Peterson darted to his right and gained 18 yards through the middle of the Buffalo Bills defense.

Peterson went left on the next play, squeezing through tacklers for 17 yards. He hit the same spot after the next snap, and by the time the Bills could finally bring him down, Peterson had gained 28 more yards.

As he watched the scene unfold at New Era Field in Buffalo on that frigid November afternoon, Leslie Frazier could only shake his head. The defensive coordinator for the Bills had held the same title with the Minnesota Vikings in 2007, when Peterson was in his debut season as the team's prized first-round pick. Now, 12 years later, Frazier was getting a taste of what it's like to be on the other side when the running back had entered one of his zones.

"Here he is at this stage in his career, and he's still able to really embarrass you if you don't shore up what you're doing," Frazier said. "We had to adjust because he was on his way to having one of those days."

Peterson made a career out of making even the most prepared defenses look silly. In 15 seasons, Peterson ranked fifth on the NFL's all-time rushing list at 14,918 yards, just 351 yards behind Barry Sanders. His path to a spot among the game's greatest figures at his position has been paved by a relentlessness that defined his most memorable moments, whether it was his record-setting rookie season or his NFL MVP campaign in 2012 that came on the heels of ACL surgery.

"When you're coaching against Adrian, teams are stacking the box to stop him," said Frazier, who became the Vikings head coach from 2011 to 2013. "They are going to get some negative runs on him, some stops along the way where it's 1 yard, 2 yards. But there were so many times where it looked like the play was done and he'd find a crease, and instead of it being a 4-yard gain, it would turn into a 50-yard touchdown. That's demoralizing because they all went into the game saying, 'We're going to stop Adrian Peterson. He's not going to get 100 yards on us.' So when he would break one of those runs, you'd see the air go out of the defense, and it happened often."

From 2007 to 2015, Peterson carried the ball a league-leading 2,381 times. He accounted for 38.1 percent of his team's touches during that span, which also led the NFL. He was one of the league's last true workhorse backs, serving as the engine of an offense even as the league moved toward its current pass-happy existence. What made Peterson different is that he was both battering ram and Bugatti during his prime. His career highlight reel is peppered with shoulder-lowering runs that propelled defenders into the grass, backside first. But the real beauty was in the breakaways.

If geometry scholars studied Peterson's work, they would be con-founded by his ability to erase the right angles like some kind of anti–Pythagorean theorem. Frazier saw it from the time the rookie stepped onto the field for his first training camp. Peterson would cross the line of scrimmage with a burst and by the time the deep safety could calculate the path he needed to take to cut him off, it was too late.

"You think of a guy like Barry Sanders who was a ballet dancer, so elusive," said Frazier, who was teammates with the late Walter Payton for five seasons with the Bears. "Adrian had a little bit of both. You saw that in that rookie year with some of those outside runs. His breakaway speed is one of the things that separated him for me, along with his heart and his passion. Those things were ev-ident throughout his career. They were there from his rookie year, the passion, the hunger, and the anger he ran with. It was differ-ent than anything you saw in the backs we faced from a defensive standpoint."

In 2014, Peterson played just one game when he pleaded no con-test to a charge of misdemeanor reckless assault after police said he used a wooden switch to discipline his 4-year-old son. The NFL suspended him, and commissioner Roger Goodell told him at the time he had "shown no meaningful remorse" for his conduct.

"I did a lot of praying," Peterson said at the opening of training camp in 2015. "With time, I was able to sit back and think about things and smooth things out."

Nearly every day of the 2020 season, as he went through rehab for a torn ACL, Broncos wide receiver Courtland Sutton would press play on another video sent to his phone by teammate Von Miller. The brief clips often told the story of an athlete overcoming some kind of setback to return to his or her respective sport. Sutton consumed them all as he worked his way through the recovery process, but there was one video that resonated more than the rest.

"The video Von sent me of Adrian Peterson, when he tore his

ACL, that's the video I keep on me," Sutton said. "It was very inspirational. The mindset he had of, 'I'm working my butt off to be able to come back and go play,' he firmly believed that the work he was putting in was going to allow him to come back and play the game at a very, very high level. He went off for 2,000 yards and was nine yards short of the NFL record. It was all about how you see the situation and how you see yourself having success and not dwelling on the negatives of anything."

On December 24, 2011, Peterson tore both the ACL and MCL in his left knee during a game against Washington. There was immediate doubt as to whether he would be able to return for the start of the 2012 season. Some medical professionals, Frazier remembered, voiced concerns over whether Peterson would ever be able to regain the same form that made him the league's most electrifying running back.

"He was telling me along, throughout the offseason, 'Coach, I'll be back. I'll be better than I was before. It's just a minor setback,'" Frazier said. "Yeah, you hear that, but you're still thinking, 'We gotta take this slow.' A lot of guys, even to this day, it's the following season, not the initial season coming off the injury, that you capture what you were before. So, we all kind of tempered our expectations. But not Adrian."

Peterson rushed for 499 yards during the first six games of the 2012 season. He was averaging just under 19 carries per game as the Vikings' coaching staff sought to ease Peterson back into his typical workload.

"But the more we gave him the football, man, the better and stronger he got as the year went on," Frazier said.

In eight of the next nine games, Peterson rushed for at least 108 yards, twice eclipsing 200 yards. It left him needing 208 yards in the Week 17 finale against the Packers to break Eric Dickerson's single-season record of 2,105 yards, a mark that has stood since 1984.

"Going into that last game, I told myself I was just going to go out there and play," Peterson recalled in 2020. "I wasn't thinking about the record at all. In Houston the week before [when Peterson rushed for 86 yards on 25 carries], I was thinking about it too much. I didn't have a good performance and I told myself, 'You know what, man, if it's going to happen, it'll happen.'"

The Vikings needed a victory over Green Bay that day to secure a playoff spot. With the game tied 34–34 late in the fourth quarter, Peterson took a second-down carry at the Packers' 37-yard line and rumbled for 26 yards. There was enough real estate left for Peterson to break the record with one more run. But a game-winning field goal was the only play. So Peterson finished with 2,097 yards, still the second-highest total in league history. His average of 6.03 yards per carry that season is by far the highest ever for any high-volume running back.

"It epitomized Adrian's heart," Frazier said of the 2012 season.

Seven years later, on that field in Buffalo, Frazier could still see those MVP flashes as Peterson tore through the Bills' defense. The coordinator made his adjustments—Peterson finished with 108 yards—and Buffalo cruised to a 24–9 win. Afterward, coach and player embraced on the field. Frazier told Peterson how much he appreciated that he could still sense "that heart and passion" every time he took a handoff.

53.
Bobby Bell

His speed and versatility made Bobby Bell a transformative player for the Chiefs during the 1960s.

Position: Linebacker

Team: Chiefs (1963–1974)

By Nate Taylor

Bobby Bell's 12-year career with the Kansas City Chiefs was full of great plays, but one of his greatest is one in which he didn't even record a statistic.

The highlight occurred early in the fourth quarter of the 1969 AFL divisional playoff game. Facing the great Joe Namath and the New York Jets, the Chiefs' defense was trying to protect a 6–3 lead. A pass interference penalty in the end zone committed against receiver George Sauer by cornerback Emmitt Thomas, a future Hall of Fame inductee, gave the Jets a first-and-goal at the Chiefs' 1-yard line. The following two plays featured the Chiefs stonewalling the Jets' rushing attempts.

Bell, the Chiefs' star outside linebacker, anticipated a different tactic from the Jets for the pivotal third-and-goal play.

"It's a play-action play on Bobby's side," Hall of Fame middle linebacker Willie Lanier recalled in 2021. "He plays it eloquently."

At 6-foot-4 and less than 230 pounds, Bell demonstrated on the play just how freakish an athlete he was compared to his peers at the time. Bell didn't bite on the fake handoff from Namath, and he deftly executed three assignments in a span of nine seconds, showing the agility to reach running back Matt Snell in the flat, the patience to cover Snell as Namath scrambled, and the tenacity to then hit Namath and force an incompletion.

"He was out there with Snell, and he had no right being there," Namath told reporters of Bell after the game. "If he's not there, it's a touchdown. I think the Fifth Army hit me."

The defending Super Bowl champion Jets settled for a game-tying field goal at windy Shea Stadium in New York. The Chiefs needed just two plays on the ensuing drive to score the game's lone touchdown and win, 13–6. Since that game, every prominent member of the 1969 Chiefs has referenced Bell's play as the most important of several highlights during the team's postseason run, which ended in an upset victory in Super Bowl IV over the Minnesota Vikings, the last game before the AFL-NFL merger.

Bell recalled that every part of his career prepared him for that impactful moment.

"I gave it all I had," Bell said. "I thank God every day that I could make the adjustment, from my high school to college and college to the pros."

Bell was so successful because his intelligence matched his rare athleticism. Growing up in Shelby, North Carolina, Bell was the quarterback of the six-man team at all-Black Cleveland High School. He also played safety, running back, and cornerback before his body fully developed. When it did, he was able to become a two-way lineman in college at Minnesota.

Bell said Minnesota had just five Black players when he arrived. Encouraged and inspired by his father, Pink Lee Bell, who worked picking cotton and chauffeuring bosses at a textile mill, Bobby Bell promised his family that he would excel as America's society became more integrated.

A two-time All-American as a tackle and defensive tackle—who also played snaps at quarterback and center—Bell finished third in the Heisman Trophy voting in his final year at Minnesota in 1962.

"I could play just about any position, which I did, basically," Bell said, laughing. "My thing to coaches was, 'If you can coach me, I can play anything.' I liked to know what everybody's doing around me. It helped me because I learned the defense from being a quarterback."

The Vikings selected Bell with the 16th pick in the 1963 NFL Draft. But the Dallas Texans, during their final season in Texas before relocating to Kansas City, also selected Bell with the 56th pick in the AFL Draft.

"I picked the Chiefs because of Lamar Hunt," Bell said of the Chiefs' founder who helped form the AFL in 1959 and spontaneously invented the phrase "Super Bowl" for the sport's grandest game.

Hunt met Bell on Minnesota's campus and the two discussed their future together while eating ice cream. Bell, who didn't have an agent, wanted a no-cut, guaranteed contract. The Vikings declined to offer Bell such a deal. The Chiefs gave Bell the contract he wanted, which also included more years.

Bell's Hall of Fame statistics and résumé with the Chiefs were remarkable: nine Pro Bowls, six-time All-Pro, two-time AFL champion, Super Bowl champion, and a spot on the 1970s all-decade team. He recorded 40 sacks (according to Pro Football Reference), 26 interceptions, and nine fumble recoveries. In 1969, Bell was *Pro Football Weekly*'s inaugural winner of the NFL's Defensive Player of the Year Award.

"He was the only player in my 30 years of coaching who had the ability to play any position on a football team and that team would still win," late Hall of Fame coach Hank Stram said of Bell as the presenter during Bell's 1983 Hall of Fame induction. "He played for three coaches: his coach [John Weston] in Cleveland High School in Shelby, N.C.; Murray Warmath, the great coach of Minnesota; and myself. And we all had the same problem. We had difficulty trying to figure out where to play him."

Bell began with the Chiefs as a defensive end before switching to outside linebacker for the final 10 seasons of his career. He was the Chiefs' long snapper, too.

"He was one of the first in the history of the NFL to be a [Black] outside linebacker," said Lanier, the NFL's first Black starting middle linebacker. "For some reason, the thought was that Black players didn't have the intelligence to play the linebacker position, just like the quarterback situation."

With an elite combination of size and speed—he ran the 40-yard dash in 4.5 seconds—and a love of studying his opponents, Bell was the perfect sweeper in the Chiefs' defense, a unit that in 1969 surrendered just 20 points in three postseason games. Bell often covered tight ends and running backs and was also effective as a blitzer.

"That's a hell of a lot of turnovers," Lanier said of Bell's 26 interceptions. "That was at a time when the ball was being thrown 16 to 18 times a game in a 14-game schedule. If you extrapolate that into what goes on today, those numbers will be off the chart."

When Bell retired in December 1974, having never missed a regular-season game, he finished with six interceptions returned for a touchdown. That's the most in NFL history for a linebacker, a record he shares with fellow Hall of Famer Derrick Brooks. Bell's nine career non-offensive touchdowns are the most for a linebacker in league history. One of Bell's favorite highlights happened in the 1969 season, when he recovered an onside kick against the Denver Broncos and outran everyone for a 53-yard touchdown return.

With the ball in his right arm, he ran past opposing players while running toward the end zone in a joyful fashion like a child in the backyard.

"You've got to make things happen," Bell said. "When I touched the ball, my mind was, 'Hey, you've got to score.' I loved playing defense. It's fun. I loved to make tackles. I loved to sack the quarterback. I just loved it."

Bell never left Kansas City. He owned a barbecue restaurant chain in his name in the city for almost 30 years, one of his proudest achievements since he spent his teenage years in Shelby working at Red Bridges Barbecue Lodge as a carhop during segregation.

From the moment the two teammates met, knowing they both came from segregated backgrounds in high school, Lanier has always loved Bell's highly inquisitive demeanor.

"His skill set was more than just football," Lanier said of Bell. "He was a lifeguard. He learned to swim at a time when a lot of Blacks did not learn to swim because there were not many pools for you to learn."

Bell was a motivational speaker for many years. Bell often mentioned in speeches what his father did for him. By 2014, Bell was in the basement of his home with Pamela Held, his companion, when he looked at all his awards and achievements. But Bell felt like something was missing: his college degree.

A few weeks later, Bell was shocked when he learned he needed to complete just 13 credits to earn his undergraduate degree in parks and recreation and leisure services. One of the first people Bell told was Lanier.

"We don't go a week," Bell said, "without talking to each other."

Once again, Bell had to make the proper adjustment, as he took his laptop with him everywhere for months to ensure he passed his online courses.

On May 14, 2015, Bell, at age 74 and more than 50 years since he left Minnesota to start his pro football career, returned to Minneapolis to receive his diploma at the school's graduation ceremony. With Lanier in attendance, Bell walked across the stage wearing a gold Bulova watch, a gift given to him by his father in 1959 just before he left Shelby to head to Minnesota.

"That," Bell said, "was one of the highlights of my career."

52.
O. J. Simpson

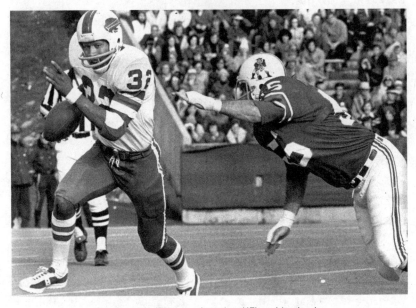

O. J. Simpson (32) was a four-time NFL rushing leader and an All-Pro every season between 1972 and 1976.

Position: Running Back
Teams: Bills (1969–1977), 49ers (1978–1979)

By Tim Graham

O. J. Simpson is halfway through his second Bloody Mary when he turns philosophical.

Exasperated and laughing, his brow furrows and his palms flip upward.

"How many Americans, even today, wouldn't like to live my life?" Simpson asks. "I don't work. I play golf four or five days a week. I go out to dinner a couple of nights with friends. People want to buy me drinks. I'm always taking pictures with people. Ladies hug me.

"People truly care for me. You don't know who truly cares about you until you've gone through some serious stuff, and I've gone through serious stuff. The media won't say it, but that is my life. I'm living a good life now."

Nicole Brown Simpson, the mother of Simpson's two children, essentially was decapitated and her friend Ronald Goldman slashed to death. The industries that brought him fame excommunicated him. Over a decade after the "trial of the century," he served nine years in prison over an armed memorabilia heist.

That all feels far in the past to Simpson, who, in July 2021, is finally speaking on the record about the arc of his complicated legacy, from football megastar to delightful pitchman/broadcaster/actor to accused double-murderer to dark, pop-culture obsession.

He just turned 74. "I'm in the fourth quarter of my life," Simpson says.

Two days after his birthday, Simpson is in a private room at the southwestern Las Vegas sports bar where he holds court Sundays for fantasy football, with the temperature outside climbing to 116 degrees. He alternates between Bloody Marys and cups of coffee to resurrect his hoarse throat. "He was running for mayor last night," says one of Simpson's two associates, neither of whom wants to be named.

Dressed in a light gray golf shirt, dark gray slacks, and black Cole Haan sneakers, he spends three hours discussing his life's imprint. He knows two homicides and the subsequent trial drive the public's fascination with him.

"I'm an entire TV genre," Simpson says, shaking his head. "I've always been content. So I accept the fact now they constantly show these O.J. shows.

"But how often can they show it? You'd think they'd be tired of talking about it by now. I saw a new one was coming out. Jesus, what else is there to say?"

Simpson has made it a point not to advance the conversation. But he agrees to speak about his legacy, and he knows the conversation involves far more than football.

"For years, I thought when I die," Simpson says, "the first thing they're going to say even before they talk about the Heisman and football is that he is the guy that ran through the airports for Hertz. Everybody knew me for that. Hertz, I felt, superseded my football. And then the younger kids got to know me through the Naked Gun movies and called me Nordberg."

All was eclipsed in the summer of 1994. The celebrity known for his graciousness was accused of committing a grisly double murder and became a nationally televised fugitive.

Simpson was the only person arrested for the June killings of ex-wife Nicole Brown Simpson and her friend Ronald Goldman. The sensational criminal trial mesmerized America for eight months and ended with O. J. Simpson's acquittal. At a 1997 civil trial, he was found liable for the deaths, the verdict so anticipated it was broadcast via split screen just as President Clinton began his State of the Union address.

Simpson has been averse to revisiting those times, certainly not with a tape recorder running. On this particular day, however, he can't avoid those topics or the nine years spent inside Lovelock Correctional Center as Nevada inmate No. 1027820. They always will be integral to his legacy.

Simpson is asked how he thinks his obituary will be presented.

"Wow," Simpson replies. He looks away. His eyes widen. He inhales deeply. "I hope it starts out with football. I know they're going to add the other stuff.

"The L.A. thing, unfortunately, some people wrongfully believe something, but I moved on. I still think I'm a good guy. I didn't let it change me. It did for a while. I was angry for a while, but I treat everybody the way I want to be treated."

The L.A. thing . . . The L.A. stuff . . . That L.A. crap . . .

Those are Simpson's all-encompassing references to the murders and his legal problems. He's still in Nevada on parole for the Vegas crap, but even with fully unrestricted travel, he says he has no desire to return to Los Angeles, the town he first electrified as a Heisman Trophy, national championship running back for USC.

"I have trouble with L.A.," Simpson says. "People may think this is self-serving, but I might be sitting next to whoever did it. I really don't know who did this."

Many people believe Simpson ostensibly confessed when he gave a hypothetical account of the murders for an ill-conceived book called *If I Did It*. Goldman's family seized publishing rights to the book to help satisfy the $33.5 million civil judgment.

Does Simpson think the world ever will learn for sure what happened the night Nicole Brown Simpson and Ron Goldman were stabbed to death?

"You've got to look to learn," answers Simpson, whose NFL and Screen Actors Guild pensions are shielded from the civil judgment. "I figured eventually somebody would confess to something, you know?

"I had one suspect I told my lawyers to look at. I still think he might be involved, but I can't talk about it."

When they were USC teammates, Ron Yary was Simpson's fiercest blocker. Perhaps no one helped pave the runway for Simpson's football ascent more than Yary did.

Yary loved playing with him. Their collaboration launched Pro Football Hall of Fame careers. In 1968, a year before the Buffalo Bills took Simpson with the first overall draft choice, the Minnesota Vikings took Yary with the top pick.

But Yary stopped standing up for Simpson a long time ago.

"The thought of taking a knife and plunging it into another person that you love and care about—or even that you're angry with—takes a hell of a lot," Yary says when phoned for his thoughts about Simpson's legacy.

"Even in war, to kill a person with a knife is intimate. I don't know if there's a harder way to kill someone. You have to be out of your mind to commit a crime like that."

Yary is convinced Simpson committed the murders, a leap not all of Simpson's former teammates and friends will make.

Simpson maintains support from many old pals. They regularly laugh over the phone about old times. They visit Las Vegas for golf and meals with one of the cheeriest, friendliest people they've met.

"He loves to be loved and went out of his way to make other people feel special," former Bills receiver J. D. Hill says. "He wouldn't shun anyone. Didn't matter where you were from, what color you are. He wants to make everyone happy."

Joe DeLamielleure, the Pro Football Hall of Fame guard, recalls stopping for gas on the way to Bills practice and seeing Simpson follow a school bus for disabled children into the parking lot. DeLamielleure watched Simpson board the bus, speak with the kids, and sign autographs until everybody had one.

"There's not a soul in the world who would have noticed it," DeLamielleure says, "except I happened to be at the gas station. That was impressive to me. He had a good heart."

Simpson captured imaginations with his majestic running style. That plus his high-wattage charm are how Simpson became one of the first Black athletes to transcend sports and become a celebrity, an achievement made all the more remarkable by the fact that he played for a bad team in a small market.

When Simpson retired after the 1979 season, he ranked second to only Jim Brown on the NFL's all-time rushing list. Simpson won the rushing crown four times and in 1973 became the first to surpass 2,000 yards. The NFL played only 14 games then, so his 143.1 rushing yards per game still is the record by a whopping 10 yards. Simpson's best season might have been 1975, when he ran for 1,817 yards but scored 23 combined touchdowns.

"Without a doubt, he's the best player I've ever played with," DeLamielleure said. "Nobody could do what O.J. could do.

"He also practiced as hard or harder than anyone I ever played with. I couldn't believe a superstar like that worked that hard. He taught me what effort was."

While still playing for Buffalo, he starred in a Hertz commercial campaign, was a spokesman for Oldsmobile, Schick razors, Foster Grant sunglasses, RC Cola, and Wilson Sporting Goods, called events for ABC Sports, and hosted *Saturday Night Live*.

He had high-profile roles in action films such as *The Towering Inferno, Capricorn One, Killer Force,* and *Firepower* and the seminal miniseries *Roots*.

People magazine in October 1975 called him "the first Black athlete to become a bona fide lovable media superstar."

"Buffalo was such a punch line of a city," comedy writer and Buffalo native Nick Bakay says from his Los Angeles home. "The one shining light we had was O.J.

"There was the horrible joke that expat Michael Bennett put in *A Chorus Line*, that 'to commit suicide in Buffalo is redundant,' which made the whole world laugh, but if you're from Buffalo? I hated that joke so much.

"O.J. was our one ambassador to the world. You can make all the jokes about us you want, but we have the greatest football player on the planet, who also happens to be kind of a Hollywood star. So, ha ha, suck on that."

The Bills went 43-81-2 during Simpson's nine seasons and appeared in a single playoff game. A trade to his hometown San Francisco 49ers didn't provide success. His magnificent career ended with a whimper, knee injuries limiting him to 45.8 yards per game over two feeble seasons.

Simpson remained relevant in retirement. He thrived as a sportscaster, produced movies for NBC, and landed more acting roles.

He says one of his greatest post-retirement joys was covering the Bills when they reached the Super Bowl after the 1990, 1991, 1992, and 1993 seasons.

"You would think that losing four consecutive Super Bowls was more than any fan could or should endure," says Bakay, who has "Go Bills" etched inside his wedding band. "But wait for it: greatest player in franchise history, crime of the century.

"I am absolutely and forever ripped in half by this whole experience."

Margaret Sullivan is another child of Buffalo, growing up at a time when Simpson was everyone's darling. She was the features editor for the *Buffalo News* at the time of Simpson's criminal trial and eventually became the paper's editor in chief.

Sullivan, now the *Washington Post*'s media columnist, doesn't see Simpson as a football player anymore. Similar to the contradictions of Michael Jackson, Woody Allen, and Bill Cosby, she simply cannot separate the art from the artist.

"I can't think of him as anything except a terrible criminal," Sullivan says. "I don't think I'm typical. I'm reacting to it as a newsperson, as a woman, maybe not the way someone fully immersed in the football world would think about it. I can't separate out all of it.

"To me, his legacy changed irrevocably with an incredible fall from grace."

In the USC huddle, Yary remembers looking into Simpson's eyes and being deeply impressed. Simpson, despite his otherworldly talents, viewed himself as one-eleventh of the offense, no better than anyone else.

Yary, convinced of Simpson's guilt, tries to comprehend how the admirable teammate he knew back then could become a killer.

"How could such a great guy turn into a slashing murderer of two innocent people?" Yary asks. "What drove him to that point?

"I wonder, is that inside of me? Could I raise within me that kind of monster? Is that inside of you? Is that inside of everybody? Because, I'll tell you what, my perceptions of O.J. were that it could never get to that point."

Yary speculates Simpson's personality changed because instant fame opened up unprecedented doors before playing an NFL snap. The Juice strolled to the front of every line, was inundated with job offers and business opportunities, enjoyed his pick of the ladies, got showered with perpetual praise.

"He was never checked," Yary says. "Nobody ever said no to O.J.

"That's what put him in a situation that he'll never be able to live down."

Hill doesn't see it that way. The Pro Bowl receiver played five seasons with Simpson in Buffalo and makes regular trips to Las Vegas to spend time with him.

An ordained minister who battled crack cocaine and alcohol addictions in retirement, Hill founded Catch the Vision, a youth mentoring program in Chandler, Arizona.

Forgiveness, second chances, and redemption are real to Hill.

"There are people who don't agree with my philosophy, but O. J. Simpson is my friend," Hill says. "If God's not going to quit on him, who am I to quit on him?"

When they're together, Hill says they don't discuss what happened in Los Angeles or Las Vegas. They reminisce about the good old days and what brings them happiness today.

But, by chance, they were headed to a golf course on October 3, 2020, the anniversary of Simpson's controversial acquittal. The date hadn't registered for Hill until Simpson began to cry.

"He brought it up," Hill recalls. "We spent time. God, just to be there, just to talk. I didn't ask questions. I just listened to the pain of his loss.

"There was no celebration of a victory or joy of being set free. He just shared his pain. I don't have any idea of that kind of pain. Can you imagine what goes through his mind?

"Whenever they talk about him, it's attached to the tragedy more than anything. They don't talk about his football career or his acting or how he gave to charities. He lived to please people."

Hill's voice cracks.

"I'm sorry," Hill continues. "That's painful for me and most of us who played with him and love him and put our efforts into his career. I can't fathom or come to accept that he could do what he was accused of doing."

Yary is unsympathetic.

"That tragedy," Yary says, "is going to follow him throughout eternity.

"He's paid for it a thousand times over privately in his mind. If he's got any soul at all, he's got to be in agony for what he did."

Simpson eventually went to prison. A jury in 2008 found him guilty of all 12 charges stemming from an attempt to forcibly take back memorabilia he claimed had been stolen from him. Simpson had assembled a group of men, some of whom were armed, to storm a Las Vegas hotel room where the memorabilia was.

On the 13th anniversary of his murder acquittal, Clark County District Court Judge Jackie Glass sentenced Simpson to nine to 33 years. He was released on parole in 2017.

"The judge saw what happened in California and gave me a punishment I didn't deserve," Simpson says.

Simpson takes a sip of coffee and laughs about what he's about to share next.

"There's a guy I met in prison who sent me a message on my birthday," Simpson says. "We called him Bellagio because he robbed the Bellagio and another casino. He played first base on my softball team. Intelligent guy.

"In the message, Bellagio said he was taking his girlfriend to the Dominican Republic. I asked my lawyer, 'How the hell can he leave the country?' He's on parole, but it's looser than mine. He did less time than I did. He robbed two casinos!"

Simpson has gone on trial twice while the world watched, mocked, scrutinized, and rationalized. Given the stakes of each case, one can argue he came out ahead by serving only nine years.

He doesn't declare that as any kind of victory. But in connecting the two verdicts, he reconciles that the legal system is good.

"I did my time better than anybody can do time," Simpson says. "I got out, and you'll never hear me dog the jury because I believe in the system.

"How can you tell me you believe in the goddamn system, but you got problems with me living my life now? Because your attitude was different than the jury, who heard all the evidence and didn't have the media influence? Then you try to present yourself as a good American. Bullshit, you're not. You don't believe in the American system."

Reasons may have changed over the years, but people still want to pose for pictures next to Simpson. They still want to shake his hand, snag his autograph. They can't wait to talk about how they met The Juice.

There is no lack of companionship.

"I have loyal, terrific friends," Simpson says. "The only people that abandoned me are the ones who were asking me for favors all the time. I don't need them. I couldn't care less. The general public, despite what the media says, treats me well.

"I prayed for fame as a kid. I wanted people to chase me like I chased Willie Mays. The Lord gave it to me. I can't bitch about it now."

Mortality has been on his mind. No matter how many years he continues to mark the anniversary of his 39th birthday rather than his actual age, he doesn't deny the inevitable anymore.

He mentions that he never thought about his death until he contracted COVID-19 in 2020. The experience frightened him enough to discuss final arrangements with his children.

"When I had COVID, I almost couldn't get out of bed," Simpson says. "I made it to my balcony, trying to breathe. I couldn't catch my breath.

"I felt vulnerable and for the first time thought I might be near the end. Since that day, I have wondered. Do I want to be buried? Do I want to be cremated? Years ago, I would have left it up to Nicole because I know she would have done the right thing.

"I know what I want my kids to do, but I don't want to discuss it here."

He has a daughter and son with his first wife, high school sweetheart Marguerite. Their youngest child was 2 when she drowned in a swimming pool in 1979. He also has a daughter and son with

Nicole. Although the Brown family contested, he was awarded custody after her death.

"Have you read anything about them?" he asks about his children with Nicole. "Heard anything negative about them?

"Judge me by the job I did with my two kids."

Simpson knows his plea doesn't have to be honored and probably won't be.

His legacy will be decided by the public that adores him, loathes him, ridicules him, can't get enough of him.

"A lot of people think of me as a legend," Simpson says, "especially younger guys because they've heard of me their whole lives—no matter what it was for. Most people who weren't around, anybody younger than 25, they just see a celebrity.

"Fame is a weird thing. Doesn't matter if you're a good person or a bad person in this day and age. If you're famous, you've got an edge in America. Fame supersedes whether you're good or bad, and everybody is after the fame."

51.
Dick "Night Train" Lane

Dick "Night Train" Lane (81) intercepted 14 passes in twelve games
as an NFL rookie and got even better from there.

Position: Cornerback

Teams: Rams (1952–1953), Cardinals (1954–1959), Lions (1960–1965)

By Stephen Holder

For a man who would go on to enjoy a transcendent career
and later be enshrined in the Pro Football Hall of Fame, Dick
"Night Train" Lane's NFL career could not have begun in a more
unremarkable manner.

After one season of junior-college ball and four years in the
Army—he earned All-Army honors in 1949 and '51 as a member of
the Fort Ord (California) football team—Lane found himself work-

ing in an L.A.-area aircraft factory during the Korean War. Let's just say the job wasn't what he thought it would be.

"They told me I'd be a filer," Lane once said. "I thought they meant a file clerk in an office. I was a filer, all right. I filed big sheets of metal into bins with oil dripping off the metal onto me.

"Each night, my wife would have to shampoo my hair a couple of times just so I could get clean enough to ride the bus to work the next day."

So unfulfilled was Lane with his new employment, he went looking for alternatives. Among them, a return to football. Convinced to give him a shot based on his small-college résumé and his Army club-team experience, the Los Angeles Rams granted Lane a tryout—as a wide receiver—with no guarantees. But the week before the season opener, all but one of the Rams' defensive backs were hit with injuries, so Lane was moved to cornerback.

Soon, one of the most improbable starts to a career in NFL history commenced. Lane went on to become a star by the end of his rookie season in 1952, setting a league single-season record that still stands with 14 interceptions in a 12-game season.

He would compile 68 career interceptions (fourth all time) with the Rams, Cardinals, and Lions, becoming a feared tackler and a seven-time Pro Bowl selection.

He impacted games, whether by returning his many interceptions for chunks of yardage, brutally upending ball carriers, or, oftentimes, with his mere presence.

As Packers coach Vince Lombardi told his quarterback, Bart Starr, during Lane's years with the Lions, "Don't throw anywhere near him. He's the best there is."

Patriots coach Bill Belichick, describing Lane's game during NFL Network's all-time team unveiling in 2019, said of Lane, "He was a great tackler. He usually played over on the left side, left cornerback. You didn't really want to run over there, especially outside."

Just imagine if Lane had been actually hired to, well, file. The NFL record books might look vastly different.

Everything about Lane's story is utterly implausible, so much so that his status as one of the greatest undrafted players in history is arguably not the most notable part of his journey.

To truly convey the unlikely nature of his path, you must begin with Lane's earliest years.

Lane, who died in 2002 at 73, was abandoned in a trash heap at three months old by his biological parents, a prostitute and a pimp. Ella Lane, a widow with four other children, heard the child's cries and went over to investigate. He was hers from then on. She adopted the boy and raised him in Austin, Texas.

She fostered a child who grew to become a player who showed the NFL a breed of defender it had rarely seen. Truth is, Lane is the kind of player who theoretically could compete today.

Given the importance of cornerbacks in the modern NFL, having a player like Lane would be a coach's dream. He was a multidimensional player who could smother receivers, but he also played with anticipation, showing an ability to instinctively feel where quarterbacks would throw before they actually did. That skill would have served him well in a league now dominated by the quick passing game.

He also was a physical player who reveled in defending the run. And when he tackled you, he did it with a certain level of violence. His signature tackling technique was so unique that it gained a nickname of its own, the "Night Train Necktie." Lane would famously use his gangly arms to wrap ball carriers around the shoulders and slam them to the ground. His brand of takedown was not the timid tackling you might associate with some cornerbacks.

Lane was quite proud of that.

"My objective is to stop the guy before he gains another inch," he once said. "I'm usually dealing with ends who are trying to catch passes, and if I hit them in the legs, they may fall forward for a first down. There is nothing I hate worse than a first down."

Another area where Lane literally measures up to today's premier corners is in his size. He stood 6-foot-1 and weighed around 200 pounds, a profile that would be tantalizing to current teams on a draft board.

"This is a big, physical corner," Belichick said. "A forerunner to Mel Blount and Rod Woodson."

Packers Hall of Fame cornerback Herb Adderley once described Lane like this: "I've never seen a defensive back hit like him. I mean, take them down, whether it be Jim Brown or Jim Taylor."

The Rams initially viewed Lane as a receiver in his first training camp with the team. But when he failed to make a mark there, they tried him on defense.

Lane was a natural. His length was a particularly key attribute.

"In a big pileup once, I reached out and grabbed somebody's ankle," Lane told the *New York Times* in 1974. "It happened to be the ball carrier. Another time I got flipped up in the air, but in my somersault, I made a tackle. The coach, Joe Stydahar, came running out on the field, yelling, 'That's the kind of player I want!'"

No retrospective on Lane would be complete without a refresher on the origin of his nickname. It stems from Lane's relationship with Rams teammate Tom Fears, who initially tutored Lane as a receiver during his first camp.

"Fears liked to play records, and his favorite was 'Night Train,'" Lane once said. "Every day I'd be going to his room and he'd be playing it. He roomed with a guy named Ben Sheets, and whenever I'd walk into the room, Sheets would say, 'Here comes Night Train.' He started calling me that, and it stuck."

The song was a big-band blues and jazz hit first recorded by Jimmy Forrest in 1951. Buddy Morrow released another version in 1952 that sold more than a million copies.

Initially, Lane was uncomfortable with the racial overtones of the nickname, especially as it had been given to him by his white teammates. But he grew to embrace it after a newspaper reported on his performance against then-Washington star Charlie "Choo-Choo" Justice with the headline, "Night Train Derails Choo-Choo."

Lane gained his nickname because of his connection to the work of a particular artist, and it ended up being attached to a player who brought a level of artistry to his game. Watching Lane pluck footballs from the air, run with long strides toward the end zone, or employ the perfect angle to take down a runner could only be described as art. And his aggressive athletic style and out-of-nowhere playmaking were akin to a night train as well.

Had Lane been content to hang around that factory filing sheets of metal, had he not had the nerve to think he could do the unthinkable, NFL fans would have been robbed of watching one of the best players of all time.

50.
Steve Young

Steve Young was a two-time MVP and was hard to stop
as both a highly accurate passer and an effective runner.

Position: Quarterback

Teams: Express/USFL (1984–1985), Buccaneers (1985–1986), 49ers (1987–1999)

By David Lombardi

It was March 2015. The city of San Francisco was midway through its demolition of Candlestick Park. NFL Films was working on a project about Steve Young, so producers brought the 49ers' Hall of Fame quarterback to the ruins of the hallowed old stadium.

"Holy cow!" Young exclaimed on the documentary as he walked out of Candlestick's dilapidated tunnel and onto what remained of its playing surface. "Great memories coming out of here. How many games? How many moments?

"Right here is where we threw the pass to Terrell [Owens]. This is about the spot, too, right here, for the ol' Viking run. They had that planned out perfectly, didn't they?"

Just like that, Young had naturally reminisced on the two legendary plays that had essentially bookended his career with the 49ers: 1988's frenetic 49-yard touchdown run against Minnesota and the dramatic 25-yard touchdown pass to Terrell Owens that slayed Green Bay in the January 1999 NFC wild-card game.

The two plays, aside from notable stumbles that are defining features of each one, couldn't have been any more different stylistically. That's because Young had evolved into a markedly more complete player throughout the 1990s. By the time he threaded the pristine dart to Owens against the Packers, Young—37 at the time—had become the most efficient passer in NFL history and an embodiment of the West Coast offense's celebrated aerial precision.

But as a 28-year-old against the Vikings, Young was anything but that. He was a supremely talented yet very raw scrambler. His frantic weaving dash, while it would become a symbol commemorating Young's place as one of the best running quarterbacks in NFL history, was the essence of unscripted entertainment.

"It was as if I was a cartoon character," Young said in a 2018 interview. "One door closed, so I turned around and ran in another direction. And then another door closed, so I turned around in another direction.

"And suddenly, it was like water running downhill."

Aesthetically, the run indeed was beautiful. But to 49ers coach Bill Walsh, the architect of the West Coast offense and therefore a fierce proponent of finely choreographed and structured movement, it was the epitome of freewheeling frustration.

"Pretty good job," Young remembered Walsh telling him on the sideline. "Glad you know what you're doing."

There was a method to the chaos. Young's first four professional seasons, two with the USFL's Los Angeles Express and two with the

Tampa Bay Buccaneers, were distinguished by necessitated self-preservation. The painstaking process of refinement that would ultimately send Young to Canton didn't truly start until after Walsh traded for him in 1987.

"You'd see flashes in those early days," former 49ers tight end Brent Jones, who also joined the team in 1987, said of Young. "I think his natural inclination coming from the USFL and Tampa was, at the first sign of trouble—get out, because it was only gonna get worse."

But excellence from within the pocket would be necessary for Young to successfully follow Joe Montana as the 49ers' starter. And his eventual blossoming in that regard would lead to a remarkable extension of the 49ers' dynasty into the 1990s.

"Think about the coaches that Steve had, from Bill Walsh to Mike Holmgren to Mike Shanahan," Jones said. "It's remarkable, at least in those early stages, to think, 'Can you really make a guy whose instinct is to run into a pocket passer?' He had to trust his line, his footwork. And he did it. He accomplished it. And it took a lot of discipline on his part."

The path to the pinnacle, which Young reached at the end of the 1994 season by leading the 49ers to a title in Super Bowl XXIX, was anything but a cakewalk. Young has even likened the journey, which featured chapters of distinct challenges, to "climbing Everest."

The first part of the ascent involved escaping Montana's shadow.

"Our strength is at quarterback," Walsh said in what's now a famous interview entering the 1988 season, one that ended with the 49ers winning their third of four Super Bowls in the decade. "But our problem is that we have two, and there's a quarterback controversy developing. We're gonna have to select between Steve Young and Joe Montana."

It was a debate that took the 49ers' fan base by storm and would be even more feverish now, in this age of social media and all the corresponding hot takes. But Montana silenced the noise by guiding the 49ers to consecutive Super Bowl titles, leaving Young and his fierce demeanor restless on the bench even after that sensational run against Minnesota.

"It was a tease in a lot of ways, because Joe started playing again not long after that," former 49ers center Randy Cross said. "But to the fans, on that day, they knew what they had in that left-hander, No. 8. And for a lot of people, it was like, 'God, how can you have that as a backup?'"

After Montana was hurt in an NFC Championship Game loss to the New York Giants that ended the 49ers' 1990 season, Young finally entered the spotlight for good.

Shanahan took over as the 49ers' offensive coordinator in 1992 and Young won his first MVP award. He broke the NFL record for passer rating and won another MVP and the Super Bowl in the 1994 season. He excelled over four more years after that, finishing his career as the highest-rated passer in NFL history.

For Young's 49ers, the 1990s were neatly divided into two epochs: the first came in the front half of the decade against the mighty Cowboys, and the second came over the back part of it against the powerful Packers.

In both cases, Young swallowed bitter playoff defeat multiple times before ultimately conquering the nemesis of the time.

Jones had a front-row seat to the process. In 1987, Holmgren had picked Jones to be Young's training camp roommate (the tight end was initially planning to room with his friend, 49ers fullback Tom Rathman). Jones and Young formed a unique bond that would traverse the intense years ahead.

"During the regular season, everyone did have their own hotel room—except me," Jones said, laughing. "[Young] would get some anxiousness, especially before games. He said, 'I need you to be my roommate during the season, too.' We'd sit and talk football, go through the game plan, and talk about what to look for in the game. And we'd watch the same movies over and over and over again. He didn't like to watch live TV. He didn't want to watch football on Saturday.

"And that kept him focused and free from having to obsess or worry over the game."

Back-to-back losses in NFC title games to Dallas that closed the 1992 and 1993 seasons devastated Young and the 49ers.

"There's a late interception by me," Young said of that first defeat, "I'm sure if I watched it, I'll want to throw up in my mouth again."

But 1994 would be different, and Jones could sense that at the San Francisco Airport Marriott the night before the epic championship game.

"The Cowboys had taken a couple championships away from us," Jones said. "But this time we came in and we felt like we were prepared. We felt like we had a plan. I think when you check all the boxes, you have that much more confidence in the end. Steve just had to go out and execute to his ability level."

The 49ers vanquished the Cowboys in the most star-studded contest in NFL history.

"Life is experiential, right?" Young asked rhetorically. "When you've gotten kicked in the teeth twice, you understand. We sharpened the saw, and that's the best part of it: we beat one of the great teams ever at the height of their greatness. We had to be greater, and that was one heck of a thing."

Jones's favorite memory of his friend's career comes from after that game, when Young sprinted joyously around Candlestick's muddy field. He pumped his fist while clutching the game ball. He even accidentally barreled over a cameraman, much to the delight of Fox broadcaster John Madden.

"I think it's hard to not see Steve running around the stadium with his arms up resembling a heavyweight boxer who just got the knockout," Jones said. "He's just so emotional and committed to the game and excellence. I can still see the cameraman going down. It was awesome."

The subsequent Super Bowl served as a coronation. Before the 49ers walloped the Chargers 49–26 and Young threw a Super Bowl–

record six touchdown passes, Shanahan unveiled an ambitious and supremely confident game plan.

"I remember Mike in the pregame, looking me in the eye and saying, 'You're more ready than ever,'" Young said. "He said I would throw eight touchdown passes, and that really helped me because Mike didn't really say that unless he really meant it. He and I just poured ourselves into that football game to make sure it got done. I remember that peaceful sense of confidence, that we're in great shape.

"I loved him. I loved him. So many guys talk a big game on Wednesday and don't call plays on Sunday. So many. Mike called plays that meant something. They were connected. He didn't take a break. He didn't panic and jam the ball up the middle. He loved to beat the crap out of defenses. He loved to just punish 'em, and I loved that. 'Cause I did, too. I loved that about him."

The next season, Shanahan left to be Denver's head coach and Green Bay replaced Dallas as the perennial thorn in the 49ers' side.

For Young, three consecutive playoff losses to the Packers—who were led by Holmgren, previously Young's QB coach both in college at BYU and with the 49ers—were painful reminders that even an exhilarating climb could be followed by a discouraging descent.

"Dallas was a rivalry, but it wasn't like playing your brother," Young said. "This was a family fight. The Hatfields and the Mc-Coys, that was us and the Cowboys. But those Packer fights, it was incestuous. Everyone who was over there, I knew, they knew, we all knew—we ran the same plays.

"It was like losing to your brother in the street."

That made Young's final triumph all the more sweet.

Though the stakes of the January 1999 NFC wild-card game against Green Bay weren't as high as those against Dallas four years earlier, they remained massive on a personal level. Time was running short on the dynastic 49ers. There was a desperate itch for them to grace Candlestick with at least one more memorable win.

Center Chris Dalman stepped on Young's foot as he dropped back with seven seconds left and the 49ers trailing. Whereas 1988's stumble before the goal line against the Vikings was built of exhilarated exhaustion, this one ignited momentary dread.

But Young avoided the catastrophe of a potential game-ending sack and straightened up.

"Think of the athleticism he showed to stay upright even after 300 pounds fell on his foot," Dalman said in 2021.

Young then spun a picture-perfect encapsulation of his football journey: a pinpoint pass from the pocket to Owens, who was open in a sliver amid quadruple coverage.

The quarterback Young had striven so hard to become over his career was on display. Candlestick of the '90s indeed roared at full throttle one last time.

Early the next season, a seismic hit from Arizona cornerback Aeneas Williams concussed Young. And though doctors would later clear Young to return, he never played again.

John Elway retired in Denver after 1999, so Shanahan attempted to lure Young into a reunion with the Broncos.

"I was hoping I was going to get him again before he really retired," Shanahan said in 2018. "I thought Steve might come back for one more shot, but it didn't work out."

Young was eager to start his family. The time felt right to step away from football, even if the 38-year-old was still capable of playing at a prime level. So the ending of Young's career presented a paradox of sorts: he still clearly had gas left in the tank, but he had also left all of his football self out on the field.

Perhaps nothing illustrated this more poetically than a 1995 preseason game against the Chargers.

Young had already netted Super Bowl MVP honors by that point, so he had every reason to take cover when safety Rodney Harrison ripped his helmet off on a blitz.

Instead, Young bolted downfield for a 9-yard gain, head fully exposed in what has become an iconic image of his determination.

"I was just tired of us being kind of lackadaisical," Young told the Associated Press after that exhibition game.

Said Jones: "That was the ultimate John Wayne play, running around without your helmet on. I remember just laughing, saying it'll be impossible to top that John Wayne. But that was Steve. He played banged up like nobody's business. When he'd get hit, it would be a big hit. He ran the ball. He wasn't typically stepping out of bounds. He'd take guys on. He was bruised up, battered. He played with cartilage issues in his knees. He had broken ribs in a playoff game. His desire to be on the field was relentless."

That yearning was Young's constant pillar, and it was apparent even after he had perfected his craft and earned his hardware. Since time is often connected, it certainly had been on display during that initial Vikings run.

Consider the stumble at the end of that score a metaphor for the effort Young poured into every second of his football career.

"I promise you, my legs—just because the rigor of playing when Joe was hurt and what it meant to me, I was doing everything I physically could," Young said. "I didn't stumble. My legs went out. I was like a marathon runner on the last mile, and my legs collapsed. I didn't trip. I didn't stumble. My legs were finished.

"But I said, I just can't go down here. If I go down here—I just have to get to the end."

49.
Sid Luckman

Sid Luckman (42) was the first successful T-formation quarterback, and he led the Bears to four NFL championships.

Position: Quarterback
Team: Bears (1939–1950)

By Dan Pompei

Sid Luckman led the Bears to four championships in the 1940s. He was named All-Pro five times and averaged 8.4 yards per pass attempt in his career, which still is tied with Patrick Mahomes for second best in NFL history.

None of that seemed conceivable for a boy from Brooklyn whose parents were Jewish immigrants. It wasn't even a dream.

Luckman was more interested in education than the gridiron after winning two city football championships at Erasmus Hall in Brooklyn, so he attended the New College for the Education of Teachers and gave up the sport. Football's lure was powerful, however, so he returned to it after one year and eventually transferred to Columbia University. By his senior season, he was on the cover of *Life* magazine with the headline "BEST PASSER."

Still, Luckman doubted he had what it took to play in the NFL. In the book *What Bears They Were*, he said, "I, as an Ivy League player, probably was not good enough or could possibly get good enough to play pro football."

The way Luckman saw it, his football days would end after college. His brother Leo ran a trucking business, and Sid's intent was to be his partner. There were problems at home, as Luckman's father, Meyer Luckman, and two others with ties to organized crime were convicted for strangling and beating Meyer's brother-in-law to death. Meyer was sentenced to 20 years to life at Sing Sing prison.

Luckman dedicated his own book in 1949 to his father, saying he "played the toughest game of all."

Meyer Luckman's trouble wasn't George Halas's trouble, however. The owner and coach of the Bears envisioned a new style of offense, the T formation, and he thought Meyer's son was the ideal quarterback for his system even though Sid had been a single-wing tailback at Columbia. In what was termed "Operation Luckman," Halas went after Luckman hard. He told Luckman he would help him get involved in the laundry truck business in Chicago if trucking appealed to him so much.

Halas enlisted the help of anyone he thought would be beneficial to help sell Luckman on the Bears. Among them was Benny Friedman, the Jewish quarterback who had been Luckman's hero when he played for the New York Giants and Brooklyn Dodgers. Luckman said Freidman pitched him on the advantages of playing in the T formation and told him, "You'll have great years ahead, if you bear down."

Operation Luckman worked, and Halas traded end Edgar "Eggs" Manske to the Steelers for the second choice of the 1939 draft to select Luckman.

Upon becoming a Bear, Luckman was stunned to open a playbook with 396 plays and thousands of variations. Halas thought it would take him two years to learn, but Luckman had it down well enough to play in five months.

Luckman spent hours working on the finer points of the game in an era when few others did. According to *The Chicago Bears* by Howard Roberts, Luckman practiced pivots, feints, handoffs, and ballhandling in the locker room, at his home, and in hotel rooms. He had his wife, Estelle, quiz him, and he and Halas would talk on the phone about any questions he had from the day.

"It was a very difficult transition from playing tailback at Columbia to quarterback for the Bears," Luckman said, according to the book *Bears: In Their Own Words*. "The signal calling was diametrically opposite. The spinning was very difficult because you had to be so precise and so quick. . . . We had counterplays and double counters and fakes."

Luckman's dedication, Halas said, was the reason he was successful. He was more than successful—he was a pioneer.

"In Sid, we created a new type of football player—the T quarterback," Halas said. "Newspapers switched their attention from the star runners to the quarterbacks. It marked a new era for the game. Colleges changed from the single and double wing to the T, using Luckman as their model in molding quarterbacks. In Sid's 12 years with the Bears, football was completely revolutionized."

Luckman wasn't as gifted a passer as his forever rival, Sammy Baugh. But no one could match Luckman's intangibles. In his book *Pro Football's 100 Greatest Players*, Hall of Fame coach George Allen said, "[Luckman] called his signals brilliantly and was a master tactician, maybe the smartest quarterback I ever watched work. He was the best ball-control quarterback ever."

Luckman was exceptionally tough. His big toe was mangled so severely that it required three shots of Novocain every week, and he had to wear a larger shoe on the injured foot. He broke his nose seven times.

Luckman wasn't just a quarterback. He also punted and played defensive back, covering the likes of Don Hutson and Tom Fears.

Above all, Luckman was a leader. And not an accidental one.

"It was more than a job of calling signals," he wrote in *Luckman at Quarterback*. "It was a job that required a quarterback to know his club backward and forward, from end to fullback, almost to the point of knowing their pet habits and how they wanted their eggs fried for breakfast."

According to Bears tackle George Connor, Luckman was able to get more out of his teammates because he made it a point to know them.

"He knew how to handle each man," Connor said. "He might plead with one man or scold another. But none of them resented him because they knew that he was a great team player himself."

Pleasing was important to Luckman. In a *New York Times* obituary of Luckman, guard Ray Bray recounted he told Luckman his dream was to score a touchdown. With the Bears were on the 1-yard line, Luckman gave the big man a handoff. Bray was stopped short, but Luckman responded kindly. "Get back where you belong, chum," he said, before handing the ball off to a running back who powered ahead for a touchdown.

According to *Halas by Halas*, Halas's wife, Min, repeatedly asked Luckman to kick on an early down. Her husband forbade this, but one day when the Bears had a safe lead and the wind at their backs, Luckman quick kicked from the Bears' 8. Everyone in the park heard Min yell, "That's my play! He did it for me!" After the game, Sid gave her a kiss and confirmed she was right.

He once lost $25,000 when a friend asked him to invest in his restaurant, which eventually went under. "I had to," he told New York columnist Jimmy Cannon. "The guy who owns the place was nice to me when I first came to Chicago. This is a great fellow. He had to be, to be nice to a kid like me. Nobody knew me then."

Later in his life, his investment in another restaurant—the renowned Chicago steak house Gibsons—was much more fruitful. It also was advantageous to anyone who called Luckman a friend, because the tab always was on Luckman.

Those who visited his Chicago home on Lake Shore Drive almost always left with a gift. He gave away scores of ties with the label "Custom made for a friend of Sid Luckman." There was Sid Luckman perfume for the women.

Luckman is believed to be the third Jewish player in NFL history after Friedman and Marshall Goldberg. Anti-Semitism was common during Luckman's playing days, and he dealt with his share. Luckman sometimes joked his name was "That Jew."

Opponents often reminded him of his heritage before a snap, usually with language you wouldn't hear in a Disney movie. Fans in visiting stadiums gave him more of the same. In *Tough Luck: Sid Luckman, Murder, Inc., and the Rise of the Modern NFL*, his son Bob Luckman relayed how Luckman nearly hit teammate George Musso with a chair after Musso said something that offended Luckman. Musso and Luckman eventually became roommates and friends.

Football's ability to bridge divides was one of its most appealing qualities for Luckman.

"What affected [Meyer Luckman] most about my rise in football was the democratic attitude he saw throughout the game, and especially the unbiased ways of my coaches," Luckman wrote in *Luckman at Quarterback*. "Irish coaches and Italians and Bohemians, who brought a Jewish boy out of Flatbush and worked their heads off to make a high-priced football man out of him."

Luckman's four championships are equal to or more than all but three quarterbacks—Otto Graham and Tom Brady, who have seven apiece, and Bart Starr, who has five. Two more titles were within Luckman's grasp. The Bears won it all in 1941. They went into the 1942 championship game on an 18-game win streak, favored by as many as 20 points over Washington. Their smallest margin of victory during the regular season in 1942 was 14 points. They lost the championship game 14–6—one of the biggest postseason upsets in history.

The Bears won the championship in 1943, and after the season,

Luckman signed with the Merchant Marine. He received permission to play for the Bears on game days in 1944 but sat out three games. The Bears won only one of those games, finished 6-3-1, and missed the playoffs.

In the service during World War II, Luckman made trips to England and France for over a year and a half. On one of the trips in June 1944, he took part in the Normandy Invasion by delivering oil to the troops in Europe and then bringing back the wounded.

One of the highlights of his playing career came during that championship season of 1943. An injury to his throwing shoulder that later required surgery nearly prevented him from playing against the Giants at the Polo Grounds. But he was determined to play because it was "Sid Luckman Day." After a painkilling injection, Luckman threw for 433 yards and seven touchdowns in a 56–7 victory. His passing yards and passing touchdowns set NFL records. Wrote William D. Richardson in the *New York Times*, "His was passing artistry of a kind probably never before witnessed on any gridiron, and although his wizardry sent the Giants down to depths they never had explored, the fans gave the black-haired star a tremendous ovation when he trotted from the field after chucking his final toss to Hampton Pool a trifle more than five minutes before the game ended."

Fans from Brooklyn pooled their money to buy Luckman a $1,000 war bond, and the Bears matched the gift.

Luckman was beloved in a way few athletes have been beloved. "He was popular till the day he died," his son said. "Everybody knew who he was in Chicago, and anywhere he went it was, 'Hi, Sid' and when people come up and ask for his autograph, they'd walk away feeling better than when they came. You know, he made them feel special."

Halas considered Luckman his son. Bears fans and broadcasters bring up his name regularly, 70-plus years after his last snap. The private dining room upstairs at Gibsons still is called Club 42, after Luckman's jersey number.

Luckman was a special source of pride for the Jewish community. At his funeral service in 1998, Rabbi Jonathan Magidovitch spoke of Luckman's impact as a Jewish football player in the 1940s.

"At the time Sid Luckman played for the Bears, Jews in Europe were regularly murdered, regardless of their humanity or talent," Magidovitch said, according to the *Chicago Tribune*. "Sid Luckman was the embodiment of judging people for what they do. He carried the hopes of a generation."

48.
Randy White

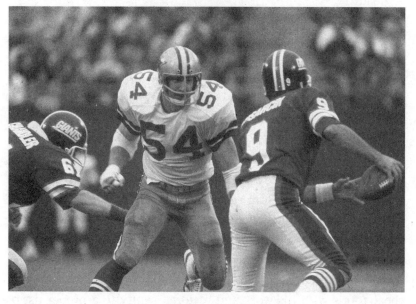

Defensive tackle Randy White (54) earned
co–Most Valuable Player honors in Super Bowl XII.

Position: Defensive Tackle

Team: Cowboys (1975–1988)

By Bob Sturm

However good you believe Randy White was, he was probably even better than that. That's because he played during an era when record-keeping was not quite where it needed to be. The NFL started counting sacks as an official statistic in 1982. Therefore, when you search the career sack leaders of the Cowboys franchise, you will be led astray with nonsense that would suggest Jim Jeffcoat, Greg Ellis, and Tony Tolbert have more sacks than White. This claim might then be interpreted by younger generations that they had a more destructive impact on the line of scrimmage than the Manster, who somehow was able to manage that awesome nickname with only 52 career sacks.

Absurd.

John Turney of ProFootballJournal.com used play-by-play records dating to 1960 and searched for the lost 22 years of sacks. He concedes that he is depending on those records to be accurate. They are not always perfect, but those manual records work much better than suggesting some of those pre-1982 moments never happened. They did, and they should be counted.

According to the NFL's official records, the great Harvey Martin and two-year edge George Selvie both have 10 career sacks as Cowboys and are tied. You certainly must know Martin had that in a single season several times over—he even had 20 in one season. The top five sack leaders in Cowboys history, according to the "official" stats, would be DeMarcus Ware (117), Jeffcoat (94.5), Ellis (77), Tolbert (59), and Ed "Too Tall" Jones (57.5).

Turney, after studying tape, records, and statistics, has adjusted those totals with his work and restored sanity to a proper list of all-time Cowboys sack leaders: Ware (117), Martin (114), White (111), Jones (106), and George Andrie (97). You can now find those unofficial numbers posted on Pro Football Reference so that fewer young football enthusiasts are led astray.

The key here, though, is that everyone on that list rushed off the edge except for White. Feared so widely that he was known as "Manster" as in half-man, half-monster, he was an inside and undersized defensive tackle. No defensive tackle in the history of this franchise approached his 111 career sacks: Jethro Pugh had 96.5, Bob Lilly 95.5, and after that the list drops off considerably. That 111 is the third-best total all time at his position regardless of franchise. The only two men ahead of him—Alan Page (148.5) and John Randle (135.5)—are also Pro Football Hall of Famers.

By today's standards, we know what a dominant defensive tackle looks like. Modern-day Aaron Donald is unlike anything we have seen, with 20.5 sacks in 2018 from the defensive tackle position.

His size, quickness, and motor should remind people of what White once was. Donald weighs less than 285 pounds. But, again, White was 265—tiny even for his era.

That is because he entered the league as a linebacker. White was originally supposed to succeed Lee Roy Jordan at middle linebacker when he was drafted at No. 2 in 1975 (behind Steve Bartkowski and two picks in front of Walter Payton). But that didn't quite work out due to Dallas's flex defense. White felt off-kilter. "[It] went against your natural instincts," he said.

That's when Tom Landry came up with an unconventional solution.

"Coach Landry called me in his office and told me, 'Randy, we're thinking about moving you to defensive tackle. What do you think?'" White said. "I told him, 'Coach, I just want to play football. I will play wherever you put me. Just give me a chance to play.'"

That eagerness from a man still wearing that linebacker's No. 54, though, quickly turned into trepidation.

"I'm looking and I'm going, 'OK, we have Ed Jones and Harvey Martin and the middle linebacker job, I didn't do too good there, so if I don't make it at the tackle spot, where am I going to go?'" he said. "So it was kind of desperation mode for me."

White immediately got to work, putting in extra sessions before and after practice with defensive line coach Ernie Stautner, himself a nine-time Pro Bowl pick at the position. Then he applied whatever lessons he could from his middle linebacker days to make the new position his own.

White certainly had the ability. He had the work ethic. But he needed more to rise to the very top of the league and become an All-Pro every single year from 1977 to 1985. If you talk to any player who played with or against him over those years, they would tell you that without question, White was ahead of his time with his hand skills. The ability to shed blocks, defeat his opponent, yet keep his hands from holding is an art form that was barely birthed in the 1970s.

"I don't think there is any question that he was ahead of his time with his hands," said Kurt Peterson, a Cowboys guard from 1980 to 1987 and, consequently, a frequent practice opponent of White's.

Yes, there were the hands. But there was more.

What was it that gave him the edge that allowed him to dominate for a decade? If you asked him, it went back to what happened outside the lines. It was his preparation, his training, and his incredibly unorthodox approach to football.

White had these sharpened trench skills in his arsenal that he utilized as early as anyone in football and they took him quickly to the top. That is where Dr. Bob Ward, the Cowboys' strength and conditioning coach as well as a sports scientist, comes into the picture.

"Dr. Bob" was an innovator. Back then, the Cowboys figured plenty out about the National Football League before their opponents when it came to all facets of the sport. What probably doesn't get enough credit for those dominant teams and players is the training methods and programs that shaped them.

Landry and Tex Schramm gave Ward carte blanche to mold their teams in whatever ways he saw fit. He took advantage.

What would this mean for the training of White, Jones, Charlie Waters, and the rest of the players who bought into the value of this form of training? In a nutshell, daily work built on a wide range of martial arts. Ward believed in varied techniques and specialties. There is no wisdom in spending too much time in a single direction.

For White, that meant leveraging Ward's connection with Danny Inosanto, Bruce Lee's old training partner and a master of Jeet Kune Do, a Cantonese hybrid martial art largely credited to Lee. The usual bag and sled drills were now accompanied by various drills holding a pair of Filipino fighting sticks. It was seemingly antithetical to how the position was played; you can't shed blocks with your hands occupied. But White came to understand the larger gains the technique brought him.

"Some players were like, 'We can't play football with sticks,' but the whole point was you develop the skills with the sticks in your hands, and when you drop the sticks, everything you do with the sticks you would do with your hands while playing," White said. "So you're training your hands and body to move, and it makes you use your left hand and left side as good as your right side. Your footwork, your timing, your distance—it's not the absolute, but it was one ingredient that I had the opportunity to be exposed to, and really it helped me take it to a different level and helped my career to be as successful as it was."

Ultimately, Ward says that every one of his ideas and concepts was about controlling the mind. And, he said, "Randy embraced it more than anyone. . . . He worked through that physically to a point where he could make it unconscious—an artless art."

White credits Ward for his success. The Manster has no doubt that he and his Cowboys teammates were exposed to techniques unheard-of elsewhere in the NFL.

"I don't think we were, I know we were," he said. "I don't think anyone else even had the thought of bringing martial artists in to help you with becoming better at playing football. . . . Coach Landry allowed Dr. Bob to implement all of these different ways of training into our football, but in doing so, he was way ahead of everybody. Everybody was playing catch-up to the Cowboys."

Then there was the persona. A review of White's career makes it clear that the Manster moniker was based largely on the pure fear he inspired among his adversaries. Intimidation was an art form, and the popular memories seem largely based on his ability to terrify his opponents with a skill set and disposition that kept those unlucky foes up at night.

"Before you played the Cowboys, you heard it from everyone in the league: Randy White, he is the intimidator of football," Washington offensive lineman Mark May, a longtime opponent, told NFL Films. "He was a fierce competitor . . . he was half-monster. Most tackles didn't have the tenacity and the athletic ability that he had."

What wasn't clear, though, is what made up the totality of White's greatness. Was it a ridiculous God-given athletic ability we had seldom seen? Was it his advanced pass-rush techniques? Was it his intimidation? Was it his work rate, motor, and endurance that allowed him to excel when others were tired?

The answers vary because defining greatness is never simple and those categories bleed into each other. But when someone has better skills and is willing to work harder and longer to win the battles, signs of weakness aren't often evident. This is where Hall of Fame–level careers can be found.

Then, White's conditioning and that relentless motor would allow him to do something that always benefited him: it put him inside the heads of his opponents.

"When a guy gets tired—I don't care how big, strong, and fast a guy is—when he gets tired and you are not, you can beat him," White said. "That was one of my plans. I always trained hard. I wanted to go in the fourth quarter when my opponent gets tired."

All of it made for one heck of a show.

"One thing that made him different was that we as offensive linemen had to take a knee on the sideline and watch him play. We only did that for a couple guys like Walter Payton and Earl Campbell," said Peterson, citing White's signature play of chasing down Eagles receiver Scott Fitzkee as a prime example. "Randy, on game day, was just relentless."

His name is Randy White. His nickname—Manster. If offensive guards could peer into his eyes and read his mind, they would all quit the game. For no one man can keep No. 54 from his appointed rounds.

47.
Rob Gronkowski

Rob Gronkowski retired with the third-most career touchdowns among tight ends.

Position: Tight End

Teams: Patriots (2010–2018), Buccaneers (2020–2021)

By Jeff Howe

Rob Gronkowski was a different breed from the moment he walked through the doors at Gillette Stadium in the spring of 2010.

And took a nap.

On the floor.

In a $1,500 suit.

During his pre-draft visit. The New England Patriots were well aware of the entire Gronk experience before selecting him in the second round of the draft. They recognized the immense talent and potential along with the unique personality that would surely stick out in Foxboro.

It all came home to roost during his nine seasons with the Patriots and another two years with the Tampa Bay Buccaneers. Gronkowski is a four-time Super Bowl champion and four-time First-Team All-Pro who ranks 10th all time among tight ends with 621 receptions, sixth with 9,286 yards, and third with 92 touchdowns.

He did it the Gronkulean way, without too much need to cater to cookie-cutter expectations, and that's part of what made him special.

During a meeting at the combine, Gronkowski professed his love of *SpongeBob* to former Patriots director of college scouting Jon Robinson. Then during his visit to Gillette, while awaiting a meeting with three coaches, Gronk folded up his suit jacket into a pillow and fell asleep on the floor outside director of scouting administration Nancy Meier's office.

"The initial visits left something to be desired," said Brian Ferentz, who was the Patriots' assistant tight ends coach at the time. "His best qualities—it's like any interaction you've ever had with Rob—always find a way to shine through. It's why he's a charismatic guy. He can't help it. He's a terrible poker player. He can't lie. He can't deceive. He is who he is. That's not an act. That's not a show.

"I always say that Rob is dumb like a fox. He plays up certain aspects of his personality for effect, but it's not an act. It's genuine. It's who he is. But he is much smarter than he lets on. When you're around him for an extended period of time, you get a sense of that."

Gronkowski scored 20 touchdowns by his 26th game—a record-setting pace for a tight end—and that night highlighted another side of his portfolio. In a 34–3 blowout victory against the Kansas City Chiefs on *Monday Night Football*, Gronk leaped past linebacker Derrick Johnson's low tackle attempt, flipped into the Gillette Stadium end zone, and awkwardly landed on the side of his head, twisting his neck in squeamish fashion and requiring a concussion test on the sideline.

It was both his national coming-out party and a reminder of a hulking menace of a performer who had back surgery at the University of Arizona and would constantly be under even more duress due to his physicality.

Gronkowski was asked that week if he would ever consider changing his style of play to preserve his body.

"I'm blessed that I'm fine from it and everything," Gronkowski said, "but I definitely don't feel like I'm going to change anything."

Even as the surgeries mounted—nine in his career—Gronk's style undeniably worked. He set a positional record with 18 total touchdowns in 2011, tore his ACL in 2013 but had the second-best season of his career in 2014 when he had 82 catches, 1,124 yards, 12 touchdowns, and was an on-field blocker for all 17 of their touchdown runs, including the playoffs. Gronk also caught a touchdown pass in each of the Patriots' three postseason victories on their way to a title in Super Bowl XLIX.

"When it comes time to determining how good he was compared to the history of the game," former New York Giants tight end Mark Bavaro once said, "you're going to have to remember the little things that he did—the fact that he could get open, the fact that he could catch balls with people on him, the fact that everybody in the world is trying to stop him and they couldn't.

"He's not just catching balls when nobody is looking or when someone is focused on something else or it's a trick play. He is catching balls when everybody knows they're going to throw to him. He's catching balls when it's third-and-5, and everyone says, 'Just make sure Gronkowski doesn't catch a ball,' and he still does with two or three guys on him.

The 6-foot-6, 265-pound Gronkowski had an impact at tight end that the best running backs of the 1980s and '90s had at their position or the best wide receivers of the '90s and early 2000s had at their position. He was a player an offense could be built around at a position around which the offense had never been built.

And then there was the personality, which was as large as it was genuine. He carried the party-boy reputation from Tucson to the

NFL, twerked, spiked beer cans, and never passed up an opportunity for a goofy joke.

In the week leading into Super Bowl XLIX, Gronk was asked why he partied so hard, and he replied without missing a beat, "Because I'm a baller." His teammates repeated that line every chance they got.

They adored Gronkowski because they knew his personality was real and essentially harmless. He was a big kid who just wanted to have fun with his friends.

Gronkowski famously kicked Indianapolis Colts safety Sergio Brown "out the club" by blocking him through the end zone during a 2014 regular-season victory, but there was another moment that flew way under the radar. After his wild 26-yard touchdown, Gronk stormed back to the sideline out of breath, eyes popping out of his skull, shrieking like a hyena and yelling at anyone who would listen.

"How did I do that?"

"Did you guys see what I did?"

"Did it look cool?"

Gronkowski wasn't as dominant over the second half of his career due to the injury toll, but he was still a force in the biggest moments. He caught nine balls for 116 yards and two touchdowns in a Super Bowl LII loss to the Philadelphia Eagles, then six for 87 yards, including a 29-yarder to set up Sony Michel's game-winning touchdown in the fourth quarter of Super Bowl LIII. After a one-year retirement, Gronkowski reunited with Tom Brady in 2020 and the pair connected six times for 67 yards and two scores in a Super Bowl LV for Tampa.

There isn't enough room on the internet to run through every other big play or performance of his career.

"There's no doubt in my mind Rob Gronkowski is the greatest to ever play that position," Ferentz said.

Gronk didn't reach Tony Gonzalez's positional record of 1,325 catches for 15,127 yards. He had a remote opportunity to make a charge for Antonio Gates's 116-touchdown mark before retiring in June 2022.

The greatness of Gronkowski won't be defined so much by those numbers. Rather, he won unlike any great tight end in history. His dominance at the position in his era was unmatched.

"I guess he's a throwback, but I hate that it's being called a throwback now when it's actually the definition of the position," Gonzalez once said. "You're supposed to block, and you're supposed to catch. It's frustrating, but I guess that's me being nostalgic and old school, being that old, disgruntled man like, 'Back in my day, you had to block, and we had to walk 20 miles to school.' That's the way the position is going, so I love the tight ends who can come in and both block and catch because it helps [the team]."

A modern-day throwback, there was only one Gronk.

And yeah, it looked cool.

46.
Gale Sayers

Though he played just seven seasons,
Gale Sayers gained 9,435 total yards and scored 336 points.

Position: Running Back
Team: Bears (1965–1971)

By Dan Pompei

More than 50 years after his last run, Gale Sayers is revered not for yards, records, nor championships, certainly not championships.

He is revered for style.

No one has played the game like Sayers did—not before him, not after him. He was Fred Astaire in cleats, with grace, subtlety, and savvy that was not of this world. "It was a gift," he told *Sports Illus-*

trated in 2010. "And trust me, it was easy. It was so easy, I can't even explain it."

Teammate Johnny Morris said Sayers was the only player he has seen who could change directions in midair. It was as if his feet didn't need the ground for him to propel himself.

Most running backs make rounded cuts. Sayers's cuts were sharp and hard, like the corners of a square hickory table. And he could make those cuts at full speed, physics' laws be damned.

"Every runner I know, deep down, would like to run the way Gale Sayers did," Jim Brown wrote in his autobiography, *Out of Bounds.* "No one has ever run prettier."

Runners usually have a plan. Sayers? He was all instinct.

"Really, I don't know where I'm going," he told the *Chicago Tribune.* "I go where my feet take me."

His feet took him where defenders couldn't get a hand on him, let alone a hit or a tackle. He said he never was hit solidly on a kick return or punt return because of his peripheral vision.

Sayers could make defenders, even some of the best defenders who ever lived, look like they were playing in slow motion while he was on fast-forward. One of Sayers's cuts on a 63-yard run left Lions hall of famer Lem Barney on the ground.

"I never looked forward to playing him," Hall of Fame defensive tackle Merlin Olsen told the *Los Angeles Times.* "Every time Gale got the football, he made me sick to my stomach."

In his book *Pro Football's 100 Greatest Players*, longtime NFL coach George Allen wrote, "Sayers was the most exciting running back I ever saw, the best long-gain guy I ever saw. . . . He was the quickest at hitting a hole. If there wasn't a hole, he was the best at finding a place to slide through. When he was going wide and found a crowd, he was the best at reversing his field and getting loose."

It was quickly evident Sayers was not like the others. In his first preseason game, he returned a punt 77 yards, returned a kickoff 93 yards, and threw a 2-yard touchdown pass. During his first season, he broke an NFL record by scoring 22 touchdowns. Fourteen of those touchdowns were rushing, six were receiving, one was on a punt return, and one was on a kick return. Along the way, his teammates started calling him "Magic."

Saying Sayers was a running back is like saying a mobile device is a telephone. When Jim Dooley took over as head coach of the Bears in 1968, he considered Sayers at flanker to replace the retiring Morris, and very well might have moved him there if he had been more confident in his running backs.

What Sayers probably did best was return kicks. His 30.6-yard average per kick return remains the best in NFL history.

It is possible, maybe probable, that no one in the history of the National Football League ever had a better performance than Sayers did on December 12, 1965, against the 49ers at Wrigley Field. The rain was steady and the playing field was gray, as grass had stopped growing months prior and dirt had become mud. Everyone struggled with their footing—except Sayers. He once said on that day, he cut on the back part of his feet instead of the balls of his feet. He slipped one time, however—on the last play of the game, he fell at midfield on a punt return just as he was about to break free for what could have been a touchdown. It would have been his seventh. As it was, he tied an NFL record. Sayers took nine handoffs and scored on four of them. One of his two receptions went for an 80-yard touchdown. He fielded five punts and scored on one of the returns. He said he was hit on only one of them, as he was going into the end zone. Oh, and he totaled 336 yards.

Sayers could have scored another touchdown if head coach George Halas had not pulled him in the fourth quarter with the Bears about to score. Halas said he had a premonition Sayers would get hurt on the next play. Sayers's backup, Jon Arnett, ran it in from two yards out and was vigorously booed.

The 49ers had come up with a special scheme for Sayers called "The Chicago Defense." It called for defenders to be disciplined in their run gaps and double-team Bears blockers. "I just wonder how many Sayers would have scored if we hadn't set our defense to stop him," 49ers assistant coach Y. A. Tittle said.

In November 1968, Sayers took a pitch on a play called 49 Toss Left and planted his right leg. San Francisco safety Kermit Alexander drove his shoulder into Sayers's knee, which bent sideways. Teammates Ralph Kurek, Rudy Kuechenberg, and Mike Reilly carried Sayers off the field, and Halas, known as impervious, wept on the sidelines.

Just three and a half years into his career, the great Sayers as we knew him was no more. But he showed his greatness was multidimensional the following year when his will became more imposing than his skill. Sayers changed his running style, bullying his way to an NFL-high 1,032 rushing yards. He also led the league with a career-high 236 rushes. He was named UPI's Comeback Player of the Year.

He could not have been blamed if he had been distracted that season. His fullback Brian Piccolo was fighting for his life in a New York hospital for much of the season, and Sayers was visiting him weekly. They had become close after Halas's son-in-law Ed McCaskey made them room together early in their careers.

Piccolo passed away in June 1970. Sayers's autobiography, *I Am Third*, became the template for the made-for-TV movie *Brian's Song*, which lifted Sayers to a higher level of fame. Sayers said fans throughout his life wanted to talk about the film and his friendship with Piccolo more than anything he accomplished in football. The movie's most remembered scene was the depiction of Sayers's speech at a New York banquet, in which he said he was accepting the most courageous player of the year award on Piccolo's behalf.

When Sayers gave his speech, he spoke fluidly. It was an accomplishment because Sayers was a stutterer, and yards usually came easier to him than words. He often responded to questions early in his career with one-word answers, leaving the impression he was arrogant. Sayers, at the suggestion of Halas, signed up for a Dale Carnegie course. In his book *Sayers: My Life and Times*, he wrote it was one of the best things he ever did for himself.

A couple of months after Piccolo's passing, Sayers injured his good knee in a preseason game. He played just four more games and, after the fourth knee surgery of his career, told coach Abe Gibron he had reached the end. At the age of 28, he had spent himself completely. When he retired in 1972, the *Chicago Tribune* called it "one of the blackest days in Bears history."

It was a black day in part because it was understood then that the Bears never would capitalize on his greatness. During his career, the Bears never played in a postseason game. Their record with Sayers was 29-36-3.

After football, Sayers returned to his alma mater, the University of Kansas, to work in administration. He later was the athletic director of Southern Illinois University and then founded Sayers Computer Source, a supplier that once did $360 million in sales in one year.

He credited his second wife, Ardie, with helping him come out of his shell in the 1970s when he was at Kansas.

"At that time of my life, it was difficult for me to meet and converse with strangers, even though I knew it was an important part of my job," he wrote. "Ardie was a much better conversationalist, and I counted on her to carry the conversation at the many social events where I was asked to appear. Ardie often impressed upon me the importance of communicating with people. . . . I used to practice giving speeches in front of Ardie."

Sayers had every right to have a star mentality, but his humility was rare. When Halas caught him speeding in a Corvette and told Sayers to get rid of it, he did it. He later followed his coach's request to stop riding his Honda motorbike, and another to stop playing in offseason charity basketball events. In *Sayers: My Life and Times*, published in 2007, he wrote that he hoped players who followed him wouldn't destroy the game.

"When I see players like Terrell Owens making all of that money and then acting foolish most of the time, it really turns me off and makes me ashamed at the way some players disrespect the game. It's a team game, simple as that. . . . We are supposed to be role models."

Instead of his greatness being diminished by playing in only 68 games and what amounted to five seasons, Sayers's mystique was heightened by it. He is remembered as the one who transcended his brutish sport.

As with Marilyn, Hendrix, and Tupac, we are left to wonder what could have been if Sayers had not been stopped too soon.

"If he hadn't gotten injured, if he could have played 10 or 11 years, Gale might hold every legitimate record there is," Brown wrote. "His performance never will be forgotten by anyone who understands football."

At the age of 34, Sayers was inducted into the Pro Football Hall of Fame. He remains the youngest enshrinee ever.

45.
Larry Allen

Larry Allen (73) played every position on the Cowboys' offensive line except center and is on two All-Decade teams (1990s and 2000s).

Position: Offensive Line

Teams: Cowboys (1994–2005), 49ers (2006–2007)

By Bob Sturm

I magine a player so feared that you actually had to turn to a bear to find an opponent that would make him an underdog—mostly because bears won't play within the NFL rulebook.

That is probably the best way to describe Larry Allen to those who need a description.

To properly express Allen's legend among those who played with him, played against him, and viewed him from close range, one must recognize that his ability was routinely discussed in terms that made comparisons somewhat pointless.

For instance, modern Cowboys All-Pro guard Zack Martin is an amazing player and one of the very best in the modern era. He will likely join Allen in the Hall of Fame someday. Yet, you never hear him compared to Allen. It is unfair to him to have to stack up to the legend. People don't even do it.

The same goes for any player in that position in Cowboys history, and to a certain extent, most feel the same way in the NFL. His dominance preceded him with such terrifying and ominous effects that opponents dreaded the meetings.

The comparisons often stopped, save for local radio entertainers who would canvass teammates about how Allen would do outside the confines of the NFL in feats of strength and dominance.

Could he win in a Battle Royale that included all of humanity?

Could he win a squaring off with a fairly sized black bear? How about an irate chimpanzee? Or maybe a middleweight lion?

Teammates would certainly not claim Allen could take out any and all wild animals, but they would also not completely rule out his chances.

He was that big, strong, and mean.

He entered the league in 1994. By his second season, he would run off a streak of seven consecutive years of making the first-team All-Pro squad and would go to 11 Pro Bowls. He played in an era when almost all the tape has survived and you can see him put on absolute clinics in critical spots, perhaps best demonstrated by his two-game masterclass in the 1995 NFC Championship Game against Green Bay and Super Bowl XXX two weeks later against Pittsburgh in Arizona.

Brad Sham, in his 2003 book *Stadium Stories*, made the claim that Allen is the greatest draft pick in the history of the Cowboys franchise. Sham eliminated those who were taken particularly high and were supposed to be great, arriving at his answer in a way that is defensible but also subjective. The Cowboys have made some superb picks over the years, and Jason Witten's third-round selection in 2003 certainly can't be far behind. Yet Sham's opinion makes sense. No team should be able to get what many suggest is the best guard ever with pick No. 46, and the team selecting someone that special should never be coming off back-to-back Super Bowl wins.

Yet, this is precisely what happened. Just 27 days after Jimmy Johnson and Jerry Jones divorced, the Cowboys traded up to select Shante Carver with pick No. 23 by sending the 49ers their first- (No. 28) and second-round (No. 62) selections. But with the NFL introducing compensatory picks for the loss of free agents in 1994, Dallas was awarded another Day 2 pick: No. 46.

Describing Allen with words can become difficult when hyperbole is thrown around with such routine for every player who comes along. If everyone is "special," the truly special players have their value diminished. But to those who played with and against him, the dominance and fear of Allen is something this sport has rarely seen. He is one of the few players who left foes resorting to such hushed tones of reverence when speaking their name.

John Randle is a Hall of Fame inductee and one of the best defensive tackles to ever lace them up. Randle put up 14 years of superb play and his bust has resided in Canton, Ohio, at the Pro Football Hall of Fame since 2010. To hear him speak of Allen should tell those who didn't see him in his prime all they need to know:

"When a man can bench-press 692 pounds, that man can launch you," Randle told NFL Films. "It's like going against a bear; I mean, he's just humongous. He'll grab you, pick you up, and start laughing. And there is nothing you can do. It's like going against a car; you are trying to stop him, and you are just sliding.

"I've seen him take linebackers and just drive them 20 yards. Not 5, not 10. And you go back to the huddle and that linebacker is looking at you like, 'What am I supposed to do?' Do the best you can. Do the best you can.

"You didn't taunt him. You were nice to him. Give him a hand up and smile at him. Sometimes he'd smile back. But don't get him mad. He is one of the most powerful men to ever play the game."

Allen's excellence is unmatched. The elite company he shares is evident by simply looking at his seven first-team All-Pro selections and his 11 Pro Bowl berths. As far as offensive linemen across the league, over five and 10 in those categories, only Anthony Muñoz (1980 draft), Bruce Matthews (1983), and Randall McDaniel (1988) qualify.

What if the same standard was applied to any Dallas Cowboys in the 5/10 club? What would that list look like?

It would include nobody but Larry Allen. Randy White would have enough All-Pro teams and Jason Witten would have enough Pro Bowls, but only L.A. checks both boxes. It is remarkable to consider what a player from Butte Junior College (a place that also produced Aaron Rodgers) and Sonoma State (a place that produced seemingly no other athletes of note and no longer has a football program) became on Sundays at Texas Stadium.

Justin Tuck would tell a story in retirement that would put the picture in the frame about how Allen would love to get inside your head by walking to the line of scrimmage and looking across the line at the defense, put up his right hand to pull down the string on an imaginary train whistle, and yell "whoot-whoot!" to let you know the train is coming.

That, of course, meant so was Emmitt Smith right behind him.

"He would love to signal that here was where the hole was that Emmitt is about to run through, and there is nothing you can do about it. Imagine that. What are you going to do about it? It was like playing football with your son," Tuck said. "It wouldn't matter if your young boy was told your play. Dad is going to make a hole here."

This, of course, is why to this day Smith can be the all-time leading rusher in NFL history and still be underrated in some circles. Because Allen was so devastating that many would attribute that rushing record largely to him. Think about that.

There are so many other stories that would be listed as his feats of strength.

- Week 16 in 1994. As a rookie, Allen was forced to play tackle because Erik Williams had been injured. The Cowboys led 7–0 in the second quarter when a pass was deflected at the line of scrimmage. Darion Conner picked it off and was running it the other way. Allen ran with him down the sideline and tackled him to save a pick-six as announcer Dan Dierdorf lost his mind at the marvel he just saw. "This guy has a rocket booster strapped to his back. . . . Look at this, folks—6-3, 325 pounds! I'm telling you, that is one of the most impressive athletic feats I have ever seen!"
- The time he really did bench 700 pounds in the Cowboys' weight room. To see the pandemonium and euphoria that he created was the result of a man bench-pressing more weight than NFL players can possibly conceive. It then became part of his name during games, as in "Larry Allen of the Cowboys— who once benched 700 pounds—just made a great block there."
- The time in San Francisco when Allen did not appreciate the kicker chirping at him after an extra point (for an unknown reason) and quickly smacked said kicker in the face mask hard enough to produce more stars than José Cortez was used to seeing on the sides of helmets.

He was an awesome player who seldom lost a snap. He did lose one or two, by the way—including a famous one to the late, great Reggie White in a moment where young Allen was playing tackle and Reggie got under him with a hump move, proving that when two Hall of Famers do battle, the other guy might win once in a while.

But that is the thing about offensive linemen. They can win

98 percent of the snaps, give up two sacks, and everyone thinks they had a bad game. The defensive guy can lose 98 percent, get a sack, and leave the game feeling great. It is a slanted battle, but Allen seldom showed himself to be human.

He was huge. He was nasty. He was confident. And he was also reserved in his talking. But there was never any question about what the incredibly gifted and talented players in the NFL thought about him. They were reverent and respectful. Careful to choose their words so as not to upset him. In a game where mouths run with no harness because talking trash is an art form, even the best talkers would nod at Allen and try to get out of Dodge without any significant damage.

He was simply incomparable among his fellow man. The only bears with a chance did not play for Chicago.

44.
Bruce Matthews

Upon his retirement, no one had played in more NFL games (296) than Bruce Matthews.

Position: Offensive Line
Teams: Oilers (1983–1996), Titans (1997–2001)

By Joe Rexrode

Warren Moon wouldn't pick anyone but Bruce Matthews to block for him on the football field, and Moon also played with Walter Jones, Will Shields, Randall McDaniel, and Mike Munchak—Hall of Famers all.

But none of those other guys played every position on the line, as Matthews did, extensively and expertly. None of them covered more than 1,000 punts as an NFL long snapper while also serving as the team's emergency punter. And emergency quarterback. And resident creator and winner of a variety of athletic competitions—including launching plastic hotel balcony furniture into the pool during training camp—in a 19-year NFL career with the Houston Oilers/Tennessee Titans that saw him make 14 straight Pro Bowls, play in 296 games, and miss none because of injury.

"He'd be out there throwing better passes than the quarterbacks," Moon said of Matthews, who got occasional practice reps under center during his career but never got the call on game day. "He's out there making one-handed catches. He's out there catching punts. He could do anything. But the amazing thing is he could play all those [offensive line] positions for that long, at that level. People just don't do that."

Matthews did, which is why longtime *Houston Chronicle* columnist and Hall of Fame voter and honoree John McClain believes Matthews has a case as the best offensive lineman to ever play the game.

"Not the best guard or center," McClain said of the positions Matthews played the most, though he had 39 combined starts at left and right tackle. "The best lineman, period."

Steve Watterson, Matthews's strength coach from 1986 until Matthews's 2002 retirement, who previously worked for Dick Vermeil's Philadelphia Eagles and at the Olympic Training Center during offseasons, takes it a step further.

"Steve McNair is a close second, but Bruce was the greatest pure athlete I've ever been around," said Watterson, who retired in 2018. "I know that's the type of hyperbole that usually gets a lot of rancor and challenges, but I'm telling you, play him in basketball. Kick a soccer ball with him. Didn't matter. He takes on all challenges."

Hockey, for example. Matthews decided to give ice skating a try in the early '90s, because why wouldn't a 6-foot-5, 305-pound man who has played in the NFL for nearly a decade and has never been near a rink decide to plant himself on a pair of 1-millimeter-wide blades and see how fast he can go? Speed skating, as it turns out, was an effective and low-impact offseason workout for Matthews. Trying hockey, as those close to him knew, was inevitable. And then-Oilers equipment manager and Montreal native Gordon "Red" Batty just happened to be in a beer league with other staffers.

Imagine the scene, and what the contractual and social media ramifications would be today, when Matthews took the ice.

"I mean, it was straight out of a movie with Will Ferrell or something," Watterson said. "It didn't make sense. He's got all the accoutrements—all the pads, shin guards, shoulder pads—and he's simply the biggest human being any of us had seen. Everyone froze for a moment. I don't know how they even got a hockey helmet for that 8-plus head. So, he gets out there and of course he's not used to the stopping and going and pushing and stick work. But just like everything else, he got it after about 10 to 15 minutes. I know he knocked the crap out of me. And he quickly became a pro at hooking and tripping if you got by him."

Said Matthews: "You develop that as an offensive lineman. Some call it holding. I call it being smart."

And you do things like this only if you have extraordinary physical gifts.

"I'll never forget talking to the late Bob Young about Bruce one time," McClain said of the Oilers offensive line coach from 1990 to '94, "and he told me, 'Bruce is like a ballerina. All he's missing is the tutu. We teach these guys techniques, and he just ignores me. Then he gets there faster than anyone because he's so damn talented.'"

Matthews had that in abundance, and variety. He played piano. He dreamed of being the biggest catcher in Major League Baseball history as a high schooler in Arcadia, California, though it eventually became clear he should emulate his father, Clay Sr., and older brother Clay Jr., and work toward the NFL.

After starring at USC and being selected in the first round, just as his brother had five years earlier, Matthews got the rookie treatment with the Oilers in 1983. Munchak, the No. 8 overall pick a year earlier out of Penn State, was eager to see this No. 9 overall pick humbled in front of the team. Matthews was told to stand up and sing something.

"He had held out and missed the first week, so I think he felt bad about that when he came in, and he was as quiet as can be for the first three or four days," Munchak said. "He's the first-rounder, the veterans can't wait to abuse him, so he has to stand on a chair in front of everybody. He starts singing an Elvis song and it's like 'Oh my God. This guy is good.' He's entertaining the room like he's got the most outgoing personality ever. And it just went from there."

Matthews and Munchak became best friends, opening holes for Earl Campbell at first, protecting Moon, dominating for years even in the run-and-shoot offense that does little to satisfy a lineman's urge to fire off the ball and set a tone. Matthews's Elvis-like singing (and dancing) became a Sunday evening attraction for patrons of a Houston bar called Sams Boat.

Matthews's play became the standard in the NFL. His versatility allowed him to excel at every position, which is almost as unheard-of today as an NFL lineman on ice skates, and his durability allowed him to have longevity usually reserved for kickers and quarterbacks.

"That's the thing that really amazes me, and Bruce still has all his faculties today," Moon said. "Because, let me tell you, those guys were going at it. We had real two-a-days. Sometimes three-a-days. And there was a lot of hitting. For him to come out of that OK after all those years, that's another tribute to how great he was."

Or to God, in the mind of Matthews, a husband to Carrie, father of seven—including Falcons left tackle Jake Matthews—and giving presence of nearly 40 years now in the Houston community. It's not that Matthews never got hurt. Jeff Fisher, his teammate at USC and later his head coach with the Oilers and Titans, told *Pro Football Weekly* in 2000 of a knee injury that was not going to keep Matthews out of a big game with Jacksonville: "If it were you or I, we wouldn't drive a car."

But Matthews, who had knee replacement surgery in the summer of 2021, said the only real difference between him and Munchak was that he was able to avoid lasting ailments. That allowed him to put his experience and mental grasp of the game to use long after most players can.

"You come to Year 7, 8, 9 in this league, that's when your experience and feel for the game and knowledge are peaking," Matthews said. "Unfortunately, there's such a small window for a lot of guys where they have that knowledge, and they aren't physically declining yet. And that's where I was blessed. I mean, I'd get blown up, rolled up by three guys in a pile and it looked like it was going to have to be a double amputation, like it was going to be the ugliest injury ever. I'd get up, no worse for the wear. [Munchak] has one guy falling on his leg and he'd need to have knee surgery. God blessed my brother and I with bodies that could just take the pounding in the NFL."

And that brings up the last, but no less important, element that made Matthews great. The Clay-Bruce driveway basketball games growing up—finally won at times by Bruce after he got to USC and Clay, five years his elder, was in the NFL—made other folks' tackle football games look tame. Clay reached a lifting milestone. Bruce would exceed it. Clay starred at USC. Bruce starred at USC. Clay played 19 seasons. Bruce played 19 seasons. Starting in the home and extending to wherever he was in the world, Bruce wanted to beat someone at something.

"Most competitive guy I've ever been around," Munchak said. "In every phase of life. For example, we argued all the time, and it didn't matter if he actually agreed with me or not. He would take the other side of an argument just to see if he could change your mind, just to see if he could win."

One of these arguments famously happened at the team hotel in San Antonio during training camp in 1994, after Munchak had retired from playing and had started his coaching career as an offensive assistant. So they could say they followed the rule of players and coaches not drinking together, Munchak and Watterson sat on one side of the hotel room and Matthews on the other. A cooler full of beer sat between them with a string that divided the room. No one can remember what the debate was about that night, only that it got so loud at around 3 a.m. that then–head coach Jack Pardee yelled up from his balcony into their room to see what was going on.

"Just finishing up bed check, Jack!" Watterson yelled back.

Practice that day, like every day, started at 6 a.m.

"That was a rough morning for him, I think," Munchak said of Matthews. "He actually had to practice, and I got to coach. A little easier on my end."

But Matthews still won when it came time to see who could land more plastic balcony furniture in the pool. On Mondays after games, most players at the facility were getting treatment, resting up.

Matthews was out on the field starting up games of "Helmet Ball." This was one of many games he made up around the facility and locker room to keep things interesting. Players would stand in a circle with helmets on the ground and get points for hitting a helmet with the football. Catch the ball as it bounced off a helmet and that's double points, with the thrower eliminated. Stick the ball in the helmet and you win automatically. As with many games he devised, he would come up with rules on the fly, often rules that helped him win.

"He was like Dewey from *Stripes*," Watterson said of Matthews, an enthusiastic tormentor of rookies who shaved many a hairstyle into something unrecognizable. "Like, 'Since we're in Italy, the rules mean this' or 'Since it's Wednesday, you owe me all your money.' He would be the king of any game in that locker room."

In a car, he'd turn on the radio and immediately start barking out song titles and artist names as fast as possible.

"Bruce Springsteen, 'Glory Days'!" Munchak recounted in his 2007 speech as Matthews's presenter at the Pro Football Hall of Fame.

"And the thing is, he keeps doing it and he's making you feel bad that he knows something you don't know," Munchak said. "So then obviously you start playing. And then he starts singing the songs. And, unfortunately, he sings very well."

Matthews called himself a "nasty competitor," which obviously served him well as he tried to block players such as Bruce Smith, Howie Long, Tim Krumrie, and Warren Sapp. But it was deeper than that, he said, going back to USC, when he was blocking for Charles

White and Marcus Allen, learning from Anthony Muñoz, watching defensive teammates such as Ronnie Lott and Joey Browner fly around.

"The thing is, I was always very skeptical of my abilities," Matthews said. "I was very insecure about it. I talk about that with Jake now all the time. I tell him, 'I was playing my 19th year in the league and still scared to death they were gonna find out I suck and cut me.' I carried that insecurity with me my whole career. So there was never really any contentment. I was always on edge, always had a lot of anxiety and stress. But I think that kept me sharp and working hard."

Even now, Matthews said he's skeptical that he should be mentioned among the game's all-time greats. He grew up "an almost nerdish fan," he said, reading media guides and watching every pregame show. So the day he ended his rookie holdout remains fresh in his mind. Archie Manning, one of his football heroes, was with the Oilers then. Manning introduced himself to the rookie and offered to take him out after practice.

"We got pizza and beer," Matthews said. "It was the biggest thrill of my life. I immediately called home and said, 'You'll never guess who took me out and paid for me.'"

As was obvious by the time Matthews and Peyton Manning shared a Pro Bowl, and that story, in 1999, these are the two most accomplished families in football history. That said, the Matthews family's three generations of NFL players (Bruce and Clay Jr. each had two sons who played in the league) trump the Mannings' two—so far. Bring that up and Matthews's competitiveness overcomes all reverence and self-doubt.

"Are we the first family?" he said. "Oh, heck yeah."

43.
Drew Brees

Only Tom Brady has more passing yards,
passing TDs, completions, and attempts than Drew Brees.

Position: Quarterback

Teams: Chargers (2001–2005), Saints (2006–2020)

By Jeff Duncan

I n 2009, the TV show *Sports Science* wanted to gauge Drew Brees's renowned accuracy for one of its episodes. So the show's producers had him throw footballs at an archery target 20 yards away and compare his strike rate to Olympic archers.

With the cameras rolling, Brees put on a show. He didn't just hit the target. He peppered it. Over and over. Pass after pass.

Brees hit the 4.8-inch bull's-eye 10 out of 10 times, an astonishing display of biomechanic wizardry that amazed the producers.

Brees's consistent fundamentals were the secret to his accuracy. The show's scientists determined that he threw each of his passes with the same 6-degree launch angle, 600-revolutions-per-minute spin rate, and 52-mile-per-hour launch speed.

The Olympic archers paled in comparison.

Other quarterbacks won more Super Bowls than Brees. Some were more prolific deep throwers. Others were more dangerous runners and scramblers.

But when it came to the simple art of throwing a catchable, accurate, on-time pass, there has never been anyone better than Brees.

"What Drew did, he made it look easy, but it's not—the window is that big and he hits it," said Tom House, Brees's longtime performance coach and throwing specialist. "Drew would have a spectacular play or two, but he was not a spectacular quarterback. He was just the best fucker who has ever thrown a football."

House is biased, of course. But there is little argument to his bold proclamation.

When Brees entered the league in 2001, a 60 percent completion rate was considered the gold standard. By the time Brees retired in 2021, he had almost single-handedly raised the bar to 70 percent. Brees led the league in completion percentage six times and recorded the three highest completion rates for a season in league annals. His 67.7 career completion percentage remains the highest in NFL history among players who played five or more seasons. There have been 17 seasons in which an NFL quarterback completed 70 percent of his passes or better. Brees owns seven of them.

"You could put every quarterback in the league on the same field and tell them to throw all of the same routes, and you're just going to notice something different about the way Drew places the football, when and where," said former NFL quarterback Luke McCown, who served as Brees's backup for three seasons from 2013 to 2015. "It's just different. The hand of God reached down and touched Drew and said, 'You're going to be the most accurate guy to ever throw a football.'"

Saints coaches attributed Brees's historic accuracy to his unusually large hands and flawless mechanics. His hand width of 10.25 inches ranked among the top 11 percent of quarterbacks at the NFL Scouting Combine, while his 6-foot height ranked among the bottom 8 percent. Because of his large grip, Brees could control the ball and deliver it with maximum rotation. It's one of the reasons he excelled in the windy, cold conditions of West Lafayette, Indiana, as a college star at Purdue.

"I've always felt that accuracy is [about] trust and anticipation," Brees said. "You have to trust the guys that you're throwing it to, and you have to anticipate where they're going to be before they're there. . . . I don't care how well everyone's covered. There's a place where I can get a completion. There's a place where I can throw the ball, where my guy can get it and nobody else can. And it's my job to figure out how to do that."

Brees was an accurate quarterback in high school, college, and early in his pro career with the San Diego Chargers. But he took it to a different level under the tutelage of House, a former Major League Baseball pitcher and pitching coach.

After his second season as a starter for the Chargers, Brees's career was going nowhere. He won only 10 of his first 28 games as a starter and threw more interceptions (31) than touchdowns (28). He knew he needed to overhaul his entire life if he wanted to reach his potential. In the 2004 offseason, he changed his diet, his strength training, his approach, and his attitude. He worked with a performance specialist on conditioning and balance work and consulted with House about throwing mechanics as part of a broad-based overhaul. That season, Brees led the Chargers to a 12-4 record and a division title while earning the first Pro Bowl berth of his career.

"He realized he had more in the tank and went out and found a way to get more out of his gene pool," House said.

When Brees arrived in New Orleans as a free agent two years later, he brought his renowned preparation regimen with him and continued to perfect it. He knew he needed to maximize everything within his control—conditioning, nutrition, game prep, mental stamina—to compensate for what he couldn't control—his lack of prototype height, speed, and strength. To that end, he developed a strict daily regimen, one for the season and one for the offseason. And from day one, he committed himself to always being the first and last player in the building.

In New Orleans, Brees joined forces with Saints coach Sean Payton to form one of the most successful quarterback–head coach tandems in NFL history. In Payton, Brees found the perfect aggressive, play-calling yin to his cerebral, calculated passing yang. The Saints blitzed opposing defenses with a dizzying array of formations, receiver splits, and personnel groupings. The league had never seen anything like the complexity of the attack. And each offseason, Payton and Brees went into the X's and O's lab and added to the system.

With Brees calling the signals and Payton calling the plays, the Saints offense took off. During their tenure in New Orleans, the Saints gained more yards (95,655) than any offense during any other 15-year period in NFL history. From 2006 to 2020, the Saints led the league in scoring or total offense eight times and never ranked lower than 12th in either category.

During that span, the tandem brought unprecedented stability and success to the once-moribund Saints organization. In the four decades before Brees and Payton arrived in New Orleans, the Saints managed to win just 40.3 percent of their games, two division titles, and one playoff game. In the Payton-Brees era, the Saints went 150-88 (.630), won six division titles, and went 9-8 in the playoffs.

The high-flying, Brees-led offense transformed the Saints from a perennial also-ran into one of the most popular, high-profile teams in the league. Every home game at the Superdome has been sold out since 2006, and the city of New Orleans annually tops all U.S. markets in television ratings for Saints and NFL games, according to Nielsen Company and the NFL.

"He's clearly the best quarterback I've been around," said Mark Brunell, who played behind Brett Favre in Green Bay to start his career. "He did everything very, very well. It wasn't just one aspect of being a quarterback. He was good at everything: the locker room, off the field, his study habits, his work ethic, his family, the media. I've never seen anything like it."

Over time, Brees transformed himself into the Greg Maddux of NFL quarterbacks, a passing surgeon who beat opponents not with his fastball but by repeatedly painting the black with pinpoint passes. The back-shoulder throw became a staple of modern passing offenses because of Brees's almost telepathic connection with go-to receivers like Marques Colston, Michael Thomas, and tight end Jimmy Graham.

"Drew was the first guy that meticulously took you apart with how he played the position and made you bleed out by a thousand cuts," former NFL quarterback Trent Dilfer said. "It was about being a surgeon, not a butcher."

Statistically speaking, Brees is in a class almost by himself. He retired with more passing yards (80,358) and completions (7,142) than any quarterback in NFL history and was the fastest quarterback ever to reach the 50,000-, 60,000-, and 70,000-yard thresholds. He set records for the most consecutive games with a touchdown pass and the highest completion percentage in a game by connecting on 29 of 30 passes in a 2019 game against the Indianapolis Colts.

Brees is widely considered the best player to never win the NFL's Most Valuable Player Award, having finished second four times. He won nearly every other major individual honor in his distinguished career: 13 Pro Bowl invitations, two NFL Offensive Player of the Year awards, and the Super Bowl XLIV MVP award. He also was incredibly durable. He missed just 10 games because of injury during his 20-year NFL career.

"Over the years, his durability and availability were quite amazing," Payton said. "I think he is as courageous and tough a player as I have ever been around. Not only physically but mentally. There is a grind mentally, a physical wear-and-tear each week of getting ready to play at that level and the level he expects himself to play at. So, nothing that he ever did surprised me because you've just seen it time and time again. And he's [not only] one of the best players of all time, but one of the best teammates and one of the best guys to be around and coach."

For all his records and success, Brees only won one Super Bowl during his 15-year tenure. Part of that was due to bad luck (NOLA No-Call, anyone?). Mostly, though, it was because of leaky defenses. Brees drove his team to leads in the final 2 minutes of playoff games in 2011, 2017, and 2018 only to see the defense fail to preserve the leads each time. In the 2010 and 2011 playoffs, Brees led the Saints to scoring outputs of 36 and 32 points against the Seattle Seahawks and San Francisco 49ers, and neither was good enough to produce a win.

In a way, Brees's partnership with Payton might have hurt his status among his peers. Because of Payton's play-calling aptitude, Brees often was labeled a "system quarterback," a tag that hounded him throughout his playing career, from Westlake High School in Austin, Texas, to Purdue to the NFL.

Optics were part of the problem. Brees executed so efficiently, he made the job of playing quarterback look easy. His greatness was more nuanced than that of big-armed peers like Favre, Dan Marino, or Patrick Mahomes. To fully appreciate Brees's greatness required time and a sophisticated football mind. It also required an appreciation for intangible traits like work ethic, leadership, and attention to detail.

"When you watch Aaron Rodgers run around the backfield for 25 seconds and throw a 70-yard pass across his body on the money for a touchdown, there's a wow factor that is easy for the casual fan to appreciate," former Saints right tackle Zach Strief said. "Drew throws 35 passes in a game, and all 35 of them are within two feet of where they were intended to be. You will walk away from that game going, 'Man, that guy is efficient.' But you don't necessarily walk away going, 'That guy is a freak of nature.' Now, in reality, he is absolutely a freak of nature. But the flash is not there for him."

Athletically, Brees was not Lamar Jackson. He might have lacked elite straight-line speed, but the rest of his athletic skills were way above average, even by NFL standards.

One of the most enduring memories of the Saints' 2009 Super

Bowl season was Brees, in helmet and full pads, using his 32-inch vertical leap to dunk the ball over the goalpost while celebrating a touchdown he scored on a quarterback sneak in a comeback win against the Miami Dolphins in Week 6.

"He was a rare athlete," Payton said. "When you look at his foot agility, his release, his accuracy, and the fact he has hands as big as mitts, he's got a skill set that is perfect for the position."

Few quarterbacks were more adept at maneuvering in the chaotic phone booth of an NFL passing pocket. His extraordinary footwork and pocket presence were big reasons why the Saints annually ranked among the least-sacked teams in the league.

The Saints incorporated Brees's athletic skills into their offense. Bootlegs and rollouts, which took advantage of his mobility and uncanny accuracy as a passer on the run, were a staple of the system.

"There's a lot of things to playing quarterback that are not necessarily about being fast or strong," former Saints quarterback coach Joe Lombardi said. "He had an awareness that was uncanny. He had a sixth sense."

Brees's sixth sense was on full display in a 2008 game against the Chargers at Wembley Stadium in London, England. In the fourth quarter, Brees completed a clutch 15-yard pass to tight end Billy Miller to convert a third-and-5 and help the Saints hold off a late rally by the Chargers. On the surface, there was nothing particularly spectacular about the pass—until the coaches watched the video from the end zone and were able to see it from Brees's perspective.

From behind, the field was a maze of crisscrossing chaos, with four Saints receivers running crossing routes at various depths, creating a scissors action for the Chargers secondary. Miller, aligned to the left side of the formation, ran a 12-yard in cut to the right behind the underneath receivers. As Brees reached the top of his three-step drop and climbed the pocket to avoid the pass rush, four Chargers defenders converged in man-to-man coverage downfield, stacked one by one between the hash marks, right where Miller's route was taking him.

"It should have looked like a stop sign to the quarterback," Lombardi said. "It's just a cluster of defenders."

But as Brees cocked his right arm and fired downfield, something magical happened: the Chargers defense parted, each defender vacating the middle of the field to follow his man in coverage. Brees's pass zipped into the void, right into the waiting arms of a cutting Miller at the 30-yard line.

In the film room, the Saints coaches were dumbfounded.

"Who throws that ball?!" longtime Saints offensive coordinator Pete Carmichael asked incredulously while rewinding the video of the play. "There's no way you throw that ball."

Few quarterbacks would have the audacity to even attempt such a pass, much less complete it. The throw never made the *Sports-Center* highlight reel or went viral on the internet. But it remains the stuff of legend around Saints headquarters. The team's offensive coaching staff regularly shows video of the play to new quarterbacks that enter the program. In their minds, it is the quintessential Brees completion, a shining example of his otherworldly anticipation, awareness, and accuracy.

"People can say and think whatever they want," Strief said. "Put that guy [Brees] in any system in the NFL, and he was going to excel. To claim that [Brees] is a product of the system because we threw the ball a lot and he got a lot of yards is preposterous. He was the system. The stuff that we ran was the same stuff that other teams ran. We were not running magical plays. We had a quarterback that on the last step of his drop already knew where the ball needed to go and when, and could put it in a window twice the size of a football. That is the system."

42.
Jim Parker

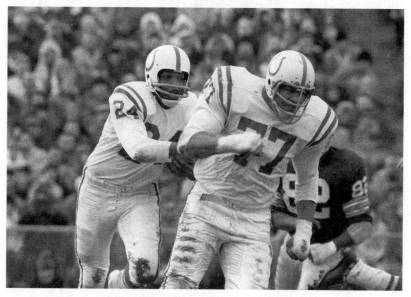

Jim Parker (77) was equally elite at guard and tackle
and played in eight consecutive Pro Bowls.

Position: Offensive Line

Team: Colts (1957–1967)

By Katherine Terrell

Jim Parker's last act with the Baltimore Colts was one that summed up his entire career. Parker, a team player to the end, made a surprise announcement in December of his final season that he was retiring with two regular-season games left to play. The undefeated Colts had a shot at the postseason, and Parker, who felt like he couldn't contribute in the same way, wanted them to have every opportunity to get there.

"The injury to my leg has not progressed in the way it should,"

Parker announced. "By leaving now, the club may be able to add somebody who will help them down the stretch."

He added: "It's like walking away from your family. It's something I feel I have to do, but it hurts. It's the hardest thing I've ever had to do in my life."

It was only a few years after that day that Parker was inducted into the Pro Football Hall of Fame. Yet a player who ranks as one of the NFL's greatest offensive linemen may have never realized his true potential if he had his way coming out of Ohio State.

Parker, who was considered a mammoth of a man at 6-foot-3, 260 pounds when he entered the draft in 1957, would have preferred to play defense. He was a two-way player for the Buckeyes under coach Woody Hayes, playing all along the offensive line and the defensive line, too. He thought he could play linebacker or defensive end in the NFL.

But the Baltimore Colts, who took him with the eighth overall pick, were convinced he had the ability to play offensive tackle.

"Weeb [Ewbank] said he had the three greatest linebackers in the game," Parker, who died in 2005, recalled in a 1977 interview. "And at defensive end, I saw they had Gino Marchetti. So that left me with tackle."

As Parker spent part of that summer preparing to play defense in the Chicago College All-Star Game (a preseason game that pitted college all-stars against the NFL champions), the team said it would try him and the other draft picks on defense "if they lack the speed and blocking ability to work on the attack."

Parker never got to play defense again after that game, and the league was better for it.

Described as "an old softy" by his wife after he got teary upon the retirement of his Colts jersey in September 1968, Parker was a monster on the field to opposing defenders but was jolly and light-hearted off the field. He was the kind of player who understood how to help the team any way he knew how, even if it took him a few years to accept that doing so meant giving up his own wishes about where he might play.

"I'll play anywhere," Parker said shortly after signing his first contract with the Colts in 1957. "Defense is my preference, but as long as I play, I will be happy."

It would be the first of many times in his career that Parker would put aside his own preferences for the sake of his teammates.

What defines Parker aren't his accolades, although there are many: nine first-team All-Pro selections, one second-team All-Pro nod, eight Pro Bowl berths, selections on the NFL's 75th and 100th anniversary teams, and selections into both the Pro Football Hall of Fame and College Football Hall of Fame. That's in addition to All-American honors at Ohio State and the 1956 Outland Trophy, given to the best interior lineman in college.

In 1982, Paul Zimmerman, who would go on to write *The New Thinking Man's Guide to Pro Football*, polled 25 old-timers in the NFL, asking them their thoughts on the greatest lineman of all time. Zimmerman wrote that a number of those polled pointed to Parker, whom Zimmerman referred to as "the best pure pass blocker that ever lived."

Parker's talent was obvious from day one, although he admitted in later years that he had a suitcase packed for 11 years, just in case. Ewbank, then the Colts coach, was singing his praises after just one season.

"He is going to be, if he isn't already, one of the best offensive tackles in the league," Ewbank said in early 1958.

But talent didn't make Parker unique, and it wasn't what endeared him to his coaches. It was his attitude.

At times Parker drove his coaches nuts with his sweet tooth and hatred of weekly weigh-ins that lasted until retirement, but as a player, he had few other vices.

"Physically, he was in a class by himself," Hayes said when presenting Parker at his Pro Football Hall of Fame induction in 1973. "Attitude-wise, he was even greater. You only had to tell him once."

Most players excel at one position, and in some instances a player will change positions late in his career, with tackles sometimes moving inside to guard or cornerbacks switching to safety after experiencing some decline. But Parker, who played only left tackle for his first five seasons, was asked to move to left guard after teammate Palmer Pyle suddenly went down for the year right before a midseason game against the Packers in 1962.

The best tackle the Colts had quickly proved himself to be the team's best guard as well. Parker bounced between guard and tackle for the rest of the season, thoroughly dominating All-Pro defensive tackles including Pro Football Hall of Famer Henry Jordan and College Football Hall of Famer Roger Brown. He so completely controlled Brown that the six-time Pro Bowler pleaded with a reporter to not bring up Parker again.

"Don't mention his name," Brown said in a 1962 interview. "I don't want to meet him no more. One of the toughest in the league? He is the toughest."

Parker earned All-Pro honors at guard in 1962 even though he played in only four games at the spot that season. But that was where he'd stay for the next three seasons for a variety of reasons: incoming rookie Bob Vogel, a fellow Buckeye, was better suited at tackle. The defensive tackles in the conference at the time were particularly good pass rushers. Parker, the best pass blocker on the team, bolstered the inside with his presence.

Parker, who was the biggest guard in the NFL at the time, could do it all. A move to guard wasn't a slight. To him, it was a challenge.

"A guard has to block any man on defense—tackles, ends, linebackers, halfbacks and safetymen," he told the *Baltimore Sun* in 1964. "And there's a lot more running than at tackle."

Parker continued to rack up honors until his final two seasons, when in 1966 he was asked to move spots one more time, this time to right tackle in case rookie first-round pick Sam Ball didn't work out.

Parker showed up at that camp with an aching knee and a weight issue, trying to adjust to a position he admitted felt "awkward" because he had never played it in the NFL.

"I'm a little overweight and I feel weak, but old Jim will be ready, and I can still block," he told the *Baltimore Sun* that July.

And true to form, within weeks, he was back in his element, harassing defensive ends again for the first time in years, much to their disappointment.

"Henry [Jordan] can have him back," Packers All-Pro defensive end Willie Davis told the Associated Press after a 24–3 Packers win on September 10, 1966.

But it had become clear that despite his high standard of play, Parker didn't have many seasons left. He admitted before the 1966 season that he was ready to retire by the next year but would come back if the team wanted him back. He said he wasn't going to stick around if he couldn't live up to his own standards.

"The moment I can't play the kind of football I feel I have played, then I hope I'm in a position to really get out of the game," he said that year. "I would like to walk out of this league like a Gino Marchetti, like a guy on top."

Parker was playing on tired and injured legs during the 1966 season, but he never missed a game. It wasn't until the second game of the 1967 season that a new injury to his knee sent him to the sideline for the first time. He appeared in only one more game that season.

Parker's retirement was a gesture that Colts coach Don Shula proclaimed to be "maybe the most unselfish act in sports history." And when Parker was quickly voted into the Hall of Fame alongside teammate Raymond Berry in 1973, it was no surprise that Hayes spent most of his speech focusing on Parker's attitude.

"He had a rule that when he came through the iron gates of the south end of the stadium to go in to take his shower, he would look at the iron gate and look up to the stadium, and if he didn't feel that he was better than he was the day before he would turn around and go back to the practice field," Hayes said.

"He'd never leave that field unless he felt that he was better than he was the day before. His ability to give himself to the team happened long before he came to the Ohio State University . . . this is the thing to me that is so outstanding with Jim Parker in pro ball. Sure, he was All-Pro for eight years. He played in the Pro Bowl game every year he was in the league. But to me the biggest thing of all, right in the middle of his career when the Baltimore Colts needed a guard because they got a brand-new tackle from Ohio State [Bob Vogel], he was a pretty good tackle but couldn't play guard. So, what did Jim do? He didn't stand around and say that 'I've earned that tackle position—I'm a tackle.'

"He said, 'I'll play where the team needs me.'"

41.
Marshall Faulk

Marshall Faulk was the second NFL player to gain 1,000 yards both rushing and receiving and the first with four consecutive 2,000-yard seasons.

Position: Running Back

Teams: Colts (1994–1998), Rams (1999–2005)

By Jeff Duncan

Marshall Faulk was almost too talented for his own good.

As a senior at George Washington Carver High in New Orleans, he was so proficient on the football field that coach Wayne Reese employed him like a latter-day Taysom Hill. Faulk played cornerback, running back, quarterback, and receiver. He also punted, returned punts and kickoffs, and was the place holder on extra points and field goals. His teammates called him "The 48-Minute Man" because he never came off the field.

Faulk's multidimensionality helped the Rams to respectability on the field. But it undermined his own cause off it. He was left off the *Times-Picayune*'s 1990 All-Metro team as a senior largely because he failed to amass enough statistics in any one area to distinguish himself against the competition. (The oversight was so egregious the paper's sports editor felt compelled to write an impassioned mea culpa to Faulk in 2011.)

College coaches also were unsure about Faulk's best fit as a prospect. They knew he could play. They just weren't sure where. Because of his athleticism and relatively slight 5-10, 180-pound frame, most major schools recruited him to play cornerback. But San Diego State, which had St. Rose, Louisiana, native Curtis Johnson on its staff as lead recruiter, liked him as a running back. So Faulk turned down blue bloods such as LSU, Miami, Nebraska, and Texas A&M to head across the country and join coach Al Luginbill's high-flying offense.

For a teenager from the Desire Housing Complex in New Orleans's impoverished Ninth Ward, it was a bold move. Faulk worked odd jobs to help his mother make ends meet for her six children. He sold popcorn at the Superdome as a teenager to get into Saints home games for free. When he left for San Diego State, it was the first time he'd ever been out of Louisiana or flown on a plane.

"It was easy to underestimate Marshall," said Johnson, who coached the Aztecs' wide receivers at the time. "He was this little, short, dumpy kid with narrow shoulders, coming out of Carver High School, which didn't have a very good team at the time. But when you watched the film, you realized he could play. Marshall was a phenomenal athlete, and he could do everything. And he knew exactly what he wanted to do. He was smart and confident in his abilities."

It didn't take long for Faulk to make an impact at San Diego State. In the second game of his college career, starter T. C. Wright bruised his thigh late in the first quarter against Pacific. The backup—Wayne Pittman—couldn't find his helmet on the sideline. So Faulk, who had fumbled twice in his college debut against Long Beach

State, got the call. He answered by rushing for a then-NCAA-record 386 yards and seven touchdowns on 37 carries.

Faulk's first carry came with less than four minutes left in the first quarter. By the end of the quarter, he had three carries for 12 yards. But he carried 13 times for 117 yards in the second quarter, 11 times for 194 yards in the third, and 10 times for 63 yards in the fourth.

"No one expected something like that," Johnson said. "The rest was history."

Faulk was on everyone's radar. And no one questioned his ability to play running back.

He went on to record one of the most impressive freshman seasons in college football history. He rushed for 1,429 yards and a 7.1-yards-per-carry average, while finishing ninth in the Heisman Trophy race. He rushed for 1,630 yards as a sophomore and finished second in the Heisman race to Miami quarterback Gino Torretta. As a junior, he rushed for 1,530 yards, while adding 47 receptions for 644 yards. The Indianapolis Colts made him the No. 2 pick in the 1994 NFL Draft.

"Marshall was one of the smartest players I've ever coached," said New Orleans Saints coach Sean Payton, who served as Faulk's position coach during his sophomore and junior seasons at SDSU. "And he knew not only offensive football, but also the defensive protections. He knew the quarterback play. He studied it hard."

In the NFL, Faulk's versatility, once a hindrance, became his calling card.

During his 12-year NFL career with the Colts and St. Louis Rams, Faulk redefined the running back position and became the archetype for modern-day backs such as Alvin Kamara and Christian McCaffrey. With his cat-quick elusiveness and sprinter's speed, Faulk routinely made defenders look silly in the open field. Yet, he also had the power and toughness to run between the tackles, as evidenced by his 91 career red zone touchdowns. He caught passes out of the backfield long before it became the norm for NFL backs. And he could pass protect like a sixth lineman.

"I don't think there was anyone better in the all-around game," said longtime NFL personnel executive Gil Brandt. "Marshall is a Hall of Fame running back. But if you had lined him up at wide receiver for his career, he would have caught 1,000 passes. He would have been a Hall of Fame wide receiver."

Faulk was so smart, the Colts considered him a coach on the field. When Indianapolis selected Peyton Manning with the No. 1 overall pick in the 1998 draft, Faulk helped ease the rookie's transition to the NFL by teaching him the playbook.

"Marshall's ability to read defenses was as good as any quarterback," Manning said. "He was a tremendous presence for me, and I always will be grateful to him for helping me that year. I loved watching him play, and there will never be another like him."

Faulk's career went to another level after the Colts traded him to St. Louis in 1999. With the Rams, he joined forces with quarterback Kurt Warner, receivers Isaac Bruce and Torry Holt, and offensive coordinator Mike Martz to form the "Greatest Show on Turf" offense, which took the league by storm in the late 1990s and early 2000s.

The results were incredible: an NFL record three straight seasons with 500-plus points, two Super Bowl appearances in three seasons, and an improbable Super Bowl title in Faulk's first season in St. Louis. Warner and Faulk combined to win the league's MVP award three consecutive years: Warner in 1999 and 2001; Faulk in 2000.

But opponents would tell you that Faulk was the guy they worried about the most.

Before facing the Rams in Super Bowl XXXVI, New England Patriots coach Bill Belichick called Faulk "the hardest player to match up against" in the NFL.

"When I think back to when he was in Indianapolis, they would split him out a lot, and I thought he was better than their other receivers," Belichick said. "For him to be the best wide receiver and the best running back really puts you in a bind defensively."

In an effort to try to combat Faulk, opponents would regularly change their defensive game plans and personnel when they played the Rams.

"Once you found out what the matchups were, you could make an adjustment on the sideline with Marshall and he could take care of that immediately," Martz said. "In fact, he'd come to the sideline and understand it and say, 'Hey, here's what they're doing. How about this?' Pretty unusual."

Warner calls Faulk "the most complete player I've ever been around." Faulk was so smart and so talented that Warner believed he could have played quarterback in the NFL if given the chance.

"He was a highlight waiting to happen," Warner said. "He could do everything. Mentally, he was the sharpest player that I've ever been around."

Faulk will go down in history as one of the most multitalented players in league history. He is the only NFL player with at least 12,000 yards rushing and 6,000 yards receiving. He caught more passes in his career (767) than 20 Hall of Fame wide receivers.

"He could block, he could run inside, he could run outside, and he could catch the football," Hall of Fame coach Tony Dungy said. "He was a versatile, talented player and a very cerebral guy, as well. Marshall did everything. He just was a complete football player."

Faulk retired in 2007 and was a first-ballot inductee to the Hall of Fame in 2011. His career accomplishments speak to his multidimensional game:

- Faulk and Jim Brown are the only backs in NFL history to average more than 5 yards a carry over three consecutive seasons.
- Among backs, Faulk has the most receiving yards (6,875) in NFL history and the second-most receptions (767).
- Faulk, Roger Craig, and Christian McCaffrey are the only backs in NFL history to have 1,000 yards rushing and 1,000 yards receiving in the same season.
- Only four players in NFL history produced more yards from scrimmage than Faulk.

Not bad for a kid from New Orleans's Ninth Ward who couldn't even make the All-Metro team in high school.

"My father told me this: if you are ever traveling on a road and there are no speed bumps, you are headed for a dead end," Faulk said. "I didn't make the All-Metro team, so I went all the way to San Diego State to become the best player in the country and the No. 2 pick in the draft. Life is a challenge. God gave me talent. Football gave me an opportunity. I made the commitment."

40.
Eric Dickerson

Eric Dickerson (29) was the first NFL player to rush
for 1,000 or more yards in seven consecutive seasons.

Position: Running Back

Teams: Rams (1983–1987), Colts (1987–1991), Raiders (1992), Falcons (1993)

By Bob Kravitz

Viola Dickerson was Eric Dickerson's great-great-aunt and adoptive mother, and she was the valedictorian of her high school class in Sealy, Texas. Despite her academic accomplishments, she was like so many Black women in her place and time; she went on to clean houses for White people on the other side of the tracks, never fulfilling her promise, never earning what she believed she was worth.

Eric, her adopted son—his biological mother, Helen Johnson,

had him at 15 and was more of an older sister than a mother—saw all of that and it informed his behavior and his approach to the business of football as his gifts as a running back opened up a whole new world to him.

Eric knew how smart his adoptive mother was. It didn't seem right that she had to work long hours for little pay.

There are two Eric Dickerson stories to be told here.

One focuses on his otherworldly rushing skills, which landed him in the Hall of Fame.

The other is the never-ending contract disputes that marked— some would say sullied—his marvelous career, his tenures with the Rams and Colts ending because of disagreements over money and, in Dickerson's mind, basic fairness.

Dickerson, who declined an opportunity to speak for this story, was cast as a malcontent, an ingrate, and worse. Many of the criticisms of the time had "shut up and run the ball" undertones. The racial component of the commentary was hard to ignore.

Greg Hanlon, who cowrote the book *Watch My Smoke: The Eric Dickerson Story*, said Dickerson was a victim of his time and was, in many ways, ahead of his time.

"You've got to look at it in context: this was the 1980s, an age of exploding sports salaries," Hanlon said. "And when guys asked for more money, especially Black athletes, it was not looked at kindly by the establishment—White sports ownership, White sports management, White sports media. And a largely White fan base."

On the field, Dickerson had few rivals. To start, he looked different; he wore a neck collar, normally reserved for linebackers, which he got from old SMU teammate Craig James. He wore rec specs—he had myopia—because contact lenses kept popping out. In an era when players were wearing as few pads as possible, Dickerson wore the biggest, boxiest pads imaginable, looking like a cross between a hockey goalie and the Michelin Man. And that running style: Has anybody ever had Dickerson's almost-regal gait, his ability to get his pads low through the hole and then explode into space running straight up like an Olympic sprinter? He was a long strider, someone who made the difficult seem perfunctory. He was the personification of athletic grace.

"I blocked for 37 different running backs," said Jackie Slater, the Hall of Fame offensive lineman for the Rams, during his Hall of Fame introduction of Dickerson. "And you know, all these guys had unique talents. They had a gift that kept them in the league. It could have been their vision, it could have been their quickness, their power or their speed. And most of these guys kept their jobs because of one or two of these talents.

"But in my opinion, Eric Dickerson was the original freak in that he possessed all of these, and the greatest of them was his speed. You know, they say speed judges speed better than people who don't have it, and I've found that to be true. We were playing the Tampa Bay Buccaneers in Tampa and I remember we ran the 47-Gap. And I kicked out on a guy and rolled around, and all I could see was two defensive backs with an angle on him. All they had to do was keep running. Close right in on him. But, you know, speed judges speed better than people who don't have it, and they adjusted those angles, and they tried to head him off at the pass. But they couldn't head him off at the pass. Forty-two yards later, he went into the end zone untouched. I'm telling you, the man was great."

The production was undeniable. He set rookie records for most rushing attempts, most rushing yards, and most touchdown runs. His second season, he set the single-season rushing record with 2,105 yards. In fact, Dickerson had more rushing yards than the Rams' quarterback, Jeff Kemp, had passing yards that year. He reached 10,000 rushing yards faster than any other back in history, doing so in 91 games, faster than Jim Brown, Barry Sanders, and Emmitt Smith, among others. Even after a substandard third season in 1985, Dickerson went for 248 yards in a playoff game against the Cowboys. One year later, in 1986, Dickerson rebounded with 1,821 rushing yards.

John Robinson, the longtime USC and Rams coach, desperately wanted Dickerson to join the Trojans back when the running back was considered the top recruit in the country. He went to tiny Sealy, Texas, and tried to work his magic with Eric and his family, but no luck. He ended up at SMU.

"He came out for a visit, but I think L.A. was too big for him at the time," said Robinson, who is now retired and living in Baton Rouge, Louisiana.

"I remember seeing him in high school. He was bigger and faster than everybody and had more moves than anybody. We went after him as aggressively as we possibly could. He was clearly the best player I had seen that year—in many years—and we tried hard. As a senior, shoot, he was around 6-2, 215 pounds. He was in a league by himself."

Four years after that failed recruitment, Dickerson was available to the Rams with the second pick in the 1983 NFL Draft (John Elway went first).

"Took some time, but I finally got him," Robinson said, laughing. "I convinced our ownerships this guy was unique. I'd always wanted to have a good running game, and we already had a good offensive line.

"He could outrun everybody and on third-and-short or by the goal line, he had the ability to get down really low and punch his way in, and nobody could stop it. He had all the ingredients, he really did. He wasn't a good receiver at the beginning, but he worked hard at it and became very good. If you didn't hug him in man-to-man, he was going to catch the ball in front of you and get yards after the catch. He was just a complete back. And he never got hurt, it seemed.

"He'd come off the field, I'd say, 'You OK? You OK?' and he'd just look at me and say, 'Just give me the ball.'

"And we did."

It wasn't just what Dickerson could do, but how he did it. He ran with that unique style.

"He ran upright, almost like he was leaning backwards, but he would get lower when the tackler came; he'd get his pads low and hit you with his pads," Robinson said. "Remember, he always wore all the pads he could find. He could do everything. And the physical power—everybody thought of his speed and acceleration, but power was a big facet of his game."

But there was trouble beneath the surface. Contract discussions, which began all the way back in 1985, had become extremely contentious by 1987. The Rams had enough of the give-and-take and the holdouts, ultimately executing a three-way deal with the Colts to send Dickerson to Indy.

It still rankles Robinson how the Rams let Dickerson get away.

"Oh, I absolutely regret that," he said. "It was a terrible decision on our part. And we had a really outstanding offensive line and the passing game was coming along, so I felt he could really have maximized his ability had he stayed in L.A. It was just really unfortunate we were unable to keep him."

The move put the Colts, relatively new to Indianapolis, having moved in 1984, back on the NFL map. At least for a while.

"I remember the feeling we had in the locker room after we made the trade," said Colts Ring of Fame wide receiver Bill Brooks, who played in Indianapolis from 1986 to 1992. "It was a sign that Jim [Irsay, the owner and then-GM] was committed to putting a winning team together. Bringing Eric in, a big name and a big talent like him, it put us on the map as a franchise and put us in a position to reach the playoffs. Remember, we'd just moved to Indy a few years earlier, so we were in our infancy at that time. I felt like Eric brought big-time football to Indianapolis."

There were some good moments in Indianapolis—a playoff appearance in 1987—and one year later, Indy had a Monday night moment on the national stage, beating the Broncos 55–23 with Dickerson scoring four touchdowns on Halloween night. But Dickerson's production slowly dimmed and the constant demands for better pay became tiresome. Finally, in April 1992, the Colts traded him to the Raiders for fourth- and eighth-round picks.

Hanlon said Dickerson remains sad about the way things went

down in L.A. He loved the city, loved his teammates, and enjoyed playing for a team that was closing in on the two NFC powers of the day, the Niners and Giants.

Indianapolis, not so much.

In the Hanlon book, Dickerson recounts how a high-ranking team official used the N-word in his presence. Once, during contract negotiations, he saw a banner in the Hoosier Dome that showed him as a baby with a 29 jersey, holding fried chicken and a watermelon. His cousin, who lived in Indy at the time, told him to turn on the TV one day, where the news was covering a Ku Klux Klan rally in Market Square, which was being treated like some kind of American Legion group.

The experience of his mother informed his actions throughout his football life. He would not accept a penny less than he felt he was worth. And he was castigated for that.

According to Hanlon, people who consumed the media depiction of Dickerson got a misrepresented version of him.

"He's a very thoughtful, interesting, warm, generous man," he said. "It's a shame much of his career was spent with the press trashing him for daring to stand up for himself.

"But here's the thing: he's not bitter because he thinks he was in the right. He doesn't have any regrets. He doesn't."

39.
Ed Reed

Ed Reed, a former NFL Defensive Player of the Year, led the Ravens in interceptions in seven of eleven season and had 64 in his career.

Position: Safety

Teams: Ravens (2002–2012), Texans (2013), Jets (2013)

By Jeff Duncan

Ed Reed defined the *free* in free safety.

During his 12-year Hall of Fame career, Reed was known as a wandering genius, a master at gridiron subterfuge, routinely freelancing before the snap to confuse the enemy and frustrate opposing quarterbacks. He was rarely where opponents expected him to be. At times, he would line up in spots that even surprised his own teammates and coaches.

It was all by design, part of the chess game Reed orchestrated from the center field position in the dominant Baltimore Ravens defenses in the 2000s.

"You could never be sure where he was going to be, and I say that in a good way," said John Harbaugh, who served as the head coach for five of Reed's 11 seasons in Baltimore. "It wasn't like he was back there guessing and taking chances, because you'd take advantage of that and a pattern would probably occur. But Ed knew what he was doing and why he was doing it."

Wherever Reed lined up, opposing quarterbacks were sure to note it. Locating No. 20, the most dangerous playmaker in the Ravens secondary, was a pre-snap priority. He was the rare defender capable of changing a game with an impact, momentum-turning play. And his infectious swagger and keen instincts emboldened his teammates, inspiring them to another level of execution.

"Ed Reed was one of those guys that you had to know where he was as a quarterback because he was such a ball-hawk safety and had such great fielding instincts," former New Orleans Saints quarterback Drew Brees said. "Balls that you could throw and fit in against everybody else, that just wasn't going to happen against Ed Reed unless he was way out of the picture."

During a behind-the-scenes look at the Patriots years ago, NFL Films cameras captured quarterback Tom Brady and Belichick studying the Ravens defense before a matchup with Baltimore. When Reed's image popped on the video screen, Brady told his coach, "Every time you break the huddle, that's who you're looking at."

In the 2011 AFC Championship Game, network television cameras caught an image of Brady's left wristband with a telling reminder scribbled under the play list: "Find [No.] 20 on every play."

"He's pretty much ingrained permanently in my mind," Brady said later when asked about the message.

There was good reason for Brady's and Brees's obsession.

Reed, along with Paul Krause and Ronnie Lott before him, is considered one of the greatest ball hawks in league history. His rare combination of intellect, athleticism, instincts, and daring helped redefine the safety position. His 64 career interceptions rank seventh in NFL history, and he holds the league record for total interception return yards with 1,590. He also had nine postseason interceptions, tying the NFL record shared by Lott, Bill Simpson, and Charlie Waters.

Reed set an NFL record for the longest interception return for a touchdown with a 106-yard score in 2004 and eclipsed it with a return of 107 yards in 2008.

Reed also blocked four punts in his career, returning an NFL-record three for touchdowns. He was so dominant on special teams that Patriots coach Bill Belichick said he would have never taken him off the punt return/block team if he'd been his coach.

"Shoot, you can kind of go on and on: unbelievable ball skills, unbelievable range, great hands, great range," former NFL quarterback Peyton Manning said of Reed. "You could tell what kind of athlete he was because of what he did once he's got the ball in his hands, returning them for touchdowns. He was such a smart player, too."

A play Reed made against Manning in 2009 was a prime example of Reed's extraordinary moxie. On second-and-10 from the Ravens' 40, he baited Manning into an ill-advised pass to Reggie Wayne, who ran a go route on the weak side of the formation. On the snap of the ball, Reed abandoned his pre-snap alignment on the weak side, intentionally opened his hips, and turned his back to Wayne's side of the field as he retreated in coverage toward the middle of the field. Then, as Manning began to uncork his pass to Wayne, Reed wheeled around with his back to the offense and outsprinted Wayne to the ball for the interception.

Reed knew the entire time where the ball was going. Through his film study, he knew that Manning's primary read on the play was the free safety, so Reed knew he needed to be one step ahead of Manning to fool him. He also knew Manning habitually followed up a pump fake with a pass in the same direction.

"Reed knew that when he went to the middle of the field, Peyton would come back to the X, so he ran to the middle of the field, and without even looking at the quarterback, turned and ran back over to the sideline and intercepted it," Belichick said years later. "Best play I've ever seen a free safety make. One of the greatest plays I have seen in the NFL."

It was not the way the Ravens defense drew it up, but Reed was allowed to improvise because coaches and teammates knew they could trust him to make plays and not compromise the rest of the defense. More often than not, Reed delivered, because the risks he was taking were calculated and informed by hours of film study.

"Ed did some unique things that kind of changed the safety position," former Ravens defensive backs coach Bennie Thompson told the *Baltimore Sun* in 2015. "Ed would play on instinct. He knew the game so well and studied so much film, he knew what the other team was going to do."

Reed led the NFL in interceptions in 2004, 2009, and 2010. His 139 passes defensed ranks second among safeties in NFL history.

"I've seen him pick off a slant on the opposite side of the field when he was playing as a Cover 2 safety and take it to the house," said former Ravens cornerback Lardarius Webb, who teamed with Reed for four seasons in Baltimore. "He'd do things that seemed unorthodox, but he trusted what he studied."

Reed was just as unconventional off the field as he was on it. He listened to old-school R&B, was fond of wearing a fedora, and occasionally dozed off during meetings. At times, he could be prickly and guarded with teammates and reporters who covered the team.

When Jim Leonhard first arrived in Baltimore in 2008, he was taken aback at Reed's seemingly nonchalant attitude toward position meetings. Then he learned about Reed's intense late-night film sessions at home, saw how they translated to the playing field, and never questioned his teammate again.

"He had his process," said Leonhard, who today calls Reed "the smartest football player I've been around."

Reed's knack for playmaking also showed in his penchant for stripping ball carriers of the football. He forced 11 fumbles and recovered 13, returning two for touchdowns.

An amazing seven of Reed's 13 touchdowns were on returns of 30 or more yards. The Ravens were 12-2 in the games in which he scored a touchdown. He remains the only player in NFL history to score return touchdowns via interception, fumble, punt, and blocked punt.

"Football was in my blood," Reed said. "I was born to play football. I studied and prepared so we could be our best. I just wanted to be a great football player for my teammates. My philosophy was simple: I was trying to score when I got the football in my hands."

Reed developed this mindset on the playing fields of his neighborhood in St. Rose, Louisiana, about 30 minutes north of New Orleans. His father, Ed Sr., and older brother Wendell Sanchez introduced Reed to sports at an early age and regularly took him to a nearby park to compete in whatever sport was in season. Reed said he learned his ball-tracking skills as an outfielder in Little League baseball. He adopted his scoring mentality as a youth-league quarterback and standout guard in basketball.

He was a do-it-all performer for the Destrehan High School football team, playing quarterback, running back, defensive back, kick returner, and punter. Fellow St. Rose native Curtis Johnson, a former assistant coach with the New Orleans Saints, said he once saw Reed play fullback, quarterback, and defensive back in the same game.

Johnson recruited Reed to the University of Miami in 1997 because of his all-around athleticism. At the time Reed only ran a 4.6 40-yard dash, which scared off some of the elite programs in the SEC, but he was a standout long jumper and a state finalist in the javelin. He signed a track scholarship with Miami because the probation-idled Hurricanes were only allowed 15 scholarships.

"Ed was a tremendous athlete," Johnson said. "We didn't know what we had when we signed him. He turned out to be our Michael Jordan."

Reed blossomed into an All-American at Miami and helped lead the Hurricanes to the 2001 national title. His 21 career interceptions and 389 interception return yards are still school records there.

The Ravens took him with the No. 24 pick in the 2002 draft, but only after a handful of their preferred targets were off the board. Owner Steve Bisciotti famously wanted to select Florida cornerback Lito Sheppard instead but ultimately yielded to general manager Ozzie Newsome's wishes.

Reed proved to be the best player in the entire draft. In Baltimore, he teamed with defensive stars like Ray Lewis, Terrell Suggs, Haloti Ngata, Jimmy Smith, and Chris McAlister to form one of the most dominant units of the era. During Reed's 11-year tenure, the Ravens won four AFC North titles and the franchise's second Super Bowl, a 34–31 upset of the San Francisco 49ers in New Orleans.

With the Ravens, Reed was selected to nine Pro Bowls and earned All-Pro honors five times. In 2004, he became the first safety in two decades to be named the NFL Defensive Player of the Year. Dick Anderson, Kenny Easley, Bob Sanders, and Troy Polamalu are the only other safeties to win the award. Reed was inducted into the Hall of Fame in 2019.

"Ed Reed is the best safety in the history of the game," former Ravens defensive coordinator Rex Ryan said. "And I don't think it's close."

38.
Randy Moss

Randy Moss set a single-season NFL record with 23 TD receptions in 2007 and was named to the All-Decade team for the 2000s.

Position: Wide Receiver
Teams: Vikings (1998–2004), Raiders (2005–2006), Patriots (2007–2010), Vikings (2010), Titans (2010), 49ers (2012)

By Mike Sando

Randy Moss's first NFL position coach, Hubbard "Axe" Alexander, won two national championships at the University of Miami and three Super Bowls with the Dallas Cowboys before the Minnesota Vikings hired him as part of Dennis Green's staff in 1998. Alexander, then nearly 60 years old and a 35-year coaching veteran, was delivering a scouting report on the upcoming opponent when a 21-year-old rookie from Marshall University moved to adjourn the meeting.

"I just remember Randy, he said, 'Axe, sit your ass down. It don't matter what coverage they got, it don't matter who they got. I'm going to go right by them and we're going to light them up like a tiki torch,'" former Vikings quarterback Brad Johnson said. "Randy was not disrespectful, but it was like, hey, the coaches are putting too much thought into this thing. Just throw it up. For a rookie to speak up like that and back it up . . ."

Moss dominated from the moment he stepped on an NFL practice field, reducing the game's elite to awe while immediately tipping the balance of power from Green Bay to Minnesota in the old NFC Central Division. Defensive backs remain reverent to this day.

LeRoy Butler relished competing against the NFL's great offensive players as an acclaimed safety for the 1990s Packers. With one exception.

"When I played Jerry Rice, I was excited—oh, man, I'm playing the GOAT," Butler said. "Cris Carter, OK, we have to be smart about how we are going to double. Herman Moore, he is going to catch a lot of passes, we gotta get him on the ground because he is so big."

Moss triggered a more visceral reaction.

"Randy Moss, your heart is on an EKG machine and it explodes," Butler said. "Your heart is thinking, 'I'm going to be on *SportsCenter*, he is going to jump over me and catch it and I just got Mossed.'"

A two-time finalist for the Pro Football Hall of Fame, Butler and his Packers were coming off consecutive Super Bowl appearances when Gene Washington, then the NFL's director of football operations, stepped to a microphone at the Theater in Madison Square Garden on April 18, 1998, to make an announcement that would rock the Packers from their perch atop the division.

"The Minnesota Vikings have selected wide receiver, from Marshall University, Randy Moss," Washington announced.

The Vikings changed starting quarterbacks every season from 1998 to 2000 and still led the NFL in points and touchdown passes over that period. They did it with Moss setting receiving records for yards (4,163) and touchdowns (43) over the first three seasons of a career. They did it at the expense of the Packers, who had dominated the division through most of the 1990s.

"Jerry Rice is the GOAT, you can't even argue that in no barbershop," Butler said, "but Randy Moss is the most feared player in NFL history, in my opinion."

Butler's Packers had traded up 10 spots to select a defensive lineman, Vonnie Holliday, two slots before the Vikings took Moss at No. 21.

Moss's talent warranted a much higher selection, but before flourishing at Marshall, he had pled guilty to misdemeanor battery and tested positive for marijuana, leading Notre Dame and Florida State to reject him. The Vikings were going through an ownership transition at the time, which some in the league thought cleared the way for Minnesota's football decision-makers, Green chief among them, to select a player whose off-field résumé scared off some team owners.

"We would all watch like *SportsCenter* in the locker room, and we always saw his film at Marshall," former Vikings running back Robert Smith said. "He was one of those guys that everybody knew, and when he got drafted, we had Cris Carter and we had Jake Reed and I thought, 'This is going to be unfair.'"

Has there ever been another receiver possessing Moss's combination of 6-foot-4 height, 210-pound size, 4.2-second speed, acrobatic jump-ball artistry, fluid movement, elevated football IQ, and ability to catch from basically any platform, sometimes with a single hand, while enduring to play 218 games?

Smith, twice a Pro Bowl choice with the Vikings from 1993 to 2000, qualified for the 1992 U.S. Olympic Trials in the 400 meters. He once ran an anchor leg against Carl Lewis while subbing on a 4x100 relay team at the Mt. SAC Relays. Smith, more than most, knows the difference between football speed and bona fide track credentials. While he contextualized Seattle's DK Metcalf clocking a 10.36 in the 100 by noting that high school students in Texas have run 10 flat, Smith said he would have loved to see Moss run the 200 in an Olympic setting.

"The very first day in camp, my agent called me after the first practice and he said, 'What do you think of Randy Moss?'" Smith recalled. "I said, 'Shit, I've never seen anything like this.' Not just with the speed, but elite athletes and people that move differently. Randy moved so differently than everybody else and he caught the ball so smoothly, I told my agent, 'He's going to be a Hall of Famer if he stays healthy.'"

Moss, a first-ballot Hall of Famer in 2018, ranks fourth in all-time receiving yards and second to Rice in receiving touchdowns. But stats aren't what anyone remembers about him.

"Randy changed how other teams drafted," Johnson said, "and he changed coverages. Some people, like in Cover 2, they started using safeties as the corner guys because they could press, and then they used the corners at safety because they had more speed to catch up to him."

Moss dominated so thoroughly as a rookie, especially against the Packers, that Green Bay selected defensive backs in the first, second, and third rounds of the 1999 draft. It remains the only time in 86 Green Bay drafts that the Packers took defensive backs in Rounds 1, 2, and 3. They could have used a few more.

"It's one of those things that you say to yourself, 'My God, if I had this to do over again, I'd draft him,'" said Ron Wolf, the Packers' GM from 1991 to 2000 and a Hall of Famer. "He was just a sensational football player, especially against us. And that is true, we did take three DBs the next year in the draft—one, two, and three. We had to find somebody to cover that guy or at least eliminate him, and we could never do that."

Moss totaled 30 catches for 753 yards and seven touchdowns in his first six games against the Packers. "He came to the league with talent that we really haven't seen since," former Packers linebacker George Koonce said.

The Mossing of the Packers began with a five-catch, 190-yard, two-touchdown performance in Moss's fifth career game, an epic 37–24 Vikings victory in a Monday night rainstorm at Lambeau Field. The victory ended the Packers' 25-game home winning streak, which was two short of the regular-season league record for consecutive home victories set by the 1971 to 1974 Miami Dolphins.

Packers quarterback Brett Favre entered that Monday night matchup as the reigning MVP for three years running. Moss exited the game as the new star of the NFC Central.

"I remember Denny Green and I talked before the game, and the league was going through some goofy stuff just prior to the game, like they were having crummy games," said Mike Holmgren, the Packers' coach from 1991 to 1998. "I said, 'Denny, they really need this Monday night game between you and me. This is going to be pretty good.' And I knew about Randy Moss, but I didn't know that."

Moss finished the game with touchdown receptions of 52 and 44 yards, plus catches for 46 and 41 yards. A holding penalty nullified another 75-yard touchdown grab.

The Packers had not ranked lower than fifth in points allowed over any of the previous four seasons, but their secondary was going through some transition following safety Eugene Robinson's departure. Moss wrecked the transition. The Packers, NFC Central champs from 1995 to 1997, would watch the Vikings win division titles in 1998 and 2000. Moss was a catalyst.

"I remember after that Monday night game, calling the secondary into my office and I said, 'Let's talk about this, how can one guy have one game like that against us?'" Holmgren said.

Johnson, a Vikings quarterback from 1994 to 1998, offered some insights. According to Johnson, a two-time Pro Bowler and a Super Bowl champ with Tampa Bay, Moss told him he would run full speed on deep routes against Darrell Green, Deion Sanders, and Dale Carter, but rarely against lesser corners.

"The rest of them, he said, 'If you will just throw it as far as you can, I'll go get it,'" Johnson said. "That is unique for someone to say that. Usually, they are full tilt all the way. What is really cool about it was, if it was a jump ball, the defender was running at 100 percent at the tail end of the catch, and Randy would be at 80 percent and more under control for the jump ball."

While Holmgren left Moss behind to some extent when he departed Green Bay for Seattle in 1999, Dick Jauron proved less fortunate. Jauron, the Chicago Bears' head coach from 1999 to 2003, was one year into a head-coaching stint with Buffalo in 2007 when Moss signed with the AFC East–rival New England Patriots. As a result of that transaction, Jauron became the opposing head coach for more of Moss's starts (16) than anyone else. His teams held Moss to 13.3 yards per catch, but Moss still had 103 receptions for 1,367 yards and 11 touchdowns in what amounted to a regular season's worth of games against Jauron-coached defenses.

"The biggest issue was him, but he was on really good teams," Jauron said. "You had to pick your death because the odds of you beating them, unless you had equal talent, was not great. Then you put him on the field and if you let him get going, the game got out of hand fast. Real fast."

Moss scored four touchdowns against Jauron's Bills during a 56–10 Patriots victory in 2007, when New England was blowing out just about everyone. Moss had a 204-yard game against Jauron's Bears in 1999. It wasn't always that way. Moss averaged less than 10 yards per catch in four of the matchups.

Moss's Minnesota teams were indeed loaded with talent: Carter, Reed, Smith, Randall Cunningham, Randall McDaniel, Ed McDaniel, and John Randle. The Patriots had Tom Brady, Logan Mankins, Mike Vrabel, Wes Welker, Vince Wilfork, Richard Seymour, Asante Samuel, Ty Warren, Rodney Harrison, and Junior Seau. Even the 2012 San Francisco 49ers were stacked when Moss came out of retirement to finish his career with them.

Not that anyone would ever call Moss the product of any system.

The Vikings would sometimes call two plays in the huddle: go routes on the outside against single-safety looks, some sort of running play against Cover 2. These were only general guidelines when Moss was on the field.

"One time, Randall [Cunningham] was the quarterback and it's

Cover 2 and he goes to the max protection, double go routes and Brad is on the sideline going, 'What's he doing?'" said Norv Turner, who coached Moss with the Oakland Raiders. "And Randy runs right through the Cover 2 coverage, runs by the safety by 5 yards and Randall throws it out of there and Randy tracks it down and it's a touchdown and Brad says, 'That's not really the way we drew it up, but it looked pretty good.'"

Brian Billick, the Vikings' offensive coordinator when Minnesota broke the league's single-season points record while going 15-1 in 1998, once challenged his quarterbacks to overthrow Moss off five-step drops. Johnson said the quarterbacks struggled to do so. Moss ran under just about everything. It's all part of the Moss legend.

"I was watching tape one day and I said, 'Wow, this man just ran through Cover 2,'" former Packers cornerback Tyrone Williams said. "I watched him split a safety and a corner, and the safety was already 20 yards back. There are a few guys who can run like that, but they always had one or two weaknesses. This guy had none."

When players are as talented as Moss, it's easy to overlook aspects of their games that are more difficult to see from the outside. Teammates and opponents describe Moss as exceptionally knowledgeable about the game. Turner described Moss as highly competitive, recalling unusually physical battles in practice with Charles Woodson. Moss also showed toughness by playing through a painful tailbone injury at that time. He could sometimes be challenging to manage, as Minnesota discovered during Moss's short second stint with the Vikings, but concerns raised in the 1998 pre-draft process proved overblown.

"Deion Sanders and Randy Moss are the two best athletes I was ever with," said Johnson, who played with Sanders at Florida State, "but they were extremely smart and extremely competitive as well."

When former teammates gathered in recent years for Moss's annual fishing tournament in Minnesota, some of them told stories about the late receivers coach Moss interrupted as a rookie years ago. They remembered "Axe" Alexander, who died in 2016 at age 77, as one of the funniest coaches they ever encountered.

"Axe was like my dad, straight Mississippi, would talk shit about anybody and tell tales," Smith said. "One time at practice, he told us he saw a 100-foot snake down there in Louisiana—stuff like that."

If Axe were still around, there's no telling what tales he might spin about his legendary former receiving pupil. There isn't much need for embellishment in this case, which is why it didn't take the veteran coach long to realize Moss spoke the truth, even as a rookie.

"Axe would sit down, he wouldn't go over the coverages, he wouldn't go over the guys on the other team," Johnson said. "He said, 'All right, let's ride.' That's the way it was."

37.
Jack Lambert

Jack Lambert was the NFL Defensive Rookie of the Year in 1974 and won Defensive Player of the Year honors two years later.

Position: Linebacker

Team: Steelers (1974–1984)

By Mark Kaboly

They called him "Jack Splat" (it was a nickname Myron Cope gave him that Jack Lambert didn't necessarily like).

"Dracula in Cleats," he was called (there's an entry on Urban Dictionary about it).

The scariest-looking player in NFL history and a downright frightening middle linebacker for the league's most storied defense; the guy who body-slammed Cliff Harris in Super Bowl X because he tapped his kicker on the head after a miss; the guy who once told

Howard Cosell that quarterbacks should wear dresses; the guy who "Mean" Joe Greene once said was so mean he didn't even like himself; and the guy who once sat at his locker wearing a black Stetson and a black T-shirt that said "I'm a Fuckin' Maniac" in orange bubble letters on his back is everything you would think the middle linebacker of the Pittsburgh Steelers should look like.

Toothless. Mustached. Menacing. Before being drafted by the Steelers in 1974, the scouting report on Lambert, a marginal player at Kent State, noted that while he didn't have ideal size for a linebacker, he had a "lust for contact."

Nearly 40 years after Lambert retired because of a toe injury, he's still talked about in the same way—one mean SOB whom Steelers fans adore to this day.

But there was much more to Lambert than being an undersized badass of a middle linebacker. He was the Defensive Rookie of the Year in 1974, an All-Pro eight times, a nine-time Pro Bowl player, the Defensive Player of the Year in 1976, and a Super Bowl winner after the 1974, '75, '78, and '79 seasons.

Lambert was a funny dude (at times), something he showed when he appeared in a series of commercials for Kennywood Park, a Pittsburgh-area amusement park, near the end of his storied 11-year career.

But Lambert was all about ruthless aggression during practices and games and wasn't ever about to apologize for that. Lambert's persona was a perfect fit for the 1970s "Steel Curtain" defense, which featured tough guys like Greene, Jack Ham, Mel Blount, L. C. Greenwood, Dwight White, Donnie Shell, and others.

"Jack was the most intense player I played with on the Steelers," Shell said. "He had the intensity every week. It is very hard to stay at that level for 16 games. At practice and in the game, he always had that intensity. It was just one of his gifts. He was very intimidating and didn't take any stuff from anybody, and he would stand up for our teammates."

Lambert did that plenty of times over his career, but none was more memorable than Super Bowl X. It is a clip that might be most associated with Lambert—and Harris.

The Steelers were trailing the Cowboys and struggling to set a tone in the game. Trailing 10–7 in the third quarter, Roy Gerela missed a 33-yard field goal—his second miss of the game. Harris, who trash-talked Lynn Swann all week about being scared to get hit, turned to Gerela and patted him on the head.

Lambert saw that and tossed Harris to the ground. That's all the Steelers needed. They outscored the Cowboys 14–7 over the final 25 minutes on the strength of two field goals by Gerela. Lambert led everybody with 14 tackles.

"I think in the first half, we were intimidated a little bit," Lambert told reporters after the game. "The Pittsburgh Steelers aren't supposed to be intimidated. We are supposed to be intimidators. I was a little excited, and after the second field goal Gerela missed, Harris slapped him around the head a little bit, and that's just not going to happen when I am out there, as far as I am concerned."

In 1976, Terry Bradshaw was hurt when he was sacked by the Browns' Turkey Jones, and the Steelers started the season 1-4. Mike Kruczek replaced Bradshaw the next week against the Bengals, and Bo Harris clobbered him out of bounds early in the game. Lambert raced down the sideline to smack Harris around because of what he thought was a late hit.

"It wasn't something that I sat down and planned to do," Lambert said to NFL Films. "I didn't think about things out there. I reacted. The Cliff Harris incident in the Super Bowl, I never thought about doing that. I saw him whacking Roy in the helmet, so I turned around and grabbed him and threw him to the ground.

"Sometimes I got the feeling that people thought I was a dirty football player, and that bothered me. I never went out there and tried to hurt anybody or anything like that. I could play anywhere you wanted. We had some guys out there from time to time that wanted to do some things that weren't legal, and I could do that too if I had to, but I'd rather play by the rules."

. . .

Lambert was a bit of an anomaly coming out of Kent State in 1974.

Many scouts and coaches believed he was too small to play linebacker in the NFL. Lambert, whose front teeth were knocked out as a teenager, was a quarterback at Crestwood High School in suburban Cleveland before switching to defensive end in college. Art Rooney Jr., who scouted Lambert and was responsible for drafting him, knew Lambert was small but loved his toughness.

"I scouted him on a day when the fields were muddy," Rooney told ESPN in 2003. "They were practicing on a cinder parking lot. They're out there in their underwear, not going hard, and Lambert launches himself at the running back, takes him down. He's picking cinders out of his arm and I'm thinking, 'If he could just gain a little weight, his toughness will put him over the top.'"

Despite his being 6-foot-4 and 204 pounds, the Steelers selected Lambert in the fourth round. He was called "a fifth linebacker at best" by a local sportswriter after the draft. The Steelers didn't expect much more out of Lambert, either. They picked him to back up Andy Russell and Jack Ham at outside linebacker. When middle linebacker Henry Davis was injured, Lambert was moved inside as a rookie and the rest was history.

Lambert was a defensive captain for eight years. He played in six AFC Championship Games and had 28 interceptions, 1,479 tackles, and 23.5 sacks.

"To look at Lambert, he doesn't look like a middle linebacker," Greene once said. "He didn't pass the eye test. But he could play."

Lambert couldn't use his size or strength to his advantage, so he used his determination and his smarts. His ability to anticipate and his knowledge of the game were greatly underrated and underappreciated.

"He was smart and he was physical," said Keith Butler, the Steelers' former defensive coordinator and a middle linebacker for the Seahawks when Lambert played. "He didn't give a crap about his body. He would throw his body around all over the place. I used to watch him before I got drafted, and as a youngster in college, you always look at guys you think you can emulate when you get in the league, so I watched him a lot. He was a tall and skinny guy just like me. I loved how he played because of him being physical and a smart football player."

Known for his durability, Lambert missed only seven games during his first 10 seasons, but his career came to an end after a serious toe injury in 1984.

"Probably one of the best linebackers in the modern era was Ray Lewis, and what made Ray Lewis so great was his ability to beat the blocker to the point of interaction with the running back," said Craig Wolfley, Lambert's teammate from 1980 to 1984. "That is exactly the way it was with Jack. He could read an offense like you can read a book. He was so intelligent and so quick to react. His ability to see the traffic and not being influenced by shiny things that could persuade you was phenomenal. He was a tough little bump. He earned his respect, that's for sure."

Lambert was inducted into the Pro Football Hall of Fame in 1990. He hasn't been heard from much since as he stays almost completely out of the spotlight. Lambert has spent his retirement years serving as a volunteer deputy wildlife officer, coaching youth baseball and basketball teams, and taking care of his area's local athletic fields. He also played for a men's hockey team for a while.

He never returns for Steelers events, let alone takes part in the yearly Hall of Fame ceremonies. Lambert did make a rare public appearance in 2019 for a memorabilia signing, but that was unusual.

"I never looked at professional football as a popularity contest," Lambert once said. "I looked at it as my job. I don't care if my opponents liked me. I cared if they respected me."

36.
Forrest Gregg

Forrest Gregg set an NFL record with 188 consecutive games played
and was named to the 1960s All-Decade team.

Position: Offensive Tackle

Teams: Packers (1956–1970), Cowboys (1971)

By Jay Morrison

Forrest Gregg played with Barbie dolls, held teacups with his pinky finger extended, and, on most days, would rather knock back a sugary grape soda than a beer.

But for 15 or 16 Sundays out of the year, Gregg was an intense destroyer of souls as one of the greatest offensive tackles to ever play in the NFL.

Even future Hall of Fame defensive ends such as Deacon Jones and Carl Eller were most often sentenced to 60 minutes of frustration and futility whenever they faced the Green Bay Packers, the team Gregg led to five NFL championships, including the first two Super Bowls, while earning seven first-team All-Pro selections and nine Pro Bowl nods.

Gregg, who earned the nickname "Iron Man" for playing in a then-record 188 consecutive games, wasn't even halfway through that run when Packers coach Vince Lombardi bestowed an even more meaningful moniker upon his right tackle, calling him "the finest player I ever coached" in his 1963 biography, *Run to Daylight*.

A Birthright, Texas, native, Alvis Forrest Gregg won a third Super Bowl in 1971—his sixth NFL championship—when he delayed retirement by a year to return to his home state and play for the Cowboys in what would be the final entry on a Pro Football Hall of Fame résumé.

"In his heyday, there wasn't anybody he couldn't block one on one," Packers Hall of Fame center Ken Bowman said. "I'm talking about first-rate defensive ends, guys who are in the Hall of Fame. Forrest didn't have much trouble with any of them."

Bowman said he fondly recalls Gregg taking him under his wing as a rookie in 1964, but his favorite memory came during a game against the Bears, their hated rivals, when he raised his teammate's hackles.

In those days, every defense was a 4-3, so Bowman's job after snapping the ball on pass plays, if the middle linebacker didn't blitz, was to help whichever lineman was having trouble with his assignment to help protect star quarterback Bart Starr.

"On this one play, I backed up, [Dick] Butkus didn't come, and everybody was doing a good job, so I snuck over there to the right to stick Ed O'Bradovich, and I drove him into the ground," Bowman said. "Forrest leaned down and helped O'Bradovich up, and then with that drawn-out Texas dialect of his, he says, 'Bow, me and Mr. O'Bradovich here were getting along just fine, so you don't have to come out here again, OK?' And I rarely ever had to go out and try to help him again."

But as great as Gregg was in pass protection, it was an era dominated by the run. And Gregg was the key blocker for Lombardi's favorite play, the sweep, clearing the way to daylight for tailback Paul Hornung.

Gregg was elected to the NFL's all-decade team of the 1960s, its 75th anniversary team in 1994, and its 100th anniversary team in 2019, with the latter honor coming just a few months after his death at age 85 following a bout with Parkinson's disease.

Upon hearing of Gregg's death, O'Bradovich was one of his former rivals who wrote a letter to Gregg's widow, Barbara, and the couple's children, Forrest Jr. and Karen, to express his condolences and share details of his respect and admiration.

Following his retirement in 1971, Gregg went straight to the sideline, coaching the Chargers offensive line in 1972 and '73. He coached the Browns offensive line in 1974 before taking over as coach from 1975 to 1977.

After one season in the CFL as coach of the Toronto Argonauts, Gregg returned to the NFL as coach of the Bengals from 1980 to 1983, leading them to their first Super Bowl, where they fell 26–21 to the 49ers in January 1982.

In the AFC Championship game that sent the Bengals to Super Bowl XVI, they defeated the Chargers 27–7 in the "Freezer Bowl" with a temperature of minus-9 degrees and a windchill of minus-59 in the second-coldest game (by temperature) in NFL history.

Gregg also was on the field for the coldest, the 1967 Ice Bowl with an air temperature of minus-13 and a windchill of minus-36. With Gregg and the Packers' offensive line plowing the way, Bart Starr scored on a 1-yard sneak with 13 seconds remaining to send Green Bay to Super Bowl II.

But it was the other end of the thermometer and summer days in the blazing Texas sun that truly defined Gregg's commitment to success. In an era when the offseason was a time players typically would take off, Gregg never did.

"He had a work ethic that a lot of guys wished they had," Forrest Jr. said, recalling many summer days as a young boy when he'd climb into his dad's Rambler and head to the Gainesville High School football field.

"He'd put these legs weights on, and he'd get out there. He would pull [block] over and over again," Forrest Jr. continued. "He'd pull right, I swear, 100 times. Then he'd do it left 100 times. And after that, he'd run sprint after sprint after sprint. He worked out religiously. He took it seriously, and he never thought he was too good to work."

At the end of the day, father and son would hit the gas station for an ice-cold grape soda before heading home, where Gregg would make time to play dolls and drink fake tea with Karen.

And on a summer night in Canton, Ohio, in 1977, when he was enshrined in the Pro Football Hall of Fame, the memories of those times—as well as all the moves between Wisconsin falls and winters to Texas spring and summers and all the sacrifices from cross-country relocations as a coach—no doubt were racing through Gregg's mind more than a Deacon Jones head slap or a third-and-goal trap block.

"My dad is an emotional guy, and I knew he was going to cry," Forrest Jr. said. "We all knew he was going to cry. We were sitting there not more than 10 feet away from him, and he's looking at us trying to make the speech, and he couldn't do it. He didn't last more than a minute or two."

Gregg regained his composure after that night and quickly restored his fiery reputation as a taskmaster and disciplinarian, but some cracks in the facade eventually developed.

Gregg's first draft pick as Bengals coach was Hall of Fame tackle Anthony Muñoz. During a pre-draft visit to work out Muñoz at USC, Gregg tried a couple of pass-rush moves against Muñoz, and the big tackle jammed him in the chest and knocked him on his ass.

"He looked at me and said, 'Coach, coach, are you all right?'" Gregg later recounted. "I know that he thought, 'There goes my chance in the draft.' But I just smiled and said, 'I don't need to see any more.'"

The Bengals drafted Muñoz with the No. 3 pick and, under Gregg's tutelage, he went on to play 13 seasons and ended up joining Gregg in Canton in 1998.

"He was strict in the way he ran things, but he had been through all of it and there was credibility in that, and it was an amazing experience to play for a Hall of Fame tackle who won championships and was one of the top players of all time," Muñoz said. "I used to watch his highlights and just be in awe. For an era where you couldn't use your hands like we could, the athleticism and the ability to maintain contact with guys was just phenomenal. You watch his intensity and how he kept after guys by moving his feet because your arms couldn't leave your body."

Early in the 1981 season, a player prank left many Bengals worrying Gregg's arms would indeed leave his body.

"For the rookie skit they were putting on that year, Cris Collinsworth had snuck into Forrest's office and stolen this loud pair of plaid pants he sometimes wore," said Ken Anderson, the quarterback who led the Bengals to the Super Bowl that season and was named the NFL MVP.

When Collinsworth walked into the room wearing Gregg's pants and started impersonating the no-nonsense coach, there was an audible gasp from the veterans.

"But we actually saw Forrest smile," Anderson laughed.

In his first season as Bengals coach, Gregg mandated that all players wear suits for road trips. Pat McInally, the free-spirited, Harvard-educated punter, went to a thrift store and threw together an ensemble that in no way matched. Gregg wasn't pleased and laid into McInally, said former Bengals offensive lineman and current radio analyst Dave Lapham.

"The next road game, McInally arrives in a limousine, dressed in a tuxedo with all the trimmings, top hat, cane," Lapham said. "Forrest cracked up."

Gregg left Cincinnati to replace Starr, his quarterback in Green Bay for each of the five titles they won, as Packers coach from 1984 to 1987. That marked the end of his run in the NFL. He returned to

SMU, his alma mater, in 1989 to lead the Mustangs out of the darkness after the NCAA-imposed death penalty. Gregg later would call that team "the finest bunch of players I was ever around. That was the most enjoyable time of my football life."

His football life, of course, is mostly known for his time with the Packers. But that final season with the Cowboys in 1971 offered a poignant picture of what Gregg was all about as a football player and a man. While he only appeared in six games that season, Gregg played a huge role in bringing the Cowboys locker room together to set the stage for an incredible run of success that would last into the '90s.

Gregg wasn't the first former Packers player Tom Landry had called to bring to Dallas. Herb Adderley, who played nine seasons with Gregg in Green Bay, had joined the Cowboys the year before in 1970.

"From the way the story has been told to me, my dad walked into the locker room and he saw Herb, who was a Black defensive back, and my dad was a southern Texas guy, and he walked up to Herb, and they hugged each other and kissed each other like long-lost brothers," Forrest Jr. said. "A lot of the Cowboys players, and in particular a lot of the Black players, said that had a big effect on them because at that time they didn't really see themselves as a team. They talked about that years later. Roger Staubach mentioned it to me one time on Hall of Fame weekend, how that incident really brought that team together.

"That's one of my favorite stories I've heard about my dad because it showed what was really important to him and to those guys," Forrest Jr. added. "It doesn't matter what you look like or what you believe or where you come from. You're all family and family comes first."

35.
J. J. Watt

A five-time All-Pro, J. J. Watt twice led the NFL in sacks
and once tied for the lead in forced fumbles.

Position: Defensive End

Teams: Texans (2011–2020), Cardinals (2021–2022)

By Aaron Reiss

After another Texans season ended without a playoff berth, the team's coaches turned their attention to the NFL Draft and quickly identified a difference of opinion between themselves and the scouting staff. It pertained to a Wisconsin defensive lineman named J. J. Watt.

According to then–head coach Gary Kubiak, Texans scouts viewed Watt as a late-first-round prospect, maybe even an early second-rounder. But Kubiak's staff thought Watt needed to move up the board. Way up the board.

Watt was a menacing pass rusher and run stuffer, but his 14 pass breakups in two seasons at Wisconsin signaled to then–Texans defensive coordinator Wade Phillips that Watt had an unstoppable motor and a special feel for the game.

The Texans drafted Watt at No. 11, to a chorus of boos from fans at a watch party back in Houston. Longtime *Houston Chronicle* writer John McClain thought the Texans would select edge rusher Aldon Smith out of Missouri—the prospect many fans wanted—but when the 49ers traded up to No. 7 to select him, Houston had to pivot to Watt. Luckily for the Texans, they only felt better about their pick the next day.

As the Texans brass assembled inside their war room to prepare for the subsequent rounds of the draft, Watt, who had just arrived in Houston, stopped in to greet everyone. When the Watt family exited the room a few minutes later, the defensive end's father lagged behind to thank the group "for seeing in my son what I've seen in him his whole life."

"I'll never forget that," Kubiak said in a 2021 interview. "When his dad left, I was like, 'Holy shit, we got a good one here.'"

What Watt's father realized, and what Kubiak would come to understand, is that Watt's penchant for overachieving wouldn't stop in the NFL. It's part of why Watt ranks so high on this list 12 years into a career that has included five All-Pro seasons, three Defensive Player of the Year awards, and equally impressive charitable accomplishments.

Watt's motto—Dream Big, Work Hard—has been his brand since before he was a brand. Once a scholarship tight end at Central Michigan, Watt walked on at Wisconsin and worked as a maintenance man at the school's Camp Randall Stadium before ever playing a down as a Badger. He daydreamed about future football success during his lunch breaks, and his supervisors for that gig still laugh recalling Watt slapping a paintbrush out of a slacking coworker's hand.

"He's got great ability, but a lot of his greatness came from his work ethic," said Phillips, who has worked with plenty of legends. "That's how most of the great ones I had were."

The gift for batting down passes that attracted Phillips to Watt ultimately changed the way Kubiak coached. As an offensive mind, Kubiak used to not like when defenders would disrupt practices with such plays, but Watt's first NFL position coach, Bill Kollar, told Kubiak that if he didn't let Watt get his hands on balls, then Watt wouldn't do it in a game. Kubiak listened, and it's a good thing he did, because late in Watt's rookie year in 2011, he got his mitts on the football in what was then the biggest game in franchise history.

Near the end of the first half of the Texans' first playoff game, a wild-card matchup against the Cincinnati Bengals, Watt snagged a pass out of the air for a pick-six that gave Houston a halftime lead and helped secure the win. The play remains one of the most iconic in the Texans' mostly lackluster history, and it represented a turning point in Watt's journey to becoming the most dominant defensive player in the NFL.

"He came into that offseason very confident and never looked back," former Texans edge rusher Connor Barwin said.

Over the next four seasons, Watt made four All-Pro teams and won his three Defensive Player of the Year awards. He ranked first in sacks, QB hits, and tackles for loss, all by a wide margin. He also broke up 41 passes, 20 more than the next-closest defensive lineman.

"He just frustrated offensive linemen," Barwin said. "They had no idea where he was going to go ever because he was so unpredictable. That's what made J.J. such a challenge. Both Aaron Donald and J.J., you prepare for them the same way. They're both game-wreckers on every single snap."

Former All-Pro Texans receiver Andre Johnson was still elite when Watt arrived in Houston, but the defensive end quickly became the new face of the franchise, thanks as much to his skill as his willingness to engage with fans. He spent a Christmas visiting a children's hospital without a media cadre, posed for a pregnancy announcement for a couple he never met, and used a Ring Pop to propose to a 6-year-old girl who went viral for crying that she'd never get to marry the Texans superstar.

When Hurricane Harvey devastated Houston in August 2017, Watt used his platform to raise more than $41.6 million in recovery aid, the biggest crowdsourced fundraiser in history. Details of where the money went remained pinned to the top of Watt's Twitter account for years.

"I'd put him in the Hall of Fame as a person for all the things he's done in Houston," said Phillips, who has spent much of his life in the city. "He's made it his home. He's an honorary Texan, as far as I'm concerned."

As Watt emerged as the NFL's most feared defender, the Texans graduated from an unaccomplished expansion franchise to a team that more consistently competed for a spot in the postseason. After the team's first nine seasons all ended in Week 17, three of Watt's first five years in Houston included a playoff berth—two under Kubiak, and one under coach Bill O'Brien.

"You have to have star players," Phillips said. "You can be a good coach, but you have to have star players that can make a difference, and he's certainly a difference-maker."

But even Watt could only make so much of an impact. In 10 years in Houston, he never made it past the divisional round. The Texans spent much of Watt's prime employing a rotating cast of subpar quarterbacks, and Watt suffered back, leg, and pectoral injuries that limited him to eight or fewer games in three of the past five seasons. That made Watt playing in all 16 games in 2020, his final year in Houston, bittersweet. He was healthy, and the Texans had one of the league's best quarterbacks in Deshaun Watson, but poor roster construction under O'Brien made them one of the NFL's worst teams.

During one of many post-loss rants in the Texans' 4-12 season, Watt said he felt the worst for disappointed fans.

"That sucks as a player, to know we're not giving them what they deserve," he said.

After that season, Watt asked for his release and signed with the Arizona Cardinals. On his way out of town, Watt sent signed No. 99 Texans jerseys to many people, from reporters and radio personalities to former coaches, including the now-retired Kubiak, who believed his former star defensive end still had "plenty of good football left in him."

But as was so often the case in Watt's career, individual accomplishments did not translate to team success. In 2021, Watt returned from a shoulder injury to play in the Cardinals' first playoff game in six seasons, but they were blown out in the wild-card round. In 2022, even at age 33, Watt was Arizona's top pass rusher, tallying 12.5 sacks and 25 QB hits. But the Cardinals failed to sniff the playoff picture.

Rather than join a different team in the offseason and continue to chase a Super Bowl, Watt, a new father, opted to retire at the end of the 2022 season. "I know I still can [play]," Watt said after he recorded two sacks against the 49ers in the final game of his career, "I'm just choosing not to."

After all, Watt's 12 years in the NFL showed not just how much he can accomplish on the field, but off it. At 33 years old and with career earnings north of $120 million, Watt can pursue whatever other passions he has.

As Kubiak learned from the defensive end's father in the Texans' war room many years ago, it's best never to underestimate what J. J. Watt can do.

34.
Gino Marchetti

Gino Marchetti (89) was a highly effective defensive end
who was elected to eleven consecutive Pro Bowls.

Position: Defensive End
Teams: Texans (1952), Bears (1953–1966)

By David Lombardi

Keith Carter has precious memories of Gino Marchetti, one
of the most dominant defensive linemen of all time and—to
many—the epitome of the Greatest Generation. Marchetti fought in
World War II, made a stand for racial equality more than a decade
before the civil rights movement, and even became a successful
restaurateur in the decades after his powerful football career.

Carter was an NFL offensive line coach with the Tennessee Titans, and Marchetti—a Pro Football Hall of Famer—was his grand-father.

"I can remember being a kid, and the guy would take me to my doctor's appointment and then buy me a Happy Meal on my way back to school," Carter said. "He would do that, and he'd let me sit in his lap and drive. He came to every one of my games. He was such a crucial part of my life. I was the luckiest guy alive to have him in my life."

When Marchetti died at age 93 in 2019, the legacy he left behind was certainly larger than life.

Marchetti was born to Italian immigrants in West Virginia, where his father was a coal miner. He moved to Antioch, a town outside of San Francisco, as a youngster. He forged documents so that he could join the U.S. Army as a 17-year-old in World War II, where he fought as a machine gunner in the Battle of the Bulge—which saw nearly 90,000 American casualties.

That all happened *before* Marchetti enrolled at the University of San Francisco, where he captained the Dons' 1951 football team that finished 9-0 but ultimately refused an invitation to that season's Orange Bowl because it came on the condition that the team's two Black stars—future Pro Football Hall of Famer Ollie Matson and Burl Toler—could not play.

Marchetti began his NFL career in 1952 with the New York Yanks. They immediately became the Dallas Texans, who moved and turned into the Baltimore Colts in 1953. Marchetti played for Baltimore until 1966, becoming an 11-time Pro Bowler and 10-time All-Pro, including nine first-team selections.

Though the NFL didn't track sacks as an official stat until 1982, recent historical tabulation work by Pro Football Reference has unofficially made totals since 1960 available. The new data says Marchetti, who was 33 in 1960 with five full seasons still ahead of him, racked up 56 more sacks from that point until his retirement.

If sack numbers from Marchetti's first eight seasons in the 1950s—when he was in his actual prime—ever become available, they'd likely dwarf multiple official NFL records.

According to the *Washington Post*, Baltimore's coaching staff once counted 43 sacks for Marchetti over just one 12-game season (Michael Strahan holds the official NFL single-season sack record with 22½ in a 16-game season). And that, of course, happened during a much less pass-happy era of football history.

"I've been asked the most sacks I've had in one game," Marchetti said in a 2010 NFL Films documentary. "I know I had nine. It's a great feeling, because it was a great challenge to me, to feel like, 'Man, I got him. I got him.'"

That same clip featured a story shared by former NFL general manager Ernie Accorsi. It came from Marchetti's prime, when he terrorized the 49ers at San Francisco's Kezar Stadium—which also happened to have been his home field during college in San Francisco.

Marchetti squared off that day against fellow future Hall of Famer Bob St. Clair, a 49ers offensive tackle who had been his college teammate and co-captain at USF.

After the game, St. Clair sprinted across Kezar's field to find Marchetti.

"Bob St. Clair came up to him, put his hand on his shoulder, and said, 'I just want to say I touched you once today,'" Accorsi said.

That moment of respect encapsulated Marchetti's devastatingly elusive speed rush, which he actually tailored during a one-year position switch to left tackle at the beginning of his career. That's when Marchetti learned the offensive line's tricks of the trade, knowledge he'd later leverage to deliver those countless sacks from the defensive edge.

Carter, Marchetti's grandson, was born in 1982. Though that was nearly 16 years after Marchetti played his final down for the Colts, Carter remembers how Marchetti ported his attention to detail into the realm of supporting his grandson.

"He'd be at my high school football games and he'd refuse to sit in the stands, just so he could be by the fence," said Carter, who went on to play defensive end and tight end at UCLA before starting his coaching career. "He wanted to hear the sound of the game more than be up in the bleachers and watch it.

"I would always study the guy I was going against and find his move first depending on what movement and twitch gave his move away. [Marchetti] was all about speed off the ball and trying to find whatever visual cue he could get from those guys to let him know it's time to rock and roll."

During his NFL career, the 6-foot-4 Marchetti towered over most of his opponents. Colliding with Marchetti, former Detroit Lions quarterback Bobby Layne once told the *Los Angeles Times*, was "like running into a tree trunk in the dark."

Since Carter never saw his grandfather play in person, he instead learned to cherish the gentle giant that Marchetti was off the field.

"He's considered larger than life, but that's hard for me to imagine, because he was so modest and humble," Carter said. "He drove the same car. He had a Ford Bronco up until I was in junior high. It had 280,000 miles on it. He refused to give it up. He had a Ford Explorer that he took to the used car dealership, and they gave him a great deal because its gold, orange color was so bad.

"He did not live in the limelight or the spotlight whatsoever. To me, he was larger than life just as my grandfather."

Marchetti worked offseason jobs during his career, just like most players of his time. He even worked at a Baltimore iron mill. Marchetti ventured into the restaurant industry late in his career, opening a successful chain called Gino's Hamburgers that grew to more than 300 locations. Even as Marchetti approached his 90s, he stayed active in the business world, working as a consultant to help launch a new group of restaurants.

"He didn't want to be in a suit and tie all day," Carter said. "He wanted to go work in the kitchen and get a feel for what was going on in the company at ground level. That's just the type of worker he was. Here he is, a part-owner of Gino's franchise, and it wouldn't be uncommon for him to be in there cooking the burgers, getting kitchens organized, and getting the food consistent.

"He did everything on the ground floor. He was never above anybody or anything. No job was ever too small."

That attitude was certainly apparent in two of Marchetti's most iconic moments as a football player. Both, like the fervor he showed when enlisting as a 17-year-old to serve his country in World War II, illustrated how Marchetti naturally prioritized teammates over self.

Stakes were astronomical when the 1951 USF football team faced that decision regarding its Orange Bowl bid. Accepting the invitation, besides giving the team a chance to complete a 10-0 season with national-level glory, would mean a financial windfall for a cash-strapped USF program that was struggling to remain operational.

But no matter the cost, Marchetti and the rest of the Dons were absolutely unwilling to leave two of their teammates behind.

"For him, it was no big deal," Carter said. "We're all sitting here looking at it and saying, 'Man, that was such a strong powerful moment of how sports and camaraderie can bring people together from different backgrounds.' To him, that was a no-shit moment. It wasn't a hard decision. The coach came in and said, 'What do you want to do?'

"And he said that, 'We all together at the same time unanimously said, *We ain't goin'! If they can't go, we're not going!*' And that was it. That's just how he rolled."

Two days later, USF's football program folded. That undefeated 1951 team starring Marchetti, Matson, and St. Clair remains the Dons' last hurrah. USF would later return as a Division II team, but the program folded again for good in 1982.

Seven years after the 1951 season, Marchetti played in the 1958 NFL Championship Game, which became widely known as the greatest game ever played. Marchetti's Colts beat the New York Giants 23–17 at Yankee Stadium in the first NFL playoff battle decided by sudden-death overtime.

Baltimore would've likely lost in regulation had Marchetti not stopped star New York running back Frank Gifford short of a first down with less than three minutes remaining. But in the pile, the full weight of teammate Gene "Big Daddy" Lipscomb crushed Marchetti. A stretcher took Marchetti, who'd suffered a broken ankle, to the sideline.

Though he was in agony, Marchetti refused to immediately be taken to the locker room. Propped up on the stretcher, he watched his Colts drive for the game-tying field goal that forced overtime.

"Him not wanting to leave the field until the game was finished, him and his teammates refusing to go to the bowl game because the whole team wasn't invited, it speaks volumes—especially to the period of time," Carter said. "It just makes me proud. He was the lifeblood of the team.

"Here's the ironic thing: He was a great leader who never wanted to be a leader. I try to find ways to be a good leader, but he was a good leader without trying. Sometimes, less is more. He just led by example and people followed."

33.
Bronko Nagurski

Bronko Nagurski (right) was one of the most powerful, versatile, and effective players in NFL history.

Position: Fullback
Team: Bears (1930–1937, 1943)

By Dan Pompei

With most heroes, there are legends, and then there are realities.

With Bronko Nagurski, there are legends. Only legends.

If Homer, Vince McMahon, and Stan Lee could have collaborated to create a hero, they would have come up with the Bronk. The story would have included passages about a young man lifting a plow overhead, a head cracking a brick wall, a horse being knocked on its back, and a ring that could have been used as a bracelet.

It would have told of modest beginnings.

Nagurski grew up in International Falls, Minnesota, one of four children of Polish-Ukrainian immigrants. His given name was Bronislau, but a teacher who couldn't pronounce it called him Bronko instead, as if she knew what he would become.

Nagurski learned how to work from his father, Mike, who ran a 240-acre farm and sawmill, and later a corner grocery store. His son helped by chopping wood, pulling wagons, pushing plows, and delivering groceries. He ran two miles back and forth to school—of course he did—often in freezing or below-zero temperatures.

From his mother, Michelina, the Bronk learned not to give an inch. According to *Monster of the Midway*, she often told him in Ukrainian: *Ty moz'esz robyty tse.* "You can make it." Throughout his football career, when facing his most daunting challenges, Nagurski repeated the phrase silently to himself.

Opportunity found him when he was working on the family farm as a high school student.

"I was driving past a farm when I noticed this big, strong boy plowing a field—without a horse," Minnesota football coach Clarence "Doc" Spears said. "I stopped to ask directions. The boy pointed—with the plow. That's how I happened to discover Bronko."

Spears told the story many times over the years, but Nagurski never did. When he was pointedly questioned about it later in his life, Nagurski said, "It wasn't a very big plow."

At Minnesota, Nagurski was a force from his first practice, when he defeated two all–Big Ten linemen in a nutcracker drill. By the time Nagurski was a senior, he had two spots on the All-America team of famed sportswriter Grantland Rice—at fullback and defensive tackle.

Nagurski continued playing fullback and tackle after signing with the Chicago Bears in 1930, and he continued dominating on both sides of the ball. They say he knocked out more than a dozen opponents in his rookie season alone.

Nagurski was different from almost everyone he played with or against. Sid Luckman, once his quarterback on the Bears, said his rival Sammy Baugh told him Nagurski was the most powerful human being he ever encountered.

He was 6-foot-2, 235 pounds in an era when the average lineman weighed 210. His neck, size 22, had the girth of some of the logs he used to chop. When the Pro Football Hall of Fame presented him with a ring upon his induction in their charter class of 1963, it was a size 19.5—still the largest ring ever made for a Hall of Famer.

Hall of Famer John "Blood" McNally told sportswriter Ray Didinger about Nagurski trampling two Steelers on his way to the end zone in 1937. One of them was knocked out for 10 minutes, the other suffered a broken shoulder. "It was as if they were run over by a locomotive," McNally said.

There can be no mention of Nagurski without the story that would make today's concussion spotters cringe. In a 1930 game against the Packers in front of a crowd at Wrigley Field that included nearly every Chicagoan of status, including the notorious Al Capone, Nagurski was given a handoff in the final minutes on the 2-yard line. He rammed through two Packers with his head down. His momentum carried him through the end zone and his leather helmet crashed into the outfield wall, which was about one step past the end line. When Bears trainer Andy Lotshow asked if he was OK, Nagurski replied, "Who the heck was that last guy?"

Nagurski apparently walked away with less damage than "that last guy." Wrote George Halas in his autobiography *Halas by Halas*, "Some people will today show you a crack in the south wall at Wrigley Field they say was made by his helmeted head."

It was not Nagurski's only collision out of the boundary of play. The year after he cracked Wrigley's wall, he had a sideline crash with a mounted policeman who was there to prevent fans from coming on the field. Nagurski sent both the horse and policeman airborne. He helped the cop to his feet, brushed the grass off his uniform, and said, "I'm sorry, Officer. I didn't mean to hit you. But you really should get out of my way when I'm running." He then turned his attention to the horse, patting his nose. "I'm sorry, horse," he said.

There were no recorded apologies to the cop car he barreled

into on the sideline during another game, even though Nagurski knocked off the front fender.

Nagurski won most of the collisions he was involved in, but his game was about more than power. In his early years, he was the second-fastest player on the Bears after Red Grange. Nagurski was timed at 10.2 in the 100-yard dash at Minnesota.

Some think he was a better defensive player than an offensive player. On offense, he could also throw the ball and was one of the premier blockers of all time.

In 1934, Beattie Feathers became the first player to rush for 1,000 yards in NFL history. "I had the greatest blocker who ever lived," Feathers said, referring to Nagurski. Feathers averaged 8.4 yards per carry, still an NFL record for a running back. Wrote Stanley Frank in *Collier's* magazine, "Every inch was made behind Nagurski's interference."

In the 1932 title game against Portsmouth that had to be played in Chicago Stadium because of a blizzard, Nagurski threw the key touchdown pass to Grange. The following year, in the first official championship game, he threw for two touchdowns against the Giants, including the game winner.

In addition to playing football on both sides of the ball, Nagurski was a pro wrestler for a portion of his career, putting unthinkable stress on his body. This is what a 21-day stretch during 1937 looked like for Nagurski, according to the book *The Chicago Bears*, by Howard Roberts.

- Sunday, Sept. 19—played with Bears in Green Bay.
- Tuesday, Sept. 21—played an exhibition with Bears in Duluth, Minn.
- Wednesday, Sept. 22—wrestled in Portland, Ore.
- Thursday, Sept. 23—wrestled in Vancouver, B.C.
- Friday, Sept. 24—wrestled in Seattle.
- Monday, Sept. 27—wrestled in Phoenix.
- Wednesday, Sept. 29—wrestled in Los Angeles.
- Thursday, Sept. 30—wrestled in Oakland, Calif.

- Friday, Oct. 1—wrestled in Salt Lake City.
- Monday, Oct. 4—played with Bears in Pittsburgh.
- Wednesday, Oct. 6—played an exhibition with Bears in Erie, Pa.
- Friday, Oct. 8—wrestled in Philadelphia.
- Sunday, Oct. 10—played with Bears in Cleveland.

When Nagurski signed with the Bears as a rookie in the days before the draft, he agreed to a one-year contract worth $5,000. It was the richest contract in NFL history at the time. It also was the high point of his NFL earnings. His salary was cut every year because he played during the Great Depression. His salary was down to $3,700 by 1932. And he often didn't even collect his money on time, as Halas didn't have the cash to pay his players.

In 1938, Nagurski demanded $6,500. Halas countered with an offer of $6,000. Nagurski was confident he could make more if he were wrestling full-time, so he retired from football at 31 at the peak of his abilities.

In 1943, the Bears, depleted by World War II, made a pitch for him to return. After some hesitation, Nagurski agreed to play for $5,000 with the stipulation he had to be paid up front.

Nagurski was available only because he had been rejected medically by Army physicians after trying to enlist for the war the day after the Pearl Harbor bombing. A doctor told him there were six reasons he failed his physical.

He was healthy enough to play in the NFL, however, and at the age of 35, Nagurski made a comeback with the understanding he would not be used as a fullback because he couldn't run like he once did. Nagurski had to wear a metal brace on his back because he had broken two vertebrae earlier in his career. He also had a degenerative hip condition.

It was evident quickly he still had his power, however. In training camp, he broke several teammates' noses and another's clavicle.

The Bears' roster had changed considerably, as only six of his previous teammates remained and many of his new ones were more than a decade younger. Opponents called him an old man, and teammates treated him with reverence. At practice one day, he told a group of Bears players, "If one more of you guys calls me Mr. Nagurski, I'm going to lay you out."

Nagurski went through most of the season playing tackle. In the final game of the regular season at Wrigley, the Bears needed to beat the Cardinals to win the Western Division title. They trailed 24–14 entering the fourth quarter when Nagurski lined up at fullback for the first time since 1937 to the chants of "Bronko! Bronko! Bronko!"

Snow began to fall.

In the final quarter, he carried 16 times for 84 yards and a touchdown as the Bears won 35–24. Fans stormed the field afterward and carried him off on their shoulders.

Nagurski played fullback again in the championship game and scored a touchdown as the Bears beat Washington 41–21.

"Bronko is the one man that I never wanted to see again," said Baugh, who opposed him as both a quarterback and defensive back. "I still have nightmares about that big monster."

Nagurski retired again after the game and returned to wrestling. He became a heavyweight champion before stepping away from his second sport in 1960 at 52. He was inducted into the National Wrestling Hall of Fame in 2009 with a class that included Nick Bockwinkel and Ricky Steamboat. It was his fourth Hall of Fame, as he previously had been inducted into the Pro Football Hall of Fame, the College Football Hall of Fame, and the Minnesota Sports Hall of Fame.

Nagurski never stopped coming home to International Falls. He and his childhood sweetheart, Eileen, raised six kids there, and when he was done with wrestling, he bought a gas station at 217 Third Avenue. But he wasn't just the administrator at Nagurski Pure Oil Service Station. Wearing overalls and flannel shirts, the Bronk pumped the gas. The story goes that he screwed the gas caps on so tightly that people had to return to him to have them taken off.

Nagurski turned down most requests to make public appearances in the years leading up to his death in 1990. But he was convinced to toss the coin for the Super Bowl in 1984. By the way he moved at that time, it was clear his opponents weren't the only ones who felt the impact of all those collisions.

Those collisions defined him until the end.

"How good was he?" Grange said in a WGN radio interview in 1978. "On defense, he was equal to Dick Butkus in Butkus's prime. On offense, he was faster and equal to Larry Csonka. Put the two together and you got Nagurski."

32.
Alan Page

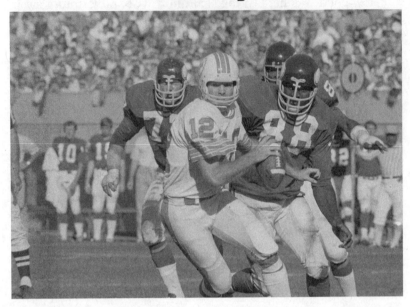

In 1971 Alan Page (88) became the first defensive player to be named NFL MVP.

Position: Defensive Tackle

Teams: Vikings (1967–1978), Bears (1978–1981)

By Stephen Holder

There were moments in the careers of players like Warren Sapp and Aaron Donald, two of the most dominant defensive tackles in history, where we let out a collective gasp and realized they were doing things we've perhaps never seen.

Except, we have. Because Alan Page exists.

The things that the likes of Sapp and Donald have done, the feats that moved us to marvel at their pass-rush prowess, those are plays Page made with regularity.

For 15 seasons with the Vikings and Bears, Page was an unblockable, gap-destroying, game-wrecking force who did nothing less than redefine his position. In 1971, he became the first defensive player to win the Associated Press Most Valuable Player award. Just one other defensive player, Lawrence Taylor in 1986, has done it. He anchored one of the greatest defensive lines ever, the Vikings' "Purple People Eaters," along with fellow Hall of Famer Carl Eller and multi-time Pro Bowlers Jim Marshall and Gary Larsen.

There is little doubt that Page himself is well aware of these facts. But try getting him to address his greatness out loud. He has always preferred to leave that task to others—and they often oblige.

Take it from Packers Hall of Fame offensive lineman Jerry Kramer, who after his retirement in 1968 briefly considered a return to the game.

Very briefly.

"Any time I consider coming out of retirement and then I think of Alan Page," Kramer once said via NFL Network, "it makes retirement a little bit easier."

Page, who retired after the 1981 season at age 36, played in an era before sacks were an official statistic. But historians like John Turney have intervened, compiling the totals of the top sack artists prior to 1982.

What Turney found was that no defensive tackle has produced more sacks than Page (148.5). The research also determined Page had eight seasons with 10 or more sacks, including a career-high 18 in 1976.

Page's response? Meh.

Surprised? Don't be. After losing the Super Bowl in 1977, Page told a reporter, "How on earth can otherwise sensible people get so involved in a football game? You could measure the lasting impact on the lives of the people who played in it and those who watch it at just about zero."

Page had such a humble view of himself while playing that he rarely signed autographs—not because he was arrogant but because he thought the idea of someone admiring him on the basis of his athletic talents was silly.

He is, however, exceedingly proud of his post-football pursuits.

Page, who famously attended law school while playing in the NFL, went on to a law career and served 22 years on the Minnesota Supreme Court. He also has been an unwavering champion of education; the Page Educational Foundation, created in 1988, has awarded more than $16 million in grants to more than 7,700 Page Scholars.

If Page had been forced to choose between being an NFL star of historic import or the arbiter of justice and promoter of education he eventually became, there seems to be little doubt which path he would have followed.

When he was elected to the Pro Football Hall of Fame in 1988, Page uttered more than 1,600 words in his speech. Precious few had anything to do with football.

"Football was very good to me, and my good fortune has continued in my chosen career as a lawyer," he said in his speech. "But in that world where I now work, professional accomplishment is measured on a far different scale over a much longer period of time. So, I find it a bit strange to again be the object of this much attention for what I accomplished many years ago, in a very narrow field of endeavor called football."

He went on to speak in depth about his post-football passions and what drives his important work.

"I don't know when children stop dreaming," he said. "But I do know when hope starts leaking away, because I've seen it happen. Over the past 10 years, I've spent a lot of time speaking with school kids of all ages. And I've seen the cloud of resignation move across their eyes as they travel through school, without making progress. They know they are slipping through the net into the huge underclass that our society seems willing to tolerate."

He continued, "We are at a point in our history where Black teenagers constitute the most unemployed and undervalued people in our society. And instead of making a real investment in education that could pay itself back many times, our society has chosen to pay the price three times: once when we let kids slip through the educational system; twice, when they drop out to a street life of poverty, dependence, and maybe even crime; and a third time when we warehouse those who have crossed over the line and have gotten caught."

You could know nothing of Page's football success and still come away in awe of his life's work. He tends to have that effect on people. People like, say, President Bill Clinton, who knew Page only for his on-field talents before meeting him years later and becoming a close friend. Clinton wrote the foreword of Page's biography, *All Rise: The Remarkable Journey of Alan Page*, noting that he was struck by the contrast between the man he watched terrorize quarterbacks in the NFL and the man he came to know.

"He wasn't a 'Purple People Eater' at all!" Clinton wrote. "Alan Page is more than a gentleman."

It is quite amazing that a man who never missed a game, was selected to nine consecutive Pro Bowls, and was the best player on one of the best defenses in NFL history could easily argue his non-football résumé is superior. It's not a very difficult argument, to be honest.

He tackled racial disparities as an employment lawyer. He adjudicated critical issues facing the public as a jurist, one who received more than 70 percent of the vote on two occasions. And he changed the lives of many Minnesota youth by empowering them through education.

Now *that* is autograph-worthy.

"I came across some research that suggested that, while we put athletes and entertainers on a pedestal and treat them as heroes, the people that really influence us are those that we can reach out and touch," Page told the *Pioneer Press* in 2015. "So, the notion that our scholars come from the neighborhood of the children they work with, they're someone who looks like them . . . If we could get them back in the community, we could actually change the future."

A lofty goal for some, but probably not for someone who once changed the way his very position was played—not that he'd ever tell you about it.

31.
Bob Lilly

Bob Lilly (74) was the Cowboys' No. 1 draft choice in 1961, and he was one of the franchise's and league's most outstanding players for the next fourteen seasons.

Position: Defensive Tackle

Team: Cowboys (1961–1974)

By Jon Machota

Third-and-9 from the Dolphins' 38-yard line with 13 seconds remaining in the first quarter of Super Bowl VI. The Cowboys were clinging to a 3–0 lead when Dolphins quarterback Bob Griese attempted to draw the Dallas defensive line offside with multiple hard counts.

It nearly worked. Cowboys left defensive end Larry Cole flinched, but never crossed the line of scrimmage.

As soon as Griese took the snap, he was in trouble. Cole immediately darted past Miami's right tackle.

The Cowboys knew the Dolphins would be looking to pass, so on the right side of the defensive line, tackle Bob Lilly and end George Andrie ran a stunt. Lilly's job was to get into the left tackle, creating some space for Andrie to loop underneath. Andrie didn't get much penetration, but Lilly wrecked the play by quickly getting the left tackle off balance. The center tried to help, but he was too late. Lilly was already seven yards upfield.

Lilly and Cole had Griese running for his life. The Miami QB had his own end zone closing in quickly, so he attempted setting up to at least throw the ball away. Cole had the best chance at getting the sack until he jumped while trying to knock down Griese's pass fake. Lilly never lost contain, so when Griese attempted to spin away from Cole, Lilly was there to finish him off.

Here's how CBS play-by-play voice Ray Scott and color commentator Pat Summerall called what happened next.

Scott: "Griese forced to scramble. . . . He's down inside the 10-yard line! And Bob Lilly has him!"

Summerall: "Griese, of course, is a fine athlete, but here's one of the best ones around, No. 74 is Lilly."

Griese lost 29 yards on the play, a Super Bowl record.

"It was amazing because I got there quickly," Lilly told the *Fort Worth Star-Telegram* in 2019. "My goal was to grab my guy and grab George's tackle before he could set up. Jethro [Pugh] would get his guard, and Larry was going to come through, but we both [Lilly and Cole] got through there just like that.

"Cole was over there, I was here, and it was kind of like a rodeo deal. We had him in the middle. Pretty soon, Bob Griese just turns around and took off fast, and I caught him and dragged him down. So I give Larry Cole a big part of the credit.

"Bob always says, 'How'd you get me?' Well, I had Larry Cole. He said, 'I took off.' Well, I said, 'Bob, I'm faster than you are.'"

The sack became the signature play of Lilly's Hall of Fame career.

The Cowboys went on that day to win their first Super Bowl in franchise history, 24–3.

From 1966 through 1970, Dallas made the playoffs every season. The Cowboys reached the conference championship game three times and the Super Bowl once during that time. But they failed to win it all, so they were assigned monikers like "Next Year's Champions" and "Bridesmaids of the NFL."

Both bothered Lilly.

Another signature moment from his career occurred at the end of the Super Bowl the year before Dallas beat Miami. Many costly mistakes led to the Cowboys losing 16–13 to the Baltimore Colts. Lilly was so frustrated at the end that he flung his helmet at least 20 yards.

Legendary Cowboys coach Tom Landry mentioned that moment while presenting Lilly for the Pro Football Hall of Fame in 1980.

"He almost threw his helmet out of the Orange Bowl," Landry recalled. "Well, that demonstrated how much it hurt him to lose, and I knew right then that we had a great chance to win Super Bowl VI."

After he finally won the Super Bowl the following year, the video of Lilly smoking a cigar in the postgame locker room became one of the most famous images in team history.

Lilly was the first draft pick in Cowboys history, going No. 13 overall in 1961. He played 14 seasons in Dallas, missing only one game. He had a career-high 15 sacks in 1966 and finished with 95.5 in 196 regular-season games. He made 11 Pro Bowls, was named All-Pro nine times, and made the NFL's All-Decade teams for the 1960s and 1970s. Lilly was also a member of the NFL's 75th anniversary and 100th anniversary all-time teams.

Landry played Lilly, the face of the original "Doomsday Defense," early in his career at defensive end before eventually moving him to defensive tackle in 1964. Landry would call it the best decision of his coaching career. Lilly would go on to become one of the greatest defensive tackles in NFL history.

"When you have a guy that's that big and that much of a player, whatever he wanted to do, he could do it," former Cowboys teammate Dan Reeves said in an NFL Films interview. "Nobody could beat him off the ball. Centers would try to choke-block him and then the guard would pull and they couldn't reach him. He'd be in the backfield and just cause so much havoc."

Lilly was the first Cowboys player to be named All-Pro, the first to make a Pro Bowl, the first to be inducted into the Ring of Honor, and the first to be enshrined in Canton, Ohio. It's pretty easy to understand how he got the nickname "Mr. Cowboy," which Lilly says was given to him by legendary Cowboys quarterback Roger Staubach.

"I take it as an honor," Lilly told the *Star-Telegram*, "but I do think there's a lot of other players that certainly deserve that title if there's going to be a title like that. I really don't . . . I don't know that I really like it. It makes me feel kind of weird because I've got so many friends that I think are great."

The Cowboys don't retire jersey numbers, but Staubach's No. 12, Troy Aikman's No. 8, Emmitt Smith's No. 22, and Lilly's No. 74 are the only ones players are not allowed to wear in the regular season.

"Regardless of whether Bob was double-teamed or even triple-teamed, he'd still beat you," Staubach said in the book *A Cowboy's Life*. "There were times when he didn't even confront the opposition at all. He would either jump over them, go around them or strategically outsmart them by making the play."

"A man like that comes along once in a lifetime," Landry added in the book. "He is something a little more than great. Nobody is better than Bob Lilly."

Another key to his success was his eyes. He had 20/12 vision during his playing career. He used it to identify the smallest details, giving him an edge over his opponent. He'd look for offensive linemen tightening their chinstraps, a sign that they were preparing to pass block. He'd look at their fingertips while on the line of scrimmage—the tighter they were pressed into the ground, the more likely they were going to run block. He'd notice the amount of space between a guard and a center, which gave him a good idea if he would be double-teamed.

And while his eyes presented advantages on the field, they also led to one of his greatest passions off the field: photography.

Lilly began experimenting with the hobby in 1961 as he was coming off an All-American senior season at TCU. As a member of the Coaches' All-American team, he was gifted a Kodak Motormatic camera, 200 rolls of film, and prepaid mailers to send the pictures in to get developed.

The interest stayed with him throughout his Cowboys career. Lilly photographed everything from empty stadiums and meeting rooms to teammates and their families.

"Some of my old teammates have told me, 'If we didn't have those pictures, we wouldn't have any pictures of our kids when they were little,'" Lilly said.

Following his playing career, Lilly became so involved with photography that he eventually opened a photography and fine art gallery in New Mexico. He sold it in 1989 before moving back to Texas, where he lives today.

"Football is like a triple-chess game," Lilly said. "Once you get about three or four years, if you're very astute, you not only know what your defense is, but you know what they're going to do. I think that's the way photography is. It's the little things. It's the little things that catch your interest. It's details. . . . You learn all these things over a period of time, just like football."

30.
Merlin Olsen

Merlin Olsen (74) was a ten-time first- or second-team All-Pro.

Position: Defensive Tackle
Team: Rams (1962–1976)

By Jourdan Rodrigue

Most remember Merlin Olsen as the Hall of Famer, the five-time first-team All-Pro defensive lineman who anchored one-quarter of the "Fearsome Foursome" in the 1960s and '70s, who quietly accumulated 14 Pro Bowl berths, who sat offensive linemen up out of their socks, who held the wall and occupied the space that allowed the swords and arrows to fly all around him and at the poor quarterback on the other side.

Others may recall his work in television and film, his car dealership, or the fact that he was a kind, gentle guy, an "everyman." Others remember him simply as Uncle Merlin. But his career on the gridiron is why he's on this list.

"Back in the mid-'70s I had a teacher in junior college, became a friend, named Leon Donahue," Rory Copeland wrote in an email. "He played offensive guard for the 49ers and the Cowboys in [the] '60s," said Copeland. "I once asked him, 'Leon, who was the toughest defensive lineman you ever played against?'

"Without hesitation he said, 'Merlin Olsen. It was like wrestling a bear—a bear that never got tired.'"

Olsen, who was inducted into the Hall of Fame in 1982, finished his 15-year career with 91 sacks—as an interior defensive lineman. Olsen ate up and maneuvered space with an artist's creativity, which allowed the others in the "Fearsome Foursome"—Deacon Jones, Roosevelt Grier, and Lamar Lundy—to become one of the most revered position groups in history. Olsen did his job with a certain joy and calmness that centered the rest of his counterparts.

"I love the game of football, I liked playing the game—*more than liked* playing the game," said Olsen in his Hall of Fame enshrinement speech. "There was some special magic out on that piece of grass out there on that field. And win or lose, when I came off that field, it was always coming down. I am sure that the thing I miss most about the game is the people, the very special people and those incredible highs and lows."

Joe Marciano, a native New Yorker and lifelong Rams fan, once caught a game against the New York Giants deep in enemy territory at Yankee Stadium in 1970. The Rams were out of playoff contention that year, while the Giants just needed to beat the Rams to cement their first playoff berth in seven years. That week, the New York City newspapers were out for blood. They splashed the headline "All I Want for Christmas Is Rams Soup," as Marciano recalled.

"I was with a close high school friend who was a huge Giants fan," he wrote. "What we witnessed in Yankee Stadium was Olsen totally dominating the entire Giants offense. He harassed [Fran] Tarkenton unmercifully all day long and shut down the middle of the line of scrimmage. This, all in a game that meant nothing to the Rams and everything to the Giants. The final score was 31–3 Rams.

"On the way home after the game, my dejected friend was very quiet, but he made one observation. He said: 'It was all Merlin Olsen.' I said, 'What about Deacon Jones?' And my friend said, 'Not today. Today it was all Merlin Olsen. He's the best I've ever seen.'"

In those days, the players in Los Angeles felt very close to the fans. They were in the community, eating at the same restaurants and shopping at the same stores and markets.

Many remember Olsen through his illustrious acting career, with roles as the title character on the show *Father Murphy* in the 1980s, or as Jonathan Garvey in *Little House on the Prairie*.

"He was always portrayed as a gentle giant off the football field," wrote Rams fan P. C. Lehmann. "On the football field, by all accounts, he was still a gentleman—but as my father used to say, 'Until the whistle blew, he was a relentless man on the hunt, driven from something beyond.' As a kid, I didn't even know what that meant, but it stuck with me."

Copeland said that his friend, Donahue, agreed about Olsen's quiet persona, but he knew he could flip a switch when he needed to.

"He didn't say much because he didn't have to," Copeland said. "But, once, by the end of the third quarter, Leon was dragging and before a snap, Merlin quietly said to him, 'Leon, you gotta stop drinking so much beer.' That's all he said. And Donahue knew he was right."

Olsen gravitated toward people, just as he pulled them into his own gravity. Jimmy Marchini used to bring his brand-new portable television (the 1970s model that plugged into his car's cigarette lighter, thanks very much) to the Coliseum parking lot before Rams games so that fans waiting to catch sight of the players coming in could also catch that morning's games. Olsen stopped by so often to talk football and get the scores and matchups himself that he came to know Marchini and his wife by name. Olsen loomed over everybody's heads but was soft-spoken and kind-eyed—until it was time to head into the tunnel.

"There would come that moment when the smile would fade, his eyes would narrow, and he'd head toward the Coliseum; always with a gracious goodbye and a 'See ya next home game,'" Marchini recalled. "You could easily see the transition in his countenance when he turned to enter the Coliseum. Game prep for Merlin began long before donning the uniform. . . . The one thing my wife and I could be sure of, as sure as the sun coming up, was that Merlin was going to give it 100 percent that day."

Jeff Vandee, a third-generation Rams fan, recalled his grandfather's favorite Olsen story.

"It was the late '60s early '70s and he was on his way home from work and decided to stop for a beer [at] a local watering hole in Long Beach [California] called Mr. C's," he said. "During these years, Long Beach was a popular hangout location for many Rams players. My grandfather, while having a drink, got into a heated discussion with former Rams linebacker Myron Pottios. Not sure who started the fight, but it turned into 'Let's take it outside.' As both men stood to head for the door, Merlin, now aware of the situation, stepped between the two men to calm the situation and have them separated. From my understanding, Merlin was highly respected amongst his NFL peers. . . . Merlin was a gentle giant and peacemaker."

Tom Bradford, a Rams fan since he was 15 years old, remembers a night at the old Palomino Club in North Hollywood, California—where Bradford and his wife were celebrating her birthday.

Lisa Olsen, Merlin's niece on her father's side, carries many memories of him with her. Merlin Olsen passed away from cancer in 2010 at age 69.

"He was just Uncle Merlin," she recalled. "Just super sweet to his kids, never ever acted like he was ever anything more than the rest of us . . .

"I remember his hands. He'd go to show us something as a kid, and it was just like, 'Dang . . . they're just massive.' But he was so kind and gentle and warm and genuine—you just felt that more than the physical feeling of [him]. He would always make sure, if he was talking to you, that he'd always get down right by you. . . .

He was so huge that he could have felt scary, but never. And his smile . . . oh, it could just completely melt your heart in an instant."

Merlin Olsen opened a Porsche/Audi dealership in Encino, California, and when Lisa moved from Boise, Idaho, out to Southern California in her 20s for her first big job, Olsen looked out for her. One of her prized possessions from that time? A license-plate frame that Merlin gave her from the dealership with his name on it.

Olsen, now in her mid-50s and the CFO of a gasket company in Long Beach, keeps the license plate frame on every car she owns to this day. Sometimes, she'll be at the grocery store, and every so often, someone older will stop her, having watched her drive in.

"I haven't seen one of those in a long time," they'll say, and Lisa will tell them a little bit about her uncle. She said whoever approaches her also usually has a memory of her uncle, from watching him play or even meeting him by chance.

She said they'll always smile—she knows the one—that wistful smile people get when they're missing somebody, their uncle, their pal, their colleague, their favorite player who just happened to be a good person, too.

It's a smile of sweet, sad nostalgia that comes when people who love this game miss the way they felt back then, when they watched one of the greatest to ever play dig his cleats into the Southern California grass.

29.
Emmitt Smith

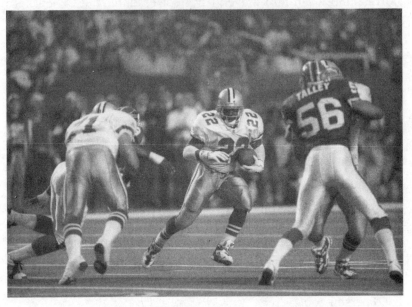

Emmitt Smith (22) retired as the NFL's career leader
in rushing yards and rushing touchdowns.

Position: Running Back

Teams: Cowboys (1990–2002), Cardinals (2003–2004)

By Bob Sturm

Any time you talk about someone who holds all of the records in their given pursuit, there is an instinctive reaction from those who back others in the conversation to try to cheapen those records by saying it is merely a product of longevity.

He just played longer.

He wasn't necessarily the better player—he just did it for longer.

The reaction for an NFL running back, especially someone like Emmitt Smith, who has run for more yards and touchdowns than anyone who played the sport, the same in the postseason, won league MVP, been named the MVP of the Super Bowl, and had more consecutive 1,000-yard seasons than *anyone*, is quite simple.

You're exactly right. Part of what makes him special is exactly that. He absolutely did it better because he did it for longer.

Perhaps some people don't believe in the long-standing truth in athletics that "the most important ability is availability." But they might not be football fans.

Football people know that some of the most special careers were only seen for a flash. What separates Jerry Rice, Tom Brady, and Smith from the others is not just flashes of greatness. It is at least a full generation of greatness. That is how records are broken and greatness is cemented.

In the case of Smith, it is best demonstrated by a number of accomplishments:

- From 1991 to 2001, he had 11 consecutive seasons of 1,000 yards. In 1990, he fell 63 yards short of that mark. And in 2002, he fell 25 yards short. Otherwise, he might have had 13 consecutive. Still, his 11 seasons in a row are more than any other player has ever had—in consecutive fashion or not.
- He ran for 18,355 yards in the regular season during his career and another 1,586 in the postseason. Both of those marks are unlikely to be approached again given the direction and brevity of careers at running back in the modern game.
- In his career, he has over 500 more touches than any other player, with 4,924. In 2020, Derrick Henry led the NFL with 397. It would take more than 12 seasons at that league-leading rate to catch Smith.

"They will say he had a passing game, they will say he had a great offensive line. They will come up with a lot of different reasons as to why it was not just him," Daryl Johnston said.

To understand Smith's place in football's historical archives is to understand the team he played for is often thought of as one of the most unbelievable dynasties of recent memory. The early '90s Dallas Cowboys were the only team to have won three Super Bowls in four years until the Patriots did it from 2001 to 2004. What made the Cowboys the better of the two teams, though, would be the year they *didn't* win. New England did not even make the 2002 playoffs, while the Cowboys lost a close 1994 NFC Championship Game in San Francisco that would have opened the door for an unprecedented four consecutive titles in a sport that has never seen such a thing. They were close enough that a late-game pass interference no-call on future team member Deion Sanders still gets cited routinely around town.

The sum of the parts was the key to the Dallas dynasty being so great. Yes, there was a huge amount of Hall of Fame greatness on display, but the full complement was so destructive as a unit that to break into smaller pieces to measure the individual parts missed the point. You could not separate fully the strength of Troy Aikman from that of Michael Irvin or Smith. Nor could you separate their impacts from the performances of Larry Allen or Nate Newton or Mark Tuinei or Jay Novacek. Broadcasters would routinely marvel at the simplicity of the playbook. They seemingly needed fewer than 10 plays in the game plan to destroy and overwhelm opponents. There are stories of even declaring what play was coming to a defense and it not mattering. The result was secured before the snap occurred.

This brought wins and ultimately titles, but individual accolades were often marginalized. The greatness of the quarterback was talked down because of all the weapons around him. The offensive line was minimized because of the weapons. The weapons were undervalued because they had such great offensive line play. And what about the great coaching staff? Of course, it was a great team with all of these benefits.

This resulted in even more noise around the team. How great would Aikman have been if he had to live in Dan Marino's reality, where not everything was so rosy? What about Smith? Surely Barry Sanders would love to play with this team. And could Smith do all of this in Detroit? Come on.

But all of those conversations are unresolvable and utterly unfair to those who accomplished the climbs up the mountain. Yes, they required teammates and support staff, but to consistently claim that "anyone" could do what they did robs from those who actually did it.

Smith did it. He did it all. And he did it over and over again.

And because of his ability to do what he did down after down, week after week, and season after season, he was able to deliver dependability that was often not appreciated until it was over.

No player saw it from a closer distance than Aikman, and no player is more closely tied to his accomplishments and their partnership. I asked him: What stands out when he thinks back on the NFL's all-time leading rusher? Aikman didn't care as much about the miles of yardage for its absurd achievement as much as he did for its signifying traits.

"If you play long enough, you're gonna put up big numbers," Aikman said. "But with Emmitt, the reason that his numbers are significant to me is that in order to do what he did, you have to play at a high level for a long time. You can't miss games. You have to be on the field. So the records speak to his availability and durability. That's what I think of all those years and numbers.

"Had Emmitt gone down, there was no plan B, and there just wasn't really a 1A and 1B with these runners. It was just Emmitt. We just got so spoiled with his durability and remaining healthy that it was just—it was overlooked. We just took it for granted."

Aikman thought a moment and continued.

"And then the other part that when I think of Emmitt as a runner and this is not hyperbole: I just honestly don't ever recall the first man in the hole making a play on him. He had an uncanny ability to just make the first guy miss. It was crazy how good he was at doing that."

That should not be lost in a study of Smith. A quick trip through his vast highlight film verifies this dozens of times. A deeper dive that involves charting key games during that dynasty will prove the large percentages of loaded boxes he would face. Opponents knew the Cowboys had immense talent, but they also started their game plans by trying to stop No. 22. Easier said than done. Especially since he would not let the first guy ever get him. At least that is what Aikman said.

Smith was honored to hear his quarterback suggest such a thing—even if he remembered it slightly differently.

"I've always tried to develop this in terms of being able to make the first guy miss and calculate two or three moves ahead," he said. "That was just something that I believe just started to unlock as I played and got more game experience. As a running back, I started seeing things on the football field before they actually happened and where guys were coming from."

But, when I spoke to him about the ability to play so many years while missing so few games, despite playing a position that takes collisions more than anyone on the field, I asked if he consciously ran the ball in a way that might prolong his career.

"I think my running style suited me well because I had a low center of gravity and had a great balance with great vision," he said. "I can be the low player and get leverage on other players and protect myself at the same time. And so I think the gift of being able to be 5-9 and only weigh so much, and when I'm running the ball, I probably get smaller and when you tried to tackle me, I knew how to just shield my body naturally. I mean, this is not something that I developed, this is something that just came naturally."

Smith played 13 years in Dallas and during that stretch, the Cowboys played 208 games in the regular season. He played in 201 of them and had a contract disagreement (he resists the term *holdout*) to start the 1993 season for two of those seven missed games. He never played in fewer than 14 games in a season in Dallas and had perfect attendance eight times during that era. He famously played with a shoulder separation in a key stretch in the 1993 finale and through the Super Bowl against Buffalo when he dominated and won MVP.

NFL insiders tell us to cautiously look at the "Curse of 400." Four hundred touches in a season is usually followed with the disappointment of a career drop-off of significance that should be avoided by a valuable resource. Christian McCaffrey was the most recent victim after a huge 2019 followed by a barren 2020.

Smith had 400 touches in 1991, 1992, 1994, and 1995. The year he fell short in 1993 was because of his contract absence or he would have done it five consecutive years. During those seasons, his worst yardage total was 1,821. He evidently wasn't subject to curses any more than he was subject to injuries or tacklers in the hole.

"You didn't get the message?" he asked me with a laugh at the end of our visit.

I didn't know the message I was supposed to receive.

"That I was Superman? Didn't nobody tell you that?"

Nobody did tell me, but it was obvious. The record books said it all. There have been many amazing runners in the history of this sport and the beauty and ranks will be in the eyes of the beholders.

But only one of them is the all-time leading rusher in both the regular season and the playoffs, as well.

This one.

28.
Rod Woodson

Rod Woodson (26) was elected to eleven Pro Bowls,
a record for a defensive back at the time.

Position: Defensive Back

Teams: Steelers (1987–1996), 49ers (1997), Ravens (1998–2001), Raiders (2002–2003)

By Mark Kaboly

When you think of Rod Woodson, you think of a Hall of Fame defensive back who was as fast as he was athletic. If you are a Steelers fan, you might also think of one of the few times the organization was wrong when it came to letting a player leave prematurely—because that's still a sore subject.

Few would bring up Woodson's name when talking about the

greatest defensive back in league history, right there with the likes of Deion Sanders. But maybe they should.

"Deion and I just had different games," Woodson said. "I was a physical corner, and Deion liked to use his speed. The difference was he would tell you how it was, and I wouldn't say anything."

Woodson, who is now the head coach of the Vegas Vipers in the XFL, enjoyed a storied 17-year NFL career in which he played 164 games at cornerback and 74 at free safety. His total of 238 games played as a defensive back ranks fifth all time.

Statistically, Woodson's numbers were better across the board than Sanders's—71 interceptions to Sanders's 53, 1,158 tackles to 512, 13 defensive touchdowns to 10.

"Deion gets so much credit for who he was during that era, which he should," said Ryan Clark, a 13-year safety who's now an ESPN analyst. "But Rod Woodson was on the same level, and then you add to that basically two Hall of Fame careers at two different positions. When you look at a guy like Rod from an athleticism standpoint, he's before his time. But . . . the reason it wasn't as talked about as it should have been was because of the physicality of the style of play of that era."

But this isn't about comparing who was better, Woodson or Sanders. It is about Woodson being, quietly, one of the best players who ever played. He made 11 Pro Bowls—the third most ever by a defensive back—at three positions (including kick returner) and was a six-time first-team All-Pro, also at three positions. He was a three-time team MVP and one of only five active players named to the NFL's 75th anniversary team in 1994. He was selected to the Steelers' 75th anniversary team and named the Defensive Player of the Year after the 1993 season.

Yet when you hear debates about the best defensive backs who ever played, it's Sanders, Ronnie Lott, Darrell Green, and Charles Woodson (of no relation) who are typically mentioned.

Rarely is Rod Woodson.

"I don't believe in any way that he is underrated because he is a Hall of Famer," Clark said. "However, his input to the game isn't talked about as profoundly as it should [be]."

It could be because of Woodson's lack of flash.

Woodson grew up in a small Indiana town and was greatly influenced by his hardworking, never-complaining father. So it is no surprise that Sanders, whose career somewhat paralleled that of Woodson's, got the publicity (and rightfully so) while Woodson went about his daily business.

"Deion is his own creation. He is a great brander. I am not a brander. I am a blue-collar, Midwest football player," Woodson said. "That was my dad. He worked [as a laborer] with his hard hat on and he went to work. He didn't complain about it, he didn't talk about it—he just went to work, and that's how I played football. I was a blue-collar football player.

"One thing that Chuck Noll told me when I got there in 1987 was that if I don't tackle, I don't play. I told him we don't have to worry about that. I used to play tackle football in the streets."

Woodson would not be overlooked if he were coming out today. He stood 6 feet and 202 pounds with long arms. At the combine, he ran a 4.33-second 40-yard dash and had a 36-inch vertical leap. He also had the athleticism to be a world-class, 110-meter hurdler at Purdue—and for a few months on the European track circuit, where he competed as he held out the first half of his rookie year with the Steelers. Woodson qualified for the Olympic trials in the hurdles in 1984, but he was far from being a prototypical track guy.

When Woodson ran the 4.33, he was immediately labeled a cornerback. Until then, he had been a safety—except for his final year at Purdue, when he moved around just about everywhere. In his final college game, a 17–15 win against Indiana, Woodson started at running back and rushed for 93 yards, caught three passes for 67 yards, made 10 tackles, broke up a pass, forced a fumble, and returned two kickoffs for 46 yards and three punts for 30 yards. He played 137 snaps, roughly 90 percent of the game.

"Rod Woodson was actually before his time," Clark said. "When we talk about the long corners and having the length on the outside with speed, Rod Woodson was that. We just didn't go goo-goo eyes over the measurables at that time."

Woodson was widely pegged as a top-five prospect in the 1987 draft. With the Steelers selecting 10th that year, Noll was convinced there was such little chance of Woodson falling to Pittsburgh that he told defensive coordinator Tony Dungy not to even bother scouting him.

When draft day came, the Steelers were stunned Woodson was still around and wasted no time selecting him. Surely, they thought, the Browns were going to take Woodson or Penn State linebacker Shane Conlan at No. 5, but they decided on Duke linebacker Mike Junkin, who played 20 games over three years before he was out of the league.

That decision allowed the Cardinals to take quarterback Kelly Stouffer and the Bills to select Conlan. The Lions and Eagles passed on Woodson, and the rest, as they say, is history.

"I never talked to them, and as a matter of fact, on draft day, the Saints called me and told me that they were drafting me at 11 if I was there, it's not even a question," Woodson said. "Once the Browns took Junkin, the draft board shifted a little bit in my favor because I was able to drop a little, because the teams ahead of the Steelers already had corners.

"I never talked to the Steelers, but when they did call, I was pretty excited because we only had three channels [on television], and all the good teams were on, so I could be a part of a team I watched a lot."

Woodson's time with the Steelers didn't start well. Because he held out for the first half of the season in a contract dispute, there was some concern he didn't want to play in the NFL. There were whispers he'd forgo the start of his pro football career for an opportunity to compete in the 1988 Olympics in track and field.

When he finally signed, he was a return man and backup defensive back for the final eight games of the 1987 season. He continued to learn the cornerback position the following year.

"He just had a presence about him," Steelers Hall of Honor wide receiver Louis Lipps said. "He showed it every day in his work and his game and his play."

When Woodson showed up, Lipps was already an established veteran on the team, being named Offensive Rookie of the Year in 1984 and a Pro Bowler in 1984 and 1985. Even though Lipps didn't match that production throughout his career, he was one of the best receivers in the game. So naturally, when Woodson arrived, a battle ensued.

"We fought each other every day, man," Lipps recalled. "We bettered each other. We put money in the bucket, and at the end of the year, we would go have dinner or go have drinks somewhere. It helped me so much because come Sunday, it was a piece of cake. Nobody else would come even close to what Rod could do."

It wasn't until 1989 that Woodson finally broke out, becoming the best shutdown corner in the league.

"Moving to corner took every bit of three years to feel comfortable," Woodson said. "I was able to play corner and still have my eyes in the backfield. That wasn't a good thing when you play corner, which I didn't know at the time."

When Noll's successor, Bill Cowher, took over in 1992, Woodson really blossomed. But it wasn't so much Cowher's impact as it was his hiring of two other influential coaches: defensive coordinator Dom Capers and defensive backs coach Dick LeBeau.

"The attacking-style mentality Capers had as the defensive coordinator, the entire Steelers Nation had," said Pro Football Hall of Famer Kevin Greene, who signed with Pittsburgh in 1993. "They wanted us to come after folks and crush people. They didn't want to see soft zones. They wanted to see 'Pin the ears back and turn the Steelers loose. Let them go.' That's what we did. And we did it well."

In 1992, Woodson was second on the team in both tackles (100) and sacks (six). The next season, he had eight interceptions (one returned for a touchdown), 28 passes defended, two forced fumbles, two sacks, a blocked field goal attempt, and a team-high 79 solo tackles. For his effort, he was named NFL Defensive Player of the Year. He and Sanders were the only defensive backs to win the award from 1984 to 2004.

Woodson was arguably the best cornerback in the league from 1989 to 1994, when he made six Pro Bowls and earned five All-Pro nominations. He had 27 interceptions and returned three of them for touchdowns, and he was an asset as an outside tackling corner.

In 1995, the Steelers were primed to rebound from a devastating AFC Championship Game loss to the Chargers, and Woodson was going to be one of the catalysts to make that happen. However, it all came crashing down late in the first quarter of the opener against the Lions thanks to Barry Sanders and the artificial turf at Three Rivers Stadium.

Woodson tore the ACL in his right knee while trying to stop Sanders, and his standing as the NFL's best cornerback ended. Woodson also injured his MCL, complicating issues.

Still, he immediately thought he could be back by the end of the season.

"It was my idea," Woodson said. "I was with Cowher, and the team doctor gave the prognosis of four to six months recovery, and I was like, 'Whoa, wait, four months? That's the end of the season.' I said, 'I can get back by then.' Cowher is looking at me like I am crazy, and I am like, 'No, I can be back.' We were so good, and Carnell [Lake] was so good at corner and no other injuries happened in our secondary, [so that] allowed me to stay on the active roster."

Cowher thought about it for a day or two before tentatively agreeing to it. It helped that Cowher was able to move Lake from safety to corner a couple of games later and Lake played at an All-Pro level. It also was imperative that nobody in the secondary got hurt, so the Steelers didn't need Woodson's roster spot. He was back on the field just shy of five months after the injury in Super Bowl XXX, playing 12 snaps as a backup and deflecting one pass in the loss to the Cowboys.

"It was one of those times when you lose a Rod Woodson, you kind of wonder where we are going to go," team owner Art Rooney II said. "To be honest with you, I didn't think Carnell was going to do what he did when he stepped in there. You don't always think of your safety stepping in at cornerback and think it is going to be a good thing."

Five months later, Woodson's return marked the first time a player has played following an ACL injury in the same season, an achievement that earned him the Ed Block Courage Award in 1996.

"I was maybe 60 percent," Woodson said. "It felt great leading up to it, practicing on it felt great. I thought it was good enough."

Woodson played one more season for the Steelers in 1996 and became an unrestricted free agent in 1997. He was plagued by injuries in 1996, including a strained Achilles, a sprained knee, and an ailing back. He declined the Steelers' contract offer and signed with the 49ers.

During the 10 years he played in Pittsburgh, the Steelers finished with a winning record eight times. They made six playoff appearances, won four division titles, and claimed one AFC championship.

Woodson spent one season with the 49ers before being a salary-cap casualty. He signed with the Ravens and spent one year at corner before making the switch back to safety under defensive coordinator Marvin Lewis, after Baltimore chose cornerbacks Duane Starks and Chris McAlister in the top 10 in back-to-back drafts.

While in Baltimore, he made three Pro Bowls and was second-team All-Pro in 2000 as a 35-year-old safety, helping the Ravens win Super Bowl XXXV with one of the best defenses in NFL history. He played his final two seasons for the Raiders and returned to the Super Bowl in the 2002 season, when he again earned Pro Bowl and first-team All-Pro honors after tying for the league lead with eight interceptions (two returned for touchdowns).

"Just listen to Rod and let him talk defense with you, and he has a masterful mind," former Steelers teammate Craig Wolfley said. "Besides the great and almost unbelievable athletic skills of his physical attributes of strength and speed, but his mind. . . . If you are talking top shutdown guys in the league, if he is not top three in the conversation, then somebody is [mistaken]."

27.
John Hannah

Peers of John Hannah (73) voted him the league's top offensive lineman four times, and he was All-Pro for ten consecutive years.

Position: Offensive Guard
Team: Patriots (1973–1985)

By Steve Buckley

How appropriate, how fitting, how on brand, that a telephone call placed to John Hannah did not arrive at a fancy-schmancy country club, or the sushi bar on some cruise ship.

No. Hannah, then age 70, was sitting atop a tractor somewhere out on his Alabama cattle farm, taking in hay.

"If you can hear me, I can talk for a little bit," he said, speaking over the steady hum of farm machinery. "We've been attacked by armyworms, and they basically destroy your hay. We've had so much rain down here—about three times the amount of rain in July that we normally get—so I'm trying to salvage what little hay I have left in this field."

The purpose of the call was celebratory, of course, to talk about Hannah's place among the NFL's best players, and inquiring minds wanted to know how he felt about that.

"I enjoyed the game," he said. "I'm glad I got to play, hope I gave it everything I had."

That's too easy an answer for too good of a career. Selected as the fourth pick of the first round by the Patriots in the 1973 NFL Draft, Hannah made a smooth transition from Bear Bryant's perennially powerful Alabama Crimson Tide to the perennially trying-to-get-their-act-together Patriots. He played his entire 13-season career in New England, during which he was a seven-time All-Pro and named to nine Pro Bowls. He was later named to the All-Decade Team for the 1970s and '80s and was elected to the Pro Football Hall of Fame in 1991.

Though offensive linemen seldom get the spotlights and parades, he was, quite simply, the first Patriots megastar. *Sports Illustrated* put an exclamation mark on this period in Pats history, when, for the cover of its August 3, 1981, issue, Hannah was proclaimed THE BEST OFFENSIVE LINEMAN OF ALL TIME. The words appear over a head shot of a helmeted Hannah delivering a no-nonsense peer into the lens, the look on his face suggesting the coin toss has been executed and the game is about to begin.

Reminded of that cover proclamation, Hannah said, "I'll leave all that other stuff for everybody else. You always enjoy, miss, and love what you're best at, you know what I mean? It was a lot of fun, but you can't play it after you're 34, 35 years old if you play it the way we played it."

Fair enough. But there was another reason for the telephone call. It had to do with a comment from former Patriots quarterback Steve Grogan, Hannah's longtime teammate in New England. Hannah was known to be famously intense—as in 100 percent intensity 100 percent of the time, leaving no room for the occasional light moment or other displays of in-game levity—and Grogan took a stab at softening that reputation.

"Every once in a while," said Grogan, "John would come back to the huddle, and he'd be giggling. And you'd watch the film the next day and find out why he was giggling."

So why would he be giggling?

"It was always because he pulled on a sweep and some little defensive back didn't see him coming, and John would roll him end over end," said Grogan. "And he got the biggest kick out of that. And he'd come back laughing. That's the only time I ever saw him laugh, or basically talk, on the football field."

How funny, how perfect, that the example Grogan chooses to submit of Hannah's ability to yuk it up on a football field involves the leveling of some little defensive back. But that was probably Grogan's point all along.

Hannah wasn't just old school; he was nineteenth-century, one-room-schoolhouse, potbelly-stove-burning-in-the-corner old school. He played each game with a grim determination, too caught up in putting up a wall between opposing defenders and his own backfield to trifle with such hood ornaments as marching bands, cheerleaders, and ceremonial coin tosses.

Hearing of Grogan's anecdotes about taking out defensive backs, Hannah laughed a little and replied, "Steve's one to be talking about being serious. He was every bit as serious, if not more than me."

Raymond Berry, the Hall of Fame receiver with the Baltimore Colts and later head coach of the Patriots, offered an assessment of Hannah that was devoid of yuks and banquet stories.

"John Hannah was the most suited offensive lineman—ever," said Berry. "He had everything it takes to be an offensive lineman. Size. Strength. Mentality. He had no weaknesses at all. He was the complete offensive lineman.

"He was easy to coach because you didn't need to coach him much," Berry said. "He could do it all without too much instruction. When you have great players, you don't have to do too much other than point them in the right direction."

So, what propelled John Hannah to top-100 greatness? The easy answer is that he had the basics: size, talent, football smarts . . . the list goes on and on. But according to former Pats linebacker Steve Nelson, Hannah had something else going for him: practice. And Nelson's not talking about garden-variety, nose-to-the-grindstone, practice-makes-perfect practice . . . you know, the kind of stuff that famous athletes used to preach on the back of cereal boxes.

With Hannah, said Nelson, it was something more.

"I don't know if you'd call it an *insecurity*, but he just had this need to keep proving himself," said Nelson, who was teammates with Hannah for 12 seasons. "The greatest players, there's something diffident about them.

"He was as committed to practice as he was to the actual game," said Nelson. "You'd look at him at practice and talk with him, and he really did act like we were in a game."

Nelson recalled a practice in which Hannah, banged up a little from a recent game, was asked to wear a red jersey, indicating he wasn't to be jostled.

"It was a trainer who determined that he was injured, and John was so upset about having to wear that red jersey," Nelson said. "It drove him crazy."

But former Patriots safety Tim Fox, while agreeing with Nelson that Hannah brought a game-day mentality to practice, points out that there was one big difference.

"On practice days," said Fox, "you could talk to him. But on game day, you'd walk into the locker room and John Hannah would be sitting in his locker, just staring straight ahead. He was the most intense player I've ever played with. There was no talking to him. You didn't even want to approach him on the bus. He scared me, to be honest with you."

And then there was film study, which Hannah used as part of his preparation for the next team on the schedule. When he watched film of his own performances, said Nelson, Hannah would often come away upset by what he'd just seen.

"He never thought he played well," said Nelson. "You'd watch film with him, you'd watch him battle [longtime Jets defensive lineman] Joe Klecko all day long, and Klecko, of course, was a great football player also. John would win most of the battles and then he'd pick things out he thought he did wrong. He wouldn't be satisfied.

"His standards were so high," said Nelson. "Unreasonably high."

These days, Hannah's direction isn't pointed much to football, though he's seen enough games to make this observation: "For an offensive lineman, the way we'd pass protect, it'd be a lot harder [today] because those quarterbacks are moving around so much," he said. "The only guys that really stay in the pocket and understand the offensive lineman's situation that I've seen are guys like [Tom] Brady. He kind of sits in the pocket and understands that the safest place for him is up front . . . because the offensive lineman doesn't have eyes in his ass and he doesn't know where the quarterback is unless he's where he's supposed to be. You're blocking an area and if he doesn't stay in that area, it makes it awfully hard. A lot of these quarterbacks are dancing around and moving around."

And yet Hannah says he doesn't watch a lot of football. Asked why that is, he said, "You want the honest answer, or the fabricated answer?"

We chose Door No. 1.

"I think the game's lost a lot," he said. "A couple things: One, I don't like all the politics. They ought to just play ball and quit trying to friggin'—they don't know what's going on anyway, and they're all making good money and they bitch about the country. So I don't understand that.

"And another thing, heck, I don't like the rules changes," he said. "I think it's gotten to be a real wussy sport."

26.
Aaron Donald

Aaron Donald (99) has a record three NFL Defensive Player of the Year awards.

Position: Defensive Tackle
Team: Rams (2014–2022)

By Jourdan Rodrigue

The iconic image is now etched forever in football history: Aaron Donald, jogging around the field after a game-sealing hit on Cincinnati Bengals quarterback Joe Burrow in the final minutes of Super Bowl LVI, and pointing to his ring finger.

"Ring me," he roared. "RING ME."

It was just about the last item possibly left for Donald, then 30, to accomplish in his career. The star defensive tackle and cornerstone for the Los Angeles Rams for almost a decade had already been the

Defensive Player of the Year three times, an eight-time Pro Bowler, a seven-time All-Pro, and Defensive Rookie of the Year when he was drafted by the Rams 13th overall in 2014 out of Pittsburgh.

The stories from that time are also iconic. Team after team passed on one of the greatest football players in history because he was "too small" for a defensive tackle despite eye-popping college production. The Rams now consider themselves lucky Donald fell to them at No. 12—they even skipped over him with the No. 2 pick (they took Greg Robinson, an offensive tackle from Auburn), thinking others between that pick and their next one would do so as well.

"That's one I'll never forget," former Lions defensive line coach Jim Washburn famously told the *Detroit Free Press* in 2018. "They had one guy there that said, 'What in the world are we going to do with a little guy like that? I thought we were trying to get away from little guys.' I said, 'Well, you make the exception to the exception,' and then I went off and stood up and Kris Kocurek did, too. We went on and on about Aaron Donald."

Of course, everyone knows better now that a future Hall of Fame berth for Donald is all but inevitable. Entering the 2022 season, Donald had 98 sacks and in 2022 became the fastest defensive lineman in history to reach No. 100. He's the 10th-fastest to hit that milestone among all non-blitzing pass rushers, according to Elias Sports Bureau. Donald recorded the most sacks of any player between 2014 and 2021—and the most quarterback hits (135)—all from the interior defensive line, minus a couple of snaps here or there as an outside linebacker (because, yes, he can do that, too).

It doesn't matter that Donald is technically "undersized" at his position. He's stronger, gets better leverage, wins with speed, wins with his hands, and will beat an offensive lineman with moves he's never seen before.

"I think this is what is not talked about him enough—he never misses with his hands," Rams head coach Sean McVay said. "He's got such good leverage, quickness, and explosion—but his hand placement, he always wins.

"It's a joke," McVay added, cackling. "He is unbelievable. As good as you think he is, he's even better. . . . He makes pros look so bad—it's hard to even explain. I mean, he does this so frequently I can't even tell you. It's a joke.

"He's the epitome of everything that's right."

For years, opponents have had to dedicate entire days of offensive meetings to try to slow Donald down. And still, Donald has ranked among the top players in the league in pressure rate, despite also annually leading the NFL in double- and triple-team rate.

Raheem Morris, the Rams' defensive coordinator since 2021, calls Donald "the boogeyman" for other teams.

"He doesn't miss. He's very accurate with his hands. His hand placement goes exactly where he wants it all the time, [and] that allows him to use all of his power," said Morris. "If you ever see him in the weight room, it is absolutely astonishing to watch. If he can get his hands in the right position, he can catch you off-balance. He uses his height to his advantage, where most players can't."

Emotionally, Donald became a fixed point of motivation for the Rams in their storybook 2021 season. McVay opened the year by saying, "I love this guy. This guy is as much motivation as anybody for why, if we don't win a Super Bowl—if this guy doesn't get one—then shame on me."

In the weeks leading up to the Super Bowl, teammates privately became aware of Donald's consideration of retirement, should they win. It was the last thing left for him to do, the last territory left unclaimed by his stardom.

Battered and depleted on both sides of the ball, Rams teammates rallied for Donald as they went on their postseason run. Von Miller, another future Hall of Fame pass rusher, started bringing his replica of the Lombardi Trophy (from 2015) into the Rams' practice facility where he knew Donald would walk by it each day. Miller also left Donald notes as if the trophy were speaking to him. "Win me, and you'll live forever," one of them said.

Donald had always been a quiet leader for the team, preferring to do so by example.

"We're here to play!" Donald roared at his teammates, in a now-famous sideline speech as the Rams mounted a comeback against rival San Francisco in the NFC Championship Game. "We're one game away! Bow up! We're playing for something, man! It's got to mean something to you! Everything we got! Everything you got! Let's finish this!"

In the end, and in the fourth quarter of the Super Bowl, Donald met the moment in the only way he could: by wrecking the game, breaking it wide open, at exactly the right moment.

The player who had done unbelievable things for almost a decade had one more tool in his bag. He set up his own pass rush by correctly diagnosing a Bengals run play on third-and-1 and made a one-armed stop for no gain on running back Samaje Perine. That dictated the Bengals' next play—in addition to the protection they would set and the type of formation in which they'd line up. He knew it the whole time. McVay knew what Donald would do next.

"I said, 'Aaron is going to close the game out right here,'" McVay said. "He is the effing man."

On that fourth-and-1, with the Super Bowl on the line, Donald did what he does—what he's always done, what he's the best in the world at doing, what history will note he's among the best ever to do:

He rushed.

25.
Sammy Baugh

Sammy Baugh set a record with six NFL passing titles and led the league in punting four times.

Position: Quarterback
Team: Washington (1937–1952)

By Dan Pompei

If in a single game, a team were to throw four touchdown passes, intercept four passes, and pin an opponent on the 1-yard line with an 81-yard punt, that would be impressive, very impressive.

If one player did it? Beyond imagination. And in many ways, Sammy Baugh was.

"Slingin' Sammy" was one of the most accomplished passers of all time. But he also was a safety and punter who performed at a Hall of Fame level at both positions for Washington, then known as the Redskins. And he did it all with the flair of a western hero, which he played in a film series.

The range of his abilities was most evident in a game against the Lions in November 1943. His number of touchdown passes—four— matched the number of passes he intercepted on defense. According to the *Detroit Free Press*, he played every snap until the final 35 seconds of the game. In addition to the 81-yard punt, Baugh also had three consecutive quick kicks, one of his specialties.

He led the league in yards per punt that season—one of five times he had the highest average. Baugh's average of 51.4 yards per punt in 1940 set a record that still stands. The four interceptions in that game against Detroit contributed to his total of 11 for the year, which also led the league.

Baugh was 6-3, 180 pounds. If you saw him today, you'd think he must be the kind of guy who skips leg day. But the look, as it often is, was deceptive. He was not averse to contact.

"He had that tough, prairie strength," Steve Sabol of NFL Films told the *Washington Post*. "He was a leathery kind of guy."

He made two touchdown-saving tackles on kickoff returns during that 1943 season.

He did have an advantage that year. NFL rosters were depleted because many players joined the American effort in World War II. As a married father of two and a rancher who provided beef for the armed services, Baugh was not drafted. The NFL competition, subsequently, was not what it was in other years. He led the league in 1943 with a 55.6 completion percentage. What's telling is that the rest of the passers in the NFL completed 42.6 percent that season.

But he was no one-season wonder. He played 16 seasons, led the league in completion percentage eight times, and finished in the top 10 in passer rating 10 times. He subsequently is considered the league's first great passer.

In the 1982 book *Pro Football's Greatest Players*, Hall of Fame coach George Allen wrote that he had "absolutely no doubt" Baugh was the No. 1 quarterback in history. "He was tall and thin but very wiry, and he had long arms and large hands, and he threw the ball better than any passer I ever saw," Allen continued. "He had a whip-like motion and he could throw soft and hard, short and long as well as anyone ever."

Baugh's abilities helped change the very idea of offense. Instead of going through defenders, teams realized they could also go over them and beyond them. It was Baugh who was the first to pass regularly on first down.

"Baugh demonstrated that the forward pass could be an effective weapon instead of an act of desperation," Sabol said.

Before Baugh, defenders could hit quarterbacks as long as the ball carrier was not on the ground and the whistle had not blown. Partly because of Baugh and the new style of play he ushered in, the NFL made it illegal to hit quarterbacks after they had thrown the ball.

Most passers of his era held the ball by the laces; Baugh held it by the seam. He also didn't wear the same shoulder pads that most of the other passers did. Baugh wore thin pads with no straps because he thought he could throw better. He wore the same pads throughout his entire career while going through 100 pairs of shoes by his team's estimation. He even had a name for his shoulder pads—blue jays.

Baugh didn't take a direct path to become a great quarterback. Baseball was his first love. He played third base at Texas Christian University and was a shortstop in the St. Louis Cardinals' minor-league system. In fact, his nickname—Slingin' Sam—was given to him by Fort Worth sportswriter Flem Hall because of the way Baugh threw a baseball.

Baugh could hit the out route better than he could hit the curve-ball, so football became his sport, and Washington chose him with the sixth pick of the 1937 draft. He played tailback in the single-wing offense for his first four seasons and moved to quarterback in 1941 when Washington switched to the T formation that the Bears made popular with Sid Luckman.

Much of Baugh's career was linked with Luckman's, and the passers defined their era. Any time one of them was asked who the best quarterback in the NFL was, they named the other. On the day Baugh threw four touchdown passes and intercepted four passes, he was overshadowed by Luckman, who threw seven touchdown passes.

They met three times for the NFL championship. Luckman's Bears won 73–0 in 1940—"the most humiliating thing I've ever gone through in my life," Baugh said. It was humiliating, in part, because Baugh considered the 1940 team the best he ever played on. In 1942, Washington beat Chicago 14–6. And Luckman's Bears won 41–21 in 1943. Baugh intercepted Luckman in the 1942 championship game while Luckman intercepted Baugh in the 1943 championship game. A collision with Luckman in that game knocked out Baugh.

"I was still in there but I was calling plays we'd used the year before," Baugh said in *What a Game They Played*. "Then they took me out and at the half were asking me all of these questions about all kinds of damn things, and I don't remember if I could answer them or not. I finally went back in during the fourth quarter. I had a concussion, they told me later."

Baugh's most memorable championship game was a 28–21 victory over the Bears in his rookie season before Luckman entered the league. He threw for 355 yards, which stood as a postseason record until Russell Wilson threw for 385 against Atlanta in the 2012 playoffs. Afterward, Washington coach Ray Flaherty called it "the greatest one-man show ever put on in pro football."

The Bears' strategy was to try to injure Baugh, according to the book *Slingin' Sam: The Life and Times of the Greatest Quarterback Ever to Play the Game*. When Baugh and fullback Bronko Nagurski shook hands after the game, Baugh said, "Did you know that when you'd break through the line and head towards me [at safety], nobody ever blocked me?" Nagurski laughed and said, "No one was supposed to block you. Hey, I was supposed to run over you and get you out of the game."

It did not work.

"The only time I got hurt was when I got a broken rib from a young steer's horn," Baugh once said.

Born and raised in West Texas, Baugh was promoted as a cowboy. He wore a Stetson and cowboy boots when he was introduced to the press. With a pinch of tobacco in his lip, his Texas drawl, and his colorful language, Baugh was a natural for the role. Later in his life, he rode a mare named Bluebonnet and became a champion roper.

"He looked like the personification of every cowboy star who ever straddled a bronc, only more so," Washington owner George Preston Marshall once said.

Hollywood thought so, too. In 1988, Robert Duvall visited Baugh in Texas and played dominos with him. He then modeled his *Lonesome Dove* character, Gus McCrae, after Baugh. Forty-seven years earlier, during the height of Baugh's playing career, he starred in the 12-episode serial film *King of the Texas Rangers*.

While filming in California, he did not live the Hollywood life, however.

"Ah, shit on celebrity," he said in 1999. "It didn't make sense to be showboating all over Hollywood and spending a lot of money for a steak when I could take that money back to Texas and buy a whole cow."

That's pretty much what he did in 1941, using the $4,500 he made from *King of the Texas Rangers* to buy a cattle ranch on 7,500 acres in the panhandle of Texas, not far from the Double Mountain fork of the Brazos River. According to Texas Co-op Power, the house, built in 1902, had no electricity or running water initially, and Baugh and his wife took baths in a horse trough.

Shirley Povich of the *Washington Post* wrote that Baugh never learned to act like a big shot. Late in his career, when his skills were waning, Baugh asked to have his salary cut—twice. When Baugh retired, Marshall had to talk Baugh into taking the trophies, plaques, and awards he had been given.

Teammate George Buksar said Baugh was without a doubt the most popular man in football. Baugh never publicly criticized a teammate or complained, even though he never had a star receiver to throw to, played for eight head coaches, and his team's owner was considered by many to be the worst in the NFL.

"Sammy would still have all the passing records in football if he had the receivers they had today," Washington center Al DeMao said. "Sam never had that luxury."

On Sammy Baugh Day at Griffith Stadium on November 23, 1947, 2-6 Washington took on the 7-1 Cardinals, who had the best defense in the NFL and would win the NFL championship that year. Before the game, Washington tight end Joe Tereshinski spoke to his teammates. "There's the best football player in the world," he said, pointing to Baugh. "Let's show him what we think of him. Let's see that he doesn't get any mud on his pants today."

An inspired Washington team won 45–21 as Baugh completed 33 of 35 passes for 355 yards and six touchdowns. The Touchdown Club of Washington collected donations to purchase a Packard station wagon and presented it to Baugh. It was burgundy with gold-colored wood paneling. The license plate number was 33, Baugh's jersey number. On the side of the car was the inscription "Slinging Sam."

24.
Brett Favre

Brett Favre set an NFL record with eighteen consecutive 3,000-yard passing seasons.

Position: Quarterback

Teams: Falcons (1991), Packers (1992–2007), Jets (2008), Vikings (2009–2010)

By The Athletic Staff

Brett Favre's first regular-season pass attempt didn't go quite as Falcons offensive coordinator June Jones had drawn it up.

"We were getting beat down and June tells me, 'Hey, we are going to let the kid finish this one out, get him some film and stuff like that,'" said Billy Joe Tolliver, Atlanta's backup quarterback behind Pro Bowler Chris Miller in 1991.

Favre retired from the game 20 years later after a legendary run that included three MVP awards, two Super Bowls, one championship, and a record 297-game starting streak, but the beginning of his career was doomed to failure.

Falcons general manager Ken Herock had overruled head coach Jerry Glanville and the coaching staff in drafting Favre over Louisville's Browning Nagle, creating internal strife. Favre wasn't interested in being anyone's backup, but instead of dedicating himself to winning over the coaching staff, he checked out, resigned to the fact the staff wasn't invested in his success.

"So Favre goes out there and June calls, I want to say it was Mike Pritchard, on a shallow cross," said Tolliver. "Favre drops back there, and that head is down and he just lets go of this fricking missile. It's 100 miles an hour on like a 7-yard route."

Pritchard had no shot at making the catch. Washington linebacker Andre Collins picked him off and raced 15 yards for a touchdown. Favre had been on the field for one play, and the deficit had widened from 49–17 to 56–17.

Glanville barked at Favre along the sideline after the play, while Jones tried to summon his young third-string quarterback to a sideline meeting.

"Hey, how about that, my first pass in the pros was a touchdown," Favre told Glanville.

"Yeah, but it was for the other team," Glanville replied.

"Hell, 30 years from now, no one is going to remember that," Favre cracked.

Pritchard walked by just as Jones finally tracked down Favre.

"Mike, you learn to catch that ball right there, I'll make you famous," Favre told his wideout.

Jones looked at Tolliver. Tolliver looked at Jones.

"I think the kid gets it," Tolliver told his offensive coordinator. "Me and June just walked off in different directions, and Favre is sitting there saying, 'Hey, what did you guys want?'" Tolliver recalled. "That was pretty much the moment when I knew for a fact that this guy's got it."

Favre finished that loss to Washington with zero completions and two interceptions in four attempts, his only four attempts in live game action for the Falcons, although he did sometimes impress during competitive periods in practice.

"I knew he had the talent," Glanville said. "You could not disguise what was laying there in the weeds. But he did things that you have to decide, is one individual bigger than the team? I'll just say this, I've been coaching since '64, and he is the only guy I ever coached that is not in the team picture."

Favre could not be found as the Falcons prepared for their 1991 opener at Kansas City. He failed to show for the walk-through, missed the team picture, and hadn't checked in with anyone.

Glanville was furious. Tolliver, acquired days earlier so the staff could have a more experienced and reliable backup behind Miller, was conferring with Jones when a frazzled Favre suddenly drove up in a rush, emerged from his car, and ran over to his head coach.

Favre told Glanville he'd been involved in a car accident on the way to the facility. It was a difficult sell, to say the least, with Favre's undamaged car parked in plain view. Favre took another run at an alibi, explaining that his buddies from home were visiting, and the group had been involved in an accident while delivering Favre to the facility, leading them to return home so that Favre could retrieve his own vehicle.

"Is that your final story?" Glanville asked.

"Well, would you believe I *saw* a wreck?" Favre answered.

Glanville stared down his young quarterback.

"Favre, you *are* a wreck," the coach said.

The Falcons traded Favre to the Packers for a first-round pick on February 11, 1992. Atlanta VP of player personnel Jeff Herock hated to do it, but he felt there was little choice under the circumstances. Defending Favre at that stage of his career was a losing proposition, even though the talent was obvious.

Packers GM Ron Wolf and Herock were close friends and former coworkers, so Wolf knew how much Herock loved Favre as a talent. Wolf had planned to draft Favre with the Jets in 1991 only to have

Herock select the quarterback one spot before New York went on the clock.

There were other competitive tie-ins. Herock, who had played for Bill Walsh with Oakland and Cincinnati, had wanted to hire Walsh's top assistant, Mike Holmgren, to the Falcons, but the organization didn't want to wait through the 49ers' playoff run. Herock also made a hard pitch for Reggie White in free agency, only to have the Packers land him.

"Some friend Ron Wolf is," Herock said. "We always laugh about it. I say, 'You son of a bitch.' I couldn't get White signed. I couldn't get Brett to stay here. I wanted Holmgren, but I get Jerry Glanville."

Wolf was so eager to consummate the deal for Favre and so fearful the trade might collapse, he neglected to insist upon standard language making the deal contingent upon Favre passing a physical examination. That led to stressful moments for the newly hired Wolf when a Packers team doctor failed Favre on his initial physical, citing injuries sustained in an actual car accident Favre had suffered in college.

"I'd just bought a house," Wolf said, "and I'm thinking, 'Shit, I'm fired,' but it worked out. Brett never missed a game for the Packers, ever."

Holmgren's hard coaching and structured, timing-based offense provided Favre with a foundation that was lacking in Atlanta. Still, Favre's evolution took time.

"One thing I'll always remember with Brett was the first practice seeing him live," said Seahawks GM John Schneider, who was with the Packers at the time. "We were on the sideline, Brett threw an out route that got away from him, threw it over our heads. It hit the side of the indoor facility and it sounded like a fricking shotgun went off, it was so loud. And we're like, 'Holy cow, we gave up a first-round draft pick for this guy.'"

"God gave all of us gifts and some of us multiple gifts," former Packers linebacker George Koonce said, "but when Brett was standing in line to receive his gifts from God, God told him, 'I want you to go back around and get in line again, because I got some more to give you.' The way the ball came out of his hand, we as defensive players used to just marvel."

It wound up being the greatest trade the Packers ever made.

In January 1994, Favre led the Packers to their first postseason victory in more than a decade, 28–24 against the Detroit Lions in a game featuring an incredible play in the final two minutes.

Favre had by then already thrown two touchdown passes to Sterling Sharpe, including a 28-yard missile that might have punctured the Pontiac Silverdome if Sharpe hadn't snared it at the goal line with a defender on his back. Favre, 25 at the time, had also thrown a pick-six interception that day, not that he would have dwelled on such a thing.

Favre had about a minute remaining in his first playoff start, following a 1993 regular season in which he tossed an NFL-high 24 picks, including four against these same Lions with playoff seeding on the line a week earlier. The Packers were within a few yards of attempting the tying field goal.

Chris Jacke blasted practice kicks into a sideline net, but this game wasn't coming down to the kicker, not with the dice in Favre's hands. The most prolific of the gunslinger quarterbacks would have shocked no one if he'd thrown his second pick of the game or coughed up his 15th fumble in 17 games that year.

What actually happened helped send Favre hurtling toward three successive MVP seasons.

Favre rolled to his left, well outside the hash, and launched the ball at an awkward angle to the right corner of the end zone, more than 50 yards in the air, with pinpoint accuracy to Sharpe for the winning touchdown.

In the chaos that ensued along the Packers' sideline, Favre hoisted into the air an older member of the team's support staff who apparently hadn't quite processed the outcome.

"It's OK, kid, we'll get 'em next time," the staffer told Favre, thinking the Packers had lost.

So many extreme outcomes were possible when Favre had a football in his hands. No one could be too certain what might happen, or sometimes even what had actually happened. It's what made Favre the most compelling quarterback of his era, perhaps of any era.

There were some certainties. Favre would play every week for 297 consecutive starts, no matter how many shades of purple, green, and yellow various joints might have turned. It's an absurd streak accomplished during a rougher era. The streak began a year before Mosaic (later Netscape) introduced the first commercially popular web browser. It ended nearly two decades later with a team announcement sent to millions of smartphones via Twitter. Favre's palpable joy for the game and for competing was another constant.

Favre tossed 112 touchdown passes from 1995 to 1997, his MVP seasons. John Elway ranked second in the league over that stretch with 79. No one else had even 70.

The Packers, led not only by Favre but also elite defenders such as LeRoy Butler and Reggie White, dominated during their 1996 championship season especially. They won by lopsided margins through the playoffs: 35–14 against the San Francisco 49ers, 30–13 against the Carolina Panthers, and 35–21 against the New England Patriots.

Favre was at his peak, and so were the Packers.

"I loved the guy because it wasn't about him," Butler said. "Brett used to be embarrassed talking about MVPs around his teammates because he knew how important we were to him. I think that is why we won. We would run through a wall for him."

Holmgren and an offensive staff featuring multiple future head coaches—Andy Reid, Jon Gruden, and Steve Mariucci were a few— had reached Favre through a combination of tactics. They made it clear to the quarterback that they believed in him, that their own careers hinged on his performance. They also coached him hard, and sometimes harshly. Favre also got healthier through reduced partying and professional rehab to conquer a reliance on pain-killers.

"There are a lot of fabulous quarterbacks, but not everyone has the locker room like he did," Holmgren said. "All his teammates loved him. Now, he was a knucklehead sometimes with me, but they loved him and they played hard for him and he had so much fun playing. And they recognized that."

If Holmgren provided the old-school discipline and structure in the Walsh mold, Favre provided the irreverent counterbalance to keep the Packers loose.

"He was the only guy in the history of the NFL who had the guts to prank the head coach, the team president, the GM, Reggie White," Butler said. "Every time there was a joke, Brett did it."

Favre has disclosed past struggles with drugs and alcohol, but episodes later in Favre's career and in his post-playing life have cast a shadow on his congenial, devil-may-care persona. He was accused of sending inappropriate messages to a staffer while a member of the Jets in 2008, then fined $50,000 for failing to cooperate with the league's investigation into the matter. In 2020 and again in 2022, he was implicated in a massive welfare fraud scheme in his home state of Mississippi.

Wolf said he'd take Favre over any quarterback, including his successor, Aaron Rodgers, because he knew if there was a game tomorrow or anytime, Favre would be in the lineup, guaranteed. During the 297-game starting streak, 238 other quarterbacks started games in the NFL.

"The thing about Brett Favre is that he had to play the game," Wolf said. "That was so important to him. He had to play. And what a great mindset that is."

In the end, Favre walked away from the game with 71,838 passing yards, 508 touchdowns, and, yes, 336 interceptions.

23.
Barry Sanders

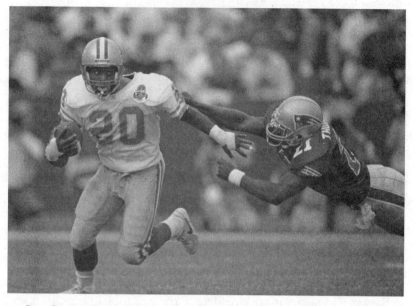

Barry Sanders (20) made first- or second-team All-Pro for ten consecutive seasons.

Position: Running Back
Team: Lions (1989–1998)

By Chris Burke

How does one describe the indescribable?

It's not just that Barry Sanders was elusive and shifty and nearly impossible to bring down. It's that he did things that no player, before him or since, could even think to replicate.

Perhaps his most famous run came in the 1991 postseason against the Cowboys, the Lions' lone playoff win to date of the Super Bowl era. Sanders took a handoff near midfield, ran full speed into a pileup of five defenders (and two or three of his own blockers), bounced off, and came out the other side. He then turned line-backer Ken Norton Jr.—a three-time Pro Bowler and Super Bowl champ with nearly 1,300 career tackles—absolutely inside out before racing to the end zone.

Stunning. Impossible.

And yet, Sanders's greatest moments probably didn't come on those highlight-reel plays. Instead, they were found in his ability to turn the mundane into the remarkable: a 5-yard gain on which he had to juke an unblocked defender in the backfield; a 2-yard run that saw him cut back across the entire width of the field just to pick up a few extra inches.

"What I like to tell people is that [it was] the runs that people didn't see," said former Lions left tackle Lomas Brown, a seven-time Pro Bowler. "Every Monday [in team meetings], there were three or four runs that we'd sit back and say, 'Oh my goodness, how did he do that?' Every Monday, you'd see three to four plays you'd probably never see from another running back. Some of those short losses were some of the best runs I've ever seen."

Sanders's knack for making defenders look foolish was so supernatural that the Lions even built it into their playbook. Detroit's run-and-shoot attack typically spread the field and left minimal blockers in to protect Sanders and his quarterback. If a defense overloaded the box to stop the run, well . . .

"[If] we had six guys, we'd block six," said former Lions guard Mike Compton. "If there was a seventh guy, it was 100 percent a coined phrase: 'That's Barry's guy.' Barry would have to make him miss."

"We had one of the most unsound blocking schemes, I think, probably in the history of the game," Compton said. "When have you ever heard [of] a run play where you were outnumbered out front but you keep the play on? That's how we would block some of our runs: Barry would be responsible for that free guy."

Almost without fail, Sanders could handle that free guy. He wouldn't so much change directions with the ball in his hands as he would teleport. A defender would line him up, break down for the tackle, and—poof!—Sanders was somewhere else, setting up another opponent for a demoralizing whiff.

He might have been the only sideline-to-sideline-*to-sideline* player in NFL history.

"If you miss him the first time," Dolphins defensive lineman Daryl Gardener told the *Miami Herald* before facing Sanders in 1997, "stay right there, because he's coming back at you."

At one point, in just the fifth game of his 1,470-yard, 14-touchdown rookie season, Sanders had the Vikings defense so flustered that Minnesota's coaching staff asked the refs to check Sanders's jersey for silicon spray.

"Guys have to do something to save their jobs," the Vikings' defensive coordinator at the time, Floyd Peters, told the *Minneapolis Star-Tribune*. "We weren't the first team to think that. Sometimes, you miss enough tackles, you want to believe he has something on."

Sanders wound up being named the NFL's Offensive Rookie of the Year in 1989, after he made what was, at the time, a groundbreaking decision to enter the draft early. The Lions selected him No. 3 overall, behind only Troy Aikman (Dallas) and Tony Mandarich (Green Bay).

He followed up that ROY award with a rushing title in 1990, then led the NFL in rushing TDs (16) and rushing yards per game (103.2) in 1991. He'd claim three more rushing titles (1994, '96, and '97). During the last of those seasons, Sanders became just the third running back in league history to eclipse the 2,000-yard mark, reaching that height with a 184-yard showing in the regular-season finale to help Detroit clinch a playoff berth.

In 1999, Sanders's 10th season in the NFL and with the Lions, he carried the ball a career-high 343 times for 1,491 yards. But he scored just four touchdowns, and Detroit finished a disappointing 5-11. A few months later, on the eve of training camp, Sanders retired.

The story of his career cannot be told without some time spent on the end. That retirement announcement came via a letter faxed to his hometown newspaper, the *Wichita Eagle* (Kansas).

"The reason I am retiring is simple," Sanders wrote. "My desire to exit the game is greater than my desire to remain in it. I have searched my heart through and through and feel comfortable with the decision."

Sanders was just 31 at the time and, with 15,269 career rushing yards, needed just 1,457 more to break the NFL's all-time record, held then by Walter Payton. (Emmitt Smith, with 18,355 yards, later topped Payton.) It was a startling decision, and it took the Lions more than a decade to fully recover.

Even once the franchise became semicompetitive again, the running game remained an albatross. In fact, the Lions once endured a stretch of nearly five years (November 23, 2013, to October 21, 2018) without a 100-yard rusher. Sanders went over the century mark 76 times during his career, roughly half of his regular-season appearances.

Of course, before any of that, Sanders had to break through as a potential superstar. You can't tell Sanders's story without the beginning, either.

For the first three-plus years of his prep career at Wichita North High, Sanders primarily played defense. Before Sanders's senior season, though, Wichita North hired a new head coach, Dale Burkholder. He saw something in the undersized, underutilized Sanders that no one else had.

"I was still playing defensive back," Sanders said during his Pro Football Hall of Fame enshrinement speech in 2004. "Actually, I was playing cornerback and sort of wingback, second-string wingback. And Coach noticed that: 'You know, I probably should put this kid at running back and see what he can do.'"

Sanders rushed for 1,417 yards on 10.2 yards per carry over the final seven games of the season, enough to earn him a scholarship offer from Oklahoma State. There, he backed up the great Thurman Thomas for two years before turning in what might be the most impressive season in college football history as a junior: 2,628 yards rushing at a staggering 238.9 yards per game, 37 touchdowns, and

3,250 all-purpose yards. Later, after capturing the Heisman Trophy, Sanders rushed for 222 yards and five touchdowns in a Holiday Bowl win over Wyoming. (At the time, the NCAA did not count bowl game stats toward a player's official totals.)

The next season, he was a Detroit Lion.

A holdout through all of his rookie training camp, Sanders did not sign a contract and join his new team until the Wednesday before Detroit's 1989 season opener against the Cardinals. Lions head coach Wayne Fontes wasted no time in getting Sanders onto the field in Week 1, anyway.

"His first carry, Mike Utley was playing right tackle, I was playing right guard, Kevin Glover was the center," former Lions guard Ken Dallafior recalled. "We ran a '36 slant,' which was off the right tackle. Barry ran off Mike and I, then cut behind the double-team block and went for [18] yards. Mike and I looked at each other, and I won't say what words we used, but we sprinted over and picked Barry off the turf and pushed people away from him.

"You knew at that minute he was extraordinarily special. Our eyes were as big as saucers. Like, 'I can't believe what I just saw.' That was his first run from the line of scrimmage."

That air of wonderment never faded for Sanders's teammates over his next 3,061 career rushing attempts (and 352 receptions). Blocking for Barry was a singular experience. Brown estimated that 30 percent of Sanders's runs were complete ad-libs by the remarkably talented running back—plays that started off in one direction and wound up somewhere else entirely. Former Lions guard Jeff Hartings put that number at 50 percent.

"I know one time," said offensive tackle Ray Roberts, who spent five seasons in Detroit (1996–2000), "we were talking about a new contract—as an offensive lineman, you don't have a whole lot of stats—and we went to the Lions, like, 'This percentage of runs started out to the left side. We don't know where they ended up, but [Barry's] first step was to the left side.'"

Because of Sanders's running style, the Lions' offensive line as a collective group never received much credit (in fact, it was usually the opposite) for their running back's accomplishments. During his Detroit career, though, Sanders ran behind several accomplished blockers. Brown, a seven-time Pro Bowler, arguably has a Hall of Fame case; Glover, over a 15-year career, was among the NFL's steadiest players up front; Hartings made two Pro Bowls and was an eventual Super Bowl champion in Pittsburgh.

Being cast as an afterthought to one of the game's greatest shows still nags at some of those linemen.

"I hate that," Brown said. "I hate it. . . . They always say, 'If Barry had Emmitt [Smith]'s offensive line, he'd have had 20,000 yards rushing.' And I tell people all the time that's not true. Barry's style was just totally different than Emmitt's style. . . .

"Regardless of whether he had our offensive line or Emmitt Smith's offensive line in front of him, Barry was going for the big play. And we loved it."

Sanders's sudden retirement aside, it would've been difficult to begrudge him much. On top of everything else, he also happened to be perhaps the most humble player in the Lions' locker room. His own father, William Sanders, barely even acknowledged Barry's career while presenting him for Hall of Fame enshrinement. He brought Barry to the podium by calling him the "third-best running back that ever lived."

Many of those who watched Barry Sanders play, those who lined up as his teammate or tried to tackle him, might disagree.

On the final day of the 1996 regular season, Sanders needed 160 yards to claim the league's rushing title. In the first quarter, he broke loose for a 54-yard touchdown run, juking an unblocked defender at the line, running through an arm tackle, spinning away from two more defenders, and then using a block from receiver Brett Perriman to pull away.

"As he passed me running down the field," Hartings recalled, "I was thinking, 'I'm in a video game. Someone's hitting buttons and making him spin and jump cut.' I don't know if anybody blocked anybody."

"Quintessential Barry Sanders!" ABC *Monday Night Football* announcer Al Michaels exclaimed as Sanders reached the end zone. "Highlight-film star."

"Oh, wow," color commentator Frank Gifford added. "I love to watch him."

What else is there to say?

22.
Deion Sanders

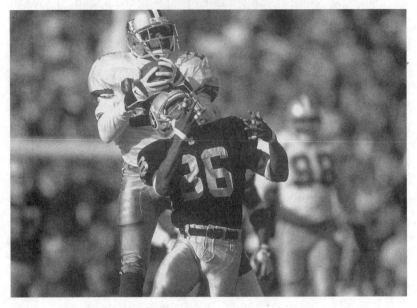

Deion Sanders (21) had nine career touchdowns on kick or punt returns
and matched that with interception-return TDs.

Position: Cornerback

Teams: Falcons (1989–1993), 49ers (1994), Cowboys (1995–1999), Washington
(2000), Ravens (2004–2005)

By Mike Sando

Deion Sanders smashed a home run and two doubles and totaled four RBIs for the New York Yankees on a September
Tuesday in 1989.

One day later, Sanders signed his rookie contract with the Atlanta Falcons.

Four days after that, Sanders scored a touchdown just five minutes into his first NFL game.

This wasn't just any touchdown. Sanders broke two tackles, eluded two other defenders, and outran a final helpless Los Angeles Ram during a 68-yard punt return. A teammate would call the moment as electric as anything he witnessed on a football field, but these were not even the most entertaining particulars. Terry Bradshaw, working the game for CBS, affirmed on the broadcast Sanders's status as the NFL's ultimate showman from the very beginning.

"Deion Sanders told us yesterday that for every touchdown he gets on a punt return, he will give the blocking people three choices: a Gucci watch, a bunch of money, or a gold chain," Bradshaw told viewers. "He can afford it and that's excitement and that's Prime Time and that's why he was their No. 1 draft choice."

Sanders remains the only person to score an NFL touchdown and hit a Major League Baseball home run in the same week. He's the only one to play in both a World Series and a Super Bowl. But he was so much more than an accomplished two-sport athlete. No other superstar in NFL history has combined Sanders's two-sport athletic range with such a deliberately flamboyant public persona, all while remaining one of the guys in the locker room.

"Sometimes guys make it on fame, sometimes guys make it on talent," said former Falcons linebacker Jessie Tuggle, a five-time Pro Bowl choice. "Deion made it in for both. He was a special individual on and off the field."

Describing Sanders as an eight-time Pro Bowler, six-time Associated Press First-Team All-Pro, 1994 Defensive Player of the Year, two-time Super Bowl champ, and first-ballot Pro Football Hall of Famer is insufficient. Calling him the greatest cover corner, or at least one of the top few, is only part of the evaluation.

"I don't know who all the corners are in the Hall of Fame, but in his era, there wasn't anybody any better than Deion Sanders," Hall of Fame general manager Ron Wolf said.

Sanders knew how to cover. He also knew even before his arrival in the NFL how to get the media to cover him. He was trending when the metrics to measure such things were primitive.

"He was ahead of the curve in those days, branding himself as Prime Time with the fur coats and limousines coming to the games," former Falcons assistant coach Jimmy Raye said. "It was a spectacle. He talked the talk, but he could walk the walk. He was accepted into the fold immediately."

When Sanders played at Florida State, the Seminoles would spend the night before a game across the Georgia border in Thomasville, then bus to the stadium in Tallahassee the next day. Buses would drop off players near the football dorm, where players would drop their bags in their rooms and then walk a short distance, perhaps a couple hundred yards, to the fieldhouse and locker room. This was a perfectly fine arrangement for most players.

"On the big games, Deion, he'd get off that bus, he would have a limousine take him around to the front of the stadium, probably a half-a-mile limousine ride on game day," former FSU and NFL quarterback Brad Johnson said. "That's how Prime Time was built. He made a name for himself. Obviously, he backed it up on the field in college and then in the pros playing baseball, football, riding helicopters from World Series games, Atlanta Braves to Falcons games."

Sanders's style of personal branding could easily be construed as selfish, but teammates and coaches at every level say it wasn't so.

"One of the nicest human beings I've ever been around," former Falcons receiver Mike Pritchard said. "After I was drafted, Deion actually picked me up and showed me around Atlanta. He wanted me to feel welcome. It just settled me down and allowed me to be more confident once I did get signed and delivered and out there for training camp my rookie year. He was the best teammate a player could ever have."

Johnson called Sanders "a great locker room guy" at FSU and said antics such as the limo rides were mostly for show. And what a show it was.

"We draft him, he comes in with gold chains on, and I said, 'This guy, he's going to set this city on fire,' which he did," former Falcons executive Ken Herock said. "He comes in and he just automatically lights everything up. Everybody loved him. He's infectious. When you're around him, you want to do well, you want to play well."

The Falcons had selected Aundray Bruce first overall in 1988 and had built their marketing around him. That changed a year later when Sanders fell to Atlanta with the fifth pick.

"I'm sitting at home watching TV," Tuggle said, "and every station in Atlanta was at the airport when they got there and I was thinking, 'They didn't do this big of an uproar when we had the No. 1 overall pick and picked Aundray Bruce.' They had a big interview and Prime Time came in like Prime Time: the curly hair and the dressy shirt, the suit and the sunglasses. You would think he was a character right out of Hollywood."

The 1989 draft had four Hall of Famers in the first five picks, and the Packers' ill-fated decision to select Tony Mandarich at No. 2 saved the Falcons, who wanted one of the Sanderses, Barry or Deion.

"Deion was so dynamic," Herock said. "Barry was on the quiet side. We needed someone to excite the fan base. I was around football a long time with some great Raider players and never saw anybody else who can really get everything—the city, the town, the team—that excited."

The Falcons' 87-game streak without a punt return for a touchdown ended less than six minutes into Sanders's first game.

"I played with 93 Pro Bowl players in my career, and I have never felt anticipation in a stadium like when Deion played that first game against the Rams," said Hugh Millen, a Falcons quarterback from 1988 to 1990.

Millen was working out at the Falcons' facility one offseason day in 1989 when his usual routine turned into a spectacle. Prime Time was making his first appearance at the facility. Sanders wasn't there to spot Millen on the bench press.

"He had this entourage that was going around the facility and all these cameras following him like, 'Here is Deion in the new facility,'" Millen said. "I'm the only one in the weight room lifting and now it is like this opportunity, like Deion meets his first teammate, right? Five cameras are watching us do the bro hug or whatever the hell we were doing, and the owner and GM and everybody is there, like it was this almost staged thing."

Say the words "Neon Deion" or "Prime Time" without mentioning "Sanders" and generations of U.S. sports fans can instantly form a vision of him in their minds—so dynamic, so talented, so versatile, so confident, so productive, so media savvy, so Deion.

"What you see is what you get, and what you don't see is what you get," said former 11-year NFL cornerback Toi Cook, who won a Super Bowl with Sanders on the 49ers and was a national champion as a baseball player at Stanford. "Deion could have attended Stanford, Deion could have attended Princeton, Deion could have attended Yale. Most people don't know that. They only see what they want to see. But beyond all of that glitz is a super CPU that was blessed with super speed. He is like the perfect DB."

Sanders always made a distinction between cockiness and confidence. He wanted to project the latter, which he saw as based in reality and therefore more substantive.

"There's no question he has as much confidence as anybody that I've ever seen play sports," Hall of Fame quarterback Warren Moon said.

Moon finished the 1990 season as the NFL leader in passing yards per game (312) and touchdown passes (33) with the Houston Oilers. In Week 1, Moon was throwing into coverage during the final minute of a game his Oilers trailed 40–27 when Sanders took the ball back in high style, 82 yards along the Houston sideline.

"Deion put his hand behind his helmet and he started Cadillacking at the 50 with Warren Moon chasing him," said Jerry Glanville, who coached Moon in Houston before becoming the Falcons' head coach in 1990.

Sanders barely acknowledged Moon's diving attempt at a tackle. He began high-stepping before he even reached midfield. After the play, the Falcons celebrated in the end zone boisterously enough to incur a penalty. When Sanders finally returned to the Atlanta side-line, the head coach was waiting for him.

"I said, 'Deion, I love that Cadillacking,'" Glanville said. "He goes, 'You do?' And I said, 'But let's do it from the 10-yard line in.' He did it from the 50!"

Even the perfect quarterback throwing to the perfect receiver with the perfect play call wasn't always good enough against Sand-ers, as the 49ers discovered when trying to close out a 19–13 victory against the Falcons in 1990. San Francisco started that season 10-0 on its way to a 14-2 record, but only after surviving a scare on third-and-3 with 1:12 left in regulation.

Mike Holmgren, the 49ers' offensive coordinator at the time, was one of the preeminent play callers for a two-decade period begin-ning in the late 1980s. He cites that 1990 finish against Sanders for making him conservative at times later in his career.

"We had sprint right option, which was a great play for us," Holmgren said. "We got Joe Montana as the quarterback, Jerry Rice is the primary receiver. You couldn't ask for a better situation. It got down to third-and-short and we could ice it with a first down, or I could run a running play and move the clock."

Holmgren called for the pass.

"So we run sprint right option, Deion is the corner, and he is sup-posed to do something else," Holmgren said. "Joe throws the ball to Jerry, but Deion had broken coverage and come up. It hit him right in the chest. He could have caught it and gone, we would have lost the game. We were lucky that he dropped it. It always stuck with me, thinking nothing could go wrong with the greatest quarterback in the game, the greatest receiver. But because of Deion Sanders's ability, he almost beat us with that play."

Some corners are elite in coverage. Others have rare speed. Some catch the ball well. A few threaten the end zone with the ball in their hands. Sanders achieved the highest level in all those areas. He was also special for his ability to bait quarterbacks.

Along those lines, Glanville connected Sanders to another Hall of Fame corner he coached decades earlier in Lem Barney of the

Detroit Lions. Barney had carried on the tradition from another legendary Lions cornerback, Dick "Night Train" Lane.

"All three did something nobody does in football: let a receiver get open intentionally," Glanville said. "When I had Lem Barney, we are playing the Vikings to win the game and his guy is running through the post and Fran Tarkenton sees what I see, lets it go, and Lem Barney picks it off. When I got Deion, he let the guy get away from him too far, I thought. But both Deion and Lem Barney said the same thing to me: 'If I don't let them get open, I won't get any work.' Who invented that? Night Train Lane."

As Glanville put it, all three would have been Hall of Famers regardless of who was coaching them. Sanders once dozed off during a Falcons film session, only to have an angry coach spot him and order the lights turned on.

"Deion said, 'Hey, listen, I play corner. Does my guy ever catch a ball?'" Tuggle recalled. "He didn't say that disrespectfully, but if you go out there on Sunday and you shut your guy down week in and week out, what else can they say? Nothing else was said."

Michael Haynes, who played with Sanders on the Falcons and against him as a member of the Saints, was a receiver who had clocked 4.4-second times in the 40.

"I was a speed guy who used to always think, you get a step on somebody, ain't no way they're going to catch up," Haynes said. "Not with Deion. We were playing the 49ers one time, the receiver ran a post route and Deion let him get into the post. As soon as the ball was thrown, he turned it on and undercut the pass and he tipped the ball with one hand to himself. It was a well-thrown ball. He just turned it on, went and got the thing."

When Sanders was with the Cowboys in 1995, the Raiders' Raghib Ismail had a step on him and was headed deep. Quarterback Jeff Hostetler delivered the ball for what could have become a long touchdown. Ismail had run 10.2 in the 100 meters and had a season-best 6.07 in the 55 meters during the 1991 NCAA indoor season. "Rocket" was his nickname.

Sanders reeled in Ismail, leaped over him to intercept the ball over his shoulder, held up the ball to the crowd as if showing off his loot, and commenced a long return before stepping out of bounds to avoid a hard hit. The play showcased Sanders's speed, ball awareness, hands, showmanship, and smarts.

"In *Mortal Kombat*, there is a guy that throws the spirit—not a spirit, like a javelin—and ropes you in, brings you in," Cook said. "Deion had that ability, but without grabbing you."

Also in that game, Sanders got deeper than Ismail's teammate, former Olympic gold medalist James Jett, on a pass to the end zone. Jett clocked 10.1 in the 100 and once beat Carl Lewis in an Olympic prelim.

"Deion had pull-over speed like the highway patrol—get over here, pull over," Cook said. "James Jett and guys like that don't have to double-move anybody. They can just run by people, like Willie Gault or Randy Moss. If those guys are double-moving you, you got some skills."

Sanders finished his career with 53 interceptions and a 25-yard average return distance. He collected one of his most memorable picks in his lone season with the 49ers, against the team that drafted him, in the Georgia Dome. The game became famous for Sanders's second-quarter brawl with former teammate Andre Rison, a 93-yard Sanders interception return for a touchdown, and a postgame news conference that Atlanta media replayed all week, and then some.

"I've got one thing to say: This is my house!" Sanders told reporters after the 49ers' blowout victory. "I built this, and this is my house! I don't care if I'm with the Falcons or not. This is my house and it will always be my house."

By then, Sanders had already addressed his former team, looking back over his shoulder and shouting toward them as he returned the ball along the Falcons' sideline.

"He is running by me and everyone on the sideline with his hand behind his head, high-stepping, yelling out, 'This is my house!'" Tuggle said. "Man, the fans in the Georgia Dome went crazy. Everybody on the bench for the 49ers came to the end zone, and Deion literally put on a show for them. That almost felt like the perfect movie script if a person wanted to write one for him to come back to the Georgia Dome. It was really unbelievable."

That 93-yard return helped Sanders finish his career ranked fourth in interception return yardage (1,331). He's first among cornerbacks who did not convert to safety. The total includes yardage from games where Sanders himself did not pick off a pass. Others who intercepted passes knew to get the ball to the cornerback who posed a scoring threat from anywhere on the field.

The get-it-to-Deion mandate unfolded most conspicuously during the final moments of a 27–20 playoff victory over the Saints on December 28, 1991. Cornerback Tim McKyer picked off a pass and could have ended the game by kneeling. Instead, he lateraled to Sanders, who ran 32 yards before pitching to Joe Fishback, who scored. All the while, Sanders's friend and special guest, superstar rapper MC Hammer, celebrated on the Falcons' sideline. The touchdown was nullified when officials determined Sanders had pitched the ball forward. Still, the Falcons won the game.

"You gotta be really good to have antics in this league because your opponents generally don't like it," former two-time NFL head coach Dick Jauron said. "Deion could do whatever he wanted."

Sanders is tied for fifth with nine interception returns for touchdowns. He scored nine additional times on returns (six punt, three kickoff).

"Deion could cover like nobody I've ever seen and gambled more than any corner I've ever seen, only because of his confidence and his speed to recover," Moon said. "I think Mike Haynes was the second-best corner that I ever played against, just a very long corner who was hard to throw over. But I don't remember Mike letting anybody beat him on purpose. Deion had the speed to catch up and either knock the ball down or maybe even intercept it if the quarterback didn't lead the receiver, so you almost had to throw a perfect ball if you were going to beat him."

If Sanders had a weakness, it was long said to be his unwillingness to tackle, but many who have studied Sanders say he was much better than advertised in that aspect of the game. They say he wouldn't seek out contact if a teammate could make the tackle instead, but if a tackle needed to be made, Sanders would make it, sometimes emphatically.

"We went down there to Dallas [in Week 7 of the 1999 season], and we were a really good offensive football team that year," former Washington coach Norv Turner said. "The mentality was, you could run at Deion because he'd pick his spots."

Washington opened the game with an outside handoff to 230-pound halfback Stephen Davis, who led the NFL that season in rushing touchdowns (17) and rushing yards per game (100.4) for a team that ranked second in scoring. Sanders shot underneath his blocker and launched himself into Davis's legs for a 4-yard loss. Message sent.

"Deion hit him with a really, really physical tackle," Turner said. "We weren't counting on that. That mentality that he wouldn't tackle, he is like a lot of these real good players. He picked his spots, but he was as competitive a person as you are going to see."

With the Falcons, Sanders would stay after practice and challenge wide receivers to a role reversal. Sanders would run routes against the receivers. Hugh Millen would throw pass after pass to the greatest cornerback he ever saw. Oh, and how did those post-practice battles go?

"How do you think it went?" Millen said. "Deion is as fast as he wants to be. Ninety-five percent of the guys you watch on Sunday are only 5 percent better than the guys who just got cut at the end of August and are laying your tile, but there are a few exceptions to that where you say, 'This guy is a man among boys in the ultimate theater of men.' Deion was one of those guys. Twitchiest dude I have ever seen."

Sanders finished his career with 60 receptions for 784 yards and three touchdowns. He regularly lobbied offensive coaches for playing time. That included the night before the 49ers' Super Bowl

XXIX victory against the San Diego Chargers, when Sanders called offensive coordinator Mike Shanahan in an effort to secure snaps late in the game.

Shanahan said Sanders was not only a great competitor but also adept at identifying which teammates and opponents truly loved the game. Those skills were valuable to Sanders in his role as head coach at Jackson State, and they continue to be in his first FBS job at Colorado. "Coach Sanders" might be more than three decades removed from offering Gucci watches, cash, and gold chains to teammates who spring him for touchdowns, but the legend endures.

21.
Aaron Rodgers

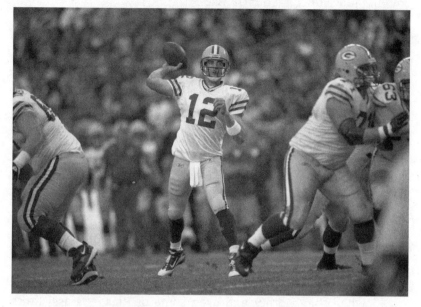

His outstanding passing accuracy put Aaron Rodgers (12)
atop multiple season-leader lists in his career.

Position: Quarterback
Team: Packers (2005–2022)

By Matt Schneidman

Not long after Craig Rigsbee named a true freshman as his starting quarterback at Butte Community College in Oroville, California, in 2002, the coach received a scathing two-page letter from the mother of the quarterback who lost the job.

Rigsbee chose a quarterback from nearby Pleasant Valley High School (in Chico, California) who stood only 6 feet tall and weighed a mere 165 pounds. He was smart and had a quick release, but he lacked arm strength.

The mother wrote in the letter that Rigsbee didn't know football. That he didn't know what he was doing because he was an offensive lineman in college. That he was the worst coach ever because he couldn't judge talent at quarterback.

"Probably the worst letter that I've ever received in my life as a coach," Rigsbee remembered almost 20 years later.

The quarterback he started? The one who this fuming mother thought her son should play over?

His name was Aaron Rodgers.

It may seem like hyperbole given everything he has accomplished, but Rodgers has been overlooked more than you'd imagine for a quarterback of his stature.

Such as . . .

. . . when he received almost no interest from Division I colleges in high school and settled for Butte after Illinois wanted him only as a walk-on. Illinois head coach Ron Turner's nephew was Rodgers's high school quarterbacks coach, and Rigsbee maintains, "He still is very upset about that . . . Aaron was crushed."

. . . when that mother and even some of Rigsbee's assistants thought Rodgers should ride the bench at Butte.

. . . when he endured arguably the most infamous draft-day plummet in history in the 2005 NFL Draft before the Packers picked him at No. 24.

. . . when Packers fans mercilessly booed him at Family Night in 2008 inside Lambeau Field ahead of his first season as a starter after taking over for Brett Favre.

. . . when the Packers traded up to select another quarterback, Jordan Love, in the first round of the 2020 draft with four years remaining on Rodgers's contract.

Through it all, Rodgers has proven one thing: if you slight him, overlook him, doubt him, he will prove you wrong. Rodgers will deny that he needs extra motivation, and maybe he's being truthful when he says that, but three of Rodgers's four MVP Awards came directly after the only three times players voted him outside the top 10 on the NFL Top 100 list.

"I would never bet against him coming off a year where he thinks that maybe he got slighted or maybe he didn't get respected like he should," Rigsbee said, "because his whole life has been like that."

If not for Rigsbee, Rodgers might not have made it to his first year at community college, let alone his 18th year in the NFL.

No Division I schools sought his football skills, so why not put his genius to work in another field? Law school was an option, perhaps a more viable one than sports. Football clearly didn't want him like he wanted it. One letter said no, then another, then another.

"He wasn't getting anything," Rigsbee said, "and he thought about quitting."

But Rigsbee wouldn't let Rodgers's talent go to waste. He knew there was something in him, even if nobody else saw it. So he called Rodgers, asked where he lived, and realized Rodgers's family home was only about 120 yards from his own in Chico.

Rodgers's mom, Darla, answered the door.

"No kid of mine is gonna go to JC," Rigsbee recalls her saying because of how smart Rodgers was. "I just want to let you know."

Rigsbee pitched her on why she should let her son play football at junior college, the type of team they had at Butte, the role he'd have, the competition they'd face, the exposure to Division I programs he'd get.

He spent an hour and a half convincing her. He was there so long that she made cookies during the visit. He explained to young Aaron that he had two quarterbacks returning, one that was good and one that was *really* good. He'd have his work cut out for him.

"Hey coach, I'll stop you right there," Rodgers, then a high school senior, interjected. "I don't really care who you got coming back. Only thing that I'll ask is you give me a legitimate chance to start."

Rodgers asked if Rigsbee would let him go to a four-year college if he played well enough his freshman year. Rigsbee thought that was ambitious, perhaps too ambitious, because of the quarterback room Rodgers would join at Butte and because of the reality that players typically spend two years at junior college before going to Division I.

But he obliged, ignored those assistants who wanted Rodgers on the bench, and sure enough, Rodgers spent only one season at community college before then–Cal coach Jeff Tedford caught wind of him while recruiting Butte tight end Garrett Cross.

In two years at Cal, Rodgers completed 63.1 percent of his passes for 5,469 yards, 43 touchdowns, and only 13 interceptions while helping the Golden Bears to an 18-8 record during that span. He cemented himself as one of the top quarterbacks in the 2005 draft class and hoped to join the team he grew up rooting for, the 49ers, with the No. 1 overall pick.

But the 49ers selected Alex Smith instead. Rodgers waited and waited. Was it the elevated height at which he held the ball before he threw? The perceived lack of deep-ball prowess?

"There was no doubt in my mind he was much more prepared to be an NFL quarterback," Tedford said, comparing Rodgers to Smith. "He played from under the center. You got certain people who say something about how he held the ball, but there was nothing to say he couldn't throw a long ball. He was flawless, really. I believe it just came down to a personality preference. Aaron had a lot of confidence in himself. . . . Alex never took one snap under the center and really, in my mind, even though Alex was a very good player, in my mind, being NFL-ready, Aaron was much further ahead."

No quarterbacks were taken from pick 2 to pick 23, but look at some of the names drafted before him: wide receiver Troy Williamson, defensive end Erasmus James, cornerback Fabian Washington. If you thought Rodgers would just brush off his hours-long wait in the greenroom that left him stranded as the last one there, you were sorely mistaken.

He felt slighted, overlooked, doubted.

In an interview with San Francisco's CBS TV affiliate that night, Rodgers was asked how disappointed he was to not be a 49er.

"Not as disappointed as the 49ers will be that they didn't draft me."

• • •

Local TV crews and fans staked out Austin Straubel International Airport in Green Bay on Family Night in 2008.

While Rodgers prepared for his first appearance in front of a packed Lambeau Field as the full-time starter, cameras awaited Favre's arrival in a private jet 10 minutes away. Favre wanted to play for the Packers after officially retiring not long before, and he was inside the stadium to hear the fans who wanted him back jeer Rodgers when the young quarterback struggled, albeit not mightily, in a glorified exhibition.

The Packers stuck with Rodgers at some fans' behest, eventually trading Favre to the Jets, and Rodgers set out to prove the organization made the right choice.

"For him to get that chance and turn out to be the player he is, it's surreal," Tramon Williams, a longtime teammate of Rodgers, told the *Wisconsin State Journal* in 2018. "But that summer? It takes a courageous, strong-minded guy to do what he did. Because most people would not be able to do that. Obviously, he's the quarterback he is today because of that."

What those fans didn't know is they were booing someone who'd grow to be as good as or better—in our collective mind, considering he's ranked higher in our NFL 100—than Favre.

After a playoff-less 6-10 campaign his first season as a starter, Rodgers and the Packers went 11-5 and lost in the opening round of the playoffs in 2009. In just his third year at the helm, he carried a 10-6 team that sneaked into the playoffs as the NFC's No. 6 seed to a Super Bowl championship. In what still stands as his only appearance in the game—the biggest knock on his otherwise prolific legacy—Rodgers completed 24 of 39 passes for 304 yards and three touchdowns without an interception in a 31–25 win over the Steelers en route to MVP honors.

He and the Packers have appeared in the NFC Championship Game four times since then and lost all four, twice in excruciating fashion in one-possession games against the Seahawks (2014) and Buccaneers (2020) and twice via blowouts against the Falcons (2016) and 49ers (2019).

Rodgers's status as one of the greatest to ever play the position, and quite frankly the sport itself, is already solidified. He has earned a reputation as someone who makes the impossible look mundane.

Remember that ESPY-winning throw to Jared Cook against the Cowboys in the 2016 playoffs? What about those Hail Mary passes against the Cardinals, Giants, and Lions? And the 34-yard touchdown pass to Davante Adams that didn't count against the Bears after Rodgers somehow evaded three pass rushers and dropped a dime while getting chopped in half? Who else can do all that, not to mention the list of superhuman throws that would resemble a CVS receipt if we took the time to list them all?

"Being with that guy," Adams said, "it's allowed me to know what true greatness is."

"I was having a discussion with Robert Tonyan last night," Packers wide receiver Allen Lazard said. "[Rodgers] is not a quarterback. He's a professional thrower of the ball. And if you really watch and kind of study his film, just the way that he's able to throw the ball, especially in the body positions that he's in, it's not recommended by a lot of coaches. . . . Jumping, twisting, looking off defenders, the timing of things, he's just like a kid back there playing backyard football, and it's a blessing to be able to play with him, alongside him, and something that I don't take for granted because all the passes that he makes are unbelievable."

Late into his 30s, Rodgers still can make any throw, at any time, from anywhere on the field. You'd be hard-pressed to find a quarterback who is smarter, has better manipulated defenses before and after the snap, turned his hard count into a lethal weapon and cut years off the lives of defensive coaches who endured sleepless nights before and after facing him.

He's already proven them wrong: that mother who mailed an angry letter to Rigsbee and those Butte assistants, the Division I schools that didn't recruit him, the 49ers and those frustrated Packers fans in August 2008.

And if you think he's finished after following up two MVPs with what for him was a down season in 2022, that's all right. That's just how he wants it, just how he has thrived his entire life.

"Here's just this kid from a small town that wanted a chance and proved everybody wrong every step of the way," said Rigsbee, the coach who might've saved Rodgers' career 20 years ago. "When you doubt him is when he's gonna be his best."

20.
Bruce Smith

Bruce Smith (78) was named to two All-Decade teams
and set an NFL record with thirteen seasons of 10 or more sacks.

Position: Defensive End

Teams: Bills (1985–1999), Washington (2000–2003)

By Tim Graham

Y ou know you're a big deal when Dennis Hopper huffs the insoles of your dirty shoes.

Younger Buffalo Bills fans might think Josh Allen has western New York by its blue collar with his various commercial roles, but in the early 1990s, the franchise's greatest player was the subject of an iconic advertisement, starring an iconic actor for an iconic company.

"It's hard to describe the magnitude of what that meant in that moment of time for the Bills, for the generation that was watching and for my career," Hall of Fame defensive end Bruce Smith said. "It took on a life of its own.

"It's pretty damn cool. It has stood the test of time."

Smith was such a diabolical force that advertising firm Wieden & Kennedy chose him to be an obsession of fictitious, mentally unstable referee Stanley Craver (played by Hopper) in a famous Nike commercial loaded with highlights of Smith terrorizing helpless blockers and quarterbacks.

"You know what Bruce does in these shoes, man?" the demented Craver says after sneaking into the Bills' locker room to whiff Smith's cleats. "Bad things, man! I mean bad things!"

New York Jets left tackle Jeff Criswell couldn't escape bad things. Eighteen seconds into the commercial, Smith ragdolls him.

With the commercial in high circulation, Criswell was demolished dozens of times a day on national television.

"You had to bring your best game, or else you were going to have your ass handed to you," Criswell said from his home in Greenwich, Connecticut. "He could literally throw you on your head and make you look bad. Not many guys could topple a 300-pound tackle the way that he could."

Smith was an unprecedented combination of pass rusher and run stuffer, who finished his career with the most sacks in NFL history and the most tackles by any defensive lineman.

He was an eight-time All-Pro and was named to 11 Pro Bowls. He was Defensive Player of the Year twice. The Pro Football Hall of Fame voted him to its All-Decade teams for the 1980s and 1990s.

Over his 19 seasons, Smith amassed 200 sacks, two more than his contemporary Reggie White. Sacks weren't officially counted until 1982, but when Pro Football Focus recently published its findings of unofficial sack records, Smith still stood at the top. Deacon Jones was credited with 173.5 sacks.

Smith forced 43 fumbles and recovered 15. He recorded 1,224

tackles, an unofficial number but illustrative of his three-down dominance.

"You can look at his sacks, but it's bigger than that," seven-time Pro Bowl left tackle Richmond Webb said. "Those pass-rush specialists get to rest on first and sometimes second down and come in fresh.

"This guy didn't leave the field until it was time to punt. He was out there for 10 or 12 plays straight. That's what is so rare."

In 20 postseason games, he produced 14.5 more sacks, including a safety in Super Bowl XXV. In four AFC Championship Game victories he had 16 tackles, 3.5 sacks, a forced fumble, and two pass deflections.

The ongoing debate back then was between Smith and White for the NFL's best pass rusher. Webb and Criswell are admittedly biased because they had to face Smith twice a year, and White played on the opposite side. But both left tackles called Smith the best player of any kind they went against.

As a defensive end in a 3-4 scheme and without a dominant complementary component like other legendary sacksmasters enjoyed, Smith might deserve extra credit.

"It's like when you're diving off the Olympic platform," Smith said from his home in Virginia. "There should be something into the equation for degree of difficulty. For those things to have been accomplished, you have to take a step back to really soak it in."

White, for instance, starred alongside two-time All-Pro Clyde Simmons and two-time Pro Bowler Sean Jones in 4-3 setups.

Deacon Jones's entire defensive front is legendary. He played with fellow Hall of Fame defensive tackle Merlin Olsen and Pro Bowl linemen Rosey Grier, Coy Bacon, and Lamar Lundy.

"When you stick your hand in the dirt," Smith said, "it's a man's world. And in our era, the double teams . . ."

And the chops, and the chips, and the peel backs . . . In Smith's era, tight ends were required to be more proficient blockers, and teams still deployed fullbacks.

Yes, the Bills featured fabulous linebackers in Shane Conlan, Darryl Talley, Cornelius Bennett, and Bryce Paup, but none of Smith's linemates went to a Pro Bowl while with the Bills.

"You could slide to him and chip him all you wanted to," Criswell said, "but he could break through two guys just as easy as one sometimes.

"He was always there. There were times it felt like Bruce was in our huddle, listening to our play as we called it."

Even more impressive regarding Smith's production is that throughout his heyday the AFC East boasted mainstay left tackles. That made for terrific rivalries with Webb, Criswell, six-time Pro Bowler Bruce Armstrong with the New England Patriots, and seven-time Pro Bowler Chris Hinton (and then Zefross Moss) with the Indianapolis Colts.

Smith averaged nearly a sack per game against the AFC East. He recorded 31 sacks against the Jets, the most against any opponent. He had 25 versus the Colts and 21 versus the Patriots and 15 on the Dolphins.

The Kansas City Chiefs, trying to find a way past the Bills, signed Criswell as a free agent in 1995 because of his familiarity with Smith.

"Most times you'd say you're playing the Raiders, playing the Colts," said Criswell, who started 146 games over his career. "Whenever we were playing Buffalo, I called it 'Bruce Smith Week.' That's not to take away from how talented they were in the 1990s as a defensive unit, but we were always trying to account for Bruce. And he knew that.

"That's why they moved him around. He would play nose. He would stand up. He would do all kinds of things that made it tough to game-plan."

In retirement, Smith advocates for former players struggling with health and wellness issues.

Smith has done well financially, but he considers himself blessed. He has quietly helped former teammates pay their bills and find assistance for manifold problems. He said he recently reviewed his benefits package and came away frustrated for those who must pay "a psychological price" while dealing with the NFL's retirement system.

"With these accolades comes an obligation to speak up for those voices we don't always hear from," Smith said. "I just think the process it takes to get the benefits, the jumping through hoops to qualify, is so difficult. You're almost making former players suffer more when they already need surgeries and treatment. A percentage of guys get depressed and frustrated and just give up. It should be streamlined and accessible. It's dead wrong with all the resources and monies that are flowing today."

19.
Ronnie Lott

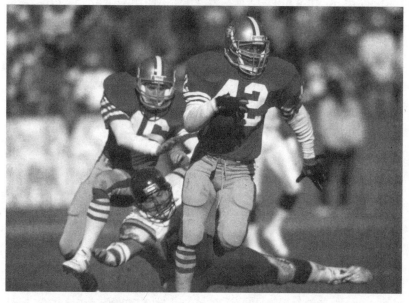

Ronnie Lott (42) made 63 interceptions during his career—twice leading the league in that category—while playing three positions in the secondary.

Position: Defensive Back

Teams: 49ers (1981–1990), Raiders (1991–1992), Jets (1993–1994)

By Matt Barrows

G et off my grass!"

Grumpy old men have been hollering that since suburban lawns began dotting the American landscape following World War II. A teenaged Ronnie Lott got the treatment in a tony Los Angeles area neighborhood in the late 1970s and, as tough as he was, it sent a shiver down his spine.

That's because the message didn't come from a codger with a

pair of pruning shears. It came from a towering football legend, Jim Brown.

Lott had just started out at USC. He and roommate Marcus Allen had heard about a huge party Brown was throwing in Beverly Hills and decided to see if they could get in. Lott remembers waiting outside with a throng of wannabe partygoers hoping to bathe in the glow of Brown, who'd been out of football for more than a decade and who more recently had starred in films with the likes of Raquel Welch and Jacqueline Bisset. That's when Lott felt a hard tap on his shoulder. He looked up, and there was Brown.

"And he said, 'Hey, get off my grass!'" Lott recalled.

Two things happened. Lott took in the sheer magnificence of the man—the huge hands, the boulder-like shoulders—and had a sudden and sobering realization of the work it would require to become an NFL great in his own right. *How could he ever possibly be mentioned in the same breath as Brown?*

"And I'm positive that Jim Brown could've played at that time," Lott said. "That's how great he looked, how amazing he looked. And that's when I was, '*Woooow!*' Because I had never seen a back that big. I had never seen anybody who was put together like that."

It also started a lifelong relationship with Brown, who invited the young men into his house. From that point, Lott said, he never passed up a chance to visit with, and learn from, Brown.

"I believe some things are meant to be," he said. "And that was meant to be because Jim at that time, not only was he one of the best athletes in the world, Jim was also one of the great activists, one of the great spokespeople for all of sports, for all of humanity. You just don't see it. He was one of a kind."

For Lott, the meeting was both a chance encounter and, looking back at his life, not all that unusual. That's because Lott has been having Forrest Gump–like brushes with football greatness since he was a kid, with each leaving permanent marks on the soulful safety.

When he was 13, he sat transfixed as Rams defensive end Deacon Jones spoke to a group of kids at a sports banquet and still remembers what Jones said that evening.

"He said, 'I want you to be the best,'" Lott recalled. "'I don't care if you're the garbageman, I want you to be the best garbageman you can be. You know what the best garbageman is? It's being able to do that job and still smile at people.'"

At football camps, he met James "Shack" Harris, the first Black quarterback to open a season as a team's starter, as well as then–Rams running back Lawrence McCutcheon, with Lott sitting in awe and taking mental notes of what they told the campers. At USC, he was exposed to past Trojan greats as well as future stars such as Allen, Dennis Thurman, and Anthony Muñoz, who were on his late 1970s teams.

At one point, Lott met former Packers star Ray Nitschke and was stunned when the longtime linebacker, whom Lott had grown up watching, whispered in his ear: "I wish I could have played with you."

The parade of football legends telling him stories, offering him advice, and sharing their wisdom never seemed to end. Lott opened his ears and eyes and took everything in.

"I met some guys that are part of this top 100 group, and I still hear their voices," Lott said, his own voice cracking with emotion. "I still hear the voices talking to me."

Those voices were like jet fuel for a career in which Lott became perhaps the best safety to play the game. His 63 interceptions are tied for eighth all time, and he had 16 forced fumbles over his career. He won four Super Bowls with the 49ers, reached the Pro Football Hall of Fame in 2000, and was a member of the NFL's 100th anniversary team.

Lott's high school stadium is named after him, as is the Lott IMPACT Trophy, which is given annually to a college defender who both excels on the field and shows great character off it. Of all the stars from the 49ers' glory years in the 1980s, perhaps none have given back to the community and to younger players as much as Lott.

"There have been multiple occasions where I've called Ronnie and said, 'Hey, would you be willing to have a cup of coffee with a particular player?'" said former teammate and current 49ers senior advisor to the general manager Keena Turner. "And he's never said no. And I mean *multiple* times over the years. He's always had that in him—an understanding of the leadership piece and how he views the game and historically how he wants to have a place in that."

Mostly, Lott was known as one of the most devastating hitters of all time. He badly wanted to channel Brown and Nitschke and Jack Tatum and everyone he met along the way. And because of that, he played with a throwback's tenacity and toughness. When you crossed the field in front of Lott, you did so at your own peril.

"He was a destroyer," his buddy, Allen, once told NFL Films.

Lott was infatuated with sports from the time he could walk.

Born in Albuquerque, New Mexico, in 1959, the first team he cheered on was the Albuquerque Dukes, a minor-league baseball team at the time. When he was 5, his father, a master sergeant in the Air Force, moved the family to Washington, D.C., where Lott rooted for Charley Taylor, Pat Fischer, Billy Kilmer, and the Washington teams of the 1960s and early '70s.

He memorized the rosters, gobbled up newspaper stories, and ran pass patterns down the street, pretending to be Taylor. Younger brother Roy fired him passes as if he were Kilmer.

"I couldn't wait to play in RFK Stadium," Lott said.

At age 10, the family moved again, this time to San Bernardino, California. Around that time, Lott recalls his father taking him to see a friend's son play football. Lott saw the glittering helmets, heard the sharp crack of shoulder pads, and asked if he could play, too. The following season, he got his own set of equipment and started making plans about the type of player he'd become.

Lott remembers Bears linebacker Dick Butkus appearing in a television commercial for Prestone at the time and growling into the camera: "I'm Dick Butkus, and plugging holes is my business."

Lott read everything he could about Butkus and decided he'd make plugging holes his business, too.

And that's what he did.

When Allen first arrived at USC in 1978, he was a defensive back along with Lott, who had started there the year before. Allen, of course, soon was moved to running back, which meant he had to go against the hard-hitting Lott in practice.

"We roomed together and stuff, and Ronnie tried to kill me at practice," Allen recalled. "And I actually admired that because he was trying to bring the best out of me. . . . Ronnie obviously showed no quarter. He brought it every single day and he made me a better player."

The position switch was a brilliant move for Allen. He'd go on to win the Heisman Trophy in 1981, the year the 49ers drafted Lott with the No. 8 pick. The running back played 16 NFL seasons, had one of the most famous runs in Super Bowl history—74 yards against Washington in Super Bowl XVIII—and made the Pro Football Hall of Fame in 2003.

If Allen turned into a star, however, his roommate became a supernova.

Lott was a swift and savvy cornerback to begin his career with the 49ers, collecting 17 interceptions—and scoring four touchdowns off of takeaways—in his first four seasons, all of which ended with Lott in the Pro Bowl.

His reputation truly erupted with a move to safety in 1985. Lott weighed only a little more than 200 pounds throughout his career but put himself in a pair of oversized, butterfly-style shoulder pads and—with the speed of a cornerback—launched into ball carriers like a cannonball through wooden ships.

"There was just this ferocity and intensity," Turner said. "And he was constantly confrontational on the field—with opponents and teammates. There was always this bubbling kind of boil with him that wasn't always under the surface. It was always riding right on top."

Linebacker Bill Romanowski felt that boil after a preseason game during his rookie season in 1988. A Raiders tight end shoved him in the back following a play, which Romanowski ignored, choosing instead to run back to the huddle. He regretted doing so when the 49ers defense reviewed the film the next day. Wearing his trademark scowl, Lott aggressively told the rookie he couldn't let an opponent get away with that kind of cheap shot.

"He said, 'Romo, if I ever see anybody push you in the back and you don't do something about it, I will personally kick your ass!'" Romanowski recalled. "'This is a game of respect! And if you're gonna let somebody punk you, they will punk you right out of this league!'"

That was the essential ingredient to the 49ers' success in the 1980s. They had Joe Montana pushing the offense during practice and Lott making sure his defensive mates matched every bit of fire thrown at them. The result was a practice pace no one had seen at the time.

"One of Bill [Walsh]'s greatest strengths was teaching a team how to practice against each other," said Paul Hackett, the team's quarterbacks coach from 1983 to '85. "What happens when you have a scout team? The tempo goes down. And Ronnie wasn't going to let that happen. No way. Because he knew the way to make the offense better and to make himself better was to keep the tempo high. And that's where it all began for those teams. It was an energy level that was incredible for that time in football."

Lott, of course, wasn't allowed to lower his big shoulder pads and wallop Jerry Rice, Roger Craig, and crew in practices. Opponents weren't as lucky.

Lott's thunderous hits usually came in one of two scenarios. The first was when pass catchers dared to cross the field in front of the roving safety, who would usually stop their momentum cold, dislodging the ball in the process. Washington receiver Art Monk once told the *Sporting News* that Lott hit him so hard in a game that it essentially knocked him out of football for good. Former 49ers defensive coordinator Ray Rhodes called Lott's blows "woo licks" because they would instinctively elicit a sudden "WOO!" from crowds, opponents, and the 49ers' sideline.

The other type of big hit came when Lott shot in from the secondary to fill a gap on a running play. That famously happened in the first quarter of Super Bowl XXIII after Bengals running back Ickey Woods gained 27 yards on his first four carries.

Woods was a 231-pound rookie who entered the game with freight-train momentum. He'd rushed for 1,066 yards in the regular season and another 228 yards—and three touchdowns—in Cincinnati's two playoff wins. Early on, it seemed like he'd keep rolling against San Francisco.

Between series, however, Lott told teammates they had to send a message to the rookie. In fact, the defensive captain vowed to deliver it himself, which he did when Woods took off to his left, then planted to move upfield. One moment there was an open hole, the next Lott was shooting through it from the other side. He collided with the running back, thumping Woods with his oversized left shoulder pad and sending him backward in the opposite direction.

It was a "woo lick" teammates said they felt as much as heard. To them, it was the feeling of reassurance, that everything would be fine for the 49ers' defense that evening. And it was. Woods, who averaged 6.8 yards a carry on his first four runs, had a 2.9-yard average on his next 16. The Bengals gained only 229 yards against Lott's defense that night, didn't score an offensive touchdown, and fell 20–16.

"It was definitely a tone-setter," Turner said of the hit. "I would think if I'm on the offensive side of the ball, I'd want to know where that No. 42 is the rest of the game, right?"

If that was Lott's most well-known hit, the most defining moment of his career came three years earlier. Lott was filling an open running lane when Cowboys running back Tim Newsome lowered his head and caught Lott's left pinky between his helmet and Lott's shoulder pads. Blood spurted from the digit and Lott, a grimace on his face, walked off the field with trainers on either side.

He had the hand taped and finished the game. He did the same a week later in a wild-card playoff loss to the Giants.

A few months later, when doctors unraveled the gauze and took another look at the pinky, it remained mangled. They told Lott he had a decision to make. They could operate on the finger, graft a piece of bone from his wrist, and rebuild the tip of the digit, a process that would put Lott in a cast for two months and perhaps keep Lott out of the lineup when the 1986 season began.

Or they could simply cut it off.

That's when Lott heard Nitschke whispering in his ear and started replaying Butkus's Prestone commercial from 1970 in his head. He recalled conversations with former 49ers running back Joe Perry, who served in World War II before his professional football career and with other NFL greats who worked a second job in the offseason because they made only a few thousand dollars a year playing the game.

He remembered Larry Wilson, the Cardinals safety who once intercepted a pass with two broken hands. And he thought of Brown and his realization, when he was still a teenager, of what it would take to become an NFL giant like Brown.

To Lott, who idolized these men since he was a little boy and who wanted nothing more than to uphold their legacy, a lengthy rehabilitation that would save the tip of his pinky and eat into the 1986 season felt like a betrayal.

"If you've got Ray Nitschke whispering in your ear saying, 'Hey, man, I wish I could have played with you,' how could you not play in a game?" Lott asked. "Those guys weren't playing for a paycheck. They were playing for something more than that."

So Lott had the damaged pinky removed at the first joint.

He started the opener of the 1986 season and wasn't affected by the missing tip of his finger. In fact, he set a career high with 10 interceptions that year. Mostly, he sealed his reputation as someone worthy of being mentioned along with Butkus and Brown, Nitschke and Wilson. He became one of the NFL's all-time tough guys.

"Right at that moment," Allen said of the instant a steel blade cut through flesh, bone, and gristle, "that's where heroes are born and legends never die."

18.
Dan Marino

Over the course of his long career, Dan Marino became
the NFL career leader in passing attempts, completions, yards, and TDs.

Position: Quarterback

Team: Dolphins (1983–1999)

By Dan Pompei

The temptation is to paint Dan Marino by numbers because his numbers are so vibrant.

Passing yards: 61,631.

Touchdown passes: 420.

Completions: 4,967.

Touchdown-interception differential: 168.

Each was an NFL record when Marino retired. He finished his

career with more than 40 of them, though many have been broken in the evolving NFL.

But the statistics, as spectacular as they might have been, couldn't come close to capturing all of him any more than words could capture a striking sunrise. There was the ability to see a play unfolding like a psychic, to understand where his receiver would be and where the defender would not be.

"People talk about the quick release, but what made Dan special was his vision," said Ron Jaworski, who backed up Marino for a season late in his career. "He was going to find the hole, see that hole, and make the accurate throw. That's just an intuitive talent that Dan had."

The arm could have been a military weapon. His throws made everyone else's look ordinary, if not soft. Jimmy Johnson, who coached Marino for the final four years of Marino's career, said, "I would have loved to have had Dan when he was in his prime, because when he was in his prime, he threw the ball better than any quarterback probably who has ever played the game."

There was the deep grunt when the ball left his hand. Then the furrowed brow, the pursed lips, the hard steps upfield after a first down. Nobody competed like Marino.

"When the game was on the line, he didn't shy away from it," his longtime receiver Mark Duper said in *A Football Life*. "He wanted the ball."

There was the lick of the fingers at the line of scrimmage and the blue-eyed glare through the heart of a defense. Marino believed there was nothing he couldn't do, and usually, he was right.

According to the *Miami Herald*, he once told Mark Clayton, who caught 79 of his touchdown passes, that he could throw a football through a hurricane. Another time, he told Clayton he could put a pass through the eye of a needle.

"There's no feeling quite like seeing a receiver and a defender running downfield with so little space between them that it wouldn't fit under a door—and still thinking you can put a pass right in there,"

Marino wrote in his autobiography. "Knowing it, actually. And then throwing the football like a fastball so the defender can only shake his head as it zips by."

There was the medieval-looking knee brace he wore with straps and buckles sticking out. And the ankle splints and rib protectors. In the second quarter of a 1995 game against the Colts, Marino tore cartilage in his knee. He missed one series and came back. He then bruised his hip badly. Marino refused to sit out another snap, but he had surgery on the knee the next morning. The contusion drained blood for 10 days.

There was the finger pointed in the air after a touchdown pass. Then there was the little boy hop. Marino wasn't as expressive as some, but his fierce love for the game—the satisfaction he derived from it—was on display every time he touched a football. Dolphins games, he said, were some of the best days of his life. When he received a signing bonus after being drafted by the Dolphins and had money for the first time in his life, he bought a stereo and a satellite dish for his parents so they could watch him play. That's all.

"You can see what mattered to me, right from my start with the Dolphins," he said. "Football is what I loved. Football is what drove me. Football always has been my singular passion and constant companion."

He could have been a baseball player. The Kansas City Royals drafted him in the fourth round in 1979, and for an eye blink, he thought about playing two sports professionally. But he was too good at football. Or too good at quarterback. He never played another position, even in pickup games as a kid.

Marino led the University of Pittsburgh to a 33-3 record over his first three seasons and was considered one of the best players in the country. But his last season in college was his worst. Marino's draft stock dipped, and it continued to fall when rumors spread that he liked to party.

Marino was the 27th pick in 1983, the sixth quarterback taken after John Elway, Todd Blackledge, Jim Kelly, Tony Eason, and Ken O'Brien. Marino said he never resented being passed over by so many teams—he was grateful he fell to Miami, where head coach Don Shula brought out Marino's best, in part by giving him the freedom to do what he thought was best with play calls.

Marino didn't start the first six games of his rookie season but still made the Pro Bowl. In his second season, at the age of 23, he led the Dolphins to a Super Bowl, broke the NFL record for touchdown passes with 48—12 more than anyone had previously thrown and 16 more than second-place finisher Dave Krieg—and was voted NFL Most Valuable Player.

In his third season, he played what would be remembered as the game of his life, leading an upset of the 12-0 Bears on a Monday night. Facing a defense with three Hall of Famers employing one of the most disruptive blitzing schemes ever, Marino threw quick darts that beat pressures and exploited open spaces.

It was the only loss for the 1985 Bears, which was especially significant to Shula, as it allowed the 1972 Dolphins to continue to call themselves the only undefeated team in modern NFL history.

Marino seemed indestructible at the time. He had a streak of 154 straight starts, not including four games when he was on strike in 1987. In *My Life in Football*, he wrote he was prouder of that streak than anything else.

He was Pittsburgh tough, but he was human. In a 1993 game at Cleveland Municipal Stadium, he slipped on a loose patch of grass and tore the Achilles tendon on his right leg.

The surgery didn't repair the tendon as hoped. Marino said the tendon atrophied and elongated, so he couldn't push off his back foot when throwing. To this day, he cannot stand on his toes.

He was not himself in the preseason, and some wondered if they had seen the last great Marino. But in the regular-season opener, on a muddy field against the Patriots, he threw for 473 yards and five touchdowns—the fifth coming on fourth-and-5 from the Patriots' 39 with the Dolphins trailing by three with 3:19 remaining in a 39–35 Miami victory.

He ran a 5.1 40-yard dash before the 1983 draft and rushed for negative yards in 12 of his seasons. In 17 years, he ran for a total of 87 yards. But he was sacked an average of just 16 times per season, and he led the league in lowest sack percentage 10 times. Marino said he developed quick feet from jumping rope when he was young, but avoiding sacks was more about his quick mind and quick release.

"I've always had a knack for knowing where defensive players are when I'm in the pocket," he wrote in his autobiography. "I might not see them, but I've always been able to feel their presence."

The man with the golden arm had tarnished legs. Marino had six knee surgeries during his career and was forever getting one of them drained. After he retired, he said he couldn't even walk around comfortably because of his lower body.

He probably could have found a group of Dolphins fans happy to carry him on their shoulders. To them, and to his opponents, Marino was beyond a great quarterback.

"Going against him, I felt like baseball players must have felt playing against [Joe] DiMaggio," Bills defensive end Bruce Smith told *Sports Illustrated*.

While DiMaggio won nine World Series championships, Marino never won a Super Bowl. He never made it back to one after his second season. Even though he had the second-most wins of any quarterback in history at the time of his retirement and made it to the playoffs in 10 seasons, Marino never won a championship at any level, all the way back to Pee Wee football. As inconceivable as it seems, his Dolphins were 8-10 in the playoffs.

"The cool part is I played 17 years, I had a great career, I'm in the Hall of Fame, I won a lot of football games and did a lot of things, but that's the one thing that's not cool—I don't know what that feeling's like to walk off the field Sunday and be a Super Bowl champion," he said.

But that might be what captures Marino best. He played so spectacularly that he didn't have to play on a championship team to be considered one of football's greatest quarterbacks ever.

17.
Ray Lewis

Ray Lewis was a two-time NFL Defensive Player of the year and eight-time All-Pro.

Position: Linebacker
Team: Ravens (1996–2012)

By Jeff Zrebiec

It was the whole experience. For 17 years, his pregame dances, passionate speeches, and punishing hits defined a football Sunday in Baltimore.

When Ray Lewis was drafted by the Ravens in 1996, the nascent franchise didn't have a logo, uniforms, a state-of-the-art football stadium, or a modern training facility. By the time his "last ride" ended under a sea of confetti in February 2013, the Ravens had become one of the most respected and reliable brands in the sport.

The two sparkling Lombardi trophies displayed in the entrance of their stately training facility serve as the proof.

One of the players responsible for what the franchise has become is now celebrated in bronze in front of its downtown stadium, beckoning a fan base that has embraced the organization's blue-collar and defensive-minded approach.

There stands Lewis, 9 feet tall and 1,200 pounds—posing, preening, and prodding his teammates to follow his lead—a fitting portrayal of a player who had a larger-than-life persona.

"He could inspire not only a defense but an entire city," said former Tennessee Titans running back Eddie George, one of Lewis's longtime rivals. "When you go up against a player like that, you've got to bring something substantial to the table as well. You have to prepare during the week for 60 minutes of battle, not just physically but mentally and spiritually because he could take your spirit and he'll suck it right out of the team."

Lewis is considered by many pundits to be the best middle linebacker in NFL history and one of the top defensive players of his generation. He was inducted into the Hall of Fame in 2018 on his first try. In 17 seasons, he was selected to 13 Pro Bowls and garnered first-team All-Pro honors seven times. He was a two-time league Defensive Player of the Year. Only Jack Ham had more takeaways as a linebacker than Lewis, who is the only player in NFL history to have at least 40 career sacks and 30 career interceptions.

"He was the best linebacker I've ever played against and maybe the best defensive player I ever played against as well," said Peyton Manning.

Lewis was both the engine and the enforcer for the Ravens' 2000 defense, one of the most dominant units ever assembled. That unit posted four shutouts and set a record for fewest points and rushing yards allowed before steamrolling through the postseason, allowing just one offensive touchdown in four playoff games. Lewis was named MVP in the Ravens' Super Bowl XXXV thrashing of the New York Giants, capping one of the best seasons ever for a defensive player.

Twelve years later, he played the final game of his career in the Ravens' 34–31 victory over the San Francisco 49ers in Super Bowl XLVII, which Baltimore clinched on a late goal-line stand, sending Lewis out in fitting fashion. A few days later, he rode through Baltimore in a military Humvee and was celebrated by throngs of fans for the impact he had on the city and its football team. The post–Super Bowl parade felt like a coronation for Lewis, an iconic figure in Baltimore on a par with Johnny Unitas and Cal Ripken Jr.

Lewis is fond of saying "Baltimore is my city," but his NFL career seemed destined to begin elsewhere. He wanted to stay in Miami, where he was a two-time All-American for a loaded Hurricanes program. The Dolphins, who had the 20th pick, selected Baylor defensive tackle Daryl Gardener instead. The Packers, who were picking 27th, had vowed to take Lewis, but they never got the chance.

Having already taken offensive lineman Jonathan Ogden with the fourth pick, the Ravens badly wanted to select a linebacker with their second first-round pick at No. 26. The guy they coveted, Texas A&M's Reggie Brown, was selected 17th by the Detroit Lions. When the Ravens were on the clock, Lewis was the highest-rated linebacker remaining on their board.

He proved to be quite a consolation prize.

Baltimore did have concerns. Lewis was only 6-foot-1 and 235 pounds, less than the ideal size for a linebacker. But Ravens linebackers coach Maxie Baughan went to Florida to work Lewis out before the draft and gushed about him to the team's decision-makers.

"He can go all day," Baughan told Ozzie Newsome, the Ravens' longtime vice president of player personnel.

Lewis wasted no time in making a strong impression. He stepped up to the pull-up bar during physical testing at rookie minicamp and asked a Ravens official what the team record for repetitions was. He was told there wasn't one, because the Ravens were a new franchise. Lewis took it upon himself to establish a record. There was a presence and confidence to Lewis that had teammates flocking to him.

The Ravens released veteran starting middle linebacker Pepper Johnson shortly after the minicamp, installed Lewis in his place, and handed him the reins of the defense. Lewis never gave them back.

"He was this fireplug of energy," said former Ravens linebacker Jamie Sharper, who was drafted the year after Lewis and lined up alongside him for the next five years. "You could say that Ray was a smaller linebacker because of his height, but he had those broad shoulders and he was always carrying around 235. And Ray could run.

"He was the guy who brought that new mentality of a smaller linebacker who could get sideline to sideline. He got no respect coming into the league because they said he was undersized, but he transformed the idea of what linebackers could be in terms of size and speed."

Lewis averaged 146 tackles over his first six NFL seasons and missed only four games during that span. In 2003, Lewis's eye-popping stat line included 163 tackles, six interceptions, 14 passes defended, 1.5 sacks, two forced fumbles, two fumble recoveries, and a defensive touchdown. He was a dynamo, running sideline to sideline, making plays all over the field and hitting everything he encountered. He left his mark, too. It was widely reported that Cincinnati Bengals star running back Corey Dillon declined to go back on the field in a 2000 game against the Ravens because Lewis and his teammates were hitting him so hard and so often.

"He never took a play off," said former Jacksonville Jaguars running back Fred Taylor, who faced Lewis twice a season for a good chunk of his career. "He was just flying around. He was going to be near the ball. In the film room before the game, you'd never see Ray loafing. He would always get around that pile, some way, somehow.

Even if he didn't make the tackle, he would go up to the ball carrier and grab the ball and say, 'I'm going to get this next time.'"

Lewis did it all for the Ravens, who built their team around a hard-hitting and ball-hawking defense. He stopped the run, blitzed, covered, and forced turnovers. He was relentless and intimidating. And he led with his words and his actions. When he was at Miami, teammate Warren Sapp challenged Lewis to lead the defensive huddle. In Baltimore, Lewis was further emboldened by veterans Shannon Sharpe and Rod Woodson to take ownership of the team. Ravens owner Steve Bisciotti called Lewis "the greatest leader in NFL history."

Some teammates grew tired of Lewis's pregame speeches and the attention given to them, especially later in his career. But it was impossible for them not to admire how he played and not to want to follow his lead on the field.

"He brought the fire and the energy, and it was contagious," former Ravens defensive end Michael McCrary said. "It spread throughout the whole unit."

"From the moment he woke up, it was all football. It was literally like watching a lion get prepared to go out and hunt," said former Ravens linebacker Jameel McClain, who spent five seasons playing alongside Lewis. "There was the intensity in his eyes, the seriousness of his focus. My locker was next to Ray, and if you could just walk in the room, you'd feel an energy like, 'Geez, what is this guy about to do?' I don't think I've seen anyone who was able to flip a switch like Ray flipped a switch."

Other teams wanted what the Ravens had. They couldn't have Lewis, so they plucked everything around him. A long line of Ravens defensive assistants from the Lewis era, including Marvin Lewis, Jack Del Rio, Mike Singletary, Rex Ryan, Mike Nolan, and Chuck Pagano, got head coaching jobs. Ravens defensive free agents got huge money to play elsewhere.

Baltimore had plenty of defensive talent, but everything started with Lewis, on the field and off. He was the pied piper.

"There have been some guys that were athletically gifted, like

Junior Seau, Derrick Thomas, Reggie White. I played against those guys, and they were awesome. But Ray was lethal in the fact that not only did he have the physical attributes, but his spirit, his ability to lead and his football IQ were off the charts," George said. "He was just a perfect combination of all of that. He understood the game. He had all of it. He was the perfect defensive player in my mind."

George was on the other end of perhaps the most impactful play of Lewis's career. During the Ravens' Super Bowl run in 2000, Lewis caught a ball that deflected off George and returned it 50 yards for a touchdown, putting away the favored Titans in the AFC divisional round.

But there were plenty of other highlight-reel plays to choose from. There was the hit he put on the Pittsburgh Steelers' Rashad Mendenhall, breaking the running back's shoulder. There was the crushing block he put on Denver Broncos linebacker Keith Burns on Chris McAlister's 107-yard touchdown return of a missed field-goal attempt. There was the time he shot the gap on fourth-and-2 to spill San Diego Chargers running back Darren Sproles and save a Ravens victory. On that day and so many others during his career, Lewis was the Ravens' closer.

"Before he even did that against the Chargers, he was talking about it on the sideline. We were in the game and it was like, 'OK, what is Ray talking about?' He knew it was coming down to it and he knew their play, and he knew he was going to shoot the gap and make the play," McClain said. "That's what makes great people great. Great people take calculated risks. But he couldn't take all those risks without the preparation that he had. He wasn't a blind man running out on the field dreaming of making a play. He was a man that knew the play coming and knew what play he was going to make. When the game was on the line, with the way Ray prepared and the way he cared about the game, you wanted that last place to come down to him versus them."

. . .

More than anything else during his time as Lewis's teammate, Mc-Clain remembers the Tuesday and Wednesday meetings. Defensive coaches would install the game plan for that Sunday's game, going over scouting reports and player and coach tendencies. McClain. said Lewis could have run the meetings. He'd tell his teammates what was coming next, instruct them on where they needed to be on a certain play and what they needed to look for. Lewis kept a detailed notebook on opposing players and offensive coordinators. Not long after the previous Sunday's game ended, he was deep into that notebook or tape as he prepared for the next challenge.

He was the rare non-quarterback who could beat teams with his brain and brawn, never mind his physical skills, passion, and leadership ability.

"He knew the plays. He'd be able to call the plays out at the line of scrimmage based on film study, which was phenomenal to me," said former Bengals receiver Chad Ochocinco. "Ed [Reed] would be able to do the same thing. They'd call the plays out before they would happen. I'd be like, 'God damn,' and they'd be right every time. Ray would see things before they even happened, which is what Peyton and Tom [Brady] are able to do at the quarterback position. To be able to do that as a linebacker speaks volumes on the work he put in.

"He is the best linebacker period to ever play the game. No disrespect to those who came before him, Dick Butkus, Mike Singletary, guys like that. Ray was a different type of animal. He was a quarterback on defense."

16.
Deacon Jones

Deacon Jones (75) was an unstoppable pass rusher
who was voted to eight consecutive Pro Bowls.

Position: Defensive End

Teams: Rams (1961–1971), Chargers (1972–1973), Washington (1974)

By Dan Pompei

Some say Deacon Jones created the sack by giving it a name. This is disputable. What is indisputable is Jones mastered the sack like no one before him and arguably no one since. Then he turned it into entertainment.

To understand how that happened, we need to go back to his hometown of Eatonville, Florida, where what he saw as a child gave him the purpose and determination that helped make him one of pro football's all-time greats.

Jones was with Black friends after a church service when a car filled with young White people drove by. One of the passengers threw a watermelon out of the window and hit an elderly Black woman in the head. Jones said he could hear the people in the car laughing, and he chased the vehicle for as long as his lungs allowed. The woman died of the injuries she suffered, and Jones said there was no police investigation.

At South Carolina State University in 1958, Jones took part in a demonstration after a group of Black people were arrested for eating at a lunch counter designated for Whites. Police tried to stop the protestors by chasing them with German shepherds and high-powered water hoses. "I ran right up into that alley," Jones told *Pro Football Weekly*. "Had no out to it. And they turned the hose loose right up in that alley on me, pinned me up against the wall, and it ripped the back of my [suit], right down the back. I almost drowned, man. I almost drowned, and I was a well-conditioned athlete. I couldn't move a muscle. It had me pinned up against that wall, and I couldn't move."

Jones saw his scholarship at South Carolina State revoked for participating in the protest, and he went to Mississippi Vocational College, where he encountered more racism.

It was football that enabled him to deal with all of it. "Thank God I had the ability to play a violent game like football," he said, according to the *New York Times*. "It gave me an outlet for the anger in my heart."

Jones, by admission, was malicious as a defensive end. He said the harder he hit, the more he released his hostilities. "I ain't helping you up off the ground," he said in an interview with NFL Films. "I'm gonna step on your hand."

Or slap your head. As a 14th-round draft pick by the Rams in 1961, Jones needed every possible edge. He came to the NFL without refinement—his defensive line coach with the Rams, Jack Patera, told ESPN that his stance initially was like a frog squatting with a hand between his legs. But Jones learned.

Jones was not the first to use the head slap—some say he took it from teammate Rosey Grier—but he used it better than anyone. "Rembrandt, of course, did not invent painting," he said.

Jones used the maneuver so effectively that by 1974 almost every lineman in the NFL was copying him, and by 1977 the NFL made it illegal.

"I have a mean streak, and in my business, I needed it, or I never would have made it," Jones said in his autobiography, *Headslap*. "Pro football is, after all, a pain-giving game. My head slap gave pain. It made you not want to hold me at the line, which is the one illegal move offensive linemen get away with over and over in every game, today more than ever. My head slap was the right hand of Joe Frazier and Muhammad Ali rolled into one."

Jones had scars on his hands from the maneuver. Opponents had worse.

"Our right tackle Cas Banaszek had ice bags on his head after every game against the Rams," 49ers tight end Bob Windsor said, according to the *Los Angeles Times*.

Jones didn't head-slap just to punish opponents. He did it to win games. He was a thinking man's pass rusher, and the head slap was a way to gain an advantage.

"Football is a game of moves, a game of edges," he wrote. "I aimed to create a weakness; I would slant, go for the angles. That way, even against two men, it wouldn't be a Mexican standoff. With my quickness, I'd make a move. The guy setting up across from me goes for it, but he's already beat. Now he's got to move backwards. That's when I take him on. I'll go outside or reverse and cut inside."

The great Jim Murray of the *Los Angeles Times* wrote that Jones was to defensive football what Babe Ruth was to offensive baseball. "He was a genius at it," he said.

When Jones was paired with Merlin Olsen in 1962 on the left side of the Rams line, he had another advantage. The pair became one of the most effective in NFL history at stunting.

"[Olsen] and Deacon had to be the best defensive duo ever and they'd work stunts beautifully," said former Rams coach George Allen.

Jones was voted NFL Defensive Player of the Year in 1967 and '68. Olsen won the Bert Bell Award as the NFL MVP in 1974. Both were five-time first-team All-Pros, and both were voted to the NFL's 100th anniversary team. Jones and Olsen were the heart of the Fearsome Foursome. Rounding out the quartet were Grier and Lamar Lundy. Roger Brown then replaced Grier from 1967 through '70.

At 6-5 and 270 pounds, Jones had physical gifts that were rarely seen in his era. Allen said he was the quickest defensive lineman off the snap he had ever seen and also said he had better footwork and faster hands than any other defensive lineman. Jones was so athletic, Allen said, that he could have been an outstanding linebacker or even a defensive back. He also was extremely durable, missing just five games over a 14-year career that concluded with two seasons in San Diego and one in Washington.

And there was more.

"He was the single-best practice player I ever coached," Allen wrote in *Pro Football's 100 Greatest Players*. "He went as hard in practice as in games. He drew blood from his teammates in practice."

Jones was outstanding in practice, but more so in games. Especially games that meant something.

"He was at his best in big games because he had a big ego, and he loved being known as the best and loved being in the spotlight," Allen said.

Jones, whose given name was David and who became known as the Secretary of Defense, would not argue. He changed his name because Deacon had more pizzazz. The first time he met the press in Los Angeles, he told them of the change. "My name is Deacon Jones," he said. "I've come to preach the gospel of winning football to the good people of Los Angeles."

He loved to talk, whether he was entertaining the public, demeaning opponents, or lobbying officials. Cowboys offensive lineman Rayfield Wright was a verbal victim in a 1969 game.

"As an offensive lineman, you're taught only to hear the quarterback's voice, nothing else," Wright told *Sports Illustrated*. "I'm listening in case there's an audible, and in the pause between 'Huts!' I hear a deep, heavy voice say, 'Does yo' mama know you're out here?' It was Deacon Jones."

Jones's swagger, loquaciousness, and charisma made him one of the all-time great interview subjects.

"I wouldn't want to be a lawyer, I wouldn't want to be a doctor, I wouldn't want to be the president of the United States," Jones said in an NFL Films interview. "I was destined. Just like Ray Charles was born to sing the blues, Deacon was born to rush quarterbacks."

But he did more than that. Jones sang R&B in nightclubs with the band Nightshift, which later became War. While he wasn't always treated well in his hometown, Hollywood loved him. Jones portrayed a Black Viking in *The Norseman*, gave fatherly advice to an alien in the TV show *ALF*, and recited poetry in Miller Lite ads.

"Blue is the violet, red is the rose, and if you don't believe me, I'm gonna break your nose."

A showman at heart, Jones once brought down Washington's Bobby Mitchell, known as one of the NFL's fastest men. But before the tackle, he ran with him for 10 yards or so, matching him stride for stride. Later, he said he didn't bring him down earlier because he wanted everyone to see that he was as fast as Mitchell.

Whatever he did, an audience formed.

"He was a storyteller," said Hall of Fame defensive end Michael Strahan, whom Jones took under his wing. "I've never heard a guy tell stories the way Deacon told stories, from his head slaps to how they basically changed the game for him."

If Jones couldn't talk about himself, others stepped up.

"What was it like to play against Deacon Jones?" Packers quarterback Bart Starr said. "How did people feel about Attila the Hun?"

Strahan called Jones the founding father of defensive ends.

"Deacon made the position glamorous, which was hard to do," he said. "Quarterbacks are glamorous, not defensive linemen . . . until Deacon came along."

Jones played before sacks were officially kept, but unofficial records indicate he had 173½, still the third most in history even though he played before the passing era. He also unofficially had 26 sacks in a 14-game season in 1967, which would still be the NFL record even for a 16- or 17-game season. A recently published study of sacks before 1982 says Jones led the league in sacks five times—three more times than anyone else.

After Jones died in 2013 at the age of 74, the NFL started giving the Deacon Jones Award to the player who finishes each season with the most sacks.

Said Olsen: "There has never been a better football player than Deacon Jones."

15.
John Elway

John Elway was legendary—and feared by opposing fans—
for his 47 winning or tying fourth-quarter drives.

Position: Quarterback

Team: Broncos (1983–1998)

By Lindsay Jones

For all the thousands of yards and hundreds of touchdowns John Elway threw in his 16 years with the Denver Broncos, there is one play, one perfectly iconic moment, that remains frozen in time.

"The Helicopter."

You can picture it, can't you?

It's the third quarter of Super Bowl XXXII, and Elway's Broncos are tied 17–17 with Brett Favre's Green Bay Packers. Denver is facing a third-and-6 from Green Bay's 12-yard line.

In photos of the moment, Elway is suspended in air, his body parallel with the grass, his right hand gripped tightly around the tip of the football. His eyes are wide, his teeth gritted.

On video, it feels like the play happens in slow motion. The pigeon-toed Elway, then 37 years old, lumbering forward, then launching himself headfirst. He's hit by three Packers, and the force of the collision sends Elway's body spinning, just like the propellers of a helicopter. When he landed on his backside, Elway was a half-yard past the first-down marker.

"You tell me that 37-year-old man doesn't want to win this game!" KOA 850 radio analyst Scott Hastings said at the moment. "That's sacrifice. Oh, man!"

Two plays later, the Broncos scored a touchdown to break the tie, and they never trailed again. Elway's Super Bowl heartache was over, as team owner Pat Bowlen handed him the Lombardi Trophy and said the four most memorable words in franchise history: "This one's for John."

Elway had unrivaled arm strength, impressive athleticism, and an insane level of competitiveness that carried the Broncos to five AFC championships. He likely would have been a first-ballot Hall of Famer even without a Super Bowl ring. But the Helicopter and the Broncos' upset of the Packers in January 1998, followed by Denver's repeat Super Bowl title the next season, catapulted Elway into a different quarterback stratosphere.

When he retired after the 1998 season, only seven other quarterbacks had won at least two Super Bowls. (The list has since grown to 12.)

"I watched all the talking heads that week before the game, and I remember watching Terry Bradshaw and him saying something like, 'John Elway won't be considered elite because he hadn't won any Super Bowls.' That pissed me off to hear that about my guy," former Broncos receiver Rod Smith said. "We really did want to give him one."

And to Smith and other teammates from the 1997 Broncos, the Helicopter showed just how much Elway wanted it, too.

"He could have slid, he could have not run at all," former Broncos fullback Howard Griffith said. "He chose to do the thing to win the game."

"That moment showed me that John was all the way in," former Broncos safety Steve Atwater said. "I knew that already, but him making that sacrifice, diving in the air like Superman and getting spun around, he's leaving it all out here. Made me feel confident and think, 'Oh, we have to do the same thing.'"

(Atwater was serious about the personal sacrifice: He was knocked from the game late in the fourth quarter after a collision with teammate Randy Hilliard and Packers receiver Robert Brooks.)

Elway's final coach with the Broncos, Mike Shanahan, laughs now when he thinks about the Helicopter. Because if Elway had gotten his way, it never would have happened.

"He hated it. He told me before the game he didn't like it," Shanahan said recently.

The Broncos had practiced the play earlier in the week as part of a goal-line package, designed to be a fade route for the X receiver— lined up on the outside left of the formation—against man coverage. Shanahan and offensive coordinator Gary Kubiak assured Elway that in the red zone, the Packers would show zone coverage and the play would be there for Elway to make.

But Elway was wary of running a pass play from inside the 5-yard line in theory, then was incensed when Shanahan radioed in the call when the Broncos were at the 12-yard line.

"He looked at me, just disgusted," Shanahan said, laughing.

When Elway saw the Packers in man coverage, not in zone as his coaches had promised, he knew the only play available would be to try to run for a first down. Shanahan realized it, too.

"So the first thing I'm looking at [after the snap] is: Are the linebackers going to drop deep?" Shanahan said. "Being on the 12-yard line, the first thing they do is go to cover the pass. And John goes back, makes the right read, and the rest of it is his desire to make the first down."

Elway was a gifted scrambler in his early playing days, rushing for more than 230 yards in eight consecutive seasons from 1984 to

1991 and scoring 33 rushing touchdowns in his career. But at age 37, running wasn't his first, or desired, option.

Elway took a three-step drop, all the way to the 20-yard line. Then he raced forward, crossed the 10-yard line, and saw the first-down marker off to his right at the 6, just as three Packers came charging at him.

"They thought I was going down. The only way I could get the first down was if I put my 6-inch vertical on them and go over the top," Elway told NFL Films in 2019. "I can still feel the adrenaline that was going through my veins at that moment in time."

Smith remembers scrambling around past the 5-yard line, trying to get open after the play broke down. He was facing Elway when the quarterback made his leap, and he remembers making eye contact with Elway almost immediately after he landed.

"The energy was already high, but it shifted completely after that. You could see everyone pumping their fist like they made the play," Smith said. "We were just so fired up to see him go for it and throw your body on the line for the group. He didn't do it for him, he did it for us."

Atwater, on the sideline with his defensive teammates, remembers holding his breath to make sure Elway wasn't injured and didn't fumble.

"It was so crazy, because I'm wondering if he's even OK, because three guys hit him," Atwater said. "But he popped up, raised his arm up, and it was like, 'Aw, yeah, this is it. This is it.'"

It set up a first-and-goal at the 4, and two Terrell Davis runs later, the Broncos were up 24–17. They would go on to win 31–24.

Elway threw for only 123 yards that day. Davis, with his three rushing touchdowns, won Super Bowl MVP. A year later, Elway would throw for 336 yards, including an 80-yard touchdown to Smith, in Super Bowl XXXIII against the Falcons. The quarterback was named Super Bowl MVP in the final game of his career.

He was elected to the Pro Football Hall of Fame in 2004 after what longtime Denver sportswriter Woody Paige likes to describe as the shortest presentation in the history of the selection committee. It was just five words: "Ladies and gentlemen, John Elway."

14.
Joe Greene

Joe Greene started his career as the NFL Defensive Rookie of the Year and added two NFL Defensive Player of the Year awards.

Position: Defensive Tackle
Team: Steelers (1969–1981)

By Ed Bouchette and Mike DeFabo

On January 28, 1969, NFL commissioner Pete Rozelle stepped to the microphone at the Belmont Plaza Hotel in New York City and—between drags of his cigarette—announced the Steelers' first-round pick . . . and also the dawning of a new era.

"Joe Greene," he said. "G, R, double-E, N, E. Defensive tackle, North Texas State."

In that moment, Greene became the fourth player off the board and the first-ever draft pick in what would become a storied tenure under coach Chuck Noll. The selection of a relatively unknown defensive tackle from an almost unheard-of school was met with waves of skepticism from fans and media alike. A headline in the *Pittsburgh Post-Gazette* the next day read, "Who's Joe Greene?"

While so many questioned the draft pick, Greene himself was skeptical of his destination. He's admitted on numerous instances that he did not want to join a hapless franchise defined by losing seasons and empty seats. In the Steelers' 36 seasons of existence before Greene arrived, they had reached the playoffs just once—losing 21–0 to the Eagles in 1947. To many, Greene figured to be another bust, continuing a streak of irrelevance.

But over time, "Mean" Joe Greene transformed the image and identity of the Pittsburgh Steelers. A franchise that was once a punch line evolved into a powerhouse dynasty that would hoist the Lombardi Trophy four times from 1974 to 1979.

Greene, widely considered the best player for a franchise that has 29 Hall of Famers, was the cornerstone of it all. Iconic Steelers running back Franco Harris has called Greene "the greatest Steeler of all time." When former Steelers chairman Dan Rooney was inducted into the Pro Football Hall of Fame, he chose Greene as his presenter. And after Noll's passing, Greene was selected as one of the pallbearers.

Physically dominant at 6-foot-4 and 275 pounds, he was virtually unblockable. He was selected to the Pro Bowl 10 times, including each of the first eight years of his career. He was a five-time first-team All-Pro selection, 11-time first-team All-AFC selection, and twice the NFL Defensive Player of the Year (1972 and 1974).

But Greene was also more than that. His temperament and determination infused the Steelers with a passionate distaste for losing, helping set the standard for many generations to come—even if he was initially reluctant to join the franchise in the first place.

"My feelings on that changed probably around my third year," Greene said of his displeasure at landing with the Steelers. "Chuck used to make these speeches and gave us a set of benchmarks and said, 'If you do these things—quality three-and-outs, hold a team to

17 points or less, no foolish penalties, three turnovers or something like that a game—we'd have a chance to win.'

"That first year, we didn't see any evidence of that, and our second year, we didn't see much. But that third year, I started to see gradual progress, and when we did match those benchmarks, we won the ballgame. I was one of those guys complaining all the time, 'Why don't we change what we're doing because we're not winning?' But eventually, I became a believer in what Chuck was preaching."

Raised by his mother in Temple, Texas, Greene's given name is Charles Edward. But to Greene's aunt, something about the kid's stocky build reminded her of heavyweight boxing champion Joe Louis. She nicknamed him "Joe"—and the moniker stuck.

The "Mean" part would come along later. After he was bullied in middle school, the kid named after a heavyweight boxer began taking matters into his own hands. He recounted on NFL Network's *A Football Life* the time he beat up his bully to get back $5 that was stolen. That same fiery competitiveness and quick temper made Greene a standout at Dunbar High School.

"I look back at my time playing football," Greene said. "In high school, we didn't win. I got thrown out of just about every game I played in high school. I think I got thrown out of all of them my senior year and nine of 10 my junior year. . . . I did so poorly that I was embarrassed. I didn't want my girlfriend to see me get beat up. That's when I became a bad actor at linebacker. No. 1 was not looking bad for my girlfriend, No. 2 was winning."

Greene's on-field prowess earned him an opportunity at what was then called North Texas State University (now University of North Texas). Initially, he planned to be an educator. While it's fun to imagine what kind of discipline Greene might have doled out to class clowns, his aspirations changed.

"The instructor was telling us about getting an education, and if you do well here, you can become a teacher and probably make $6,000 a year," Greene said. "This was the year Dick Butkus, middle linebacker from Illinois, was drafted by the Bears. I read in some paper where Dick Butkus signed for $50,000. That was the worst thing from the standpoint of me losing my interest in getting a degree. I said, 'My goodness! $50,000! I need to play some football.' That's when I got my mind toward being a better football player."

In the two seasons before Greene joined the North Texas varsity team, the football team was a combined 5-14-1. In the three seasons Greene played, 1966–68, they went 23-5-1. He'd change more than just the school's football reputation. The official nickname of the university was the Eagles when Greene arrived on campus. When the star defensive lineman began taking over games, fans chanted "Mean Greene! Mean Greene!" To this day North Texas athletic teams bear the name "Mean Green."

He sparked a similar transformation with the Steelers. As a rookie, Greene played well enough to earn the Defensive Rookie of the Year award and make the Pro Bowl, but the Steelers went 1-13. It marked the first of three consecutive losing seasons to kick off the Noll era.

The losing ate at Greene. He became so angry in one game over a perceived lack of holding calls against the opposing O-linemen that he rifled a football into the stands. Another time, he whipped his helmet into the air in disgust. It hit the goalpost and shattered. Later in his career, he was caught kicking an opponent in the groin and punching another in the belly to get him to stop holding him.

The tide began to turn for the Steelers thanks to years of successful drafts led by Bill Nunn, Noll's football genius, and Greene's determination. Fans and opponents would take the Steelers seriously—or else Greene would make them. He became the centerpiece of a dominant defensive front that also featured L. C. Greenwood, Ernie Holmes, and Dwight White. Together, they earned the nickname the "Steel Curtain," a moniker that would eventually come to describe the entire defense as a whole.

"He was the greatest third-down player you ever saw in your life," said Art Rooney Jr., who headed the Steelers' player personnel department when it drafted Greene.

In Super Bowl IX, Greene backboned a defense that held the Minnesota Vikings scoreless (the team's only points came on the recovery of a blocked punt), allowed just 17 yards rushing, and intercepted Fran Tarkenton three times (one by Greene on a tipped pass). Just a few short seasons removed from irrelevance, the Steelers had ascended into a class of their own. They stayed there to establish their dynasty, winning four Super Bowls in six seasons.

Greene, along with defensive coordinator George Perles, later became the impetus for innovation. The star defensive tackle would line up in a titled position between the guard and center and attack quickly off the line, in a tactic that would eventually come to be called the Stunt 4-3. Greene's disruption demanded double teams, and he selflessly ate up blockers to allow teammates to feast.

In the latter stages of Greene's career, he endured a nerve issue that caused weakness in his left arm. While age and injury took their toll, he remained the same single-minded competitor. He did not just dominate on the field but in their locker room as well. Once, when a player decided to turn on a stereo in the locker room during a week of practice, Greene quietly walked over and yanked the cord out of the wall.

Former Steelers offensive lineman and longtime color commentator Craig Wolfley remembers one particular incident during his rookie season in 1980. The Steelers lost to the Oakland Raiders on *Monday Night Football*, 45–34, in a game full of penalties, missed assignments, and self-inflicted wounds.

"Joe hates the Oakland Raiders, hates losing to the Oakland Raiders, and hates losing stupidly on *Monday Night Football* to the Oakland Raiders," Wolfley recounted.

As Wolfley was struggling to take off his shoulder pads, like a turtle burying his head in his shell, he remembers hearing a loud crash.

"There's a helmet rattling around in his locker," Wolfley said. "I look up and it's Joe Greene. All of the sudden I hear this growling."

"'A little too [dang] happy,'" Wolfley remembers Greene saying. "It got silent as a church. He quieted the entire room. That's a lot of alpha males on those 1980 teams. And that's the type of respect he earned. When Joe talked, people listened. In my 12 years of playing, the only guy that ever called a players-only meeting that meant anything."

Over time, Greene's public image began to evolve, as the father of three and grandfather of many more began to show his softer side. "Mean Joe" appeared in a Coca-Cola commercial that debuted in October 1979 and aired during Super Bowl XIV a few months later. After chugging a youngster's Coke, Greene tossed his jersey to the kid with a now-famous phrase, "Hey kid, catch." For his work he won Best Actor in the Clio Awards, the Oscars of the advertising world.

Greene would later be part of a TV program with Kermit the Frog's nephew Robin and make other television appearances that revealed a different off-field persona.

At his retirement press conference following the 1981 season, Greene said, "Just remember Joe Greene as being a good football player. And not really mean."

Even though Greene wasn't terrorizing quarterbacks or threatening linemen, the game kept calling him back. He coached the defensive lines of the Steelers, Dolphins, and Cardinals. He boomeranged back to Pittsburgh as a special scout until his retirement in 2013. Greene earned four Super Bowl rings as a player and two more as a scout, appropriately—as the player most credited with turning them into winners—owning all six of the Steelers' championship rings.

"He's the greatest of the great," Wolfley said. "That's what everybody said. He started the whole turnaround. If there was a Mount Rushmore of Steelers, he's at the pinnacle."

13.

Don Hutson

Don Hutson is credited with creating the wide receiver position thanks to his incomparable play.

Position: Wide Receiver

Team: Packers (1935–1945)

By Dan Pompei

When Don Hutson lined up on the first play from scrimmage on the Packers' 17 against the Bears at City Stadium in Green Bay 86 years ago, nobody knew he was about to change a team, a rivalry, a position, and the way the NFL played offense.

It was Hutson's second game as a pro. He had been a first-team All-American at Alabama and was made the highest-paid Packers player with a paycheck of $300 per game, but he didn't catch a pass in his NFL debut the previous week against the Chicago Cardinals.

Some suspect he was intentionally minimized in the game plan because Packers coach Curly Lambeau wanted to catch the Bears off-guard.

The Bears had won 17 consecutive regular-season games and had beaten the Packers six consecutive times. They always have been the team to beat for the Packers, but never more so than that day.

The Bears elected to cover the tall, thin rookie with Beattie Feathers, at one point considered the fastest man in football. Most of the other Bears defenders had their eye on star halfback Johnny "Blood" McNally. When Feathers backpedaled and glanced at Blood, Hutson loped past him, caught a pass from Arnie Herber, and scored an 83-yard touchdown, the only points in the Packers' 7–0 victory.

"That was a very, very important game for me because there were some people around Green Bay that thought Lambeau made a mistake by paying me," Hutson said years later, according to the book *Mudbaths and Bloodbaths.* "So that took care of that."

The Packers visited Chicago five weeks later. The Bears led 14–3 with three minutes remaining, and most of the fans who had been at Wrigley Field had started for home. Hutson then scored two touchdowns in the final three minutes to lead the Packers to a 17–14 victory.

The Bears would have started the season 7-0 if not for Hutson. As it was, they didn't qualify for the postseason. Hutson's Packers won their first championship in five years the following season. They would win two more and play in another championship game during Hutson's 11 years in Green Bay.

According to Hall of Fame defensive back George McAfee, the Bears eventually designed two or three defenses especially for Hutson. But it really didn't matter. "I just concede him two touchdowns a game, and I hope we can score more," Bears head coach George Halas said.

Before Hutson, ends were primarily blockers for halfbacks. Hutson was the first modern wide receiver. But he was more than that. He was the first great wide receiver. The case could be made that he was the greatest wide receiver. He is the only wide receiver in history to be named most valuable player twice. It was one of many things Hutson accomplished that no other receiver did. He led the league in receiving yards seven times, receptions eight times, and receiving touchdowns nine times. Hutson led the NFL in scoring five consecutive seasons. He held 19 NFL records when he retired in 1945.

No one would have guessed it by looking at him. Hutson stood 6-1 and weighed maybe 180 pounds. Before he made that 83-yard reception against the Bears, the skeptics said he was too thin to hold up in the NFL. The research of Packers historian Cliff Christl revealed only one other end in the NFL weighed less than Hutson in 1935, and the other 44 averaged nearly 200 pounds per man.

Wearing a helmet that looked like it was a couple of sizes too small, no hip pads, and mini-shoulder pads, Hutson hardly was intimidating by sight. He didn't care what he looked like, however.

"I had my shoulder pads cut down so they were pretty small and less restrictive," he said in the book *What a Game They Played*. "I didn't wear hip pads. It was to give me a little more speed, a little better maneuverability; it gave me a little edge, I believe."

Speed was his thing. He said he ran a 9.7-second 100-yard dash.

"Hutson was so darn fast," Bears lineman George Musso said in *Mudbaths and Bloodbaths*. "He'd lull you to sleep. You'd think he was coming full speed, and he'd be coming about three-quarters speed. Then, when he got to you, he'd leave you. He was that kind of ballplayer—he could fake you out of your jockstrap. Oh, hell, he was the best."

The "fake you out of your jockstrap" skill was an underrated part of his toolkit.

"Hutson is the only man I ever saw who could feint in three different directions at the same time," Eagles coach Greasy Neale said, according to the *New York Times*.

Former Packers general manager Ron Wolf has studied films of Hutson. "What made him special was his ability to maneuver once he got in the open field," Wolf said.

Hutson believed his quickness came from playing with snakes. As a Boy Scout in Pine Bluff, Arkansas, Hutson had a collection of 35 to 40 snakes that he caught and kept in cages in his yard.

Reptiles had nothing to do with the graceful way he moved. Nicknamed "The Alabama Antelope," Hutson was the first player associated with the phrase "poetry in motion," according to NFL Films legend Steve Sabol.

Hutson wasn't so natural playing defensive end, but he lined up at the position during his first three seasons. He struggled at defensive end taking on larger players. So in 1938, he was moved to defensive back, a position at which he would excel. Hutson led the league in interceptions in 1940.

"If he never caught a pass for us, he would have [still] been one of our most valuable men," Lambeau said in the book *Packers Versus Bears*. "I have never seen him miss a tackle."

Hutson also was an outstanding kicker, and he led the league in extra points three times and field goals once. He was even a player-coach in his final two seasons.

But what he did on offense was groundbreaking. As much as he was a wide receiver, a defensive back, and a kicker, he was a pioneer. Hutson was fortunate to catch passes from Herber, a Hall of Famer, and later Cecil Isbell, who played like a Hall of Famer in a five-year career. Together, Hutson, Herber, and Isbell worked with Lambeau to transform the sport.

Hutson and Lambeau drew up pass patterns used to this day, including the stop-and-go, the straight-line slant, and the post route.

In one game against the Cleveland Rams, Hutson ran the post route and grabbed the right post with his left arm, then swung around it with his feet off the ground to the other side, where he made a one-handed touchdown catch of Isbell's pass.

Hutson scored 29 points in a single quarter against the Lions—still an NFL record—despite being double-teamed. He attributed it to having the wind at his back.

Three days before the Packers opened the 1943 season against the Bears, Hutson learned that his father passed away and his little brother was killed in action in the South Pacific. He played that Sunday. His 26-yard touchdown catch in the fourth quarter gave the Packers a 21–21 tie. After the game, Hutson took the train from Green Bay to Chicago, then flew to Memphis, where he was picked up for the 150-mile drive to Pine Bluff. He buried his father the next day.

In the 1944 NFL championship game, Giants coach Steve Owen was so concerned about Hutson that he triple-teamed him, which opened up lanes for running back Ted Fritsch in a 14–7 Packers victory.

Hutson's most productive seasons were 1942 through 1945, when the NFL was diluted from players serving in World War II. Hutson was not drafted because he had three daughters. Critics say his statistics were skewed because he wasn't playing against the usual caliber of competition.

But it's not like those were his only dominant years. He was an All-Pro for eight of his 11 seasons. Hutson retired with 488 receptions and 7,991 yards. The next-closest player in NFL history at the time had 190 catches and 3,300 yards.

Hutson never missed a game with an injury, but that doesn't mean he never was hurt. He tried to retire at least three times before actually doing so after the 1945 season.

"It was damn near impossible for me to quit football in Green Bay," he said. "You know what the Packers meant to the town, and I'd been having some good years. I got the feeling they wanted me to play forever."

They could not be blamed. In Peter King's 1993 book *Football: A History of the Professional Game*, he named Hutson the greatest player of all time. He was not out on a limb.

Former Bears assistant coach Clark Shaughnessy wrote this in 1943: "In the years to come whenever forward-pass catching is mentioned, one name will always be mentioned first—Don Hutson, without a doubt the greatest pass catcher the game of football has ever known and probably the greatest it will ever know. No one but Superman could perform the feats Don Hutson has performed in catching passes."

Bears Hall of Fame lineman Clyde "Bulldog" Turner told the *Milwaukee Journal-Sentinel* that Hutson was the best he had ever seen. "I don't like to compare players then with players now. But he was head and shoulders above the ones in that era."

The Packers opened a new indoor practice facility in 1994. The Don Hutson Center, they called it. At the dedication, Wolf declared Hutson, who died three years later at age 84, the greatest of all the Packers.

Said Wolf: "He must have been an era ahead of himself."

12.
Anthony Muñoz

His peers voted Anthony Muñoz the NFL's best lineman four times.

Position: Offensive Tackle
Team: Bengals (1980–1992)

By Paul Dehner Jr.

There's little debate among those who follow the NFL and understand offensive line play that Anthony Muñoz represents the gold-jacket standard.

Eleven consecutive All-Pros. Four-time NFL lineman of the year. Two Super Bowl appearances. Member of the 100th anniversary team. NFL Man of the Year in 1991. First-ballot Hall of Famer and the only player in Canton who spent the entirety of his career with the Bengals.

Understanding what made Muñoz such a dominant offensive tackle starts with recognizing what a gifted athlete he was. This wasn't just a meat-and-potatoes big guy who could simply eclipse oncoming defenders; he was an agile, athletic force who could match skills beyond just size and strength.

That athleticism can be rooted to Muñoz's skills in other sports in his younger days. His page on ProFootballHOF.com points out that Muñoz was too big as a kid to play Pop Warner football, so he turned his attention to baseball. He rode that all the way to the University of Southern California, where he was a pitcher on the 1978 Trojans squad that won the College World Series.

In a 2020 oral history of the 1979 USC football team, Trojan teammate Ronnie Lott told The Athletic's Bruce Feldman that Muñoz's skills certainly went beyond the gridiron.

"Anthony was an incredible athlete," Lott said. "I played against him in football, basketball, and baseball, where he was a pitcher and played third base. Guys would try to bunt on him but he was so athletic, he was like a much larger Brooks Robinson."

Bengals teammates got a taste of Muñoz's skills on the diamond as well and were equally impressed.

Teammate and wide receiver Cris Collinsworth pointed out on the *NFL 100* show on NFL Network that the Bengals had a softball team in those days. At shortstop for those teams, the most athletic position on field, wasn't one of the lightning-quick wide receivers, explosive defensive backs, or even a quarterback.

It was their left tackle, Muñoz.

"I'm talking one of the great athletes that has ever put on a helmet in the National Football League," Collinsworth said on the show. "There's 100 unbelievable players that are going to be on this board. There's not one guy that's going to be on this board that I would trade for him."

Muñoz told Feldman that baseball was his first love and it was a deciding factor on committing to USC, because they would let him play on the baseball team as well as football. But make no mistake, football was always going to be his destiny. All of those skills combined with his size were too much for him not to be a major NFL prospect.

He was the third overall selection in the 1980 NFL Draft by the Bengals. The reason he didn't go first overall was because of concerns about a knee injury he suffered during his final season with the Trojans.

When he returned to play in the Rose Bowl for his final college game, Bengals president and legendary coach Paul Brown was in attendance with his sons, Mike and Pete.

Muñoz put on a show that would serve as an appetizer for one of the great careers in league history.

"The three of us sat there and laughed out loud," said Mike Brown, now Bengals president, 11 years later to *Sports Illustrated*. "The guy was so big and so good it was a joke."

At 6-foot-6, 278 pounds in his playing days, his combination of size and strength overpowered most defensive ends of the 1980s NFL. Yet, that wasn't what set him apart. His pure athleticism was what elicited the belly laughs that filled the Bengals' meeting rooms for over a decade.

"It was crazy," Bengals offensive linemate Joe Walter said. "You see how big of a guy he is, he was just so light on his feet."

The Bengals even made sure to use those skills for more than just run blocking and pass protection as Muñoz caught seven passes and four touchdowns during his career, becoming a red zone favorite of quarterback Boomer Esiason.

To see a sack given up against Muñoz was the rarest of sights, though it did happen. Buffalo's Bruce Smith was the most notable to ever give him trouble and the two met up in multiple big games, none bigger than the 1988 AFC Championship Game, where the Bengals advanced to Super Bowl XXIII.

"There are no comparisons between him and other tackles," Smith told *Sports Illustrated* two years later. "He's proven it year after year that he's the best."

Line up a list of the best defensive ends from Muñoz's career and you'll have a list of players declaring him the best offensive lineman they've ever seen. The play on the field stood on its own merit and was nothing shy of consistently dominant.

"He wouldn't just block people," Bengals offensive linemate Dave Lapham said. "He would totally embarrass them. Finishing wasn't the word. It was destroying them."

Walter added, "It was magical to watch. It's crazy how smooth he was in run game, pass protection, everything, never was over-extended, never got in trouble, always was that level player. And he just destroyed guys."

What was happening behind the scenes, however, made an impression on a franchise that would win two AFC Championships (1981, '88) during his career and end up two narrow losses to Joe Montana away from being viewed as team of the decade.

Not often would an offensive lineman be credited with lifting a team to the Super Bowl in the same way quarterbacks are discussed. But with Muñoz, there was truth to his presence lifting the entire team, including an offensive line that ranked among the best of their era across the board.

"You go in on Mondays after a game and he's finishing running five miles, already got a workout in and then when we get there to do our workout, he's working out with us again," Walter said. "He was always prepared, always in shape, and wanted to be the best."

Walter, who played right tackle, said he would eventually sit directly next to Muñoz so he could copy his notes, which were extensive and meticulous and full of items he hadn't always thought about.

"I don't think it's a coincidence the two Super Bowl teams he was the left tackle because when your best players are your best people and your best workers, you have a chance to raise the whole ship," Lapham said. "When your best players are malcontents and don't work, you don't have a shot. There's not a better example of your best player being your best person than Anthony Muñoz."

His unparalleled legacy played out in every aspect of the football team. In every way imaginable, Muñoz was the complete package. The best the game has seen.

"When he's all-in on something, he is ALL-IN and he's going to give every ounce of effort," Lapham said. "Attack and dominate."

11.
Otto Graham

Otto Graham (14) led the Browns to ten consecutive title games and was a nine-time first-team all-league QB.

Position: Quarterback
Team: Browns (1946–1955)

By Dan Pompei

If, as Bill Parcells was fond of saying, you are what your record says you are, then Otto Graham was the best that ever was. And probably the best that ever could be.

The quarterback took legendary coach Paul Brown's Cleveland teams to championship games in every one of his 10 seasons, and the Browns won seven of them—the first four in the All-America Football Conference and the last three in the NFL. He lost only

17 games in a decade. His winning percentage of .810 remains the highest in history.

It didn't matter what he was playing, he just won. The son of music teachers, Graham was an Illinois French horn champion at the age of 16. He also played in a brass sextet that won a national championship. Graham went to Northwestern University on a basketball scholarship but played football on an intramural team. When Northwestern football coach Pappy Waldorf watched Graham's championship-winning intramural team, he invited him to join his Wildcats. As a member of the Rochester Royals of the National Basketball League, a forerunner to the NBA, Graham played on the 1945–46 championship team.

Graham was fortunate to always seem to be surrounded by excellence. With the Royals, he played with Bob Davies, Al Cervi, and Red Holzman, who are basketball Hall of Famers. In Cleveland, he was coached by Hall of Famer Brown. He threw to Hall of Famer Dante Lavelli. He handed off to Hall of Famer Marion Motley. And he had Hall of Famer Lou Groza blocking and kicking field goals and extra points for him.

Graham and Lavelli were the only two players to start in all 10 championship games the Browns played in that era, however.

Graham was in a class alone.

"He was head and shoulders above everybody," Browns receiver Dub Jones said in the book *Brown's Town: 20 Famous Browns Talk Amongst Themselves.*

"Otto was my greatest player," said Brown, who later coached Jim Brown. "He had the finest peripheral vision I had ever seen, and that is a big factor in a quarterback. He was a tremendous playmaker. He had unusual eye-and-hand coordination, and he was bigger and faster than you thought."

Graham was a single-wing tailback coming out of Northwestern. But with Lavelli and outstanding receivers Mac Speedie and Jones as his targets, Graham took passing to another level, throwing sideline routes like no one before him and perfecting the art of anticipatory throws and rhythm passing. He averaged 8.63 yards per attempt for his career, still an NFL record more than six decades after his last pass.

"I could throw a pass to a spot as well as anyone who ever lived," said Graham, who also averaged 11.4 yards as a punt returner and played defensive back for the Browns. "But that's a God-given talent."

They called him "Automatic Otto." Lavelli said Graham's throws were so perfect, he caught many one-handed. "I'll always remember how he never got excited and maintained his cool," Lavelli said.

As much as the quarterback benefitted from Lavelli and the other receivers, it was his synergy with Brown that shaped Graham's legend. While at Northwestern, Graham beat Brown's Ohio State teams twice, which led Brown to make Graham the first player he signed when he left Ohio State and took over in Cleveland.

A creative tension existed between coach and player, but it was a tension that enhanced focus and determination.

Graham led through encouragement; Brown through fear. Graham appreciated the value of putting on a show for fans; Brown was stoic and rarely expressed emotion publicly. Graham said he would "rather risk losing some games by, say, 35–28, and have the fans on their feet with excitement" than win every game 3–0. Brown said he would rather win in an empty stadium than lose in front of 80,000.

Graham said he called his own plays for the first four or five years of his career, as did all quarterbacks in that era. Brown then decided to take over, shuttling in plays by alternating guards and disallowing audibles. Sportswriters started calling Graham "Mechanical Otto" because of Brown's heavy hand.

Graham bucked his coach on occasion, including in a 1951 game against the Bears. Graham wanted Jones to score his sixth touchdown and tie an NFL record, but Brown wasn't calling plays to tie the record. Graham described what happened in *Brown's Town*.

"[Browns guard] Abe Gibron said, 'Fuck Paul Brown. Call your own goddamn play,'" Otto said. "I called a deep pattern and hit Dub for the sixth touchdown. It was a touchdown, so Paul couldn't say anything."

Graham didn't appreciate Brown's strict approach, which included intolerance for tardiness, bed checks, and a rule that players could not have sex with their wives from Tuesday through game day during the season. Graham once jokingly challenged his coach on the rule about sex. "What about the single men?" he said, even though he was married.

Brown once took Graham out of a game late in his career because he thought he was scrambling too much and loudly announced on the sideline, "I want a quarterback who's got the guts to stay in the pocket."

Graham was furious. "I could have strangled him," he said.

In *Brown's Town*, Graham said of his coach, "Irritating is not strong enough a word for him. He could really get to you sometimes. He didn't give a damn if you were one of his coaches or one of his players. If he felt like a jab at you, with somebody else listening in, would help the team, he'd do it."

Graham, who served two years in the Navy's V-5 program while attending Northwestern during World War II, was mostly a good soldier when it came to dealing with his coach.

"A lot of people in this world have great egos, but on the Browns, there was room for only one ego, and it wasn't mine," Graham told *Sports Illustrated* when he was 76 years old. "I never openly criticized the coach. . . . He was the admiral, the general, the CEO."

Through it all, Graham appreciated Brown's brilliance.

"Paul Brown was just light years ahead of everybody," Graham said. "I'm grateful I got to play under him. I learned a lot about football, about organization, about life. There were times when I hated his guts. I could have killed him. Other times I felt something close to love."

Because of Brown, Graham became the first football player at any level to wear a face mask.

Graham slid out of bounds after a run in the first half of a game against the 49ers in 1953. San Francisco linebacker Art Michalik hit him late, knocked him out, and split the corner of his lip toward his cheek. Graham was given 15 stitches inside and outside of his mouth, all without an anesthetic.

Graham, as tough as he was accurate, made it clear he was not done for the day. "There was no way I wasn't going to play in the second half," he wrote in the book *OttoMatic*.

Legend has it that Brown quickly designed a face shield with quarter-inch-thick Plexiglas, and equipment man Morrie Kono attached it to Graham's helmet. Graham returned in the third quarter and, despite having difficultly seeing and breathing through the Plexiglas, connected on 9 of 10 attempts in a 23–21 Cleveland victory.

The hit on Graham started a conversation about violence in football, and Graham became an advocate for rules changes. What bothered him most was defenders being allowed to pile on ball carriers, partly because ball carriers in those days were allowed to get up and run with the ball if they had not been held down for a sufficient amount of time. Graham wrote an essay for *Sports Illustrated* decrying NFL violence, which brought criticism from the league, the media, and opponents. Graham never missed a game in his career because of injury, but some started calling him "Touch Me Not Otto."

"All I really wanted was an end to gang tackling," Graham wrote in *OttoMatic*. "In response to my mouth injury, [NFL commissioner Bert] Bell defended brute force, saying, 'We are going to continue to play the hard-hitting type of football which has brought the pros national popularity and made them a better gate attraction now than at any time in the past.' I was upset that the commissioner trivialized my injury, and it became clear that someone had to speak out for my peers."

The league adopted a rule in 1955 that said the play was over when the ball carrier touched the ground with any part of his body other than his foot or hand.

By that time, Graham had become a giant in the NFL. But he started out as an outsider when the Browns jumped from the AAFC to the NFL in 1950.

In January of that year, Graham was given the AAFC most valuable player award at the Washington Touchdown Club's annual banquet. While accepting the award, he looked over at the Washington team's owner, George Preston Marshall, who made his money in the laundry business, and jokingly said, "You'd better buy back a piece of that laundry business if we play [Washington] next year." From his seat on the dais, Marshall shot back, "Son, you couldn't drive one of my trucks and probably won't even have a job next year."

Marshall wasn't the only doubter. Bell predicted the Browns would be lucky to win three games, and then he tried to give them a schedule so difficult that his prediction would come true. In their first game, the Browns played on the road in front of the largest crowd in professional football history at the time against the defending champion Eagles. Graham's first pass was a 59-yard touchdown to Jones, and he passed for two more touchdowns and 346 yards in a 35–10 victory. He would call it the highlight of his career.

The Browns won the NFL championship that year. Graham probably would have been named MVP, but there was no award that year.

He won the MVP the following year and again in 1953 even though the Browns lost in the NFL championship game for three straight seasons. Graham took those losses hard.

"Emotionally, I was so far down in the dumps those three years," he said, according to ESPN. "I was the quarterback. I was the leader. It was all my fault."

Graham finished out his career with two straight NFL championships and won his third NFL MVP award in his final season in 1955. He retired at the age of 33.

We learned more about Graham from the 1956 Browns, with whom he had no affiliation.

One year after Graham led the Browns to his final championship, the Browns finished 5-7.

10.
Dick Butkus

Dick Butkus (51) is considered a prototype and ideal of middle linebackers.

Position: Linebacker
Team: Bears (1965–1973)

By Dan Pompei

S ome of the best-ever football players were on a different level as athletes.

Some ran faster than almost everyone else.

Some had an overpowering combination of size and strength.

Some could outsmart their competition.

Dick Butkus checked each of those boxes, but what really made him different was fear. He mastered fear like no one ever, making it work for him and against his opponents.

Paul "Dr. Z" Zimmerman in 2001 called Butkus the best middle linebacker in NFL history. Thirty-one years earlier, Butkus appeared on the cover of *Sports Illustrated* with the headline "The Most Feared Man in the Game."

You can almost envision the sweat beading on the forehead of Lions running back Mel Farr when he said, "He terrifies you when he comes charging in like a madman." And you can almost see the trembling lower lip of Cardinals and Packers running back MacArthur Lane when he said he prayed he could get up every time Butkus hit him.

In his 1997 book, *Butkus: Flesh and Blood*, Butkus wrote that he never was afraid of another player. His only fear was injury. He knew every other player had the same fear, so he found ways to make that fear work for him.

"Let me explain how I feel about fear," Butkus wrote. "For one thing, we all have it. If you don't, you're an idiot. In fact, every player who has ever put on a jersey and pads has experienced fear. The trick is to feel the fear and rise above it. The only way I know to do that is to get good and mad. The anger defeats the fear every time. This technique is as old as warfare itself. From the Romans to the Native Americans to the U.S. Marine Corps, the battle cry remains the primary method of pushing the fear down so far the whimpering can't be heard. On the football field, there was no one louder than me."

For Butkus, the games in his head preceded the games on the field. It began in pregame warm-ups when he went to the other team's side of the field, where he didn't belong. Lions center Ed Flanagan once found Butkus wiping his muddy cleats on his warm-up jacket. Vikings center Mick Tingelhoff was practicing his snaps one day when he noticed his hands were wet. Then he saw Butkus standing over him, spitting.

If he saw an opponent laughing, Butkus imagined he was laughing at him. Bears coach George Halas played along. Once, on the field, before the Bears played the Lions, he asked Butkus, "Did you hear what Flanagan said about you?" Flanagan had not said anything, but that was information Butkus didn't need to know. Butkus stewed, and Flanagan paid the price that day.

Hall of Fame coach George Allen is credited with drafting Butkus. In his book *Pro Football's 100 Greatest Players*, Allen wrote that Butkus "played with the ferocity of an angered animal." He added, "He was mean."

In his autobiography *Out of Bounds*, Cleveland running back Jim Brown wrote that Butkus was "Unequivocally out of control. The ideal linebacker." He also noted that no middle linebacker ever did it better than Butkus. "When football players sit around, discuss guys they admire, they talk about Butkus. Football is hitting. Butkus was the ultimate hitter."

Bears teammate Ed O'Bradovich recalls that as O'Bradovich tackled ball carriers, Butkus charged from behind, yelling, "Hold him up!" Butkus wanted a free shot. The Lions once were blowing out the Bears and running out the clock. Butkus perplexed teammates and the opponent by calling all the Bears' remaining time-outs. His reasoning? He wanted more shots at Flanagan—all with a running head start.

Butkus never saw the benefit of shaking hands with opponents after a game or helping them up. In fact, after a tackle, he typically either kicked the ball carrier or shoved him down as he was trying to get up. If he was in an especially advantageous position, he took a bite out of a stray limb or finger.

Being portrayed as a brute offended Butkus, he claimed, but he played the role, probably in the event that the enemy was paying attention. He once told an interviewer, "I sometimes have a dream where I hit a man so hard his head pops off and rolls downfield." When sportswriter Jerry Magee asked him how he felt about quarterbacks in 1970, Butkus said, "I don't personally like anybody."

The fear Butkus inspired was never more apparent than in the eyes of Lions running back Altie Taylor, who had been foolish enough to tell a reporter he thought Butkus was overrated. During a subsequent game, he saw Butkus charging at him full speed. Taylor stepped out of bounds before he could be hit. This angered Butkus so that he kept chasing Taylor out of bounds. In fact, he chased him into the stands at Soldier Field.

Butkus could back up his threats with the ability to strike with stunning force. And he did. Whereas fears often are worse than the realities that follow, the fears of Butkus's opponents almost always ended up justified. When the Lions used an I formation against the Bears at Tiger Stadium, every player in the I—center, quarterback, fullback, and halfback—was knocked out of the game by Butkus.

In another game against Detroit, Hall of Fame tight end Charlie Sanders hit Bears linebacker Doug Buffone with a forearm on a crackback block, knocking out three of Buffone's teeth. Butkus vowed payback on behalf of his friend. Later in the game, when Sanders tried to catch a pass over the middle, Butkus was waiting for him. "Cold-cocked me," Sanders said. "Hardest I ever was hit."

Bears running back Gale Sayers, who was drafted fourth overall and one pick after Butkus in 1965, said the hardest he ever was hit was by Butkus—in practice.

"Dick hit you with his head and shoulder, and that gave you enough of a jolt," Sayers said. "But then he'd rake you over with his whole body, elbows, knees—nothing dirty, mind you—it was just great tackling form."

His was a distinct tackling style that most coaches do not teach. When Butkus was playing fullback at Chicago Vocational High School on the city's South Side—a period when he and his four brothers also worked for a moving company strapping refrigerators to their backs, lifting armoires overhead, and carrying pianos up flights of stairs—it bothered him most when he was hit high and the tackler wrapped his arms around him so Butkus couldn't break his fall. As a result, Butkus began tackling that way.

"I'm going to put my head in someone's sternum, and it won't be picture-perfect, but I'll tell you what—they won't come back," he said. "I'll put them on their backs and somewhere along the line, they'll cough up the ball and that's the whole thing. The idea of hitting somebody hard is not for your ego. It's to make them forget about the ball."

He was as adept at stripping the ball from opponents as he was stripping their courage. They didn't keep track of forced fumbles in Butkus's day, but he might hold the NFL record if they did. He had 27 fumble recoveries—an NFL record at the time—to go with 22 interceptions. His 49 takeaways in 119 games speak to his rare ability to impact games.

Pete Elliott, Butkus's coach at Illinois and Butkus's presenter into the Pro Football Hall of Fame, said Butkus had the best instincts he ever saw. He honed those instincts. Allen wrote about how Butkus was a student of the game who wanted scouting reports on upcoming opponents before Allen could complete them. He said on plane rides to road games, while teammates played cards, Butkus studied his game plans.

Butkus weighed 13 pounds, 6 ounces at birth, and at 6-foot-3, 245 pounds as an adult, Butkus was huge for a linebacker in his era. His head and hands were enormous, and his arms were longer than any shirt sleeves off the rack. Teammates nicknamed him "Paddles" because he wore 12EEE shoes. His legs, however, were short—which he said was a benefit to the position he played. With short-area quickness, Butkus couldn't beat many teammates in a race, but he could beat any of them to a ball carrier.

Butkus once thought he would transition to center at the end of his playing career and then coach the Bears. But by 1973, his right knee would barely allow him to walk, let alone play football. At one point, coach Jim Dooley asked him to start a game and come out after the first play just so the opponent could feel his presence.

Butkus told the Bears he was finished, but Halas insisted he play. Four independent doctors told Butkus they thought he should retire. Butkus consequently filed a lawsuit against the Bears. The suit eventually was settled with the Bears agreeing to pay him the total value of his contract, but Butkus and Halas did not speak for five years.

When they finally reconciled, Butkus asked his coach to sign a copy of his autobiography. Halas signed it, "To Dick Butkus. The greatest player in the history of the Bears. You had that old ziperoo."

By then, it was clear Butkus was more than, as Halas called him, "the greatest player in the history of the Bears." He was a cultural phenomenon whose name was synonymous with toughness.

In the Rocky motion pictures, the boxer had a bull mastiff. "Butkus," he called him. He was one of the thousands of dogs who shared the name.

A series of popular beer commercials led to opportunities in acting for Butkus. He appeared in some 250 commercials, 40 television series, and many movies.

One of those movies was the 1976 comedy *Mother, Jugs & Speed*. Raquel Welch, who starred in the film, told the director she couldn't understand why people thought Butkus was vicious. The director's response, according to the *Los Angeles Times*, "Just don't pick up a football around him, honey."

9.
Johnny Unitas

Johnny Unitas's record of 47 consecutive games
with a touchdown pass stood for more than half a century.

Position: Quarterback

Teams: Colts (1956–1972), Chargers (1973)

By Bob Kravitz

I t was 97 degrees, a moist 97 degrees, at the Baltimore Colts' training camp facility in Westminster, Maryland. Bill Curry, the former Packers center who had just arrived in Baltimore in 1967, was
walking down a hill toward the practice field, the oppressive heat
and humidity awaiting him in the valley below, when he caught up
to Johnny Unitas.

The veteran Colts quarterback was wearing a sweatsuit.

And he was singing.

"So, me being a smart-ass, I walk up to the legend and say, 'What are you so happy about, old man?'" Curry recalled. "He turned to me and said, 'Billy, you're a long time dead. You know that, don't you?' I said, 'What?' 'Yeah, you don't understand what I'm saying. You don't get very long on this earth; if you're not happy about where you're going today, maybe you need to go somewhere else. I love football practice. I can't wait to get down there.'"

Curry hesitated briefly.

"From that point on, my practice habits immediately became the best they'd ever been," said Curry, who played for the Colts from 1967 to 1972. "It gave me goose bumps, and still does. He just turned and walked on down, and he was still humming his happy tune."

Unitas lived the game, lived *for* the game. A Pittsburgh-area kid whose father died when he was 5 years old and whose mother had to work multiple jobs to make ends meet, Unitas was forever told he was too skinny, lacked the requisite arm talent, couldn't make it in the big leagues. What the NFL didn't know, and would come to find out during his Hall of Fame career, was that he was preternaturally tough and had a beautiful mind for football. Even during a time when quarterbacks were calling some of their own plays, Unitas was a step ahead of the rest, calling everything, revealing himself as the ultimate field general.

"If the coaches sent someone in with a play, Johnny sent him off the field," Curry said. "He would say, 'Don't send plays. I'm the quarterback and I'm calling the game, period.' And that's why he and Don Shula clashed at times. He said, 'If you let me call the game, we're going to win every time and they can't stop us, so don't mess with me.'"

Ernie Accorsi, a former journalist, NFL PR man, and team executive, grew up in Hershey, Pennsylvania, where the Eagles and Colts played during the preseason. Unlike all his buddies, he became a head-over-heels Colts fan before going on to a notable career working for the Colts, Browns, and Giants. He remembered a typical Shula-Unitas moment. Shula sent in a play, and Unitas called timeout and walked to the sideline.

"Did you call 30 Smash?" Unitas asked his Hall of Fame coach.

"Yeah," Shula replied.

"Well, then you go run it," Unitas said.

End of conversation. Unitas ran his chosen play.

In the end, he was one of the greatest quarterbacks of all time, leading his Baltimore teams to three NFL titles (1958, 1959, and 1968) and one Super Bowl championship (1970). He was named the league MVP three times, was named to the Pro Bowl 10 times, and was first-team All-Pro five times and second-team three times. Between 1956 and 1960, he set the record for most consecutive games with a TD pass (47), a mark that would stand for 52 years until it was broken by Drew Brees in 2012. He led the league in passing yards four times, led the league in passing touchdowns four times, made the league's 1960 All-Decade team, and has his numbers retired at the University of Louisville (No. 16) and the Baltimore Colts (No. 19). Honestly, we could fill up this entire story with all of his statistical accomplishments, but those would not tell the full scope of the story. To see him, as Accorsi did through Unitas's entire career in Baltimore, was to appreciate not only how he played the game, but how he *thought* the game as well.

"Is he the greatest of all time?" Accorsi wondered. "I don't know how you can say that; it's a totally different game now. I could make the case for [Tom] Brady, but I'll tell you this: if I had my career on the line for one drive after all the football I've seen in my life, John Unitas would be the guy I want."

Talk to players of that era and their admiration for Unitas borders on the mystical.

"I remember walking up to the Pietà in Rome and before I knew it, tears were streaming down my face; I had never seen anything like that," Curry said. "I've seen grown men watch Unitas play football and have the same reaction. I'm not suggesting he's Michelangelo's product, but if the Almighty cared about football, He wanted folks to see someone who didn't have the talent, didn't have the arm strength or foot speed or anything beat opponents to death with his brain and his work ethic.

"He was a marvel. It's not like he didn't have any God-given gifts, although he'd tell you that. What he had was the gift of anticipation. He had the ability to throw the ball to the spot where the receiver would be. And if the receiver wasn't where he was supposed to be, he'd go back to the huddle and tell the sidelines, 'Get his ass out now.'"

Unitas was not highly recruited and ended up at Louisville at a time before the school began playing big-time football. He often thought of transferring, and even took a trip to Bloomington, Indiana, to check out Indiana University. But he remained loyal to the one school that took a chance on him and he had a strong career despite playing for a losing program.

Unitas was drafted by the Steelers in the ninth round, but the Pittsburgh coach at the time, Walt Kiesling, thought he was too dumb to execute the offense effectively. As one of four quarterbacks vying for a job, Unitas never got a practice rep or a chance to throw a pass in a preseason game and was summarily cut, a slight that he never forgot or forgave.

Left without any good NFL options, Unitas worked construction while playing semipro ball on the weekends for the local team, the Bloomfield Rams, playing quarterback, safety, and punter for $6 a game.

Then, in 1956, he joined another Rams player for a tryout with the Colts, borrowing gas money to make the trip.

He made the team as a backup to quarterback George Shaw and got some garbage-time work before Shaw broke his leg early in the season. Given the opportunity he never received in Pittsburgh, Unitas emerged and Shaw never got his job back. In 1957, Unitas's first full season behind center, he led the league in passing yards and touchdown passes, and a legend was born.

Unitas was a central character in the "Greatest Game Ever Played," the much-chronicled 1958 NFL title game between the Colts and Giants, won in overtime by Baltimore 23–17. It was the game that put the NFL on the national map, securing the special relationship between pro football and TV. It was the game that changed everything, although it was par for the course for Unitas as he led the Colts to victory with running back Alan Ameche scoring the game winner in the league's first championship overtime game.

"He took them on a long drive and I always felt like he could do that any time he wanted, and he did," Accorsi said. "The great slogan in Baltimore was, 'Take us in, John.' He had that mentality that he could perform a miracle every time he touched the ball.

"[Former Giants linebacker] Sam Huff told me, there's a famous trap draw in that [1958] game where Ameche runs about 35–40 yards right by Huff. I told him John said he checked to that play because you took one step to the right. He said, 'Yeah, I did. [Receiver Raymond] Berry was killing us, our corner was begging for help. Every time I thought he was going to run it, he threw it, and every time I thought he was going to throw it, he ran it.' He was always one step ahead."

Unitas's football mind existed on a higher plane of consciousness.

"He could look at all 11 players and see everything, everybody's feet, and that's a gift; you don't train somebody to see the game that way," Curry said.

But Unitas did train. As much or more than any Colts player.

"One day, I was feeling sorry for myself, I'd lost about 12 pounds to dehydration, I'm dragging myself up to the hill to take a shower, I can't stop sweating, and I realize in the near darkness that somebody was still on the practice field," Curry said. "The first thing I thought was, those are high school kids playing. But no, it was Unitas and Berry. After five hours of camp practice. Shula's camps were unbelievable, twice as hard as [Vince] Lombardi's, and if you could survive that, you would win a lot of games.

"They were down there together, Berry running outs and digs and flies and curls, one after another after another. John's greatness wasn't about talent; it was about the most unbelievable work ethic I've ever seen."

Berry said of Unitas, "He had a very durable arm. You couldn't work him too much. He had tremendous endurance that allowed us to stay after practice and work on our routes. He could throw as long as he wanted to. One of the great things is, physically and mentally, he was very tough. He would have made a great linebacker."

Greatness, however, has an expiration date. The last game of the 1968 preseason, Unitas tore some tendons in his right arm. He would go on to have some productive seasons thereafter, but he wasn't the same, throwing more interceptions (64) than touchdowns (38) from 1968 to 1973. His career ended unhappily and ignominiously in San Diego, where he was a shell of himself, much like Joe Namath when he joined the Rams.

"John Mackey was not given to hyperbole, but he once said being in a huddle with John was like being in a huddle with God," Curry said. "I'm not sure I'd go quite that far, but he wasn't completely wrong. Johnny U. was different. He was special."

8.
Walter Payton

Walter Payton won the NFC rushing title in five consecutive seasons
and is one of the most beloved players in NFL history.

Position: Running Back
Team: Bears (1975–1987)

By Dan Pompei

I n the latter stages of Walter Payton's career, the strangest thing
happened when the Bears played on the road. Fans who were
there hoping the Bears would lose started to clap when Payton ran
out of the tunnel during pregame introductions. First, it was softly,
politely. But the noise they made became a rumble and then a roar.
Soon, tens of thousands of people who wanted Walter Payton to lose
were on their feet, showing their appreciation for what he had done
and who he was.

It didn't matter if their colors were green and gold, purple and yellow, Honolulu blue and silver, or creamsicle orange and white. People who loved this game loved this player.

He was an average-sized human, just 5-foot-10, 202 pounds. He played for the franchise that defined toughness, the franchise of George Halas, Bronko Nagurski, Ed Sprinkle, Mike Ditka, and Dick Butkus. So it was left to Payton to redefine toughness.

The essence of the game he played was contact, and no running back ever was better at contact. It wasn't just run-into-you, run-over-you contact. It was explosive, check-your-teeth contact. "I love the contact," he once said. But he didn't have to say it because every highlight video said it better.

The kind of contact he loved was supposed to be associated with a linebacker with a nickname like "Killer," not a running back they called "Sweetness." In his 1978 autobiography, *Sweetness*, he said, unsurprisingly, "I've never had an opponent call me Sweetness."

Payton had 4,330 touches in his career, and he ended almost every one of them with a violent collision—the lowering of the shoulder, the firing of the hips, the ramming of a forearm. Payton never sought the safety of the sideline. He never went down to avoid a hit. He rarely ever fell backward at the end of a play. He made defenders think his skin was armor and his hands were morning stars.

"I was probably the runner who wouldn't go down easy," he said in his second autobiography, *Never Die Easy*, which was published after his 1999 death at the age of 45 from primary sclerosing cholangitis, a rare liver disease. "Like one of those cowboy movies where a guy is coming at him and he gets shot once and he gets shot again, and again and again, and he's still walking and then all of a sudden a big explosion goes boom, an arm over here, arm over there, leg over there and they're still trying to get him down. That's the type of runner I was."

In addition to being the runner who wouldn't go down easy, he also was the runner who would spring back up easy. Payton didn't drag himself to his feet or roll over and push himself up against the ground. He popped up like a whack-a-mole. Even from the bottom of a pile of linemen, he somehow was the first to his feet. And he did it with a smile, never a grimace.

What happened after the whistle with Payton was more dispiriting to his opponents than what happened before it. *He took my best shot, and it hurt me more than him.*

Payton wasn't always that way. He started his first training camp with an elbow injury. Teammates questioned his toughness and work ethic during his rookie season. He begged out of practice before a game against the Steelers because his ankle was bothering him, and head coach Jack Pardee told him he couldn't play in the game because he didn't practice. Backup Mike Adamle performed so well in Payton's place that he replaced Payton in the starting lineup in subsequent games. Missing that game was one of the only regrets of his career.

Depending on perspective, either it was the worst thing that happened to him or the best.

He reported to training camp the following year after an intense training regimen that included high-stepping through the sands along the Pearl River in his native Mississippi. He worked so hard, he said, that he struggled with dizziness and nausea throughout training camp in 1976.

"He was in the best condition I've ever seen anybody in," Bears receiver Bo Rather said, according to Jeff Pearlman's book *Sweetness: The Enigmatic Life of Walter Payton.*

From then on, he refused to sit out a game.

Payton's mystique of invincibility didn't just happen. He created and fostered it. He played with fractured ribs on four separate occasions. He was undeterred by a turf toe that required weekly injections. He played with several knee injuries and more than one shoulder separation. A nerve injury in his shoulder didn't prevent him from taking the field.

Payton refused to allow his opponent to see him in pain. Bears trainer Fred Caito said he had to go out on the field only once for Payton, when he injured an ankle. Bears center Jay Hilgenberg said Payton insisted Caito not touch his leg because he didn't want to reveal what was bothering him. Payton eventually walked off the field by himself. He wouldn't allow anyone to examine him on the sideline either.

"Fred [Caito] would walk alongside and put a Darvon painkiller in his hand and he'd go over and get a Gatorade," longtime Bears strength coach Clyde Emrich said.

He probably shouldn't have played in the most productive game of his career. In the days leading up to a game against the Vikings in November 1977, Payton had a fever of 104 degrees. As teammates warmed up on the field, he was queasy and weak and experiencing hot and cold flashes.

Payton didn't think he would be able to play, but did he ever, running for a then-single-game record 275 yards.

Bears offensive tackle Ted Albrecht said he and receiver James Scott had to prop Payton up in the huddle.

What made the performance even more remarkable is it came against a division-winning team that featured the legendary "Purple People Eaters" defense.

"He had one of the best days I've ever seen a running back have," defensive lineman Jim Marshall said in 2000. "Especially against our defense. We were, at the time, at the peak of our game. There weren't any players we couldn't stop. And he was virtually unstoppable that day."

It's not like the Vikings didn't know what was coming. The Bears ran it 63 times (40 times by Payton) and threw it seven that day, and used only three running plays. Bears offensive coordinator and renowned passing guru Sid Gillman took such affront to the conservative play calling by fellow assistant Fred O'Connor that Gillman quit after the season.

The day after the game of his life, amid a season in which he would be voted the NFL's most valuable player, Payton could have been under the covers sipping chicken soup. Instead, he was practicing with the scout team.

"I don't think anybody played with as much heart as Walter Payton," Hall of Fame tight end Ozzie Newsome once said.

With rare commitment and competitiveness, Payton raised the bar for every group of men with whom he ever went to battle. It was nearly impossible to wear the uniform he was wearing and not try to give more, dig deeper, and care more.

Payton usually was the first Bear out to practice every day and the last to head home. He wanted every edge he could get. Payton took the insoles out of his KangaROOS cleats and wore only a thin baseball-style sanitary sock so he could feel the seven cleats on the ground against the sole of his foot.

In an era when look-at-me became popular, Payton handed the ball to the referee after every touchdown and jogged back to the sideline. On the other hand, he arrived at training camp in Platteville, Wisconsin, in a helicopter and stayed in his own trailer while teammates slept in dorm rooms.

Many of his teammates found him mysterious and distant. His childish pranks—pantsing and goosing the unsuspecting, throwing M80s in the bathroom, pouring drain opener in jockstraps—were annoying, but Payton always seemed to be there with a hand on a shoulder when it was most needed. He routinely was kind to players who had no chance of making the team. Payton wept with Bob Thomas after the kicker was cut after 10 seasons. He was one of the only Bears who tried to make Doug Flutie feel welcome when the Bears acquired the quarterback in 1986.

In many ways, Payton was the adhesive that held the great Bears of 1985 together, a leader through spirit and example. But he also was moody. After the Bears won Super Bowl XX by the score of 46–10, Bob Costas wanted to interview him for the network postgame show. Payton couldn't be found initially because he was pouting in a closet over not scoring a touchdown. After some time, he gained his composure and fulfilled his media obligations.

Like always, he popped back up.

Payton was difficult to get a feel for, even in his running style. Most runners try to beat defenders the same way over and over, playing to their strengths. Payton could go any which way on any given handoff. His runs were more staccato than melodic.

Stutter step.

Glide.

Small step.

Big step.

High step.

Twist.

Hurdle.

Pause.

Sideways shift.

Burst.

And then a power finish.

The extra yard was his, always.

Most can only play one instrument. Payton played them all. He was the Bears' emergency quarterback, kicker, and punter. He threw eight career touchdown passes on 34 attempts. He also averaged 31.7 yards on 17 career kick returns. In practice, he used to field punts—behind his back. Payton hoped for a chance to play defensive back. Pardee once said one of the things he did best was tackle defenders after the Bears quarterbacks threw interceptions.

He could have been a Pro Bowl receiver—when he retired, he had caught more passes than any running back in history. During the 13 years he played, only nine men in the NFL had more receptions than his 492. Five of them are Hall of Fame wide receivers, and two are Hall of Fame tight ends.

Payton took as much pride in clearing holes as he did in running through them. Jim Finks, who drafted Payton, called him the best blocker in the NFL. Bears running backs coach Hank Kuhlmann told Pearlman that Payton was a better blocker than runner. One of the plays Payton was proudest of was stoning Lawrence Taylor on a blitz pickup.

Hall of Fame coach and longtime commentator John Madden said Payton was the greatest football player in history and that every player in the league should be given a video or book that details Payton's approach to the game.

That's why Walter Payton was applauded, even by the enemy.

7.
Peyton Manning

A five-time MVP, Peyton Manning (18) set the record
for single-season passing TDs (55) and yardage (5,477) in 2013.

Position: Quarterback

Teams: Colts (1998–2011), Broncos (2012–2015)

By Jeff Duncan

During the spring of 2012, Peyton Manning was trying to work his way back from a neck injury that sidelined him for the 2011 NFL season and was several weeks into his on-field training program at Duke University in Durham, North Carolina.

At the time, Manning was 12 years into his NFL career and a four-time NFL MVP. But at that moment, his future hung in the balance.

The spinal fusion procedure Manning underwent the previous September was his third neck surgery in 19 months and the riskiest and most complicated of the three. The Indianapolis Colts, the only team Manning had played for since being drafted with the first pick in 1998, had made it known they planned to release him. But before Manning could find another team, he first had to regain his old form, which was not a given.

Manning was at Duke because of David Cutcliffe, the Blue Devils' head football coach. Cutcliffe knew Manning as well as anyone, having coached him for four years as the offensive coordinator at the University of Tennessee. One of the most respected quarterback coaches in the nation, Cutcliffe was a longtime friend and trusted confidant of the Manning family.

For the first two months of 2012, Cutcliffe rebuilt Manning's game from scratch. He sent him through hour after hour of fundamental drills, catching shotgun snaps, taking snaps from center, handoff drills, and footwork. Day by day, throw by throw, Manning gradually started to regain his form. By March, the velocity and accuracy of his throws were almost back to 100 percent.

On March 3, Manning conducted the ultimate litmus test: a play-by-play simulation of the Colts' 30–17 win against the New York Jets in the 2009 AFC Championship Game.

True to form, Manning left no stone unturned in his effort to authenticate the simulation. He flew in former teammates Jeff Saturday, Austin Collie, Dallas Clark, and Brandon Stokley to help recreate the game and recruited a couple of Cutcliffe's Duke players to fill out the lineup.

As he'd done for the previous 13 seasons in Indianapolis, Saturday handled the center snaps. Collie and Clark played themselves. Depending on the play, Stokley was either Reggie Wayne or Pierre Garcon. Duke tight end Cooper Helfet played Jacob Tamme or Gijon Robinson. Former Duke running back Jay Hollingsworth played Joseph Addai. Former Colts offensive coordinator Tom Moore called the plays. Cutcliffe charted the plays and called out the defenses.

Using the play clock in Duke's indoor practice facility, Manning mimicked his entire 26-of-39, 377-yard, three-touchdown performance play by play, pass for pass, second by second. No detail was overlooked during the three-hour workout. Manning called plays in the huddle and made his trademark "Omaha!" checks at the line of scrimmage. They ran each play at full speed from the exact yard line and hash mark as the real game. The receivers ran the same routes, and Manning completed the passes to the same targets. When the script called for the Jets to be on offense, Manning and company retreated to the sideline and waited for the exact time of possession to expire on the play clock before retaking the field. They even scripted a 12-minute break for halftime. The only thing the game didn't have was defenders.

"Our tempo and the amount of energy we expended was identical," Saturday said. "Everybody went down there knowing we were going to work. We knew he [Manning] was taking this very serious."

The Duke video crew recorded the game from both sideline and end zone angles. Cutcliffe and Manning then evaluated the game film from the workout and compared it side by side with the 2009 game, gauging his footwork, the velocity and trajectory of his throws, and the speed of his drop-back and release.

The consensus: Manning was back.

"I knew from the moment I caught his first pass that he was back," said Stokley, who teamed with Manning for five seasons in his 15-year career. "It was pretty impressive."

It also was classic Manning. He might get outplayed. Someone might have better God-given athleticism. But no one was going to outwork or out-prepare him.

"[The Duke workout] showed you exactly what kind of detail Peyton went to in trying to get back," Stokley said. "Who does that? Most people would never even think about doing something like that. It was another example of his attention to details. Everything mattered to Peyton, and there was a standard of excellence there. His commitment and work ethic never slipped."

Four days later, the Colts released Manning, vaulting him into free agency, where he eventually signed a five-year, $96 million contract with the Denver Broncos.

Manning rewarded Denver by leading the Broncos to a pair of

13-3 records and AFC West titles in his first two seasons. Two years later, he quarterbacked Denver to a 24–10 upset of Carolina in Super Bowl 50, completing one of the great comeback stories in NFL history.

"It was the first time I'd been hurt, which was bad enough," Manning said. "Then, I had to learn how to be an effective quarterback again, even though it meant adjusting my game. To be able to come back with a new team and be part of an organization that won another championship was very special."

Tony Dungy's favorite story about Manning also focused on something that happened during the offseason.

During the summer of 2007, Dungy's Colts were coming off the franchise's first Super Bowl title in nearly four decades. Two months earlier, they had selected Ohio State receiver Anthony Gonzalez in the first round of the NFL Draft.

Gonzalez, though, couldn't attend the Colts' spring workouts because Ohio State's quarter session lasted until late June. This did not sit well with Manning, who did not want his rookie receiver playing catch-up during training camp. So the 10-year veteran, eight-time Pro Bowler, and two-time MVP called an audible.

He hopped in his car twice a week and made the five-hour round trip to Columbus, Ohio, where he schooled Gonzalez on the playbook and threw passes to him on a nearby field. All this for a first-year player who wasn't even going to start.

"He didn't tell anyone he was doing it, either; just went on his own, five hours round-trip," Dungy said. "He figured, that's what it takes, so I'm going to do it. And he was like that with everything."

When asked about the story, Manning laughed.

"Yeah, it's true," Manning said. "But they also had some pretty good golf courses in Columbus. So there was a dual purpose in mind."

At 6-foot-5, Manning had the prototypical build NFL coaches and scouts seek in a franchise quarterback. He was not as athletic as his father, former NFL quarterback Archie Manning, but he compensated with size, strength, and an intuitive awareness in the pocket. But what separated Manning from his peers was his beautiful mind. Few quarterbacks in NFL history could process information as quickly and voraciously as Manning. When it came to reading coverages and making split-second decisions on where to throw the ball, he was a gridiron supercomputer.

"Football is a team game, but when you're the quarterback and your teammates and coaches are counting on you so much, above all else, you want to be prepared to do your job," Manning said. "I loved to play the game, of course, but I always looked forward to the preparation part, too. If there was some kind of edge I could get on the competition, I wanted to find it.

"There are a lot of talented players who don't work hard and some who do work hard but maybe don't have the physical ability. But if you can combine the two and have a passion for the game, well, then you have a chance to be really good."

As the son of an NFL quarterback, Manning was raised in the sport. He, along with his brothers Cooper and Eli, spent countless afternoons with his father in the New Orleans Saints locker room and developed a passion for the game at an early age. As a tyke, he could rattle off the alma maters of every NFL starting quarterback and famously memorized the Ole Miss starting offensive line and their hometowns: Buddy Mitchell from Columbus; Billy Coker from Clarksdale; Wimpy Winther from Biloxi; Kip Jernigan from Jackson; and Worthy McClure from Hattiesburg.

During his recruitment as a senior at Isidore Newman School in New Orleans, Manning famously asked as many questions of the coaches recruiting him as they did of him.

"Peyton was a quarterback from the get-go," Archie said. "He was always a leader, always curious, always asking questions. He made lists and kept notes. He had notebooks galore."

Manning carried his maniacal preparation habits to Tennessee, where he enjoyed a decorated career that saw him win the 1997 Maxwell Award as the top player in the nation. His Volunteers teams went 40-5 with Manning as a starter and he left Tennessee as the SEC's all-time leader in passing yards (11,201), completions (863), completion percentage (62.5), and total offense.

Manning was one of the last great quarterbacks to play all four years in college. The Colts drafted him with the No. 1 pick in 1998. After a rough rookie season, Manning turned the Colts into a juggernaut. The Colts posted double-digit wins in 11 of the next 12 seasons while winning eight division titles.

In 17 NFL seasons with the Colts and Broncos, Manning won more MVP awards (five) than any player in NFL history and retired as the league's all-time leading passer. He was the first NFL quarterback to win Super Bowls with two franchises (longtime rival Tom Brady became the second). At the time of his retirement, Manning held NFL records in career passing yards (71,940), passing touchdowns (539), and consecutive seasons with at least 25 passing touchdowns (13). He earned Pro Bowl honors 14 times and All-Pro honors seven times. And in 2021, he was enshrined in the Pro Football Hall of Fame after being elected on the first ballot and a presentation to the voting committee that required less than five seconds.

"I always looked up to Peyton because he was a little bit older than me, and he was always doing things the right way," Brady said. "His team was always in it. I know our teams had a rivalry against one another. When you went against a Peyton Manning–led team, you were going against [one of the best teams] in the league. It's no real surprise that he'd be a first-ballot Hall of Famer. An amazing player."

Manning was at his best with the game on the line. His 54 game-winning drives are the most in NFL history, more than contemporaries Brady and Drew Brees, who played more games and seasons in their careers.

"You knew you had a chance to win no matter who you were playing against every week," Stokley said. "You always felt confident that you were going to score a touchdown and it was always going to work out because you knew your guy at the most important position in sports was prepared like no one else."

6.
Joe Montana

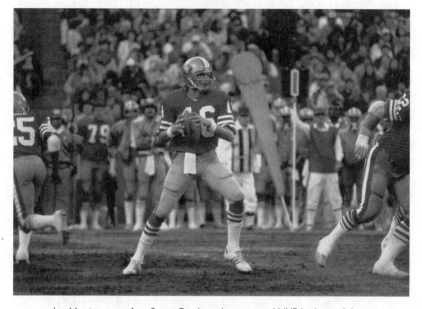

Joe Montana won four Super Bowls and was named MVP in three of them.

Position: Quarterback
Teams: 49ers (1979–1992), Chiefs (1993-1994)

By Matt Barrows

You think it's hollow?"

Three 49ers quarterbacks were standing beneath a goalpost at practice, necks craned and eyes trained on the top of the upright some 40 feet above them. They tapped on the metal, then reasoned that because the contraption gets hauled on and off the field during practices it couldn't possibly be solid. It would be too heavy to move.

"There's gotta be an opening on top, right?"

They continued to look up. There was only one way to find out.

"So Steve, Joe, and me started flipping these rolls of athletic tape up to the top of the pole to see if we could get it in there, if there was a cap on it or not," Steve Bono recalled. "I don't remember who made the first one, but one of us flipped a roll up there and it disappeared. And it was, 'Oh shit! There's no cap on this thing!'"

And with that, the most unique quarterback time-waster in the history of the NFL was born. During the 1990 season, Bono, Joe Montana, and Steve Young invariably would be the first 49ers out of the locker room and onto the practice field. It wasn't to hone their craft. It was to see if anyone could toss a half-spent roll of tape perhaps three inches in diameter into a hole four stories above them that was perhaps 4½ inches in diameter.

It became part sport, part science. Here's a brief oral history of the tape roll game:

MONTANA: "The tape had to be a certain size. It couldn't be a full roll of tape. So you had to go in and get some from the trainer that they'd already used."

BONO: "I'm sure Lindsy [McLean] the trainer didn't like us taking all his tape. We literally did it for a whole season."

YOUNG: "The hard part is, the smaller the tape roll, the better the chance but the more unstable it was. The bigger the tape, the more weight—so you'd get some sort of consistency to get a shot at it. But how many lip-outs did we have over the years? Hundreds."

BONO: "It was an underhanded flip. There couldn't be any wobble. It had to be a tight spiral to get it in there."

YOUNG: "Every once in a while [another player] would come over. Then they'd throw a couple and be like, 'You guys are idiots. That's impossible.'"

MONTANA: "The closer you were to the pole, the easier it would be. You had to slide it up the pole and drop it over the top. If you went like that you could do it. You had to play the wind and all that stuff."

YOUNG: "If they still have those goalposts from all those years ago, you could take them apart and all the tape rolls would come shooting out. I bet you there's 30, 40 in there. That's after 10,000 attempts."

Try to pinpoint why the Montana-led 49ers offenses were so successful and you'll come up with several answers.

There was Montana's brain that could flash through five reads on a single drop back. There was his touch and accuracy, a perfect match for Bill Walsh's precision offense. Montana led his team to four Super Bowls and never threw an interception or took a loss in any of them. His passer rating in those four victories: 127.83.

There was his icy poise—what former 49ers assistant equipment manager Ted Walsh calls "that death stare"—whenever he stepped onto the field. Walsh remembers acting as the snapper during seven-on-seven drills, tossing the ball back to Montana and seeing the locked-in look on No. 16's face.

"I just remember how his eyes were," Walsh said. "He had those blue eyes. And he'd scan the whole defense, and his lips would move like he was processing information. He'd say things like, 'I hate this fucking play' or 'Like stealing candy from a baby.' It was a different comment each time."

But there also was an entirely different side of Montana, a warmth, wit, and love of mischief that kept everyone around him loose. The NFL's comeback king also was a renowned bicycle thief, swiping teammates' rides at training camp in Rocklin, California, and depositing them in creative spots. Like in the limbs of a live oak tree. Or tethered together with a 30-foot chain and lock.

One evening Montana, Young, and Bono got out of their quarterback session early. They snuck over to Sierra College's science building, where the linebackers met. One quarterback quietly crawled out of a hallway window onto the space above the building's entrance. His partners in crime handed up bicycles, one after the other. When the linebackers emerged they found their bikes piled one on top of the other 15 feet above them.

"People thought we were always at each other," Young recalled of the caper. "We never argued in our whole lives. We never had a cross word. In training camp, he and I would spend hours trying to figure out the greatest pranks to pull. I mean, I loved hanging out with Joe because it was always fun."

The game with the athletic tape was part of that fun. In 1990, in the midst of one of Montana's best seasons with the 49ers, he appeared on the cover of *Sports Illustrated* as the magazine's sportsman of the year. The image catches Montana in golden California sunlight, his head thrown back and a broad smile on his face. It's a portrait of a man on top of the world.

Look closely and you'll see he's holding something in his right hand. It's a roll of athletic tape. The photographer took the shot while Montana, Young, and Bono were in the midst of one of their goalpost challenges. The game isn't mentioned in the accompanying story. But as it turns out the photo perfectly captured a critical ingredient to the 49ers' dominance: Montana's breezy charm.

"That was his great skill. He had the ability to lift up everyone who played with him on both sides of the ball," Paul Hackett, the team's former quarterbacks coach, said. "There was nothing uptight about him. He could use humor at the right time to allow people to be their best."

The 49ers started looking at Montana in the winter of 1979. Walsh, who had recently been hired to resurrect a two-win team, was intrigued and asked another newcomer, executive John McVay, if he knew anyone at Notre Dame with an inside scoop on the school's fair-haired quarterback.

McVay had just the guy. He was close with the school's running backs coach, Jim Gruden, who had served as an assistant under McVay at the University of Dayton. So McVay flew to South Bend, Indiana, treated Gruden to lunch at a restaurant just off campus, and asked about Montana, who was getting only tepid interest from the NFL.

"All those teams always had a question about Joe and whether he had one of those rocket, gunslinger arms," Gruden said. "And I said, 'Well, you should get one of those machines, those Jugs machines, that fire long passes.' I said, 'All I know is when the game's on the line, he completes every pass that he throws.'"

Gruden, after all, had been one of the few people remaining at the Cotton Bowl just months earlier when Notre Dame found itself in a hopeless situation against the University of Houston. A wicked ice storm had descended on Dallas the previous night. The temperature at kickoff was 20 degrees with a windchill of minus-6.

"I mean, no one was left in the stands," Gruden recalled. "If it hadn't been the Cotton Bowl, they probably would have postponed it. They chipped ice off the field to play the game. It was extreme, freak weather."

Early in the telecast, CBS cut to sideline reporter Frank Glieber, who told viewers that he'd just spoken to Montana and that "he says he's never been this cold during a football game in his life."

It would get worse. Joe Cool was turning into Joe Frigid.

By halftime, his teeth were chattering, his body temperature had fallen to 96 degrees, and all color had drained from his face. While the team doctor plied him with chicken bouillon, Notre Dame opened the third quarter with its third-string quarterback.

He struggled against the fierce wind as Houston opened up a 34–12 lead. Notre Dame's players and coaches kept nervously looking toward the tunnel entrance to see if Montana would emerge. With a little more than a minute left in the third quarter, he finally did.

"When he came back the whole team—offense, defense, everybody—changed," Gruden said. "That was the effect he had on the team. We knew we had a chance. If we could stop 'em, he would score points. The third-team quarterback ain't gonna do it. We ended up scoring 23 points in seven minutes against a really good team."

In South Bend, Montana had a reputation as the Comeback Kid heading into the 1979 Cotton Bowl. It swelled that day and continued to grow over the next decade and a half.

When he announced his retirement in April 1995, Montana had amassed 31 fourth-quarter comebacks, beginning with one against the Saints in 1980 in which he and the 49ers overcame a 28-point deficit, which at the time was the biggest comeback in NFL history.

His most famous rally came the next season on an improbable back-of-the-end-zone throw to his best friend—and regular bicycle-theft accomplice—Dwight Clark against the Cowboys. Montana drove his team 89 yards late in the fourth quarter and hit Clark with 58 seconds remaining, Two weeks later Montana led the 49ers to their first-ever Super Bowl win, 26–21 over the Bengals.

Cincinnati was the foil for more Montana heroics seven years later in Super Bowl XXIII. The 49ers trailed 16–13 with the ball on their 8-yard line and 3:10 remaining when Montana trotted onto the field during a television timeout.

Most sports fans know what happened next. More than 80 million were watching, camera strobe lights were flashing, and the moment was crackling with tension. Montana's reaction: to point out to his offensive linemen that comedian John Candy—*see him over there by the tunnel?*—was watching from the stands.

"And sure enough, the whole huddle turns around, and looks down there, and there's John Candy eating popcorn at the other end of the stadium," tackle Harris Barton recalled in an NFL Films documentary. "We're like, 'Yeah, that is John Candy. Look at that.' And then, the official blows the whistle and the play starts."

Montana then completed seven of his next eight passes, including a game-winning, 10-yard dart to John Taylor in the middle of the end zone with just 34 seconds left.

What's not as well known about that game is that Montana had been lightening the mood hours before his famous Candy comment. He was one of the first players to arrive at Joe Robbie Stadium, and not because he'd had trouble sleeping or so he could go over the playbook one last time.

It was so he could remove the nameplates from his teammates' lockers and paste them on the doors to the bathroom stalls. And so he could wad up strips of athletic tape and pelt unsuspecting teammates as they walked by with their headphones on.

"That's typical Montana right there," Hackett said. "When everyone else was nervous and the most tense—'Oh my God, what are we going to do?'—he was at his best. This was his world. He knew how to have his teammates at their best. He really did. And they performed for him and with him because of it. They loved him."

Bono said he made the mistake of shadowing Montana before a noon game in Minnesota in 1990. They arrived at the stadium at 7:30 a.m., at which point Montana had his usual pregame meal.

"Coffee and a Snickers bar," Bono said. "He called it the breakfast of champions. It's all he ever ate."

Then they spent the rest of the morning wandering around the stadium pulling pranks and chatting up whomever they bumped into.

"By the time the game came, I was worn out," Bono recalled with a laugh. "We were doing all kinds of nonsense."

There was a similar low-key wind-up for a big game in Kansas City in 1994. Montana had been traded to the Chiefs a year earlier, the 49ers and the heir to Montana's crown, Young, were visiting in Week 2 and the media were frothing like it was a Super Bowl. The Chiefs issued 500 media credentials, and the crowd that day was the second largest in Arrowhead Stadium history.

The day before the big grudge match, Montana played golf with his dad, then invited a few former 49ers teammates and friends from the 49ers' equipment and training staffs to his house for a barbecue dinner. The group ate ribs and raced go-karts—including Montana, according to those on hand—slamming into one another and tearing around the cul-de-sac where the Montanas lived.

The next day, Montana embarked on his usual, pregame ramble, including a midfield chat with Young, the protégé with whom he was supposedly feuding.

"In fact, I remember a conversation on the field beforehand that was kind of funny," Young said. "He had a couple of jokes about how intense it was."

There were also the usual capers.

Walsh, the equipment staffer, remembers trying to make his way with his bulky equipment tackle box through the huge crowd that had assembled on the sideline during pregame introductions. At one point, he was held up by someone who was tugging on the back of the tackle box. Walsh looked behind him.

"And it's Joe just dicking around," he said.

Then, of course, Montana stepped onto the field, his blue eyes turned icy and serious, and he led his new team to a 24–17 win against his old team.

"He was always in the locker room four or five hours before [the game] started and there was always some sort of prank," Bono said. "Then the game would begin and he'd methodically pummel you."

5.
Reggie White

Reggie White (92) retired as the NFL's career sack leader
and was a member of two All-Decade teams.

Position: Defensive End
Teams: Showboats/USFL (1984–1985), Eagles (1985–1992), Packers (1993–
1998), Panthers (2000)

By Bo Wulf

Typically, Phil Simms spent his final moments in the locker
room before a game making sure his knowledge of the week's
playbook was buttoned up. The former New York Giants quarterback made sure he knew all the checks he'd have to make at the line
of scrimmage. But sometime in the mid-1980s, in the underbelly of
Veterans Stadium before a game against the Philadelphia Eagles,
Simms did something different. He gave himself a pep talk.

"I didn't even look at my playbook," Simms remembered. "I just sat there and I'd go, 'OK, now. Hang in there.' I'm talking to myself: 'Just gotta hang in there. You're gonna get hit, don't worry about it. Just make your reads, throw the ball.' All this stuff. And that was truly my thought process. I never did that against anybody else."

That's because nobody else had Reggie White.

"I never saw the kind of fear in the eyes of a lineman the way they used to be afraid of blocking Reggie," said former Eagles linebacker Garry Cobb, "because they knew this guy is just tossing people."

For most of those unfortunate enough to line up across from White, there were two ways of handling that fear. One way was to follow Simms's lead. Accept the dread and find a way forward. Or you could go the opposite direction and confront the beast head-on, as one poor Detroit Lions offensive lineman did during a preseason practice against the Eagles in 1986.

"The O-line and the D-line were doing one-on-one pass rush," remembered Jeff Fisher, who was the Eagles' defensive backs coach at the time. "And Reggie literally just shook and hip-tossed and blew by him. And the player came back and he just was MF'ing Reggie. . . . After the tirade was done, I'm told Reggie just looked around and said, 'Jesus is coming.' And so Reggie patiently waited in line for his turn and then stepped out of turn and lined back up on this same player and literally destroyed him. I mean, just shook and tossed him. Then he bent over and reached down to help him and said, 'Jesus is here.'"

Over the course of his 15 NFL seasons, White made lasting impressions on everyone he played with, against, and for. To his opponents, he was the bare-armed, bare-handed best defensive lineman in the game. To his coaches, he was the skeleton key to great defense. To his teammates, he was a leader, a spiritual advisor, and a class clown.

After two years with the Memphis Showboats of the USFL, White arrived in Philadelphia in 1985 and quickly proved himself with 13 sacks. A year later, Buddy Ryan took over as head coach and brought along his vaunted 46 defense. It was a match made in heaven or hell, depending on which side of the ball you were on.

"The 46 defense basically covers the center and both guards," said Fisher. "At that time protection-wise, the league hadn't caught up. What happens is you can create one-on-one matchups."

Lined up either at left defensive end or directly over the center, White was unblockable by one player alone. His sack total rose to 18 in 1986 and then to 21 in the strike-shortened 1987 season.

"People always ask me, because I've coached so many great players, who was the best?" said Wade Phillips, the Eagles' defensive coordinator from 1986 to '88 before he went on to coach the likes of Bruce Smith, J. J. Watt, and Aaron Donald. "I always say Reggie had the best year that anybody's ever had. . . . We only had 12 games, he had 21 sacks. I don't think anybody will ever come close to that."

Off the field, White was both a philosopher and a comedian. He would stage full-length wrestling matches in the locker room, dump water jugs onto a coach's head in the middle of practice, and playfully tease everyone in his orbit with his unmistakable raspy voice. His secret weapon was impressions.

"He was the best," said former Eagles wide receiver Mike Quick. "He was as good as anybody I've ever seen who's not onstage making money doing impressions."

"Macho Man" Randy Savage, Elvis, Muhammad Ali, Buddy Ryan, every other coach in the building, and on and on the list went, including his pièce de résistance, Rodney Dangerfield.

"That dude, Reggie had him down to a T," said Quick, laughing at the memory.

While White acted like a "big kid" at times, being the locker room cutup also helped him become a leader. It made the best player on the team seem approachable, not above everyone else.

Those late-'80s, early-'90s Eagles defenses are among the greatest ever, but they were "a tough group to lead," according to Cobb. White was more playful than hotheaded, which was an asset on a unit that featured several players with "strong personalities," like middle linebacker Seth Joyner, safety Andre Waters, and defensive tackle Jerome Brown.

"[White] was always even-keeled," said Cobb. "And he was always a leader."

There were Pro Bowlers at each level, with Eric Allen and Wes Hopkins in the secondary and Joyner and William Thomas at linebacker. Up front were Brown in the middle and Clyde Simmons on the right side. "You'll never assemble a defensive line like that ever again," said Fisher.

For the opposition, though, everything was still about White.

"He was unselfish in the sense that he knew that people were gonna double-team him and Clyde and those guys would have one-on-one opportunities, but that never fazed him," said Quick. "And when Reggie decided that he wanted to make a play, you could put two people on him if you wanted to, but you're just wasting them because he's gonna make a play. That's how good Reggie was."

Often, that play was made on account of his patented hump move. Listed as 6-5, 291, though he topped 300 pounds for most of his career, White "moved like a linebacker," as Phillips described it. The speed and power he generated coming off the line of scrimmage meant offensive linemen had to account for him bursting off the edge. But if they leaned too far in that direction, White's thunderbolt of a right arm came across to knock them out of the way.

"To be able to stop him, you had to try to get in front of him," said Phillips. "And then when you start moving that way, he would come with that hump move and throw you out of the way."

"Domination," said Fisher. "There's no better way to describe it, utter physical domination."

"He could take a 320-pound man and just toss him like it was nothing," said Quick, laughing again. "The funniest thing is to see a 320-pound man just being tossed, and I've never seen anything like that."

Adding to the presentation of his dominance was the stylistically naked way he went about it. Most of the time, White wore nothing on his arms or hands. No extra pads, no tape on his fingers. Just a country-strong man who looked like he rolled out of bed ready to go to work on the assembly line discarding misfit linemen.

In eight years with the Eagles, White finished with 124 sacks in 121 games. As dominant as he and those teams were, there's still a tinge of disappointment for Eagles fans looking back. For one, there is the bitterness of being regarded as among the best teams never to have won a Super Bowl. For two, there was the heartbreak of his departure.

When White signed with Green Bay in 1993, it was a seminal moment for the league. He charted the course for free agency in the generation that followed and may have saved a Packers franchise that was viewed as borderline unworthy in the decades since their Vince Lombardi–led glory years. During his six seasons in Green Bay, White found the football salvation he'd been searching for.

In his 15 seasons, White finished with fewer than 10 sacks only three times, including his 8.5 for the No. 1 Packers defense in 1996. That year, he saved his best for last.

In Super Bowl XXXI, White had been largely held in check during the first half, but the Packers carried a 27–14 lead over the Patriots into halftime. In the second half, New England decided it was time to play catch-up on offense. They began passing on nearly every down and removed tight end Ben Coates's secondary responsibility of chipping White on every pass play to get him out on routes quicker. The result was a one-on-one matchup for White against right tackle Max Lane and a green light to pin his ears back.

"One time I set on Reggie, he decided to bullrush me and literally my feet came off the ground because he came in low and . . . picked me up into [quarterback Drew] Bledsoe's lap," Lane remembered. "I'd never felt that before. And I never felt it afterward. There's a lot of things that get blurry over the years, but that feeling did not. It was that naturally freaky strength."

In terms of trying to quantify how often a defensive player wrecked a game, you can do worse than counting three-sack games. White and Lawrence Taylor are tied for the all-time lead with 12 three-sack games apiece in the regular season. But in the second half of Super Bowl XXXI, White made it 13 as he helped deliver the Packers their first Super Bowl trophy in over 30 years. When the game was over, White was the one who paraded around the field with the aptly named Lombardi Trophy as if it had always belonged to him.

Looking back, Lane figures he's in good company at least.

"He even tea-kettled Larry Allen, so I didn't feel so bad," he said.

There are so many ways to slice White's dominance as the greatest sack artist of all time. Here's one. His 13 sacks as a rookie are tied for the third-most ever. His 31 sacks through two seasons are the second-most. After that, he's atop the leaderboard for most sacks through three years all the way up to 19, when Bruce Smith finally surpassed the total White finished with in 15. (Of course, sacks only became an official stat in 1980. Pro Football Reference has done the work to account for unofficial sacks before 1980, in which case Deacon Jones would overtake White for a few of those seasons. Then again, if White hadn't spent the first two years of his career in the USFL, who knows how many more he'd have.)

White's death in 2004 at the age of 43 still registers as a shock nearly 20 years later. His life was about so much more than football and he had so much more to do.

"Reggie was a spiritual leader for a lot of people," Quick said. "I think that he was wise beyond his years. A lot of the things he told us that we should be doing were a lot of the things I learned later in life. To me, it's hard to find a better man."

"I think he was so important that God just wanted to bring him home early because he needed him."

If there is solace in White's absence, it's that his legacy is very much alive. When J. J. Watt was drafted by the Houston Texans in 2011, Phillips was the head coach. He decided to play Watt on the edge because he remembered how well it worked for White to have one-on-one matchups with the offensive tackle.

Any time an offense uses slide protection, that's a vestige of the invention bred by the necessity of trying to stop White. When a defensive player is penalized for landing on the quarterback with the full weight of his body, blame White. Whenever a player signs a big-ticket deal in free agency, they have White to thank. And then there's the trickle-down effect of the lessons White imparted directly.

In 2000, after one year of retirement, White came back for one last season with the Carolina Panthers. Mike Rucker was a second-year defensive end trying to learn how to be a pro. His locker was next to White's.

"When you're able to locker next to Reg, you've got history on your side," he said. "For me to be able to sit there and allow him to pour into me spiritually, from a football perspective and just how to carry yourself off the field, that's invaluable. . . . How do you carry being successful? How do you carry yourself when someone asks you for an autograph and you're sore and you're icing your knees and maybe the season's not going the way we want it? How do you react? I got to see that firsthand."

From Rucker's perspective, he passed on the lessons he learned from White to Julius Peppers, who passed it on to Charles Johnson, who passed it on to Mario Addison, who passed it on to Brian Burns. It's easy to draw the same line in Philadelphia all the way to Brandon Graham, or to someone like Rashan Gary in Green Bay.

"How do you take that type of character, take what you can use and be able to pass that on? . . . Those characteristics that Kevin [Greene] had, that Reggie had that they gave to me," Rucker said. "That, to me, is worth more than any sack total, than any Super Bowl. Your legacy is still living on. Reggie White's legacy is still living on at the Carolina Panthers because of that lineage. And that's on the field and off the field."

4.
Lawrence Taylor

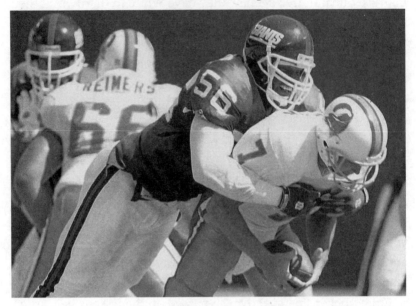

In 1986 Lawrence Taylor (56) became the first defensive player
since 1971 to be named league MVP.

Position: Linebacker
Team: Giants (1981–1993)

By Dan Duggan

Washington quarterback Joe Theismann was lying in a hospital bed two days after having his right leg shattered by New York Giants linebacker Lawrence Taylor during a game in 1985. As Theismann dealt with the pain from his broken tibia and fibula and grappled with the impact of the injury on his career, a nurse entered his room and told him Taylor was on the phone.

Theismann vividly remembers the conversation more than three decades later.

"Joe, how you doing?"

"Not very well."

"Why?"

"Why?! You broke both bones in my leg, for crying out loud!"

"Joe, listen, I don't do things halfway. I've got to go to practice. Talk to you later."

The play and that exchange with Theismann encapsulate the man who terrorized quarterbacks from 1981 to '93. No one would accuse Taylor of doing anything halfway, especially with his combination of unparalleled athleticism and ferocious competitiveness.

"There isn't another Lawrence Taylor," Theismann said. "To me, he's the standard by which you measure everything."

Brian Baldinger played offensive line for the Cowboys, Colts, and Eagles from 1982 to '93. He never slept as poorly on a Saturday night as when a matchup with Taylor loomed the next day.

"You just never knew when he was going to erupt, whether it was power, speed, some array of moves," Baldinger said. "When he wanted to get to the quarterback, some days you just felt like you were helpless."

The anxiety started much earlier than Saturday when offenses game-planned for Taylor.

"You're sitting in a meeting and the coaches will put up defensive teams. What you do is V's are usually defensive linemen, B's are backers, S's are safeties, and C's are corners," Theismann said. "So when you look at a defense, everybody is designated that way. But when we played the Giants, there was one big No. 56 with a circle around it. He was not a B. He was No. 56, and he was the one you had to pay attention to."

Taylor's game-wrecking ability caused coaches to alter their schemes.

Washington coach Joe Gibbs kept a tight end in to help Pro Bowl left tackle Joe Jacoby block Taylor. When that invariably failed, Gibbs created the H-back position, essentially another tight end lined up in the backfield who would often get sent in motion to chip Taylor.

"We completely changed our blocking patterns to try to block him," Baldinger said. "We never put a back on LT. We put our Pro Bowl left tackle Pat Donovan on him and we fanned to his side. The whole game plan was LT. Otherwise, he was going to ruin you."

The schematic changes did little to slow the Hall of Famer.

"If he saw it once, it was over," former Giants linebacker Carl Banks said. "He was just so relentless that he just wouldn't be blocked anyway."

There was an acceptance that there was a limit to the effectiveness of any game plan against Taylor.

"You just wanted to slow him down a little bit," Theismann said. "At least make him halfway human, as opposed to playing Superman."

Harry Carson played inside linebacker next to Taylor for eight seasons. A 2006 Pro Football Hall of Fame inductee, Carson saw firsthand the impact Taylor had on opponents.

"You're in the Vet [Veterans Stadium], and when [former Eagles quarterback] Ron Jaworski breaks the huddle, you can see the fear in his eyes as he's looking for where Lawrence Taylor is," Carson said. "Not just in his eyes, but other quarterbacks that we played at that time, whether it's Joe Theismann or Danny White—they're looking, 'Where is Taylor?' To see that fear is something that you can't buy."

Having missed the playoffs for 17 consecutive seasons, the Giants desperately needed some good fortune in 1981. Holding the second pick in the draft, they got their break when the Saints took running back George Rogers at No. 1. The Giants took Taylor and immediately realized they had acquired a game-changer.

"Back then, rookies and quarterbacks went to camp a week earlier, and we had a scrimmage," former Giants quarterback Phil Simms said. "They had to take Lawrence out of the scrimmage after no more than 10 minutes—I don't even think it got that far—because he sacked the quarterback on every single throw. Not *some—every* throw. I can remember the quarterback was Cliff Olander and he was going crazy, 'Can somebody block him?!'

"No, Cliff. Nobody can block him."

The Giants had a talented veteran linebacker corps at the time featuring Carson, Brad Van Pelt, and Brian Kelley. But they didn't have anyone like Taylor.

"Opponents couldn't treat Lawrence as just another outside linebacker," Carson said. "They had to treat him as a lethal force who could disrupt the entire offensive scheme of what they're trying to do."

Taylor's unique skill set was deployed expertly by Bill Parcells and Bill Belichick, the Giants' head coach and defensive coordinator, respectively, for most of his career. Instead of dropping Taylor into coverage, which was the norm for 3-4 outside linebackers at the time, the coaches freed the 6-foot-3, 237-pounder to hunt opposing quarterbacks. The trio revolutionized the game in the process.

Middle linebacker had long been the glamour position on defense. Dick Butkus, Ray Nitschke, and Chuck Bednarik were the stars from the generation that preceded Taylor. But Taylor's dominance sent every team searching for pass rushers who could attack the quarterback's blind side.

"Lawrence came along and changed the approach from inside to outside more," Theismann said.

Taylor won NFL Defensive Player of the Year in each of his first two seasons and again in 1986, when he recorded a career-high 20½ sacks and became just the second defensive player to win league MVP. No defensive player has won the award since. Taylor and the Big Blue Wrecking Crew defense then led the Giants to a Super Bowl victory.

"I think he saw the game differently than just normal really good football players," Banks said. "You're like, 'How'd he do that?' You look at film, nothing looked perfect, but here he is in the backfield. It's almost like he sees when things are going to happen and how they're supposed to happen. He just did everything differently than everybody else."

Taylor had 15½ sacks in the final 12 games of the 1988 season after returning from a four-game suspension for violating the NFL's substance-abuse policy. He maintained his elite level of play for two more years, culminating in a second Super Bowl win in the 1990 season. The eight-time first-team All-Pro retired after the 1993 season with 142 career sacks, which ranks ninth all-time.

"I got to see greatness firsthand," Carson said. "He just elevated the play of everybody else. It gave us the opportunity to do some things defensively that we might not have been able to do had it not been for the talent, the speed, the quickness, the agility of Lawrence and what he brought to the table."

The Giants made the playoffs seven times in Taylor's 13 seasons, twice winning the Lombardi Trophy. It's easy to trace the genesis of the Giants' transformation from doormats to champions.

"He turned the franchise around," Giants senior vice president of player personnel Chris Mara said. "We went from there and got a lot of great players, but it all really started with LT."

Born in Williamsburg, Virginia, in 1959, Taylor was known as "Lonnie" growing up. He accepted one of his few scholarship offers from the University of North Carolina and developed into the best defensive player in the country. Taylor's off-field exploits in college didn't concern NFL scouts.

"Thankfully for LT, this was before social media and cell phones and stuff like that," Mara said. "There were reports of him being a little bit crazy. But back then, that didn't come into play. When you talked about a player in the draft room and he had gotten in a barroom brawl or he had beaten somebody up, [head coach] Ray Perkins wanted to move the guy *up* on the board."

Taylor vaulted to A-list celebrity status in New York City after winning Defensive Player of the Year as a rookie, and Lonnie quickly morphed into "LT," with Taylor partying as hard as he played.

"I saw him leave [practice] and he had a black leather outfit on with a bright red shirt and I just go, 'Wow, going out tonight, huh, big boy?' He laughed and he left," Simms said. "The next morning, the first team meeting was at 9. The steel door that comes into our locker room at Giants Stadium swings open. You hear this noise, I turn and look and Lawrence takes a step in—same outfit on, looks at me, and I just smile and go, 'Rough night, big guy?' He goes, 'You wouldn't believe it.'

"We're walking to the field and I just go, 'How you feeling?' I'm having fun. I'm enjoying this. He said, 'Man, there's only one thing to do.' I said, 'What's that?' He goes, 'I'm just going to go crazy today.' And he literally went out and dominated practice. It ruined everything. He is just going nuts, knocking people around, throwing them, sacking the quarterback—doing everything."

Taylor's hard-partying lifestyle created a misconception that he didn't practice hard. Banks quickly discovered the opposite was true after getting selected by the Giants with the third pick in the 1984 draft.

"It was the most eye-opening experience I ever had from a standpoint of just how fast he practiced," Banks said. "My first day of minicamp, we take the field and Lawrence practiced faster than I ever played a college football game. His tempo and his effort, I was like, 'Whoa! This is what it's like.'"

Taylor didn't bring that same intensity to the meeting room. He was notorious for catching up on the sleep he missed the previous night during film sessions.

"We were doing our pass-rush installation for a big game against Washington. He came in in the middle of the meeting, crawled under a table, and went to sleep with sunglasses on," Banks said. "Our defensive line coach, Lamar Leachman, basically had had enough. He said, 'God damn it, Lawrence! We're trying to put this pass rush in. You'd think you would be awake for at least this part of the meeting.'

"Lawrence was grumpy, and he gets up and he says, 'What are you talking about?' He says, 'Cut the lights off and put the film on.' He looked at two plays and he cut the lights on, went to the chalkboard, and drew up our entire pass-rush scheme for that game. We had been doing this for about 45 minutes, an hour. This guy wakes up, he looks at two plays—literally, two plays—draws it up, tells us what we should be doing and why we should be doing it.

"Then he looked at the coach, and he says, 'Can I fucking go back to sleep now?'"

Taylor was simultaneously dominating the NFL and abusing cocaine and crack. He checked into a drug rehabilitation center months before winning the 1986 MVP award. Taylor had avoided punishment from the league by switching his urine samples with those of teammates, but his drug use finally caught up to him in 1988, when a second positive test led to a four-game suspension.

"It was something that hurt his heart, to be suspended," Carson said. "There were other things going on in his personal life. It wasn't just the drugs thing. It was television trucks parked outside of his home in Upper Saddle River. That has a profound impact on you and your family. He wasn't just Joe Blow. He was one of the best players to ever play the game and he's suspended for drugs."

Taylor's personal demons followed him into retirement. He continued to battle drug addiction and was arrested multiple times. He was sentenced to six years' probation in 2011 after pleading guilty to sexual misconduct and patronizing a prostitute after allegedly having sex with a 16-year-old girl.

"I call him Lawrence," Carson said. "'LT' is the one thing that always got him in trouble. This was true way back then, but also in more recent years.

"I've told him flat out, 'You really need to let LT commit suicide and just be Lawrence Taylor.' Lawrence is an altogether different individual. He's the guy people like and can be jovial [with] and he's a good guy. But when you throw in that LT thing, LT is what gets him in trouble."

It's one of the most iconic clips in NFL Films' vast library: Taylor is stalking the Giants' sideline and imploring his teammates to "go out there like a bunch of crazed dogs and have some fun!"

For as many times as that clip has aired, it may not be well known that Taylor was speaking that intensely during a 1985 *preseason* game against the Jets. A mic'd up Taylor also famously said, "Son, y'all got to do better than this," after sacking Jets quarterback Ken O'Brien in that exhibition game.

It didn't matter that it was the preseason. There was no off switch to Taylor's competitiveness.

"He could do anything that he wanted to do once he felt challenged," Carson said. "If it was chess, he would try to beat your ass."

When Carson missed a 1988 game against the Saints with a knee injury, Taylor was forced to move to inside linebacker. Playing through a torn muscle near his shoulder, Taylor had three sacks and two forced fumbles in a Giants win.

"Guys will light it up when they're healthy and they're fast and they don't have any injuries," said Theismann, who was a television analyst for the game. "But when you can do what he could do when he was hurt, it takes it to another level."

Taylor's athleticism transcended football.

"He could play basketball, baseball, he was a golfer—loved golf," Carson said. "If you wanted him to play quarterback, he probably could. He was just overall very athletic. Regardless of what position you asked him to play, he could do it."

Taylor even played tight end in one game after crossing the picket line during the 1987 strike.

"Even though it was against replacement players, it was a pretty amazing thing," Giants co-owner John Mara said. "He had a skill set and a drive that really was unmatched by anybody in my lifetime."

Belichick isn't inclined to provide sound bites. But the Patriots coach couldn't avoid delivering when asked if then–Bears linebacker Khalil Mack was in Taylor's class ahead a 2018 matchup with Chicago.

"Wait a minute, we're talking about Lawrence Taylor now," said Belichick, seemingly offended by the mere suggestion. "I'm not put-

ting anybody in Lawrence Taylor's class. Put everybody down below that. With a lot of respect to a lot of good players, we're talking
about Lawrence Taylor."

Simms had a front-row seat for the LT experience as a teammate
for Taylor's entire career. Having witnessed the wild Saturday
nights and the dominant Sunday afternoons, Simms is left with a
simple conclusion.

"That guy is never to be seen again."

3.
Jerry Rice

Jerry Rice set NFL records for receptions, receiving yards, 1,000-yard seasons, and more.

Position: Wide Receiver

Teams: 49ers (1985–2000), Raiders (2001–2004), Seahawks (2004)

By Matt Barrows

"Can you come up to the room?"

Bill Walsh was excited. The 49ers were in Houston to play the Oilers and Walsh had flipped on the television in his suite. A local team, Texas Southern, was hosting Mississippi Valley State and Walsh couldn't take his eyes off the Delta Devils' star receiver. Plays and formations mushroomed in his mind. He was eager to share his ideas.

He picked up the phone and started dialing numbers. Then he

propped open the door with the security latch and pulled a dining room chair in front of the TV to more closely study the receiver, a senior named Jerry Lee Rice.

First into the room was Michael Lombardi, a member of the scouting staff.

"He said to me, 'Michael, make sure you get me tape on this player,'" Lombardi recalled. "So I had to call Mississippi Valley State and I got three canisters of tape eventually delivered to the offices."

General manager John McVay, receivers coach Paul Hackett, and public relations director Jerry Walker filed in later that evening and gathered around the TV. Mississippi Valley State had a wild offense, stacking three, sometimes four, receivers in a straight line on one side of the formation with Rice on an island on the other.

"Then they'd drop back and throw to Jerry no matter how many people were covering him," Hackett said. "That fascinated Bill."

The date was October 20, 1984. The 49ers would go on to beat the Oilers, 34–21, the next day. In fact, they went undefeated the rest of the season, routing Dan Marino and the Dolphins in the Super Bowl. With Walsh calling plays, Joe Montana tossing touchdowns, and Ronnie Lott patrolling the secondary, they seemed unstoppable.

But in his mind, Walsh already was figuring out ways to go faster. He wanted to start using more three-receiver sets in his famous offense. He leaned forward in his chair to get a closer look at Rice. He was transfixed. *Look how he moves. Look how he uses his hands. Get ready—this next one's coming to him*, he told the others.

"Bill was wild about him," McVay recalled of the gathering. "And he wanted to share his joy with the rest of us."

Said Hackett: "I remember Bill getting very excited."

As the group left the hotel room, Walker turned to McVay.

"I said, 'That guy was pretty good. Is he for real?'" Walker said. "And John said, 'I think Bill knows talent when he sees it.'"

As it turned out, Rice not only was supremely talented but driven like no other receiver who's played the game. How driven? After tearing his ACL in the first week of the 1997 season, a restless Rice cut off the plaster cast protecting the joint with a handsaw he found in his garage. He was back on the field for Week 15.

High standards? Rice sometimes would wash his own uniform at Mississippi Valley State. After all, the home field was practically made of dirt and if Rice didn't look crisp, how could he be expected to play crisply?

"That meant a lot to me," he said. "Because I felt that if you look a certain way, you were going to perform a certain way. And I carried that to the NFL. And I used to drive the equipment guys crazy."

He was well worth the aggravation.

Twenty years after Walsh and company watched him on a hotel-room television, Rice finished his NFL career with more receiving yards, 22,895, and more touchdowns, 208, than anyone in league history. No one was close then, and both records still seem unbreakable now.

What stands out most about Rice's career is the sustained excellence. He finished with more than 1,000 receiving yards 14 times, including 11 consecutive seasons from 1986 to 1996. When he left the 49ers in 2000 at age 38, everyone figured he was finished. Except Rice. He played four more seasons, mostly with the Raiders, before finishing his final season with the Seahawks. He gained another 3,648 yards and scored another 21 touchdowns. At age 40, with the Raiders, he made another Pro Bowl appearance and helped them reach the Super Bowl.

"We're talking about maybe the greatest football player who ever lived," Hackett said. "This guy was a phenom."

It's hard to believe Walsh saw *that* amount of potential during the hotel-room viewing, but he immediately knew Rice was special. Maybe too special. The 49ers had the last pick in the first round of the 1985 draft. And after poring over the 16 mm film Rice's school mailed to California, Walsh knew the receiver wouldn't make it to pick No. 28.

When he was finished going through the reels, Walsh scribbled a note and attached it to the canister: "John Jefferson . . . with speed."

"I remember the note vividly," Lombardi said. "I regret not keeping the note."

As the offseason began, the 49ers circled four college receivers: Rice, Wisconsin's Al Toon, Miami's Eddie Brown, and Jackson State's Chris Burkett. Walsh sent Hackett to Wisconsin, Miami, and Jackson State for the school's pro days.

He told his assistant not to bother going to Itta Bena, Mississippi, the home of Mississippi Valley State.

"He said that we'd have no chance to get him," Hackett recalled. "And that's the thing I remember the most going into that year—that he was way out of our league."

Walsh, however, couldn't let go of the idea of injecting another top-end receiver into his offense. For one, the evaluators thought 1985 would be an excellent draft for wideouts, which turned out to be true. The class also included Jesse Hester, Vance Johnson, Eric Martin, and Andre Reed, who'd go on to play 15 seasons for the Bills and who was inducted into the Pro Football Hall of Fame in 2014, four years after Rice.

Walsh also was eager to use more Zebra personnel, which is what the 49ers called their three-receiver sets. To that point, his offense had leaned on two-running-back formations. The 49ers opened the 1984 Super Bowl, for example, with Roger Craig and Wendell Tyler in the backfield.

Mostly, Walsh wanted to punch the accelerator. The 49ers had a pair of venerated receivers already on the roster. But Freddie Solomon was 32 heading into the 1985 season, and for all of his franchise heroics, Dwight Clark wasn't fleet of foot. Walsh needed new blood. And he wanted another strategic piece to put on his chessboard.

So the 49ers started making inquiries about trading up in the draft. The Patriots, who had the 16th pick that season, had their sights on a cornerback, Richard Johnson. When he was taken 11th by the Oilers, New England decided to swap first-round picks with the 49ers, with the Patriots gaining some later selections in the process.

Walsh explored going even higher. The 49ers called the Bengals, whose head coach, Sam Wyche, was a former Walsh disciple in San Francisco, in a bid for the No. 13 pick. Toon already had been taken 10th by the Jets at that point.

The Bengals, however, wouldn't make a deal. They wanted a third-round pick as part of the compensation, and the 49ers would only give up a fifth. The gap wasn't bridged, and the Bengals took Brown, who had 1,114 yards for the Hurricanes in 1984, including a 220-yard game in the widely watched showdown with Doug Flutie and Boston College in November that year. They probably were happy with the pick—for a year. Brown ended up with 15 more receiving yards than Rice in their rookie seasons.

Said Rice: "I had Al Toon and Eddie Brown go before me, and I was a little upset about that. Because I just felt I was—I'm not going to say I was a better receiver, but I'll just say I thought I brought a little bit more to the table. And I was surprised about that."

While the Bengals and 49ers were on the phone, Rice was watching the draft at his brother's home in Mississippi thinking he'd be a Dallas Cowboy.

"They had the 17th pick and I had had a good showing for the Cowboys," he said. "And I just had a feeling that I was going to wear that star on my helmet."

Instead when the phone rang the voice on the other end belonged to Walsh, whom Rice had just watched win his second Super Bowl three months earlier. Walsh told him the 49ers were taking him with the 16th pick.

"I'll never forget that day," Rice said of the call. "I almost died. I could barely breathe."

The first plane trip of Rice's life was to Oakland, California, on the night he was drafted. Hackett picked him up at the airport and, a few weeks later, ushered him into perhaps the greatest meeting room in the history of the NFL.

Nowadays, quarterbacks, receivers, and tight ends have their own position coaches, and they meet and go over film in separate rooms. In 1985, Hackett coached all three groups. That meant the first faces Rice saw when he entered a tiny classroom in Redwood City belonged to Clark, Solomon, and Montana, who already was a two-time Super Bowl MVP.

Montana said he remembers Rice hardly uttering a word as a rookie. What could he say?

"It's Joe Montana. *Joe Montana!*" Rice remembers thinking. "And now he's sitting across from you. It's like, what do you say to legends?"

If that wasn't intimidating enough, Hackett's classroom was like an advanced trigonometry course with lines, arrows, and squiggles heading every which way on the overhead projector.

There were more than 120 pass routes in the West Coast playbook, and the 49ers receivers had options on most of those routes. There were verbal audibles. And Montana had a set of hand signals his pass catchers had to know, too. The 49ers wanted to go fast and weren't going to slow down for a rookie. They pushed Rice to keep up.

"It was going to school," receiver Renaldo Nehemiah said. "Usually the night before we'd have an exam. And you had to do well on that exam to show them you had the aptitude to play the next day. So it was challenging. It wasn't just playing the game."

If a receiver ran the wrong route in practice, Walsh merely would shake his head. Hackett—whom Nehemiah called Walsh's sergeant at arms—was more demonstrative.

"Paul might throw down his playbook or notes or whatever they were and his hat would fall off and he'd say, 'OK, let's run it again!'" Nehemiah said.

The press was even more unforgiving. When Rice suffered a bad case of the drops to begin the season, including some prominent flubs on deep balls, the *Mercury News* ran a story with the headline: "Snap, Crackle, Drop."

"There was just so much going on in my head," Rice said. "Because it was complicated, man. You had to be like a quarterback when you got to the line of scrimmage."

Inside the Mount Rushmore of meeting rooms, however, no one panicked.

Clark, the funny, charismatic, easygoing southern boy who three years earlier made the greatest snag in franchise history, watched Rice effortlessly move in and out of his routes during a minicamp practice that year, then turned with a smile.

"That boy is smooth, and he's gonna be rich," Lombardi remembers Clark saying.

Said Montana: "The first couple of days were rough on him. But everybody has those. I threw two interceptions in the first preseason game I was in that got run back for touchdowns. It takes time to settle down. And then once he did that, it was, 'Look out.'"

Solomon, who was the oldest player in that meeting room, also was funny, warm, affectionate, one of the 49ers' best storytellers and biggest characters. After games, he and defensive end Fred Dean would sneak cigarettes in a tiny space tucked away beneath the Candlestick bleachers that was out of view from both reporters and Walsh.

Solomon and Clark also were the ones who usually doled out nicknames. Nehemiah was "Noodles" because he got hit so hard in a game against the Falcons he collapsed like a wet noodle. Rice's rookie nicknames included "Fifi."

"Because of my haircut," Rice explained. "It was like a poodle—I had my hair shaved close on the sides. They gave me a hard time about that."

For the same reason, the veterans also called him "Bert"—after the *Sesame Street* character. Clark and Montana, in fact, once came into work with a Bert doll they found at a local Kmart. They dressed it in a No. 80 jersey and placed it on the lip of a blackboard that was behind the screen Walsh used to show game film. When the head coach finished his film session that day, the screen went up—and, cue the laughter—there was Bert wearing Rice's number.

It was affectionate teasing.

"They needled him but also showed him the way at the same time," Hackett said.

Solomon, who had been with the team since 1978, knew why the 49ers brought in Rice. Instead of being resentful, he took the rookie in and became his mentor. Solomon had been a quarterback at the University of Tampa, and in pre- and post-practice sessions the aging veteran not only taught Rice the finer points of being an NFL receiver but usually was the one throwing him passes.

"He'd show Jerry how you look the ball in, make sure you have a good grip on it, tuck it in between your elbow and your hands," Walker said. "They would go over that all the time. . . . The two of them were kind of inseparable."

The 1985 season ended up being Solomon's last.

Said Rice: "There was no hesitation at all with Freddie. He knew the reason why they brought me in. And he was willing to pass his knowledge on to me and really coach me and take me under his wing. And that's something I'll never forget. Because it became almost like a traditional thing where if you'd been there a long time you passed that knowledge on to the next player coming up."

Once Rice caught on to the offense, he caught fire. He began to not only see the ball into his hands, but he was also so calm, so focused, he could pick up the rotation of the ball and would watch it spin into his palms. When the ball was in the air it belonged to him.

He ended his rookie season with three of his best games of the year, a 241-yard effort against the Rams on *Monday Night Football*, 82 yards versus the Saints, and 111 yards against the Cowboys, the team he thought was going to draft him.

The next season, Rice led the NFL with 1,570 receiving yards. He was off and running toward the record books.

"And I think we all thought the sky's the limit for him at the time," Hackett said. "And it turns out there was no limit to the guy."

2.
Jim Brown

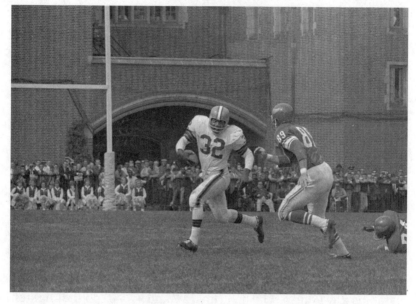

Jim Brown (32) won four MVP awards and retired at age thirty.

Position: Running Back
Team: Browns (1957–1965)

By Dan Pompei

I n the second quarter of a game in 1963, Jim Brown caught a screen pass from Frank Ryan. The fullback burst past Washington defensive back Jim Steffen, put a move on defensive back Johnny Sample, broke a tackle attempt by defensive back Dale Hackbart, spun away from cornerback Lonnie Sanders and linebacker Bob Pellegrini, and then ran away from defensive lineman Andy Stynchula and Hackbart for an 83-yard touchdown.

The play told us everything about Brown. He had the athleticism to make the catch, the steps as quick as fingers on a keyboard, the body control to leave a defender lunging at air, the violence to trample, the light-footedness to whirl out of trouble, and the sixth gear to separate.

Which is to say, he lacked nothing.

"Guys that are extremely strong may not be as agile," former Raiders running back Marcus Allen said in the documentary *Jim Brown: A Football Life*. "Some guys have all the speed in the world but may not have the balance. Jim had it all."

His physique could have been carved in Florence, Italy, during the Renaissance. Befitting a player who was called a fullback but ran like a halfback, Brown was 6-foot-2, 230 pounds, with a 32-inch waist. With the ball in Brown's hands, alleged tacklers looked like hobbits at his ankles.

Patriots coach Bill Belichick told *Sports Illustrated* that Brown moved as if he weighed 185 pounds. Legend has it in 1958, he ran a 4.5-second 40-yard dash wearing pads and starting from a three-point stance. Cleveland's fastest player before Brown joined the team was Ray Renfro, who had run a 4.7 and was 40 pounds lighter.

Said Brown's teammate Paul Warfield, "The creator said, 'I'm only going to do this one time in a very special player.'"

The son of a professional boxer, Brown stood out in any sporting arena. In addition to being a Hall of Famer in football, he also was inducted into the National Lacrosse Hall of Fame. Brown excelled at the sport at Syracuse, as he did in basketball and track. The fifth time he tried golf, he shot a 77. So confident was he in his abilities that he proposed a boxing match against his friend Muhammad Ali when Ali was the 24-year-old heavyweight champion.

But in football, he separated himself from every other who played the game. In 1958, Rams defensive tackle Glenn Holtzman told *Sports Illustrated* that tackling Brown was like tackling a locomotive. "Fast as the fastest, hard as the hardest," Holtzman said. "He gets off to the quickest start of any big man I've ever seen."

In that 1963 game against Washington, Brown also had an 80-yard run and accounted for 262 scrimmage yards. He was voted first-team All-Pro that season—one of eight times he was so honored in his nine-year career. He made the Pro Bowl, as he did in every season he played. He also led the league in rushing, as he did seven other times. His 1,863 yards in 1963 were the most in a season in NFL history up to that point.

But really, it was just another year for Brown, who won the NFL MVP award in three other seasons but was beaten out in 1963 by Giants quarterback Y. A. Tittle.

Brown averaged 104.3 rushing yards per game in his career— still the most in league history by nearly five yards. He did it in an era when defenders could get away with doing almost anything they wanted to ball carriers—and usually did. He dominated even though he was the focal point of every defensive game plan in every game of his career.

"Keep in mind, third-and-8, third-and-9 was not a passing down in Cleveland," Browns guard John Wooten said. "It was just a case of whether we were going to flip the ball to him, or throw a little flare pass."

At the 1957 College All-Star Game, Browns great Otto Graham, serving as an assistant coach, told Brown, who had just been picked sixth in the draft, that he never would make it in the NFL. The comment probably made Brown more resolute, but he did not need extra motivation.

"I'll tell you why I'm the way I am," Brown said. "It doesn't start on the field. It starts as a person. I was dealing with race since I was born. And in my inner self, my strength was unbending when it came to accepting that BS, racial discrimination. Because I was never going to let anybody make me feel like I was not top-shelf. And that was the battle that raged. And I could use a lot of that on the field."

Brown attended mostly white Manhasset High School in Long Island, New York.

"Race was always an issue everywhere, and I was the only African American on the team," he said. "That was very difficult based upon the racial attitudes of some people."

The NFL Brown played in was primarily White, and Black players dealt with segregation issues when traveling. His coach Paul Brown separated the Black players from White in the team cafeteria. In interviews with sportswriters, Brown often steered the conversation to racism and civil rights. In 1966, he created the Negro Industrial Economic Union to help Black-owned businesses, and 22 years later started Amer-I-Can, a program to guide gang members.

Brown's will was evident in everything he did.

"He probably has the spirit of a 350-pound man," Wooten said in a 2002 documentary by Spike Lee, *Jim Brown: All-American*. "And sometimes Jim would just make up his mind. He would not go down."

Brown refused to drink water during games because he believed it would make him feel satisfied and diminish his drive. He never missed a game in his career. Len Dawson, who played with him for two years, said he never even saw Brown in the training room.

"He stayed away because he didn't want people to think he was weak, and he would just fight through pain," Dawson said in a 2006 biography of Brown, *Jim Brown: The Fierce Life of an American Hero*. "I mean, he never got his ankles taped."

When it came to pain, Brown undoubtedly gave more than he got. Lions defensive end Bill Glass said getting blasted with Brown's forearm was like getting hit with a lead pipe.

"Some of the biggest, toughest guys in the NFL got pretty scared when they saw Jim swinging that arm of his," Glass said. "Jim Brown could knock you senseless."

Hall of Fame coach George Allen said because Brown was stronger and more determined than his opponents, he wore them down. In his 1989 autobiography, Brown wrote, "The key in the NFL is to hit a man so hard, so often, he doesn't want to play anymore."

Brown sneered at runners who were averse to contact. Eighteen years after he retired, Brown threatened to make a comeback at the age of 47 because Franco Harris was nearing his career yardage total, a record at the time. Brown thought Harris, who frequently ran out of bounds, was an unworthy successor as rushing king.

"A fullback running out of bounds is like a Hell's Angel driving a Rabbit," Brown wrote. "Bogie smoking a Swisher Sweet. It just isn't right."

Brown probably would have dominated if he relied strictly on brute force. But he also was a thinking man's runner. He spent hours before every game visualizing where each run would take him and how he would counter every defender's move. Wooten spoke of Brown's "great analytical knowledge" and said Brown watched film with the offense and told blockers how to align on plays.

"He is incredibly perceptive about running the football," said Belichick, who enlisted Brown's help when he was coaching the Browns. "Tremendous understanding of how to beat defenders, how to attack their leverage to give them a two-way go. He has great insight into what a runner sees, and he could explain it in very simple terms. Here is the tackler, here is your leverage point."

Brown may have been a little too perceptive for the good of his first coach, the legendary Paul Brown. When Paul Brown's offense became stale and predictable in the early 1960s, Jim Brown sought to change the team, just as he sought to change race relations. Jim Brown led a player movement that led to Paul Brown's firing. New coach Blanton Collier and assistant Dub Jones sought Jim Brown's input on the playbook. As Brown had wished, they subsequently relied more on sweeps, option blocks, and passes to the fullback.

In Collier's second season, Cleveland won its only championship during Brown's career.

"I felt . . . potent," Brown wrote in *Out of Bounds*. "Sentimental. Grateful. Whole. My goddamn melon hurt from smiling. I also felt intense relief. Unless he wins a championship, even a superstar is never fully accepted."

After the championship season, Brown commenced an acting career, appearing in the 1964 motion picture *Rio Conchos*. In 1965, he won the Most Valuable Player award but wasn't sure if he wanted to return the following season. Brown had signed a three-movie deal with Paramount that paid him more than he was making in the NFL. And there were other perks. "I knew when you went from

Sam Huff to Raquel Welch, it wasn't exactly bad shit," said Brown, who had a love scene with Welch in *100 Rifles*.

When Brown was filming *The Dirty Dozen* in London in the summer of 1966, Browns owner Art Modell told the press he would fine Brown heavily if he did not report to camp on time. It was enough to push Brown to walk away when he still could have run for who knows how many thousands of yards.

With a movie tank as a backdrop and wearing military fatigues, Brown, ever the revolutionary, announced his retirement at 29.

"I want more mental stimulation," he said at his retirement press conference. "I have a hand in the struggle of what is happening in our country and I have an opportunity to do that now."

In addition to spending his time as an actor and activist, Brown also spent time behind bars. He was jailed in 1978 for beating up a golf partner, in 1986 for allegedly beating his fiancée (she eventually refused to press charges), and in 1999 after vandalizing his wife's car. Brown was charged with a number of other crimes against women but never convicted.

Just as Brown was many things as a running back, he was many things as a human being.

Now, and as far as we can see, he will be more than a human being. In 2016, the Browns unveiled an 8-foot, 2,000-pound bronze statue of Brown off Al Lerner Way in front of FirstEnergy Stadium.

The great Jim Brown cradles the football in his left arm and extends his right as if he is ready to deliver one of those lead-pipe stiff-arms. His calves are enormous. The helmet is extra wide, as was the custom-made helmet Brown used to wear.

From the looks of it, neither a microburst nor a bulldozer could bring down that statue very easily.

As it should be.

1.
Tom Brady

Tom Brady did this seven times in his incomparable career.

Position: Quarterback
Teams: Patriots (2000–2019), Buccaneers (2020–2022)

By Jeff Howe

Julian Edelman had never seen the board.

During the 2013 offseason, he uncovered Tom Brady's greatest source of motivation. The teammates had been working out together in Los Angeles when Edelman saw a prominently displayed whiteboard in Brady's home gym, scripted with a sole objective.

SUPER BOWL XLVIII: FEB. 2, 2014, METLIFE STADIUM.

At the time, Brady had three Super Bowl rings—modest, by his standard. That's because Brady's standard, as Edelman would find out in that moment, was well beyond the scope of anything he could imagine.

"Bro, how crazy is it that you're going after Montana?" Edelman asked Brady.

"I ain't going for Montana," Brady responded with an unmistakable air of confidence. "I'm going for Jordan."

For as long as anyone can remember, Brady kept a Super Bowl countdown clock in each of his home gyms—Brookline, Massachusetts; L.A.; and most recently Tampa—as a way to remind himself of his eternal sacrifice. It's been said the boards have been updated as early as the day after each year's Super Bowl.

New year, new mission. Same chase.

It's why Brady's daily routine made other hard workers feel insufficient, why he stuck to a diet that many mock, why he pushed pliability over strength training, why he began to scout his next opponent before even leaving the parking lot where he played that day's game.

When Edelman first uncovered the whiteboard, Brady was nearing the end of a decade-long Super Bowl title drought. He didn't ultimately match Joe Montana's fourth ring that year at MetLife Stadium, but Brady persisted.

He finally tied Montana in 2015. Passed him in 2017. Year after year. Championship after championship.

"He was my idol growing up," Brady said of Montana. "I thought he was the greatest player I've ever seen. He and Steve Young were my two guys I dreamed about being someday."

He's won more titles than both. Combined.

Seven titles spanning three different decades. Michael Jordan—and his six rings—are in the rearview mirror.

"When you talk about GOATs and the legends of the league, the alpha GOAT, that's Tom Brady," said Ty Law, a Hall of Famer who was Brady's teammate for three titles in New England from 2001 to 2004. "That's the alpha GOAT, and there should be no debate about it. He's in the same breath as when you talk about Michael Jordan, LeBron [James], Wayne Gretzky. When you're talking about the Mount Rushmore of sports, Tom Brady's face is up there.

"[What he's done], it's something," Law added, "we'll probably never see again in our lifetime."

To put just a few of his achievements into proper perspective, consider: Brady has more Super Bowl victories than any individual franchise. He has more rings than the Vikings, Bills, Bengals, Cardinals, Falcons, Panthers, Titans, Chargers, Browns, Lions, Jaguars, Texans, Eagles, Seahawks, Bears, Saints, and Jets have combined (five). He has played in more Super Bowls (10) than nine franchises combined. Fourteen teams have played in fewer playoff games than Brady has won.

"When you talk about what he's been able to do in his career," former Patriots defensive coordinator Romeo Crennel once said, "I don't know that anyone will be able to do it again."

There's no mystery to his success. The drive for each Lombardi Trophy consumed every moment of his life.

He lived every day with the necessary vengeance to accomplish feats of greatness the likes of which the NFL has never seen—and will probably never see again. He stoked that fire at Michigan when the coaching staff rotated him with Drew Henson. He harnessed it when he was bypassed 198 times in the 2000 NFL Draft and stuck as the fourth quarterback on the depth chart as a rookie.

Shortly after Brady took over for an injured Drew Bledsoe in 2001—and before Patriots head coach Bill Belichick named him as the full-time starter—Brady was out to dinner with some teammates when he looked at Law and safety Lawyer Milloy and said, matter-of-factly, "I ain't giving [the job] back."

Law and Milloy loved the attitude but also knew team owner Robert Kraft—who earlier that year had handed Bledsoe the richest contract (10 years, $103 million) in NFL history—wasn't paying Bledsoe all that money to sit on the bench.

Brady proved the money didn't matter. Seven months after he'd signed that contract, a fully healthy Bledsoe was relegated to second string.

Brady relit that fiery passion when the Patriots drafted Jimmy Garoppolo in the second round in 2014. Brady, 37 at the time, was at an event with friends shortly thereafter when he questioned the strategy to find his successor. "I don't know why they drafted a quarterback," Brady told them. "I'm gonna play until I'm 45."

Brady might have sold himself short. During his age-45 season he threw (733 attempts) and completed more passes (490) than any quarterback in NFL history. He led yet another team to the playoffs.

But Brady's Buccaneers lost. And he hated it. He's always hated it.

The greats always seem to despise losing just a little more than they enjoy winning, don't they?

Rob Gronkowski got a taste of Bardy's abhorrence of losing during the 2014 offseason as the future Hall of Fame tight end recovered from a torn ACL that kept him out of the playoffs.

It had been nearly a decade since Brady and the Patriots last won a Super Bowl.

"[Brady] knew he was going for it back in the day," Gronkowski said of Brady's Super Bowl record chase. "When I got injured, he wished I was out there in the playoffs, and he was excited for me to come back the following year. He was like, 'You owe me a couple more Super Bowls.' I'm like, 'Why is that?' He's like, 'Because you got injured this year. I need you out there.' I'm like, man, this guy is incredible. He's excited to have his teammates out there and to get to Super Bowls year in and year out.

"And it wasn't like one Super Bowl. It was Super *Bowls*. Because I got hurt one year and couldn't finish out the season. It clicked in my head. I was like, 'I do, for sure.'"

Four games into the 2014 season, the Patriots got embarrassed by the Chiefs on *Monday Night Football*, and Belichick was asked whether he'd consider starting Garoppolo. Brady felt the sting of such an ugly defeat, and as the Patriots' buses pulled into Gillette Stadium before the Tuesday sunrise, the players poured into the parking lot, got in their cars, and drove home. All except Brady.

He walked alone into the football offices to dissect the film and prepare for the Bengals. The Patriots won their next seven games and eventually dethroned the Seahawks in one of the greatest Super Bowls ever played. It was also the first of four Super Bowls that Brady and Gronk would win together.

Brady's whiteboard is as legendary as it is symbolic. He doesn't need to be reminded of the date of the Super Bowl any more than he needs to remember to breathe.

It's merely a glimpse into what makes him tick. Brady didn't become the greatest player in NFL history over the past 22 seasons just because of a peripheral desire. That drive consumed him.

"It's his inner soul," Edelman said. "It's his competitiveness. It's his ability to go out and stay motivated year in and year out without letting acknowledgments, winning, adversity affect him. It's unreal. It's a killer instinct.

"When you hear people talk about Michael Jordan, how competitive he was, Tom is just like that. Those special, special people have the chemical makeup for greatness, and that's what Tom Brady has."

On the eve of Super Bowl XLIX, as the Patriots walked through their final preparations for the Seahawks, Brady and offensive coordinator Josh McDaniels anticipated an added dose of man-coverage looks as they got closer to the goal line. So they added a new play design—one they never got a chance to practice.

It nearly worked the first time. With the Patriots trailing 24–14 midway through the fourth quarter, Edelman was singled up against cornerback Tharold Simon at the 4-yard line and broke loose on an in-and-out route, but Brady's throw was high and incomplete.

"After the one we didn't complete," Edelman said, "Tom gave me that big deep breath and that, 'My bad, bro.' You could tell that hurt him. I remember sitting next to him [between possessions], and him saying, 'We're getting a lot of man coverage. I'm going to come back to you, babe. We're going to get that again.'

"His attitude and his charisma right before those big drives— growing up, you heard about how Joe Montana was always so calm, cool, and collected. Tom was calm, cool, and collected, but he had a fierce [look] in his eye. You saw that killer instinct in his eye."

Brady called the play again on the next series, and he connected with Edelman for the winning touchdown.

The résumé is unparalleled. Brady's 251 regular-season victories are not just the most ever, they are more than two of the greatest winners in the history of the sport—Montana (117) and Terry Bradshaw (107)—have combined. The 65-win gap between Brady and those at No. 2 (Brett Favre and Peyton Manning, 186) is more than Joe Namath's entire career (63).

His 34 playoff wins more than double Montana's 16, which rank second all time.

"He's a winner," former Buccaneers coach Bruce Arians said. "Everywhere he goes, he wins. He's not the biggest, fastest, all that stuff, but he's the winner of all winners. He has a burning desire in him to compete."

Even beyond the wins, Brady's statistical achievements are legendary. He's a three-time MVP, including the first to win it unanimously (2010). He is the NFL's all-time leader in passing touchdowns (649), passing yards (89,214), and completions (7,753).

Brady's record 89,214 passing yards are 8,856 clear of Drew Brees and more than 26,000 more than the next active player (Matt Ryan). He's thrown 649 touchdown passes—78 more than Brees and 172 more than the next active player (Aaron Rodgers). To put those numbers in further perspective, if Chiefs quarterback Patrick Mahomes avoids injuries, slumps, and roster reconstructions to maintain his career averages, he wouldn't eclipse Brady's touchdown record until 2034 and the yards mark until 2035—at the age of 40.

Among his other records, Brady ranks first in:

- Starts (333)
- Pro Bowls (15)

- Super Bowl MVPs (5)
- Associated Press MVP top-five finishes (10)
- Three-touchdown games (104)
- Four-touchdown games (39)
- Fourth-quarter comebacks (46)

"Look, I'm in the [Hall of Fame] club, and I've still got to pinch myself to this day," Law said. "But if there is any time that you bend the rules, you do that for Tom Brady. Give him his gold jacket while he's still playing. That's how great, that's how dominant he's been."

There's been so much history between his first confetti shower—when a still-green 24-year-old had the "aww, shucks" gaze of disbelief as he clasped his hands to his head—and the last, when the 43-year-old raised the Lombardi with the assuredness of a gladiator and his sword.

"That's just confidence," Edelman said. "That confidence isn't false confidence. That confidence is earned confidence."

There were the records, the comebacks, and the iconic moments. It was the Snow Bowl, the drive against the Rams in New Orleans, and the duels with Peyton Manning. It was the defiance of time, be it 28-3 or the postseason masterpieces against a (much) younger challenger to his throne in Mahomes.

It's not supposed to look this easy. But that's because Brady handles the difficult stuff out of sight.

"It's his competitiveness and determination," Gronkowski said. "It's his commitment. It's not just his commitment to the game. It's his commitment to himself, his discipline, taking care of himself, eating the right way, getting the body treatment. That's hard to do, no doubt about it. It may look easy because it's him doing it. But to be just as good as you were the day before, and be able to recover and wing it again the next day, it's not easy to do. That's why the average NFL career is 3.5 years. You've got to figure out a system to be ready to go the next day or the next game. He's mastered that to a T. . . . That's what makes him so great."

It's gotten to the point that Brady is the undisputed greatest of all time. He has pursued this title for so long, crossing the likes of Joe Montana and Michael Jordan off his list.

He's done it all. He was the sixth-round draft pick who, according to Kraft, called himself the "the best decision this [Patriots] organization has ever made" as a rookie—and was right. He's the undisputed greatest of all time.

Yet even with every milestone set, every record shattered, he came back for more.

He walked away once, only to feel that familiar, irresistible pull back to doing what he does best—better than anyone in NFL history ever has. Competing. Working. Winning. He spent 40 days in retirement before recommitting himself to the chase for more greatness.

Brady once said he'd retire, "When I suck. I don't plan on sucking for a long time."

He never sucked. And unlike so many of his contemporaries, Father Time didn't come for him by 40. He won an MVP at that age and finished second at age 44.

So again, what was left for Brady to do—why, at his age and as the greatest ever, did he keep playing? To pad his lead. Tom Brady didn't spend a lifetime chasing this title just to give it back.

The Shooting Stars

By Dan Pompei

Who was the most talented quarterback in NFL history?

Many would say John Elway.

Some might go with Brett Favre, Patrick Mahomes, or Aaron Rodgers.

But another quarterback should be in the conversation.

Bill Walsh, perhaps the most astute quarterback evaluator ever, would say the most talented was Greg Cook.

"Those who saw Cook would have to say that physically, he was the best ever to step on the field," Walsh wrote in his 1990 book, *Building a Champion*. "He wasn't just a big Adonis who could throw the ball 100 yards. This was a quick, graceful athlete with a lightning-fast delivery and great instincts."

Cook is one of several players who, while they did not make The Athletic's list of the top 100 players of all time, showed the promise to be an all-time great.

Walsh, who helped make Hall of Famers of Joe Montana and Steve Young and worked wonders with Ken Anderson, was an assistant coach for Paul Brown on the Bengals in 1969 when the team drafted the 6-4, 220-pound Cook with the fifth pick. It was clear from Cook's first days that he had something special.

Walsh told NFL Films that Cook threw "by far" the best deep ball of any quarterback he saw and said Cook combined Terry Bradshaw's size and strength with Montana's feel and instincts.

Cook won his first three starts. In his third game, Walsh called for a rollout pass, with halfback Paul Robinson responsible for picking up the blitz. Chiefs linebacker Bobby Bell, a future Hall of Famer, overwhelmed Robinson and combined with fellow linebacker Jim Lynch for a brutal hit on Cook that slammed him to the ground, shoulder first.

Cook felt a pop. "I was hit from behind, stretched out, and landed on my arm," he told the *Cincinnati Enquirer* after the game. "I pulled a muscle, but I think it will be OK by next week."

MRIs were unavailable in 1969, so no one knew Cook tore his rotator cuff and partially detached his biceps. After sitting out the better part of four games, Cook, with some help from ice and cortisone shots, started the rest of the season.

And he didn't just play. He excelled. Cook was voted AFL Offensive Rookie of the Year and led the league in passer rating, yards per completion (9.4), and yards per attempt (17.5)—the latter two marks remain the best in modern NFL history for a rookie.

But by the time Cook's injury was diagnosed in the offseason, calcium had formed around scar tissue. Cook sat out the 1970 and '71 seasons. In January 1972, he announced his retirement. In 1973, he tried again with the Chiefs, completing one pass before retiring for the second time. In 1976, Walsh, then with the Chargers as offensive coordinator, pushed to bring Cook out of retirement. He wrote that he thought it would have been a "real battle" between Cook and future Hall of Fame quarterback Dan Fouts. But Cook would only play for a guaranteed contract, and the Chargers refused.

Three surgeries couldn't bring his arm back. His career lasted 12 games.

Cook passed away in 2012 at the age of 65 from complications from pneumonia. At the time, Bengals president Mike Brown said, "Greg was the single most talented player we've ever had with the Bengals. . . . Had he been able to stay healthy, I believe he would have been the player of his era in the NFL."

Walsh took it further, saying Cook "could very well have been remembered or noted as the greatest quarterback of all time."

• • •

It was a third-and-1 from the Seattle 2 in the third quarter of a Monday night game when Raiders running back Bo Jackson took a pitch from Marc Wilson and ran left. At the 1-yard line he was met by Seahawks linebacker Brian Bosworth, who was unblocked and had played his position perfectly up to that point. It was a rare one-on-one, open-field collision between two of the highest-profile athletes in America.

Jackson lowered his right shoulder and exploded into Bosworth, carrying him to six points and leaving the flashy "Boz" on his back. "He and Bosworth one-on-one, and Jackson just shoves him into the end zone," Al Michaels said incredulously on the broadcast. It wasn't even Jackson's most remarkable play of the night. That would have been the 91-yard run that ranked 25th on the list of the greatest plays in history compiled by NFL Films in 2019.

Save for that Monday night when he left his tire tracks on Bosworth and ran for 221 yards, Jackson's football legacy is more about what he could have done than what he did.

We've been left to wonder since the 39th game of his career, when Jackson, playing in the postseason for the first time, was hit by Bengals linebacker Kevin Walker on a 34-yard run. As was often the case, the hit did not initially stop Jackson, but Walker held on and slid down his body, clenching Jackson's right calf until Jackson went down.

"The momentum of my body kept going, and my left leg was extended to the point where I couldn't bend it and fall," Jackson told Dick Schaap in an interview for the book *Bo Knows Bo.*

Jackson knew something was wrong with his left hip. He later said it dislocated and he popped it back in. It was initially diagnosed as a pulled muscle, and after the game, he told reporters, "It's a hip pointer. I'm going to play next week."

Doctors later found a small fracture in the hip socket and a loss of blood supply to the femur head, known as avascular necrosis. That led to deterioration of the cartilage and bone, which prompted a 1992 hip replacement and the end of Jackson's football career.

Jackson never rushed for 1,000 yards or scored more than six touchdowns in a season. He never was an All-Pro. Yet there is no doubt he was a world-class running back. His 5.4 average per carry is the second-best in the modern era among running backs with at least 200 attempts.

After a legendary career at Auburn that culminated with a Heisman Trophy, Jackson was the first pick of the 1986 draft by the Bucs. But he had his heart set on playing baseball, and the Bucs told him they wanted all of him. Jackson subsequently threw his first NFL stiff-arm, signing with the Kansas City Royals instead.

The Bucs forfeited his rights, and it appeared Jackson never would play in the NFL. But the Raiders dug up a scouting report on Jackson written by director of player personnel Ron Wolf. It was seven words long—the shortest Wolf ever wrote. In the Raiders' scouting system, a "1" was the highest possible grade, and Wolf gave Jackson a "1" grade in every category except blocking. Wrote Wolf, "I don't know if he can block."

In 1987, the Raiders chose him in the seventh round, and owner Al Davis told Jackson he was willing to allow him to play two sports. The idea appealed to Jackson, so he signed a deal with the Raiders that called for him to report 10 days after the end of baseball season and play as few as eight games a year. Davis paid Jackson the highest salary of any non-quarterback in NFL history up to that time.

"Everybody was in awe of him," Chiefs all-pro defensive tackle Bill Maas said. "Everybody in every other locker room was talking about him."

According to Jeff Pearlman's biography of Jackson, *The Last Folk Hero*, Jackson, who played at nearly 240 pounds, was asked to run the 40-yard dash on a wet field wearing full pads and a helmet. Raiders coach Tom Flores and two assistants timed him at 4.19. Thinking they might have been too quick on the stopwatch, they asked him to run it again. In the do-over, he ran a 4.17.

"He hit the hole extremely fast," Maas said. "His speed was unprecedented for a running back. You might have had a receiver or two as fast as he was. But nobody that big was that fast."

Wolf said he observed Jackson lie flat on his back and spring to his feet without using his hands. "As far as pure athletic ability, Bo Jackson had the most I've seen in a running back," said Wolf, whose talent evaluating skills earned him a place in the Pro Football Hall of Fame.

As gifted as Jackson was in football, baseball always appeared to be his first love, and some never forgot that he once called football a "hobby." In Pearlman's thoroughly reported book, he wrote that Jackson still didn't know his playbook four years into his career. He also pointed out Jackson was a disinterested blocker and receiver, refused to lift weights, wouldn't play hurt in the opinion of teammates, and fell asleep during meetings.

Despite that, Jackson, for a brief time, was one of the most feared runners in the game. Said Wolf, "If he had stayed healthy, he probably would have rushed for 4,000 yards in a season."

In a memorable 1988 game, two defensive linemen, one a Minnesota Viking and the other a Philadelphia Eagle, dominated with identical statistics—eight tackles and four sacks. The Viking, Keith Millard, was particularly proud because the Eagle, Reggie White, was—and is—regarded as one of the greatest ever.

Millard stood shoulder to shoulder with White that day, but history does not remember him as White's equal.

"Had he played for 10 or 12 years, hell, he'd have been a Hall of Famer easily," Vikings middle linebacker Scott Studwell said. "What he had was special."

Millard's intensity was rare. In 1991, he told *Sports Illustrated* he worked himself into a violent rage before games. "I look like a monster and I feel like a dog with rabies," said Millard, who was the 13th pick of the 1984 draft but spent one season with the Jacksonville Bulls of the USFL before joining the Vikings.

The intensity was never more noticeable than in 1989, which

might have been the most impressive season by a defensive tackle in modern NFL history. In his first game against the Oilers, Millard lined up against a future Hall of Famer at left guard in Mike Munchak and a future Hall of Famer at right guard in Bruce Matthews. Millard had three sacks. One month later, Millard had a combined seven sacks in back-to-back games against the Lions and Packers.

"I felt early that season I couldn't be blocked," Millard said. "It didn't matter who we were playing."

Millard finished with 18 sacks and probably would have had more if he had not played with a separated left shoulder the last six weeks of the season—15 of his sacks came in the Vikings' first 10 games. No defensive tackle in history had as many sacks until Aaron Donald 29 years later. Millard was voted NFL Defensive Player of the Year, beating out Hall of Famers White, Chris Doleman, and Bruce Smith, among others.

In 1990, Millard appeared ready to take his game to another level. But in the fourth game of the season, Millard jumped over Bucs center Randy Grimes and came down awkwardly, tearing the ACL and MCL and damaging cartilage in his right knee. Millard didn't play for two years. He started only six more games in his career and had three more sacks.

"His snap count anticipation and get-off were two of his strong suits," Studwell said. "He lost that. As strong as he was with his upper body and getting his hands into people's pads as quickly as he did, he had lost a little bit of that, which took away a big piece of his game."

Still, Millard was a first-team All-Pro twice, a second-team All-Pro twice, and a member of the 1980s All-Decade team.

"I never thought I'd go out like that, but I don't focus on the what-ifs," said Millard. "I try to focus on if I accomplished what I set out to do, which was to play in the NFL at the level of some of the guys in the league that I respected most, like Reggie White, Howie Long, Dan Hampton, and Jack Youngblood. I feel I did."

. . .

On his first carry of a game against the Vikings on October 21, 1984, Billy Sims became the all-time leading rusher for the Detroit Lions.

The first pick of the 1980 draft, Sims already had been the NFL's Offensive Rookie of the Year and a three-time Pro Bowler, but he was in just his fifth season, playing in his 60th game. At 29 years old, it seemed likely he would make his rushing record untouchable in the coming years.

Sims had rushed for 101 yards midway through the third quarter of that game at the Minneapolis Metrodome when he took his 22nd handoff of the day from Gary Danielson. Sims went right, planted to turn upfield, and was hit high by Vikings linebacker Walker Lee Ashley.

It was the last run of his career.

"I was complaining about the turf," Sims told the *Detroit Free Press* in 2015. "It was terrible. . . . I didn't really get a direct hit on my knees. My foot got caught in the turf and then I got tackled and I went down. I'm thinking, 'Oh, a bad knee sprain. I'll be OK. I'll be back.'"

Dr. Robert Teitge, who performed surgery on Sims's knee, said Sims tore multiple ligaments and cartilage and had "fairly extensive" fractures around his knee joint. Sims spent two years rehabbing the injury before announcing his retirement in 1986. In 1989, when he was nearly 34 years old, Sims told the Lions he wanted to play again, and even offered to come back for a blank check. The Lions did not accept.

Sims was a powerful contact runner whose explosiveness made him play bigger than his 6-foot, 212-pound frame. Lions defensive end Al "Bubba" Baker said that Sims was the strongest player on the team in the seated shoulder press.

"He saw the hole, he put his foot in the ground, and I'm not kidding you, he was going 100 miles an hour," Baker told the *Eye Test for Two* podcast. "I gotta tell you, no one—maybe [Eric] Dickerson—but no one could plant their foot and be going in a different direction like Billy Sims. And that's including Barry Sanders. . . . He was a different kind of runner. And the one thing I respected Billy for was: if the hole was clogged, he made a hole."

Sims didn't always plant his foot in the ground. Bears Hall of Fame defensive lineman Dan Hampton recalls his defensive co-ordinator Buddy Ryan showing players a clip of Sims against the Oilers five times—and Ryan never showed a clip five times. "Billy put his foot on the back of a player trying to tackle him and leaped forward about 5 yards, and then he kicks this safety and keeps going for more yards," Hampton said. The play inspired a nickname from ESPN's Chris Berman, who henceforth called the Detroit runner "Kung Fu Billy Sims."

Baker believes if Sims had stayed healthy, he would have become the leading rusher in NFL history. As it is, his 85.1 yards-per-game average is eighth highest in NFL history among players with at least 1,000 carries.

"Everyone asks me who the best running back I played against was," Hampton said. "I played against a bunch of 'em: Earl Campbell, Barry Sanders—broke some fingers trying to tackle Barry—but Billy might have been the best of all of them. As far as running backs with natural running ability, he was as great as anybody I ever saw."

The Cowboys needed a play to neutralize Washington safety Sean Taylor, so they called for a naked bootleg. With a crossing route on the second level to defend, Taylor theoretically would be unable to prevent a sizable gain on a pass to the running back in the flat.

But somehow, Taylor tackled the back after a gain of a yard. Afterward, a coach approached Cowboys tight end Jason Witten, who ran the crossing route.

"Were you open on the deep crosser?" he asked.

"No," Witten said. "Sean Taylor was the deep safety on that side, and he saw me sneaking over there."

Said the coach, "But he made the tackle in the flat. What do you mean?"

Witten: "He had both of us covered."

A safety isn't supposed to be capable of having both players covered. But Taylor was no ordinary safety.

Defensive coordinator Gregg Williams, who worked three decades in the NFL, called Taylor the best athlete he ever coached. The argument can be made that Taylor was gifted to do everything a safety can be tasked to do in a way that no other player has been before or since.

"What made him so different is he could play as a two-high safety, the single-high safety playing deep, come down in the box, cover tight ends, cover backs, and stop the run," Witten said. "That was what made him rare."

Taylor could do it all. He just didn't do it for long.

On the night of November 26, 2007, Taylor was sleeping in his Palmetto Bay, Florida, home with his fiancée and their 18-month-old daughter when five intruders broke in searching for money. Taylor clutched a machete as his bedroom door burst open and a teenage gunman opened fire, shooting Taylor in the upper leg and severing his femoral artery. Taylor was airlifted to a local hospital but died the next day.

Taylor was 24 years old and in his fourth NFL season. His jersey No. 21 was retired by his team. The only other Washington players with retired jerseys are Hall of Famers Sammy Baugh and Bobby Mitchell.

Taylor is remembered for many things, including his fierceness. One of his most talked-about hits came during the 2007 Pro Bowl, when punter Brian Moorman fielded a snap and took off running instead of kicking. Taylor got to Moorman before the punter could reach the sidelines—and hit him as hard as if it were the Super Bowl.

"It didn't matter if it was a Pro Bowl, a practice, if his team was 5-10 in the last week of the season, Sean didn't care," Witten said. "That was one of the things I always thought was most rare about him."

The fifth pick of the 2004 draft, Taylor was nicknamed

"Meast"—he was half-man, half-beast. "Every game, he'd do something to let you know he wasn't from this planet and all of us were," former teammate Ryan Clark said on *A Football Life*.

Witten says Taylor was "by far" the most talented safety he ever played against: "There wasn't anything he couldn't do."

The Future Top 100?

By Mike Sando

The Pro Football Hall of Fame requires a five-year waiting period from retirement before players can be considered for enshrinement. The delay allows time for reflection so that recency bias doesn't influence decisions. Some players are so special, almost from the beginning, that they seem destined for Canton—or, in this case, possibly destined to appear on later versions of The Athletic's Top 100.

Travis Kelce, TE, Kansas City Chiefs: Kelce arguably belongs on the Top 100 already.

He has more receiving yardage than four of the five tight ends on the list (Tony Gonzalez is the only one with more). Kelce is the only tight end in league history with 1,400 yards in a season. He needed only 15 games to reach that milestone in 2020.

Kelce also owns the most productive three-year stretch for a tight end in league history, with 3,918 receiving yards gained from 2018–20. To adjust for eras, The Athletic divided every tight end's top three-year yardage total by the total for the NFL leader regardless of position. Kelce's yardage from 2018–20 was 96.1 percent of wide receiver DeAndre Hopkins's league-best total over those seasons. Kellen Winslow (1980–82, 1981–83) and Charle Young (1973–75) are the only other tight ends to reach 90 percent of the leader's total over a three-year period.

Justin Jefferson, WR, Minnesota Vikings: Jefferson needed only 15 games of his third NFL season to break Randy Moss's single-season team record for yardage. He has also set the NFL record for receiving yards through the first 49 games of a career. The top five players on that list include one fast starter who fizzled (Odell Beckham Jr.) and three bona fide all-time greats in Julio Jones, Moss, and Jerry Rice.

That is the sort of company Jefferson is keeping early in his career. It's the elite of the elite, and it's not as though Jefferson landed in an incredibly favorable situation as far as scheme, quarterback, or any of those variables that can make a difference.

T. J. Watt, OLB, Pittsburgh Steelers: Watt's 77.5 sacks through the first 87 games of his career ranks second since 1960, according to Pro Football Reference, which has unofficial sack totals going back that far. That is also the second-best total since the NFL made sacks an official state in 1982. Only Reggie White (94) had more through 87 career games.

White, Smith, and the elder Watt are already in the Top 100. The younger Watt has a shot at joining them if he can hold up physically. He missed only four games in his first five seasons before missing seven in 2022.

Myles Garrett, DL, Cleveland Browns: The best pass-rushers can contort their bodies, getting low and wide as they turn the corner on offensive tackles on their way to the quarterback. When Garrett was only a rookie in 2017 and teammate Joe Thomas was a 10-time Pro Bowl left tackle entering his final NFL season, the veteran blocker called Garrett "twice as good" as Miller, then the runner-up in Defensive Player of the Year balloting, at this differentiating skill.

Only Reggie White and the Watt brothers had more sacks than Garrett through the first 84 games of a career. Garrett had 74.5, putting him just ahead of luminaries such as Derrick Thomas, Von Miller, Bruce Smith, Andre Tippett, and Richard Dent.

Only a six-game suspension in 2019 and a car accident suffered in 2022 have managed to interrupt Garrett as he continues to set a Hall of Fame production pace through his first six seasons.

Tyreek Hill, WR, Miami Dolphins: Hill has been arguably the

NFL's most-feared player over the course of his career. A seven-time Pro Bowl choice in seven seasons, he reached 75 touchdowns faster than every wide receiver but Jerry Rice and Randy Moss. Hill has 10 touchdowns on receptions, rushes, or returns covering at least 75 yards. Only Devin Hester (14), Ollie Matson (13), Bobby Mitchell (12), and Dante Hall (11) have more. Of those players, all but Hall played *at least 40 more games* than Hill has played to this point in his meteoric career.

Instead of experiencing a drop-off in productivity after being traded away from Mahomes and Kansas City in the 2022 offseason, Hill established career highs with 113 catches for 1,632 yards in Miami, both totals ranking behind only Jefferson.

Micah Parsons, OLB, Dallas Cowboys: Parsons is only two seasons into his career, so we are very premature when including him on such a list. But none other than Lawrence Taylor called Parsons "special" early in the Dallas star's second season.

Parsons, like Taylor, was Defensive Rookie of the Year. Taylor was Defensive Player of the Year in each of his first two seasons, and again after his sixth season, when he was also league MVP. Parsons was second in Defensive Player of the Year voting and a first-team All-Pro as a rookie after collecting 13 sacks and 20 tackles for loss months after being selected with the No. 12 pick out of Penn State.

Parsons leads the NFL in Pro Football Focus pressure rate over his first two seasons. But, as Taylor reminded, it's early.

"Let's see if he can keep it up for daggone 13 years," Taylor said, referencing the length of his own Hall of Fame career.

Trent Williams, LT, San Francisco 49ers: Williams has earned Pro Bowl honors in each of the past 10 seasons he has played, and he seemed to get better with age. The 6-foot-5, 320-pound Williams is widely regarded as the best in the league at his position two years after Washington traded him to the 49ers entering his age-32 season, which came after Williams missed the 2019 season following the removal of a rare, life-threatening cancerous growth on his scalp.

"You just watch every single game, every single clip, he just physically dominates every single person that's across from him, and the fact that he's not talked about more, I think it's outrageous," San Francisco teammate George Kittle told reporters in 2021, Williams's 11th in the league. "He's a hell of a football player who needs way more recognition."

Appendix: The 100

1. Tom Brady
2. Jim Brown
3. Jerry Rice
4. Lawrence Taylor
5. Reggie White
6. Joe Montana
7. Peyton Manning
8. Walter Payton
9. Johnny Unitas
10. Dick Butkus
11. Otto Graham
12. Anthony Muñoz
13. Don Hutson
14. Joe Greene
15. John Elway
16. Deacon Jones
17. Ray Lewis
18. Dan Marino
19. Ronnie Lott
20. Bruce Smith
21. Aaron Rodgers
22. Deion Sanders
23. Barry Sanders
24. Brett Favre
25. Sammy Baugh
26. Aaron Donald
27. John Hannah
28. Rod Woodson
29. Emmitt Smith
30. Merlin Olsen
31. Bob Lilly
32. Alan Page
33. Bronko Nagurski
34. Gino Marchetti
35. J. J. Watt
36. Forrest Gregg
37. Jack Lambert
38. Randy Moss
39. Ed Reed
40. Eric Dickerson
41. Marshall Faulk
42. Jim Parker
43. Drew Brees
44. Bruce Matthews
45. Larry Allen
46. Gale Sayers
47. Rob Gronkowski
48. Randy White
49. Sid Luckman
50. Steve Young
51. Dick "Night Train" Lane
52. O. J. Simpson
53. Bobby Bell
54. Adrian Peterson
55. Jack Ham
56. Julio Jones
57. John Mackey
58. Mike Webster
59. Herb Adderley
60. Joe Schmidt

61. Jonathan Ogden
62. Bart Starr
63. Junior Seau
64. Steve Largent
65. Walter Jones
66. Ray Nitschke
67. Earl Campbell
68. Gene Upshaw
69. Charles Woodson
70. Terry Bradshaw
71. LaDainian Tomlinson
72. Mel Blount
73. Marion Motley
74. Chuck Bednarik
75. Lance Alworth
76. Art Shell
77. Ted Hendricks
78. Mike Haynes
79. Roger Staubach
80. Willie Lanier
81. Tony Gonzalez
82. Kellen Winslow
83. Leo Nomellini
84. Mel Hein
85. Clyde "Bulldog" Turner
86. Buck Buchanan
87. Champ Bailey
88. Darrell Green
89. Bobby Layne
90. Willie Brown
91. Willie Davis
92. Lenny Moore
93. Elroy "Crazylegs" Hirsch
94. Steve Van Buren
95. Jim Otto
96. Paul Warfield
97. Mike Ditka
98. Patrick Mahomes
99. Marcus Allen
100. Fran Tarkenton

Appendix: The 100 by Team

(Note: Players listed under a team in bold reflects the team for which they played the most games. Players listed under a team in regular type spent at least one season of their career with that team.)

49ers

Larry Allen
Ronnie Lott
Joe Montana
Randy Moss
Leo Nomellini
Jerry Rice
Deion Sanders
O. J. Simpson
Rod Woodson
Steve Young

Bears

Dick Butkus
Mike Ditka
Bobby Layne
Sid Luckman
Bronko Nagurski
Alan Page
Walter Payton
Gale Sayers
Clyde "Bulldog" Turner

Bengals

Anthony Muñoz

Bills

O. J. Simpson
Bruce Smith

Broncos

Champ Bailey
Willie Brown
John Elway
Peyton Manning

Browns

Jim Brown
Willie Davis
Otto Graham
Marion Motley
Paul Warfield

Buccaneers

Tom Brady
Rob Gronkowski
Julio Jones
Steve Young

Cardinals

Dick "Night Train" Lane
Emmitt Smith
J. J. Watt

Chargers

Drew Brees
Lance Alworth
Deacon Jones
John Mackey
Junior Seau
LaDainian Tomlinson
Johnny Unitas
Kellen Winslow

Chiefs

Marcus Allen
Bobby Bell
Buck Buchanan
Tony Gonzalez
Willie Lanier
Patrick Mahomes
Joe Montana
Mike Webster

Colts

Eric Dickerson
Marshall Faulk
Ted Hendricks
John Mackey
Peyton Manning
Gino Marchetti
Lenny Moore
Jim Parker
Johnny Unitas

Commanders

Champ Bailey
Sammy Baugh
Darrell Green
Deacon Jones
Adrian Peterson
Deion Sanders
Bruce Smith

Cowboys

Herb Adderley
Larry Allen
Lance Alworth
Mike Ditka
Forrest Gregg
Bob Lilly
Gino Marchetti
Deion Sanders
Emmitt Smith
Roger Staubach
Randy White

Dolphins

Dan Marino
Junior Seau
Paul Warfield

Eagles

Chuck Bednarik
Mike Ditka
Steve Van Buren
Reggie White

Falcons

Eric Dickerson
Tony Gonzalez
Julio Jones
Deion Sanders

Giants

Mel Hein
Fran Tarkenton
Lawrence Taylor

Jets

Brett Favre
Ronnie Lott
Ed Reed
Aaron Rodgers
LaDainian Tomlinson

Lions

Dick "Night Train" Lane
Bobby Layne
Barry Sanders
Joe Schmidt

Oilers/Titans

Earl Campbell
Julio Jones
Bruce Matthews
Randy Moss

Packers

Herb Adderley
Willie Davis
Brett Favre
Forrest Gregg
Ted Hendricks
Don Hutson
Ray Nitschke
Aaron Rodgers
Bart Starr
Reggie White
Charles Woodson

Panthers

Reggie White

Patriots

Tom Brady
Rob Gronkowski
John Hannah
Mike Haynes
Randy Moss
Junior Seau

Raiders

Marcus Allen
Willie Brown
Eric Dickerson
Mike Haynes
Ted Hendricks
Ronnie Lott
Randy Moss
Jim Otto
Jerry Rice
Art Shell
Gene Upshaw
Charles Woodson
Rod Woodson

Rams

Eric Dickerson
Aaron Donald
Marshall Faulk
Elroy "Crazylegs" Hirsch
Deacon Jones
Dick "Night Train" Lane
Merlin Olsen

Ravens

Ray Lewis
Jonathan Ogden
Ed Reed
Deion Sanders
Rod Woodson

Saints

Drew Brees
Earl Campbell

Seahawks

Walter Jones
Steve Largent
Jerry Rice

Steelers

Mel Blount
Terry Bradshaw
Joe Greene
Jack Ham
Jack Lambert
Bobby Layne
Marion Motley
Mike Webster
Rod Woodson

Texans

Ed Reed
J. J. Watt

Vikings

Brett Favre
Randy Moss
Alan Page
Adrian Peterson
Fran Tarkenton

Photograph Credits

All photographs were licensed from Getty Images. Additional photographer and rights credits follow:

p. 1, Fran Tarkenton: Focus on Sport; p. 9, Marcus Allen: *Sporting News;* p. 18, Patrick Mahomes: Kirk Irwin; p. 27, Mike Ditka: Robert Riger; p. 33, Paul Warfield: *Sporting News;* p. 39, Jim Otto: Michael Zagaris; p. 43, Steve Van Buren: Bettmann; p. 49, Elroy "Crazylegs" Hirsch: Vic Stein; p. 53, Lenny Moore: Robert F. Kniesche/*Baltimore Sun*/Tribune News Service; p. 58, Willie Davis: James Drake; p. 63, Willie Brown: Heinz Kluetmeier/*Sports Illustrated;* p. 67, Bobby Layne: Hy Peskin/*Sports Illustrated;* p. 72, Darrell Green: George Gojkovich; p. 77, Champ Bailey: Mike Ehrmann; p. 82, Buck Buchanan: James Flores; p. 86, Clyde "Bulldog" Turner: *Sporting News;* p. 92, Mel Hein: Tom Watson/NY Daily News Archive; p. 97, Leo Nomellini: James Drake/*Sports Illustrated;* p. 108, Kellen Winslow: Focus on Sport; p. 113, Tony Gonzalez: David E. Klutho/*Sports Illustrated;* p. 120, Willie Lanier: *Sporting News;* p. 125, Roger Staubach: Walter Iooss Jr./*Sports Illustrated;* p. 130, Mike Haynes: Miguel A. Elliot; p. 135, Ted Hendricks: George Gojkovich; p. 141, Art Shell: Focus on Sport; p. 151, Lance Alworth: Charles Aqua Viva; p. 157, Chuck Bednarik: Robert Riger; p. 165, Marion Motley: Bettmann; p. 169, Mel Blount: Focus on Sport; p. 174, LaDainian Tomlinson: Robert B. Stanton/NFL Photo Library; p. 180, Terry Bradshaw: George Gojkovich; p. 185, Charles Woodson: Tom Hauck/Allsport; p. 189, Gene Upshaw: Focus on Sport; p. 194, Earl Campbell: Rich Clarkson/*Sports Illustrated;* p. 200, Ray Nitschke: Robert Riger; p. 206, Walter Jones: Otto Greule Jr.; p. 213, Steve Largent: Focus on Sport; p. 219, Junior Seau: John W. McDonough/*Sports Illustrated;* p. 226, Bart Starr: Bettmann; p. 231, Jonathan Ogden: Mitchell Layton; p. 237, Joe Schmidt: Marvin E. Newman/*Sports Illustrated;* p. 241, Herb Adderley: Fred Roe; p. 248, Mike Webster: *Sporting News;* p. 253, John Mackey:

Index

NOTE: **Bold page references** indicate top 100 players; *italic page references* indicate photographs

Accorsi, Ernie, 158, 163–64, 403, 554, 555, 557
Adamle, Mike, 561
Addai, Joseph, 566
Adderley, Herb, xiii, 31, *241*, **241–47**, 298, 395
Adderley, Toni, 241–42, 246–47
Aikman, Troy, 126, 421, 430–32, 465
Alabama Crimson Tide, 227, 261–62, 442, 530
Albrecht, Ted, 562
Albuquerque Dukes, 496
Alderman, Grady, 3
Alexander, Hubbard "Axe," 377–78, 383–84
Alexander, Kermit, 329
Ali, Muhammad, 215, 604
Allen, Eric, 582
Allen, George, 31, 139–40, 195, 310, 327, 451–52, 516–17, 549, 551, 606
Allen, Harold "Red," 13–15
Allen, Jeff, 24
Allen, Josh, 488
Allen, Kyle, 22
Allen, Larry, *332*, **332–37**, 430, 584
Allen, Marcus, 9, **9–16**, 54, 115, 224, 344, 494–97, 501, 604
Allen, Paul, 207–8, 212
Allen, Woody, 290
Allman, Mike, 210, 211, 212
Alworth, Lance, 31, *151*, **151–56**
Alzado, Lyle, 136
Ameche, Alan, 557

Anderson, Dave, 93, 95
Anderson, Dick, 376
Anderson, Edwin J., 67, 70
Anderson, Ken, 139, 394, 617
Andrie, George, 316, 419
Arians, Bruce, 614
Arizona Cardinals, 78, 88, 236, 412, 437, 455, 467, 634; Watt, 400
Arizona State Sun Devils, 130–31, 134
Arkansas Razorbacks, 152, 153, 533
Arnett, Jon, 328
Ashley, Walker Lee, 623
Atkinson, George, 65, 188
Atlanta Braves, 472
Atlanta Falcons, 635; Gonzalez, 118–19; Jones, 260–68; Sanders, 470–80
Atwater, Steve, 522, 523
Auburn Tigers, 447, 620
Austin, Stephen F., 197

Bacon, Coy, 490
Bailey, Champ, 75, *77*, **77–81**, 242
Bakay, Nick, 289
Baker, Al "Bubba," 623–24
Baldinger, Brian, 587–88
Ballard, Chris, 25
Baltimore Colts, 634; Hendricks, 137–38; Mackey, 253–58; Marchetti, 402–3; Moore, 53–57; Parker, 353–58; Unitas, 53, 54, 55, 553–58; Super Bowl V,

Baltimore Colts (*cont.*)
253–54, 420; 1958 Giants game, 54–55, 56, 405, 556–57
Baltimore Ravens, 636; Lewis, 507–13; Ogden, 231–36; Reed, 371–76; Woodson, 440; Super Bowl XLVII, 509; Super Bowl XXXV, 440, 508–9
Banaszek, Cas, 516
Banks, Carl, 588, 589, 591
Barney, Lem, 327, 475–76
Barr, Michael, 87, 91
Bartkowski, Steve, 317
Barton, Harris, 576
Barwin, Connor, 398
Baugh, Mike, 206–7, 210, 211
Baugh, Sammy, 86–87, 91, 93–94, 310, 408–9, 412, *450*, **450–55**, 625
Baughan, Maxie, 509
Bavaro, Mark, 323
Beathard, Bobby, 74
Beckham, Odell, Jr., 628
Bednarik, Chuck, 47, 98, *157*, **157–64**, 589
Behring, Ken, 207–8
Belichick, Bill, 127, 220–21, 261, 264, 296, 298, 362, 372–74, 589, 593–94, 604, 607, 611, 612
Bell, Bert, 517, 545
Bell, Bobby, 204–5, *279*, **279–83**, 618
Benirschke, Rolf, 112
Bennett, Cornelius, 491
Bennett, Michael, 289
Berman, Chris, 624
Berry, Raymond, 254, 255, 357, 443, 557–58
Bieniemy, Eric, 19, 274
Bierman, Bernie, 101
Biles, Ed, 198
Billick, Brian, 232, 383
Bisciotti, Steve, 376, 511
Bisset, Jacqueline, 494
Blackledge, Todd, 504
Blank, Arthur, 263
Bledsoe, Drew, 611

Bleymaier, Joe, 19
Bloomfield Rams, 556
Blount, Mel, *169*, **169–73**, 298, 386
Bockwinkel, Nick, 412
Bono, Steve, 221, 572–74, 577–78
Boozer, Emerson, 144
Boselli, Tony, 234
Bosworth, Brian, 619–21
Bowlen, Pat, 521
Bowman, Ken, 391
Bradford, Tom, 426
Bradshaw, Terry, 171, *180*, **180–84**, 248–49, 251, 252, 387, 471, 521, 614, 617
Brady, Tom, ix, xi, 20, 79–80, 170, 191, 227, 312, 372, 429, 445, 555, 570, *609*, **609–16**
Branch, Cliff, 188
Brandt, Gil, 34–35, 38, 211, 362
Bray, Ray, 311
Brees, Drew, 20, 79, 178, 224, *345*, **345–52**, 372, 555, 570, 614
Brian's Song (movie), 329
Bridgewater, Teddy, 274
Brooks, Bill, 369
Brooks, Derrick, 282
Brooks, Robert, 522
Brookshier, Tom, 161
Brown, Eddie, 598, 599
Brown, Jerome, 582
Brown, Jim, 35, 56, 93, 158, 196, 239, 288, 298, 327, 331, 363, 367, 493–94, 500, 549, *603*, **603–8**
Brown, Lomas, 464, 467, 468
Brown, Mike, 167–68, 538
Brown, Paul, 52, 165–68, 538, 541–45, 606, 607, 617
Brown, Pete, 538
Brown, Reggie, 509
Brown, Roger, 356, 517
Brown, Sergio, 324
Brown, Troy, 79
Brown, Willie, *63*, **63–66**, 188, 191
Browner, Joey, 344
Bruce, Aundray, 473
Bruce, Isaac, 217, 362
Brunell, Mark, 348–49

Bryant, Bear, 442
Bryant, Kobe, 247
Buchanan, Junious "Buck," *82*,
    82–85, 191
Buck, Jack, 3
Buffalo Bills, 274–75, 633;
    Simpson, 287–89, 291; Smith,
    488–92
Buffone, Doug, 550
Burkett, Chris, 598
Burkholder, Dale, 466
Burns, Brian, 585
Burns, Jerry, 2
Burns, Keith, 512
Burrow, Joe, 446
Butkus, Dick, xiii, 98, 196, 201,
    391, 413, 496–97, 500, 501, 513,
    526–27, *547*, **547–52**, 560, 589
Butler, Keith, 388–89
Butler, LeRoy, 378–79, 461–62
Butte College Football, 481–84
Byner, Earnest, 233
Byrd, Gill, 216

Caito, Fred, 561–62
Calhoun, William Dee
    "Haystacks," 106
Campbell, Earl, *194*, **194–99**, 320,
    341, 624
Candy, John, 576
Cannon, Jimmy, 311
Cantrell, Dylan, 21
Capers, Dom, 438
Capone, Al, 409
Carolina Panthers, 504, 635;
    White, 585
Carr, Jimmy, 159
Carr, Joe F., 93
Carter, Cris, 378
Carter, Dale, 381
Carter, Keith, 401–6
Carver, Shante, 334
Casares, Rick, 28, 29
Cason, Wendell, 198–99
Cervi, Al, 542
Chamberlain, Wilt, 247
Chicago Bears, 239, 453, 505, 633;

Butkus, 496–97, 500, 526–27,
    547–52; Ditka, 27–30; Luckman,
    90–91, 308–14, 408–9;
    Nagurski, 99–100, 407–13, 408,
    453–54; Page, 414–17; Payton,
    276, 559–64; Sayers, 326–31;
    Turner, 86–91; 1943 Packers
    game, 533–34
Chicago Cardinals, 44–45, 88, 530
Chicago Rockets, Hirsch, 49–51
Christl, Cliff, 245–46, 532
Cincinnati Bengals, 138–39, 203,
    392, 393–94, 398, 599, 633;
    Muñoz, 536–40; Super Bowl LVI,
    446; Super Bowl XVI, 142, 392,
    576; Super Bowl XXIII, 499, 538
Clark, Dallas, 566
Clark, Dwight, 576, 598, 600, 601
Clark, Ryan, 435–37, 626
Clayton, Mark, 503
Cleveland Browns, 158, 239, 392,
    633; Brown, 603–8; Davis, 58,
    62; Graham, 541–46; Motley,
    165–68; Warfield, 33–38
Cleveland Rams, 533
Cline, Tony, 138–39
Clinton, Bill, 286, 417
Coates, Ben, 583
Cobb, Garry, 580, 581–82
Coker, Billy, 569
Cole, Larry, 418
Coletto, Jim, 233
Collie, Austin, 566
Collier, Blanton, 35, 607
Collins, Andre, 457
Collins, Nick, 188
Collinsworth, Cris, 394, 537
Colston, Marques, 349
Compton, Mike, 464
Concannon, Jack, 30
Concussion (movie), 250
Conerly, Charlie, 60
Conlan, Shane, 437, 491
Conley, Chris, 24
Conner, Darion, 336
Connor, George, 311
Cook, Greg, 617–18

Cook, Jared, 486
Cook, Toi, 474
Cope, Myron, 385
Copeland, Rory, 424, 425
Corey, Walt, 84
Cortez, José, 336
Coryell, Don, 52, 109–11
Cosby, Bill, 290
Cosell, Howard, 196–97, 386
Costas, Bob, 563
Cowher, Bill, 438, 439
Coyer, Larry, 79–80
Craig, Roger, 15, 54, 363, 498, 598
Crennel, Romeo, 611
Criswell, Jeff, 489, 490, 491
Crockett, Davy, 197
Cronkite, Walter, 127–28
Cross, Garrett, 484
Cross, Randy, 303
Csonka, Larry, 36, 37, 202, 413
Cumbie, Sonny, 21–22
Cunningham, Randall, 4, 6, 166, 382–83
Cuozzo, Gary, 256
Curry, Bill, 55–56, 137, 255, 256, 553–58
Curtis, Paul, 115
Cutcliffe, David, 566, 567

Dallafior, Ken, 467
Dallas Cowboys, 116, 305, 499–500, 576, 634; Adderley, 241, 244, 246; Allen, 332–37; Alworth, 154–56; Ditka, 31–32; Gregg, 391, 395; Lilly, 418–22; Sanders, 476–77; Smith, 428–33; Staubach, 2–3, 125–29, 203, 395, 421; Taylor, 624; White, 315–20; Super Bowl V, 253–54, 420; Super Bowl VI, 31, 37, 126, 154, 244, 418–20; Super Bowl X, 3, 172, 386–87; 1967 Packers game, 227–28; 1975 Vikings game, 1–4; 1994 49ers game, 304
Dallas Texans, 281, 636; Marchetti, 401–6; Watt, 396–400
Dalman, Chris, 306

Daly, Dan, 50, 51–52
Danielson, Gary, 623
Davies, Bob, 542
Davis, Al, 16–17, 40, 65, 66, 139, 142, 147, 149–50, 191
Davis, Duane, 59, 60–62
Davis, Ernie, 255
Davis, Henry, 388
Davis, Stephen, 479
Davis, Willie, xiii, *58*, **58–62**, 245, 357
Davis, Wyatt, 60
Dawson, Len, 84, 125, 606
Dayton Flyers, 574
DeLamielleure, Joe, 288
Del Rio, Jack, 511
Dempsey, Jack, 181
Denver Broncos, 633; Bailey, 77–81; Brown, 64; Elway, 520–23; Manning, 567–68, 570; Super Bowl XXXII, 520–21; 1969 Chiefs game, 282–83; 1988 Seahawks game, 214–16; 1997 Chiefs game, 116
Detroit Lions, 89–90, 451, 509, 549–50, 635; Lane, 296; Layne, 67–70; Sanders, 463–69; Schmidt, 237–40; 1966 Baltimore game, 256; 1994 Packers game, 460
Dial, Buddy, 35
Dickerson, Eric, 277, *365*, **365–70**
Dickerson, Viola, 365–66
Didinger, Ray, 44–48, 160–63, 409
Dieken, Doug, 168
Dierdorf, Dan, 336
Dilfer, Trent, 349
Dillon, Corey, 510
DiMaggio, Joe, 506
Dimitroff, Thomas, 118, 262–67
Dirty Dozen, The (movie), 608
Ditka, Mike, viii–ix, *27*, **27–32**, 255–56, 560
Do, Jeet Kune, 318
Doleman, Chris, 622
Doll, Don, 238
Donahue, Leon, 424, 425

Donald, Aaron, 316–17, 398, 414, *446*, **446–49**, 581
Donzis, Byron, 195
Dooley, Jim, 328, 551
Dorenbos, Jon, 163
Dorsett, Tony, 73, 75, 195
Douglas, Harry, 260
Duke Blue Devils, 437, 565–66
Dungy, Tony, 271, 363, 437, 568
Duper, Mark, 503
Duvall, Robert, 454

Easley, Kenny, 376
Eason, Tony, 504
Edelman, Julian, 609–10, 613–15
Edgerson, Booker, 155
Edwards, Brad, 76
Eller, Carl, 390–91
Elliott, Pete, 551
Ellis, Greg, 315, 316
Elway, John, 222, 306, 368, 461, 504, *520*, **520–23**, 617
Emrich, Clyde, 562
Ertz, Zach, 108
Evergreen State Geoducks, 94
Ewbank, Weeb, 54, 354, 355

Farr, Mel, 548
Faulk, Kevin, 80
Faulk, Marshall, 54, *359*, **359–64**
Favre, Brett, 19, 229, 348, 350, 381, *456*, **456–62**, 482, 485, 520–21, 614, 617
Fears, Tom, 51, 298, 311
Feathers, Beattie, 410, 531
Fencik, Gary, 195
Ferentz, Brian, 322, 324
Ferentz, Kirk, 236
Ferguson, Nick, 79–80
Finks, Jim, 564
Fischer, Pat, 496
Fishback, Joe, 478
Fisher, Jeff, 341, 580, 581, 582
Fitzkee, Scott, 320
Flacco, Joe, 6
Flaherty, Ray, 453
Flanagan, Ed, 548–49

Flores, Tom, 15, 142, 148–49, 192, 620
Florida State Seminoles, 208–10, 379, 383, 472
Flutie, Doug, 563, 599
Fontenot, Terry, 267
Fontes, Wayne, 467
Fordham, Todd, 209
Forrest, Jimmy, 298
Fouts, Dan, 109–12, 618
Fox, Tim, 444
Foxworth, Domonique, 79, 80
Frank, Stanley, 410
Frazier, Joe, 516
Frazier, Leslie, 274–78
Friedman, Benny, 309, 312
Fritsch, Ted, 534
Fry, Dick, 94

Gable, Clark, 46
Gagne, Vern, 102
Garcon, Pierre, 566
Gardener, Daryl, 465, 509
Garoppolo, Jimmy, 611–12
Garrett, Myles, 628
Gary, Rashan, 585
Gates, Antonio, 108, 174–75, 176, 179, 324
Gault, Willie, 477
George, Eddie, 508
George, Phyllis, 126
Gerela, Roy, 387
Gibbs, Joe, 73, 587
Gibron, Abe, 330, 543
Gifford, Frank, 51, 159, 161–62, 405, 469
Gilliam, Roosevelt, 143–44
Gillman, Sid, 153–54, 562
Givens, David, 80
Glanville, Jerry, 457–59, 474–76
Glass, Bill, 606
Glass, Glenn, 28
Glass, Jackie, 292
Glieber, Frank, 575
Glover, Kevin, 467, 468
Goldberg, Marshall, 312
Goldman, Ronald, 285, 286–87

Gonzalez, Anthony, 568
Gonzalez, Tony, 108, 112, *113*, **113–19**, 324–25, 627
Goodell, Roger, 204, 258, 276
Graham, Brandon, 585
Graham, Jimmy, 108, 118, 349
Graham, Otto, 312, *541*, **541–46**, 605
Grambling State Tigers, 59, 84, 143
Grange, Red, 93, 181, 410, 413
Grant, Bud, 98, 101, 102, 103, 105
Green, A. J., 263
Green, Darrell, 13, *72*, **72–76**, 242, 381, 435
Green, Dennis, 377–78
Green, Denny, 381
Green, Jerry, 70
Green, Roy, 74
Green, Trent, 115
Green Bay Packers, xiii, 162, 522–23, 635; Adderley, 241–47; Davis, 59–62; Favre, 229, 348, 350, 381, 458–62, 482, 485, 520, 614, 617; Gregg, 390–95; Hendricks, 138; Hutson, 530–35; Nitschke, 200–205, 495, 496, 500–501; Rodgers, 481–87; Starr, 138, 162, 226–30; White, 583; Woodson, 186–88; Super Bowl II, 227, 242, 392; Super Bowl XXXI, 583–84; Super Bowl XXXII, 520–21; 1930 Bears game, 409; 1950 Lions game, 69; 1999 49ers game, 301, 305–6
Greene, Joe, 42, 171, 172, 181, 183–84, 190, 195–96, 203, 270, 271–72, 386, 388, *524*, **524–29**
Greene, Kevin, 438, 585
Greenwood, L. C., 171, 386, 527
Gregg, Forrest, xiii, 31, 245, *390*, **390–95**
Gregg, Forrest, Jr., 392–93, 395
Gretzky, Wayne, 610
Grier, Roosevelt, 424, 490, 516–17
Griese, Bob, 36–37, 38, 418–19
Griffin, Blake, 117
Griffith, Howard, 521–22

Grimes, Randy, 622
Grogan, Steve, 442–43
Gronkowski, Rob, 108–9, *321*, **321–25**, 612, 615
Groza, Lou, 542
Gruden, Jim, 574–75
Gruden, Jon, 186, 461

Hackbart, Dale, 603
Hackett, Paul, 498, 574, 577, 596–600, 602
Hadl, John, 154
Halas, George, ix, 52, 92, 94, 239, 531, 560; and Butkus, 548, 551–52; and Ditka, 28–29, 32; and Luckman, 309–11, 313; and Nagurski, 409, 411; and Sayers, 328–30; and Turner, 87–91
Haley, Dick, 183
Hall, Dante, 629
Ham, Jack, *269*, **269–72**, 386, 388, 508
Hampton, Dan, 196, 622, 624
Hanlon, Greg, 366, 369–70
Hannah, Charlie, 12
Hannah, John, *441*, **441–45**
Hanratty, Terry, 181
Harbaugh, John, 372
Harden, Mike, 214–18
Hardwick, Nick, 175, 176, 177
Hardy, Kevin, 236
Harper, Alvin, 217
Harris, Bo, 387
Harris, Chris, Jr., 80–81
Harris, Cliff, 31, 195, 385, 387
Harris, Franco, 181, 182, 248–49, 525, 606–7
Harris, James "Shack," 236, 495
Harrison, Marvin, 216
Harrison, Rodney, 219, 222–23, 224, 306, 382
Hartings, Jeff, 467, 468
Haskins, Dwayne, 274
Hayes, Bob, 31
Hayes, Lester, 10, 13, 15–16, 65, 216–17
Hayes, Woody, 34, 354, 355, 357

Haynes, Mike, 65, *130,* **130–34,** 216, 476, 478

Heard, Jerrod, 22

Hein, Mel, *92,* **92–96**

Helfet, Cooper, 566

Henderson, Gus, 89–90

Hendricks, Ted, *135,* **135–40**

Henry, Derrick, 429

Henson, Drew, 611

Herber, Arnie, 531, 533

Herock, Ken, 457–59, 472–73

Hester, Devin, 629

Hester, Jesse, 598

Hilgenberg, Jay, 561–62

Hill, J. D., 288, 291

Hill, Taysom, 359

Hill, Tyreek, 50, 628–29

Hillebrand, Jerry, 271–72

Hilliard, Randy, 522

Hinton, Chris, 491

Hinton, Eddie, 254

Hirsch, Elroy "Crazylegs," 41, *49,* **49–52**

Hirsch, Otto, 50

Holliday, Vonnie, 379

Hollingsworth, Jay, 566

Holmes, Ernie, 527

Holmgren, Mike, 302, 303, 305, 381–82, 459, 461–62, 475

Holt, Torry, 216, 217, 362

Holthus, Mitch, 25, 116–18

Holtzman, Glenn, 604

Holzman, Red, 542

Hopkins, DeAndre, 627

Hopkins, Wes, 582

Hopp, Bill, 100–101

Hornung, Paul, 227, 229, 245, 392

Hostetler, Jeff, 476–77

House, Tom, 346, 347

Houston, Sam, 197

Houston Oilers, 116, 215, 635; Campbell, 194–99; Matthews, 338–44; 1967 Raiders game, 64–65

Houston Texans, 584

Howley, Chuck, 125

Hubbard, Marv, 137

Huff, Sam, 557

Hunt, Lamar, 16–17, 121, 250, 281

Hutson, Don, xii, 93, 213, 216, 311, *530,* **530–35**

Ilkin, Tunch, 251

Indianapolis Colts, 491, 634; Dickerson, 366, 369–70; Faulk, 361–62; Manning, 566–68, 570; 1995 Dolphins game, 504; 2014 Patriots game, 324

Ingold, Alec, 65

Inosanto, Danny, 318

Irsay, Jim, 369

Irvin, Michael, 217, 430

Isbell, Cecil, 533

Ismail, Raghib, 476–77

Jacke, Chris, 460

Jackson, Bo, 16, 115, 619–20

Jackson, DeSean, 25, 263

Jackson, Lamar, 4, 6, 350

Jackson, Michael, 290

Jacksonville Jaguars, 236

Jacksonville Sharks, 138

James, Craig, 366

James, Jesse, 169

James, LeBron, 610

Jauron, Dick, 382, 478

Jaworski, Ron, 503, 588

Jeffcoat, Jim, 315, 316

Jefferson, Justin, 627–28

Jernigan, Kip, 569

Jett, James, 477

Jobe, Frank, 182

Johnson, Andre, 398–99

Johnson, Brad, 378, 380–84, 472

Johnson, Calvin, 169, 245

Johnson, Charles, 585

Johnson, Curtis, 360, 375–76

Johnson, Derrick, 322

Johnson, Jimmy, 334, 503

Johnson, Keyshawn, 236

Johnson, Pepper, 510

Johnson, Richard, 598

Johnson, Vance, 598

Johnston, Daryl, 429

Jones, Brent, 302–4, 307
Jones, David "Deacon," 4, 6, 105,
    204, 390–91, 393, 424, 425, 489,
    490, 494–95, *514*, **514–19**, 584
Jones, Dub, 542, 543, 546, 607
Jones, Ed "Too Tall," 316, 317, 318
Jones, Jerry, 334
Jones, Julio, xii, 216, *259*, **259–68**,
    628
Jones, June, 456–58
Jones, Sean, 490
Jones, Tony, 235
Jones, Turkey, 387
Jones, Walter, *206*, **206–12**, 234,
    338
Jordan, Henry, 245, 356, 357
Jordan, Lee Roy, 31, 317
Jordan, Michael, 610
Joyner, Seth, 163, 582
Junkin, Mike, 437
Justice, Charlie "Choo-Choo," 298

Kamara, Alvin, 361
Kansas City Chiefs, 322, 491,
    634; Allen, 16–17; Bell, 279–83;
    Buchanan, 82–85; Gonzalez,
    113–18; Lanier, 120–24;
    Mahomes, xiii, 18–26; Montana,
    577–78; Webster, 250, 251; Super
    Bowl IV, 83, 280; Super Bowl
    LIII, 99–100, 324; Super Bowl
    LVII, 20; 1996 Chargers game,
    221–22
Kansas City Royals, 504, 620
Kansas Jayhawks, 330
Karras, Ted, 29
Kelce, Jason, 163
Kelce, Travis, 20, 108, 109, 112,
    118–19, 627
Kelley, Brian, 589
Kelly, Jim, 504
Kemp, Jeff, 367
Kennedy, John F., 27
Kent State Golden Flashes, 386,
    388
Kiick, Jim, 36, 37
Kilmer, Billy, 105, 496

Kilroy, Bucko, 46
King, Kenny, 15
King, Peter, 534
King of the Texas Rangers (movie),
    454
Kiper, Mel, 211
Kittle, George, 108, 109, 118–19,
    630
Klecko, Joe, 445
Knox, Chuck, 217
Kocurek, Kris, 447
Kolb, Jon "Cowboy," 248, 252
Kollar, Bill, 398
Koonce, George, 380, 459–60
Kraft, Robert, 611, 616
Kramer, Jerry, 61, 415
Kramer, Ron, 255–56
Krause, Paul, 372
Krieg, Dave, 215, 505
Krouse, Ray, 238–39
Kruczek, Mike, 387
Krumrie, Tim, 343
Kubiak, Gary, 396–400, 522
Kuechenberg, Rudy, 329
Kuharich, Joe, 31
Kuhlmann, Hank, 564
Kurek, Ralph, 329

Lambeau, Curly, 531, 533
Lambert, Jack, 270, 272, *385*,
    385–89
Lamonica, Daryle, 145, 146, 191,
    242
Landry, Tom, 2, 31, 32, 35, 127, 154,
    317, 318, 319, 395, 420, 421
Lane, Dick "Night Train," *295*,
    295–99, 476
Lane, MacArthur, 548
Lane, Max, 583–84
Lanier, Willie, *120*, **120–24**, 201,
    204–5, 280, 282, 283
Lapham, Dave, 394, 539–40
Largent, Steve, *213*, **213–18**
Larsen, Gary, 191, 415
Larson, Greg, 60
Lavelli, Dante, 542, 543
Law, Ty, 610–11

Layne, Bobby, 67, **67–71**, 404
Lazard, Allen, 486
Leachman, Lamar, 591
LeBeau, Dick, 438
LeClerc, Roger, 28
Lee, Bruce, 318
Lee, Spike, 606
Lehmann, P. C., 425
Leonhard, Jim, 374
Levy, Dave, 109
Lewis, Albert, 216
Lewis, Carl, 74, 379, 477
Lewis, Ed "Strangler," 102
Lewis, Jamal, 233
Lewis, Marvin, 440, 511
Lewis, Ray, 232, 235, 376, 389, *507*, **507–13**
Lilly, Bob, 31, 316, *418*, **418–22**
Lipps, Louis, 437–38
Lipscomb, Gene "Big Daddy," 405
Liston, Sonny, 215
Lofton, James, 215–16
Lombardi, Joe, 351–52
Lombardi, Michael, 596, 598, 601
Lombardi, Vince, xiii, 59–60, 116, 162, 202, 296, 557, 583; and Adderley, 244, 245; and Gregg, 391–92; and Starr, 226, 227–29
Lonesome Dove (TV series), 454
Long, Howie, 135, 343, 622
Looney, Joe Don, 205
Los Angeles Express, 301–2
Los Angeles Raiders, 620, 636; Allen, 9–16; Dickerson, 369–70; Haynes, 131, 133; Lott, 498; Super Bowl XVIII, 11–13, 131, 497
Los Angeles Rams, 46, 194–95, 471, 636; Dickerson, 366–69; Donald, 446–49; Hirsch, 49–52; Jones, 515–19; Lane, 296–99; Olsen, 423–27
Lott, Ronnie, 9–10, 16, 17, 214, 242, 344, 372–73, 435, *493*, **493–50**1, 537, 596
Louis, Joe, 526
Louisville Cardinals, 555, 556
Love, Jordan, 482

Luckman, Bob, 312
Luckman, Meyer, 309
Luckman, Sid, 88, 90–91, 93, *308*, **308–14**, 408–9, 453
Lundy, Lamar, 424, 490, 517
Lurie, Jeffrey, 161
Lynch, Jim, 618
Lynch, John, 79–80

Maas, Bill, 620–21
McAfee, George, 88, 531
McAlister, Chris, 376, 440, 512
McBee, Ike, 133
McCaffrey, Christian, 54, 361, 363, 433
MacCambridge, Michael, 51
McCaskey, Ed, 329
McClain, Jameel, 511, 512–13
McClain, John, 339, 340, 397
McClure, Worthy, 569
McCown, Luke, 346
McCoy, LeSean, 25, 47
McCrary, Michael, 511
McCutcheon, Lawrence, 495
McDaniel, Ed, 382
McDaniel, Randall, 335, 338, 382
McDaniels, Josh, 613
McElroy, Vann, 217
McFadden, Bryant, 173
McGinn, Bob, 233
McGrath, Emily, 99–100
McInally, Pat, 394
McKay, Rich, 211, 266
Mackey, John, *253*, **253–58**, 558
Mackey, Sylvia, 253–54, 255, 257
McKinney, Odis, Jr., 11
McKyer, Tim, 478
McMillin, Bo, 69–70
McNabb, Donovan, 6, 19
McNair, Steve, 339
McNally, John "Blood," 409, 531
McVay, John, 574, 596
McVay, Sean, 447–48, 449
Madden, John, 40, 83, 136, 138–40, 142, 148, 192, 304, 564
Maddux, Greg, 349
Magidovitch, Jonathan, 314

Mahomes, Patrick, xiii, 7, *18,* **18–26**, 350, 614, 617
Mandarich, Tony, 465, 473
Mankins, Logan, 382
Manning, Archie, 344, 568–69
Manning, Cooper, 569
Manning, Eli, 569
Manning, Peyton, 79, 114, 119, 344, 362, 373–74, 508, *565,* **565–70**, 614, 615
Manske, Edgar "Eggs," 309–10
Mara, Chris, 590
Mara, John, 593
Marchetti, Gino, 5–6, 60, 354, 357, *401,* **401–6**
Marchini, Jimmy, 425–26
Marciano, Joe, 424
Marino, Dan, vii, 74, 182, 350, *502,* **502–6**, 596
Mariucci, Steve, 115–16, 461
Marshall, George Preston, 454–55, 546
Marshall, Jim, 191, 562
Martin, Eric, 598
Martin, George, 198
Martin, Harvey, 316, 317
Martin, Zack, 333
Martz, Mike, 362–63
Maryland State Hawks, 143–45
Matson, Ollie, 402, 405, 629
Matthews, Bruce, 335, *338,* **338–44**, 622
Matthews, Clay, Jr., 340, 344
Matthews, Clay, Sr., 340
Matthews, Jake, 341–42
Maule, Tex, 162
May, Mark, 319
Mays, Jerry, 121
Mays, Willie, 52, 293
Memphis Showboats, 580
Mendenhall, Rashad, 512
Metcalf, DK, 379–80
Miami Dolphins, 16, 116, 182, 196–97, 351, 381, 634; Marino, 502–6; Warfield, 34, 36–37; Super Bowl VI, 31, 37, 126, 154, 244, 418–20; 1981 Chargers game, 111–12

Miami Hurricanes, 137, 375–76, 377
Michaels, Al, 16, 469, 619
Michalik, Art, 544
Michigan State Spartans, 242–43, 246
Michigan Wolverines, 50, 187, 611
Millard, Keith, 621–22
Millen, Hugh, 473–74, 479
Millen, Matt, 140, 192
Miller, Billy, 351
Miller, Chris, 456
Miller, Von, 276, 448
Milloy, Lawyer, 611
Minnesota Golden Gophers, 408, 410
Minnesota Vikings, 98, 202, 281, 287, 636; Millard, 621–22; Moss, 377–83; Page, 414–17; Peterson, 273–78; Sims, 623–24; Tarkenton, 1–8; Super Bowl IV, 83, 280; Super Bowl IX, 528; 1975 Cowboys game, 128; 1977 Bears game, 562
Mississippi Valley State Delta Devils, 595, 596, 597
Mitchell, Bobby, 518, 625, 629
Mitchell, Buddy, 569
Moats, Arthur, 172
Modell, Art, 36, 235–36, 608
Monk, Art, 74, 498–99
Montana, Joe, viii, 181, 302–3, 498, *571,* **571–78**, 600, 610, 613–14
Montgomery, Wilbert, 47
Moon, Warren, 338, 339, 341, 474–75
Moore, Herman, 378
Moore, Lenny, *53,* **53–57**, 254, 256
Moore, Tom, 566
Moorman, Brian, 625
Morrall, Earl, 37
Morris, Johnny, 29–30, 327, 328
Morris, Mercury, 36
Morris, Raheem, 448
Moss, Randy, 216, 245, *377,* **377–84**, 477, 627–28, 629
Moss, Zefross, 491

Mother, Jugs & Speed (movie), 552
Motley, Marion, *165*, **165–68**, 542
Mudd, Howard, 210, 211–12
Mueller, Randy, 207–12
Munchak, Mike, 338, 340–43, 622
Muñoz, Anthony, vii–viii, 203, 335, 344, 393–94, 495, *536*, **536–40**
Murphy, Mark, 242
Murray, Jim, 516
Musgrave, Bill, 222
Musso, George, 312, 532
Mussolini, Benito, 99, 100

Nagle, Browning, 457
Nagurski, Bronko, 91, 99–100, 101, *407*, **407–13**, 453–54, 560
Nagurski, Michelina, 408
Nagurski, Mike, 408
Namath, Joe, 125, 126, 279–80, 558, 614
Navy Midshipmen, 126, 127, 166
Neal, Lorenzo, 175, 178
Neale, Greasy, 44–45, 89, 532
Nehemiah, Renaldo, 600, 601
Nelson, Darrin, 14
Nelson, Steve, 444–45
Nelson, Willie, 197
Neri, Phil, 210
New England Patriots, 635; Brady, 609–16; Gronkowski, 108–9, 321–25; Hannah, 441–45; Haynes, 131; Moss, 382; Seau, 220–23; Super Bowl LI, 260–61, 265–66; Super Bowl XLIX, 323, 324, 612–13; Super Bowl XXXI, 583–84; 2006 Broncos game, 79–80; 2011 Ravens game, 372
Newhouse, Dave, 41, 42
New Orleans Saints, 78, 177, 210, 569, 576, 588, 593, 602, 636; Brees, 346–51; Campbell, 198–99
Newsome, Ozzie, 232, 235–36, 376, 509, 562
Newsome, Tim, 499–500
Newton, Cam, 6
Newton, Nate, 430

New York Giants, 159, 309, 313, 424, 509, 635; Hein, 92–96; Tarkenton, 5–6; Taylor, 586–94; Super Bowl XXXV, 440, 508–9; 1958 Colts game, 54–55, 56, 405, 556–57; 1960 Eagles game, 159, 161–62; 1961 Packers game, 59–60; 1990 49ers game, 303
New York Jets, 236, 566, 635; Favre, 458–59, 462, 485; Tomlinson, 178; 1969 Chiefs game, 279–80; 2009 Colts game, 566–67
New York Yankees, 153, 470
New York Yanks, 402
Ngata, Haloti, 376
Nitschke, Ray, xiii, 6, 29, *200*, **200–205**, 245, 495, 496, 500–501, 589
Nixon, Richard, 37
Nolan, Mike, 511
Noll, Chuck, 161, 171, 182, 183, 249, 251, 252, 271, 436–38, 524–26, 527
Nomellini, Drew, 103
Nomellini, Lane, 98, 104, 106–7
Nomellini, Leo, *97*, **97–107**
Norseman, The (movie), 518
North Carolina Tar Heels, 590
North Texas Mean Green, 526–27
Northwestern Wildcats, 542, 543, 544
Norton, Ken, Jr., 464
Notre Dame Fighting Irish, 181, 379, 574, 575
Novacek, Jay, 430
Nunn, Bill, 171, 527

Oakland Raiders, 270, 528, 636; Brown, 63–66; Hendricks, 135–40; Moss, 383; Otto, 39–42; Rice, 597; Shell, 141–42, 145–50; Upshaw, 145, 146–47, 189–93; Woodson, 186, 440; Super Bowl II, 227, 242, 392
O'Bradovich, Ed, 29, 391, 392, 549
O'Brien, Bill, 399

O'Brien, Ken, 504, 593
O'Brien, Pat, 100
Ochocinco, Chad, 513
O'Connor, Fred, 562
Ogden, Jonathan, *231*, **231–36**
Ohio State Buckeyes, 34–35, 55,
    166, 207, 354, 355, 357–58, 543,
    568
Oklahoma State Cowboys, 23,
    466–67
Olander, Cliff, 589
Olsen, Lisa, 426, 427
Olsen, Merlin, 4, 327, *423*, **423–27**,
    490, 516–17, 519
Omalu, Bennet, 250
Optimist Bowl, 132–33, 134
Osmanski, Bill, 88
Otto, Jim, *39*, **39–42**, 145
Owen, Steve, 534
Owens, Burgess, 217
Owens, Terrell, 204, 217, 301, 306,
    330

Pace, Orlando, 207, 210, 211, 234
Pagano, Chuck, 511
Page, Alan, 146–47, 191, 316, *414*,
    414–17
Paige, Woody, 523
Papa, Greg, 63–66
Parcells, Bill, 211, 541, 589
Pardee, Jack, 342, 561, 564
Parker, Buddy, 70, 237–39
Parker, Jim, *353*, **353–58**
Parker, Willie, 13
Parrella, John, 219–20
Parsons, Micah, 629
Pastorini, Dan, 194
Patera, Jack, 515
Paterno, Joe, 54, 272
Paup, Bryce, 491
Payton, Sean, 348–51, 361
Payton, Walter, 98, 276, 317, 320,
    466, *559*, **559–64**
Pearlman, Jeff, 561, 564, 620, 621
Pearson, Drew, 2–3, 128
Pellegrini, Bob, 158–59, 603
Penn Quakers, 160

Penn State Nittany Lions, 54,
    269–70, 272, 340, 437, 629
Perkins, Ray, 590
Perles, George, 528
Perriman, Brett, 468
Perry, Joe, 101–2, 500
Peters, Floyd, 465
Peterson, Adrian, *273*, **273–78**
Peterson, Carl, 116
Peterson, Kurt, 317–18, 320
Peterson, Patrick, 171, 173
Petitbon, Richie, 32
Philadelphia Eagles, 634;
    Bednarik, 157–64; Ditka, 30–31;
    Van Buren, 43–48; White,
    579–83; Super Bowl LII, 324;
    Super Bowl LVII, 20
Phillips, Bum, 196, 198
Phillips, Lawrence, 235–36
Phillips, Wade, 397–98, 581, 582,
    584
Phipps, Mike, 36
Piccolo, Brian, 329–30
Pihos, Pete, 46
Pittman, Wayne, 360
Pittsburgh Steelers, 636; Blount,
    169–73; Bradshaw, 180–84,
    248–49, 251, 252; Greene,
    524–29; Ham, 269–72; Lambert,
    385–89; Layne, 70–71; Motley,
    167; Webster, 248–52; Woodson,
    170–71, 434–40; Super Bowl X,
    3, 172, 386–87; 1963 Bears game,
    27–28
Plummer, Jake, 77–78, 81
Plunkett, Jim, 12, 191
Polamalu, Troy, 376
Portis, Clinton, 77–78
positional bias, xii
Pottios, Myron, 28
Povich, Shirley, 454
Powers, Francis, 49
Pritchard, Mike, 457, 472
Providence Steamrollers, 94–95
Pryce, Trevor, 210
Pugh, Jethro, 316, 419
Pupunu, Alfred, 223–24

Purdue Boilermakers, 36, 347, 350, 436
Pyle, Mike, 29
Pyle, Palmer, 356

Quick, Mike, 74, 581, 582, 584
Quinn, Dan, 266–67

Ramsey, Jalen, 186
Randle, John, 316, 334, 382
Rather, Bo, 561
Rathman, Tom, 303
Raye, Jimmy, 472
Reagan, Ronald, 100
recency bias, xii
Reed, Andre, 203–4, 598
Reed, Ed, *371*, **371–76**, 513
Reed, Jake, 379
Reese, Wayne, 359
Reeves, Dan, 420–21
Reger, John, 28
Reid, Andy, 19, 25–26, 47, 461
Reilly, Mike, 329
Reiter, Austin, 24
Renfro, Mel, 31, 37, 254
Renfro, Ray, 35, 604
Revis, Darrelle, 171, 242, 243
Rhodes, Ray, 499
Ribary, Tag, 206–7
Rice, Grantland, 408
Rice, Jerry, 74, 115, 175, 191, 210, 213, 215, 216, 217, 378–79, 380, 429, 475, 498, *595*, **595–602**, 628, 629
Rice, John, 132
Rice, Simeon, 236
Richards, Dick, 89–90
Richardson, William D., 313
Riggs, Gerald, 14
Rigsbee, Craig, 481–84, 486–87
Rio Conchos (movie), 607
Ripken, Cal, Jr., 509
Rison, Andre, 477
Roberts, Howard, 310, 410–11
Roberts, Ray, 467
Robertson, Dale, 197
Robertson, Isiah, 194–95

Robinson, Brooks, 537
Robinson, Dave, 200–205, 242–45, 252
Robinson, Eddie, 84, 143
Robinson, Eugene, 381
Robinson, Gijon, 566
Robinson, Greg, 447
Robinson, Jackie, 168
Robinson, John, 367–69
Robinson, Jon, 322
Robinson, Paul, 618
Robiskie, Terry, 259–60, 262–64, 266–68
Rochester Royals, 542
Rockne, Knute, 100
Rodgers, Aaron, 7, 24, 187, 229–30, 335, 350, 462, *481*, **481–87**, 614, 617
Rogers, George, 588
Rohde, Len, 106
Romanowski, Bill, 191, 498
Rooney, Art, Jr., 181, 183, 269, 271, 388, 527
Rooney, Art, Sr., 181, 249
Rooney, Art, II, 439–40
Rooney, Dan, 525
Ross, Bobby, 222
Ross, Kevin, 216
Rote, Tobin, 70
Rowe, Eric, 266
Rozelle, Pete, 12, 196, 257, 524
Rucker, Mike, 585
Ruskell, Tim, 211
Russell, Andy, 388
Russell, Darrell, 207
Ruth, Babe, 181, 516
Ryan, Buddy, 580–81, 581, 624
Ryan, Frank, 603
Ryan, Matt, 118, 260, 262, 265–66, 614
Ryan, Rex, 376, 511

Saban, Nick, 261–62
Sabol, Steve, 451, 452, 533
St. Clair, Bob, 403, 405
St. Clair Veterans, 238
St. Louis Browns, 202

St. Louis Cardinals, 452
St. Louis Rams, 636. *See also*
　Los Angeles Rams; Faulk, 24,
　359–62, 364
Sample, Johnny, 155, 603
Samuel, Asante, 382
Sanders, Barry, 275, 276, 367, 430,
　439, *463*, **463–69**, 623
Sanders, Bob, 376
Sanders, Charlie, 550
Sanders, Deion, 74, 161, 242, 381,
　383, 430, 435–36, 439, *470*,
　470–80
Sanders, Lonnie, 603
Sanders, William, 468
San Diego Chargers, 79, 392, 634;
　Alworth, 151–54; Brees, 347,
　350, 351–52; Mackey, 255; Seau,
　219–24; Tomlinson, 174–79;
　Winslow, 108–12; Super Bowl
　XXIX, 479–80; 1995 Steelers
　game, 439; 2007 Vikings game,
　273–74
San Diego State Aztecs, 360–61
San Francisco Dons, 402, 405
San Francisco 49ers, 475, 484,
　633; Allen, 334, 336; Lott, 495,
　497–500; Montana, 302–3,
　571–78; Moss, 382; Nomellini,
　97–107; Rice, 595–602; Simpson,
　289; Woodson, 440; Super Bowl
　XVI, 142, 392, 576; Super Bowl
　XXIII, 499, 538; Super Bowl
　XXIX, 479–80; Young, 300–307;
　1965 Bears game, 328
Sapp, Warren, 343, 414, 511
Saturday, Jeff, 566
Sauer, George, 279–80
Saunders, Al, 109–12
Savitsky, George, 46
Sayers, Gale, xiii, *326*, **326–31**, 550
Scannella, Joe, 138
Schaap, Dick, 619
Schmidt, Joe, 201, *237*, **237–40**
Schneider, John, 459
Schottenheimer, Marty, 116,
　176–77, 178

Schramm, Tex, 129, 318
Schuh, Harry, 141
Schulian, John, 160
Scott, Clyde, 47
Scott, James, 562
Scott, Ray, 419
Seattle Seahawks, 118, 636; Jones,
　206–12; Largent, 213–18; Rice,
　597; Super Bowl XLIX, 323, 324,
　612–13
Seau, Junior, *219*, **219–25**, 382, 512
Seau, Tyler, 225
Selvie, George, 316
Sexton, Jimmy, 263
Seymour, Richard, 382
Sham, Brad, 333–34
Shanahan, Kyle, 265
Shanahan, Mike, 79–80, 149,
　302–6, 480, 522
Sharpe, Ben, 103
Sharpe, Mike, 103
Sharpe, Shannon, 511
Sharpe, Sterling, 460
Sharper, Darren, 187
Sharper, Jamie, 510
Shaughnessy, Clark, 534
Shaw, Buck, 159, 161–62
Shaw, George, 556
Sheets, Ben, 298
Shell, Art, *141*, **141–50**, 190–91, 193
Shell, Donnie, 172, 386
Sheppard, Lito, 376
Shields, Billy, 112
Shields, Will, 338
Shimonek, Nic, 23–24
Shula, Don, vii, 36, 37, 56, 137,
　172–73, 239–40, 255–56, 357,
　505, 554–55, 557
Sievers, Eric, 112
Simmons, Clyde, 490, 582
Simmons, Justin, 81
Simms, Phil, 579–80, 588–91, 594
Simpson, Bill, 373
Simpson, Nicole Brown, 285,
　286–87, 293–94
Simpson, O. J., *284*, **284–94**
Sims, Billy, 623–24

Singletary, Mike, 511, 513
Slater, Jackie, 367
Smith, Aldon, 397
Smith, Alex, 19
Smith, Arthur, 267
Smith, Bruce, vii–viii, 343, *488*,
    488–92, 506, 538, 581, 584, 622,
    628
Smith, Emmitt, 16, 175, 335–36,
    367, 421, *428*, **428–33**, 466, 468
Smith, Jimmy, 376
Smith, Mike, 263
Smith, Robert, 379–80, 382, 384
Smith, Rod, 521, 523
Smith, Timmy, 13
Smith, Will, 250
Smith-Schuster, JuJu, 18–19
Snell, Matt, 280
Snyder, Bob, 89
Solomon, Freddie, 598, 600–602
South Carolina State Bulldogs, 515
Spadia, Lou, 104
Spanos, Dean, 178–79
Spears, Clarence "Doc," 408
Speedie, Mac, 542
Spencer, Ollie, 145–46
Springs, Shawn, 206–8, 212
Springsteen, Bruce, 343
Sprinkle, Ed, 90–91, 560
Sproles, Darren, 512
Stabler, Ken, 136, 190, 191
Stallworth, John, 248
Stanfel, Dick, 238
Starks, Duane, 440
Starr, Bart, xiii, 125, 138, 162, *226*,
    226–30, 245, 246, 296, 312, 391,
    392, 394, 518
Starr, Bart, Jr., 226
Starr, Cherry, 226–27, 230
Staubach, Roger, 2–3, 31, 125,
    125–29, 203, 395, 421
Stautner, Ernie, 100, 317
Steamboat, Ricky, 412
Stokley, Brandon, 566, 567, 570
Stouffer, Kelly, 437
Strahan, Michael, 403, 518
Stram, Hank, 83, 281–82

Strief, Zach, 350, 352
Stroud, Jack, 60
Stroupe, Bobby, 20–21, 22
Studwell, Scott, 621–22
Suggs, Terrell, 376
Sullins, Payne, 23–24
Sullivan, Margaret, 290
Summerall, Pat, 419
Super Bowl I, 191, 244
Super Bowl II, 227, 242, 244, 392
Super Bowl IV, 83, 280, 555
Super Bowl IX, 528
Super Bowl LI, 260–61, 265–66
Super Bowl LIII, 99–100, 324
Super Bowl LIV, 119
Super Bowl LV, 324, 448–49
Super Bowl LVI, 446
Super Bowl LVII, 20
Super Bowl V, 253–54, 391, 420
Super Bowl VI, 31, 37, 126, 154,
    244, 418–20
Super Bowl VIII, 270
Super Bowl X, 3, 172, 386–87
Super Bowl XI, 64, 191, 415
Super Bowl XIV, 529
Super Bowl XL, 13
Super Bowl XLIII, 350–51, 485
Super Bowl XLIV, 349
Super Bowl XLIX, 323, 324, 612–13
Super Bowl XLVII, 509
Super Bowl XLVIII, 609
Super Bowl XV, 191
Super Bowl XVI, 142, 392, 576
Super Bowl XVIII, 11–13, 131,
    412–13, 497, 598
Super Bowl XX, 563
Super Bowl XXI, 73
Super Bowl XXII, 13, 73, 520, 576
Super Bowl XXIII, 499, 538
Super Bowl XXIV, 512
Super Bowl XXIX, 302, 304–5,
    479–80
Super Bowl XXV, 490
Super Bowl XXVI, 76, 463–64
Super Bowl XXVII, 432
Super Bowl XXX, 333, 439
Super Bowl XXXI, 583–84

Super Bowl XXXII, 520–21
Super Bowl XXXIII, 523
Super Bowl XXXIV, 233
Super Bowl XXXIX, 161
Super Bowl XXXV, 440, 508–9
Super Bowl XXXVI, 362
Super Bowl 50, 568
Sutton, Courtland, 276
Swann, Lynn, 248, 252, 387

Tagliabue, Paul, 256–57
Talley, Darryl, 491
Tamme, Jacob, 566
Tampa Bay Buccaneers, 367,
    620, 633; Brady, 612, 614;
    Gronkowski, 322, 324; Jones,
    267–68; Young, 301–2
Tarkenton, Fran, *1*, **1–8**, 128,
    424–25, 528
Tatum, Jack, 65, 198, 214, 217, 496
Taylor, Altie, 549–50
Taylor, Charley, 496
Taylor, Fred, 510–11
Taylor, Jim, 98, 162, 245, 298
Taylor, John, 217, 576
Taylor, Lawrence, 93, 415, 564,
    583–84, *586*, **586–94**, 629
Taylor, Sean, 624–26
Tedford, Jeff, 484
Teitge, Robert, 623
Tennessee Titans, 267–68, 635;
    Matthews, 338–44
Tennessee Volunteers, 566,
    569–70
Tereshinski, Joe, 455
Texas Longhorns, 68, 196
Texas Tech Red Raiders, 21–24, 25
Theismann, Joe, 586–89, 593
Thesz, Lou, 102–3
Thomas, Bob, 563
Thomas, Clendon, 28, 29
Thomas, Derrick, viii, 512
Thomas, Emmitt, 279–80
Thomas, Joe, 233, 628
Thomas, Michael, 349
Thomas, Skip, 65
Thomas, Thurman, 466

Thomas, Tra, 209
Thomas, William, 582
Thompson, Bennie, 374
Thompson, Ted, 215
Thorpe, Jim, 94
Thurman, Dennis, 495
Tingelhoff, Mick, 3, 548
Tittle, Y. A., 60, 106, 328, 605
Tobias, Todd, 152–53
Tolbert, Tony, 315, 316
Toler, Burl, 402
Tolliver, Billy Joe, 456, 457, 458
Tomlinson, LaDainian, 16, 54, 55,
    174, **174–79**
Tonnemaker, Clayton, 103
Tonyan, Robert, 486
Toon, Al, 598
Toronto Argonauts, 392
Torretta, Gino, 361
Trask, Amy, 65–66
Troup, T. J., 104, 239
Tuck, Justin, 335
Tuggle, Jessie, 471, 473, 476, 477
Tuinei, Mark, 430
Turner, Clyde "Bulldog," *86*,
    86–91, 535
Turner, Keena, 495–96, 497, 499
Turner, Norv, 178, 383, 479
Turner, Ron, 482
Turney, John, 316, 415
Tyler, Wendell, 598

UCLA Bruins, 231, 234, 403
Unitas, Johnny, ix–x, 53, 54, 55,
    128, 137, 254, 509, *553*, **553–58**
Upshaw, Gene, 83, 145, 146–47,
    189, **189–93**
USC Trojans, 9, 14, 15, 17, 89–90,
    95, 207, 220, 224, 286–87, 290,
    340–44, 393, 494, 495, 497, 537
Utley, Mike, 467

Valdes-Scantling, Marquez, 18–19
Van Brocklin, Norm, 50, 51, 158,
    162
Van Buren, Steve, *43*, **43–48**
Vandee, Jeff, 426

van Eeghen, Mark, 189, 191
Van Pelt, Brad, 589
Vass, George, 88, 89–90
Vaught, Johnny, 153
Veach, Brett, 25–26
Vegas Vipers, 435
Vermeil, Dick, 339
Vick, Michael, 4, 6, 19, 166
Villapiano, Phil, 39–40, 42, 190
Vitt, Joe, 214, 217–18
Vogel, Bob, 54–55, 356, 358
Vrabel, Mike, 382

Wade, Bill, 28
Walker, Doak, 69
Walker, Jerry, 596, 602
Walker, Kevin, 619
Walker, Mickey, 60
Walsh, Bill, 301, 302, 459, 462, 498, 617–18; and Montana, 573, 574, 578; and Rice, 595–601
Walsh, Ted, 573
Walter, Joe, 538, 539
Ward, Bob, 318–19
Ware, DeMarcus, 316
Warfield, Paul, *33*, **33–38**, 604
Warmath, Murray, 282
Warner, Curt, 217
Warner, Kurt, 24, 362–63
Warren, Ty, 382
Washburn, Jim, 447
Washington Redskins (Commanders), 634; Bailey, 77–78; Baugh, 86–87, 89, 91, 93–94, 408–9, 412, 450–55; Green, 72–76; Jones, 517, 518; Sanders, 479; Super Bowl XVIII, 11–13, 131, 497
Waterfield, Bob, 51
Waters, Andre, 582
Waters, Charlie, 2, 318, 373
Watson, Ben, 80
Watson, Deshaun, 399
Watson, Justin, 18–19
Watt, J. J., *396*, **396–400**, 581, 584, 628
Watt, T. J., 628

Watterson, Steve, 339, 340, 342, 343
Wayne, John, 158, 251, 307
Wayne, Reggie, 373, 566
Webb, Davis, 23
Webb, Lardarius, 374
Webb, Richmond, vii, 490, 491
Weber, Chuck, 159
Webster, Mike, *248*, **248–52**
Welch, Raquel, 494, 552, 608
Welker, Wes, 382
West, Sam, 68
Weston, John, 282
White, Charles, 14, 343–44
White, Danny, 588
White, Dwight, 183–84, 386, 527
White, Randy, 128, *315*, **315–20**, 335
White, Reggie, 336, 459, 461, 462, 489–90, 512, *579*, **579–85**, 621, 628
White, Roddy, 260, 265, 268
Wilfork, Vince, 382
Williams, A. D., 59, 62
Williams, Aeneas, 306
Williams, Clarence, 137
Williams, Damien, 24
Williams, Darrent, 80
Williams, Erik, 336
Williams, Gregg, 625
Williams, Tramon, 188, 485
Williams, Trent, 629–30
Williams, Tyrone, 383
Williams, Wally, 234–35
Williamson, Troy, 484
Willis, Bill, 166, 168
Willsey, Ray, 15
Wilson, Camp, 68–69
Wilson, Larry, 500
Wilson, Marc, 619
Wilson, Russell, 4, 127, 453
Windsor, Bob, 516
Winslow, Kellen, *108*, **108–12**, 627
Winther, Wimpy, 569
Wisconsin Badgers, 49, 50, 52, 250, 397
Wistert, Al, 46

Witten, Jason, 334, 335, 624–26
Wolf, Ron, 145, 147, 380, 458–59, 462, 471, 532–33, 535, 620–21
Wolfley, Craig, 389, 440, 528–29
Wood, Willie, 245
Woods, Ickey, 499
Woodson, Charles, 63, 65, 66, *185*, **185–88**, 383, 435
Woodson, Rod, 66, 74, 170–71, 187, 242, 243, 298, *434*, **434–40**, 511
Wooten, John, 605, 606, 607
World Football League (WFL), 37–38, 138
World War II, 90, 98, 99, 100–101, 160, 313, 402, 411, 451, 534, 544

Wright, Louis, 216
Wright, Rayfield, 31, 517–18
Wright, T. C., 360
Wyche, Sam, 599

Yary, Ron, 201, 202, 287–88, 290–92
Young, Bob, 340
Young, Charle, 627
Young, Steve, 4, 6, *300*, **300–307**, 572–74, 577–78
Youngblood, Jack, 622

Zimmerman, John G., 159
Zimmerman, Paul, 355, 548